ENCYCLOPEDIA OF
EMANCIPATION
AND ABOLITION
IN THE TRANSATLANTIC WORLD

VOLUME ONE

ENCYCLOPEDIA OF
EMANCIPATION
AND ABOLITION
IN THE TRANSATLANTIC WORLD

VOLUME ONE

EDITED BY JUNIUS RODRIGUEZ

SHARPE REFERENCE
an imprint of M.E. Sharpe, Inc.

SHARPE REFERENCE

Sharpe Reference is an imprint of M.E. Sharpe, Inc.

M.E. Sharpe, Inc.
80 Business Park Drive
Armonk, NY 10504

© 2007 by M.E. Sharpe, Inc.

Library of Congress Cataloging-in-Publication Data

Encyclopedia of emancipation and abolition in the transatlantic world / Junius Rodriguez, editor.
   p. cm.
Includes bibliographical references and index.
ISBN 978-0-7656-1257-1 (alk. paper)
  1. Slavery—History—Encyclopedias. 2. Liberty—History—Encyclopedias. I. Rodriguez, Junius P.

HT985.E53 2008
306.3'6203—dc22

2006035834

Cover images: Clockwise from top left corner, provided by Getty Images and the following: English School/The Bridgeman Art Library; MPI/Stringer/Hulton Archive; FPG/Taxi; Stringer/ Hulton Archive; MPI/Stringer/Hulton Archive; Henry Guttmann/Stringer/Hulton Archive; MPI/Stringer/Hulton Archive.

Printed and bound in the United States

The paper used in this publication meets the minimum requirements of American National Standard for Information Sciences Permanence of Paper for Printed Library Materials, ANSI Z 39.48.1984.

BM (c) 10 9 8 7 6 5 4 3 2 1

Publisher: Myron E. Sharpe
Vice President and Editorial Director: Patricia Kolb
Vice President and Production Director: Carmen Chetti
Executive Editor and Manager of Reference: Todd Hallman
Senior Development Editor: Jeff Hacker
Development Editor: Gina Misiroglu
Project Editor: Laura Brengelman
Program Coordinator: Cathleen Prisco
Text Design: Carmen Chetti and Jesse Sanchez
Cover Design: Jesse Sanchez

Contents

v

Volume 2

Topic Finder

Abolitionists, American

Allen, Richard (African American bishop)
Allen, William G.
Anderson, Osborne Perry
Beecher, Henry Ward
Benezet, Anthony
Birkbeck, Morris
Birney, James Gillespie
Blanchard, Jonathan
Bowditch, Henry Ingersoll
Brown, John
Buffum, Arnold
Burleigh, Charles Calistus
Butler, Benjamin Franklin
Channing, William Ellery
Child, David Lee
Cornish, Samuel E.
Cuffe, Paul
Dawes, William
Day, William Howard
Delany, Martin Robison
Dillwyn, William
Downing, George Thomas
Du Bois, W.E.B.
Forten, James, Sr.
Foster, Stephen Symonds
Garnet, Henry Highland
Garrison, William Lloyd
Gatch, Philip
Gay, Sydney Howard
Gibbons, James Sloan
Gibbs, Mifflin Wistar
Grinnell, Josiah B.
Grosvenor, Cyrus Pitt
Hamilton, William
Hayden, Lewis
Hopkins, Samuel
Johnson, Oliver
Langston, John Mercer
Lay, Benjamin
Lovejoy, Elijah P.
Lovejoy, Owen
Lundy, Benjamin

May, Samuel Joseph
McKim, James Miller
Miller, Jonathan Peckham
Mott, James, and Lucretia Coffin Mott
Nell, William Cooper
Norton, John Treadwell
Olmsted, Frederick Law
Owen, Robert Dale
Paine, Thomas
Paul, Nathaniel
Pennington, James W.C.
Phillips, Wendell
Pillsbury, Parker
Purvis, Robert
Ray, Charles B.
Realf, Richard
Reason, Charles L.
Reason, Patrick H.
Rock, John Sweat
Rush, Benjamin
Smith, Gerrit
Spooner, Lysander
Steward, Austin
Stroyer, Jacob
Sunderland, La Roy
Tappan, Arthur
Tappan, Benjamin
Tappan, Lewis
Torrey, Charles Turner
Vaux, Roberts
Ward, Samuel Ringgold
Washington, Bushrod
Weld, Theodore Dwight
Whitting, William
Woolman, John
Wright, Elizur
Wright, Henry Clarke
Wright, Theodore Sedgwick

Abolitionists, Brazilian

Gama, Luís
Lacerda, Carlos de
Menezes, José Ferreira de

Historical Events, Periods, and Occasions

Laws, Decrees, and Governing Documents

Newspapers, Periodicals, Editors, and Publishers

Novels, Novelists, Playwrights, and Poets

Pamphlets, Tracts, Nonfiction Works, and Writers

Philosophers and Theorists

Political Leaders, Heads of State, and Elected Officials

Religion, Religious Figures, and Cultural Movements

Slave Narratives and Narrators

Brown, Henry "Box"
Brown, William Wells
Bruce, Henry Clay
Clarke, Lewis G.
Cugoano, Quobna Ottobah
Douglass, Frederick
Equiano, Olaudah
Federal Writers' Project, Slave
    Narrative Collection
Fedric, Frances
Grandy, Moses
Gronniosaw, James Albert Ukawsaw
Henson, Josiah
Jacobs, Harriet
Northup, Solomon
Pennington, James W.C.
Roper, Moses
Stroyer, Jacob
Truth, Sojourner
Tubman, Harriet
Veney, Bethany
Zembola, Zamba

Slave Rebellions and Rebel Leaders

Barbados Revolt (1816)
Berbice Slave Revolt (1763)
Bogle, Paul
Cinque, Joseph
Curaçao Slave Revolt (1795)
Demerara Revolt (1823)
German Coast Rebellion (1811)
Gordon, George William
Haitian Revolution (1791–1804)
Hausa Uprising (1835)
Jamaica Rebellion (1831–1832)
Maroon Wars, Jamaica (1729–1739,
    1795–1796)
Maroon Wars, Suriname (1600s–1800s)
Morant Bay Rebellion (1865)
Pritchard, "Gullah" Jack
Prosser, Gabriel
Sharpe, Samuel
Stono Rebellion (1739)
Tacky's Rebellion (1760–1761)
Tailors' Revolt (1798)

Toussaint L'Ouverture, François-Dominique
Turner, Nat
Vesey, Denmark

Societies, Organizations, Parties, and Conventions

Abolitionist Confederation
African Institution
American and Foreign Anti-Slavery Society
American Anti-Slavery Society
American Colonization Society
American Missionary Association
American Tract Society
Anti-Slavery International
Brazilian Anti-Slavery Society
Church Missionary Society
Concert of Europe
Free Soil Party
Freedmen's Aid Societies
Freedmen's Bureau
Hibernian Anti-Slavery Society
Ku Klux Klan
Liberty Party
National Anti-Slavery Tract Society
Sociedad Abolicionista Española, La
Société des Amis des Noirs, La
Society for the Abolition of the Slave Trade
Society for the Civilization of Africa
Society for the Propagation of the Gospel
    in Foreign Parts
Sons of Africa
World Anti-Slavery Convention (1840)
World Anti-Slavery Convention (1843)

Wars and Military Affairs

African Squadron
American Revolution (1775–1781)
Beecher's Bibles
Civil War, American (1861–1865)
Maroon Wars, Jamaica (1729–1739,
    1795–1796)
Maroon Wars, Suriname (1600s–1800s)
Massachusetts Fifty-Fourth Regiment
U.S. Colored Troops

General Editor
Junius P. Rodriguez

Contributors

Wayne Ackerson
Salisbury University

Gregory Matthew Adkins
University of Dayton

Leslie M. Alexander
Ohio State University

William H. Alexander
Norfolk State University

Lena Ampadu
Towson University

Melissa Anyiwo
University of Tennessee, Chattanooga

Rolando Avila
University of Texas, Pan American

Kelly J. Baker
Florida State University

Erica L. Ball
California State University, Fullerton

Riva Berleant
University of Connecticut

Jackie R. Booker
Claflin University

Prince Brown, Jr.
Northern Kentucky University

Ron D. Bryant
Kentucky Historical Society

Dino E. Buenviaje
University of California, Riverside

William E. Burns
Independent Scholar

Kevin Butler
University of Missouri, Columbia

Malini Cadambi
The New School for Social Research

Mariana P. Candido
York University

Brycchan Carey
Kingston University

David M. Carletta
Michigan State University

Boyd Childress
Auburn University

Jorge L. Chinea
Wayne State University

Katherine L. Culkin
The Harriet Jacobs Papers

Evan M. Daniel
The New School for Social Research

Charles A. D'Aniello
State University of New York, Buffalo

LaRay Denzer
Northeastern Illinois University

David J. Endres
Catholic University of America

J. Brent Etzel
Augustana College

James C. Foley
University of Mississippi

Russell Fowler
University of Tennessee, Chattanooga

Andrew K. Frank
Florida Atlantic University

Lisa Tendrich Frank
Florida Atlantic University

Javier A. Galván
Santa Ana College

Gwilym Games
Reading Central Public Library

Steve Garner
University College, Cork, Ireland

Henry H. Goldman
Independent Scholar

Larry Gragg
University of Missouri, Rolla

Jane S. Groeper
Illinois State University

Robin Hanson
Saint Louis University

Glen Anthony Harris
University of North Carolina, Wilmington

Holger Henke
Metropolitan College of New York

Melinda M. Hicks
West Virginia University

Sharon Hill
University of Tennessee, Chattanooga

Imelda Hunt
Bowling Green State University

T.K. Hunter
Princeton University

Brian M. Ingrassia
University of Illinois, Urbana-Champaign

Michelle Jackson
Baylor University

Mary J. Jarvis
West Texas A&M University

Melinda Marie Jetté
University of British Columbia

Mitch Kachun
Western Michigan University

Jeffrey R. Kerr-Ritchie
Howard University

Stewart R. King
Mount Angel Abbey and Seminary

Timothy Konhaus
West Virginia University

Geoffrey A. Koski
Western Carolina University

Hadley Kruczek-Aaron
Syracuse University

Ethan J. Kytle
University of North Carolina, Chapel Hill

Tom Lansford
University of Southern Mississippi

Kate Clifford Larson
Simmons College

Lori Lee
Syracuse University

Kevin M. Levin
University of Richmond

Fred Lindsey
Temple University

Denise Lovett
Prairie View A&M University

David B. Malone
Wheaton College, Illinois

Eugenio Matibag
Iowa State University

Babacar M'Baye
Evergreen State University

Nathan R. Meyer
University of Louisville

Heather K. Michon
Philosophy Documentation Center

Gina Misiroglu
Independent Scholar

Hilary J. Moss
Brandeis University

Angela F. Murphy
University of Houston

Sowandé Mustakeem
Michigan State University

Caryn E. Neumann
Ohio State University

Matt Norman
Knox College

Michael Pasquier
Florida State University

Kenneth Pearl
Queensborough Community College

Kennetta Hammond Perry
University of Virginia

Luca Prono
Independent Scholar

Elizabeth Purdy
Independent Scholar

Sean Purdy
Temple University

Michelle Gammon Purvis
University of South Carolina

Mark S. Quintanilla
Bloomsburg University

Kokila Ravi
Atlanta Metropolitan College

Carole Realff
University of Sussex, England

Polly Rossdale
Independent Scholar

Walter Rucker
Ohio State University

Rosemary Sadlier
Ontario Black History Society

Margaret Sankey
*Minnesota State University,
Moorhead*

Jonathan D. Sassi
College of Staten Island

Jennifer Searcy
Loyola University, Chicago

Verene A. Shepherd
*University of the West Indies,
Jamaica*

Marika Sherwood
University of London, England

Mark G. Spencer
University of Toronto

Richard D. Starnes
Western Carolina University

Bruce Tap
Independent Scholar

Jerome Teelucksingh
*University of the West Indies,
Trinidad and Tobago*

Thomas Adams Upchurch
East Georgia College

Joel Van Haaften
*Lombard Historical Society
Museum*

Teresa M. Van Hoy
*University of Houston,
Clear Lake*

Antoinette G. van Zelm
*Middle Tennessee State
University*

Colleen A. Vasconcellos
Florida International University

Seneca D. Vaught
Bowling Green State University

Philine Georgette Vega
Independent Scholar

Barbara Schwarz Wachal
*St. Louis Community College,
Florissant Valley*

Delores M. Walters
Northern Kentucky University

J.B. Watson, Jr.
Stephen F. Austin State University

William A. Wharton
*State University of New York,
Stony Brook*

Scott Wignall
Eureka College

Heather A. Williams
Smith College

Howell Williams
Florida State University

Stephanie R. Wright
Rutgers University

Ronald E. Young
Georgia Southern University

Preface

The *Encyclopedia of Emancipation and Abolition in the Transatlantic World* is a reference work that employs a unique approach to the topic, combining elements of macro- and micro-history in its fact-filled pages. By taking a regional approach that views the transatlantic world as having common traits and characteristics that transcend the peculiarities of any particular location, this work presents a systematic examination of emancipation and abolition.

These three volumes present the complex story of emancipation and abolition by highlighting individuals, places, events, legislation, and concepts to explain the vagaries of the slave experience at specific times and locations. Taken together, this body of work provides an in-depth view of how slavery was dismantled and freedom achieved throughout the transatlantic world.

These volumes comprise nearly 450 articles prepared by a team of more than 100 international scholars who present the most current research findings in their work. Most of the entries include a brief bibliography that suggests additional books and articles about the topic being discussed.

In addition, this encyclopedia includes an impressive collection of primary source documents, many out of print for more than a century, that vividly describe efforts to abolish slavery and emancipate slaves during the eighteenth and nineteenth centuries. A concise chronology provides an overview of these efforts. A topic finder, cross-references, and comprehensive index are useful guides to the myriad interrelated topics covered in this work.

The history presented here is a story of relentless struggle to achieve freedom for the millions of men, women, and children who found themselves trapped in a dehumanizing institution that tried to rob them of their sense of personhood. Resistance efforts among the enslaved, as well as sustained campaigning by abolitionists who used the tools of political action and moral suasion, eventually helped to bring an end to one of the darkest practices in human history. The struggle to effect the abolition of slavery was a monumental achievement, and the corresponding struggle of the emancipated to attain the full liberties they were due represents a triumph of the human spirit against formidable obstacles.

The noted humanitarian Dr. Albert Schweitzer once commented, "The tragedy of man is what dies inside himself while he still lives." It is thus the fire of freedom, the fire that burned in the hearts and minds of the enslaved, that educates and empowers us still. The courage, passion, and valor of those who defied the odds and social conventions of their time to do right—simply for the sake of righteousness—transform us by demonstrating the power of what is truly possible.

The people described in these pages were not victims. Rather, their stories are monuments to heroism and achievement. In essence, the volumes of this encyclopedia tell the story of freedom and how it was achieved.

Junius P. Rodriguez

Acknowledgments

Completion of these volumes has required a collaborative venture that has pooled the talents and resources of many to produce this important reference tool. I appreciate the invaluable efforts of all who had a hand in helping to produce *The Encyclopedia of Emancipation and Abolition in the Transatlantic World.*

The work of 114 scholars who have examined the history of abolition and emancipation in the transatlantic world appears in these volumes in the form of nearly 500 encyclopedia-style entries. Having worked with many of these authors over the years, I have developed an admiration for their work, and I am pleased that they contributed their scholarship to this publishing effort. I particularly value the friendships that have formed in the development of these volumes, as many of my colleagues also have extended to me their encouragement and support.

I am tremendously indebted to my friends at M.E. Sharpe who have helped me greatly as this work has developed. I appreciate the confidence that Andrew Gyory placed in me when we first discussed tackling this project several years ago. It was a pleasure to work with Todd Hallman again—I have always appreciated his guidance when the work became especially challenging. Cathy Prisco has ably directed me toward completion of this project, and the insightful suggestions of Jeff Hacker and Gina Misiroglu have helped to fashion these volumes into a better work. Even when I may have bristled at pointed critiques, in the end, I learned that I became a better writer and editor by listening to the advice that was offered.

Throughout this project, several of my students at Eureka College have worked as research assistants and have helped me with developing portions of the manuscript. I am appreciative of their assistance and wish to express my sincere gratitude for their tremendous efforts. Special thanks are extended to Bryan Smith, Kyle Makemson, Lance Hrdlicka, Sarah Wilson, and Jon Hackler for their tireless dedication.

In addition, I must thank all my students, past and present, whose stimulating questions about slavery, abolition, and emancipation have been a valuable resource in my own intellectual growth, as I have sought to fashion and hone interpretations. Their invariable quest to learn has challenged me and sustained me through the years.

The Eureka College Faculty Development Committee generously supported start-up costs for this project and assisted in supporting research trips that were necessary to collect materials for this work. In addition, I must thank Joy Kinder who has offered expert secretarial assistance, as well as a kind word, whenever I was working intently to get mailings out on time. Eldrick Smith solved my computer problems, both great and small, which kept me on task and generally sane. In addition, the assistance of Ginny McCoy, Tony Glass, Kelly Fisher, Brent Etzel, Lynne Rudasill, and Ann Shoemaker was especially helpful in tracking down the bits and pieces that can make an editor's life challenging.

As editor, I take full responsibility for the failings and inevitable shortcomings that may appear in this work. Any attempt to examine issues as large and as perplexing as abolition and emancipation in an encyclopedia format undoubtedly requires editorial choices that will not be pleasing to everyone. It is hoped that students, scholars, and general readers alike who use this reference work will find it to be informative and insightful.

Junius P. Rodriguez

Introduction

On a basic level, the old truism that "history repeats itself" applies to many of the circumstances that we encounter when we examine the recorded past. Though we seldom find historical events replicated exactly, the search for precedent provides ample opportunities to formulate an understanding of events that are anchored within our historical consciousness.

Once such a mental construction is formed, the literary devices of simile, metaphor, and symbolism become conduits through which we can fashion a more holistic understanding of historical concepts. In this way, the modern observer can see the nascent sinews that connect the past to the present to the future. This elaborate process, which transpires within seconds in the brain, permits us to think with a sense of history.

More difficult to fathom, perhaps, are those historical anomalies that perplex us, because we cannot root them to anything in our personal experience. Because of their uniqueness, such episodes and events beguile and baffle us, defying normal processing within our historical comprehension.

Such occurrences require a more nuanced understanding of history. We must seek to measure them by considering the intricacies of cause and effect, the reflective paradigm of continuity and change, and the ever-present probability of multiple causation. Our maturity of thought can be measured by the degree to which we comprehend such rootless historical moments and grow in depth and awareness as we expand our mental landscape. In this process of fashioning understanding without the convenience of historic precedent, we become prescient thinkers.

Both of these historical thought processes occur simultaneously as we study the recorded past. Our comprehension is incomplete and our interpretations flawed if we ignore either of these approaches. The ways of knowing history always must be plural, layered, and reflective.

Slavery is likely as old as civilization itself. Though it is difficult to grasp the incongruity that war and slavery may have been the twin offspring of the elements of civilized society, this seems to be the case.

The desire to acquire property and to possess things soon fostered the notion of people as commodities. From the beginning, the peoples of Mesopotamia, Egypt, and China fashioned class-based societies in which people were acquired and owned as slaves. Subsequent societies followed this precedent and became characterized by slave ownership. The classical civilizations and cultures of the Western world all recognized slavery as legal and based their economic structures on the use of bound labor.

The institution of slavery was tacitly accepted by these societies; none questioned the morality of the practice or the intrinsic worth of human life. Neither Plato nor Aristotle questioned the wisdom of slave ownership. The prevailing moral order of the day, as it was understood through the authority of the ancients, maintained that slavery was part of the natural order of the universe. Even the gods, it seems, remained silent on the question.

Within the religious context of Judeo-Christian thought, the existence of slavery is acknowledged in scripture, but the otherworldly focus of spiritual life casts slavery as a hardship of this world that is to be endured. Slaves were urged to be loyal to their masters, echoing the paternalism of later slave masters. That advice, along with the failure of early religious leaders to condemn slavery, reads as an effective endorsement of the custom and practice. Within the pages of the New Testament, there are no recorded words spoken by Jesus that proclaim slavery to be morally offensive, and this silence would speak for more than two millennia. Proslavery apologists in the mid-nineteenth century would use the Bible to endorse the sanctity of the "peculiar institution" of slavery as part of the moral order of the universe.

Through the lens of modernity, it is difficult to imagine such a blind spot existed. It is even more disconcerting that no Jeremiah appeared on the scene to challenge the conventional wisdom of the times. Not only were the gods silent, but also humankind appeared to be blind, deaf, and mute.

Classical antiquity produced slave societies, but it produced no abolitionists. The practice of slavery

Evidence of slavery is almost as old as civilization itself. A wall painting on an ancient Egyptian tomb dating to the 18th Dynasty (16th–14th century B.C.E.) depicts the beating of a slave. *(Erich Lessing/Art Resource, New York)*

ebbed and flowed according to the rigid strictures of economic necessity in Greece and Rome and elsewhere, but it was never challenged on the basis of its moral or ethical merit. Neither faith nor philosophy nor the powers of human reason generated any groundswell of support to challenge the moral legitimacy of slavery as a social and economic institution.

The absence of historical precedent for abolitionist thought in the ancient world is perplexing to modern scholars of slavery. Nonetheless, we find an alternative understanding of the notion of emancipation. In an age of faith, the notion of liberation was perceived more as a religious matter than as a worldly concern. Saving oneself from the snares of Hell and attaining the grace that would guarantee one a place in Paradise was the truest form of emancipation that an individual might seek. Personal liberty and freedom in this world were seen as lesser concerns—transitory ephemera compared to the promise of eternal life that salvation would bring. The rhetoric of faith subsumed all relative notions of worth and worldly conditions. Thus, distinctions among the freeborn, the slave, and the freedman were comparatively insignificant in the cosmic order of things.

Secular humanism did not exist in the world of the classical civilizations. The notion that unaided reason could comprehend and direct moral authority was as heretical as claiming that men had the power of angels. Within a society rooted in scripture, there

was little opportunity for abolitionism to take hold through any grassroots moral reform initiative, and the mass of people remained powerless. Faith, custom, and tradition all maintained that a well-ordered society was one that included slaves.

Roots and Branches

The rise of abolitionist sentiment in the transatlantic world was a unique social and cultural transformation of the modern era. The paradigm shift that came to associate slavery with evil and viewed moral righteousness as a necessary first step toward personal salvation challenged all preexisting thought on the topic.

To be an abolitionist was to be a radical, to challenge the religious heritage of Judeo-Christian thought, the prevailing laws and customs of civilized society, and thousands of years of history, tradition, and practice that embraced the legitimacy of slavery. More troubling, perhaps, for an age that denied the primacy of self and denounced pride as loathsome, abolitionism not only involved abjuring all forms of preexisting authority but it also required the audacity to claim the superiority of personal philosophy fashioned from unaided reason. In truth, few were so bold to make such assertions, and the court of public opinion held such adherents to be social revolutionaries.

The historical and philosophical transformation that gave rise to abolitionist thought was born during the eighteenth century and developed slowly thereafter. It would be incorrect to attribute the rise of abolitionism to a singular cause. Only a multifaceted approach that considers all of the social, intellectual, religious, economic, and political forces undergoing transformation at the time can produce a cultural composite of the varied forces that legitimized antislavery thought.

For some, skepticism had become the order of the day. The discovery of the unfamiliar continents of the New World and the realization of a sun-centered universe diminished the preeminent position of earth—and effectively, man—and shattered the authority of the ancients. If such factual errors could be discovered within the realm of sacred knowledge, one might only speculate on the absolute certainty of moral authority. No longer satisfied with the medieval worldview, which valued inane syllogisms to fashion logic, modern thought emerged as rational people began to question the prevailing values and attitudes of their time. It would be difficult for slavery to escape notice in such an examination.

No singular purpose motivated and inspired abolitionist adherents; they were drawn to the movement by a variety of moral and ethical beliefs. For some, the greatest evil of slavery was the stain of sin that it placed on the individual slave owner and, indirectly, all who silently supported and abetted the institution. Others were drawn to antislavery by their recognition of and appreciation for the true humanity of the slave, believing that the immense pain and suffering of slavery should befall none of God's children. Still others were drawn to antislavery thought by their economic determinist views, holding that unfree labor diminished the relative value of free labor and thereby hindered the development of capitalistic free market institutions.

Though modern observers might choose to evaluate abolition on the basis of its effective outcomes, we should not fail to impugn the motives of its adherents. Perhaps Thomas Babington Macaulay's famous assertion about the Puritans—that they "hated bear-baiting, not because it gave pain to the bear, but because it gave pleasure to the spectators"—applies equally to the abolitionists.

Still, we also must acknowledge that the rise of antislavery thought helped to formulate a parallel stream of proslavery ideology that became more structured and better articulated as abolitionists' influence in the transatlantic world grew during the late eighteenth and early nineteenth centuries. Opposing ideologies may have been necessary to bring the debate over slavery to a public dialogue, but the rise of proslavery thought and the entrenched positions associated with it gave birth to even more demons than the abolitionists wished to slay.

It is possible, though tragically ironic, that conditions within the slave regime actually may have hardened as a response to abolitionist agitation, and that the "slave power conspiracy" antislavery advocates so vehemently despised in the nineteenth century may have been an indirect product of their own creation. In such a world of conflicted values, we can only surmise to what degree the slaves themselves may have been principals or pawns in the moral struggle over the merits of freedom and the promise of emancipation.

The strident voices of Africans who had endured the hardships of slavery provided new insights and added immediacy to the cause of abolitionist thought in the transatlantic world. The nameless, faceless millions who labored as slaves had long been perceived as a silent, unintelligible mass that toiled for a sanctioned reason within a divinely ordered universe. As long as one could deny the essential humanity of the slave and withhold the singular notion that men and women with names, minds—and perhaps even souls—were being subsumed within an economic system that sought to deny their very sense of personhood, then, and only then, could the system of slavery sustain itself.

Vivid narratives began to appear in print and individuals such as Olaudah Equiano, Quobna Ottobah Cugoano, and James Albert Ukawsaw Gronniosaw narrated their personal experiences of slavery from within the institution. Such accounts began to put a human face on the slave. What Equiano termed an "interesting narrative" was a persuasive tool that would help dismantle the very foundation of slavery. The power of human emotion has the capacity to transcend rhetoric, and the firsthand accounts of Africans were powerful testimony against the collective evils of slavery.

Intellectual Origins

The earliest stirrings of antislavery thought represented a radical departure from the staid conventions of reliance on the authority of the ancients and the long-standing precedent of custom and tradition.

Our present-day perception of the mutual existence of faith and reason was an idea fashioned through a very difficult birth. For many, the emergence of rationalism was perceived as the product of an ongoing cultural battle of faith versus reason, a zero-sum game in which the affirmation of one mode of thought could only be accomplished through the denial, sublimation, or outright destruction of the other. In truth, elements of both faith and reason animated and inspired the origins of abolitionist thought in the transatlantic world.

It is impossible to deny the effect of the Enlightenment upon the growth and development of the abolitionist movement. This historic intellectual revolution, which began in the early eighteenth century in Western Europe, supported not only the belief that slavery was an irrational custom and practice but also the concept that abolition was a moral imperative for all who claimed the blessings of civilized society.

It was organized religion's tacit endorsement of slavery that fueled much of the intellectual antislavery rhetoric, which, in turn, condemned any faith that would not openly equate slavery with evil. The failure of scripture to condemn slavery and the propensity of church leaders to condone the institution was understood by Enlightenment thinkers as evidence that a higher moral authority vested within the conscience of the individual was superior to the teachings and practices of Judeo-Christian thought.

Church leaders did not remain silent on the question of slavery. Neither did their pronouncements on the topic comment on the moral legitimacy of the institution; they addressed only the proper ethical relationship that should exist between master and slave. The notion of faith as an activist agent that could transform the existing structures of society was alien to most believers. It was this unquestioning reverence for the status quo—in the context of an error-filled world that was in need of ethical cleansing—that motivated Enlightenment thinkers to challenge those who practiced faith without works.

Perhaps an earlier age might have accepted the silence of the gods without question, but the growing awareness that pure, unaided reason could lead one to discern right from wrong fashioned a new understanding, a secular humanism that found a moral compass within the human capacity to think and to act on the basis of knowledge. Any institution—the church included—that sought to diminish the power of human reason and thereby limit the perfectibility of humankind was perceived as irrational and archaic. Similarly, the failure of organized religion to acknowledge the evil of slavery and to recognize it as sin was understood as a ringing endorsement of slavery and the societal ills it engendered.

Despite the best intentions of the French *philosophes* (thinkers) and others who subscribed to the principles of Enlightenment thought, rationalism was no panacea that could guarantee the moral perfectibility of human society. Notwithstanding the heady rhetoric that espoused common cause with the "brotherhood of mankind," modern notions of racial equality and the natural rights of man were not universally accepted by all who wore the mantle of Enlightenment thought. Even during the Age of Reason, a belief persisted among many that true equality was theoretical but not practical. Just as Saint Paul had admonished the early Christians to hate sin but love the sinner, some eighteenth-century rationalists readily came to hate the sin of slavery, but they could not bring themselves to recognize the true equality of the slave. From the very beginning, one finds mixed messages within the ideals and rhetoric of the abolitionists.

For many eighteenth-century European intellectuals, slavery was an artificial construct that existed in a colonial *cordon sanitaire*, out of sight and frequently out of mind of those living within the metropole. Some recognized that everyone living within a slaveholding society was sullied by the institution, but this understanding was by no means universal. Only a few writers of the Enlightenment era personally ventured to the West Indies, where they could experience and sense the true conditions of slavery and come to understand how the practice degraded the slave, the slave owner, and, by association, all who profited in any fashion from the slave-based economy. These authors, such as Abbé Raynal, offered a more realistic and candid assessment of the evils inherent in the system of slavery.

Essential to the rationalists' arguments against slavery was an understanding of the "natural rights" philosophy, which John Locke had first articulated in the late seventeenth century. This belief was both compelling and troubling to the Enlightenment thinkers, a fact suggested by Baron de Montesquieu's acknowledgment, "If they [African slaves] are, indeed, human, then we [whites] are not Christian."

Abolitionist rhetoric was troubling, because it augured a personal sense of moral blame and responsibility that was not readily accepted by a skeptical and less than introspective society. Writers such as Voltaire might proclaim their desire to "crush infamy"—*Ecrasez l'infame!*—but the will to do so was diminished by the understanding that when applied to slavery, this battle was an internal struggle within the hearts and minds of men and women. Abolition would entail an immense amount of moral courage, but it also would necessitate a humbling sense of spiritual awakening within many that would compel them to action. Thus, the battle against slavery would be joined by adherents of both faith and reason, as individuals began to understand clearly the societal costs and consequences of continued silence and inaction.

A Higher Calling

Despite the ambitious efforts of Enlightenment thinkers, the Age of Reason did not engender a more rational, morally ordered society, nor did it destroy the entrenched power of faith to motivate people to action. Indeed, the irrational calamities of their world called reason into question and beckoned many to return to theological exegesis for interpretation and solace.

Reason did not sound the death knell for faith, but it did challenge traditional religion, which responded in a variety of ways, ranging from strong affirmation of the traditional orthodoxy to more radical departures that focused on individual faith inspired by personal piety. Many of these spiritual revolutionaries believed slavery to be a social evil of this world, the tolerance of which imperiled the moral cause of their otherworldly aspirations. For some, this inner light became a passionate flame that they believed was necessary to enlighten a world that had lost its capacity to recognize such evil.

The age of religious warfare that followed the reformations of the sixteenth century spawned a multitude of new sects within the world of Western Christianity. Some of these new "mainline" Protestant denominations did not differ much from the Roman Catholic Church in their views on slavery and the slave trade. Many perceived the business of slavery as a necessary evil, needed to sustain the modern socioeconomic world that had evolved from its feudal antecedents.

Philosophical arguments such as Thomas Aquinas's concept of "just war," which had been used to defend the Crusades during the eleventh and twelfth centuries, were employed to rationalize the West African slave trade that began, somewhat modestly, in the mid-fifteenth century. Racist ideologies that presupposed the inherent superiority of some people over others viewed slavery as a paternal institution that might provide social and spiritual uplift to individuals who had not been exposed to the blessings of Christianity. In espousing these views, the orthodox religious community formed a spiritual bulwark that defended the status quo in supporting the slave trade and the practice of slavery. The notion of abolition as a spiritual calling was not a part of the theological vocabulary of most churchmen.

During the sixteenth century, the institutional structure and theological foundation of Western Christianity were challenged by a series of five religious reformations that swept across Europe and fundamentally altered the religious and political landscape. The Lutheran Reformation, the Calvinist Reformation (or Reform movement), the Anglican Reformation, the Anabaptist Reformation, and the Catholic (or Counter) Reformation were all events of profound historical importance. Of these, the Anabaptist movement, certainly the smallest and least well known of these reformations, had the most significant impact on the development of the transatlantic effort to end the slave trade and to abolish slavery.

The Anabaptist movement originated in the cantons (provinces) around Zurich, Switzerland, where reformers Conrad Grebel and Felix Manz hoped to further purify the already reformed practice of Christianity. These religious innovators believed that theological reformers such as Martin Luther and John Calvin had not taken sufficient steps to remove all of the worldly corruption from Christianity and to restore it to its biblical purity. In particular, Grebel and Manz disapproved of the Lutherans' practice of infant baptism, an action they believed was merely symbolic. The Anabaptist leaders also opposed the connection between civil and religious authority that had characterized Calvin's model community of Geneva. Fearing the religious consequences of the tyranny of the majority, Grebel and Manz advocated the separation of church and state as the only way to protect religious minorities in a pluralistic society. This view was a radical departure from the prevailing custom, which held religious singularity to be a necessary component of political power and expediency.

Because minority religious communities such as the Mennonites, the Amish, and the Quakers challenged the orthodoxy of the reformers (i.e., Luther and Calvin), they were perceived as radicals and extremists. The common tenet of pacifism that characterized these groups made their members appear less than trustworthy in a society in which militarism was understood as a test of national honor. Accordingly, the Anabaptist populations in Europe faced intense persecution during the century of religious warfare that followed the reformations. When the opportunity to start anew in the English North American colonies presented itself as a viable option during the seventeenth century, many Anabaptists, Mennonites, Quakers, and Amish emigrated to America.

Quakers on both sides of the Atlantic were among the earliest abolitionists. They were some of the first individuals to recognize that slavery was a violation of a secular ethic—involving the essential question of good versus evil—while their coreligionists of more traditional, mainline Protestant denominations still struggled with the understanding that slavery was a biblically sanctioned practice. Although the mainline denominations would divide over the issue of slavery, and religious schisms would characterize subsequent abolitionist debates, the faith communities of the Anabaptist tradition remained largely unified.

Though members of the Anabaptist tradition did not accept all that the Enlightenment supported, their personal experience with religious persecution and their willingness to speak the truth against authority made them kindred spirits with Enlightenment thinkers who could not comprehend slavery as a rational system, despite any and all political and religious sanction. The idea of nonresistance, which was universal among the Anabaptist traditions, became a key element of the antislavery movement's strategy. Although there were voices of dissent within the ranks of the transatlantic abolitionist movement— those who said that open resistance was a right and a duty—the Christ-like notion of nonviolence generally prevailed.

The antislavery impulse did not emerge spontaneously among these groups when they arrived in North America. In fact, among the Quakers, many profited from their involvement in the slave trade and ownership of slaves. It was not until 1688 that a group of Moravian Quakers would issue the Germantown Protest, a public document demanding that all Quaker brethren divest themselves of any proprietary involvement in the slave trade and the ownership of slaves.

Some abolitionists from the Anabaptist tradition were widely known as antislavery advocates and supported abolitionism in a very public fashion. Others, drawing on a more personal, pietist worldview, supported abolitionism but shunned any attention that their antislavery activities might call to themselves. Among British and North American Quakers, in particular, religious factions disputed the extent to which political involvement was a necessary part of battling the sin of slavery. For many, to be too much "of this world" was perceived as a detriment to the ultimate goal of attaining personal redemption and salvation.

Notions of inner piety were not the exclusive spiritual domain of the Anabaptists, as other groups within the mainline religious communities also came to recognize that slavery was a moral transgression that violated Judeo-Christian norms. Nor did such inner light spirituality automatically make one an abolitionist. Puritan clergymen such as Increase and Cotton Mather were certainly men of faith, but they were also slave owners, and they never chastised their fellow residents of colonial Massachusetts for holding African slaves or profiting from the riches of the slave trade.

By the mid-eighteenth century, new religious denominations such as the Methodists, the spiritual followers of John Wesley, splintered from the Anglican church and took a more active stance against the perceived sin of the slave trade. In true missionary endeavors, men such as Wesley and Thomas Coke, a member of the British Parliament, would endeavor to convert slave owners to the abolitionist perspective through persistent argument and moral suasion.

Sinners and Saints

In medicine, healing can only begin once the highest point of a fever has passed. Likewise, the strongest affirmation of antislavery sentiment could only be made once the excesses of the institution had been made manifest.

In many respects, Great Britain's experiences with regard to the slave trade and slavery within its colonial empire during the eighteenth century provided the foundation for the abolitionist impulse that would transform the transatlantic world. The Treaty of Utrecht (1713) ended the War of the Spanish Succession (1701–1714) and granted Great Britain the right to supply African slaves to the Spanish colonies in the New World. The British South Sea Company conducted this enterprise throughout the eighteenth century and amassed significant profits during this time, the height of the transatlantic slave trade.

During the eighteenth century, the transatlantic world experienced a "sugar revolution," as sugar became the dominant crop of the Caribbean. The insatiable demand for sugar cultivation created a concomitant demand for African slaves to labor on the Caribbean plantations. During the eighteenth century alone, nearly 6 million Africans were transported as slaves to the New World—more than half the entire African population shipped during the history of the transatlantic slave trade. This vast and expanding enterprise fueled British coffers, as the slave trade became the dominant industry of the era. Ships regularly departed from British ports such as Liverpool and Bristol, sailing to West Africa and ports unknown to conduct the nefarious trade, but few understood the full meaning of the flesh trade that transpired out of sight and out of mind of most Britons.

For most who lived in Great Britain, slavery and the transatlantic slave trade took place "beyond the line," and therefore true awareness of the unseemly business was limited to the merchant seamen who manned the vessels and conducted the trade. Unlike the Iberian nations of Portugal and Spain, Great Britain was home to few Africans, and thus notions of race or the humanity of slaves were concepts that were yet to penetrate the British Isles in the early eighteenth century. These ideas would be fashioned gradually, and, in the process, antislavery sentiment would begin to take root.

The relative justice or injustice of slavery was an issue that began to take form in the British courts. In a famous 1729 ruling, Attorney General Sir Philip Yorke and Solicitor General Charles Talbot issued what became known as the Yorke-Talbot decision, which stated that neither entering Great Britain nor accepting Christian baptism made an African slave a free person. The Yorke-Talbot decision established a precedent that would prevail in British thought for the next forty-three years.

The decision in the case of *Knowles v. Somersett* (1772) is generally recognized as effectively ending slavery within Great Britain. In that case, British

The rise of sugarcane as the leading crop in the Caribbean Islands during the eighteenth century led to the heavy importation of African slaves to work the plantations on Antigua, shown here, and elsewhere. *(©British Library, London, UK/©British Library Board. All Rights Reserved/The Bridgeman Art Library)*

chief justice Lord Mansfield (William Murray, first earl of Mansfield) issued his famous ruling, in which he declared "the air of England has long been too pure for a slave, and every man is free who breathes it. Every man who comes to England is entitled to the protection of English law, whatever oppression he may heretofore have suffered, and whatever may be the color of his skin."

The repercussions of Lord Mansfield's ruling were immense. Rationalists began to wonder how slavery could be tolerable elsewhere if it violated the civil norms of British society. Though there was a long-prevailing prejudice that the lands of the New World were more savage than those of Europe, the association of slavery with wilderness was no longer readily accepted by those who believed in the application of universal truths. The penchant for viewing slavery as morally permissible in some settings but not in others was irrational. The intellectual bedrock on which slavery and the slave trade had long rested began to crack.

The Natural Rights of Man

Although Lord Mansfield's ruling certainly gave impetus to the growing antislavery movement in Great Britain, efforts in Britain's North American colonies added rhetoric to the antislavery movement and ultimately brought about the first emancipation. Tensions between Great Britain and the North American colonies began to increase during the decade following the French and Indian War (1754–1763), as the British policy of ending salutary neglect within the colonies and instead raising revenues there to support colonial defense began to garner opposition.

A succession of events, including the Boston Massacre (1770) and the Boston Tea Party (1773), heightened tensions; British efforts to reestablish authority and maintain order were met with further acts of resistance by the colonial rebels. By 1776, when the delegates at the Continental Congress charged a committee with drafting a Declaration of Independence to justify open rebellion against Great Britain, freedom became the byword of the day, and slavery was its natural antonym.

In his preliminary draft of the Declaration of Independence, Thomas Jefferson, a Virginia slave owner, included a passage that directly criticized King George III for maintaining the slave trade. This language, however, was deleted from the document after delegates from the Carolinas protested, arguing that

such a statement was unwise and unnecessary. Even with this passage excluded, one cannot help but feel that the American founders viewed the struggle with Great Britain as one between the liberty of freeborn people and the slavish autocracy of a foreign monarch. Despite the irony inherent in the argument, the rhetoric was quite potent.

As Great Britain responded to the rebellion in its North American colonies, all possible contingencies for defeating the insurgency were considered. Because several colonies were home to substantial slave populations, slaves were encouraged to run away to join the British army, with the understanding that their loyal service on behalf of the British cause would win them emancipation at the end of the rebellion. Lord Dunmore, the colonial governor of Virginia, issued a proclamation to this effect, and a significant number of slaves (known as Black Loyalists) were attracted by the promise of emancipation in return for military service. In 1783, after the Treaty of Paris ended the American Revolution, British ships transported thousands of Black Loyalists out of the North American colonies to other destinations, including Nova Scotia, Jamaica, and Sierra Leone.

Although slavery had existed in all thirteen of the British North American colonies before the Revolution, it survived in only six states south of the Mason-Dixon Line after the war. Seven states in the newly established United States of America enacted gradual abolition legislation that effectively emancipated the slaves living within their borders: Pennsylvania (1780), Massachusetts (1783), Connecticut (1784), Rhode Island (1784), New York (1785, 1799), New Jersey (1804), and New Hampshire (1783 or 1789, accounts vary).

Although the rhetoric of freedom that had inspired the American Revolution remained fervent in the hearts and minds of New Englanders, the decision to emancipate slaves in these states was also motivated by economic circumstances. Slaves were few in number in all of these states, as the landscape and climate of the region were not suitable for large-scale plantation agriculture. In addition, the notion of slave labor was at odds with an incipient commercial ethic that was starting to take root in the region, as proto-industrial manufacturing sites began to mark the region's rivers and streams.

The abolition of slavery in these seven states marked the first official emancipation within the slave system of the transatlantic world. The various methods that were used to effect the mechanical aspects of emancipation, such as gradualist approaches and compensation for slave owners, would figure in subsequent debates about how emancipation should and could be achieved most efficiently.

The Society for the Abolition of the Slave Trade (also known as the Society for Effecting the Abolition of the Slave Trade) was established by British abolitionists in 1787 as an advocacy organization. Its founders were the key figures within the British antislavery establishment of the late eighteenth century: Granville Sharp, William Wilberforce, Thomas Clarkson, Josiah Wedgwood, and other notables of the day. The society came into being at the moment the British Parliament was considering legislation to outlaw the transatlantic slave trade—an odious enterprise to many, but nonetheless a business venture from which many British merchants and traders had profited handsomely throughout the eighteenth century.

The stirrings of public discussion—particularly sermons against the slave trade preached by abolitionists such as Peter Peckard, who was known for his antislavery pamphlet *Am I Not a Man? And a Brother?* (1788)—convinced British abolitionists and their sympathizers that the time had come to mount a legislative campaign against the evils of the slave trade. British abolitionists knew, however, that they would face formidable opposition from the so-called West Indian lobby in Parliament, a vocal proslavery group that defended slavery as an economic necessity of the British colonial system and vowed to impede any effort to tamper with the slave trade.

Unlike other antislavery organizations, members of the Society for the Abolition of the Slave Trade were determined to base their arguments on fact rather than mere emotion, and they began to collect data on the social and economic impact of the transatlantic slave trade. Members of the society were convinced that if they could overwhelm Members of Parliament with inconvertible evidence of the deleterious effects of the slave trade, legislation would be immediately enacted to outlaw the practice. The collection, culling, and processing of this data occupied much of the time of the society's leadership in 1787.

Researchers fanned out across Great Britain to visit the port cities of Liverpool and Bristol, where they pored over ship manifests and transcribed statistical data, all in an effort to put a human face on the flesh trade, while others visited the British West Indies to conduct further investigation. Members of the society became acquainted with the seamier side of the slave trade, as they interviewed crew members of slaving vessels and others who had firsthand experience of the business of the slave trade. They also collected personal testimonies of what transpired during the treacherous Middle Passage, as captive Africans were transported across the Atlantic Ocean. Using this documentation, the society hoped to advance the argument that the slave trade not only harmed Africans but also jeopardized the personal well-being and public morals of the crew members who were sullied by their association with such an evil enterprise.

The society's collection and processing of data were aimed at appealing to both the intellect and the reason of its eventual audience—Members of Parliament and the British public at large—so the material had to be presented in such a way as to touch both the hearts and minds of impartial observers. The society's leaders recognized that a sustained propaganda effort required sound data, but it also needed to incorporate powerful visual elements as well.

By publishing an image of a cross section of the slave ship *Brookes*, the society created one of the most powerful and lasting images of the antislavery movement. The cutaway diagram of the *Brookes* represented the system of "tight packing" that was used on many slaving vessels, as unscrupulous merchants and ship captains purposefully overloaded their vessels to enhance their profits. The stick-figure representations of the captive Africans effectively portrayed the manner in which human beings were turned into commodities that could be bought, sold, and traded, while ethical values were reduced to nothing more than the profits and losses on a balance sheet.

Another influential image was created by British potter Josiah Wedgwood, a founding member of the society. He produced cameos depicting a kneeling slave in chains with the haunting caption, "Am I not a man and a brother?" The cameos were sold to raise money to support antislavery efforts in Britain, and the image was reproduced in many forms, making it one of the most recognizable images of the abolitionist movement throughout the transatlantic world.

Having collected their data, members of the society published two pamphlets in 1788 to report their findings to the widest possible audience. Thomas Clarkson published *An Essay on the Impolicy of the African Slave Trade,* and James Ramsey published *Objections to the Abolition of the Slave Trade with Answers.* In addition to these publications and the national petition drives that followed, several British abolitionists, including William Pitt, William Wyndham Grenville, and William Wilberforce, addressed Parliament on

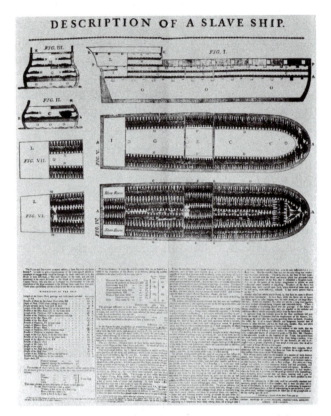

Among the most influential images of the antislavery movement was a cross section of a British slave ship depicting the severe overcrowding on the Middle Passage. The diagram was presented to Parliament in 1787 as part of the campaign to end the slave trade. (©*Wilberforce House, Hull City Museums and Art Galleries, UK/The Bridgeman Art Library*)

behalf of the society and urged the immediate abolition of the transatlantic slave trade.

Faced with such powerful evidence, Members of Parliament tried to give the appearance of enacting reform, realizing that they could not muster the support necessary to outlaw the slave trade outright. As a compromise measure, Parliament enacted Dolben's Act of 1788, a statute that regulated the conditions permitted aboard British vessels participating in the transatlantic slave trade. While this measure fell far short of the goal the abolitionists had hoped to achieve, at the same time, the Privy Council Committee for Trade and Plantations began to investigate the state of British commercial relations with Africa.

In addition to these parliamentary actions in Britain, the efforts of the Society for the Abolition of the Slave Trade had repercussions across the Atlantic Ocean. In the United States, delegates to the 1787 Constitutional Convention in Philadelphia, Pennsylvania, grappled with the perplexing question of how to end the transatlantic slave trade. The solution that emerged from the so-called Commerce Compromise became enshrined in the U.S. Constitution, as delegates promised not to interfere with the slave trade for the next two decades in exchange for a prohibition on the taxation of exported goods. However, the compromise merely postponed the date when the young republic would have to reckon with its involvement in the African slave trade.

Man and Brother

In the late eighteenth century, a new tactic was employed in the British antislavery movement as African expatriates, themselves the victims and survivors of the transatlantic slave trade, organized so that they might assist in the crusade to end the evil institution of slavery. The Sons of Africa was the first abolitionist group to be organized and led by black abolitionists.

Founded in London in 1787, the Sons of Africa was established by twelve free blacks living in Great Britain who hoped to make an important contribution to the discussion of vital issues of their time. More than just another antislavery organization, the Sons of Africa is regarded by modern historians as the first civil rights organization in the transatlantic world. Its members were revolutionary activists who were no longer willing to remain silent on the question of slavery. The black abolitionists who formed the society viewed their antislavery work as more than a mere reform-oriented pastime; it was a vital and urgent calling inspired by their own life experiences.

The former slaves turned abolitionists Quobna Ottobah Cugoano and Olaudah Equiano were the chief organizers of the Sons of Africa. In the aftermath of the famous *Somersett* case (1772), which effectively outlawed slavery by judicial pronouncement in Great Britain, free blacks became a small but significant presence in London and other British urban centers. Recognizing that the moment was right to organize in support of efforts by British abolitionists who were seeking to convince Parliament to outlaw the transatlantic slave trade, free blacks such as Cugoano and Equiano realized that they and their associates could make a significant contribution to the discussion on the merits of abolition by recounting their own experiences within the institution of slavery.

Both Cugoano and Equiano had already exerted an important influence on the antislavery discourse in Great Britain. Cugoano had published *Thoughts and Sentiments on the Evil and Wicked Traffic of the Slavery and Commerce of the Human Species* (1787), which was followed by Equiano's publication of *The Interesting Narrative of the Life of Olaudah Equiano* (1789). Both works were widely read and distributed by white abolitionists in Britain and became immensely popular.

The potent rhetoric of these first-person narratives animated the message that the Sons of Africa hoped to deliver to British society, which was not yet committed to the cause of abolitionism. The narratives were designed to effect social change. The former slaves gave powerful testimony to the inhumanity inherent in the institution and related this experience to their fellow Britons, hoping to make slavery more than an academic issue that affected others far beyond Britain's shores. In addition, they emphasized the moral dictum that one's silence on such an evil practice was tantamount to complicity in the crime.

One of the ironies of the abolitionist movement is that the efforts of groups such as the Sons of Africa were never fully appreciated or effectively utilized, a result of the fundamentally racist tendencies of many white reformers who called themselves abolitionists. Many of those who sincerely opposed the slave trade and slavery could do so because they equated these evils with sin on an intellectual level; still, on a purely social level, they could not accept blacks as their equals. This parsing of morality and personal ethics seems disingenuous by modern-day standards, but it was a fact of life within the abolitionist movement, and it often prevented the movement from mounting a singular, sustained voice against the perpetuation of the transatlantic slave trade and slavery.

Ending the Slave Trade

In the two decades preceding 1807, abolitionists in both Great Britain and the United States focused their attention on mounting legislative campaigns to outlaw the transatlantic slave trade. They believed that halting the supply of Africans transported to replenish the slave populations on plantations and farms in the Western Hemisphere would bring about the end of slavery. Abolitionists had faith that a reduction in supply, which they believed they could achieve through legislative action, would eventually result in abolition, which they knew they could not attain through direct legislation at the time.

In the United States, Congress enacted landmark legislation on March 2, 1807, that prohibited the importation of African slaves into any region within U.S. jurisdiction, effective January 1, 1808. President Thomas Jefferson signed the measure, and it became law. At the time the law took effect, there were an estimated 1 million slaves residing within the United States.

The British Parliament had defeated an 1805 effort by William Wilberforce, an abolitionist Member of Parliament, to outlaw the transatlantic slave trade, but the sympathetic government of Prime Minister William Pitt had issued an order in council that slightly reduced the annual volume of the slave trade. In 1806, upon Pitt's death, Parliament approved a resolution introduced by Charles James Fox that called for the abolition of the transatlantic slave trade, but no specific measures for implementing or enacting this policy were considered. Finally, on March 25, 1807, Parliament enacted An Act for the Abolition of the Slave Trade, commonly known as the Slave Trade Act, which outlawed the transatlantic slave trade beginning on March 1, 1808.

In the era that followed, the British government made concerted efforts to bring about the end of the transatlantic slave trade and encouraged other European powers to comply. It became a key element of British foreign policy to encourage other nations that it was in their best interest to join the United States and Britain in outlawing the slave trade.

By the 1820s, the British government would equate the slave trade with piracy, and naval patrols regularly stopped suspicious vessels at sea and searched them to see whether Africans were being shipped in violation of British law. Eventually, the United States and Britain jointly established the African Squadron, a group of naval vessels that patrolled the waters off the coast of West Africa to search for slave trading vessels.

Despite these efforts, some slave ships did manage to slip through. Yet the net effect of the 1807 legislation was the reduction of the transatlantic slave trade to a fraction of what it had been during the previous century.

Revolutionary Rhetoric

Abolitionists on both sides of the Atlantic believed that ending the slave trade was the most certain path to the eventual abolition of slavery, but slaves in the French colony of Saint-Domingue realized emancipation through other means—insurrection. When the French Revolution began in 1789, its lofty rhetoric proclaimed "liberty, equality, and fraternity" as the guiding principles of the popular uprising, and these sentiments were echoed in the Declaration of the

Rights of Man and of the Citizen, which stated, "Men are born and remain free and equal in rights."

The limits of these aspirations were tested in October 1790 when free persons of color in Saint-Domingue, led by Vincent Ogé and Jean-Baptiste Chavannes, rose up in rebellion against French colonial rule. Although the revolt was suppressed and its leaders executed, the impression of black men rising up against the authority of white Frenchmen was not lost on the massive slave population of Saint-Domingue, which made up nearly 90 percent of the colony's population.

By August 1791, the French authorities in Saint-Domingue were under assault by a large-scale uprising of the colony's slaves. Slave leader Toussaint L'Ouverture began to capture significant portions of the southern half of the colony. French commander Legér-Félicité Sonthonax issued an order emancipating the slaves in the northern portion of the colony if they would join French forces to defeat Toussaint; however, the French, tremendously outnumbered, were unable to hold on to the colony. By 1794, the National Assembly in France had declared an end to slavery throughout the French Empire on the basis of immediate, uncompensated emancipation. This policy would later be reversed by Napoleon Bonaparte in 1802.

Thus, the first emancipation effected in the transatlantic world was born of a marriage between Enlightenment-inspired rhetoric about natural rights and the unconquerable human desire for personal liberty. Although the enslaved people of Saint-Domingue may have understood this alliance of heart and mind only in rudimentary form, the leaders who inspired the rebellion understood the rhetoric. They realized that the passions of the multitude could effect more than the lofty musings of French legislators who valued ideas for their own worth but did not realize the consequences of those ideas in practical life. Years later, the American author Ralph Waldo Emerson recognized this sense of cognitive dissonance when he spoke of people who express "incredible tenderness for black folk a thousand miles off" while in reality "thy love afar is spite at home."

Although the people of France considered themselves products of the Enlightenment and recognized the intellectual rhetoric of the French Revolution as stemming from that era's lofty ideals, they could not bring themselves to recognize and accept the incompatibility between slavery and liberty. In spite of having lost Saint-Domingue, one of their most valuable colonial possessions, the French reinstated the institution of slavery throughout the remainder of the French West Indies and would not effect complete and final emancipation until 1848.

The French were not alone in their inability to associate the freedom of slaves with the values they

In the French colony of Saint-Domingue (now Haiti), a slave rebellion led by Toussaint L'Ouverture in 1791 led to the formal abolition of slavery throughout the French empire three years later. (©*Bibliotheque Nationale, Paris, France/Roger-Viollet, Paris, France/The Bridgeman Art Library*)

held so dear in their own lives. For residents of the United States, who also linked their national birth to the revolutionary philosophy of natural rights, the stirring language of "life, liberty, and the pursuit of happiness" included in the Declaration of Independence was believed to be sincere, even though it had been penned by Thomas Jefferson, a slave owner. In the minds of the French, Americans, and others who defended slavery in the early nineteenth century, a type of mental gymnastics was necessary to justify the disconnect between rhetoric and reality.

Evangelization

Abolitionists viewed the British and American actions to ban the slave trade in 1808 as a singular accomplishment that would hasten the end of slavery. Many believed that slavery could be abolished through market forces alone and that basic economic principles such as supply and demand were key to destroying slavery.

It was readily understood throughout the Caribbean region that slave populations could not sustain themselves through natural increase alone, and thus a constant supply of new Africans to replace those depleted by exhaustion and death was essential to the stability of the colonial plantation regime. The ability to maintain a closed economy without the need for slave imports might well have been the death knell for slavery throughout the Caribbean, but airtight embargoes are difficult to maintain. The same principle of supply and demand meant that as the slave supply diminished, the need for new labor increased and the prices associated with the delivery of now-illegal Africans became quite dear. Accordingly, a significant business in the smuggling of illegal Africans into the colonies of the Americas continued, despite the efforts of Great Britain and the United States to end the trade.

In Great Britain, Parliament officially declared in 1824 that participation in the illegal African slave trade was considered an act of piracy and established legal mechanisms for the enforcement of British law throughout the world. Parliament authorized the creation of special tribunals—so-called Courts of Mixed Commission—that were to be established in Sierra Leone. The purpose of these military tribunals was to decide the fate of crew members aboard captured slave vessels seized in the waters off West Africa.

The African Squadron regularly patrolled off the coast of West Africa in order to prevent the continuation of the illegal slave trade. Whenever suspected vessels were captured by the African Squadron, the captives on board were brought to colonies such as Liberia or Sierra Leone, where they were freed and the status of crew members was adjudicated.

The British government attempted to use diplomatic pressure and moral suasion in the aftermath of the Napoleonic Wars (1799–1815) and the Congress of Vienna (1814–1815) to convince other European powers to outlaw the transatlantic slave trade, but these efforts met with mixed success. Spain and Portugal were most recalcitrant in considering the cessation of the transatlantic slave trade, as the business was deemed essential to the well-being of their colonial interests in Cuba and Brazil. Even when these nations eventually agreed to outlaw the slave trade in 1817, their efforts were half-hearted at best, and enforcement of their laws was practically nonexistent. This noncompliance occurred despite the fact that the British government had paid significant cash sums to the Spanish and Portuguese governments in order to encourage them to enforce their own laws with respect to the slave trade.

In 1826, select members of the British Parliament received a packet of documents pertaining to the condition of the illegal African slave trade during the years since the British and U.S. governments had outlawed the practice in 1808. Recognizing that enforcement efforts had failed to prevent a complete embargo of the slave trade, some parliamentarians began to consider whether the total abolition of slavery might be the only effective means to end the trade; however, widespread support for such a policy of complete emancipation did not yet exist.

Firebell in the Night

In the United States, slavery ceased to be an issue of national debate in the decade following the abolition of the African slave trade. Partly because of international tensions associated with the Napoleonic Wars and the War of 1812, which was fought with Great Britain, domestic institutions such as slavery attracted little attention, even though the population of slaves in America continued to grow. Only when the expansion of slavery assumed a geographic dimension in the United States did the issue stimulate national debate that reinvigorated the abolitionist movement.

In the aftermath of the War of 1812, many Americans began to contemplate the commercial expansion of the young nation and to support a nationalistic agenda that would foster such growth. Policy initiatives such as tariff increases to protect America's "infant industries," along with the chartering of a national bank and support for developing a commercial infrastructure of turnpikes, canals, and river and harbor improvements, signaled the beginning of a market revolution that would transform the national economy. But it was increasingly difficult to reconcile this new economic vision with the stark reality of slave-based agriculture that existed throughout the southern half of the nation. This ideological divide became clear in 1819, when the Missouri Territory sought admission to the Union as a slave state.

Although some could reconcile the existence of slavery in the United States as a peculiarity of the Southern states, the extension of slavery into Western or Northern domains was unappealing to many Americans. Moreover, the admission of Missouri as a slave state seemed to portend that other areas included in the Louisiana Purchase Territory also might seek to enter the Union as slave states, thus expanding what some termed "an empire of slavery" that might spread across the North American continent. Hoping to halt the spread of slavery in the United States—and fearing the political power that the slave states might hold—politicians from the Northeastern states sought to prevent the admission of Missouri as a slave state in 1819.

For nearly two years, Missouri's admission to the Union was the focus of a national debate, as members of Congress wrangled with options to turn the territory into a free state and to effect gradual emancipation for the slaves already living in the area. These attempts drew the ire of Southern politicians, who viewed slavery as a states' rights issue and challenged all attempts to limit the sovereignty of Missouri residents to chart their own identity as a new state.

All of these debates were framed by the reality that proslavery and antislavery forces held an equal number of states at the time (ten each), and the admission of Missouri would tip the balance of power in the U.S. Senate one way or the other. With the stakes so high, the debate's intensity reflected anxiety over the larger question of what a shift in the balance of political power might imply for either side.

The debate over slavery in Missouri was so heated that former president Thomas Jefferson observed, "This momentous question, like a fireball in the night, awakened and filled me with terror." The aged founder of the nation confided to a friend that he "considered it at once as the knell of the Union" and wondered whether the civility of American political life could ever be restored. Observing that the debate pitted justice against self-preservation, Jefferson surmised, "We have the wolf by the ears, and we can neither hold him, nor safely let him go." Indeed, it would be difficult to resolve the Missouri question in a fashion that was satisfactory to all.

The Missouri Compromise of 1820 was a congressional effort to defuse the crisis by crafting a temporary solution to the key issues at hand. Under the terms of the compromise, the balance of power in the Senate was maintained as two states—Missouri and Maine, one a slave state and the other a free state—were permitted to enter the Union at the same time. In addition, the question of which lands within the Louisiana Purchase Territory would be permitted to practice slavery was decided by arbitrarily drawing a line at the point of 36°30' north latitude, the southern boundary of Missouri. According to the compromise, no states north of that line—with the exception of Missouri—would be permitted to enter the Union as slave states. For the time being, it seemed as though the Missouri Compromise had solved the vexing problem that divided the nation.

Abolitionism Unleashed

The Missouri debates had unleashed forces of abolitionism that had been silent for many years, and once the antislavery genie was out of the bottle, it was difficult to return to the days of silent acquiescence. During the height of the debate, from April to October 1820, the Quaker Elihu Embree published *The Emancipator*, an antislavery newspaper, in Jonesboro, Tennessee. One year earlier, Embree had published the short-lived *Manumission Intelligencer*, which was probably the first antislavery newspaper published in the United States.

In 1821, another Quaker, Benjamin Lundy, began publishing the *Genius of Universal Emancipation* in Mount Pleasant, Ohio. This publication was one of the earliest abolitionist newspapers in the United States to have a wide readership. Although Lundy later relocated his publication to Baltimore, Washington, D.C., and Illinois, the newspaper remained in print regularly from 1821 to 1839.

The early antislavery newspapers that appeared in the United States during the 1820s found common cause in opposing the work of the American Colonization Society, which was working to relocate free blacks to a colony in Liberia on the western coast of Africa. From the time of its founding in December 1816, the American Colonization Society was a controversial organization. The free black leader James Forten, Sr., led a protest meeting in January 1817 of 3,000 free blacks in Philadelphia who opposed the work of the American Colonization Society. Meeting at the Bethel African Methodist Episcopal Church, the group protested the efforts of the American Colonization Society, believing that the organization sought "to exile us from the land of our nativity." With criticism coming from both the abolitionist press and from groups of free blacks, support for the idea of colonization waned during the 1820s.

The growing chorus of antislavery thought that emerged at this time inspired more strident voices to join the debate. This is best illustrated by the efforts of David Walker, a free black living in Boston, who published *An Appeal to the Colored Citizens of the World* (1829). Walker's militant antislavery publication advocated active resistance by blacks to the institution of slavery. The pamphlet was distributed throughout the United States and greatly disturbed Southern slave owners, who believed that its message would incite unrest among the slave population.

Slavery and Modernity

The call for blacks to foment insurrection that was at the heart of Walker's *Appeal* may have frightened slaveholders, but it was a prescient warning that should not have been ignored. In 1831, the very foundations of slavery in the United States and the British West Indies were shaken by two massive slave revolts that produced very disparate outcomes.

Nat Turner's Rebellion, which exploded in Virginia's Southampton County in August 1831, led to a retrenchment in parts of the U.S. South, where the ordinances controlling slavery were made more stringent and patrols were increased accordingly. Some historians believe that the Christmas Uprising—also known as the Baptist War, the Jamaican Revolution, and the Great Jamaican Slave Revolt—led by Samuel Sharpe on the island of Jamaica helped to hasten the end of slavery in the British Empire.

Other forces were involved in the resurgence of abolitionist efforts during the 1830s in Britain and the United States. Both countries were witnessing the growth of democratic idealism as notions of classical liberalism in Britain and Jacksonian democracy in the United States led to an expansion of suffrage and prompted a growing activism with respect to social reform, including the antislavery impulse. In addition, the economic forces of free market capitalism were starting to emerge in both countries as the factory system expanded and new modes of industrial production began to develop; these forces were viewed as incompatible with a labor system that was still rooted in chattel slavery. In many respects, the tensions between a modern capitalist system and an almost feudal labor system such as slavery were difficult to reconcile. Time would dictate that the survival of one depended on the destruction of the other.

A new understanding emanating from the social sciences—in particular, from the new disciplines of anthropology and sociology—began to challenge the racist assumptions by which slave-based societies defined themselves. In addition, the representative success of free blacks who had been able to assimilate themselves into the society of the free, in spite of the many barriers put in their paths, eroded support for the racial exclusiveness that viewed Africans as fit only to be slaves. In many respects, the temper of the times was changing in Great Britain and the United States during the 1830s, and the rise of impassioned abolitionists in both countries was a manifestation of notions of modernity that emerged.

Triumph

Abolitionists in Great Britain had been organized in their opposition to slavery since the 1770s, and their campaign against the institution did not wane after the African slave trade was outlawed by Parliament in 1808. From the outset, British abolitionists considered antislavery agitation an outwardly focused effort that had to find resonance throughout the transatlantic world in order to be effective. Because chattel slavery did not exist in England, but it did exist in the British West Indies and elsewhere in the Americas, British abolitionists worked internally to achieve external results. Long before there was any sort of transatlantic cooperation between abolitionist groups, the British antislavery community had established a foundation for regional cooperation in a sustained campaign to bring an end to slavery wherever it existed.

Despite the level of their antislavery organization, British abolitionists were divided over the most effective means to render emancipation to the slaves. This problem was made manifest when Elizabeth Heyrick published the pamphlet *Immediate, Not Gradual Abolition* (1824). As one of the most active female abolitionists in Britain, Heyrick believed in the concept of immediate abolition, viewing slavery as a moral issue rather than an economic or a political concern. Many contemporary British abolitionists believed that a system of gradual emancipation would be more practical, because it would not produce the social and economic disruptions that immediate emancipation threatened.

British abolitionists' success in the early nineteenth century rested on their ability to transform the slavery debate from an economic argument into a moral discourse on the ethics and efficacy of owning human beings. Throughout the history of abolitionism in Great Britain, William Wilberforce was the most prominent leader of the movement, and, believing that abolitionism was a sacred calling, he worked tirelessly to end the slave trade and slavery in all British possessions. As Wilberforce, the grand old man of the British antislavery movement, lay dying during summer 1833, Parliament finally moved to address the question of slavery in the British West Indies.

On August 29, 1833, the British Parliament passed the Abolition of Slavery Act (also known as the Emancipation Act), which effectively ended slavery in all British colonial possessions. Under a system of gradual abolition that imposed a period of apprenticeship, the measure would free all slaves in the British colonies by 1838. Parliament appropriated £20 million to compensate slaveholders in the British West Indies who would suffer economic losses as a result of Britain's abolishing slavery within the empire. An estimated 700,000 slaves were emancipated in the British West Indies.

Despite their victory in the campaign to end slavery in the British West Indies, not all abolitionists were satisfied with the measure that Parliament enacted in 1833. Many believed that the system of gradual emancipation proposed by the measure would perpetuate slavery for a period of time during which West India planters could sell slaves into other markets where the practice had not yet been abolished. The British abolitionists' greatest criticism was their universal condemnation of the system of apprenticeship intended to transition emancipated slaves from slavery to wage labor. Many British reformers saw the apprenticeship system as being fraught with potential for abuse, as white planters would remain in a position of authority over their former charges and might exact revenge for the financial losses that came with emancipation.

British abolitionists also realized that the accomplishment of emancipation in the British West Indies was merely a victory in one battle in the war to abolish slavery throughout the transatlantic world. Rather than abolish their antislavery organizations after 1833, British abolitionists began to monitor the status of apprenticeship in the West Indies and established connections with other antislavery advocates in the United States and elsewhere. To this end, the British abolitionists began to publish the *Anti-Slavery Monthly Reporter* (later the *Anti-Slavery Reporter*) to chronicle efforts to abolish slavery within the British Empire and report the progress of abolitionism in other settings.

Finding a Voice

As British abolitionists were consummating their efforts to end slavery in the early 1830s, antislavery advocates in the United States were beginning to organize a large-scale campaign to agitate for the emancipation of the slaves in the U.S. South. Although autonomous antislavery societies had existed in cities and towns of the United States since the 1780s, these groups were small, poorly funded, and generally lacked visionary leadership. Until the early 1830s, no single organization spoke for abolitionism in the United States; the movement was largely faceless, with no clear leader at its helm.

The ill-organized and anonymous abolitionist movement in the United States began to change on January 1, 1831, when William Lloyd Garrison published the first issue of *The Liberator*, a weekly antislavery newspaper that would come to represent the most articulate expression of antislavery thought in the country.

Garrison had been trained in journalism through his work with Benjamin Lundy, and he believed, like Wilberforce, that there was the urgency of a moral crusade in the work to abolish slavery in American society. Garrison's style was both courageous and relentless, as he made clear that he would not back down from his views, despite any criticism they might engender. Eager and willing to be a lightning rod for the antislavery movement, Garrison vowed to fight to destroy slavery until the final objective was attained. In establishing *The Liberator*, Garrison declared, "I am

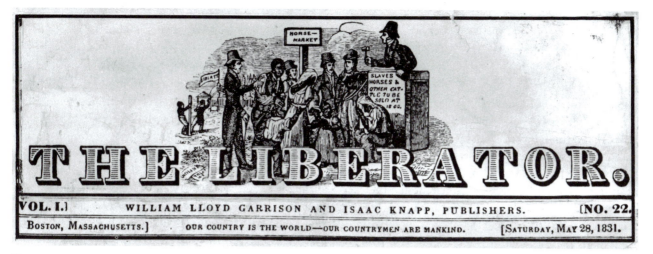

The appearance of William Lloyd Garrison's weekly newspaper *The Liberator* in 1831 helped unify the voice of the abolitionist movement in America. The Boston publication continued to promote the cause of antislavery to the end of the Civil War. *(Hulton Archive/Getty Images)*

in earnest—I will not equivocate—I will not excuse—I will not retreat a single inch—AND I WILL BE HEARD!"

The clarity of Garrison's message drew converts to the abolitionist cause. Within a few months of launching *The Liberator,* he had established a loyal following; this group included several well-heeled individuals who were able to help finance a large antislavery organization that could provide a common voice for abolitionism in the United States. On January 6, 1832, a group of dedicated white abolitionists met at the African Baptist Church on Boston's Beacon Hill to organize the New England Anti-Slavery Society. Garrison played an important role in the founding of the organization, and its members supported the concept of "immediatism," believing that gradual abolition was an inadequate response to the national sin of slavery.

Although the members of this initial group were sincere in their antislavery sympathies, Garrison found the society to be too parochial to form the basis of a national antislavery organization. Thus, in December 1833, Garrison, Theodore Dwight Weld, Arthur Tappan, Lewis Tappan, and several other black and white abolitionists met in Philadelphia to establish the American Anti-Slavery Society, the first national abolitionist society in the United States. The American Anti-Slavery Society embodied the ideals that Garrison articulated in the pages of *The Liberator*, and it was quickly dubbed a "radical association" by proslavery Southerners and some less than sympathetic Northerners.

Garrison had alienated many from the abolitionist cause through his shrill denunciation of the U.S. Constitution, which he deemed a compact with the devil because of its protection and enabling of slavery. In Garrison's opinion, the Constitution was "a compact formed at the sacrifice of the bodies and souls of millions of our race, for the sake of achieving a political object—an unblushing and monstrous coalition to do evil that good might come." Not surprisingly, Garrison was vilified for his extreme views; on occasion, he was physically assaulted. The Georgia state legislature issued a $5,000 reward for anyone who would capture Garrison and deliver him to the state for criminal prosecution.

Defending the Indefensible

The rise of an organized abolitionist movement in the United States during the 1830s came at a time when the institution of slavery in the Southern states was changing dramatically. As the federal government initiated a policy of American Indian removal during the administration of President Andrew Jackson, thousands of acres of farmland were made available for cultivation in the states of the old Southwest. Slavery was on the move in the Southern states, as a vigorous domestic slave trade began to operate to provide cotton field hands to newly established plantations and farms in Georgia, Alabama, Mississippi, and points westward. The nature and extent of slave society in the U.S. South was being transformed at the same time that antislavery advocates were organizing themselves for the monumental battle of wills that would be needed to bring an end to slavery.

Supporters of slavery fashioned a proslavery defense as an intellectual bulwark to the rise of radical abolitionism. Southerners were so certain of the righteousness of their cause that they would not retreat an inch in their defense of slavery. Their religious, intellectual, scientific, and historical justifications for slavery were perceived as superior to any abolitionist argument that could be posed to challenge the merits of the South's "peculiar institution." Moreover, Southerners assumed that their genuine belief in their own benevolence, evidenced by the spirit of paternalism that permeated the plantation South, represented a higher ethic than the money-grubbing interests of New England merchants and antislavery agitators.

Southerners also appealed to a higher authority to support their opinions. Thornton Stringfellow, a proslavery apologist from Virginia, published *A Brief Examination of Scripture Testimony on the Institution of Slavery* in 1841. Stringfellow believed that the volume of references found in the Bible supporting slavery were sufficient proof of the moral legitimacy of the practice.

With the battle lines drawn between the strident voices of radical abolitionism in the North and the reactionary rhetoric of proslavery agitators in the South, there was little space for constructive dialogue between the two sides. Political debate, one of the hallmarks of a democratic society, suffered, as diametrically opposed views, enunciated by those who were absolutely certain of their *own* righteousness, made real political discourse impossible. Not surprisingly, civil liberties eroded during the antebellum era. Southern postmasters burned abolitionist literature rather than deliver it through the U.S. mail, and members of Congress agreed to a self-imposed "Gag Rule" that forbade discussion of antislavery petitions in the U.S. House of Representatives.

The coarsening of values would continue until the 1850s, when proslavery and antislavery advocates began to murder their opponents in Kansas. Even U.S. senators such as Charles Sumner of Massachusetts were not safe from attack within the confines of the U.S. Capitol. Viewed in this context, the national bloodletting that occurred during the U.S. Civil War was merely an extension—elevated by several degrees—of the unbridled hatred that had festered for a generation.

Vagaries of Freedom

Although abolitionism in the United States originated in the Northeast, antislavery advocates also could be found in the states of the Upper Midwest. In areas such as Ohio, Indiana, and Illinois, where slavery had been prohibited by the Northwest Ordinance of 1787, there was sporadic, but not widespread, support for the abolitionist cause. These states saw much traffic in fugitive slaves who sought to escape from slavery and make their way to free states and territories in the northern United States or Canada. Many of the abolitionists who lived in the Upper Midwest were associated in some way with the so-called Underground Railroad that assisted fugitives seeking freedom.

Although they were conduits to freedom for fugitive slaves, the states of the Upper Midwest were not always friendly toward free black residents. For example, free blacks who lived in the counties along the Ohio River had to guard against being kidnapped and sold into slavery in the South. In addition, several states in the Upper Midwest enacted "Black Laws" that proscribed the rights and liberties of free blacks living there. Even before the passage of the Fugitive Slave Act of 1850, many fugitives believed that true liberty required them to make their way out of the United States and settle in Canada, where they believed they would face less discrimination.

It was Illinois that saw the first martyr to the abolitionist cause when Elijah P. Lovejoy, editor of the antislavery *Alton Observer,* was murdered in 1837. Lovejoy's death at the hands of a proslavery mob motivated many to join the abolitionist movement. In death, Lovejoy became a heroic figure who had perished in defense of his belief in freedom of the press and his firm commitment to the principles of abolitionism. John Brown, the radical abolitionist who would later come to fame in Kansas and at Harpers Ferry, Virginia, claimed that he had been called to the antislavery crusade when he had attended an Ohio memorial service to commemorate Lovejoy's death.

Methods and Means

As abolitionism grew in the United States, it became clear that the movement comprised a range of beliefs as to the best means to effect the end of slavery. Some antislavery supporters believed that gradual emancipation was the best possible method to end slavery, whereas others maintained that the sin of slavery could be absolved only through immediate emancipation.

Others debated the merits of providing some form of compensation to slave owners when emancipation was finally realized. Those who supported compensated emancipation believed that to do otherwise would impose economic ruin on the nation by severing a huge portion of capital investment from the gross national product. Those who opposed compensated emancipation believed that it was unconscionable to reward slave owners for what abolitionists deemed bad behavior.

The more radical abolitionists debated whether to offer compensation to former slaves when emancipation finally arrived. Many believed that without some type of assistance—whether in land, tools, training, or cash—the freedmen would have a difficult time making the transition from slavery to freedom as wage laborers.

Although many streams of abolitionist thought existed, it became increasingly difficult for members of the American Anti-Slavery Society to voice their opinions if they were perceived as counter to the ideas of William Lloyd Garrison. In Garrison's view, uncompensated, immediate emancipation was the only acceptable means of ending slavery; he believed that alternative strategies should not be promoted by the American Anti-Slavery Society.

In addition to his rigid stance on the proper form of emancipation, Garrison alienated other members of the society by articulating positions that many members considered extreme. Besides his attacks on the U.S. Constitution, Garrison began to discourage abolitionists from voting and taking part in the political process. Because he believed that a political solution to the slavery question could never be achieved and that the political process itself was structured and informed by the Constitution, Garrison discouraged democratic citizenship and instead promoted a form of Christian anarchism that some abolitionists saw as too revolutionary to support.

Garrison maintained that sustained appeals to reason could induce sinners to "come out" from the evil of slavery and accept the doctrine of abolitionism. He believed that such moral suasion would have more effect than the ballot box in bringing an end to slavery in the United States, and he openly advocated disunion over continued participation in a morally flawed political system that condoned and protected the flesh

trade. In addition to these views, his support for a variety of other reform causes concerned many society members who feared that the antislavery effort would be diluted by involvement in other causes of the era.

Factions already existed within the American Anti-Slavery Society by the late 1830s, and these differences would soon be exacerbated by an outright feud within the antislavery movement. The crisis became apparent in 1840 at the annual meeting of the American Anti-Slavery Society when Garrison arranged the election of Abby Kelley to the executive committee of the society over the objections of opponents who did not believe that a woman should serve in such a public capacity. This action was the opening salvo in a bitter dispute that would soon divide abolitionists on both sides of the Atlantic and hinder the progress of the antislavery movement in the United States.

Schism

In 1838, abolitionists in Great Britain celebrated the end of the apprenticeship system that had been instituted in the British West Indies as part of the Abolition of Slavery Act in 1833. Under that system of compensated, gradual emancipation, slaves in the British colonies served as apprentices for a transitional period of years before becoming totally free.

The victory in ending apprenticeship was largely the result of continual insistence by British abolitionists that Parliament investigate reports of abuse that emanated from the quasi-feudal labor arrangement. In 1836, Members of Parliament received a report from the Select Committee of Parliament, which had investigated the status of the apprenticeship system in the colonies at the urging of British antislavery advocates. Based on their success in hastening an end to apprenticeship, British abolitionists realized that they comprised a force that could continue to agitate against slavery in those areas where the practice persisted.

Buoyed by their success in the British West Indies, members of the British Anti-Slavery Society announced their intention to host a World Anti-Slavery Convention in 1840 and issued invitations to abolitionists throughout the transatlantic world to attend the gathering. Abolitionists in Britain believed that the opportunity to discuss methods and provide interregional support to ongoing antislavery efforts in the United States and elsewhere in the Americas was a natural outgrowth of a reform movement that had the abolition of slavery worldwide as its ultimate goal. Many British reformers had high expectations that the convention would usher in an era of transnational cooperation and civic consciousness, allowing abolitionists to address a host of social reforms that legislation alone had failed to remedy.

A group of abolitionists from the United States traveled to London to attend the World Anti-Slavery Convention in June 1840, but they were soon dismayed by the convention's policy of denying seats to the female abolitionists who had planned to participate in the deliberations. American abolitionists Abby Kelley and Lucretia Mott walked out of the convention in protest when they were denied seats as delegates, and Garrison showed his solidarity with the female abolitionists by refusing to participate in the meeting as well. In some respects, the poor

treatment afforded the female abolitionists encouraged the formation of the women's rights movement in the United States.

Some skeptical members of the American Anti-Slavery Society found Garrison's behavior more theatrical than substantive. Because of the timing of the World Anti-Slavery Convention, which took place in the midst of the litigation associated with the *Amistad* affair in the United States, prominent American abolitionists such as Lewis Tappan did not attend the convention. As the American Anti-Slavery Society was already experiencing internal dissension, some anti-Garrisonian abolitionists had worried that Garrison might stack the delegation with only like-minded supporters. These critics found Garrison's solidarity with the female delegates to be nothing more than showmanship at the expense of real dia-

British abolitionist Thomas Clarkson addresses the World Anti-Slavery Convention of 1840 in London. Benjamin Robert Haydon's painting of the event portrays many of the key figures among the nearly 500 British and U.S. delegates. *(Hulton Archive/Getty Images)*

logue, and a permanent schism erupted within the ranks of the American Anti-Slavery Society.

Some of the most prominent members of the abolitionist movement left the American Anti-Slavery Society in 1840. Theodore Dwight Weld broke with the Garrisonians concerning the tactics that should be used in the abolitionist movement. Weld, along with the Tappan brothers, established the American and Foreign Anti-Slavery Society, which hoped to salvage the idea of transnational cooperation that had been the centerpiece of the World Anti-Slavery Convention. Members of the new organization would work to establish close ties between the efforts of abolitionists throughout the transatlantic world.

Members of the American and Foreign Anti-Slavery Society disagreed with Garrison's position of disavowing political action and partisan politics to remedy the problem of slavery. Considering it expedient to make the antislavery cause a political issue in American national life, several non-Garrisonian abolitionists supported the establishment of the Liberty Party, a third-party political movement that was aimed exclusively at furthering the abolitionist agenda through the political process. The Liberty Party was formed during summer 1840, and it nominated James G. Birney as a candidate in the presidential elections of 1840 and 1844.

Garrison and the American Anti-Slavery Society continued to operate despite the departure of key allies in the antislavery movement. Rather than try to compromise and mend fences with the dissatisfied abolitionists, Garrison decided to move forward with his advocacy of the same unadulterated views he had expressed throughout the previous decade. In June 1840, the American Anti-Slavery Society began publishing the *National Anti-Slavery Standard* as its official journal; the publication espoused the cause of immediate emancipation for slaves.

Speaking Truth to Power

By their very nature, schisms do not strengthen a movement but instead serve to weaken it. The multiplicity of voices and positions that emerged within the ranks of abolitionists in the United States came at a time when the proslavery ideology of Southern slaveholders was being honed and fashioned into a singular expression of slavery as a benefit to society. Northern abolitionists would use a variety of tactics to counter the proslavery ideology and demonstrate the inherent evils associated with the South's "peculiar institution."

One of the most effective means of countering the views of Southerners who supported slavery and touted its benefits was to use the voices of other Southerners who presented an alternative view. This tactic was used in the publication of a tract titled *An Appeal to the Christian Women of the South* (1836), in which the South Carolina–born abolitionist Angelina Grimké urged the abolition of slavery and advocated social equality for free blacks. Her sister, Sarah Grimké, made the same appeal to moral suasion in her publication *An Epistle to the Clergy of the Southern States* (1836). In similar fashion, the Grimké sisters joined with Theodore Dwight Weld to produce *American Slavery As It Is: Testimony of a Thousand Witnesses* (1839), an attempt to present a documentary history—based on Southern newspaper accounts and eyewitness testimony—that would expose the true conditions of slavery in the South.

Another tactic that was used effectively by Northern abolitionists was the publication of slave narratives relating the first-person accounts of slaves who had endured the brutality of the system and could provide a rendering of the system from within. Several of these narratives were ghostwritten by white abolitionists who assisted illiterate fugitive slaves and injected heavy doses of the tender sentimentality that was associated with early nineteenth-century literature. The poignancy of the narrative as an abolitionist tool reached a new height when Frederick Douglass published his *Narrative of the Life of Frederick Douglass* in 1845. The autobiographical slave narrative, which Douglass wrote entirely on his own, was published with a preface written by William Lloyd Garrison and a letter by Wendell Phillips supporting its veracity.

Based on the success of Douglass's narrative, Northern abolitionists began to promote speaking tours in which articulate black abolitionists such as Douglass, William Wells Brown, and Henry Highland Garnet would recount the horrors of slavery in stark detail. Eventually, some of the black abolitionists conducted speaking tours in Britain to raise funds to support antislavery activities in the United States.

Partisan Politics

Garrison's refusal to participate in the political process set back the progress of abolitionism in the United States. By comparison, the success of British abolitionism was largely attributable to the fact that the most vocal antislavery advocates were parliamentarians who urged legislative consideration of the abolitionists' agenda. This began to change in the United States in December 1838 when Congressman Joshua Giddings took his seat in the House of Representatives; the Ohio Whig became the first abolitionist to be elected to the U.S. Congress.

Although the presence of Giddings and a few other abolitionist congressmen and senators did not tilt the balance of political power toward the antislavery cause, their participation in the political process did guarantee that all perspectives—especially the antislavery point of view—were considered within the halls of power, as national legislation was deliberated. Because the abolitionists remained a small but vocal minority in nineteenth-century America (they were considered representatives of the radical fringe), their participation in congressional debates was an achievement that was more than commensurate with their numerical strength.

In spite of the efforts of politically minded abolitionists, the dismantling of slavery in the United States appeared to be a Herculean task with little chance of success. The U.S. Constitution gave legal protection to slavery, and the mechanisms by which slavery operated were the prerogative of sovereign state governments. Within these constitutional strictures, there was little that politicians could do to influence slavery in the states where it existed legally, but they could try to limit its expansion into territories that were yet to be admitted as states. It would be in this arena that some of the greatest legislative battles of the antebellum era would be fought.

An Empire for Slavery

The U.S. government's decision to fight a war of aggression against Mexico in 1846 offered a galvanizing event for abolitionists. Upon the conclusion of the Mexican-American War in 1848, the United States acquired the vast Mexican cession territory, which amounted to one-sixth of the continental U.S. land area, and the question of the expansion of slavery suddenly became more than an academic discourse. The new lands in the Southwest offered the possibility that slavery might expand into the region. The thought of admitting additional slave states to the Union threatened the tenuous balance of power that existed in the country, and more people were drawn into the abolitionist camp by the specter of this possibility.

By shifting the focus of the debate from slavery itself to the expansion of slavery into the Western ter-

ritories, Northern politicians were able to parse the language of their positions in such a way that they did not appear to be in league with the radical abolitionists. In the simplest terms, the debate centered on power politics. Many in the North had long feared the existence of a "slave power conspiracy" that would dominate national political affairs and direct national development. For those who believed that such a conspiracy existed, the thought of adding new slave states in the Southwest portended a free state minority that would be helpless to counter the power of slaveholding interests.

The urgency of the question in 1848 could not be ignored. While the United States was considering the possible expansion of slavery into the Southwest, news arrived of France's decision to abolish slavery throughout the French West Indies. It became clear to many that emancipation was the wave of the future, and efforts to expand slaveholding territory seemed to fly in the face of reason and progress. Many also found it deeply troubling that the expansion of slavery into the Southwest, if realized, would reintroduce slavery into the area, as the Mexican government had abolished slavery throughout the region in its emancipation decree of 1829.

Democratic congressman David Wilmot of Pennsylvania had attempted to head off this controversy in 1846 by introducing a measure that would have prevented the expansion of slavery into any territory acquired as a result of the war with Mexico. Although the so-called Wilmot Proviso was defeated (on multiple occasions), it demonstrated the deep polarizing effect that slavery was having on national political life in the United States. The votes cast on the Wilmot Proviso were not based on party affiliation; rather, they were a clear indication of sectional sensibilities. Southerners, whether Whig or Democrat, tended to vote against the measure, whereas Northern politicians, regardless of party affiliation, tended to support the measure. From the point of the Wilmot Proviso onward, it became increasingly clear that the question of slavery's expansion was one of regional self-interest. The likelihood of finding a legislative compromise that would satisfy both sides was slim.

Bleeding Kansas

Northerners did fear the possible expansion of slavery into the Southwest, but those fears were largely unfounded. In the 1850s, none of the territories in the Southwest had populations large enough to seek statehood in the near future, and the climate and geography of the region seemed inhospitable to the expansion of slavery and plantation-based agriculture. Though many were apprehensive about what might happen in the Southwest, the key battleground of the debate would be the upper reaches of the Louisiana Purchase Territory, where the issue supposedly had been settled by the Missouri Compromise and the establishment of a boundary between slave and free territory at 36°30' north latitude.

In 1854, Illinois senator Stephen A. Douglas introduced the Kansas-Nebraska bill for consideration by the Congress. Douglas hoped to carve two new territories out of the upper portion of the Louisiana Purchase Territory. In order to facilitate the rapid settlement of these new territories, Douglas proposed that the question of slavery be left up to the residents who settled the territory.

Shortly after Douglas introduced his bill, six prominent abolitionists from the Northern states signed their names to a document titled "The Appeal of the Independent Democrats in Congress, to the People of the United States." The document allegedly was written by Salmon P. Chase of Ohio, and it was signed by Charles Sumner of Massachusetts, Joshua Giddings of Ohio, Gerrit Smith of New York, Edward Wade of Ohio, and Alexander De Witt of Massachusetts. The manifesto voiced strong opposition to the Kansas-Nebraska measure, which it described as a plot by slaveholders, and it is credited with galvanizing public sentiment in favor of the creation of the Republican Party.

The passage of the Kansas-Nebraska Act signaled a dangerous new turn in the debate over the expansion of slavery into the Western territories. By relying on popular sovereignty, whereby the vote of territorial inhabitants would determine the fate of slavery in the territory, the act set the stage for unparalleled lawlessness as proslavery and antislavery forces flocked to Kansas to affect the outcome of the vote that would be held there.

During the weeks and months leading up to the 1856 referendum in Kansas, the territory devolved into an area of internecine warfare, with both sides committing depredations on behalf of the supposed righteousness of their cause. As proslavery "border ruffians" from Missouri fought against antislavery "Jayhawkers" who had emigrated from Northern free states, a miniature civil war erupted in Kansas, demonstrating the failure of popular sovereignty. This volatile situation portended future danger if the United States could not resolve the divisive issue of slavery and its expansion.

Bucking the Trend

The policies that the United States enacted during the 1850s were at odds with events transpiring elsewhere in the transatlantic world. At the same time Americans were considering the expansion of slavery into the Western territories, other societies were moving away from slavery and adopting emancipation decrees. In the sister republics of the Western Hemisphere, the tide seemed to be shifting toward freedom, as nations ended the practice of slavery, which was viewed as a vestige of colonialism.

A program of gradual abolition of slavery initiated in Colombia during the early 1840s was completed by January 1, 1852, when all of that nation's remaining slaves were emancipated. Similar programs were implemented in Argentina, Ecuador, Paraguay, Peru, Uruguay, and Venezuela, as their national legislatures enacted measures to abolish slavery. It seemed as if a wave of emancipation sentiment was sweeping the Americas. After the Dutch abolished slavery in Suriname in 1863, only Brazil, Cuba, and the United States remained as large-scale slave societies in the Western Hemisphere.

In the United States, policy regarding slavery was largely driven by market forces. The value of cotton and a near-insatiable demand for the fiber by textile mills in New England, Britain, and France fueled the desire to bring more acreage under cultivation through slave-based plantation agriculture. Slavery remained viable and desirable in the U.S. South, because it was immensely profitable. Although some British abolitionists attempted to instigate a boycott of slave-produced cotton, British manufacturers did not succumb to the pressure. Moreover, small-scale attempts by some Quaker sects and other abolitionists to encourage a Free Produce movement did not gain sufficient support to change the market dynamic for Southern cotton.

The 1860 U.S. Census identified 393,975 Southerners as slaveholders, and they collectively possessed a total of 3.9 million slaves. At the same time, the average price paid for a slave field hand ranged between $1,200 and $1,800 in the U.S. South. With the profitability of cotton cultivation soaring, there appeared to be little hope that the emancipation of slaves would occur any time soon in the South.

And the War Came

Although Southern planters were enjoying immense profits from their slave-based agricultural pursuits, a growing sense of political paranoia led the region down a path of secession and disunion that would, in time, result in the abolition of slavery in the United States. By 1860, residents of the North and the South had grown suspicious of one another's political motives; each side viewed the other in monstrous form and hoped to impress its will on the nation. Northerners continued to fear the slave power conspiracy, while Southerners maintained that Northern abolitionists were bent on destroying slavery and the Southern way of life.

The election of Abraham Lincoln, the Republican presidential nominee, in November 1860 proved to be too much for proslavery Southerners, who considered Lincoln an abolitionist. Facing the imminent destruction of slavery—so Southerners believed—South Carolina was the first Southern state to secede from the Union on December 20, 1860, when it declared itself an "independent commonwealth." By February 1, 1861, six other Southern states had followed South Carolina out of the Union: Mississippi (January 9), Florida (January 10), Alabama (January 11), Georgia (January 19), Louisiana (January 26), and Texas (February 1).

The seceded states organized themselves into the Confederate States of America in February 1861. In the meantime, congressional negotiators tried to fashion a compromise that would protect slavery while dispelling the threatening specter of disunion, but all attempts to reach a negotiated settlement failed. Even as he delivered his first inaugural address on March 4, 1861, President Abraham Lincoln indicated there was still time for reconciliation, though he warned the Southern states that the threat of civil war rested on their actions.

When Confederate forces opened fire on U.S. forces occupying Fort Sumter in Charleston Harbor, South Carolina, the die was cast. The Civil War had begun.

Blue, Grey, and Black

The U.S. Civil War was a devastating conflict in which more than 600,000 soldiers were killed during four difficult years of battle. In addition, the wounds of war broke the bodies and spirits of many who survived the raging battles. In many respects, the animosities that divided the sides have not healed even to this day, nearly 150 years after the opening salvos were fired.

The war was responsible for the abolition of slavery in the United States. On January 1, 1863, Abraham Lincoln issued the Emancipation Proclamation, an executive order in which he freed the slaves in those areas that were still in rebellion against the forces of the U.S. government. The proclamation was followed by a congressional action to enact a Thirteenth Amendment to the U.S. Constitution in order to abolish slavery throughout the land. With these actions, and the successful conclusion of the war by U.S. forces, freedom came to an estimated 4 million slaves laboring in the states of the South.

The Emancipation Proclamation also authorized federal forces to begin using black recruits as soldiers during the Civil War. By the time the conflict ended, some 180,000 black soldiers had joined the U.S. Colored Troops, fighting valiantly to bring an end to slavery and free their fellow bondsmen from oppression. In many respects, the use of black troops during the Civil War was one of the most important actions that the United States could take to demonstrate its commitment to emancipation. It also provided African Americans an opportunity to prove their valor and courage by fighting for a cause that would bring liberty to millions.

Denouement: Fade to Black

Throughout the history of slavery in the transatlantic world, emancipation was achieved through a variety of means. The sustained campaigns that abolitionists mounted and the legislative enactments that followed were certainly influential in bringing freedom to the enslaved, but these formal methods were not the only actions to hasten the day of jubilee when emancipation would arrive.

For many slaves, self-emancipation was achieved through the courageous act of running away from slavery, or "stealing oneself away from slavery," as it was often described. Those who engaged in this deliberate act of emancipation were willing to risk their lives to attain the promise of freedom.

For other enslaved peoples, organized resistance was a means by which to effect an end to slavery. Although such tactics were seldom successful, they did, on occasion, produce the desired effect. The slaves who revolted in the French colony of Saint-Domingue and created an independent black republic in Haiti

The Emancipation Proclamation, an executive order by President Abraham Lincoln effective January 1, 1863, declared the freedom of all slaves in territories rebelling against the federal government. The original document is housed at the U.S. National Archives. *(Getty Images News/Getty Images)* were living proof that emancipation could be rendered through revolutionary means.

Regardless of how freedom was attained, emancipation was seldom achieved without the residual vestiges of slavery. The transition from a slave-based economy to a wage labor system was often difficult for the freedmen and freedwomen to navigate, and many became trapped in alternative modes of apprenticeship, peonage, and sharecropping that continued to exploit their labor and tax their souls. Governments that abolished slavery tended to have short memories and weak constitutions when it came to providing the blessings of liberty to the formerly enslaved.

Because slavery in the transatlantic world was largely based on racial identity—Africans and persons of African descent were enslaved by mostly white slaveholders—the badge of racial identity continued to be associated with servitude, and many freedmen and freedwomen faced racial discrimination in the aftermath of slavery. Unlike Russian serfs, who had been assimilated into mainstream society after they were emancipated in 1861, the physical attributes of the formerly enslaved in the transatlantic world did not allow such a smooth transition. Perceptions of inferiority on account of race followed many former slaves, as they made their way as freedmen and freedwomen.

The story of abolition and emancipation in the transatlantic world is one of hope and triumph, but it is a bittersweet tale. There is great promise in the realization that enlightened people came to understand the moral transgression of slavery and struggled to end it, but the society that produced the abolitionist was the same society that produced the proslavery apologist. In the broadest sense, neither could claim intellectual superiority over the other. Both individuals, though poles apart in their ideology, found common claim to history, tradition, law, and scripture in order to enunciate a position that justified their worldview, while savaging the beliefs of their opponents. The facts have a way of shattering the mythic view of self.

Junius P. Rodriguez

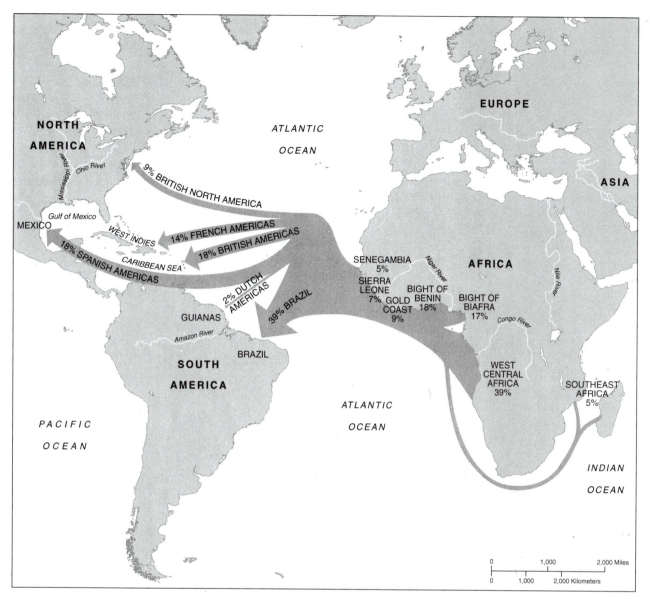

The transatlantic slave trade was a vast commercial enterprise that prospered for some 350 years, from the 1510s to the 1860s. Most of the slaves were captured in West and Central Africa, and transported by ship—the notorious Middle Passage—to South America and the Caribbean to work on plantations. Less than 10 percent were shipped directly from the African continent to the British colonies of North America or, after 1776, to the new United States. *(Cartographics)*

A–Z Entries

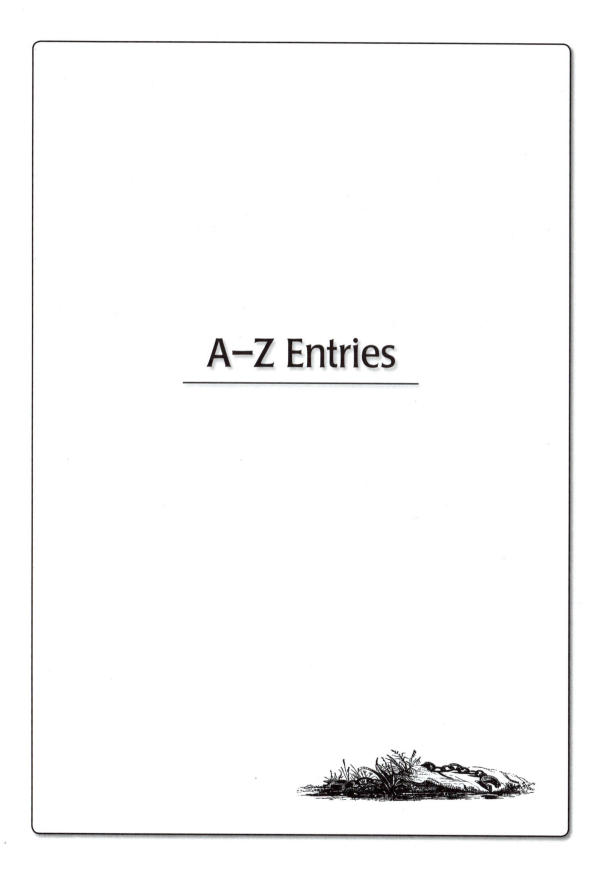

Abdy, Edward Strutt (1791–1846)

Edward Strutt Abdy, a fellow of Jesus College at Cambridge University, was a British abolitionist who visited the United States during the 1830s and recorded critical accounts of the American defense of slavery and the nation's racial attitudes. In 1835, Abdy published his observations in a three-volume work, *Journal of a Residence and Tour in the United States of North America, From April, 1833, to October, 1834.* Abdy witnessed firsthand some of the most violent antiblack and anti-abolition riots of the early nineteenth century, and his insights became especially valuable to the abolitionist movement.

The youngest son of the Reverend Thomas Abdy and Mary Hayes, Abdy knew a life of relative affluence. He was educated at Cambridge University, earning a bachelor's degree in 1813 and a master's degree in 1817, while being drawn into the growing British antislavery movement, a cause that had supporters in the halls of Cambridge. The young scholar developed a sense of radical egalitarianism that was uncommon within the abolitionist movement. Abdy felt a genuine sense of sympathy for both slaves and free blacks, and he recognized the shallow hypocrisy of many within the antislavery movement.

The primary purpose of Abdy's visit to the United States was to study the model of prison reform developed at New York's Auburn Penitentiary. Like his French compatriot Alexis de Tocqueville, Abdy used the pretense of his visit to fashion a grand tour of the United States, with travels taking him to New England, Washington, D.C., and several of the Western and Southern states. Unlike Tocqueville, however, Abdy spent much of his time in free black communities. The unique perspective that Abdy gained from this socioeconomic vantage point provided him with insights that most European visitors could never fathom.

Described by American Quaker Jacob Harvey as "our eccentric friend," Abdy spared few in his caustic commentary on antebellum American society. He criticized the trustees of the Manumission Society in

New York City for their double standard of paying black teachers less than white teachers for doing the same work in the "African" schools that the society sponsored. He found little to praise in America's democratic institutions after visiting a slave pen that was housed just half a mile from the U.S. Capitol. Abdy also criticized efforts by the American Colonization Society to relocate freed slaves to Liberia. He believed that such efforts were not in the best interest of free blacks, but only served to assuage white fears about the destabilizing effect that a free black presence might have on American society.

Though he occasionally wrote positive accounts of the way slaves were treated in some parts of the South—for example, he noted that planters and small farmers in Kentucky treated their slaves commendably—Abdy was scathing in his criticism of the manner in which free blacks were treated in the Northern states. After visiting Hartford, Connecticut, Abdy described it as one of the most disturbingly racist communities he had visited: "Some of [the blacks] told me it was hardly safe for them to be in the streets alone at night," he wrote. "To pelt them with stones and cry out nigger! nigger! as they pass seems to be the pastime of the place."

During his tour, Abdy witnessed eight days of antiblack and anti-abolition rioting that plagued New York City in July 1834. The disturbance began on the Fourth of July when a proslavery mob attacked an integrated antislavery society meeting that was being held at New York's Chatham Street Chapel, charging that the society supported racial amalgamation. Abdy was equally disturbed by the weak response that the American Anti-Slavery Society published in response to this attack, which focused on the society's defense against the charge.

Abdy later published the pamphlet *American Whites and Blacks in Reply to a German Orthodermist* (1842). In this pamphlet, he stated his view that the best solution to America's racial problem was to accept racial mixing, or miscegenation, rather than resist it.

Abdy died on October 12, 1846, in Bath, England. The unmarried scholar left his entire estate, estimated to be worth £500 (nearly $60,000 today—a large fortune at the time), to organizations promoting the antislavery cause in the United States.

Junius P. Rodriguez

See also: American Colonization Society; Anti-Abolition Riots; Racism; Tocqueville, Alexis de.

Further Reading

Abdy, Edward S. *Journal of a Residence and Tour in the United States of North America, From April, 1833, to October, 1834.* 1835. New York: Negro Universities Press, 1969.

Fladeland, Betty. *Men and Brothers: Anglo-American Antislavery Cooperation.* Urbana: University of Illinois Press, 1972.

Harwood, Thomas F. "Prejudice and Antislavery: The Colloquy Between William Ellery Channing and Edward Strutt Abdy, 1834." *American Quarterly* 18 (Winter 1966): 697–700.

Ableman v. Booth (1859)

In its decision in *Ableman v. Booth* (1859), the U.S. Supreme Court upheld the principle that state courts have no power to review or interfere with federal laws—in this case, the Fugitive Slave Act of 1850. The *Ableman* case was one of many attempts by the Northern states to protest and circumvent that legislation, which enabled slave owners to recapture runaway slaves by having them arrested under the federal law. *Ableman* was the last case in a line of state and federal legal battles—including *In re Booth* (Wisconsin, 1854), *U.S. v. Rycraft* (1854), *U.S. ex. rel. Garland v. Morris* (1854), and *In re Booth and Rycraft* (Wisconsin, 1855)—that focused on fugitive slaves.

Sherman M. Booth, the editor of Milwaukee's *Daily Free Democrat*, an antislavery newspaper, became embroiled in the *Ableman* case as a result of his perceived involvement in the escape of Joshua Glover, a slave. Glover had escaped from slavery in St. Louis, Missouri, in 1852 and fled to Racine, Wisconsin, where he lived until his capture in 1854. His owner, Benjamin Garland, was able to petition for Glover's arrest under the Fugitive Slave Act of 1850. Glover was apprehended and imprisoned.

While Glover awaited his trial, antislavery protestors in Racine, where he was being held, demanded his release. A group of Wisconsin abolitionists raided the Milwaukee jail and liberated Glover. It was believed that Booth and fellow abolitionist John Rycraft orchestrated the escape; both were arrested on March 11, 1854.

A federal marshal arrested Booth and charged him with violating the Fugitive Slave Act by abetting the escape of a slave. Because there was no federal prison in the area, the marshal placed Booth in a local jail. Booth appealed to the Wisconsin Supreme Court, believing that he would find more sympathy there for his abolitionist beliefs. (Wisconsin was one of several Northern states that had responded to the Fugitive Slave Act by passing a "personal liberty law" in an attempt to suspend the act's operation within its borders.)

Booth was released on a writ of habeas corpus (a petition to release an individual) issued by a judge of the Wisconsin Supreme Court, which ruled the federal law unconstitutional. U.S. district marshal Stephen V.R. Ableman, however, obtained a writ of error from the U.S. Supreme Court in order to have the state court's action reviewed.

The Supreme Court ruled unanimously to reverse the Wisconsin court's decision. Chief Justice Roger B. Taney's opinion denied state courts the right to interfere in federal cases, thereby upholding the supremacy of the U.S. government. Furthermore, the decision prohibited states from releasing federal prisoners through writs of habeas corpus and upheld the constitutionality of the Fugitive Slave Act.

Philine Georgette Vega

See also: Fugitive Slave Act of 1850; Personal Liberty Laws.

Further Reading

Swisher, Carl. *History of the Supreme Court of the United States: The Taney Period, 1836–1864.* New York: Macmillan, 1974.

Wiecek, William M. "Slavery and Abolition Before the United States Supreme Court, 1820–1860." *Journal of American History* 65 (June 1978): 34–59.

Abolition of Slavery Act (1833)

The Parliament of the United Kingdom, under the leadership of Prime Minister Earl Grey's Whig government, abolished slavery in the British Empire in 1833 with passage of the Abolition of Slavery Act (commonly known as the British Emancipation Act). Although the act called for slavery to be abolished, slaves were not actually freed until the following year, and some restrictions on their freedom continued to be imposed in the form of apprenticeships (periods of supervised labor designed to transition people from slavery to freedom).

The act marked the culmination of decades of struggle by British abolitionists and rebellious slaves. The abolition of slavery in the United Kingdom contributed to the dissolution of the sugar plantation economy in the British Caribbean and was a key step toward the abolition of African slavery throughout the Americas and elsewhere in the world.

Movement Toward Emancipation

Slavery and emancipation were decisive issues in the British parliamentary election of 1830, which reflected the strength of antislavery sentiment in many areas of the country. Voters elected to replace the Tories, who were generally viewed as sympathetic to slave owners, with the Whigs, led by Earl Grey.

In 1831, the new government conceded to abolitionist pressure by freeing slaves belonging to the Crown throughout the British Empire. In April of that year, however, a motion to take up the question of general emancipation, put forward by Thomas Fowell Buxton, the parliamentary leader of the abolitionists, was postponed as a result of government indifference. Prime Minister Grey's son, Henry George Grey, Lord Howick, who was then serving as undersecretary of state for the colonies and personally supported abolition, announced in Parliament that the government had no plans to carry the motion through.

The movement toward emancipation was accelerated by a revolt among Jamaican slaves in December 1831, known as the "Christmas Rebellion," and its bloody suppression by the planter-dominated Jamaican government. Some planters believed that the revolt would halt the abolitionist campaign and the activities of Protestant Dissenter missionaries in the West Indies, but instead, British antislavery forces responded by blaming the revolt on the planters' repressive measures and pressing for immediate emancipation. Antislavery pressure was rising throughout the country. Although most Whig leaders, including Grey, did not share the antislavery zeal of the abolitionist forces—indeed, some were absentee slave owners themselves—the government agreed that the West Indian situation pointed to a need for reform. Buxton responded by calling for a vote on immediate emancipation in the House of Commons in May 1832, but the motion lost at 162 votes to 90.

The Whigs' Great Reform Bill of 1832, which made the House of Commons more representative of the middle classes and the industrial towns, also decreased the parliamentary power of the West Indian interests. In the next general election, antislavery campaigners vigorously pressed their cause, distributing pamphlets and placards and breaking up proslavery meetings. Constituency groups required parliamentary candidates to pledge to work against slavery. After the election, the powerful speeches of Jamaican Baptist missionary William Knibb kept abolitionist sentiment high, particularly among Protestant Dissenters. Another important piece of antislavery propaganda, Henry Whiteley's *Three Months in Jamaica*, which detailed the atrocious ways in which slaves were treated in that country, was published in 1833.

The new Parliament, meeting in 1833, received antislavery petitions with more than a million and a half signatures. Proslavery interests were also active, organizing large demonstrations throughout the United Kingdom; however, the weakness of the proslavery movement lay in its inability to use traditional arguments to justify slavery as a civilizing or Christianizing institution. Instead, slavery apologists pragmatically argued that emancipation would destroy the West Indian sugar industry, causing untold damage to the British Empire.

The Whig government, which viewed some form of emancipation as necessary and desirable, was still not enthusiastic about the proposition, and it was particularly concerned with safeguarding the position of the West Indian planters as much as possible. Some hesitated, believing that slave emancipation was an attack on the property rights of slave owners—in the Whig view, government existed to protect property rights, not to attack them. The king's speech delivered at the ceremonial opening of Parliament on February 15, 1833, contained no reference to emancipation. (King William IV's personal opposition to emancipation was another cause of Whig hesitation.)

Outraged, Buxton responded by informing the Whig leaders that he intended to introduce another emancipation bill. The government managed to convince him to withdraw by promising to bring its own measure. In March, Buxton again threatened to bring a motion in order to prod the government. Government leaders were caught between the abolitionists in Britain and the representatives of the West Indian sugar planters and merchants, who were determined to hedge emancipation with restrictions that would ensure emancipation in name only and preserve preferred access to the British market for sugar. A committee representing the "West India interest" succeeded in blocking an emancipation plan that Howick proposed, provoking his resignation.

Formation of the Abolition Act

Britain's new colonial secretary, Edward George Geoffrey Smith Stanley, published a moderate plan for emancipation in the London *Times* on May 11, 1833. Three days later, parliamentary debate on slavery began as Buxton presented a new petition signed by 187,000 women.

The government's plan, explicated by Stanley in a speech given on May 14, attempted to achieve a balance between the need for some form of abolition and the demands of the planters. It provided the planters with a loan of £15 million as compensation for their lost property, a sum that was said to amount to ten years' profits. The newly freed slaves would be required to work for their former owners as "apprentices" for twelve years, committing three-quarters of their working hours each week. Slaves under the age of six would be freed immediately. The apprenticeship system, which was supported by the planters, had two main purposes: to ensure the continued social control of blacks and to keep a steady labor force on the sugar plantations.

The plan was unacceptable to parliamentary abolitionists, who viewed it as slavery under another name. Negotiations produced a compromise. The period of apprenticeship was cut to four years for domestic slaves and six for fieldworkers. The apprenticeships were to be overseen by salaried magistrates sent from Britain rather than local justices of the peace, who were usually drawn from the planter class. (In practice, many of the new magistrates proved more sympathetic to the planters than to the freed slaves.) To offset these changes, compensation for the planters was increased to £20 million and converted from a loan to an outright grant.

Some abolitionists were appalled by the apprenticeships and the compensation for the planters, but the parliamentary abolitionist leadership went along with these provisions to pass the bill. After receiving some minor amendments, the bill passed Parliament on August 29, 1833, to become effective August 1, 1834.

Although it was still necessary to obtain the consent of the local legislatures in colonies that possessed them, this was secured by making the payment of compensation contingent on the local legislature's passage of an emancipation act of its own. Despite the fears of many, which were encouraged by the proslavery interests, emancipation transpired without violence. (American abolitionists would later point to this as an example of how emancipation could be achieved peacefully.) Many slaves spent the day in church, and the event was recognized with public ceremonies in Britain.

William E. Burns

See also: Apprenticeship and Emancipation; Buxton, Thomas Fowell.

Further Reading

Barclay, Oliver. *Thomas Fowell Buxton and the Liberation of Slaves.* York, UK: William Sessions, 2001.

Craton, Michael. *Sinews of Empire: A Short History of British Slavery.* Garden City, NY: Anchor, 1974.

Kriegel, Abraham. "A Converging of Ethics: Saints and Whigs in British Antislavery." *Journal of British Studies* 26 (October 1987): 423–50.

Newbould, Ian. *Whiggery and Reform, 1830–41: The Politics of Government.* Palo Alto, CA: Stanford University Press, 1990.

Abolition of the Slave Trade Act (1807)

Considered one of the signature legislative achievements of the abolitionist forces in the transatlantic world, An Act for the Abolition of the Slave Trade, commonly known as the Abolition of the Slave Trade Act (or simply the Slave Trade Act), was passed by the British Parliament on March 25, 1807. Its passage set in motion a chain of events that would hasten the demise of slavery throughout the transatlantic world.

The British legislation, which was associated with simultaneous action by the U.S. Congress, announced a clear mandate to end the African slave trade, and the power and force of the Royal Navy supported the enforcement of such a policy. In the decades following the Napoleonic Wars (1799–1815), the British government would use diplomatic tact and moral suasion to convince other European powers to end the African slave trade as well.

Although Britain was not the first European power to end the slave trade—that distinction belonged to Denmark, which passed legislation banning the practice in 1803—the influence of the British action was immense, and it significantly hampered the viability of a continued transatlantic slave trade. Since the end of the War of the Spanish Succession

(1701–1714), when the British had won the *asiento* (the contract to deliver slaves to Spain's New World colonies) as a treaty concession, British slave traders had reaped huge profits from the African slave trade. This reality, coupled with an explosion in demand for slave labor associated with rising sugar cultivation during the eighteenth century, had made the British formidable participants in the nefarious trade. Parliament's action in 1807 dramatically changed the nature of the business of the African slave trade.

Abolitionists in Great Britain had been calling for an end to the African slave trade for nearly a generation before this act. Antislavery advocates such as Granville Sharp began lobbying Parliament to end the slave trade as early as 1776, but few policy changes resulted from these efforts. The West Indian lobby, an influential group of parliamentarians representing the interests of the sugar planters in the British West Indies, had enough influence in Parliament to quell any real consideration of the issues that the abolitionists raised for consideration. Although investigative committees were established to look into particular aspects of the African slave trade, few real changes resulted from these parliamentary inquiries. Perhaps the most notable action was the passage of Dolben's Act of 1788, which regulated the carrying capacity of slave ships in an effort to put a more humane face on the flesh trade.

Despite their initial failure to end the transatlantic slave trade, British abolitionists did succeed in mounting a successful and sustained propaganda campaign that educated legislators and the public about the abuses of the trade. Through public education campaigns designed to advocate the antislavery cause, abolitionists were able to inform their fellow citizens about the unseen horrors associated with the financially lucrative slave trade.

This propaganda often employed first-person accounts by Africans who had been transported in slaving vessels and described the abject horror of the Middle Passage across the Atlantic Ocean in vivid detail. Abolitionists also used compelling images, such as a schematic diagram of the slave ship *Brookes*, to reveal the less than wholesome conditions associated with "tight packing" on slave ships, as captains sought to maximize profits while paying little attention to the human misery that such practices wrought.

Over time, the campaign began to gain ground within the reform-minded segment of British society. Membership increased in the Society for the Suppression of the Slave Trade and other like-minded groups that sought to ameliorate the conditions of slavery by first abolishing the trade that transported Africans to the Americas as slave laborers. In addition, members of a growing body of parliamentarians, including many who hailed from the religious traditions of the Society of Friends (Quakers) and the Methodists, began to identify themselves as the Clapham Sect (or the Saints) and to voice opposition to the slave trade and slavery.

The West India lobby used parliamentary maneuvers to delay any legislative action against the African slave trade. Members of the opposition carefully avoided permitting a quorum in the House of Commons when they feared that antislavery legislation might be introduced. Despite these strategies, it was difficult to counter the support that Lord Grenville's government had lent to the support of the passage of a slave trade ban. The House of Lords passed the measure in a 100–36 vote during a rare 4 A.M. session, and the House of Commons gave its assent by a vote of 283–16 shortly thereafter. After both houses passed the measure, King George III gave his approval, and it became the law of the realm.

The British abolition of the African slave trade took effect on March 1, 1808, though slave trading vessels had been prohibited from leaving British ports beginning on May 1, 1807. The British abolitionist Thomas Clarkson, who had been involved in the parliamentary effort to enact the legislation, heralded the accomplishment by writing his *History of the Rise, Progress and Accomplishment of the Abolition of the African Slave Trade* (1808).

After the passage of the Slave Trade Act, British abolitionists did not relent in their advocacy; rather, they formed an organization called the African Institution to monitor the enforcement of the new law and to oversee the development of a settlement in Sierra Leone as a homeland for free blacks who chose to return to Africa. The organization also hoped to promote the development of alternative types of commerce between Great Britain and Africa.

Some abolitionists believed the abolition of the African slave trade would be the death knell for slavery, as the practice depended on a constant supply of imported Africans to sustain itself. Few believed that the slave populations in the colonies could sustain themselves through natural increase alone. Others posited that the abolition of the African slave trade might prompt slave owners in the Americas to treat their slaves better, because they would have to rely on natural increase to sustain a viable population of slaves to work on the colonial plantations and farms.

Still others recognized that the lucrative profits to be gained from transporting Africans—in spite of legislation that criminalized the practice and equated it with piracy—would tempt many to continue the trade illegally unless the parliamentary measure was strictly enforced.

Junius P. Rodriguez

See also: Clarkson, Thomas; Dolben's Act (1788); Sharp, Granville; Society for the Abolition of the Slave Trade.

Further Reading

Alvis, John. "The Slavery Provisions of the U.S. Constitution: Means for Emancipation." *Political Science Reviewer* 17 (Spring 1987): 241–65.

Carrington, Selwyn H.H. *The Sugar Industry and the Abolition of the Slave Trade, 1775–1810*. Gainesville: University Press of Florida, 2002.

Dowd, Jerome. "The African Slave Trade." *Journal of Negro History* 2 (January 1917): 1–20.

Klingberg, Frank J. *The Anti-Slavery Movement in England: A Study in English Humanitarianism*. New Haven, CT: Yale University Press, 1926.

Merrill, Louis Taylor. "The English Campaign for Abolition of the Slave Trade." *Journal of Negro History* 30 (October 1945): 382–99.

Williams, Eric. "The British West Indian Slave Trade After Its Abolition in 1807." *Journal of Negro History* 27 (April 1942): 175–91.

Abolitionist Confederation

Formed in 1883, the Abolitionist Confederation (*Confederação Abolicionista*) united a number of smaller antislavery organizations in the city of Rio de Janeiro, Brazil, and was one of the principal organizational expressions of mounting abolitionist sentiment during the late nineteenth century. It propagandized and agitated against slavery using both legal means, such as newspaper publicity and public rallies, and illegal channels, such as helping slaves flee their masters and establishing *quilombos*, or free communities of color.

Although measures that gradually restricted the scope of slavery had been introduced in 1871, the powerful slaveholding interests in the coffee- and sugar-producing regions of southeast Brazil remained intransigent, effectively blocking reform at the national level. Yet by the late 1870s, the 300-year-old system of slavery in Brazil was facing escalating challenges. The country had witnessed a significant increase in capitalist enterprises and free wage labor, and as a result, slavery had fewer and fewer defenders among the general population. Moreover, secular lib-

eral ideas of progress and civilization emanating from Europe and the United States were spreading, especially in the growing urban centers of the country. Many young urban professionals embraced these cosmopolitan ideas and formed the leadership of the abolitionist movement.

The most prominent abolitionist politicians, such as Joaquim Nabuco and Ruy Barbosa, emphasized the formal legal struggle to abolish slavery and aimed their moderate propaganda at the free masses rather than the slaves. Yet the stubbornness of the "slavocracy" and the broadening audience for antislavery ideas had encouraged a more radical strain of abolitionism by the mid-1880s. The leading black antislavery activists in Rio de Janeiro—José do Patrocínio, a fiery orator and highly respected journalist, and André Rebouças, a well-known engineer and writer—were deliberately harsher in their criticism of slavery, rejected the argument that slave owners should be compensated for freeing their slaves, and directed their messages at a much broader audience, including slaves.

The son of a white priest and a free black mother, Patrocínio was born in the interior of the state of Rio de Janeiro. He had graduated with a medical degree at the age of twenty, but his principal occupation was journalist. In 1875, he began to write for a daily newspaper in Rio de Janeiro and became involved in the abolitionist movement, penning antislavery articles and speaking at public events. In 1881, he bought the *Gazeta da Tarde (Afternoon Gazette)*, already the principal antislavery newspaper in the city, and increased its circulation through his fiery denunciations of slavery and commentary on the abolitionist movement. He gained fame as a captivating orator, drawing large audiences of blacks and mulattoes to the antislavery speeches he gave in public squares and popular meeting halls.

In the early 1880s, abolitionist organizations sprang up throughout the country within universities, professional associations, and cultural groups. In an attempt to coordinate the work of the many groups operating in Rio de Janeiro, Patrocínio, Rebouças, and the respected abolitionist João Clapp met with like-minded activists in the offices of the *Gazeta da Tarde* in May 1883 to form the Abolitionist Confederation. The organizations that made up the confederation reflected the diversity and broad-based support for the movement against slavery at the time. In addition to two general citywide organizations, the Brazilian Anti-Slavery Society and the Central Emancipation

Association, the new group brought together fifteen more organizations, including the Abolitionist Club of Employees in Commerce, the Freedmen's Club of Niterói, the Liberator of the Medical School, and the Liberator of the Military School.

Clapp was elected president of the confederation, and Patrocínio, Rebouças, and Aristides Lobo wrote the group's manifesto, which was read to an animated crowd of 2,000 people in the Dom Pedro II Theater. The manifesto was officially read in Parliament and subsequently published in the *Official Record*, which ensured it a national audience. The *Gazeta da Tarde* became the unofficial organ of the confederation until 1887, when Patrocínio's new newspaper, *Cidade do Rio (City of the River)*, became the leading publicity outlet of the abolitionist movement. Organizing frequent public gatherings, the confederation shared the Brazilian abolitionist movement's tendency to combine formal speeches with music and poetry on antislavery themes. Clapp also offered free night classes for slaves and free blacks.

Like most Brazilian abolitionist societies, the confederation's member groups and leaders had different opinions on strategies and tactics. Most of the groups in the confederation supported the abolition of slavery through legal campaigning, although their ideas had become more radical by the mid- to late 1880s. In addition to their respectable public agitations, many confederation members, including Patrocínio, were secretly involved in schemes to harbor escaped slaves in suburban quilombos.

By uniting activists and organizations in Brazil's most important city, the Abolitionist Confederation played a key role in coordinating the abolitionist movement in the crucial years before abolition was achieved in 1888. Reflecting a nationwide trend, its formal propaganda and work in condemning the ills of slavery and promoting the benefits of abolition gradually spilled over into more radical and clandestine activities.

Sean Purdy

See also: Brazil, Abolition in; Nabuco, Joaquim; Patrocínio, José do; Rebouças, André.

Further Reading

Conrad, Robert E. *The Destruction of Brazilian Slavery, 1850–1888.* Berkeley: University of California Press, 1972; 2nd ed., Malabar, FL: Krieger, 1993.
Toplin, Robert Brent. *The Abolition of Slavery in Brazil.* New York: Atheneum, 1972.

Adams, John Quincy (1767–1848)

American president, diplomat, secretary of state, and congressman, John Quincy Adams was neither an abolitionist nor an advocate of emancipation. Yet during his congressional years, Adams was a strong voice against slavery and the slave trade. In the course of his distinguished career, Adams opposed the Gag Rule in the U.S. House of Representatives and successfully argued before the U.S. Supreme Court in the celebrated *Amistad* case.

Early Life and Career

Born in Braintree (now Quincy), Massachusetts, on July 11, 1767, he was the eldest son of former president John Adams. Educated in Europe and the United States, he graduated from Harvard College in 1787. After completing studies in law, he began a career in the legal profession in 1790 in Boston.

Adams followed in his father's political footsteps when he was elected to the U.S. Senate in 1803. Though he was elected as a Federalist, Adams soon began to assert his independence, a move that eventually cost him his Senate seat.

He was appointed minister to Russia and was later sent to London as minister to Great Britain and Ireland by President James Madison. President James Monroe named Adams secretary of state in 1817, a post he filled with great distinction. Elected president in 1824, Adams advocated the American system of internal improvements; he also devoted a great deal of his administration to foreign affairs.

As president, Adams did not take a stand against slavery; in fact, during his administration, the United States signed a convention with the British to compensate Americans for confiscated slaves and property. But during the congressional debates over the Missouri Compromise in 1819 and 1820, Adams reflected on slavery as a foul stain. He considered the dissolution of the Union over the sole issue of slavery as necessary to resolve regional differences, and accurately predicted the U.S. Civil War. Known in his later years for his eloquence, Adams privately recorded his thoughts on slavery as the cause of the Civil War and applauded the eventual disappearance of slavery from the nation as its glorious consequence.

Adams abhorred slavery and the slave trade, and opposed any return of fugitive slaves; however, he found it expedient to keep those thoughts private while campaigning for the presidency. Yet he saw

ABOLITION FROWNED DOWN.

As a U.S. congressman, John Quincy Adams led opposition to the Gag Rule of 1836–1844, which barred House members from introducing antislavery petitions. He is portrayed in this 1839 cartoon lying on a pile of petitions and abolitionist literature. *(Library of Congress, LC-USZ62-9916)*

slavery as the greatest threat to the Union. Adams thought slavery immoral in light of the republican principles on which the nation had been founded. His strong belief in the U.S. Constitution and the rights of man formed the basis of what would become an intractable stance against slavery.

Congressional Years

After Adams's presidential term ended in 1829, he ran successfully for a seat in Congress in 1831 and served in the House of Representatives for the next seventeen years. As a Massachusetts congressman, Adams actively opposed slavery and the slave trade and assumed a leading role in the national struggle against the "peculiar institution." He openly attacked what he termed the "slavocracy"—those Southerners whose interest in maintaining slavery stood in opposition to his constitutional belief in the rights of man.

Once in Congress, Adams stood adamantly opposed to the Gag Rule, an 1836 congressional dictum that prevented citizens from presenting antislavery petitions in the House of Representatives. Adams felt that the Gag Rule was unconstitutional, violated the First Amendment right of petition, and violated House rules. Instead, he strongly believed in the right to petition Congress; on March 30, 1840, he presented as many as 511 separate petitions from women, free blacks, and slaves.

Associated with a group in the House that was unofficially termed the "Select Committee on Slavery," each week, Adams prepared to read petitions sent to him amid shouts of opposition and threats from proslavery colleagues. His persistence led members of Congress to consistently call for his censure and expulsion.

During his eight-year struggle against the Gag Rule, Adams earned the sobriquet "Old Man Eloquent" for his verbal attacks on the Gag Rule and on slavery in general. His sparring with Southerners Dixon Lewis of Alabama, Waddy Thompson of South Carolina, and Charles E. Haynes of Georgia was widely reported in the press. Year after year, he alone carried on the struggle until December 1844, when the congressional majority supporting the Gag Rule disappeared; by a vote of 108 to 80, the rule against the right of antislavery petition in the House was defeated.

Adams was never one to support the abolitionist movement, although he was well acquainted with many antislavery leaders. He committed to his diary his impressions of men such as William Lloyd Garrison, James G. Birney, and even Ralph Waldo Emerson, whom Adams saw as a failed preacher and schoolteacher. According to Adams, Garrison and the others were guilty of mixing religion and politics, and he viewed them as rascals. He was unimpressed with the movement, even though the abolitionists had supported Adams in his fight against the Gag Rule.

In 1841, Adams turned his attention to another antislavery cause, the *Amistad* case, which determined that a group of Africans who had been illegally abducted from Sierra Leone could not be held as slaves and had the right to return to their homeland. The Africans had revolted on the Spanish slave ship *Amistad* and were being tried in the United States for murder on the high seas.

Approached and encouraged by antislavery crusaders Lewis Tappan and Ellis Gray Loring, Adams agreed to argue on the Africans' behalf before the U.S. Supreme Court, although he had not practiced law in years. Adams once again proved his eloquence, arguing for more than four hours on February 24, 1841, and again on March 1.

Justice Joseph Story delivered the Court's decision on March 9, with only Justice Henry Baldwin dissenting. Story's decision brought an end to the *Amistad* affair, freed the slaves, and returned them to Africa. Few recognized the significance of the decision at the time, but the *Amistad* case remains a landmark decision in the annals of the Supreme Court.

On February 21, 1848, Adams suffered a stroke while speaking on the floor of the House of Representatives. He died two days later in the Capitol building in Washington, D.C.

Boyd Childress

See also: *Amistad* Case (1841); Gag Resolution.

Further Reading

Adams, John Quincy. *The Diary of John Quincy Adams, 1794–1845: American Diplomacy, and Political, Social, and Intellectual Life, from Washington to Polk.* Ed. Allan Nevins. New York: F. Ungar, 1951.

Bemis, Samuel Flagg. *John Quincy Adams and the Union.* New York: Alfred A. Knopf, 1956.

Miller, William Lee. *Arguing About Slavery: The Great Battle in the United States Congress.* New York: Alfred A. Knopf, 1995.

Wood, Gary V. *Heir to the Fathers: John Quincy Adams and the Spirit of Constitutional Government.* Lanham, MD: Lexington, 2004.

Adams, William Edwin (1832–1906)

William Edwin Adams was a radical British journalist who was drawn to the causes of republicanism, chartism, and abolitionism. Using his skills as a writer, he produced antislavery tracts to help convince members of the British working class of the solidarity between their plight and that of the sons and daughters of Africa who were enslaved.

Born into a family of humble origins, Adams grew up in the Cheltenham Spa region of southwestern England and became a self-taught journeyman printer. His rise to prominence within the radical reform movements of northeastern England was a reflection of the geographic and social mobility wrought by the industrial transformation of nineteenth-century Britain. Adams became the editor of the *Newcastle Weekly Chronicle*, a Tyneside publication that provided him with a forum in which to express his views on the pressing social questions of the day.

Adams claimed that he had been converted to the causes of republicanism and chartism, which advocated better social and industrial conditions for the working class, at the age of seventeen. The European revolutions of 1848 awakened a political consciousness in Adams, but he was not a typical radical of the period. His political philosophy was acquired more from reading than from any personal experience of the hostility of workplace conflict. In practice, Adams may have been a Cheltenham chartist, but the theoretical origins of his views were influenced largely by the revolutionary writings of American pamphleteer Thomas Paine and the political ideology of Italian patriot Giuseppe Mazzini.

Adams held a firm belief in the moral righteousness of republicanism. He believed that society could elevate itself through a system of morals and ethics emphasizing one's social duties rather than one's rights. Though many nineteenth-century radicals believed that social progress was attainable only through revolutionary means, Adams, who was often at odds with his own compatriots, held the hope that society could better itself through other means.

Chartism, a popular reform movement in Britain, supported the creation of a "People's Charter" to guarantee certain rights—universal male suffrage, ballot voting, annual parliaments, and equal representation—and to end the property requirements for Members of Parliament. Not all chartists supported the antislavery cause, though, as many perceived it to be a middle-class reform movement. On occasion, chartists disrupted the meetings of antislavery groups, arguing that British abolitionists cared more for the welfare of slaves than for the social conditions of the working poor in their own country. Adams was not alone in his support for both chartism and abolition. Joseph Sturge, a founder of the British and Foreign Anti-Slavery Society, was also actively involved in the chartist movement.

During the years of the U.S. Civil War, Adams used his editorial pen to convince readers that British support for the Southern Confederacy was not in the best interest of the working classes. In association with the Union and Emancipation Society of Manchester, Adams published the pamphlet *The Slaveholder's War: An Argument for the North and the Negro* in 1863. In this work, he argued effectively that cheap cotton would be less beneficial to British manufacturing in the long run than would the primacy of the doctrine that wage labor, freely given and duly compensated, was a universal social duty.

In addition to his views on republicanism, chartism, and abolitionism, Adams promoted other causes that were somewhat ahead of their time. Adams was an early environmentalist who held tremendous respect for the natural beauty of the countryside, and he was one of the first editors to rail against the degradation of the environment by industrial forces. He also used his columns to encourage a social movement against cruelty to animals.

Adams continued to support reform in late-Victorian Britain through his writing. After visiting the United States during the height of the Industrial Revolution, he published *Our American Cousins: Being Personal Impressions of the People and Institutions of the United States* (1883). He also wrote his autobiographical *Memoirs of a Social Atom* (1901), which discussed the various reform movements with which he had been associated.

Junius P. Rodriguez

See also: Paine, Thomas.

Further Reading

Adams, William E. *Memoirs of a Social Atom.* 1901. New York: Augustus M. Kelley, 1968.

Ashton, Owen R. *W.E. Adams—Chartist, Radical, and Journalist (1832–1906): An Honour to the Fourth Estate.* Whitley Bay, UK: Bewick, 1991.

African Institution

The African Institution was the premier national British antislavery group during the early nineteenth century. Its members included prominent lawyers, Members of Parliament, and British reformers such as William Wilberforce, Thomas Clarkson, and Zachary Macaulay. Dedicated to the abolition of the foreign slave trade, the spread of Western civilization to Africa, and the emancipation of slaves in the British colonies, the group's influence extended to Britain's diplomatic relations and the government's domestic affairs.

The African Institution carried the torch for antislavery reform from 1807 to 1823, when the Anti-Slavery Society assumed this role. The African Institution disbanded in 1827, after carrying the antislavery banner for nearly two decades and spawning a new generation of antislavery agitators.

Beginnings

In 1807, Great Britain abolished the slave trade in its colonial possessions. Hailed by abolitionists, the move nonetheless raised further questions, such as how the antislavery movement should progress. Leaders of the movement considered introducing bills for emancipation in Parliament, pushing for more direct intervention in Africa to cut off the slave trade at its roots, or establishing a naval blockade off West Africa to stop slave ships. British abolitionists could also exert moral pressure, with or without their government's approval, on countries still slaving.

In this environment, abolitionists began to discuss a new antislavery organization that would pick up the crusade from defunct groups such as the Abolition Committee. The outcome of these discussions was the African Institution.

The first organizational meeting of the African Institution was held on April 14, 1807. The leadership of the new group included virtually all of the important antislavery figures in Britain, such as Wilberforce, Clarkson, Macaulay, Granville Sharp, and William Allen. The group's purpose and plans were laid out at this gathering and then presented at its first public meeting in July 1807. Members resolved to do what they could to promote Africa's well-being, agreed to spread practical information about medical knowledge and agriculture throughout Africa, and determined to circulate information about Africa's agricultural and commercial prospects throughout Britain. Thus, the idea of "legitimate commerce" to replace the slave trade was already an issue for abolitionists.

Although it may have been naive to expect, as most abolitionists did, that the abolition of Britain's slave trade would naturally be followed by a period of development and civilization in Africa, the process of examining Africa and Britain's potential trade relationship was a reasonable one. Before legitimate commerce (as non-slave-based trade was called) could flourish, Britons needed to know the economic potential of the continent of Africa. As long as slaving was a legal enterprise, there was little economic incentive for European and American businessmen to foster any economic development within Africa.

Over the next few years, the group's focus began to change and expand. Exploiting their personal connections with Britain's top politicians, members of the African Institution managed to keep antislavery issues on (or close to) the front burner. From the beginning, however, the group was handicapped by a lack of financial resources. Although many wealthy people donated money to the organization, it simply never commanded the kind of fiscal power that was necessary to carry out its most ambitious plans. The African Institution wished to promote Western education in Africa, but it could barely afford to send books and could not support its few teachers for any length of time.

To encourage British interest in African products, the African Institution hoped to facilitate the cultivation of cash crops—hemp, cotton, and rice—in order to demonstrate Africa's potential. The group offered incentives to those who imported African products, but the quantities imported proved to be insignificant. In addition, few people even took advantage of the incentives.

Early on, the organization realized that the key to meeting its goals was the enforcement of antislavery laws that had been passed in Britain and other countries. With its key members in Parliament, the African Institution exerted considerable influence on its own government on Africa-related issues, but it was much more difficult for the group to pressure foreign governments.

Nonetheless, foreign slave trading became a major issue for the organization and for Britain; at the Congresses of Vienna (1814–1815), Aix-la-Chapelle (1818), and Verona (1822), the group kept British diplomats on task in pursuing abolition with other European countries and well supplied with antislavery literature. Some successes can be traced to the group's diligence, as other European powers slowly abandoned their slave trades and set up joint admiralty courts to try those accused of illegal slaving.

Efforts in Sierra Leone

The African Institution's efforts to support African development were most noticeable in Sierra Leone, which provided a true testing ground for development programs. Slaves freed from seized slave ships were usually landed there by the African Squadron that patrolled the waters of West Africa, providing a regular influx of new settlers. The African Institution had a voice in selecting the first governors of the colony after it came under the control of the British Crown in 1807. The group corresponded regularly with these governors, sending school supplies and books whenever possible.

As in other matters, the attention given to Sierra Leone by the African Institution meant that the British government would follow developments there carefully. Though the colony was fairly stable politically and viable economically by the late 1820s, historians debate how much credit the African Institution deserves in these areas.

The abolitionists envisioned a Sierra Leone based on individual farmers working independently on small farms. These free farmers would form the basis of a successful agricultural economy. Key to the success of this idea was the regular arrival of new settlers. If the government were to sponsor a mass transportation of free blacks from the Western Hemisphere, the hopes of the reformers might become a reality. This surely would have helped the colony, but there were no such plans.

A free black American named Paul Cuffe, however, was willing to lead such an expedition, and he had prospective colonists lined up to resettle in Sierra Leone. The African Institution supported Cuffe as much as possible, intervening on his behalf with the British government to make his efforts more fruitful and easier to complete. Ultimately, Cuffe brought thirty-four immigrants, but the War of 1812 and Cuffe's death in 1817 prevented further projects.

Shift in Focus

After Cuffe's failure to settle more than a handful of new residents in Sierra Leone, the African Institution began to turn its attention away from practical activities, such as colonization and agricultural projects, and toward political battles against the injustices of slavery and, later, the institution of slavery itself. Group members began closely monitoring slave conditions in the West Indies, advocating the creation of slave registries in all of the West Indian colonies. These registries, the abolitionists believed, would not only improve the condition of slaves indirectly but also would help stop illegal slave importing.

The African Institution also began gathering information on slave trading in East Africa and the Indian Ocean. Antislavery supporters had never paid much attention to these areas, and the group was the first to consider it. The organization carried on a detailed correspondence with Henri Christophe, Haiti's first and only black king. Political realities prevented the British government from recognizing Christophe as a legitimate ruler, but the African Institution provided moral support and even arranged for several teachers to go to Haiti. Christophe's success would have been a sizable boost to the abolitionist agenda—a successful, independent black king ruling his own territory in an "enlightened" fashion—but the king was overthrown and murdered in 1820.

The primary goals of the African Institution were only partly fulfilled, at best. The group's close personal connections with the British government did not ensure that all of its plans would be carried out, but its ties did allow the group to make its agenda a part of national planning and international concern. Its work was taken up by other British antislavery groups, including the Anti-Slavery Society, which was formed by Clarkson, Wilberforce, and Macaulay to help emancipate slaves in the West Indies, and the British and Foreign Anti-Slavery Society, which was formed in 1840.

Wayne Ackerson

See also: Clarkson, Thomas; Cuffe, Paul; Sharp, Granville; Sierra Leone; Wilberforce, William.

Further Reading

Ackerson, Wayne. *The African Institution (1807–1827) and the Antislavery Movement in Great Britain.* Lewiston, NY: Edwin Mellen, 2004.

Davis, David Brion. *The Problem of Slavery in the Age of Revolution, 1770–1823.* Ithaca, NY: Cornell University Press, 1975; New York: Oxford University Press, 1999.
Temperley, Howard. *British Antislavery, 1833–1870.* London: Longman, 1972.

African Squadron

The African Squadron was a unit of the British Royal Navy that was assigned to patrol the coast of Africa during the nineteenth century as part of that nation's broad effort to suppress the slave trade. The flotilla was established as part of the British government's 1808 decision to dispatch two vessels to the western coast of Africa in order to enforce legislation that banned the slave trade within the British Empire. The squadron eventually comprised more than thirty ships that monitored both the eastern and western coasts of the continent.

In 1807, Parliament passed An Act for the Abolition of the Slave Trade (commonly known as the Slave Trade Act) to end the slave trade within the British Empire. To enforce the new measure, a small naval force was dispatched to the western coast of Africa, the main point of departure for the slave trade. Initially, the ships were ordered to interdict only British vessels engaged in the slave trade.

Because British ships supplied the largest number of slaves, the ban on the slave trade should have led to a dramatic reduction in the transatlantic trade. With Britain's energies focused on fighting the French and its allies during the Napoleonic Wars, however, successive governments had few resources and little early enthusiasm to vigorously enforce the ban. Nevertheless, under pressure from abolitionist groups, the British government steadily increased its efforts to end the trade. In 1811, Parliament made it a felony to participate in the slave trade. In addition, a system to deal with captured vessels and newly freed slaves was put in place.

With the end of the Napoleonic Wars in 1815, Parliament authorized an increase in the size of the African Squadron. Nonetheless, until the 1840s, the flotilla averaged only six ships. This small force patrolled more than 2,000 miles of coastline along western Africa. Duty in the African Squadron was not regarded as a prestigious assignment. In fact, many officers and crew members perceived the deployment as among the worst in the Royal Navy because of the harsh climate, the threat of tropical disease, and the monotony of the patrols, with few ports or opportunities to go ashore. During the first decades of the

African Squadron
UNPARALLELED SUCCESS.

" The *Bonnetta* has been 2 years and 11 months in commission, and is now ordered to be paid off at Chatham. The Commander, Lieutenant FORBES, has been employed during the past year in negociating with the King of Dahomey, in the endeavour to establish a Treaty for the **Abolition of the Slave Trade** throughout his territory, **but which failed. His Majesty** reviewed his Troops during Commander FORBES' sojourn with him, and they are spoken of as well disciplined, though 4000 out of 10,000 of the Soldiery are Women, clothed as Men, who perform in every respect as well as their male companions in Arms'. His Majesty, as a **mark of His especial favour,** presented Commander FORBES with a **Juvenile Princess.** At the '**Customs**' (a sort of **Religious** rite), **30 Human Sacrifices** were offered to their Deity; two of these (soldiers from Attapahme,) Commander FORBES purchased for **100 dollars,** and sent to Fernando Po to be liberated.

THE SLAVE TRADE WAS VERY BRISK."

(Portsmouth Paper.)

This is in the 35th year since the Act for the Abolition of the Slave Trade passed, and after Eighty Millions of money have been spent.

These are the Majesties Queen Victoria's name is degraded by being brought into contact with.

SILLY JOHN BULL, to be gulled, and TO PAY HALF A MILLION A YEAR for a peep at FEMALE ARMIES and JUVENILE PRINCESSES! Instead of a Bonnett(a), don't you deserve a foolscap–a?

* What diplomatic tact in LORD PALMERSTON to send the commander of " *The Bonnett(a)*" as ambassador. With his usual gallantry he had not forgotten what would please female troops.

An 1842 broadside for Britain's African Squadron claims success in patrolling thousands of miles of the African coastline. The small fleet was charged with enforcing Parliament's ban on slave trading. *(Manuscripts, Archives and Rare Books Division, Schomburg Center for Research in Black Culture, The New York Public Library, Astor, Lenox, and Tilden Foundations)*

squadron's operation, from the time of its creation until 1840, some 2,200 British sailors died while serving with the unit, most as a result of disease.

The colony of Sierra Leone was the first base of operations for the African Squadron, and freed slaves were released in the territory. Sierra Leone was also home to the courts that tried those suspected of participating in the slave trade, as well as the admiralty courts that decided the fate and value of ships seized by the African Squadron. When ships from the squadron captured suspected slave vessels, a trial was held to determine whether the ship was indeed being used to transport slaves. If the crew or owners were found guilty, the officers and crew of the African Squadron received prize money from the sale of the slave ship and a bounty for each freed slave. Parliament later passed an "equipment clause" that allowed the ships of the Royal Navy to seize suspected slave vessels if they were rigged to transport slaves, even if they were not carrying human cargo at the time.

The squadron's effectiveness increased dramatically as the British government was able to negotiate treaties with other nations that allowed the ships of the Royal Navy to stop and search foreign vessels. In 1815, Portugal signed a treaty with Great Britain that allowed the African Squadron (or other British ships) to interdict Portuguese slave ships operating north of the equator. The refusal of the Portuguese to allow the British to search vessels south of the equator prompted Parliament to pass the Palmerston Act of 1839 and the Aberdeen Act of 1845, measures that gave the Royal Navy the unilateral authority to stop and seize suspected slave ships from Portugal and Brazil.

Through persistent diplomacy, by 1840, all of the world's major states had signed treaties with Great Britain—allowing them to search suspected slave ships—with the exception of the United States. In 1842, as part of the Webster-Ashburton Treaty, the United States established a system of joint patrols with the squadron, known as "joint cruising," which allowed for the interdiction of vessels sailing under the American flag. In 1863, the Washington Treaty went a step further, granting the British unconditional power to stop and seize U.S. slave ships.

Meanwhile, officers of the African Squadron began to negotiate treaties and agreements with individual African rulers to force an end to the supply of slaves. When indigenous leaders resisted British initiatives, the African Squadron used military force to destroy slave corrals on shore or to depose proslavery chiefs. In some cases, merely the threat of force or blockade was sufficient to end the trade. In 1877, for example, the British threatened a naval blockade of Zanzibar, leading the sultan there to agree to close the area's slave market. One broad result of these tactics was the tacit expansion of British influence along the western coast and, eventually, the eastern coast of Africa.

As the area the squadron patrolled increased, the size of the flotilla grew as well. By the 1840s, the Royal Navy had more than thirty ships on patrol as part of the squadron. As the size of the squadron increased, so, too, did its costs. By the 1860s, the British government had spent more than £8 million to deploy the unit. Within Great Britain, many began to criticize the high cost of the squadron, both financial and human. In 1850, a bill was introduced in Parliament to withdraw the ships, but it was soundly defeated.

It is difficult to assess the overall impact of the squadron. By the 1830s, the squadron was capturing an average of thirty slave ships and freeing more than 5,000 slaves per year on the western coast of Africa. On the eastern coast, the squadron had less success and freed, on average, about 1,000 slaves per year, until 1880, when the Portuguese established a joint naval patrol system with the squadron around their colony of Mozambique.

Some contemporary scholars estimate that the squadron captured one of every five or six slave ships commissioned. Others contend that the figure was closer to one in ten. Many have argued that once the squadron succeeded in stopping the trade in one area, slavers simply relocated down the coast.

Nonetheless, the squadron provided the main deterrent to the transport of slaves. As more nations abolished slavery and increased their cooperation with the squadron through combined patrols, the trade slowly ended. Combined with British diplomacy, the African Squadron served as the main instrument in closing down the African external slave trade.

Tom Lansford

See also: Sierra Leone.

Further Reading

Eltis, David. *Economic Growth and the Ending of the Transatlantic Slave Trade.* New York: Oxford University Press, 1987.

Fladeland, Betty. *Men and Brothers: Anglo-American Antislavery Cooperation.* Urbana: University of Illinois Press, 1972.

Howell, Raymond. *The Royal Navy and the Slave Trade.* New York: St. Martin's, 1987.

Lloyd, Christopher. *The Navy and the Slave Trade: The Suppression of the African Slave Trade in the Nineteenth Century.* London: Longman, Green, 1949; London: Frank Cass, 1968.

Miers, Suzanne. *Britain and the Ending of the Slave Trade.* London: Longman, 1975; New York: Africana, 1975.

Temperley, Howard. *British Antislavery, 1833–1870.* London: Longman, 1972.

Ward, William. *The Royal Navy and the Slavers.* New York: Pantheon, 1969.

Alexander, George William (1802–1890)

As the longtime treasurer of the British and Foreign Anti-Slavery Society, George William Alexander helped coordinate an international effort to eradicate the slave trade and slavery. According to Frederick Douglass, Alexander spent more of his own personal fortune than any other abolitionist on either side of the Atlantic to rid the world of the scourge of slavery.

A member of the Society of Friends (Quakers), Alexander was attracted to the evangelical fervor of the antislavery movement. In his zeal to bring an end to the slave trade and slavery, Alexander never wavered from the religious orthodoxy of the abolitionist crusade.

Alexander took issue with American abolitionists, whom he believed were expanding the reform agenda too much by including women's rights and "other extraneous subjects." He feared that these additional causes, worthy though they might be, took away from the primary goal of the abolitionist movement and therefore threatened to weaken it.

Upon the deaths of Thomas Fowell Buxton in 1845 and Thomas Clarkson in 1846, Alexander emerged, along with John Scoble and Louis Alexis Chamerovzow, as a leader in the British abolitionist movement. As second-generation leaders, Alexander and his colleagues faced the task of making manifest the parliamentary victories that their predecessors had obtained through earlier campaigns. The persistence of the African slave trade and the continuing presence of chattel slavery in the United States, Brazil, Cuba, and other locations made it clear that the work of abolition was far from complete.

Alexander embarked on a series of fact-finding missions to observe the successes that the abolitionists had won and to place pressure on recalcitrant governments to live up to their treaty obligations to suppress the African slave trade. Alexander visited France, Spain, and Portugal, using his personal diplomacy of moral suasion to convince those governments that it was in their best interest to enforce their own laws and satisfy their treaty obligations. In 1850, Alexander visited the West Indies to collect data on the successful implementation of the apprenticeship programs that had been established there to transition freed slaves to their new roles as emancipated free laborers. At the conclusion of each trip, Alexander presented a detailed report to the British and Foreign Anti-Slavery Society.

Upon returning from the West Indies, Alexander visited the United States as the U.S. Congress was debating a controversial body of legislation that became known as the Compromise of 1850. Alexander observed some of the congressional debates and held private meetings with antislavery advocates, including Senators Salmon P. Chase and John Hale, as well as Representatives Joshua Giddings, William Slade, and Horace Mann. Alexander also met with President Zachary Taylor at the White House. Abolitionist editor Gamaliel Bailey hosted a reception for Alexander and his colleagues before they departed for Britain.

Despite Alexander's efforts, the U.S. Congress passed the Compromise of 1850, which included the Fugitive Slave Act. The law required government officials and citizens to assist in the recovery of fugitive slaves and denied fugitives the right to trial by jury. The federal law was extremely unpopular among British abolitionists, and they protested loudly against the measure.

In 1865, Alexander responded directly to charges that had been leveled against the British abolitionists by Governor Edward John Eyre of Jamaica. Eyre had precipitated a massacre that took the lives of 400 Jamaicans when he called on the army to quell what was essentially a minor disturbance. Eyre defended his actions by placing the blame on the "pseudo-philanthropists" of Exeter Hall—the home of the British evangelical movement for many years— who had supported equal rights for former slaves.

Alexander responded to Eyre in a letter that was published in the *Anti-Slavery Reporter.* He wrote, "I think it is exceedingly unbecoming in the Governor of a Colony thus to stigmatize persons who had been, it was true, instrumental in procuring the abolition of slavery in the British West-India colonies; and, I hope, in leading to the abolition of slavery throughout the world."

Junius P. Rodriguez

See also: Jamaica, Emancipation in; Quakers (Society of Friends); Women's Rights and the Abolitionist Movement.

Further Reading

Oldfield, John R. *Popular Politics and British Anti-Slavery: The Mobilization of Public Opinion Against the Slave Trade, 1787–1807.* New York: St. Martin's, 1995.
Walvin, James. *Making the Black Atlantic: Britain and the African Diaspora.* New York: Cassell, 2000.

Aliened American, The

The Aliened American was a weekly antislavery newspaper published in Cleveland, Ohio, from 1853 to 1857. It is recognized as one of the earliest newspapers in the United States published specifically for an African American audience.

At the time of its publication, *The Aliened American* was one of only a few abolitionist newspapers published west of New York. The motto of the paper, which appeared below its masthead, identified its purpose: "To Furnish News: To Favor Literature, Science, & Art: To Aid the Development, Educational, Mechanical, and Social, of Colored Americans: To Defend the Rights of Humanity."

William Howard Day, a black abolitionist, was the founder and editor of *The Aliened American.* Other prominent black abolitionists, including James W.C. Pennington and Samuel Ringgold Ward, were frequent columnists who provided editorial insight on the issues of the day. The tone of the newspaper emphasized the self-help theme that was being popularized by the so-called National Negro Convention movement of the 1850s, which centered on the National Negro Conventions as a forum for blacks to discuss social issues. The newspaper concentrated on how the free black population of Cleveland might assist the many fugitive slaves who arrived in the city hoping to obtain passage across Lake Erie toward freedom in Canada.

Day was born and raised in a free black household in New York but moved to Ohio to attend Oberlin College, where he graduated in 1847. While he was a student at Oberlin, Day participated in antislavery activities. He drafted a resolution criticizing the governor of Maryland for failing to pardon the Reverend Charles T. Torrey, an antislavery martyr, before he died in a prison cell in May 1846. Day also took part in a sustained campaign to overturn the "Black Laws" of Ohio, which were designed to keep free blacks out of the state by restricting their liberties and freedom of movement.

Day worked as a printer on the *Northampton Gazette* in Northampton, Massachusetts, for several years before arriving in Cleveland. Motivated by the publication of *The North Star,* the antislavery newspaper edited by Frederick Douglass, Day first became editor of the *Cleveland True Democrat* (1851–1852) and later founded *The Aliened American,* which he edited for two years.

The Aliened American served a growing free black population in Cleveland during the 1850s. Day and other abolitionists railed against Ohio's Black Laws. Many free blacks who lived in southern Ohio migrated northward to cities such as Cleveland as the fear of kidnapping by renegade slave catchers became a very real danger. Many of the free blacks living in Cleveland were involved both formally and informally with the work of the Underground Railroad and efforts to assist fugitive slaves making their way to freedom.

The Aliened American appeared at a historic juncture, when it was important for Cleveland's free black population to have unfettered access to information through the black press. With the passage of the Fugitive Slave Act in 1850, conditions for fugitives in Ohio became quite tenuous. The newspaper was also able to report on important issues of the day, including the passage of the Kansas-Nebraska Act in 1854, the subsequent formation of the Republican Party, the events transpiring in "Bleeding Kansas," and the U.S. Supreme Court's infamous 1857 *Dred Scott* decision.

Junius P. Rodriguez

See also: Day, William Howard.

Further Reading

Cramer, Clarence Henley. *Open Shelves and Open Minds: A History of the Cleveland Public Library.* Cleveland, OH: Press of Case Western Reserve University, 1972.

Allen, Richard (1760–1831)

Richard Allen was a social reformer, opponent of slavery, and founder and first bishop of the African Methodist Episcopal (AME) Church, the first African American denomination. During his adult life until his death in 1831, Allen affirmed the rights of African Americans and attacked the institution of slavery.

Allen was born into slavery in Philadelphia in 1760, and when he was seven years old, his family was sold to a Delaware farmer, Stockley Sturgis. At the age of seventeen, two momentous events occurred in Allen's life: First, his mother and three of his siblings were sold. Second, he had a religious awakening and secretly joined a local Methodist group.

The young Allen was attracted to Methodism because of its opposition to slavery and its clear explanation of the Bible. Sturgis also had a religious stirring and hoped to free his slaves, but debt prevented him from doing so. Nevertheless, he allowed Allen to work extra hours to purchase his freedom and that of his brother. In 1783, Richard Allen became a free man.

Allen performed odd jobs in many East Coast communities, and he preached on the Methodist circuit in New Jersey, Pennsylvania, and Rhode Island. Based on his sound reputation, the first General Conference of the Methodist Church, held in 1784, accepted him as a "minister of promise." In 1786, he returned to his birthplace, where he preached

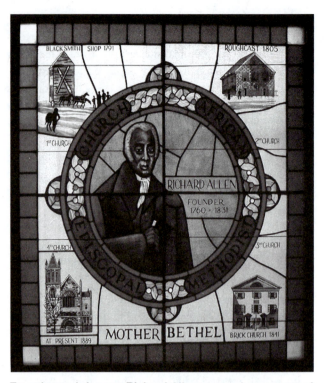

Founder and deacon Richard Allen, a vocal opponent of slavery, is memorialized in a stained glass window at the Bethel African Methodist Episcopal Church in Philadelphia. Opened in July 1794, Bethel AME was the first African American church in the United States. *(Photo by Martha E. Hall, courtesy of www.ExplorePAHistory.com)*

intermittently at the mostly white Saint George Methodist Church. Allen's preaching was effective and popular, and the number of African American parishioners soon increased.

Allen noted the need for a separate black church, independent of white authorities, but the Methodist Church rejected his request. This prompted Allen and Absalom Jones, the first black man to be ordained as a priest in the Episcopal Church, to found the Free African Society in April 1787. The organization was a nondenominational mutual aid society established to provide social services to needy African Americans. In November 1787, after being forcibly removed from Saint George's "white section" (outside the black segregated area) during a prayer time, Jones, Allen, and other black members left the church. In 1791, this group established the African Episcopal Church of Saint Thomas. Allen declined their request to be the church's first pastor because of his Methodist roots.

In 1793, a yellow fever epidemic struck Philadelphia, killing 5,000 people. Allen and Jones formed groups to help the city through the crisis, but unfortunately, the black community was criticized for "profiting" from the tragedy, since the mortality of whites was greater than that of the free black population. In *A Narrative of the Proceedings of the Black People, During the Late Awful Calamity in Philadelphia*, published the same year, Allen and Jones defended the black community.

In July 1794, Allen established the Bethel African Methodist Episcopal Church and was ordained as its deacon. After Bethel was officially initiated at the 1796 Methodist conference, white Methodist officials began to attempt to exert control over Allen's church. However, an 1816 Pennsylvania Supreme Court ruling held that because Bethel owned the property on which the church operated, it had the right to determine who would preach there.

Allen's example inspired many blacks to form AME churches in other northeastern cities. The AME Church became an important institution for both free and enslaved blacks, demonstrating that blacks could organize themselves outside the traditional white church hierarchy. The AME Church infused the everyday lives of blacks with a sense of community and helped many slaves transition from bondage to freedom. Indeed, the basement of the Bethel Church was a stop on the Underground Railroad, and the church's congregation regularly collected money to secretly assist fugitive slaves.

With the Bethel Church established and growing, Allen began to focus on antislavery efforts and published several works on the subject. In *An Address to Those Who Keep Slaves and Approve of the Practice* (1794), Allen attacked the idea of slave inferiority, arguing that slave behavior was the result of the institution of slavery, not race. He compared the slave's struggle to the struggle of the Israelites. Allen's *To the People of Color* (1794) attempted to provide hope for slaves and demonstrated that free blacks should be helping the enslaved. Another pamphlet praised key white men who had assisted the African American community.

In 1816, the AME Church was formally founded, and Allen was elected its first bishop. During this time, the American Colonization Society (ACS) proposed that all free blacks emigrate or be expelled from the United States to Africa. Allen opposed the ACS's position, believing that he had the right to stay in the country he had helped to build. As the ACS's position became more popular, Allen organized a meeting of 3,000 people at the Bethel Church to affirm that free blacks should have the same rights as other U.S. citizens. He defended his position in the *Freedom Journal*, America's first black newspaper.

By 1830, Allen's reputation in the black community was well established, and he presided over the convention of the Free Persons of Colour Congress in Philadelphia. At that meeting, black delegates from six Northern states formed what became known as the National Negro Convention movement, which sponsored yearly conventions dedicated to advancing the lives of blacks. Conventions focused on organizing boycotts of slave-produced goods, ending segregated travel in public coach transportation, and improving educational opportunities.

By the time of Allen's death in 1831, the AME Church had grown into an international institution, with members in Canada, Haiti, and West Africa.

Kelly J. Baker

See also: American Colonization Society.

Further Reading

Klots, Steve. *Richard Allen: Religious Leader and Social Activist.* New York: Chelsea House, 1991.

Walker, Clarence E. *A Rock in a Weary Land: The African Methodist Episcopal Church During the Civil War and Reconstruction.* Baton Rouge: Louisiana State University Press, 1982.

Wesley, Charles H. *Richard Allen: An Apostle of Freedom.* Ed. James L. Conyers, Jr. Trenton, NJ: Africa World Press, 2000.

Allen, Richard (1803–1886)

Richard Allen was a Dublin Quaker who became involved in a number of philanthropic reform movements in early-nineteenth-century Ireland. Although he earned his living as a draper and tailor, he spent much of his time editorializing on humanitarian issues in Irish newspapers. Chief among his reform efforts was the encouragement of Irish support for abolitionism.

Allen first became involved in the antislavery movement through his membership in the Irish Society of Friends. In 1821, Irish Quakers began to raise money to support antislavery efforts. In 1824, they sent an antislavery petition with 175 signatures, including Allen's, to the British Parliament. This activity helped spur the development of formal antislavery societies in Ireland; even after British emancipation in 1833, interest in the cause of slavery continued among Irish activists.

Allen was a member of the Irish antislavery societies from the beginning, and in 1837, he became secretary of the new Hibernian Anti-Slavery Society, which was formed to attack apprenticeship, the repressive labor system that had replaced slavery in the West Indian colonies after British emancipation. Allen was a central figure in this society during its early years. He served as a delegate to a meeting of the Central Negro Emancipation Committee in London in November and December 1837, and he organized a network in Ireland to petition against apprenticeship in Parliament. He instituted weekly meetings of the Hibernian Anti-Slavery Society at the Royal Exchange in Dublin, providing a forum for discussion of a broad range of reform topics, and he was active in corresponding with various newspapers concerning antislavery.

After the abolition of apprenticeship in 1838, the Hibernian Anti-Slavery Society began to promote the antislavery cause in America. Allen joined this effort during the early 1840s. He attended the 1840 World Anti-Slavery Convention in London and, along with other members of his society, aligned himself with the American Garrisonian abolitionists. (This approach to abolition, established by *Liberator* publisher William Lloyd Garrison, called for the immediate, uncompensated emancipation of and equal rights for blacks.)

Allen entertained various American abolitionists who visited Ireland, and in 1841, he was instrumental in the creation of the famous "Irish Address," an entreaty from Ireland to Irish Americans to support the cause of the slave. Approximately 60,000 Irish signatures appeared on the *Address From the People of Ireland to Their Countrymen and Countrywomen in America*, including those of prominent Irish leaders such as temperance advocate Father Theobald Mathew and nationalist leader Daniel O'Connell. The address failed to attract Irish Americans to the movement, but it was a significant transatlantic undertaking on behalf of American slaves.

Despite his association with the Garrisonians, Allen was less attached to them than were some of his antislavery colleagues in Dublin, and he worked to minimize divisions within the abolitionist movement in Ireland. He maintained close friendships with several members of the conservative British and Foreign Anti-Slavery Society, which had rejected Garrisonian abolitionism. In the late 1840s, Allen sent money to the British group, as well as to Frederick Douglass's Rochester Anti-Slavery Bazaar, after Douglass had broken from the Garrisonians.

Above all, Allen wished to remain true to Quaker tenets in his antislavery activity. In the early 1840s, he became less active in the Hibernian Anti-Slavery Society as Richard Davis Webb became its primary spokesman, advocating an uncompromising Garrisonian approach to antislavery. Though he served time on the Quaker Famine Relief Committee in the late 1840s and early 1850s, urging the group to reject aid from American slaveholders, Allen remained relatively quiet on the antislavery front until the U.S. Civil War.

After the war, Allen became energetic in his efforts to aid American freedmen, and he participated in the British Freedmen's Aid movement. In 1883, three years before his death, Allen visited the United States, where he toured black educational and religious institutions in the South and met with Frederick Douglass.

Angela F. Murphy

See also: Apprenticeship and Emancipation; Hibernian Anti-Slavery Society; O'Connell, Daniel; Webb, Richard Davis.

Further Reading

Harrison, Richard S. "Irish Quaker Perspective on the Antislavery Movement." *Journal of the Friends Historical Society* 56 (Spring 1991): 107–25.

Oldham, Ellen M. "Irish Support of the Abolitionist Movement." *Boston Public Library Quarterly* 10 (October 1958): 175–87.

Allen, Stafford (1806–1889)

Stafford Allen was a leading British industrialist and financier who served for half a century as a patron of the British and Foreign Anti-Slavery Society. Having earned enormous profits from his pharmaceutical business and iron foundry, Allen believed in the moral dictum that wealth must serve a higher calling. An early proponent of the social gospel, he worked tirelessly to promote the cause of abolition.

The son of Samuel Allen and Phebe Lucas, Stafford was born in Stoke Newington, Middlesex, England. Raised as a member of the Society of Friends (Quakers), Allen was attracted to the evangelical fervor of the antislavery movement. Buoyed by religious enthusiasm and blessed with business acumen, Allen devoted his time and treasury to bringing an end to the slave trade and slavery. Allen never wavered from the religious orthodoxy of the abolitionist crusade as he supported the movement for five decades.

In 1833, Allen founded the pharmaceutical company Stafford Allen and Sons in Suffolk. The business was involved in the production of flavors, fragrances, pure drugs, and essential oils, and Allen's company specialized in working with sandalwood oil and cloves. The company grew throughout the nineteenth century; in the decades following Allen's death in 1889, it became a multinational corporation. (Through mergers and acquisitions, the company became known as Bush Boake Allen in 1966 and then was acquired by International Flavors and Fragrances, Inc., in 2000.)

For a time, Allen was also involved in the operation of an iron foundry in Middlesex. Although this was never his primary business interest, the foundry did profit as railroad development in Britain grew during the 1840s.

Allen was present at the 1840 World Anti-Slavery Convention in London, which was attended by delegates from the United States and Great Britain. He was one of the abolitionists immortalized in Benjamin Robert Haydon's famous painting memorializing the event, *The Anti-Slavery Society Convention* (1841).

In addition to his work with the antislavery movement, Allen devoted himself to other social causes. During the Franco-Prussian War of 1870, he served as a member of the home Executive and Foreign Commissioners of the War Victims' Fund of the Society of Friends. In addition, medicine produced by Stafford Allen and Sons was donated to aid the victims of the conflict.

Allen's involvement in the antislavery movement reflected the stewardship and personal development associated with the crusade for social justice worldwide. The work of abolition was expensive, but donations from individuals such as Allen helped make the movement viable.

Junius P. Rodriguez

See also: Quakers (Society of Friends); World Anti-Slavery Convention (1840).

Further Reading

Fisher, Miles Mark. "Friends of Humanity: A Quaker Anti-Slavery Influence." *Church History* 4:3 (September 1935): 187–202.

Fladeland, Betty. *Men and Brothers: Anglo-American Antislavery Cooperation.* Urbana: University of Illinois Press, 1972.

Thomas, Allan C. "The Attitude of the Society of Friends toward Slavery in the Seventeenth and Eighteenth Centuries." *Papers of The American Society of Church History* 8 (1897): 263–99.

Allen, William G. (ca. 1820–ca. 1880)

Forced to flee the United States in 1853 because of the virulent racism that he faced, the abolitionist, author, and educator William G. Allen resettled his family in England. He and his wife continued their antislavery activities by teaching and lecturing throughout Great Britain.

A Virginian, Allen was the son of a mulatto mother and a Welshman. When his parents died, he was adopted by a free black couple. Recognizing the boy's intellectual abilities, Allen's adoptive parents asked for financial assistance from abolitionist Gerrit Smith to fund his education. Allen graduated from New York's multiracial Oneida Institute in 1844.

Upon graduation, Allen moved to Troy, New York, to teach school and to co-edit Henry Highland Garnet's *National Watchman*, an abolitionist newspaper. In 1847, Allen moved to Boston to study law. He became secretary of the Colored Citizens' Association and participated in the National Negro Convention movement, which centered on the National Negro Conventions, a forum in which blacks could discuss social issues affecting the African American community.

Allen began to give public lectures on the history, literature, and destiny of the African race and published his first pamphlet, *Wheatley, Banneker and Horton*, in 1849. The following year, he was appointed professor of Greek language and rhetoric and belles lettres at Central College in McGrawville, New York; he was one of only three black faculty members at this mixed-race college. Allen had become an outspoken lecturer and letter writer: He reprimanded Lajos (Louis) Kossuth, the popular Hungarian patriot who was then touring the United States, for his anti-emancipation stance, and he questioned Harriet Beecher Stowe for supporting slave immigration to Africa.

In 1852, Allen became engaged to Mary King, a white student at New York's Central College. Her father, a Baptist minister and abolitionist, approved of the marriage, but her brothers and stepmother were virulently opposed. Rumors of their engagement ignited a mob of several hundred men armed with "tar, feathers, poles, and an empty barrel spiked with shingle nails." In early 1853, the couple fled to New York City, where they married and immediately set sail for England.

Allen later detailed these experiences in two pamphlets, *The American Prejudice Against Color: An*

Authentic Narrative, Showing How Easily the Nation Got Into an Uproar (1853) and *A Short Personal Narrative* (1860). Allen's accounts, which focus on the persecution that he and Mary faced, illustrate the fears about amalgamation that often sparked violent protests in antebellum America.

With letters of introduction from Gerrit Smith, the Allens were welcomed by the British and Foreign Anti-Slavery Society, which helped them embark on a lecture tour of England. Allen spoke out on conditions in the United States, focusing on topics such as American slavery and the social and political conditions of free blacks in America's Northern states.

Despite being well received and meeting British people of influence, as well as visiting with American abolitionists, Allen was not a very successful lecturer, perhaps because of the competition he faced from other escapees, such as William and Ellen Craft and William Wells Brown. For a while, he lectured on behalf of Lady Byron's causes, including her interest in prison reform and the establishment of schools, but he could not earn enough to support a growing family.

Probably in 1855, the Allens moved to Dublin, where Allen continued to lecture and began tutoring. Although they were well received and obtained the support of Richard Webb (the Irish nationalist and abolitionist), and Allen published another book, *The African Poets Horton and Placido* (1858), the family returned to England.

Back in London, Allen joined the Emancipation Committee that had been established to aid John Anderson, another escapee, in migrating to Liberia, Africa. Allen gave an address at the farewell meeting that the British and Foreign Anti-Slavery Society held for Anderson. Through this work, he met the philanthropist Harper Twelvetrees, who helped raise funds to establish a school in which the Allens would teach.

Opened in June 1863, the Caledonian Training School, located in the working-class district of Islington, attracted many students. Assistant teachers were employed to cater to the school's 150 pupils. The venture ultimately failed, however; Allen tried merging his institution with a willing local academy, but this also proved unsuccessful.

The Anti-Slavery Association and Quaker abolitionists again organized support for the Allens. When Mary decided to open a school for girls, the British and Foreign Anti-Slavery Society printed a testimonial, and sufficient funds were raised for a new school. But the school only attracted about twenty to thirty pupils, and, in 1869, the Allens were again forced to seek support to help pay the rent. By this time, their eldest son was working for the publisher Cassell, and their eldest daughter was assisting in the school.

Evidently the girls' school also folded. By 1878, the Allens were living in a boardinghouse in the working-class district of Notting Hill, heavily dependent on charity.

Marika Sherwood

See also: Garnet, Henry Highland; Smith, Gerrit; Webb, Richard Davis.

Further Reading

Elbert, Sarah, ed. *The American Prejudice Against Color: William G. Allen, Mary King, Louisa May Alcott.* Boston: Northeastern University Press, 2002.

Alton Observer   *See* Lovejoy, Elijah P.

Alvord, John Watson (1807–1880)

John Watson Alvord is best known as the general superintendent of education for the Bureau of Refugees, Freedmen and Abandoned Lands (commonly known as the Freedmen's Bureau) and the founder of the failed Freedman's Savings Bank.

Born on April 18, 1807, to James H. and Lucy (Cook) Alvord in Easthampton, Connecticut, Alvord reached adulthood as the antislavery movement was gaining momentum, and he played an important role in its spread. After attending the Oneida Institute in Whitesboro, New York, Alvord entered the Lane Theological Seminary in Cincinnati, Ohio. There, he became a part of what became known as the "Lane Rebellion." When Lane students were told that they must disband their antislavery society, a group of them left the school in 1834.

Most of the so-called Lane Rebels went to Oberlin College in Oberlin, Ohio. Alvord helped establish the Oberlin Anti-Slavery Society and was a member of that school's first graduating class in 1836; shortly thereafter, he was ordained as a minister in the Congregational Church.

While in Ohio, Alvord became a commissioned agent of the American Anti-Slavery Society, working to recruit new members to the society. He also became an active antislavery lecturer, and he was once kidnapped by proslavery advocates who opposed his abolitionist activities. After graduating from Oberlin, Alvord served as superintendent of six black schools in Cincinnati.

Over the next decade, Alvord served as a pastor in churches in Connecticut and Boston. In 1852, he resigned as pastor of Phillips Church of Boston and became secretary of the American Tract Society. At the beginning of the American Civil War, Alvord moved to Washington, D.C., to direct the circulation of tracts among Union soldiers. He eventually began following the troops and started his educational work among freedmen and women in Savannah, Georgia, after it fell to Union forces in December 1864.

In 1865, Alvord was appointed general superintendent of education for the Freedmen's Bureau by his fellow Congregationalist and friend General Oliver O. Howard. The Freedmen's Bureau was a U.S. government agency that was responsible for helping formerly enslaved African Americans make the transition from slavery to freedom, distributing aid to the destitute, and redistributing land. Although education was not initially intended to be a part of the bureau's charge, this was the area in which it was most successful.

As superintendent of education, Alvord was responsible for all aspects of education in the former Confederate states. Believing that access to education would ensure the quick assimilation of African Americans into the larger Anglo-American society, Alvord played a central role in the establishment of a black school system throughout the South. The bureau helped build more than 1,000 schools and worked in conjunction with mutual aid societies to provide books and transportation for teachers arriving from the North.

Alvord played a key role in the establishment of the Freedman's Savings and Trust Company (also known as the Freedman's Savings Bank) in 1865 and served as its first president. In many ways, Alvord viewed the bank as a continuation of his earlier missionary work among the freedmen and women. Like the schools, the banks were established to encourage thrift, piety, and temperance among the freed slaves. However, Alvord's lack of business experience contributed to the bank's downfall, allowing speculators to gain control of the board of trustees, lobby the U.S. Congress for a change in its charter, and begin investing in real estate. Thousands of freedmen and

women lost their life savings when the bank failed in 1874 amid speculation of incompetence and fraud.

The failure of the Freedman's Savings Bank ended Alvord's long career in reform. In 1879, he moved to Denver, Colorado, to live with his sons; he died on January 14 the following year.

Stephanie R. Wright

See also: Education of Former Slaves; Freedmen's Bureau; Howard, Oliver Otis.

Further Reading

Alvord, John. *Semi-Annual Reports of Schools for Freedmen, 1866–1870.* New York: AMS, 1980.
Lesick, Lawrence. *The Lane Rebels: Evangelicalism and Antislavery in Antebellum America.* Metuchen, NJ: Scarecrow, 1980.
Osthaus, Carl. *Freedmen, Philanthropy, and Fraud: A History of the Freedman's Savings Bank.* Urbana: University of Illinois Press, 1976.

Amendments, Reconstruction

At the conclusion of the U.S. Civil War, three amendments to the U.S. Constitution were passed that pertained directly to slavery and African American civil rights. The Thirteenth, Fourteenth, and Fifteenth amendments outlawed slavery, granted citizenship to blacks, and guaranteed African Americans the right to vote, respectively. These three amendments are often referred to as the "Reconstruction Amendments," because they were drafted by the Republican majority in the U.S. Congress with the goal of extending civil rights to former slaves.

Although these amendments did represent a step forward in establishing the civil rights of African Americans, the Fourteenth and Fifteenth amendments left open the possibility of poll taxes, literacy tests, grandfather clauses (which exempted voters from restrictions if their grandfathers had voted), and racial gerrymandering (legislative redistricting) to prevent blacks from voting. These and other practices were used during and after Reconstruction to disenfranchise blacks in the South.

Thirteenth Amendment

The Emancipation Proclamation, issued by President Abraham Lincoln in 1863, had freed only those slaves who inhabited states that were still in rebellion against the Union. Because Lincoln was not legally empowered to single-handedly end the institution of slavery,

A contemporary illustration in *Harper's Weekly* depicts the celebration in Congress after passage of the Thirteenth Amendment to the U.S. Constitution—which officially abolished slavery—on January 31, 1865. Final ratification came in December. *(Hulton Archive/Getty Images)*

the document had to be followed by a constitutional amendment in order to guarantee slavery's complete abolition.

The Thirteenth Amendment, which was ratified by the states in December 1865, only eight months after the end of the Civil War, permanently abolished slavery in the United States. Section 1 of the amendment states, "Neither slavery nor involuntary servitude, except as a punishment for crime whereof the party shall have been duly convicted, shall exist within the United States, or any place subject to their jurisdiction."

Owen Lovejoy, an Illinois congressman and abolitionist and the brother of the martyred abolitionist Elijah P. Lovejoy, drafted the original language of the Thirteenth Amendment. The measure was introduced in the House of Representatives on December 14, 1863, by Ohio congressman James M. Ashley, who believed that in light of the issuance of the Emancipation Proclamation and the Union military victories at Vicksburg and Gettysburg, the time was right to remove the stain of slavery from the Constitution.

Despite such well-intentioned timing, the amendment did not easily pass both houses of Congress. Although the Senate passed it in April 1864 with a vote of 38–6, the required two-thirds majority could not be mustered, and the measure was defeated in the House of Representatives by a 93–65 vote. The Democratic minority in the House strongly opposed its passage, maintaining that the amendment would weaken states' rights.

President Lincoln took an active role in pushing the amendment through Congress, insisting that it be added to the Republican Party's platform for the upcoming presidential elections. His efforts to convince Democrats to support the amendment's passage ultimately succeeded, and the House passed the bill in January 1865 with a vote of 119–56. Lincoln supported the congressmen who insisted that Southern state legislatures adopt the Thirteenth Amendment before their states would be allowed to return to Congress with full rights.

Section 2 of the amendment authorized Congress to enact "appropriate legislation" to enforce slavery's termination. Less than a year after the ratification of the Thirteenth Amendment, Congress used its newly conferred power to pass the Civil Rights Act of 1866, giving black citizens "the same right in every state" to make and enforce contracts; to sue and be sued; to provide evidence in court; and to inherit, purchase, lease, sell, and hold personal property.

In an effort to further black civil rights, the Radical Republicans in Congress, led by Thaddeus Stevens, the party's floor leader in the House, passed sweeping legislation during the Reconstruction years, including the Civil Rights Act of 1870. They also fought for the passage of the Fourteenth Amendment, which guaranteed due process and equal protection under the law to all citizens and granted citizenship to blacks. Despite these successes, Congress failed to adopt a slavery reparations bill that Stevens proposed in 1867, thus indicating that there were limits to how far it would go in rectifying the ills of slavery.

Fourteenth Amendment

The Fourteenth Amendment, ratified in July 1868, is broken into five sections. Section 1 relates most directly to slavery and abolition, declaring that all persons born or naturalized in the United States are citizens of the United States and their state of residence. It also forbids states from making or enforcing laws that abridge the privileges or immunities of its citizens; depriving any person of life, liberty, or property without due process of law; and denying any person equal protection under the law. The remaining four sections account for the full representation of black citizens, the restriction of civil rights for particular individuals during periods of rebellion, and the recognition of public debts incurred by the states during the Civil War.

An immediate result of the Fourteenth Amendment was that it overturned the U.S. Supreme Court's decision in *Dred Scott v. Sandford* (1857), in which Chief Justice Roger B. Taney ruled that neither enslaved nor free blacks were citizens of the United States. Taney had based his decision on the original meaning of citizenship outlined in the Constitution, which he interpreted as inapplicable to all blacks, whom he described as "a subordinate and inferior class of beings, who had been subjugated by the dominant race, and, whether emancipated or not, yet remained subject to their authority, and had no rights or privileges but such as those who held the power and the Government might."

With the exception of Tennessee, all of the Southern states refused to ratify the Fourteenth Amendment. In response, Congress passed a series of Reconstruction Acts during the 1860s, demanding that the former Confederate states ratify the Fourteenth Amendment and revise their state constitutions before they could be re-admitted to the Union.

Like the Civil Rights Act of 1866, Sections 1 and 2 of the Fourteenth Amendment attempted to redress the discrimination of the Black Codes— laws passed by Southern governments during the Johnson Administration to impose severe restrictions on freed slaves, such as prohibiting their right to vote, forbidding them to sit on juries, and preventing them from working in certain occupations. The amendment empowered blacks to exercise their citizenship.

The amendment did not specifically address blacks' right to vote. It did, however, penalize those states that deprived black men of suffrage by reducing their representation in Congress in proportion to the number of male voters denied the right to vote.

Fifteenth Amendment

Most of the Democratic-controlled Southern states prohibited the vote for freed slaves and freeborn blacks, who tended to sympathize with the Northern Republicans because of their perceived antislavery policies and efforts during Reconstruction. Eager to break the Democrats' stronghold on the Deep South, Republicans in several states introduced the Fifteenth Amendment in 1869.

The Fifteenth Amendment, ratified in March 1870, made it illegal to abridge an individual's right to vote based on race or previous enslavement. Section 1 states, "The right of citizens of the United States to vote shall not be denied or abridged by the United States or by any State on account of race, color, or previous condition of servitude." The amendment granted the federal government the right to legislate qualifications for voting, a right that was formerly under the jurisdiction of the states.

Following the passage of the Fifteenth Amendment, Southern blacks began to vote in unprecedented numbers, and more blacks were elected to political office from 1865 to 1880 than during any other time in American history. Although the amendment prohibited the states from depriving any person of the right to vote because of race, it left open other types of disenfranchisement based on sex, property ownership, literacy, and payment of a poll tax. Many Southern states adopted rigorous voter qualification laws that required literacy tests (voters were asked to read a section of the U.S. Constitution) and imposed poll taxes, though voters could receive an exemption if they could prove that one of their grandfathers had been eligible to vote. It would not be until the 1960s that the full protections guaranteed by the Fifteenth Amendment would take effect. Federal courts outlawed the use of the literacy test, the Twenty-Fourth Amendment prohibited the use of poll taxes, and the Voting Rights Act of 1965 did away with all other roadblocks that local and state officials had fashioned to stymie African American citizens' right to vote.

The controversial presidential election of 1876 marked the end of Reconstruction, the restoration of white rule, and the beginning of an oppressive social system that would come to be known as "Jim Crow."

Nevertheless, the Reconstruction Amendments—especially the Fourteenth Amendment—transformed the Constitution from a document concerned primarily with federal–state relations into a vehicle by which blacks and other minorities could realize a substantive level of freedom and seek protection against misconduct by all levels of government.

Michael Pasquier and Gina Misiroglu

See also: Civil Rights Act (1866); Civil War, American (1861–1865); *Dred Scott* Case (1857); Lovejoy, Owen; Reconstruction.

Further Reading

Avins, Alfred, comp. *The Reconstruction Amendments' Debates: The Legislative History and Contemporary Debates in Congress on the 13th, 14th, and 15th Amendments.* Richmond: Virginia Commission on Constitutional Government, 1967.

Curtis, Michael Kent. *No State Shall Abridge: The Fourteenth Amendment and the Bill of Rights.* Durham, NC: Duke University Press, 1986.

Fehrenbacher, Don E. *Constitutions and Constitutionalism in the Slaveholding South.* Athens: University of Georgia Press, 1989.

Higginbotham, A. Leon, Jr. *Shades of Freedom: Racial Politics and Presumptions of the American Legal Process.* New York: Oxford University Press, 1996.

Maltz, Earl M. *Civil Rights, the Constitution, and Congress, 1863–1869.* Lawrence: University Press of Kansas, 1990.

Richards, David A. *Conscience and the Constitution: History, Theory, and Law of the Reconstruction Amendments.* Princeton, NJ: Princeton University Press, 1993.

American and Foreign Anti-Slavery Society

Formed in 1840 as a result of a schism in the U.S. abolitionist movement, the American and Foreign Anti-Slavery Society represented the conservative wing of the movement. Its members feared what they perceived to be the radicalism of William Lloyd Garrison's approach and hoped to distance the abolitionist movement from the question of women's rights.

Origins

From its founding in Philadelphia in 1833, the American Anti-Slavery Society was the only national organization in existence to lead the concerted abolitionist effort in the United States. Under the strong leadership of Garrison, the society became known for its ideological purity in dissuading Americans from relying on slavery as an economic necessity. Garrison and his supporters advocated what many considered a radical agenda that augured the emancipation of the slaves and the granting of social, political, and economic privileges to free blacks. Though the ideology of many within the movement was less radical than critics supposed, some within the abolitionist movement questioned the heavy-handed, iconoclastic style with which Garrison directed the movement.

Garrison defined the abolitionist campaign as a moral crusade and believed that direct political action could have little effect on ending the national sin of slavery. He demonstrated his distaste for political solutions by describing the U.S. Constitution as a compact with the devil, because it condoned the continued existence of slavery; to dramatize his point, Garrison occasionally burned a copy of the Constitution in public. Some in the abolitionist movement urged the creation of an antislavery political party to encourage further advocacy, but Garrison did not believe that such an effort would aid a cause that he felt would be won through moral suasion rather than political advocacy.

During its first seven years, the American Anti-Slavery Society welcomed the efforts and support of women and women's auxiliary associations to further the work of abolitionist advocacy. In particular, many women's groups were actively involved in fund-raising efforts that aided the antislavery cause. By the late 1830s, however, female abolitionists such as Angelina and Sarah Grimké were starting to speak publicly about the antislavery cause; this, too, was viewed by many—no doubt influenced by early-nineteenth-century American sensibilities—as an act of imprudent radicalism that could only hurt the antislavery movement. Despite such criticisms, Garrison and the leadership of the American Anti-Slavery Society continued to welcome the participation of women in the abolitionist movement.

These conflicts finally erupted in May 1840, as factions within the abolitionist movement made plans for a national meeting of the American Anti-Slavery Society that was to be held in New York. Fearing that his group might be outvoted by more conservative abolitionists, Garrison made efforts to guarantee that large numbers of delegates who favored his position on key issues would attend the meeting.

The most contentious item on the agenda was the proposal to elect Abby Kelley to the business committee of the society. Despite substantial opposition by those who opposed electing a woman to such a position, Kelley was elected by a vote of 557 to 451. This action triggered the defection of more conservative abolitionists to a new organization.

New Organization

The abolitionists who had bolted from the May 1840 meeting gathered at New York's Fourth Presbyterian Church to form a new organization, the American and Foreign Anti-Slavery Society. Key leaders in this schismatic movement were the brothers Arthur and Lewis Tappan and the Reverend Theodore Dwight Weld. A group of 294 seceding abolitionists signed their names as founding members of the new organization, a substantial number of them New York abolitionists. The secessionists also included a number of well-known black abolitionists, including Samuel E. Cornish, Theodore S. Wright, and Henry Highland Garnet.

On May 15, 1840, the new organization elected its officers, choosing Arthur Tappan as president, James G. Birney and Henry B. Stanton as cosecretaries, and Lewis Tappan as treasurer. The American and Foreign Anti-Slavery Society co-opted *The Emancipator,* the New York–based antislavery newspaper, as its own official organ (previously, the paper had been associated with the American Anti-Slavery Society). The new organization also established a weekly antislavery newspaper, the *National Era,* which was published from Washington, D.C.

Garrison was not dismayed by the departure of his more conservative colleagues. Rather, he believed that the schism created greater ideological purity within the American Anti-Slavery Society and made it more focused—in the eyes of many, this also made it even more radical. The departure of the New York abolitionists increased the power of the New Englanders within Garrison's group, and they recruited like-minded antislavery supporters from the Midwest to augment its rosters and help support the society's coffers.

Not surprisingly, the twin issues of political action and the place of women within the antislavery movement defined the identity of the new organization and distinguished it from Garrison's group. In April 1840, a gathering of political-minded abolitionists in Albany, New York, prompted the creation of the Liberty Party, the first political party in the United States to advocate an antislavery ideology. Kentucky abolitionist James G. Birney received the nomination of the Liberty Party as a candidate for president in the election of 1840, and the American and Foreign Anti-Slavery Society supported his candidacy.

Although the American and Foreign Anti-Slavery Society did not admit women into its leadership ranks, it did not discourage the active participation of women in the antislavery movement. In fact, the new organization encouraged the creation of women's affiliates to support the abolitionist cause, though it made it clear that only men could represent these auxiliary bodies when national meetings took place. Considering that the incipient women's movement included participants whose ideological perspectives ranged from conservative to radical, it is not surprising that some female abolitionists felt more comfortable with the role that was offered them by the new organization.

In 1848, the American and Foreign Anti-Slavery Society criticized the American Sunday School Union for allegedly pandering to proslavery interests. The union had discontinued the publication and distribution of the religious tract *Jacob and His Sons*, which benignly condemned the sale of Joseph into slavery.

Many British abolitionists, who tended to be anti-Garrisonian by inclination, found a common bond with the new organization in the United States. Some offered financial support to the group to ensure that there would be an alternative to Garrison's voice within the American abolitionist movement. Critics of the new organization often noted the term "foreign" in its name with derision, describing the group as being supported by outside interests and endorsing ideas that were contrary to the American democratic experience.

Despite the aspirations of its founders, the American and Foreign Anti-Slavery Society never achieved a powerful position within the American abolitionist movement. Relegated to being the voice of the loyal opposition to Garrisonian positions, the group never gained the traction that was necessary to chart policies of self-definition that might have redirected the antislavery movement.

Junius P. Rodriguez

See also: Birney, James Gillespie; Liberty Party; Tappan, Arthur; Tappan, Lewis.

Further Reading

Perry, Lewis, and Michael Fellman, eds. *Antislavery Reconsidered: New Perspectives on the Abolitionists.* Baton Rouge: Louisiana State University Press, 1979.

American Anti-Slavery Society

The American Anti-Slavery Society (AASS) was founded in 1833 by abolitionists Theodore Dwight Weld, Arthur Tappan, and Lewis Tappan and developed under the leadership of abolitionist and reformer William Lloyd Garrison. These men and other abolitionists met in Philadelphia in December 1833 to create the AASS.

A devout Baptist, Garrison had risen to national prominence as the publisher of the abolitionist newspaper *The Liberator,* which began appearing in 1831. Building on the success of that publication, Garrison believed there was a need for an organization that advocated immediate emancipation and equal rights for blacks in the United States. Pacifist in nature, the society determined that the best way to promote abolition was through a nonviolent Christian message. It quickly became a crucial organization in the fight for abolition during the nineteenth century.

Members of the AASS tended to come from religious or philanthropic backgrounds. The society was unique for its time because it allowed blacks unrestricted rights in the organization. Yet, while three black abolitionists—James McCrummell, James Barbadoes, and Robert Purvis—assisted in the organization of the society, African Americans were noticeably missing from the ranks of the AASS. Of the sixty people present at the first meeting, only three blacks were in attendance. Despite its liberal message, both black and white women were barred from actively participating in the AASS and were only allowed to attend its proceedings as observers. Blacks and women rarely held positions of authority throughout the course of the society's history; the issue of female involvement later caused a schism in the group's solidarity.

Early Years

During the 1830s, the AASS adopted an approach to abolition called "moral suasion." Appealing to religious sensibilities, the society argued that Christians had a moral basis for supporting abolition and racial equality. In the society's view, slaveholding was a sin that denied blacks the right to think for themselves and develop the moral conscience needed to save their souls. Moreover, according to this view, the sin of owning slaves doomed white slave owners to an afterlife of damnation and suffering. By owning

Among the largest and most active local chapters of the American Anti-Slavery Society was the one in Philadelphia. Its executive committee, posing here in 1851, included the Quaker abolitionist and women's rights advocate Lucretia Mott (front right, in bonnet). (*©Schlesinger Library, Radcliffe Institute, Harvard University/The Bridgeman Art Library*)

slaves, masters committed a myriad of sins, including brutality, sexual offenses, and laziness.

Though it argued that slavery was an economically inefficient system that benefited only wealthy slave owners in the South, the AASS also chastised Northern business interests for profiting from the raw materials and goods produced by slaves. The AASS used moral suasion to convince white slave masters to free their slaves while also persuading Northerners and other non–slave owners to support abolition.

The AASS adopted public outreach tactics to spread its abolitionist message. The society and its auxiliary groups sponsored lectures and published vast amounts of antislavery literature. In 1835, the organization initiated the Great Postal Campaign, a movement that aimed to send antislavery literature to slave owners and post offices in the South. The society also organized a petition to introduce the issue of slavery in the U.S. Congress. Female auxiliary members of the AASS often played a crucial role in the circulation and signing of the petitions. By 1836, 30,000 petitions had reached Washington, D.C.

The AASS also focused on raising awareness of slavery in the North and Midwest through publicity campaigns, employing scores of agents and lecturers to promote its cause. On the speaking tour, AASS agents usually traveled in pairs, with one white and one black abolitionist. By 1836, seventy agents were employed by the society. Former slaves such as William Wells Brown and Frederick Douglass stirred the emotions of listeners with their recollections of the brutalities they had experienced as slaves.

By 1840, the AASS had a total membership of 150,000 to 200,000. Its efforts, however, were often thwarted by mob violence and government policy. Despite the organization's sizable membership, its activities often met with physical violence and intimidation by unsympathetic audiences. Throughout the South, AASS propaganda was censored or burned. Southerners who publicly supported abolition were physically intimidated. In the North and Midwest, white mobs ransacked and burned black neighborhoods, destroyed pro-abolition printing presses, and disrupted meetings. In 1837, tensions peaked when antislavery newspaper editor Elijah P. Lovejoy was murdered by anti-abolitionists in Alton, Illinois.

In Washington, the administration of President Andrew Jackson did nothing to curb anti-abolitionism. The government refused to interfere with the tampering of mail in the South. And, in 1836, Congress instituted the Gag Rule—legislation prohibiting the introduction of petitions in reference to slavery. The rule was ultimately overturned in 1844.

Split in the Organization

Starting in the late 1830s, the AASS suffered from internal discord. From 1837 to 1840, the AASS struggled with the issue of female leadership. Garrison's increasing radicalism also made many members question his leadership: His open approval of women's equality within the organization and his public attacks on the U.S. Constitution for its endorsement of slavery were major points of contention among members. In response, Garrison balked at members' inability to embrace women's equality and continued insistence on becoming involved in electoral politics.

After failing to force Garrison out of the AASS, a majority of the organization's members left the society in 1840 to create the American and Foreign Anti-Slavery Society. Led by the Tappan brothers, both philanthropic businessmen, the American and Foreign Anti-Slavery Society adopted less radical tactics. It continued the strategy of moral suasion but also embraced the concept of political action. In 1840, the Liberty Party, the first antislavery political body, was founded.

Throughout the 1840s, Garrison controlled the AASS, which had become significantly smaller and more radical in nature since in its heyday in the 1830s. The society adopted the doctrine of "No union with slave holders" and vowed that it would never compromise on the question of slavery. The society condemned all religious denominations and their clergy for their direct support of slavery. Demanding that abolitionists peacefully renounce the American political system—which the society deemed essentially proslavery—the organization came to be seen as a mouthpiece for Garrison's radical ideas. As a result of this radicalism, the AASS's impact on mainstream politics declined.

At the start of the U.S. Civil War, Garrison parted ways with a majority of the AASS membership by supporting President Abraham Lincoln and the Republican Party. Other colleagues, such as Wendell Phillips, believed that the emancipation of the slaves must also guarantee full civil rights and suffrage for African Americans. In 1865, with the end of the war and the passage of the Thirteenth Amendment, Garrison believed that his life's work was accomplished and resigned from the American Anti-Slavery Society. The AASS carried on under Wendell Phillips's direction until 1870, when it was disbanded.

Although the American Anti-Slavery Society suffered from internal discord and strife during its existence, it nonetheless accomplished its mission: The organization helped to bring about the legal emancipation of slaves in the United States.

Jennifer Searcy

See also: American and Foreign Anti-Slavery Society; Garrison, William Lloyd; Immediatism; Phillips, Wendell; Purvis, Robert; Women's Rights and the Abolitionist Movement.

Further Reading

Duberman, Martin, ed. *The Anti-Slavery Vanguard: New Essays on the Abolitionists.* Princeton, NJ: Princeton University Press, 1965.

Filler, Louis. *The Crusade Against Slavery, 1830–1860.* New York: Harper & Row, 1960.

Kraditor, Aileen S. *Means and Ends in American Abolitionism: Garrison and His Critics on Strategy and Tactics, 1834–1850.* New York: Pantheon, 1969.

Nye, Russell B. *William Lloyd Garrison and Humanitarian Reformers.* Boston: Little, Brown, 1955.

American Colonization Society

The American Colonization Society (ACS), also known as the American Society for Colonizing the Free People of Color of the United States, was founded in 1816 by the Reverend Robert Finley, pastor of the Basking Ridge Presbyterian Church in New Jersey.

In 1815, Finley became aware of the problems faced by the free black population of his parish, particularly the social conditions of the city that made it impossible for many blacks to rise out of poverty. He believed, like many of his black counterparts before him, that returning blacks to Africa was the only long-term viable solution to America's "race problem." At the same time, he believed that colonization would aid Africa by sending Christians to "civilize" the continent, while enabling whites to rid themselves of an alien and inharmonious people. In November 1816, the minister left for Washington, D.C., with a plan for African colonization.

Origins

Once in Washington, Finley wrote to Captain Paul Cuffe, seeking his support for an American Colonization Society. In 1815, Cuffe had successfully taken a group of thirty-five blacks to the African colony of Sierra Leone. Cuffe responded positively despite his concerns about Finley's underlying aims. Finley also enlisted the help of Samuel Mills, a traveling agent for the Presbyterian Church–sponsored African Education Society, which had already agreed to train blacks for missionary and administrative duties in Finley's projected colony. Finley realized, however, that an African colony would be impossible without governmental financial aid and that federal approval was essential for the large-scale removal of blacks from the United States. Thus, the ACS was organized chiefly as a means of securing governmental assistance for Finley's plan.

Between December 21 and December 28, 1816, prominent government officials, ministers, and other important Washingtonians met at the Davis Hotel to form the American Society for Colonizing the Free People of Color of the United States. The first president was Bushrod Washington, and the illustrious list of vice presidents included such prominent Americans as Henry Clay, Daniel Webster, John Randolph, Francis Scott Key, and General Andrew Jackson.

The ACS was founded to appease two opposing groups of whites. One group, comprising abolitionists, philanthropists, and clergymen, wanted to free enslaved Africans and provide them with the opportunity to return to Africa. The second group consisted chiefly of Southern slave owners who feared the free blacks in their locales and wanted to expel them from the United States.

According to the early published writings of Clay and Randolph, it is clear that the ACS had no intention of interfering with slavery. They argued that the removal of free blacks would reduce the problem of slave control and strengthen the institution. Simultaneously, they argued that the ability to remove freed blacks from the United States might encourage slave owners to emancipate their slaves voluntarily. From its inception, it was clear that the ACS was willing to use antiblack sentiment to attract the support of slaveholders and other whites.

The society immediately made plans to establish a colony in Africa—with the aid of federal and state governments—and to garner public opinion to support the project. The federal government negotiated with Great Britain to obtain an area on the West African coast, which it established as Liberia. Its capital was given the name Monrovia, after President James Monroe. Agents were sent across the United States to raise funds and support for the project. Soon, thousands of dollars were pouring into ACS headquarters for purchasing and chartering ships to transport blacks to the new colony.

To raise support among free blacks, the ACS promoted two distinct goals: first, to plant an African American colony in West Africa that would free blacks from the degradation they experienced in the United States and provide them with new social and economic opportunities; second, to provide a means of transportation to Africa, enabling Christians to fulfill their missionary ambitions. The rhetoric worked, enticing several hundred black Americans to seek immigration to Liberia.

Early Success

The ACS was given a major boost by an act of Congress in 1819. The legislation authorized the president of the United States to restore Africans being illegally detained on American or foreign vessels to their own countries and to provide subsistence and comfort until they could return to their relatives or support themselves. Campelar, the U.S. government post on the coast of West Africa, was chosen as the place where these Africans would be received by American agents.

In February 1820, the ACS ship *Elizabeth* set out with eighty-eight blacks, two white government agents—the Reverend Samuel Bacon and Jason Bankson—and ACS agent Dr. Samuel Crozer. The group landed at Campelar. Despite the many problems of early settlement, including the deaths of twenty of the black settlers and the two white agents, the mission was considered a success. Over the next few years, several hundred blacks made the arduous journey and settled in the colony.

Though initially, only free blacks were transported to Liberia, by 1827, some slaves were being freed expressly for the purpose of removal to the African colony. By 1830, 1,420 blacks had successfully settled there. By 1832, more than thirty-two state legislatures had given their official approval for the removal of free blacks from their regions. These included slaveholding states such as Maryland, Virginia, and Kentucky. Other slaveholding states, such as North Carolina and Mississippi, had local chapters of the ACS. Despite the inability to obtain federal funds for the colonization project, many state legislatures were willing to provide financial support. In 1850, Virginia, for example, set aside $30,000 for five years to aid the ACS emigration effort.

Opposition to the idea of African colonization, however, had existed since the inception of the ACS. In 1817, 3,000 blacks, led by James Forten and Richard Allen, met at Bethel African Methodist Episcopal Church in Philadelphia. There, they unanimously opposed the idea of colonization. Forten, a prominent black merchant and initially a strong proponent of colonization, became one of the ACS's biggest detractors. He came to see the racial ambivalence of the ACS and recognized that colonization might be used to force all free blacks to leave the United States.

The famous abolitionist William Lloyd Garrison also had initially favored the idea of colonization, but he came to see Forten's point of view—that colonization did nothing but divert black Americans from the struggle for a better life in America and allow whites to ignore their responsibilities to all citizens, regardless of race or color. Garrison articulated his views in *Thoughts on African Colonization* (1831), a stinging indictment of the ACS. Using documentation from the society's own publication, the *African Repository*, Garrison destroyed the ideological foundation of the ACS and proved its underlying antiblack intent.

Legacy

These attacks prompted many of the society's most equalitarian supporters to desert, leaving the organization with proslavery supporters and those who wished to see all free blacks deported. Many local societies, which desired greater autonomy, seceded from the organization, further splintering its resources across the nation. At the same time, growing reports about corruption and the high cost of living in Liberia tarnished the idea of colonization.

During its first phase of business, the ACS successfully transplanted 12,000 people to the colony of Liberia. But it became insolvent in 1834 and went into decline in the years before the U.S. Civil War. After the Civil War, when many freedmen wanted to emigrate, financial support for the organization was not available.

By the 1890s, the problems of Reconstruction had helped to revive the colonization question. Thanks to the work of the wealthy lawyer John H.B.

Latrobe, the American Colonization Society experienced a revival, but it never again regained the success of its early years. In its later years, the ACS abandoned emigration and focused exclusively on educational and missionary efforts in Liberia. The company was finally dissolved in 1964.

Melissa Anyiwo

See also: Cuffe, Paul; Forten, James, Sr.; Garrison, William Lloyd.

Further Reading

Dickson, Bruce D., Jr. "National Identity and African American Colonization, 1773–1817." *The Historian* 58 (Autumn 1995): 15–28.

Garrison, William Lloyd. *Thoughts on African Colonization.* 1832. Introduction by William Loren Katz. New York: Arno, 1968.

Miller, Floyd John. *The Search for Black Nationality: Black Emigration and Colonization, 1787–1863.* Urbana: University of Illinois Press, 1975.

Redkey, Edwin S. *Black Exodus: Black Nationalist and Back-to-Africa Movements, 1890–1910.* New Haven, CT: Yale University Press, 1969.

Shick, Tom W. *Behold the Promised Land: A History of Afro-American Settler Society in Nineteenth-Century Liberia.* Baltimore: Johns Hopkins University Press, 1980.

Willmore, Gayraud S. *Black Religion and Black Radicalism.* Garden City, NY: Doubleday, 1972.

American Missionary Association

Founded in Albany, New York, in 1846, the American Missionary Association (AMA) became the largest abolitionist organization in the United States. Dedicated to the radical antislavery cause, the AMA promoted democratic egalitarianism and the elimination of caste. Although it was a nondenominational organization, the AMA remained committed to evangelical Christianity and always reflected the Congregationalist roots of its founders. Its organizational leadership was predominantly made up of white Americans but also included prominent African American reformers.

The AMA is best known for its educational and relief work among former slaves in the American South following the U.S. Civil War. This effort established many schools and colleges, but it had more limited success ministering to freedmen and freedwomen because of the paternalism of many AMA missionaries. During the nineteenth century, AMA missionaries also served in Africa, Jamaica, Haiti, Puerto Rico, Canada, Hawaii, Siam, the Sandwich Islands, and the American West.

Origins

The origins of the AMA lay in the celebrated *Amistad* case, in which the U.S. Supreme Court determined that a group of Africans who had been illegally abducted from Sierra Leone could not be held as slaves and had the right to return to their homeland. Abolitionist Lewis Tappan headed the Amistad Committee, which was organized to support the Africans and the lawyers representing them.

Shortly after the *Amistad* case was resolved, the committee became a part of the Union Missionary Society (UMS), a largely African American organization founded in Hartford, Connecticut, in 1841. By the mid-1840s, radical abolitionists such as Tappan had grown frustrated by the moderate stance on slavery of the American Board of Commissioners for Foreign Missions. This dissatisfaction led Tappan and fifty-one others, including four prominent African American leaders, to establish the AMA and fold the UMS into that organization.

Tappan, the guiding force behind the AMA and its treasurer for eighteen years, believed that the AMA's goal was to preach a pure gospel that made no compromises with slavery. Through moral suasion, Tappan argued, Americans could be enlightened to the glaring immorality of slavery. The AMA spread this message through ministers, missionary agents, children's anti-slavery missionary societies, and the monthly *American Missionary* magazine, whose circulation would far surpass William Lloyd Garrison's *Liberator*.

The AMA sponsored missionaries throughout the antebellum South, including the slave states of North Carolina, Kentucky, and Missouri. The association strongly criticized federal legislation supported by the slaveholding interest, including the Fugitive Slave Act (1850), the Kansas-Nebraska Act (1854), and the Supreme Court's *Dred Scott* decision (1857), and it called on the U.S. Congress to enforce laws against the importation of African slaves.

By 1859, eight AMA missionaries were working in the Kansas Territory. As elsewhere, the AMA was committed to a biracial society with free institutions that would be open to all, a stance that was opposed by some Free Soilers (members of the short-lived Free Soil political party, a pro-abolition group dedicated to opposing the extension of slavery). Missionaries in the Kansas Territory spoke out against racial injustice, urged lyceums to open their debates to blacks, taught black children in Sunday schools, and sheltered runaway slaves. The AMA blamed "Bleeding Kansas"—the violent period of Kansas history during which proslavers and abolitionists struggled over whether the state would enter the Union as a free state or a slave state—on slaveholders and their supporters in the national government.

Abroad, the AMA focused its efforts and resources on supporting the Mendi Mission in Sierra Leone, established in 1841 when the *Amistad* slaves returned to their homeland. Despite illness and death among AMA missionaries to the West African country, the association established a literary infrastructure that included two printing presses, written forms of the Mendi and Sherbo languages, and publication of the gospels and schoolbooks in these languages. The AMA also underwrote economic activities that had no connection with the slave trade, establishing a sawmill and promoting coffee cultivation.

Ministry, Social Services, and Education

Among U.S. missionary organizations, in 1847, the AMA became the first to minister to runaway slaves in Canada. Efforts there were far from successful, however, because of racial prejudice on the part of some whites, factions among the leaders of the fugitives, and resistance among some blacks to white missionaries.

At the height of its Canadian involvement in 1852, the AMA supported ten missionaries, including free black educator and journalist Mary Ann Shadd. Shadd, who had immigrated to Canada from the United States after the Fugitive Slave Act was passed, opened an integrated school in Windsor, Ontario, that received financial support from the AMA. Although Shadd and the AMA parted ways for several years, the two later joined forces again to support a school in Chatham, Ontario.

The AMA also ministered to emancipated slaves in the West Indies. James W.C. Pennington, an AMA founder and officer, as well as a former slave, emphasized these efforts. He expressed disappointment that the Europeans appeared to be losing interest in West Indian missions, and he feared that the cause of abolition in the United States would be hurt if the gospel did not take hold among freedmen and freedwomen in the West Indies.

Another AMA founder and officer, Henry Highland Garnet, also a former slave, briefly served as a missionary in Jamaica. Although the AMA provided support for native Jamaicans as teachers of the former slaves, the association encountered some of the same problems it had faced in Canada in its efforts to reach out to these people. Missionaries cited sexual promiscuity and widespread rum drinking as their greatest challenges, and without a doubt, a cultural divide existed between the evangelists and the former slaves. The difficulties that the AMA faced in its Canadian and Jamaican work would arise again in the American South after emancipation.

From the start of the U.S. Civil War in 1861, the AMA helped slaves make the transition to freedom. The AMA missionaries and teachers established a presence in Union-occupied areas such as Hampton, Virginia; New Bern, North Carolina; and Nashville, Tennessee. The organization was supporting 250 agents in the South by 1864 and 532 by 1868. Approximately 400 African Americans served the freedmen and freedwomen under the auspices of the AMA during and after the war.

For the AMA, emancipation and, by 1865, abolition did not signify the end of the association's work, but a new beginning. The AMA believed that the freed slaves needed a Christian education, not only for their moral development but also for their role as American citizens. Though education was the AMA's primary concern, the organization's agents discovered they had to focus on more practical matters first. The missionaries distributed food, clothing, and other necessities, as well as Bibles—eagerly requested by former slaves who had once been forbidden to read. Throughout the South, the AMA promoted black political and civil rights, as well as land acquisition.

Most of the AMA missionaries in the postwar South were New England Congregationalists. As such, they elicited a divided response from the newly emancipated slaves. Though the freedmen and freedwomen were pleased with the AMA schools, they routinely rejected the association's Congregationalist-style churches and Sunday schools; if the grammar schools were linked with Congregational churches, they rejected these schools as well.

Southern African American and Congregationalist worship practices were starkly different, especially with regard to conversion. Most AMA missionaries unsuccessfully sought to eradicate the demonstrative religious practices favored by most former slaves. Just a handful of the missionaries adapted their efforts to the religious culture they found among the freedmen and freedwomen.

Legacy

The most far-reaching contribution of the AMA was its role in establishing schools and colleges for Southern blacks that would become prominent institutions in American intellectual life, significant local resources for African Americans, and key training grounds for black leaders. Such institutions as Atlanta University, Hampton University, Berea College, Dillard University, Howard University, and Fisk University (alma mater of W.E.B. Du Bois) all began with AMA support. Students from these schools occasionally went on to serve as AMA missionaries, including Fisk's first missionaries to Africa.

Although the AMA gave up its foreign mission work in the 1880s, the organization continued its home mission work throughout the next century, remaining a progressive voice advocating on behalf of Southern blacks through the dark days of segregation and disfranchisement. Today, the AMA is a part of the United Church of Christ's Board for Homeland Ministries, and the AMA's archives are housed at the Amistad Research Center in New Orleans, Louisiana.

Antoinette G. van Zelm

See also: Education of Former Slaves; Liberia; Pennington, James W.C.; Shadd Cary, Mary Ann; Tappan, Lewis.

Further Reading

DeBoer, Clara Merritt. *Be Jubilant My Feet: African American Abolitionists in the American Missionary Association, 1839–1861.* New York: Garland, 1994.

Quirin, James A. "'Her Sons and Daughters Are Ever on the Altar': Fisk University and Missionaries to Africa, 1866–1937." *Tennessee Historical Quarterly* 60 (Spring 2001): 16–37.

Raines, Edgar F., Jr. "The American Missionary Association in Southern Illinois, 1856–1862: A Case Study in the Abolition Movement." *Journal of the Illinois State Historical Society* 65 (Autumn 1972): 246–68.

Richardson, Joe M. *Christian Reconstruction: The American Missionary Association and Southern Blacks, 1861–1890.* Athens: University of Georgia Press, 1986.

———. "The Failure of the American Missionary Association to Expand Congregationalism among Southern Blacks." *Southern Studies* 18 (Spring 1979): 51–73.

SenGupta, Gunja. "'A Model New England State': Northeastern Antislavery in Territorial Kansas, 1854–1860." *Civil War History* 39 (March 1993): 31–46.

Silverman, Jason H. *Unwelcome Guests: Canada West's Response to American Fugitive Slaves, 1800–1865.* Millwood, NY: Associated Faculty, 1985.

Zipf, Karen. "'Among These American Heathens': Congregationalist Missionaries and African American Evangelicals During Reconstruction." *North Carolina Historical Review* 74 (April 1997): 111–34.

American Revolution (1775–1781)

The American Revolution created unique opportunities for slaves to gain their freedom in the North American colonies. Some slaves earned their freedom by serving in either the Continental army or the King's Army, whereas others took their freedom by fleeing their plantations. Because insufficient records of African American life were kept during this time, it is impossible to determine exactly how many slaves gained emancipation. However, most historians estimate that about 50,000 slaves (some estimates run as high as 100,000) obtained their freedom one way or another during and shortly after the American Revolution.

Early Prohibitions

In 1705, a colonial law was passed in Virginia that barred slaves from military service and set a penalty of twenty lashes for slaves found in possession of any weapon. In general, British America was opposed to the arming of slaves, because the colonists feared a slave rebellion and held racist doubts about slaves' courage under fire.

During the French and Indian War (1754–1763), some slaves served in the military, but most slaves were used in backbreaking labor that supported military activities. This trend continued during the American Revolution, but a shortage of manpower forced both the American colonists and Great Britain to offer emancipation as an incentive for African American participation in the conflict.

At the start of the Revolution, one in six Americans was black, and 99 percent of African Americans were slaves. Altogether, there were about 600,000 slaves in North America, most of them living in the South. African Americans participated in most of the major battles from Lexington and Concord to Yorktown; they were present at the Boston Massacre, Bunker Hill, and George Washington's crossing of the Delaware, to name a few. They were employed in a variety of ways: as soldiers, sailors, spies, guides, and manual laborers.

More than 25,000 African Americans fought on both sides during the war. Some African American units were created, but most of these men were integrated into existing white units. By the end of the war, African Americans accounted for almost one-fifth of North American units.

At the First Continental Congress in 1774, a resolution was passed inviting free blacks to join the cause. As the colonies drifted closer to war, however, the idea of enlisting African Americans in the Continental army generated heated debate among the delegates, some of whom feared the outbreak of armed slave revolts. The debate culminated in a decision to exclude African Americans from the military. After the Second Continental Congress in 1775, newly appointed general in chief George Washington was faced with a shortage of men, the dilemma of whether to turn away African American volunteers, and the more difficult task of figuring out what to do with African Americans who had enlisted prior to the 1775 ban.

By 1777, the need for soldiers forced many recruitment officers in the North to go against official policy, and they began accepting free and slave African Americans. Southern colonies, however, remained resistant to enlisting and arming slaves.

Opportunities

In 1775, John Murray, fourth earl of Dunmore and royal governor of Virginia, promised freedom to slaves and indentured servants owned by Patriot masters in exchange for joining the British cause. Murray's Ethiopian Regiment, as it came to be called, was composed of more than 300 slaves outfitted in uniforms bearing the inscription "Liberty to Slaves." Lord Dunmore's approach encouraged other British commanders to make similar offers.

The enlistment of slaves in the British army had a threefold effect: First, slave armies fortified British forces and provided labor support. Second, fugitive slaves weakened the American military and labor support system. And third, because the slaves were fleeing their bondage, many slave owners felt obliged to stay at home and watch over their slaves, exacerbating the soldier shortage in the Continental army.

The new policy angered slave-owning Loyalists in the Southern colonies, who loudly protested to the British government. In Great Britain, many citizens complained of a policy that would arm slaves against their white masters. Therefore, in 1776, all British generals were ordered to withdraw emancipation offers that had been made without approval from the British government.

In spite of London's official stance, in 1778, Sir Henry Clinton, commander in chief of the British forces in North America, issued the Phillipsburg Proclamation, which invited all African Americans (free and slave) to join the British cause. Clinton refuted claims that he was attempting to start a race war and insisted that every slave who was won over weakened the American cause. In 1779, the British government acquiesced to the manpower needs of the British commanders in the field and officially endorsed emancipation in exchange for military service.

During the Southern campaigns of 1780 to 1782, the British carried off 20,000 African American men from South Carolina. In addition, campaigns in Georgia, North Carolina, and Virginia netted several thousand more men. Scholars estimate that more than 20,000 African Americans voluntarily joined the British side of the conflict. Despite the affirmation of liberty promised by the Declaration of Independence, most African Americans served on the British side, because they believed the British offer of emancipation to be more reliable.

The recruitment of slaves was a far less difficult task for the British than it was for the Americans because the Continental army was often constrained by the legal parameters of private property. Usually, the recruitment of slaves for the American cause required the permission of the owners, and it was sometimes obtained by monetary or land grant rewards. Occasionally, in times of extreme emergency, the colonial government took the more radical approach of impressment in order to recruit sufficient workers to build fortifications. The most effective inducement, however, was an allowance made by authorities that gave slave owners permission to send slaves as substitutes for their own military service. Historians estimate that about 5,000 African Americans served in the Continental army and navy, and 5,000 more served as labor support.

The ideals of freedom, which were proclaimed in America as sufficient reason for the Revolution, caused moral qualms among some slave owners in both the North and the South. Many Northerners had abandoned slavery voluntarily. Some Southerners had done the same, but many others wrestled with the ideological contradiction of slavery and the cause of liberty, though they could not bring themselves to give up their slave property.

George Washington, for example, who had witnessed African Americans fighting for the cause of freedom on the battlefields, owned many acres of land and hundreds of slaves. After the war and his presidency, Washington returned home to his plantation and lived the rest of his life as a slave owner, stipulating that his slaves were to be freed after his death.

Patrick Henry, who had spurred America's revolutionary zeal at the First Continental Congress by declaring "Give me liberty or give me death!" explained after the war that freeing his slaves would be too much of an inconvenience. Likewise, Thomas Jefferson, author of the Declaration of Independence (which states that all men possess the God-given right to liberty), pondered the paradoxes of slavery in his *Notes on the State of Virginia* (1785), but he, like many other slave owners in the South, could not bring himself to free his slaves.

Perhaps the most important effect of antislavery sentiment on the South was a relaxation of manumission laws. In lieu of statewide emancipation laws, manumission allowed each slave owner to free his own slaves legally if he wished. It is estimated that more than 10,000 slaves were manumitted during the 1780s in the South.

Legacy

The Revolution-fueled sentiment in the North had more profound effects on slavery. In 1777, Vermont's constitution outlawed slavery within its borders, and, in 1783, Massachusetts and New Hampshire followed Vermont's lead. Both Pennsylvania and Connecticut made similar plans for gradual emancipation. For example, Pennsylvania declared that all children born to slave mothers after 1780 would become free at the age of twenty-eight. In 1784, Rhode Island passed a similar law. The most gradual abolition plan was set by New York, which freed slave children in 1799 and all others in 1827.

This new atmosphere of emancipation encouraged many slaves to flee their plantations in the South and form African American communities in the North. Some journeyed as far as Canada to escape the nation that had enslaved them. Others fled to the Western frontier, where they joined sympathetic Native American tribes. It is estimated that about 55,000 slaves gained their freedom by running away during the war.

After the war, many slaves who had joined either the American or the British side of the conflict were repaid with their freedom. By far, however, the British army was the greater liberator, carrying off tens of thousands to Canada and the British colonies in the Caribbean. However, many slaves who had served in the war suffered great disappointment when their freedom was denied.

Some slaves were captured and severely punished by the opposing side of the conflict. In America, captured slaves were considered property to be sold, kept as servants, or returned to their owners. In some instances, slaves were publicly hanged or burned. Furthermore, Loyalists who were found guilty of encouraging slaves to join the British or to flee were tarred and feathered.

Some British commanders saw captured enemy slaves as war booty and kept them as their personal servants or sold them at a high price into bondage on the sugar plantations of the West Indies. The Treaty of Paris (1783), which formally ended the war, stipulated that the British were to return captured slaves to their colonial masters.

Rolando Avila

See also: Declaration of Independence (1776).

Further Reading

Berlin, Ira, and Ronald Hoffman, eds. *Slavery and Freedom in the Age of the American Revolution.* Charlottesville: University of Virginia Press, 1983.

Bruns, Roger, ed. *Am I Not a Man and a Brother: The Antislavery Crusade of Revolutionary America, 1688–1788.* New York: Chelsea House, 1977.

Davis, David Brion. *The Problem of Slavery in the Age of Revolution, 1770–1823.* Ithaca, NY: Cornell University Press, 1975; New York: Oxford University Press, 1999.

Locke, Mary Stoughton. *Anti-Slavery in America from the Introduction of African Slaves to the Prohibition of the Slave-Trade (1619–1808).* Boston: Ginn, 1901.

MacLeod, Duncan J. *Slavery, Race, and the American Revolution.* Cambridge, UK: Cambridge University Press, 1974.

Quarles, Benjamin. *The Negro in the American Revolution.* Chapel Hill: University of North Carolina Press, 1961.

American Tract Society

During the nineteenth century, the American Tract Society (ATS) sought to bring stability and certainty to a Protestant land by placing Christian literature, primarily in pamphlet form, in the hands of thousands of adults and children. The ATS was founded as a national organization in 1825 when the American Tract Society in Boston (formerly the New England Tract Society) merged with the New York Religious Tract Society. The new organization was formed to provide a stronger and broader base of operation in order to enter the "highways and hedges" and to reach the minds and souls of Americans. With

the goals of religious education and spiritual growth, the ATS became a driving force behind the temperance and abolitionist reform movements.

History

Unlike other voluntary groups, such as the American Bible Society and the American Education Society, the primary goals of the ATS were to spread a general and evangelical Protestant religion and to cement America's Protestant hegemony through the publication and distribution of short leaflets. The gospel it preached addressed manners and morals as important parts of the American character. A person could be considered moral, the society believed, when he or she no longer drank, gambled, or broke the Sabbath. It urged Christians to flee the social taboos of the day, emphasizing outward actions as a measure of character and downplaying the inward qualities of humility and meditation. Although the ATS shared many of the same leading members as other societies, it outstripped their influence and succeeded in reaching the masses in the North and South.

Early on, the American Tract Society led the way in religious publishing by taking advantage of new technologies. By the mid-nineteenth century, it owned numerous steam presses, whereas the leading commercial publisher at the time, Harper & Brothers, had only one. The society also used every means available for the proper and expedient printing of tracts, biographies, and devotional material. During the antebellum era, the society produced more than 6,000 distinct tracts and handbills, as well as 1,240 biographies, histories, and devotional works. The ATS also published several magazines, including the *American Messenger* and *Child's Paper.*

The modern tract was the invention of Hannah More, who had initiated the *Cheap Repository Tracts* in Britain, which were widely read and circulated in the late eighteenth century. Written in plain language, the tracts told simple stories with moral themes. More's work inspired the formation of the Religious Tract Society in London, many of whose tracts the ATS would reprint. The African American pastor and former slave Samuel Ringgold Ward lamented in his autobiography that the ATS favored slavery by producing no tract against it and edited out any references to slavery in materials reprinted from Britain.

Division Over Slavery

The main objective of the society's publishing was "to diffuse a knowledge of our Lord Jesus Christ as the Redeemer of sinners, and to promote the interests of vital godliness and sound morality, by the circulation of religious Tracts, calculated to receive the approbation of all Evangelical Christians." Because the society was no longer a partisan organization that kept a reformed Calvinistic theology before its readers—as it had been originally under the Congregationalists in Boston—the publications of the ATS needed to steer clear of all peripheral concerns. This policy was strengthened by a stipulation that each member of the publications board had the right to veto any proposed publication.

The "approbation of all Evangelical Christians" would become the central focus of the ATS's editorial efforts, and the morality of slavery was an issue that Christians in America did not agree on. As the debate over slavery raged and the abolitionist movement gained a foothold, the ATS and its six-member editorial board found themselves in a difficult position. The leaders of the society needed to maintain their editorial mandate so that they could continue their outreach efforts in Southern states, but this stance drew the ire of abolitionist leaders. Gerrit Smith, for example, noted in his address to the Jerry Rescue Convention in 1857 that pride inhibited the society from acknowledging the immorality of slavery.

The society's policy on slavery divided the national and local auxiliary societies. Abolitionists Arthur and Lewis Tappan expressed concern that the ATS and other benevolent societies were unwilling to confront slavery. In 1858, Abraham Lincoln noted during a senatorial debate with Stephen Douglas in Alton, Illinois, that the issue of slavery was beginning to tear the ATS asunder. The failure of the ATS to speak out against slavery split the society, as it had many Protestant denominations. The American Tract Society, like many of the major denominations, was in a cycle of self-deception that allowed it to believe that if slavery were ignored, then it would not affect the organization's day-to-day or long-term activities.

In 1859, after many years of objecting to the society's failure to come out against slaveholders and slavery, the Boston depository, greatly influenced by abolitionist sentiments, separated from the national organization to become known as the American Tract Society, Boston. Because it had no legal right to any of the publications of the national American Tract Society, New York, the Boston society began to publish its own tracts, books, and magazines. In an attempt to garner subscribers from the New York operation, the Boston society enhanced the quality of its publications and opened an office and distribution center in New York. Conversely, the New York society set up operations in Boston.

The existence of two American Tract Societies created confusion in many areas where materials were distributed. After many years of personal and national bitterness and strife wrought by the volatile issue of slavery, the two societies eventually reunited in 1878. The organization continues to publish religious tracts and other materials that espouse an evangelical Protestant perspective from its headquarters in Garland, Texas.

David B. Malone

See also: More, Hannah; National Anti-Slavery Tract Society.

Further Reading

American Tract Society. "The Address of the Executive Committee." In *The American Tract Society Documents, 1824–1925.* New York: Arno, 1972.

Griffin, Clifford S. "The Abolitionists and the Benevolent Societies, 1831–1861." *Journal of Negro History* 44 (July 1959): 195–216.

Thompson, Lawrence R. "The Printing and Publishing Activities of the American Tract Society From 1825 to 1850." *Papers of the Bibliographical Society of America* 35 (1941): 81–114.

Amistad Case (1841)

In the celebrated *Amistad* case of 1841, the U.S. Supreme Court determined that a group of Africans who had been illegally abducted from Sierra Leone, West Africa, could not be held as slaves and had the right to return to their homeland. The Africans had revolted on the Spanish slave ship *Amistad* and were being tried in the United States for murder on the high seas. Although the *Amistad* case did not change slavery laws in America, it drew national attention to the issue of slavery and was a victory for abolitionists, who rallied together to set the Africans involved free.

Events

On June 28, 1839, the Spanish schooner *Amistad* (the Spanish word for "friendship") set sail from Havana to a plantation in Puerto Príncipe in east-central

Cuba. On board were fifty-three West African slaves who had been purchased by plantation owners Pedro Montes and José Ruiz in direct violation of international slave trade law.

On the third day of the journey, the slaves revolted under the leadership of African Joseph Cinqué. They seized control of the vessel and killed the captain and cook. The slaves then ordered the remaining crew members to sail east in the direction of Africa. Using the rising sun to guide them by day, the crew altered course by sailing to the north at night. Ultimately, the currents and winds guided the *Amistad* to Long Island, New York.

In late summer 1839, reports began to surface about a pirate ship manned by armed blacks off the coast of Long Island. Acting on the reports, the U.S. government intercepted the *Amistad* a mile off the coast of Long Island near Culloden Point on August 26, 1839. The Spanish crew was freed, but the ship and West African slaves were seized and transported to New London, Connecticut. On August 29, the slaves were charged with mutiny and murder and imprisoned in New Haven to await their trial.

Upon learning of the *Amistad*'s interception, President Martin Van Buren favored extraditing the Africans to Cuba, where they would stand trial for the crimes of murder and mutiny under Spanish law. Although he was ambivalent on the issue of slavery, the president nonetheless depended on the support of Southern Democrats, many of whom were vehemently against emancipation. With a presidential election looming the following year, Van Buren did not want

to endorse antislavery sentiments by freeing the imprisoned Africans.

On September 11, Secretary of State John Forsyth notified William Holabird, the U.S. district attorney, that he should refuse to admit the *Amistad* case to the court docket. The motion was submitted too late, however, as the government had already charged the Africans with murder on August 29.

News of the imprisonment of the *Amistad* slaves soon attracted the attention of Northern abolitionists, who were fully aware that the foreign slave trade had been abolished in Spain and its colonies by royal decree in 1838. In the abolitionists' opinion, the slaves could not be charged with any crime, because they were free men who had been brutally kidnapped. Thus, their seizure of the *Amistad* had been an act of self-defense. As news of the case spread nationwide, abolitionists Joshua Leavitt, Simeon Jocelyn, and Lewis Tappan created the Amistad Committee to raise funds for the legal defense of the imprisoned West Africans. Connecticut attorney Roger Sherman Baldwin, who later became the state's governor, served as counsel for the Africans' defense.

The *Amistad* prisoners' legal defense strategy required the slaves to tell the story of their capture; however, none of the slaves spoke English. The imprisoned slaves had come from an area of Sierra Leone in West Africa where the Mende language was spoken. Baldwin, along with defense lawyers Seth Staples and Theodore Sedgwick, started a desperate search for anyone who could communicate with them. On September 6, Tappan brought John Ferry, an African,

Death of Capt. Ferrer, the Captain of the Amistad, July, 1839.

Don Jose Ruiz and Don Pedro Montez, of the Island of Cuba, having purchased fifty-three slaves at Havana, recently imported from Africa, put them on board the Amistad, Capt. Ferrer, in order to transport them to Principe, another port on the Island of Cuba. After being out from Havana about four days, the African captives on board, in order to obtain their freedom, and return to Africa, armed themselves with cane knives, and rose upon the Captain and crew of the vessel. Capt. Ferrer and the cook of the vessel were killed; two of the crew escaped; Ruiz and Montez were made prisoners.

In 1839, a group of fifty-three West African slaves being transported on the Spanish schooner *Amistad* escaped their chains and seized the vessel, killing the captain and the cook. The incident and the associated legal rulings created a stir in both pro- and antislavery circles. *(Library of Congress, LC-USZ62-52577)* and two other men to attempt to converse with the prisoners. Through their exchange, Ferry gained a detailed account of their kidnapping. In later investigations, the defense employed British seaman James Covey to communicate with the prisoners. A native Mende speaker, Covey successfully extracted more information. Purchased by a Spanish slave trader on Lomboko Island off the coast of Sierra Leone, the slaves had been illegally transported to Havana and sold to Montes and Ruiz.

While the abolitionists were preparing their defense, Spain also entered the legal fray over the *Amistad*. The Spanish minister to the United States, Angel Calderon de la Barca, petitioned the United States to return the slaves and the *Amistad* to Cuba, where the Africans would be tried under Spanish law.

The Case

The district court case began in Hartford, Connecticut, on November 19. Baldwin argued that according to the testimony of the West Africans, the *Amistad* captives were not Spanish subjects but free citizens of Africa, and hence they were not guilty of committing any crime. Their seizure of the *Amistad* had been an act of self-defense against their illegal capture. The decision of the district court, which was handed down on January 13, held in favor of the defense: The Africans were deemed to be neither slaves nor subjects of Spain.

Despite this judgment, an appeal by the prosecution forced another trial at the federal circuit court level in April 1840. Although the judge upheld the decision of the lower court, he nonetheless directed the case to the Supreme Court because of its growing international importance. The case was scheduled to be heard by the justices in January 1841.

The Amistad Committee was apprehensive, because five of the Supreme Court justices were Southerners. Though they were confident in Baldwin and his defense strategy, the abolitionists nonetheless believed that the team needed stronger direction. Under the leadership of Tappan, the abolitionists approached former president John Quincy Adams, then a congressman from Massachusetts, about joining the defense. Adams was sympathetic to the prisoners' cause and agreed to join, thus linking his prominent name to the case.

On February 20, 1841, the government presented its argument against the imprisoned Africans. Attorney General Henry Gilpin argued that the United States had no authority to usurp the property and laws of another country. For the defense, Baldwin and Adams continued to advance the rationale that the Africans should be granted their freedom, because they had been captured illegally.

The Supreme Court sided with the defense: Because the illegal slave trade had been abolished, it concluded, any persons escaping their captors should be recognized as free under American law. The Court ruled that the Africans were free to return to their homeland.

Aftermath

By the time the Supreme Court made its decision, it had been nearly two years since the Africans had seen their homes. Despite the court ruling, the U.S. government provided no funds for their return to Africa. To do so, the Amistad Committee transported the former prisoners to appearances at churches and lectures, raising money not only for their transportation costs but also for Christian missionary work among the Mende people. On November 27, 1841, after sufficient funds had been raised, a ship departed the United States, returning the thirty-five survivors to Africa.

Jennifer Searcy

See also: Adams, John Quincy; Cinqué, Joseph; Jocelyn, Simeon Smith; Tappan, Lewis; Van Buren, Martin.

Further Reading

Cable, Mary. *Black Odyssey: The Case of the Slave Ship* Amistad. New York: Viking, 1971.

Jones, Howard. *Mutiny on the* Amistad: *The Saga of a Slave Revolt and Its Impact on American Abolition, Law, and Diplomacy.* New York: Oxford University Press, 1987.

McClendon, R. Earl. "The *Amistad* Claims: Inconsistencies of Policy." *Political Science Quarterly* 48 (September 1933): 386–412.

Osagie, Iyunolu F. *The Amistad* Revolt: Memory, Slavery, and the Politics of Identity in the United States and Sierra Leone. Athens: University of Georgia Press, 2000.

Anabaptists

During the sixteenth century, the institutional structure and theological foundation of Western Christianity was challenged by a series of five reformations that swept across Europe and fundamentally altered the religious and political landscape. The Lutheran

Reformation, the Calvinist (or Reform) movement, the Anglican Reformation, the Anabaptist Reformation, and the Catholic (or Counter) Reformation were all events of historical importance. Of these, the Anabaptist movement, certainly the smallest and least well known, had the most profound impact on the transatlantic effort to end the slave trade and to abolish slavery.

Origins

The Anabaptist movement originated in the cantons around Zurich, Switzerland, where the reformers Conrad Grebel and Felix Manz hoped to further purify the already-reformed practice of Christianity. These religious innovators believed that Martin Luther and John Calvin had not taken sufficient steps to remove all of the corruption from Christianity and to restore it to its biblical purity.

In particular, Grebel and Manz disapproved of the Lutherans' practice of infant baptism, which they believed made the action merely symbolic. The Anabaptist leaders also opposed the connection between civil and religious authority that characterized Calvin's model community of Geneva. Fearing the religious consequences of the tyranny of the majority, Grebel and Manz advocated the separation of church and state as the only way to protect religious minorities in a pluralistic society.

The term *Anabaptist*, initially used in a pejorative sense to describe Grebel and Manz's views on infant baptism, came to identify their followers. Anabaptists who followed the religious leader Menno Simmons became known as *Mennonites*. Other dissenting religious minorities, including the Amish and the Quakers, found a common theological and ideological bond within the Anabaptist community.

Because these minority religious communities challenged the orthodoxy of the reformers (i.e., Luther and Calvin), they were perceived as radicals and extremists. The common tenet of pacifism that characterized these groups made their members appear less than trustworthy citizens in a society in which militarism was understood as a test of national honor. Accordingly, the Anabaptist populations of Europe faced intense persecution during the century of religious warfare that followed the reformations. When the opportunity to migrate to the English North American colonies became a viable option in the eighteenth century, many Anabaptists, Mennonites, Quakers, and Amish took advantage.

Abolitionist Involvement

The antislavery impulse did not spontaneously emerge among these groups when they first arrived in North America. In fact, many Quakers profited from their involvement in the slave trade and the owning of slaves. It was not until 1688 that a group of Moravian Quakers living near Philadelphia issued the Germantown Protest, a public document demanding that all Quaker brethren divest themselves of any proprietary involvement in the slave trade and the ownership of slaves.

Quakers on both sides of the Atlantic were among the earliest abolitionists. They were some of the first individuals to recognize that slavery was a violation of a secular ethic—involving the essential question of good versus evil—while many coreligionists of more traditional, mainline denominations struggled with the understanding that slavery was a biblically sanctioned practice. Although the mainline Protestant denominations were divided over the issue of slavery, the faith communities of the Anabaptist tradition remained unified during the religious schisms that characterized the 1850s.

In many respects, the abolitionist movement was an outgrowth of the Enlightenment, a secular intellectual movement that swept across Europe during the middle of the eighteenth century. Though members of the Anabaptist tradition did not accept all that the Enlightenment supported, their personal experience with religious persecution and their willingness to speak the truth against authority made them kindred spirits with Enlightenment thinkers who could not comprehend slavery as a rational system despite any and all political and religious sanction.

The idea of nonresistance, which was universal among the Anabaptist traditions, became a key element of the antislavery movement's strategy. Although there were voices of dissent within the ranks of the abolitionist movement—those who said that open resistance was a right and a duty—it was the Christ-like notion of nonviolence that predominantly characterized the tone and spirit of the transatlantic abolitionist movement.

Some abolitionists from the Anabaptist tradition were widely known as antislavery advocates who openly supported abolitionism in a very public fashion. Others, drawing on a more personal, pietist worldview, supported the antislavery effort but shunned any attention that such activity might call to them. Among

American Quakers, in particular, this distinction only widened, as religious factions disputed the extent to which political involvement was a necessary part of doing battle with the sin of slavery.

The Anabaptists, Mennonites, Quakers, and Amish, many of whom had settled in the Midwest, were essential to the work of the Underground Railroad, which assisted fugitive slaves who escaped to the Northern states and Canada in search of freedom. In addition to this work, many missionaries from the Anabaptist community served the needs of free black settlements in Upper Canada (modern-day Ontario), assisting individuals as they made the transition from slave labor to wage labor.

In addition to their many efforts as foot soldiers of the abolitionist movement, members of the Anabaptist community were also key financial contributors to the antislavery cause. Several Quaker merchants in the United States and Great Britain had great business acumen, and they shared their wealth to support the work of antislavery efforts worldwide.

Junius P. Rodriguez

See also: Germantown Protest (1688); Quakers (Society of Friends).

Further Reading

Hauerwas, Stanley. *In Good Company: The Church as Polis.* Notre Dame, IN: University of Notre Dame Press, 1995.

Kraybill, Donald B., and Carl D. Bowman. *On the Backroad to Heaven: Old Order Hutterites, Mennonites, Amish, and Brethren.* Baltimore: Johns Hopkins University Press, 2001.

Liechty, Daniel. *Early Anabaptist Spirituality: Selected Writings.* New York: Paulist Press, 1994.

Anderson, Osborne Perry (1830–1872)

A printer and abolitionist, Osborne Perry Anderson was a close associate of the radical U.S. abolitionist John Brown. He participated in Brown's 1859 raid on the federal arsenal at Harpers Ferry, Virginia, and survived to write *A Voice From Harper's Ferry* (1861), the only written account of the attack.

Born to free African American parents in West Fallowfield, Pennsylvania, on July 27, 1830, Anderson was a well-educated man, who attended Oberlin College in Ohio and later became a printer by trade. After the passage of the Fugitive Slave Law of 1850, which required citizens to assist in the recovery of fugitive slaves and denied fugitives the right to trial by jury, Anderson joined the family of abolitionist Mary Ann Shadd as they emigrated to Upper Canada (present-day Ontario), settling in Chatham by 1851.

Shadd was the first African American woman to found, write, and edit an antislavery newspaper in North America. In the pages of the *Provincial Freeman*, Shadd advocated emigration and urged free blacks and fugitives to settle permanently in Canada. Although shy and unassuming, Anderson initially served as the subscription agent for the paper and wrote several editorials in which he condemned the practices of begging agents—individuals who sought support for the "refugees" who had already managed to find housing and employment in Canada. In these editorials, Anderson sided with Shadd, who believed that such begging reinforced the idea that slavery was appropriate for black people, as it implied that they were unable to become self-sufficient. By 1858, Anderson had become the printer and general assistant for the *Provincial Freeman.*

About this time, Brown began to visit Chatham and other Canadian cities, seeking both financial support and volunteers for his plan to end slavery in America. With the support of enslaved Africans, former slaves, and other "men true to the cause," Brown intended to carry out a revolution that would overthrow the government of the United States and bring about slavery's demise. Brown initially hoped that Kansas would become a terminus of the Underground Railroad instead of Canada, and he planned on training fugitive slaves in guerilla warfare to carry out surprise attacks on slaveholding plantations. He believed he would secure the immediate support of the slaves found there, and the ranks of committed fighting men in his army would be unstoppable.

Brown had the support of many in Chatham, including the Shadd family, who provided him the use of their printing press. At the Chatham Convention of May 8, 1858, Brown revealed his full revolutionary intentions, and Anderson was chosen to join Brown's raid through a selection of straws, as only one member of the *Provincial Freeman* team could be spared. However, the action was postponed when Brown realized that news of his secret military plans had become known in the United States, and he faced the reduced financial commitment of his white supporters there.

Subsequently elected a congressman in Brown's provisional government, Anderson underwent three weeks of training at Brown's Virginia farm. By the time Brown was ready to launch his attack, many

Further Reading

Anderson, Osborne Perry. *A Voice From Harper's Ferry.* 1861. Atlanta, GA: World View, 1980.

Hill, Daniel G. *The Freedom Seekers: Blacks in Early Canada.* Agincourt, Ontario, Canada: Book Society of Canada, 1981.

Libby, Jean. *Black Voices From Harpers Ferry; Osborne Anderson and the John Brown Raid.* Palo Alto, CA: Libby, 1979.

Winks, Robin W. *The Blacks in Canada: A History.* New Haven, CT: Yale University Press, 1971.

Antelope Case (1825)

In the *Antelope* case of 1825, the U.S. Supreme Court ruled that federal courts must recognize a nation's right to engage in the slave trade if the laws of that nation do not prohibit the trade.

The *Antelope* case involved an American ship commander, John Smith, who, in pirate-like fashion, raided Spanish-, Portuguese-, and American-owned ships along the West African coast and took possession of the slaves on board. Eventually, Smith transferred 281 slaves to the *Antelope* and headed for the Florida coast. On June 29, 1820, a U.S. Treasury cutter seized the *Antelope* and delivered the crew and captives to Savannah, Georgia.

Richard Wylly Haberstram, the U.S. district attorney for Georgia, instructed U.S. marshal John Morel to house the slaves in Savannah. Acting as a legal advocate for the Africans under the instructions of President James Monroe, Haberstram sought an order that would have required the return of the slaves to Africa, under the provisions of an 1819 act stating that any enslaved Africans transported into the United States were to be delivered to the president of the United States for return to Africa at the government's expense.

However, the slave trade was legal under Spanish and Portuguese law at the time these slaves were transported from Africa. Agents purporting to represent the Spanish and Portuguese owners of the seized slaves filed claims for the recovery of their property.

In February 1821, the first trial of the *Antelope* case began. Haberstram retreated from his earlier position and appealed to the district and circuit court decisions to grant all foreign claims that could be documented. William Wirt, the U.S. attorney general, postponed the Supreme Court hearing until racial tension in America had subsided. The Missouri Compromise and the limitation of slavery were still fresh wounds in America. The election of 1824 was looming and promised to be quite heated. On February 26,

Osborne Perry Anderson, a free black and printer by trade, was one of only five participants to survive John Brown's 1859 raid on Harpers Ferry, Virginia. His book two years later is the only firsthand written account of the incident. *(Photographs and Print Division, Schomburg Center for Research in Black Culture, The New York Public Library, Astor, Lenox, and Tilden Foundations)*

Chatham men had withdrawn their support, and only two from Canada (Stewart Taylor and Anderson) joined Brown in carrying out the raid on Harpers Ferry on October 16–18, 1859.

During the attack, Anderson helped capture the grandnephew of former president George Washington, Lewis W. Washington. When Anderson realized that the raid was failing, he withdrew, following the Underground Railroad to return to Chatham, where, with Shadd's assistance, he wrote *A Voice From Harper's Ferry.* With the exception of Anderson, Brown and the other men who had fought at Harpers Ferry were either killed in the raid or subsequently executed.

Anderson later joined the Union army during the U.S. Civil War. He then settled in Washington, D.C., where he died on December 13, 1872.

Rosemary Sadlier

See also: Brown, John; Harpers Ferry Raid (1859); Shadd Cary, Mary Ann.

1825, after the election of John Quincy Adams to the presidency, the Supreme Court finally heard the case, which centered on whether the Africans were to be considered free persons or property.

Chief Justice John Marshall's opinion stated that, although he believed slavery violated natural law, many nations approved of the trade, and therefore the Court could not rule that it was a violation of international law. The Court must recognize, Marshall argued, that citizens of nations that have not prohibited the slave trade have a right to engage in that trade. The Supreme Court ordered that the valid foreign claims be paid.

By the time the Supreme Court heard the case, many of the enslaved Africans from the *Antelope* had died, and no one had a record of which survivors had originated on the ships. Thirty-nine randomly selected Africans, a number proportionate to the legitimate foreign claims, were sold by the federal government to a Georgia congressman and the proceeds delivered to the foreign slave owners. The Court ordered approximately 120 slaves, including all of those from the American-owned slave ship, to be returned to Liberia, Africa, at the U.S. government's expense.

Philine Georgette Vega

See also: Liberia; Sierra Leone.

Further Reading

Noonan, John T. *The Antelope: The Ordeal of the Recaptured Africans in the Administrations of James Monroe and John Quincy Adams.* Berkeley: University of California Press, 1977.

Anthony, Susan B. (1820–1906)

A lifelong supporter of women's suffrage and abolition, Susan Brownell Anthony helped lay the groundwork for the adoption of the Nineteenth Amendment, which granted voting rights to all American women. Although she did not live to see its passage, her activities over the course of more than fifty years made her a pioneering figure in the women's rights movement.

Anthony was born in Adams, Massachusetts, on February 15, 1820. At the age of six, she moved with her family to Battenville, New York. Although her father had married into a Baptist family, Susan and her siblings were instilled with his Quaker egalitarian beliefs. The Anthony family was active in the equal

rights movement, and such notable abolitionists as Frederick Douglass and William Lloyd Garrison frequently visited their home. Her family's activities and conversations with these visitors fueled her interest in the abolitionist and women's rights movements.

In 1850, Anthony was introduced to suffrage leader Elizabeth Cady Stanton in Seneca Falls, New York. The two women quickly became close friends and led the growing women's suffrage movement during the second half of the nineteenth century. Anthony and Stanton first worked together to form the Women's New York State Temperance Society in 1852, and they quickly learned that women were discriminated against in mainstream reform movements. Unless they obtained greater political rights, they recognized, women would never make a lasting impact on issues such as temperance.

Beginning in 1854, Anthony and Stanton focused their attention on creating an effective women's suffrage movement. They proved to be a perfect match as movement leaders. Stanton was known for her oratorical skills and writing abilities, whereas Anthony was admired for her organizational capabilities. Anthony was extremely successful at securing lecturers and raising money for women's rights conventions. Additionally, she possessed a talent for organizing women at the grassroots level. From 1854 to 1860, Anthony organized and circulated petitions to the New York State legislature demanding improved property and wage rights for women, along with the right to vote in all elections.

Although Anthony focused her attention primarily on the women's suffrage movement, she dedicated herself to the abolitionist cause as well. From 1856 to 1861, she served as the New York representative to William Lloyd Garrison's American Anti-Slavery Society. As a result of the agitation of Northern abolitionists, blacks exercised full political rights throughout New England, with the exception of Connecticut.

In an 1861 speech, Anthony argued for the full rights of citizenship for African Americans in the North, stating, "Let us open to the colored man all our schools. . . . Let us admit him into all our mechanic shops, stores, offices, and lucrative business associations, to work side by side with his white brother; let him rent such pew in the church, and occupy such seat in the theatre, and public lecture room, as he pleases . . . let him share in all the accommodations of our hotels, stages, railroads and steamboats. . . .

Extend to him all the rights of citizenship. Let him vote and be voted for; let him sit upon the judges bench, and in the juror's box."

With the onset of the U.S. Civil War in 1861, Anthony and Stanton put their suffrage activities on hold and began to work toward the emancipation of African Americans. They actively championed this cause by forming the Women's National Loyal League. Once again focusing attention on the grassroots level, in spring 1863, Anthony and Stanton circulated petitions demanding an immediate end to slavery, gathering 400,000 signatures.

In December 1865, the Thirteenth Amendment was ratified, abolishing slavery in the United States. Anthony and Stanton believed that the Republicans also would grant women suffrage in recognition of their activities during the war. However, with the proposal of the Fourteenth and Fifteenth amendments, which guaranteed citizenship and suffrage to black men, Anthony was shocked that complete equality had not been extended to women. The word "male" was inserted into the Fifteenth Amendment, boldly declaring that only men were guaranteed equal rights in America. The legislation outraged suffrage activists, and it would polarize the women's rights movement at a time when it most needed to be unified.

During the postwar era, Anthony continued to support black political rights, but not at the cost of women's rights. She believed wholeheartedly that women should not be given the vote after blacks. Fearful that the votes of black men might thwart women's suffrage, both Anthony and Stanton found themselves at odds with abolitionists, who believed that "this hour belongs to the Negro." In the abolitionists' opinion, women's suffrage should be dealt with only after suffrage was fully secured for black men.

Bitterly divided over this issue, Anthony and Stanton severed their alliances with abolitionist colleagues such as Lucy Stone and Henry Blackwell. In 1869, Stanton and Anthony organized the National Woman Suffrage Association (NWSA), an independent female suffrage society that refused to support the Fifteenth Amendment unless it granted suffrage rights to women. The NWSA stood in opposition to Stone's group, the American Woman Suffrage Association, whose leaders supported black male suffrage as defined in the Fifteenth Amendment and sought women's suffrage on a state-by-state basis. Alienated from her former allies, Anthony once again resorted to grassroots tactics. She targeted new

Susan B. Anthony, right, with friend and fellow suffragist Elizabeth Cady Stanton, began her reform work as an abolitionist. Like other notable women in the movement, she relied on "moral suasion" to persuade listeners that slavery is wrong. *(Hulton Archive/Getty Images)*

groups of supporters, such as teachers, journalists, and "social purity" activists, to join the ranks of the NWSA.

An unmarried woman for her entire life, Anthony devoted her remaining years to securing the vote for women. She and the NWSA changed tactics, arguing that the Fourteenth and Fifteenth Amendments applied to all citizens, male and female. In 1872, Anthony was arrested for attempting to vote in the presidential election. Although she received only a minor fine, she drew significant national attention to the women's suffrage movement.

After twenty years of separation and healing, the two factions of the women's suffrage movement reunited in 1890. Anthony served as vice president and then president of the newly formed National American Woman Suffrage Association until 1900.

She died from heart failure on March 13, 1906, and was buried in Rochester, New York.

Jennifer Searcy

See also: Mott, James, and Lucretia Coffin Mott; Stanton, Elizabeth Cady; Stone, Lucy; Women's Rights and the Abolitionist Movement.

Further Reading

Anthony, Katharine. *Susan B. Anthony: Her Personal History and Her Era.* Garden City, NY: Doubleday, 1954.
Barry, Kathleen. *Susan B. Anthony: Biography of a Singular Feminist.* New York: New York University Press, 1988.
Venet, Wendy Hamand. *Neither Ballots nor Bullets: Women Abolitionists and the Civil War.* Charlottesville: University of Virginia Press, 1991.

Anti-Abolition Riots

By the 1830s, a small but vocal group of radical abolitionists were advocating what they called "immediatism"—the immediate, unconditional, and uncompensated emancipation of all men, women, and children held in slavery—relying on the language of the Bible and including women in both the delivery of and audience for this argument. As the decade wore on, the immediatists became increasingly adamant that theirs was the only acceptable position.

The radical abolitionists were most active in the northeastern United States during this decade. Their message was particularly threatening to two groups: Northerners, who either tacitly accepted the slave system or preferred a less drastic plan for abolishing it, and Southerners, who saw any scrutiny of their native "peculiar institution" as a threat to their right to conduct their lives as they saw fit. Not surprisingly, the incidence of anti-abolition riots and mob activities peaked during the 1830s, although reports of such events can be found from the 1820s through the early days of the U.S. Civil War.

Radical abolitionism was banned in the slave-holding South, and quick retribution awaited radicals who dared to speak or publish newspapers or pamphlets there. In the Northern states, where anti-abolition protests took place, immediatists endured numerous varieties of harassment. Name-calling, threats, and heckling from the anti-abolition crowd, "misplaced" luggage or last-minute cancellations of speaking venues or sleeping accommodations, and physical violence were among the many weapons meted out to radical abolitionists. Because many were Quakers or pacifists, their beliefs did not allow them to effectively respond to these actions.

Two particular anti-abolition riots illustrate the nation's experience in the years leading up to the Civil War. Following a summer and fall of rising violence, the Quaker poet John Greenleaf Whittier and other abolitionists were stoned in Concord, Massachusetts, in late 1834. The next year, in October 1835, when English abolitionist George Thompson was invited to speak in Boston by the Massachusetts Female Anti-Slavery Society, an ensuing riot very nearly turned deadly. An opponent of the antislavery movement entered the group's meeting hall, intent on removing the Englishman and handing him over to the waiting mob outside, but he soon learned that Thompson was not present (having been persuaded that it was unsafe to attend). It was decided that William Lloyd Garrison, publisher of the radical newspaper *The Liberator* and one of the leaders of the immediatist movement, would be a worthy substitute to satisfy the angry throng. Garrison was violently taken from the meeting hall and led down the street at the end of a rope, presumably in preparation for hanging by the crowd. Only the quick action of Boston's mayor, who rescued Garrison and ordered him held under guard overnight in the city's jail for his own security, prevented the frenzied horde from realizing its goal of killing a prominent abolitionist that day.

Similar violence occurred in May 1838 in Philadelphia, but what is particularly disturbing about this riot is that it targeted women who were active in the immediatist movement. In response to the rising tide of anti-abolition violence, a number of men who were dedicated to the constitutional precept of free expression pooled their funds to erect Pennsylvania Hall. Intended to house the offices of a variety of social reform groups, the hall also provided a number of meeting rooms and a large assembly hall for lectures. Though the hall's stated purpose was to allow the free exchange of all ideas, because much of its financial backing and direction had come from abolitionists, it seems clear that discussion of slavery was its primary purpose.

The hall's dedication ceremonies, held in early May 1838, were given over to antislavery speakers, meetings, and rallies. At the culminating event, the abolitionist lecturer Angelina Grimké was scheduled to present the final evening's address. While Grimké spoke to a packed house, a proslavery mob became increasingly agitated outside the hall; contemporary records indicate that, although the interior shutters were quickly closed, those present in the audience could still hear the throng's shouted threats. As bricks, rocks, and bottles smashed the second-floor auditorium's windows, Grimké continued speaking, delivering the last (and, by most accounts, the most poised and powerful) speech of her brief lecturing career. Following her address, the abolitionists in attendance left the hall without meaningful police protection, choosing to simply walk through the mob with heads held high and eyes pointed straight ahead. In many cases, white women left arm in arm with free black women. Although there were certainly catcalls and threats from the crowd, no one who left the hall that evening was injured or killed.

A short time after the hall was cleared and closed down for the night, however, the alarm went up: The mob had broken in, destroyed all of the antislavery materials they could find, and set the building on fire. As the fire department watched from a distance, the magnificent structure with such grand aspirations burned to its foundations. It was never rebuilt, nor was any other structure of such a scale created to replace it elsewhere in the North or the South.

Such anti-abolition riots were indicative of a basic shift in American attitudes of the era, as many Northern whites came to view abolition as a threat to the social order. Abolitionist ideology and the right of Americans to discuss that ideology freely were under attack by violent mobs within the abolitionists' own Northern communities.

Barbara Schwarz Wachal

See also: Garrison, William Lloyd; Immediatism.

Further Reading

Curtis, Michael Kent. "The 1837 Killing of Elijah Lovejoy by an Anti-abolition Mob: Free Speech, Republican Government, and the Privileges of American Citizens." *UCLA Law Review* 44 (April 1997): 1109–84.

Gilje, Paul. *Rioting in America.* Bloomington: Indiana University Press, 1996.

Grimsted, David. *American Mobbing, 1828–1861: Toward Civil War.* New York: Oxford University Press, 1998.

Kerber, Linda K. "Abolitionists and Amalgamators: The New York City Race Riots of 1834." *New York History* 58 (January 1967): 28–39.

Morrison, Howard A. "Gentlemen of Proper Understanding: A Closer Look at Utica's Anti-Abolitionist Mob." *New York History* 62 (January 1978): 61–82.

Richards, Leonard L. *Gentlemen of Property and Standing: Anti-Abolition Mobs in Jacksonian America.* New York: Oxford University Press, 1970.

Runcie, John. " 'Hunting the Nigs' in Philadelphia: The Race Riot of August, 1842." *Pennsylvania History* 39 (April 1972): 187–218.

Anti-Slavery Advocate

Founded during summer 1852, the *Anti-Slavery Advocate* was a radical monthly newspaper edited in Dublin, Ireland, and published in London until 1863. The paper was co-edited by Bristol abolitionist John Bishop Estlin, a Dublin printer and bookseller, and Richard Davis Webb, a Scottish Quaker abolitionist and leader of the Hibernian Anti-Slavery Society. It was largely financed by Wilson Armistead of Leeds and the Bristol and Clifton Ladies Anti-Slavery Society.

The *Anti-Slavery Advocate* was an outgrowth of the Anglo-American Anti-Slavery Association, a short-lived Garrisonian group organized by Estlin, George Thompson, William Farmer, Robert Smith, and William Wells Brown. Together with the *Anti-Slavery Reporter* and the *Anti-Slavery Watchman,* this newspaper served as an example of the strength of the British abolitionist movement between 1833 and 1861.

Estlin's antislavery activities no doubt influenced his editorial decision to publish the lecture schedules and meeting reports of many black professional abolitionists who visited Britain. He was comfortable enough in the British antislavery movement that he provided room and board for many visiting Garrisonians and a number of fugitive slaves, including Frederick Douglass and Brown.

Estlin and Webb were motivated to launch the *Anti-Slavery Advocate* by their belief that the *Anti-Slavery Reporter,* the main paper of the British and Foreign Anti-Slavery Society, presented a mistaken view of the antislavery landscape in Britain and America. Thus, the objective of the *Anti-Slavery Advocate* was to provide a more balanced picture of the antislavery movement in Britain and the United States through editorials, commentaries, and articles. Indeed, as co-editor, Webb, who also contributed to the *Anti-Slavery Standard* (the newspaper of the American Anti-Slavery Society), reached a point at which "he was practically monitoring the whole exchange of men and ideas" concerning slavery "between the British and American Garrisonians." In addition to his editorial responsibilities,

Webb solidified his antislavery credentials by writing and distributing antislavery pamphlets.

With an initial circulation of 200, the *Anti-Slavery Advocate*, which was first supported by two American Quaker abolitionists, Sarah Pugh and Abby Kimber, gave antislavery proponents an opportunity to spread propaganda and generate support for the British abolitionist movement. The *Anti-Slavery Advocate* also offered those involved in the antislavery movement a reasonable chance to meet the leaders of the American movement.

The *Anti-Slavery Advocate* was distributed in Britain by the London publishers William Tweedie and Henry James Tresidder. The latter's small network of friends in Belfast, Glasgow, Liverpool, Brighton, Edinburgh, and elsewhere accounted for the *Anti-Slavery Advocate*'s success during its first eleven years. Under their editorial leadership, the paper "regularly reported on British Garrisonian meetings and other Anglo-American antislavery news" and "criticized proslavery people and organizations."

In an attempt to fashion itself as a complete antislavery newspaper, the *Anti-Slavery Advocate* also covered other issues that were important to the British abolitionist movement. These included the American struggle against proslavery factions, Britain's utilization of slave-grown American cotton, and the Irish immigrant's antipathy to free blacks in America.

The *Anti-Slavery Advocate*'s editorials, which discussed the status of American slavery and how Britain could help America, found no moral ground on which to support the American institution of slavery. The paper argued that if Britain were true to its sympathies, then it could have no compassion for proslavery advocates in the United States who wished to build a great regional empire on the enslavement of millions of their fellow men.

The desire to form a regional empire was driven by the cultivation of cotton. On the subject of Britain's use of slave-grown American cotton, the *Anti-Slavery Advocate* not only exposed the hypocritical stance of England but also persisted in its press comments. The editorial staff explained and highlighted Britain's abolitionist movement to its readers and suggested that Britain was responsible for the growth and development of America's peculiar institution "through her continued and ever larger use of slave-grown American cotton." Indeed, the *Anti-Slavery Advocate*, advancing a connection between Britain and Ireland, suggested in 1859 that Britain was in no "better position than Ireland was before the famine; for cotton is to the English more than the potato to the Irish."

The connection between England and Ireland, along with the *Anti-Slavery Advocate*'s organizational structure, led the editors to focus attention on Irish emigration to America. The *Anti-Slavery Advocate*'s print articles on the subject of Irish antipathy to the free black man in America, which appeared in the early 1860s, centered on the Irish indifference or hostility to Negro freedom. Although the principles of the British abolitionist movement had been instilled among the Irish relocating to the United States, the *Anti-Slavery Advocate* made clear that "nearly every individual of Irish emigration" supported slavery, although they were the same class of people "who have been all their lives, while in their own country, complaining of tyranny and oppression."

Glen Anthony Harris

See also: Hibernian Anti-Slavery Society; Webb, Richard Davis.

Further Reading

Lorimer, Douglas A. "The Role of Anti-Slavery Sentiment in English Reactions to the American Civil War." *Historical Journal* 19 (June 1976): 405–20.

Rice, C. Duncan. " 'Humanity Sold for Sugar!' The British Abolitionist Response to Free Trade in Slave-Grown Sugar." *Historical Journal* 13 (September 1970): 402–18.

———. *The Scots Abolitionist: 1833–1861.* Baton Rouge: Louisiana State University Press, 1981.

Ripley, C. Peter, et al., eds. *The Black Abolitionist Papers.* 5 vols. Chapel Hill: University of North Carolina Press, 1985–1992.

Turley, David. *The Culture of English Antislavery, 1780–1860.* New York: Routledge, 1991.

Anti-Slavery Bugle

The *Anti-Slavery Bugle* was founded by Abigail ("Abby") Kelley Foster in 1845 in Salem, Ohio. A "poorly printed four-page paper that lacked an editor, subscribers, press, or type of its own" at its inception, the *Anti-Slavery Bugle* would become one of the most influential antislavery newspapers in the United States. Foster, who wanted to expand the abolitionist movement into the Western United States, established the *Anti-Slavery Bugle* after she discovered that the leading Garrisonian newspapers of the day, the *National Anti-Slavery Standard* and *The Liberator,* took too long to reach Ohio's country towns.

A delegate to the World Anti-Slavery Convention in 1840 and a supporter of women's rights, Foster forged a circulation of 1,000 for the *Anti-Slavery Bugle* within a year of its start-up. Until its demise in 1861, the *Anti-Slavery Bugle* was guided by her strong sense of character, recruitment of editors, and loyalty to the abolitionist movement. The Western Anti-Slavery Society, which was affiliated with the Liberty Party, financed and published the paper.

With a masthead that read, "I love agitation when there is a cause for it—the alarm bell which startles the inhabitants of a city saves them from being burned in their beds," the *Anti-Slavery Bugle's* first editorial spelled out its promise to the Western abolitionist movement and the Southern proslavery establishment to "sound the bugle-note of Freedom over the hills and through the valleys, blowing a blast that will wake from their slumbers the tyrants at the South and their guilty abettors at the North." In pursuit of that goal, the paper carried news of the antislavery movement, but it also ran stories, essays, and opinion pieces on the temperance and peace movements and the anti–capital punishment cause.

The husband-and-wife team of Benjamin Smith Jones, a Philadelphia Quaker who had become a Garrisonian abolitionist in the mid-1830s, and Jane E. ("Lizzie") Hitchcock Jones, an abolitionist speaker and executive committee member of the Western Anti-Slavery Society, served as the newspaper's first editors. It was under their editorial leadership from 1845 to 1849 that the *Anti-Slavery Bugle* established its footing among other antislavery papers. The Joneses' own abolitionist activities gave further credibility to the *Bugle's* antislavery credentials. Benjamin gave public lectures for the Western Anti-Slavery Society; Jane denounced Ohio's enactment of the Black Laws, criticized the Fugitive Slave Law, and participated, at Foster's request, in an antislavery lecture tour of New England and western Pennsylvania during the 1840s. The *Anti-Slavery Bugle* had such a reputation as an antislavery advocate that the former slave and abolition evangelist Sojourner Truth made the newspaper's office her headquarters upon her move to Salem, Ohio.

After the Joneses gave up their editorial responsibilities—Benjamin wanted to return to his trade as a cabinetmaker and Jane was pregnant—the *Anti-Slavery Bugle* came under the editorial direction of Oliver Johnson, an antislavery journalist and trusted associate of William Lloyd Garrison, from 1849 to 1851. An important figure in the American antislavery establishment, Johnson had been a cofounder of the New England Anti-Slavery Society, editorial director of the *Pennsylvania Freeman* and the *Standard,* and co-editor of the *National Anti-Slavery Standard.* In addition, he had worked with Garrison and edited his antislavery newspaper, *The Liberator,* in his absence. With the *Bugle* in the sure hands of Johnson, Foster was able to turn her attention to spreading the abolitionist movement to eastern New York. Johnson's short two-year stint as editor maintained, but did not altogether increase, the *Bugle's* standing within the antislavery establishment.

From 1851 to 1859, the *Anti-Slavery Bugle* was edited by Marius Robinson, whose antislavery credentials had been established some seventeen years earlier when, as a student at the Lane Theological Seminary in 1834, he had helped promote Garrisonian abolitionism among Cincinnati's poor black population. Robinson continued his antislavery activity after his editorial tenure with the *Anti-Slavery Bugle.* Indeed, in 1860, he co-authored (with Benjamin and Jane Jones) the "Eighteenth Annual Report of the Executive Committee of the Western Anti-Slavery Society," which paid tribute to John Brown's rebellious raid at Harpers Ferry. Robinson's close associate, Daniel Howell Hise, a respected and successful Salem businessman who was sympathetic to the Republican Party and an ardent financial supporter of the abolitionist movement, was a faithful subscriber to the *Anti-Slavery Bugle.* Hise took great pride in entertaining antislavery leaders such as Foster and Johnson, and he went so far as to put his carriage at their service whenever it could be spared. When Robinson's tenure ended in January 1859, the Joneses returned as editors of the newspaper.

Their return, along with Foster's renewed attention to the ideological purity of the paper, was not enough to overcome the lack of financial support that seemed to always trouble the paper. The fall of Fort Sumter in April 1861, combined with President Abraham Lincoln's call for volunteers, led the Western Anti-Slavery Society to suspend publication of the *Anti-Slavery Bugle* on May 4, 1861.

Although the talented editors of the paper had been central to its success, the *Anti-Slavery Bugle* would not have survived without Foster's stewardship. Jane Jones acknowledged as much: In the final issue of the paper, she wrote that Foster's "earnestness" and "scathing rebuke of oppression" for more than a quarter century had been invaluable to the publication's overall accomplishments.

Glen Anthony Harris

See also: Foster, Abigail Kelley.

Further Reading

Pease, Jane H., and William H. Pease. "Confrontation and Abolition in the 1850s." *Journal of American History* 58 (March 1972): 923–37.

Ripley, C. Peter, et al., eds. *The Black Abolitionist Papers.* 5 vols. Chapel Hill: University of North Carolina Press, 1985–1992.

Sterling, Dorothy. *Ahead of Her Time: Abby Kelley and the Politics of Anti-Slavery.* New York: W.W. Norton, 1991.

Anti-Slavery International

The London-based organization Anti-Slavery International (ASI) has the distinction of being the oldest human rights organization in the world. Founded in 1839, the organization came into existence shortly after slavery was abolished throughout the British Empire. Its mission was to monitor those areas where slavery had been abolished to guarantee that it would not reemerge and to work diligently to advance the cause of emancipation in those areas where slavery persisted.

Members of the British and Foreign Anti-Slavery Society began this work in 1839, one year after slavery ended in the British Empire under the terms of the 1833 Abolition of Slavery Act (commonly known as the British Emancipation Act). Having succeeded in pressuring Parliament to enact this measure, British abolitionists realized that only through a campaign of sustained vigilance could they ensure that the terms of the emancipation measure would be maintained. British abolitionists were also fearful that the system of apprenticeship that was created throughout the British West Indies under the terms of the act might simply create a new form of unfree labor unless the abuses inherent in this practice were closely monitored by outside observers. They further realized that they could not rest until slavery was abolished in all settings throughout the world. (Some 165 years after that work first began, the historic mission of ASI continues.)

During the 1890s, the organization expanded its mission to advocate against the ill treatment of indigenous peoples when reports of atrocities in the Belgian Congo began to surface. As a result of this new focus, the organization merged with the Aborigines Protection Society in 1909. The Anti-Slavery and Aborigines Protection Society worked closely with the League of Nations to enact policies to eliminate slavery and unfree labor practices worldwide.

These measures included the Convention on the Abolition of Slavery (1926) and later action by the United Nations, which enacted the Supplementary Convention on the Abolition of Slavery, the Slave Trade, and Institutions and Practices Similar to Slavery (1957) in response to a sustained campaign by antislavery advocates. In 1975, ASI lobbied the United Nations to create an international panel of experts within that body that would be constantly dedicated to the elimination of modern slavery. This political action led to the establishment of the UN Working Group on Contemporary Forms of Slavery.

In keeping with the tradition of its abolitionist founders, members of ASI maintain that the power of moral suasion is one of the most potent tools for combating the institution of slavery. Throughout the years, ASI has used a combination of education and agitation to make the public aware of slavery and unfree labor practices around the world. Direct political action, in the form of sustained letter-writing campaigns and petitions, has been used to convince governments that it is in their best interest to enforce their own laws and bring an end to slavery.

ASI has registered successes in its campaign against contemporary forms of unfree labor. The creation of the Rugmark Foundation in the early 1990s was a tremendous victory in ASI's campaign against the use of forced child labor in the carpet mills of India and Pakistan. The foundation monitors the carpet mills and issues its Rugmark seal to the products of mills that are in compliance with their country's labor laws. Adding about two dollars to the cost of a carpet, the seal guarantees that the product was not produced with the use of slave labor. Similarly, ASI was successful in Brazil during the 1990s, when a sustained campaign against the use of slave laborers in the charcoal kiln mills supporting the Brazilian steel industry forced government action to eliminate forced labor practices.

Since 1840, ASI has published the *Anti-Slavery Reporter*, a quarterly journal that includes detailed accounts of abolitionist activities worldwide, legislative updates on parliamentary procedures that have led to the abolition of slavery in Britain and its colonies, details of the political action taken by both proslavery and antislavery supporters worldwide, and annual reports of the British and Foreign Anti-Slavery Society (later called the Anti-Slavery Society and today known as Anti-Slavery International). Now called the *Reporter*, the publication is a quarterly newsletter that continues to monitor antislavery efforts in all parts of the world.

Members worldwide have maintained the organization both financially and through in-kind volunteer efforts that are designed to pressure recalcitrant governments to take action against the practices of bonded labor, child labor, and human trafficking. The work of abolition and emancipation persists in the twenty-first century as human rights advocates worldwide support the efforts of organizations such as Anti-Slavery International.

Junius P. Rodriguez

See also: Abolition of Slavery Act (1833); *Anti-Slavery Reporter.*

Further Reading

Bales, Kevin. *Disposable People: New Slavery in the Global Economy.* Berkeley: University of California Press, 1999.

Anti-Slavery Reporter

The *Anti-Slavery Reporter,* the primary newspaper of the British and Foreign Anti-Slavery Society, evolved from the *Anti-Slavery Monthly Reporter* and began publication in 1840. It was during this time that British abolitionists turned to making the abolition of slavery and opposition to the apprenticeship of freed slaves a mass campaign. The *Monthly Reporter,* which first appeared in 1823, was edited off and on after 1825 by Zachary Macaulay, one of the leaders of the Evangelical Party, which helped bring an end to the British slave trade. The *Monthly Reporter* was the organ of the London Society for the Mitigation and Gradual Abolition of Slavery throughout the British Dominions.

Published biweekly, the *Monthly Reporter,* although relatively inexpensive at 3 pence per copy, ran at a financial loss. From 1841 to 1842, the paid circulation of the paper was approximately 1,200 copies. An additional 700 copies were distributed free of charge, mainly to members of the British and Foreign Anti-Slavery Society, the only antislavery organization of national stature and the major clearinghouse for black abolitionists in Britain.

The responsibility for editing the *Anti-Slavery Monthly Reporter* fell to a committee of the Anti-Slavery Society made up of Macaulay, Thomas Pringle, George Stephen, and others. Organizations, individuals, and newspapers that were sympathetic to the British abolitionist movement looked to the society—then under the leadership of John Scoble and Lewis Alexis Chamerovzow—and the *Monthly Reporter* as the best source of information about the black abolitionists who came to them requesting funds and the use of lecture halls. In addition, the paper warned local reform leaders about the occasional black abolitionist imposter who sought to raise money fraudulently.

The *Monthly Reporter* published accounts of the meetings of associations affiliated with the London Anti-Slavery Society. It also discussed the British government's policies on abolition and related these ideas to workers in the antislavery movement in the British West Indies.

Under the leadership of Macaulay, who had gained firsthand knowledge of West Indian slavery and the slave trade as an overseer in Jamaica and during a transatlantic trip on a slave ship, the *Monthly Reporter* took a leading role in publishing the literature of both the proslavery and antislavery movements. For example, the paper printed excerpts from the proslavery *West Indian Reporter* (published from 1827 to 1831), which was designed to refute the *Reporter* by giving accurate information to the people of England on West Indian affairs.

When the *Monthly Reporter* became the *Anti-Slavery Reporter* in 1840, most of the early editorial work was handled by the Reverend J.H. Hinton, an influential abolitionist and Baptist minister. As editor of the *Reporter,* Hinton represented the newspaper's evangelical dynamic and Britain's antislavery establishment. In 1841, Hinton was replaced as editor of the *Reporter* by Scoble, who, in turn, was replaced in 1852 by the novelist, social critic, and committee member Chamerovzow.

Scoble, a native of Devonshire, had been a cofounder of the British and Foreign Anti-Slavery Society and an organizer of the 1840 World Anti-Slavery Convention in London. His stint as secretary and editor of the *Anti-Slavery Reporter* was marked by tension and conflict among different groups of abolitionists. Indeed, for all the news and information the *Anti-Slavery Reporter* supplied to its readers during Scoble's tenure, the paper did not escape criticism. Former radical members of the British and Foreign Anti-Slavery Society argued that the *Reporter* "gave a distorted and very partial view of the antislavery scene in both Britain and America."

As a result, the rival British *Anti-Slavery Advocate* was established in 1852 to provide an alternative viewpoint to that presented by the *Reporter.* Founded by John Estlin, the *Anti-Slavery Advocate* eventually became the major competitor of the *Anti-Slavery Reporter.*

After 1840, the *Anti-Slavery Reporter* began to appear monthly in a condensed size and at an increased price. It focused on publishing information about newly arrived American black abolitionists and their personal histories, abolitionists' experience in the movement, and organizational ties in the United States. In addition, the paper often included American letters of introduction and visiting abolitionists' statements of purpose, as well as lecture schedules and reports of meetings.

During his stint as editor, Chamerovzow used the offices of the British Anti-Slavery Society not only to foster the further development of the *Reporter* and to mend relations among competing abolitionist groups but also to promote and distribute slave narratives. Most notably, the narrative of American ex-slave John Brown, *Slave Life in Georgia* (1854), was edited and published by Chamerovzow, and his involvement exemplified the opportunities for publishing personal accounts of ex-slaves and abolitionists offered by the *Anti-Slavery Reporter* and the British antislavery network.

Chamerovzow, in an attempt to find a common ground for British abolitionists, supported the importation of free-labor cotton from the Lancashire mills and articulated a shared desire to isolate American churchmen who were not firmly antislavery.

In 1910, one year after the British and Foreign Anti-Slavery Society merged with the Aborigines Protection Society to form the Anti-Slavery and Aborigines Protection Society, the *Reporter* was renamed the *Anti-Slavery Reporter and Aborigines' Friend*. The newspaper has been published from that date to the present.

Glen Anthony Harris

See also: Anti-Slavery International.

Further Reading

Fladeland, Betty. *Abolitionist and Working-Class Problems in the Age of Industrialization.* Baton Rouge: Louisiana State University Press, 1984.

Klingberg, Frank J. *The Anti-Slavery Movement in England: A Study in English Humanitarianism.* New Haven, CT: Yale University Press, 1926.

Ripley, C. Peter, et al., eds. *The Black Abolitionist Papers.* 5 vols. Chapel Hill: University of North Carolina Press, 1985–1992.

Turley, David. *The Culture of English Antislavery, 1780–1860.* New York: Routledge, 1991.

Apprenticeship and Emancipation

The British Parliament instituted a system of apprenticeship—periods of supervised labor designed to transition people from slavery to freedom—after the passage of the Abolition of Slavery Act (1833, commonly known as the British Emancipation Act), which abolished slavery throughout the British Empire. Though it was initially designed as a benevolent practice to aid former slaves, the system was criticized by abolitionists for its harshness. Facing mounting protests, Parliament finally abolished the apprenticeship system in 1838.

Origins

Great Britain officially abolished the transatlantic slave trade in 1807, but slavery persisted in the colonies for decades afterward. Slavery in the colonies existed as a system of racist and economic oppression. The dynamics of slavery in the British Caribbean differed from those in other parts of the Atlantic. In the United States, in many parts of the slaveholding South, blacks were still a minority population, whereas in the British Caribbean, blacks had always outnumbered the white population. Sizable numbers of free blacks lived in the Caribbean, including relatively wealthy blacks and blacks who owned slaves themselves.

The Haitian Revolution (1791–1804) spurred debate about how best to handle the slavery question. Haitian independence made the colonial powers and slaveholders very nervous. Britain decided that it would be better to allow controlled emancipation than to risk having no presence in the Caribbean. Instead of allowing the Caribbean islands to fall—and possibly losing all control of the land, resources, and labor there—Parliament began a slow process of ending slavery in the colonies. The goals were to keep the planters content by continuing to provide a laboring class, pacifying the black population temporarily with the prospect of freedom, removing abolition from the domestic British population's political agenda, and, most importantly, retaining the profitability of the islands for Great Britain.

The abolition of slavery in the British Caribbean was achieved in a much different manner than in the United States. The United States was split nearly equally on the slavery question; with half the country supporting slavery, peaceful and speedy abolition would have been hard to achieve. For Britain, however, slavery was not a matter that directly affected the British population, yet the abolitionist movement in Britain was quite strong. As the abolitionist movement grew, Parliament felt a greater need to appease its domestic population.

Equally strong, however, were the plantation interests. West Indian slave interests—the most powerful nonpolitical pressure group in Parliament—watered down all serious abolitionist attempts at emancipation. Part of the problem was that individuals other than the owners managed most of the plantations. Life in the Caribbean was not considered desirable for the British; even British subjects born in the Caribbean preferred the culture, education, and climate of their ancestral homeland.

Controlling the Caribbean became even more precarious as the British government tried to walk a tightrope between satisfying abolitionist aspirations and retaining political and financial control of the export-producing islands. London knew it could not effectively back up any emancipation legislation without the support of the planter oligarchy and the administrators of the plantations. A slave rebellion in Jamaica in December 1831 forced the British government to pursue legislative action for emancipation.

Initial Concept

The original proposal for emancipation provided that newly freed slaves would continue working on the plantations for an additional twelve years, and the British government would allocate £15 million to compensate planters for the loss of their slaves as property. Abolitionists, appalled by the length of servitude, demanded immediate freedom. The British government felt that the immediate removal of labor obligation would cripple the plantations and lead the slaves to resume what Edward Stanley, secretary of state for the colonies, termed their "primitive habits of savage life."

The Abolition of Slavery Act, which was enacted on August 29, 1833, was the product of competing interests that were determined to appease the parties involved in British colonial slavery—excepting, of course, the blacks in the Caribbean themselves. Antigua and Bermuda rejected apprenticeship and granted immediate emancipation to their islands' slaves. This move was more a reflection of those islands' larger resident proprietor class and denser black population, who had little recourse other than working on the plantations, than any humanitarian motivation.

There were two important provisions in the act, which took effect on August 1, 1834. The first was that Britain would compensate the planters for the loss of their "property," that is, the newly freed slaves. Payment amounted to about £21 per slave (a total

expenditure of £20,000,00), a sum that historian William Green notes was "incredible" for that time. But the most significant aspect of the compensation provision was not the actual amount but the reassurance given by the British government to the planter oligarchy that their private property was not being undermined.

The second important provision provided the planters with a continuing labor force that would remain under their control. This was done through apprenticeship. All slaves over the age of six were to continue working for their existing masters. The apprentices, however, were only to be paid wages for hours worked in excess of a required forty-five hours per week. Freedom would be granted to nonfieldworkers after completing the next six years of service, and field hands were to be granted freedom after eight years. Allowances to the workers were to continue as they had during slavery. All apprentices were allowed to purchase their freedom before their official release date by paying an appraised value of their worth using wages earned after the required forty-five hours were completed.

The goal of the apprenticeship system "was to foster good will between planter and freedman and to remake the culture of the former slaves." Furthermore, abolitionists envisioned the British Caribbean as a model for the ultimate eradication of slavery throughout the world. They anticipated that free labor would produce more sugar and more profits, offering an example of the benefits for eradicating forced labor. This plan, according to historian Eric Foner, was "a catastrophic failure."

Effects

Apprenticeship changed the externalities of coercive labor without altering the nature of the system. Whereas planters were still obligated to provide allowances—such as food staples, clothing, and liquor—for their workers under apprenticeship, many began charging for these provisions. Domestic workers were often threatened with demotion to fieldwork, often with the intent of extending the workers' duration on the plantation for another two years. Apprentices who desired to purchase their freedom were often appraised at exorbitant and unattainable amounts.

Children under the age of six were automatically freed from bondage. In areas where blacks were able to engage in subsistence farming or earn enough to provide for their families, this was not a burden. However, destitute parents who were unable to adequately provide for their children had the "option" of binding their children as apprentices until the age of twenty-one. Planters, meanwhile, refused to provide extra allowances, presenting a very dangerous situation for the 14,000 free children on the island. It took an act of the Assembly in 1837 to mandate that planters provide allowances for children.

The indignities and hardships that workers continued to face during the apprenticeship period were met with resistance and hostility by former slaves, who resented what they saw as a conspiracy among the powerful to deny them their rightful freedom. Legislatures that were beholden to the planter class enacted laws that varied from island to island and worked to continue the suppression of the black population. Fines and jail time for insubordination, loitering, and vagrancy severely curtailed the black population's physical and political movements and were often adjudicated arbitrarily.

The British government exacerbated this situation at the local level by inadequately providing for stipendiary magistrates. These administrators were sent to the islands to observe the planters' treatment of the apprentices and to mediate disputes between parties. The magistrates' duties and conditions, as well as meager wages, often prevented them from properly upholding their bureaucratic duties. As a result, the oversight system only contributed to the apprentices' problems.

Despite its many problems, the apprenticeship system managed to lower the number of hours that many former slaves had to work. However, this boon was often mitigated by the fact that workers lived much farther away from the plantation because the plantation owners were not obligated to furnish housing. On some of the islands, many workers were able to procure their own farmlands, often at great distance from the plantation. They used this land to provide subsistence agriculture for their families or to grow surplus produce to purchase their freedom.

The Anti-Slavery Society in Britain and other abolitionists continued to criticize the apprenticeship system as merely a masqueraded form of slavery. *The West Indies in 1837*, a report published by four anti-slavery leaders who had traveled through the Caribbean, roundly condemned the apprenticeship system as a failure. The planters' intransigency toward the former slaves and the changing social and economic relations on the islands contributed to ineffectual

governance. Furthermore, both the planters and the British government were concerned about the effects of emancipating non-fieldworkers, set to happen in August 1838, would be on field hands who were still forced to work for the planters.

Mounting domestic pressure coupled with the fear of further unrest in the colonies led the British government to move toward complete emancipation of all ex-slaves. On August 1, 1838, the British government, unable to furnish the required funds and political will necessary to transition from a slave society to a functioning free one, abandoned the apprenticeship system and fully emancipated the apprentices.

Malini Cadambi

See also: Abolition of Slavery Act (1833).

Further Reading

Bolland, O. Nigel. *The Politics of Labour in the Caribbean: The Social Origins of Authoritarianism and Democracy in the Labour Movement.* Kingston, Jamaica: Ian Randle, 2001.

Foner, Eric. *Nothing but Freedom: Emancipation and Its Legacy.* Baton Rouge: Louisiana State University Press, 1983.

Green, William A. *British Slave Emancipation: The Sugar Colonies and the Great Experiment, 1830–1865.* Oxford, UK: Clarendon, 1976.

Mathieson, William Law. *British Slave Emancipation, 1838–1849.* New York: Octagon, 1967.

Richardson, Patrick. *Empire and Slavery.* London: Longman, Green, 1968.

Arango y Parreño, Francisco de (1765–1837)

Under the economic leadership of Francisco de Arango y Parreño, Cuba sought to become the dominant sugar producer of the Western Hemisphere—a position formerly held by Haiti until revolution ended slavery there and created a black republic in 1804. His policies led to a significant expansion of slavery in Cuba.

Arango y Parreño was born in Havana, Cuba, in May 1765 to a prominent family whose wealth enabled him to obtain an excellent education. He received a bachelor of law degree from the University of Havana before going to Spain to complete his legal training. After receiving his law degree in 1789, he began a long and distinguished public career, holding many important offices, garnering frequent official commissions, and receiving many honors. The author of numerous pamphlets on agriculture and economics and volumes of memoirs, Arango y Parreño was a leading intellectual of the Americas and a key initiator of Cuba's agro-export industrialization based on sugar production.

In 1791, under Arango y Parreño's leadership, a group of prominent landowners founded the *Sociedad Económica de Amigos del País* (Economic Society of the Friends of the Land), which encouraged Cuban agriculture, industry, and commerce. Soon after, Arango y Parreño was instrumental in persuading Spain's King Charles IV to create a merchant guild in Havana. As syndic (director) of the guild from 1795 to 1809, he promoted Cuban economic development.

In 1811, he was appointed minister of the Council of the Indies, which was responsible for overseeing Spanish colonial affairs. Two years later, Havana's municipal council elected Arango y Parreño to represent the city in the Spanish Cortes (Parliament), where he sought to free Cuban goods from Spanish tariff burdens and trade restrictions and open Cuban commerce to other Spanish colonies and foreign powers.

An advocate of laissez-faire economic doctrines that sought to expand commercial liberties without extending freedom to slaves, Arango y Parreño successfully implemented free-market policies that reformed the Spanish mercantile system. Considering the island's lack of labor to be the primary obstacle to Cuba's agricultural success, he urged the expansion of slavery. In 1789, he championed the Free Slave Trade Regulation, which allowed the unrestricted importation of slaves to Cuba and ended monopoly privileges for slave importers. Slave plantations flourished, and the island's participation in the international sugar trade increased dramatically.

The slave rebellions, race wars, and social upheaval that characterized Haiti from 1791 to 1804 persuaded Arango y Parreño to remain loyal to Spain, while the Spanish American mainland waged successful wars of independence in the early nineteenth century. Many of his fellow Cuban-born white elites agreed that political liberty could prompt a social revolution that would threaten their own privileged positions, not just those of the Spaniards in Cuba, which remained a Spanish colony until 1898. The economic upheaval wrought by the Haitian Revolution inspired Arango y Parreño to propose to Spanish officials that Cuba replace Haiti as its leading sugar exporter.

When a rapid increase in Cuba's slave population caused fear of a servile uprising, Arango y Parreño adhered to the conventional practice of distinguishing the "milder" Iberian style of slavery from the harsher practices of Northern Europeans. Insurrection was un-

likely, he claimed, because Cubans under free-market conditions were loyal Spanish subjects and because slaves were treated better in the Spanish than in the French colonies.

While recommending the proper treatment of slaves under the law to protect against rebellion, Arango y Parreño justified the institution of slavery by citing the inferiority of the Africans and the civilizing effects of European culture, the lack of free labor available in Cuba to develop the economy, and historical precedents in the ancient world. He argued that English, French, and Portuguese colonists in the Western Hemisphere had imported far more slaves than the Spanish; therefore, Cubans had to procure additional slaves in order to compete with their rivals in the world market.

As for free blacks and mulattoes, Arango y Parreño distrusted them, believing they posed a danger to Cuba's social stability. He supported legislation to limit their rights until the time of his death in Havana in 1837.

David M. Carletta

See also: Cuba, Abolition in.

Further Reading

Kuethe, Allan J. *Cuba, 1753–1815: Crown, Military, and Society.* Knoxville: University of Tennessee Press, 1986.

Tomich, Dale. "The Wealth of Empire: Francisco Arango y Parreño, Political Economy, and the Second Slavery in Cuba." *Comparative Studies in Society and History* 45 (January 2003): 4–28.

Artigas, José Gervasio (1764–1850)

José Gervasio Artigas was the founder of the modern nation of Uruguay. As the leader of the incipient state during its wars of independence from Spain (1811–1820), he instituted a number of agrarian reforms that gave unprecedented land rights to ex-slaves and mulattoes. Although his radical reforms were never fully implemented, he is widely hailed as the first great agrarian reformer of Latin America.

Artigas was born on June 19, 1764, in the city of Montevideo. His family was wealthy, owning extensive rural properties in the Rio del Plata region, a Spanish colony that included large portions of present-day Argentina, Paraguay, Uruguay, and Bolivia. Like many Creoles (whites of Spanish origin born in the colonies), Artigas was influenced by the

The leading figure in Uruguay's independence movement of the 1810s—and a national hero—José Gervasio Artigas initiated radical reform measures that distributed land to mulattoes and freed slaves. *(Miguel Rojo/ AFP/Getty Images)*

liberalism and democratic reformism of the time, and he threw himself into the struggle for independence from Spain in the early 1800s.

The desire for independence in the Plata region had been growing for some time among Creole businessmen and middle-class professionals, but the movement officially launched soon after the Spanish king was deposed by the Napoleonic armies in 1808, an event that created a power vacuum in the American colonies. In 1810, a junta (revolutionary group) of prominent landowners seized power in Buenos Aires.

One of the measures enacted by the new government, as in most other former Spanish colonies, was the gradual abolition of slavery. Slavery was a minor force in the cattle-ranching economy of the Plata, but nevertheless, the government abolished the slave trade, decreed partial freedom for the children of slave mothers, and offered minimal rights to freed slaves and mulattoes. They also conscripted slaves and free blacks into the revolutionary armies fighting for independence from Spain. People of African origin would play a key role in the struggle against the Spanish colonial authorities in several parts of South America.

Artigas commanded an army of landowners from the eastern provinces of the Plata region and defeated the Spanish forces at Las Piedras in 1811, establishing the state of Uruguay. Though he had originally supported the junta in Buenos Aires, Artigas had larger plans for a confederation of provinces in the region. His plan was adamantly opposed by the centralist leaders in

Buenos Aires and by Portuguese forces that hoped to incorporate Uruguay into Brazil. In a series of battles between 1811 and 1815, effective control of the main city, Montevideo, and the interior seesawed between the Buenos Aires junta and the Portuguese. Artigas's loyal armies, composed largely of gauchos (South American cowboys), eventually prevailed.

In 1815, Artigas was elected president of the new state. In addition to affirming the partial abolition of slavery that had been decreed in 1811, he declared independence from Spain and Buenos Aires and, most importantly, passed a radical land reform law. To rebuild the war-ravaged economy, he ordered the confiscation of royal property and the abandoned ranches of wealthy landowners and the distribution of land to all who were willing to work it, including mulattoes, Indians, former slaves, and poor whites. This struck a chord among the mass of the population but threatened the wealthy landowners in the area, the conservative junta in Buenos Aires, and the slaveholders of Brazil. The reforms were only partially implemented when Portuguese armies invaded the area in 1816 and took full control in 1820. Artigas fled to Paraguay, where he lived until his death on September 23, 1850.

Artigas is still revered as a national hero and the founder of Uruguay. Historians tout his land reforms as the most creative of the postindependence measures adopted by the ex-colonies of Spain. Unlike most of his contemporaries, Artigas realized that to effectively end slavery, the government would have to confront the issues of private property. He was not a socialist or a communist in the modern sense, but his approach was unique in that it challenged the fundamental interests of the rich during a period when they were regarded as sacred.

Sean Purdy

Further Reading

Blackburn, Robin. *The Overthrow of Colonial Slavery, 1776–1848.* New York: Verso, 1988.
Bushnell, David. "The Independence of Spanish South America." In *The Cambridge History of Latin America*, vol. 3, ed. by Leslie Bethell. Cambridge, UK: Cambridge University Press, 1984.

Ashmun Institute

The biblical dictum "You shall know the truth, and the truth shall make you free" inspired the reform impulse of the founders of the Ashmun Institute in southern Pennsylvania in 1854. Recognizing that freedom in its truest sense could be attained and preserved only through educational opportunity, the Ashmun Institute was established as the first institution of higher education in the United States for young black men. It continues to follow that mission today, operating as a co-educational institution under the name Lincoln University.

The Ashmun Institute was established in the town of Oxford in Chester County, Pennsylvania. The school was named for the first president of Liberia, Jehudi Ashmun, but, on February 7, 1866, the board of trustees changed the school's name to Lincoln University to honor the martyred president and fallen emancipator. The school became the first institution of higher education in the United States to bear Abraham Lincoln's name.

The founders of the Ashmun Institute included the Reverend John Miller Dickey, pastor of the Oxford Presbyterian Church, and his wife, Sarah Emlen Cresson Dickey. A pious free black man, James Ralston Amos, had first approached Dickey in 1852 to express his desire to study for the ministry. Dickey attempted to use his influence with colleagues at two theological schools in Philadelphia to gain admission for Amos, but his efforts were rebuffed by both institutions.

Believing that capable young black men like Amos were entitled to the same educational opportunities as white men, Dickey and his wife decided to open a school that would educate Amos and other young black men who had been denied the right to an education elsewhere. When the school first opened, it had only two students—the brothers James and Thomas Amos—but its enrollment grew rapidly. By the 1920s, alumni from Lincoln University made up 20 percent of black medical doctors and more than 10 percent of black attorneys in the United States. The school has graduated more than 14,000 students in its history.

Dickey established the Ashmun Institute as an extension of his ministry, but not everyone in his community was as understanding or empathetic. Although Dickey had the moral and political support of the most affluent men in Chester County, the poorer white citizens did not condone his actions. Sensing the growing animosity within his own congregation, in 1856 Dickey resigned his position as pastor of the Oxford Presbyterian Church.

Lincoln University, in southeastern Pennsylvania, was founded in 1854 as the Ashmun Institute, the nation's first liberal arts college for African Americans. Alumni include U.S. Supreme Court Justice Thurgood Marshall and poet Langston Hughes. *(Library of Congress)*

The Pennsylvania State Assembly granted the Ashmun Institute its charter on April 29, 1854, but actual instruction at the school did not begin until January 1, 1857. In the interim, Dickey constructed the school's first academic hall and located teachers who would be willing to work at the school.

Folklore associated with Lincoln University suggests that Dickey first became acquainted with James Ralston Amos when he noticed him praying frequently in an open field near a large stone. Today, Ashmun Hall, the original academic structure built on the campus, is located on the site where Amos is said to have prayed, and the stone became the cornerstone of the building.

Alumni of the institute have conducted many noble efforts throughout the years. For example, James and Thomas Amos both traveled to Liberia, Africa, as missionaries through the sponsorship of the American Colonization Society.

The reputation of the school has grown over the years, and many have come to refer to it as the "black Princeton." Many of the young Africans who emerged as national leaders during the era of decolonization in the twentieth century were graduates of Lincoln University. The school's alumni include such notable figures as Langston Hughes (1929), a poet of the Harlem Renaissance; Thurgood Marshall (1930), the first African American justice of the U.S. Supreme Court; Nnamdi Azikiwe (1930), the first president of Nigeria; and Kwame Nkrumah (1939), the first president of Ghana.

Junius P. Rodriguez

See also: Liberia.

Further Reading

Bond, Horace Mann. *Education for Freedom: A History of Lincoln University, Pennsylvania.* Oxford, PA: Lincoln University, 1976.

Assing, Ottilie (1819–1884)

Ottilie Assing was a young German American journalist with abolitionist and feminist sympathies. In 1856, she met the famed black abolitionist Frederick Douglass when she traveled to Rochester, New York, to interview him for the prestigious German newspaper *Morgenblatt für gebildete Leser* (Morning Journal for Educated Readers). Historians suggest that Assing became romantically involved with Douglass, and their association lasted for twenty-eight years.

Assing emigrated from Hamburg, Germany, to the United States in 1852 and settled in Hoboken, New Jersey. Several factors led her to leave her homeland, including the political instability in Germany following the unsuccessful revolutions of 1848, the death of her parents, and the death of a lover. Additionally, Assing faced increasing anti-Semitic pressures in Germany; her father, a doctor and poet, had been raised as a Jew before converting to Christianity. An astute observer of society's customs and values, which she often expressed in the essays she wrote for *Morgenblatt*, Assing was satisfied with the American democratic experiment and decided to become a citizen of the United States.

Raised as an atheist, Assing considered herself a freethinking German intellectual who was moved by the power of ideas. She found rational greatness in Douglass, of whom she wrote, "everything about him is fresh, genuine, true, and good." In spite of her admiration for Douglass, Assing did not accept the notion of racial equality that was being advanced by some of the more radical abolitionists of the antebellum era.

Beyond their personal relationship, Assing developed a passionate interest in Douglass's work toward abolition and emancipation and became his most trusted confidant and adviser. She also developed an interest in the rest of Douglass's family. After first visiting them in Rochester, in 1856, she returned for the next twenty-two summers to spend time with Douglass and his family, assisting with articles, working on translations of his writings, and tutoring his five children. In 1860, she completed the German translation of Douglass's second autobiography, *My Bondage and My Freedom.*

Assing provided intellectual and moral support to Douglass and encouraged his abolitionist efforts. His first wife, Anna, was a few years older than Frederick and functionally illiterate. In addition, her health was poor, having had five children in rapid succession. Anna Douglass seemed to be uncomfortable with her husband's international celebrity and had no strong attachment to the cause of abolition.

Assing was a devoted abolitionist with the intellectual credentials to support Douglass's work. Privately, Assing believed that upon Anna's death, Douglass would marry her. However, when Anna died in 1882, Douglass married his white secretary, Helen Pitts, who was nearly twenty years younger than Assing.

Assing found it difficult to cope with this personal tragedy while also facing a recent diagnosis of breast cancer. Two years after Douglass's second marriage, Assing walked into the Bois de Boulogne park in Paris and swallowed potassium cyanide to end her life by suicide. Frederick Douglass, the only heir listed in her will, inherited her $13,000 estate.

It is difficult for scholars to assess the impact that this extended association had on Douglass and Assing, because many of the primary sources documenting their relationship no longer exist. Letters that Douglass wrote to Assing were burned after her death (Assing had requested in her will that her papers be destroyed), and only a few notes from Assing to Douglass survive.

In later years, an unrelated fire at Douglass's home in Rochester destroyed many of his personal papers.

Junius P. Rodriguez

See also: Douglass, Frederick.

Further Reading

Diedrich, Maria. *Love Across Color Lines: Ottilie Assing and Frederick Douglass.* New York: Hill and Wang, 1999.

Lohmann, Christoph. *Radical Passion: Ottilie Assing's Reports From America and Letters to Frederick Douglass.* New York: Peter Lang, 1999.

B

Backhouse, Jonathan, Jr. (1779–1842)

Jonathan Backhouse, Jr., was a successful British banker and railroad promoter who gave much of his time and financial resources to support the transatlantic abolitionist movement. Backhouse and his wife were ministers of the Society of Friends (Quakers) in Great Britain. During the 1830s, they traveled extensively, doing missionary work in the United States and trying to heal the schism that had developed among the American Quakers.

Backhouse grew up in a prosperous Quaker household in Darlington in the county of Durham in England. From the start, Backhouse had family connections that tied him to the antislavery movement in Great Britain. His mother was Ann Pease, a member of a noted antislavery family. In 1811, Backhouse married Hannah Chapman, the eldest daughter of Quaker banker and abolitionist Joseph Gurney. The marriage not only solidified the antislavery connection among the Quaker abolitionist families, but it also was good for business. Through his wife, Backhouse had ties to other prominent Quakers, including the Barclay, Birkbeck, Chapman, Church, Fox, Hoare, and Hodgkin families.

In 1826, Backhouse inherited the banking firm James and Jonathan Backhouse and Co., which his father had founded in 1774. In addition to operating this successful venture, Backhouse diversified his business interests in other lucrative and promising opportunities. Within a few years, he was involved in business projects involving quarries, coal mining, shipping, and railways. Backhouse's most lucrative venture was speculation, with his cousin Edward Pease, to promote the Stockton and Darlington Railroad in 1820.

Backhouse's many business ventures earned him handsome profits as Britain began to experience the transformation wrought by the Industrial Revolution. Both as a financier and as an industrialist, Backhouse profited, but he provided philanthropic assistance to many social causes, especially the anti-slavery movement in Great Britain. His financial success also provided him with leisure time that he could devote to conducting missionary efforts in the British Isles and in North America.

Backhouse was present at the 1840 World Anti-Slavery Convention in London, which was attended by nearly 500 delegates from the United States and Great Britain. The Quaker financier was one of the prominent abolitionists who later sat for a portrait and was immortalized in Benjamin Robert Haydon's famous painting commemorating that event, *The Anti-Slavery Society Convention* (1841).

Junius P. Rodriguez

See also: Quakers (Society of Friends); World Anti-Slavery Convention (1840).

Ball, Charles (ca. 1780–?)

The former slave Charles Ball was the author of *Slavery in the United States: A Narrative of the Life and Adventures of Charles Ball* (1837), which was initially released anonymously as *The Life and Adventures of a Fugitive Slave* (1836). The work was one of the earliest slave narratives to be published in the United States, and it was used as propaganda by abolitionists who hoped to portray the immorality of slavery and the particular conditions experienced by individual slaves. According to slave narrative scholar William Andrews, "Ball's narrative was reprinted often in the decades following its initial publication; it directly influenced the manner and matter of later fugitive slave narratives."

Born in the early 1780s, Ball served in bondage for more than forty years on a Maryland tobacco plantation and on cotton plantations in South Carolina and Georgia. After escaping from slavery, he made his way to Philadelphia, where he wrote his memoir with the help of Isaac Fischer, a white lawyer. Although the work was meant to be an abolitionist tract, Ball also provided detailed descriptions of slave religion, African cultural retention, the oppressive conditions on slave plantations—including the forced separation of enslaved families as a consequence of the domestic slave trade—and labor routines in the tobacco-, rice-, indigo-, and cotton-producing regions of the plantation South. In particular, Ball detailed the temperaments of his masters and recounted how the quality of his life depended on their character and mood.

At the age of four, Ball witnessed the first of many family breakups. Upon the death of their Maryland owner, Ball's mother and several of his siblings were sold to separate purchasers from Georgia and South Carolina. It was the last time that Ball would see his mother or any of his brothers or sisters. Ball himself was purchased by the Cox family, who lived near his father in Leonardtown, Maryland. On the eve of his impending sale to a Georgia slave buyer, Ball's father managed to escape to Pennsylvania on foot.

At the age of about twenty, Ball was hired out for three months as a ship's cook on the frigate *Congress,* and he worked at a naval yard for two years. During his time on the *Congress,* Ball became acquainted with a free black sailor from Philadelphia who told him about his life in the North. These stories, along with his father's courageous flight, encouraged Ball to plan his own escape, but circumstances delayed his effort for several years; Ball would eventually escape twice from bondage.

Ball married a slave named Judah, but when he was about twenty-eight, he once again lost his family as a result of the domestic slave trade. Mirroring the earlier breakup of his family, Ball was sold to a Georgia-based slave trader and forcibly separated from his wife and children. He was not even allowed to see or speak with his family one last time before his departure.

By making careful note of the region's topographical features and the names of towns, rivers, and streams during his passage to the Lower South, Ball managed to create a mental map of his journey to aid him in his future escape attempts. Arriving in South Carolina after a lengthy journey, the trader who had purchased Ball and several other slaves decided to sell a few of them in the state's capital. In his narrative, Ball noted the irony of being sold to yet another owner on the Fourth of July, amid the raucous celebrations recognizing liberty and the equality of men. After serving one of the most prominent slaveholding families in South Carolina for just over two years, Ball changed owners again in 1806, when he was given to his master's daughter and son-in-law as a marriage gift. Ball was transported to Georgia, where he would change hands again over the course of a two-year period.

After a brutal and unjustified whipping at the hands of his mistress and her two brothers, Ball resolved to escape from slavery. Reversing the path that had brought him to the Lower South four years earlier, he made it to northern Virginia before being captured by slave patrollers. After forty days in prison, Ball managed to escape from his captors.

Finally arriving in Maryland after a long and arduous journey, he found Judah and his three children in 1812. Four years after this reunion, his wife died and Ball remarried. In 1820, he purchased property near Baltimore, and, for the next ten years, he and his second wife raised four children in relative peace.

In June 1830, Ball was taken by slave catchers, separated again from his family, and enslaved at a cotton plantation in Milledgeville, Georgia. After another daring escape, he sought to find his new family and managed to return to Baltimore sometime between 1831 and 1832. Tragically, his family had been sold to a slave trader from the Lower South, despite the fact that they were all legally free.

Disheartened, Ball settled fifty miles from Philadelphia, where he wrote his anonymous memoir in 1836. Fearful of recapture, he concealed his identity, and the events of the rest of his life are unknown.

Walter Rucker

See also: Fugitive Slave Act of 1793; Fugitive Slaves.

Further Reading

Ball, Charles. *Slavery in the United States: A Narrative of the Life and Adventures of Charles Ball.* 1837. New York: Negro Universities Press, 1969.

Baptist War

See Jamaica Rebellion (1831–1832)

Barbados Revolt (1816)

The 1816 slave revolt in Barbados was the longest and bloodiest conflict in the history of that island. Launched by slaves who sought to expedite abolition, the revolt differed from other slave rebellions in that it was a carefully organized effort rather than a spontaneous or loosely coordinated uprising among field slaves. It did not speed abolition in Barbados, but it did lead to increased autonomy and self-rule for the island.

The Barbados Revolt had its origins in London. In 1807, Parliament abolished the slave trade, and in 1815, in order to prevent the illegal importation of new slaves, it ordered that all slaves in the colonies be registered. Slave owners in Barbados resented the registration order, because they believed that it eroded their political autonomy. As the sugar plantation owners and island leaders met to develop their response, house slaves misinterpreted the controversy as a debate over the coming abolition of slavery. Slaves across the island came to believe that officials in London were trying to free them but local planters were resisting the effort.

A group of slaves formulated a plan for an island-wide revolt as a means to force abolition. The group that organized and led the revolt included Bussa, a first-generation African slave, and Joseph Franklin Washington, a slave of mixed descent who held a high position on a neighboring plantation. Other leaders included Nanny Grigg, the senior house slave on the Simmons Plantation, and a group of skilled slaves who were thought to be loyal to their owners because of their privileged positions and less brutal lifestyles. Washington, like many of the other leaders, was aware of the successful Haitian Revolution of 1791–1804 and believed that Great Britain, like France, would abandon the island once the slaves took over. The leaders were able to plan and coordinate their revolt at weekend dances and festivals, events attended by both slaves and free blacks.

The planners decided to launch the revolt on Easter Sunday, because they knew that the white owners would be relaxed and unready, and many plantation owners would be away in town. On April 14, 1816, the rebellion began when Bussa and a group of slaves set fire to the sugarcane fields. Throughout several parishes, slaves set fire to plantations and attacked white plantation owners. Almost 5,000 slaves took part in the revolt. Ultimately, some forty estates were burned or looted and an estimated 20 percent of the island's sugarcane crop was destroyed. The revolt failed to spread across the island, however, as the British were able to muster troops and the militia to contain the violence.

The main combat lasted four days, although sporadic fighting continued for two months as the militia sought to capture all of the slaves involved in the revolt. The revolt reached its climax on April 16, when Bussa led a force of about 400 slaves against the soldiers of the First West Indian Regiment at the Bailey Plantation. Bussa was killed during the battle, and his force was routed by the superior firepower of the British troops. Officially, 176 slaves were killed

during the rebellion, 214 were subsequently executed (including Washington), and 123 were deported from the island. Unofficial observers later speculated that the number of slaves killed was closer to 1,000, as the soldiers and plantation owners had taken revenge on rebel slaves as they were captured. Only one white person was killed during the revolt.

In the aftermath of the uprising, the British Parliament granted Barbados the right to pass its own legislation, including a slave registry law. This action was the first step toward self-government for the island. Bussa became a popular figure in local folklore and inspired the descendants of slaves as they sought independence from Great Britain in the twentieth century.

Tom Lansford

See also: Haitian Revolution (1791–1804).

Further Reading

Beckles, Hilary. *Black Rebellion in Barbados: The Struggle Against Slavery, 1627–1838*. Bridgetown, Barbados: Antilles, 1987.

Craton, Michael. *Empire, Enslavement, and Freedom in the Caribbean*. Princeton, NJ: Markus Wiener, 1997.

Genovese, Eugene D. *From Rebellion to Revolution: Afro-American Slave Revolts in the Making of the Modern World*. Baton Rouge: Louisiana State University Press, 1979; New York: Vintage Books, 1981.

Higman, B.W. *Slave Populations of the British Caribbean, 1807–1834*. Baltimore: Johns Hopkins University Press, 1984.

Beattie, James (1735–1803)

James Beattie was a Scottish poet, essayist, and professor of moral philosophy and logic at Marischal College, Aberdeen University. Born in Laurencekirk, Kincardineshire, Scotland, he is best known for his celebrated "common sense" critique of fellow countryman David Hume, the prominent philosopher and historian who regarded Beattie as a "bigotted silly Fellow." Beattie is most often remembered for his poetry, especially *The Minstrel* (1771, 1774), but his *Essay on the Nature and Immutability of Truth in Opposition to Sophistry and Scepticism* (1770), written against Hume, was also widely known to contemporaries. Slavery was a frequent topic in Beattie's lectures and writings.

At Aberdeen, Beattie gave a lecture *On the Awfulness and Expediency of Slavery*. It included denunciations popularized in his *Essay on Truth*, a work that was reprinted four times within two years of the publication of its first Edinburgh edition and was soon translated into Dutch, French, German, and Italian. The evils of the slave trade, that "diabolical commerce," were a frequent subject in Beattie's correspondence with leading abolitionists such as William Dickson and William Wilberforce, who sought his support to strengthen the antislavery cause in Scotland. During these years, Beattie also worked on *Discourse on Slavery*; it was never published but parts of it made their way into later works. In the late 1780s, Beattie wrote and circulated a petition at the university to abolish the slave trade, a position he supported in subsequent essays.

Beattie's most extended discussion of slavery can be found in his two-volume *Elements of Moral Science* (1790, 1793). In it, Beattie offered something of a history of slavery, which he prefaced with the often-quoted comment that "slavery is inconsistent with the dearest and most essential rights of man's nature; it is detrimental to virtue and industry; it hardens the heart to those tender sympathies, which form the most lovely part of human character; it involves the innocent in hopeless misery, in order to procure wealth and pleasure for the authors of that misery; it seeks to degrade into brutes, beings whom the Lord of heaven and earth endowed with rational souls, and created for immortality; in short, it is utterly repugnant to every principle of reason, religion, humanity, and conscience."

Beattie aimed to challenge the traditional defenses of slavery, such as those proposed by the Romans. Drawing on the French political philosopher Baron de La Brède et de Montesquieu, he discussed the "origin, lawfulness, and expediency, of the slavery of the Negroes" in the West Indies. He thought it "impossible for a considerate and unprejudiced mind, to think of slavery without horror" and suggested this was especially so for the British mind, which cherished liberty. Beattie believed that the first step toward ending slavery was "to prohibit under the severest penalties the importation of slaves from Africk into the British colonies" and argued for more humane treatment of slaves everywhere.

Condensing the arguments in favor of the slavery of blacks into five main ones, Beattie gave an extended, point-by-point refutation of each. Authors who followed him in the late eighteenth and early nineteenth centuries, including the Reverend William Goodell and Saint George Tucker, frequently cited Beattie's arguments.

Mark G. Spencer

See also: Montesquieu, Baron de La Brède et de.

Further Reading

Beattie, James. *Elements of Moral Science.* 2 vols. 1790, 1793. London: Routledge/Thoemmes, 1996.

Fletcher, F.T.H. "Montesquieu's Influence on Anti-Slavery Opinion in England." *Journal of Negro History* 18 (October 1933): 414–26.

Robinson, Roger J., and William Forbes. *An Account of the Life and Writings of James Beattie.* 2 vols. 1806. London: Routledge/Thoemmes, 1996.

Beecher, Henry Ward (1813–1887)

The Reverend Henry Ward Beecher was one of the most prominent figures in nineteenth-century American religion and society, and he played a major role in the abolitionist movement. Speaking out against slavery and other sociopolitical issues of the day, he used the pulpit as a means of communicating his thoughts on abolitionism, evolutionism, women's rights, and temperance.

Born on June 24, 1813, in Litchfield, Connecticut, Henry Ward Beecher was a member of a prominent family with long-standing ties to abolitionism. His father was Lyman Beecher, a renowned Congregationalist minister, and his sister was Harriet Beecher Stowe, the author of *Uncle Tom's Cabin* (1852). He received his early education at the Mount Pleasant Classical Institute in Amherst, Massachusetts, and graduated from Amherst College in 1834.

Three years later, Beecher received a degree from Lane Theological Seminary in Cincinnati, where his father was president. While at Lane, Beecher studied under the tutelage of his father, who had strong Calvinist ties, as well as under Calvin Stowe, who later became his sister's husband. Beecher also contributed to an antislavery newspaper until its offices were mobbed and destroyed, and he patrolled the streets of Cincinnati when a temporary police unit was called on to protect free blacks from threats.

During his apprenticeship at a Presbyterian church in Lawrenceburg, Indiana, in 1839, Beecher began to develop the oratorical skills that would later distinguish him. From 1839 to 1847, he served as pastor of the Second Presbyterian Church of Indianapolis. In 1847, he moved to the Plymouth Congregational Church in Brooklyn, New York, where he was pastor until 1887.

His charismatic preaching style attracted large audiences who traveled from across the nation to hear his dramatic messages: Every Sunday, crowds of 2,500 regularly attended the church to listen to his spirited sermons. Although Beecher regarded slavery as a

Known for his eloquence and appeal to ordinary people, the Reverend Henry Ward Beecher—posing with his sister, novelist Harriet Beecher Stowe, in about 1870—was one of the most prominent religious figures and antislavery advocates of his time. *(Hulton Archive/Getty Images)*

sin, and its opposition was the cornerstone of his ministry, he also denounced such issues as U.S. arrogance toward Mexico and the mistreatment of Indians.

Plymouth Church soon gained a reputation as a center of political activism and liberal causes. In 1854, Beecher's congregation vehemently objected to passage of the Kansas-Nebraska Act, a controversial bill that Stephen A. Douglas had introduced into the U.S. Senate. The bill proposed that each territory be allowed to decide whether it would be a slaveholding state or a free state once it entered the Union. Beecher assisted efforts to block the bill by raising money to supply weapons to those who opposed slavery in these territories. The rifles purchased as a result of Beecher's fund raising were referred to as "Beecher's Bibles."

Beecher's progressive political agenda included support for black causes in spite of public outcry and criticism. Beecher obtained the chains with which the militant abolitionist John Brown had been bound after his raid on the federal arsenal at Harpers Ferry, Virginia, trampling them in the pulpit. He also held mock "auctions," during which the congregation purchased the freedom of real slaves. The most famous of these former slaves was a young girl named Pinky, who was auctioned during a regular Sunday worship service at Plymouth on February 5, 1860. A collection taken up that day raised $900 to buy Pinky from her owner. The Plymouth congregation also hosted the Fisk Jubilee Singers, young college singers who traveled the country and the world to raise money for their college, and the New York press criticized Beecher for inviting the "Nigger Minstrels" to give a concert. The abolitionist leader Frederick Douglass lauded Beecher as an exceptional member of the clergy whose ministry was free of the contradiction of practicing Christianity while upholding slavery.

Beecher and his Brooklyn church often housed fugitive slaves and later became known as the "Grand Central Depot" of the Underground Railroad, an elaborate, secret system of safe houses that assisted fugitive slaves in their journey to freedom in the North. Oral tradition and published memoirs reveal that slaves seeking passage to Canada may have hidden in the tunnel-like basement beneath the church sanctuary. T.J. Ellinwood, Beecher's stenographer, quoted Beecher as saying, "I opened Plymouth Church, though you did not know it, to hide fugitives. I took them into my own home and fed them. I piloted them, and sent them toward the North Star, which to them was the Star of Bethlehem."

From his first pastorship to the start of the U.S. Civil War in 1861, Beecher's opposition to slavery deepened. Although he never formally joined the abolitionists and was generally regarded as a moderate, Beecher denounced the compromises and atrocities that escalated to war. During the decade from 1850 to 1860, in lectures and in contributions to various periodicals, he never hesitated to voice his opinion. *Freedom and War* (1863), a collection of his sermons and addresses delivered in his Brooklyn church, illustrates the evolution of Beecher's antislavery stance, culminating in his belief in immediate abolition, which he expressed just prior to Abraham Lincoln's issuance of the Emancipation Proclamation in 1863.

In 1863, Beecher traveled to England, where he used his speaking platform to address British audiences on the U.S. Civil War. His talent for argument and persuasion swayed hostile, doubting British audiences in Manchester, Glasgow, Edinburgh, Liverpool, and London to sympathize with the Union cause. As editor in chief of the *Independent* from 1861 to 1863, Beecher voiced his support for the abolition of slavery. In 1870, he founded and became editor in chief of the *Christian Union*, later called the *Outlook*, a nondenominational religious weekly.

Beecher wrote lectures on topics other than slavery. His *Seven Lectures to Young Men* (1844), influenced in tone by Benjamin Franklin's *Poor Richard's Almanack* and the *Industrious Apprentice*, was addressed to young working-class men who acted as clerks, mechanics, salesmen, and apprentices. His writing style was influenced by naturalism, which inspired much of the imagery in his work. This influence is especially apparent in his *Plain and Pleasant Talk About Fruit, Flowers, and Farming* (1859).

After the Civil War, Beecher championed such causes as women's suffrage, temperance, and evolutionism, and he condemned anti-Semitism. He was sued by a former friend and congregant, Theodore Tilton, who alleged that the reverend had committed adultery with Tilton's wife. Although the trial resulted in a hung jury, Beecher was acquitted of all charges. His reputation suffered from the event, but he remained a popular writer and speaker. He continued raising his voice against slavery and other societal ills until his death on March 8, 1887.

Lena Ampadu

See also: Stowe, Harriet Beecher.

Further Reading

Cooper, Anna Julia. *The Voice of Anna Julia Cooper: Including "A Voice from the South" and Other Important Essays, Papers, and Letters.* Ed. Charles Lemert and Esme Bhan. Lanham, MD: Rowman & Littlefield, 1998.

Douglass, Frederick. "Oration, Delivered in Corinthian Hall, Rochester, July 5, 1852." In *Black Writers of America*, ed. Richard Barksdale and Keneth Kinnamon. New York: Macmillan, 1972.

Robinson, William H. *From Log Cabin to the Pulpit; Or, Fifteen Years in Slavery.* Eau Claire, WI: W.H. Robinson, 1913.

Rugoff, Milton. *The Beechers: An American Family in the Nineteenth Century.* New York: Harper & Row, 1981.

Beecher's Bibles

Henry Ward Beecher was a Congregationalist minister, son of the highly influential preacher and theologian Lyman Beecher, and brother of Harriet Beecher Stowe,

author of the antislavery classic *Uncle Tom's Cabin* (1852). Educated at the Lane Theological Seminary in Cincinnati, a hotbed of social reform in the 1830s, Beecher was an outspoken critic of American culture. Dubbed "America's Chaplain" because of his personal charisma and his power in the pulpit and as an orator, Beecher often used his position to speak out about his disdain for alcohol and drinking, his support for a greater role for women in American life, and his vehement opposition to slavery. He also became known for his "Beecher's Bibles"—Sharps rifles sent alongside Bibles to individuals who opposed slavery in the Kansas-Nebraska Territory.

By the mid-nineteenth century, a growing number of Americans were convinced that the owning and employing of slaves was a moral issue and a manifestation of grievous sin. With the passage of the Kansas-Nebraska Act in 1854, these detractors of the slave system sprang into action. According to the legislation, the slave or free status of the region included in the Kansas-Nebraska Territory was to be decided by popular sovereignty—that is, the inhabitants who populated the new holdings of the United States would be allowed to decide for themselves whether they wanted to allow slavery in their states. Not surprisingly, this pronouncement by the U.S. Congress, coupled with mounting tension between pro- and antislavery forces, led supporters of both positions to immigrate to these Western regions of the expanding nation.

It was not only the inhabitants of surrounding states and territories who were apprehensive about what might happen in the Kansas-Nebraska Territory; remarkably, New Englanders and New Yorkers took a deep interest in the distant region as well, largely because antislavery rhetoric had been widely argued in the Northeast for some two decades before the Kansas-Nebraska Act's passage, and the organizing efforts of the American Anti-Slavery Society had been fruitful in that area.

Some New Englanders were particularly smitten with "Kansas Fever," so much so that about sixty people from New Haven, Connecticut, decided to uproot themselves and go to Kansas to raise their voices and votes for the "free" cause. Learning of this, a Yale College professor was so moved by the group's sacrifice that he offered $25 to purchase Sharps rifles for the New Englanders so that they could defend themselves in this area, which had become known as "Bleeding Kansas."

Not wanting to miss an opportunity to demonstrate his own and his congregation's antislavery fervor, the Reverend Beecher took the idea one step further. Beecher pledged that his Brooklyn congregation would match his audiences' purchases of rifles for the defense of Free Soil abolitionist settlers in Kansas.

Ever the pragmatist, Beecher was sure to see that Bibles, as well as weapons, were sent to support the Free Soilers in their cause. The rifles were packed in crates marked "Bibles," on the assumption that such a label would not arouse the suspicion of the settlers' opponents. In addition, concealing the identity of the contents kept the aid companies from any conflicts with the federal and state authorities, which had forbidden shipments of arms to the bloody region.

Though the minister's advocacy of violence seems philosophically inconsistent, Beecher's logic was simple and clear: According to the *New York Evening Post*, Beecher claimed that there was more moral power in a rifle than in a hundred Bibles, so far as Bleeding Kansas was concerned.

Barbara Schwarz Wachal

See also: Beecher, Henry Ward.

Further Reading

Abbott, Lyman. *Henry Ward Beecher.* Cambridge, MA: Riverside Press, 1904; Miami, FL: Mnemosyne, 1969.

Etcheson, Nicole. "Black Slavery, White Liberty." *North and South* 3 (September 2000): 42–58.

Ewy, Marvin. "The United States Army in the Kansas Border Troubles, 1855–1856." *Kansas Historical Quarterly* 32 (Winter 1966): 385–400.

Fellman, Michael. "Rehearsal for the Civil War: Antislavery and Proslavery at the Fighting Point in Kansas, 1854–1856." In *Antislavery Reconsidered: New Perspectives on the Abolitionists,* ed. Lewis Perry and Michael Fellman. Baton Rouge: Louisiana State University Press, 1979.

Isely, William H. "The Sharps Rifle Episode in Kansas History." *American Historical Review* 12 (April 1907): 546–66.

Ryan, Halford R. *Henry Ward Beecher: Peripatetic Preacher.* New York: Greenwood, 1990.

Behn, Aphra (ca. 1640–1689)

Aphra Behn was the first English woman writer to live entirely by her pen and one of the most prolific playwrights of the Restoration, second only to John Dryden. She is best known, however, for her prose narratives, particularly the slave novel *Oroonoko, or the History of the Royal Slave* (1688). Although abolitionists stressed the importance of Behn's *Oroonoko* to their cause, contemporary critics have questioned whether the novel is, in fact, a rejection of slavery. Behn is re-

membered today not for her advancement of the antislavery cause, but as the mother of women's writing. Indeed, Virginia Woolf underlined Behn's importance to English literature, declaring in *A Room of One's Own* (1929) that "all women together ought to let flowers fall upon the tomb of Aphra Behn, which is, most scandalously but rather appropriately, in Westminster Abbey, for it was she who earned them the right to speak their minds."

Controversy and mystery surround Behn's biography. Born about 1640 in Harbledown, Kent, England, she was most likely the second daughter of Bartholomew Johnson and Elizabeth Denham and was baptized at Harbledown in Canterbury. In her twenties, she probably spent two years in Suriname and married her husband, a merchant of Dutch origins who is believed to have died a year after their marriage. In the late 1660s, Behn served as a spy for King Charles II of England at Antwerp, but, as a result of the debts she incurred during her service for the Crown, she was briefly jailed in a debtor's prison.

In the 1670s, Behn began a literary career that would bring her public and critical acclaim from the start. Until the mid-1680s, she produced almost one play each year, typifying the dramatic production of the Restoration era. After the failure of her play *Like Father, Like Son* in 1682, she began to publish poetic collections and prose, including the three-volume *Love Letters Between a Nobleman and His Sister* (1683–1687), the first epistolary novel in English literature; *The Fair Jilt* (1688); and her most famous work, *Oroonoko.* Behn died on April 16, 1689, and was buried in Westminster Abbey.

The popularity of *Oroonoko,* long considered the first antislavery novel, was boosted by Thomas Southerne's highly successful 1696 stage adaptation, which was performed throughout the eighteenth century. The book became part of the propaganda of the anti–slave trade movement, as late-eighteenth-century and nineteenth-century commentators saw it as casting its sympathy for the cause of outcasts and slaves. When Harriet Beecher Stowe's *Uncle Tom's Cabin* was published in 1852, many regarded *Oroonoko* as its forerunner.

Behn's novel received more critical scrutiny in the last decades of the twentieth century. Since then, critics have pointed out the novel's racism, as well as Behn's concern being more with gender rather than race. Her depiction of the female heroine Imoinda, who is sold into slavery because she is in love with the fallen-king-turned-slave Oroonoko, seems to parallel her characterizations of other female figures in her plays: Women are considered the property of their husbands and are themselves traded. Though such parallels encouraged the view that Behn was a liberal antislavery writer, modern critics point out that her position as a marginalized white woman does not necessarily imply that she also took the side of the black slave.

Luca Prono

See also: Novels, Antislavery.

Further Reading

Duffy, Maureen. *The Passionate Shepherdess: Aphra Behn, 1640–89.* London: Jonathan Cape, 1977.

Goreau, Angeline. *Reconstructing Aphra: A Social Biography of Aphra Behn.* New York: Dial, 1980.

Greer, Germaine. *The Uncollected Verse of Aphra Behn.* Essex, UK: Stump Cross, 1989.

Link, Frederick M. *Aphra Behn.* New York: Twayne, 1968.

Plasa, Carl, and Betty J. Ring, eds. *The Discourse of Slavery: Aphra Behn to Toni Morrison.* London: Routledge, 1994.

Benezet, Anthony (1713–1784)

Beginning in the 1750s, Philadelphia schoolmaster Anthony Benezet was a highly effective antislavery activist, advancing a critique that integrated his Quaker beliefs in equality and justice with the natural rights philosophy of the Enlightenment and his readings about Africa. A prolific writer and correspondent, Benezet worked within an extensive transatlantic network while lobbying skillfully in the halls of government and Quaker meetings. Pennsylvania's Gradual Abolition Act of 1780 was one of his greatest achievements, but Benezet also had a broad influence on both sides of the Atlantic in the second half of the eighteenth century.

Benezet was born on January 31, 1713, in northern France. His Huguenot parents fled persecution in France when he was two years old. After six months in Holland, the family settled in England and then moved to Philadelphia in 1731. Benezet married Joyce Marriott in 1736, and three years later, he left the family mercantile business to become a teacher.

Around 1750, he began to hold evening sessions in his home for the instruction of African American children. He continued to do so for the next two decades until a school for blacks was organized in 1770; he served as an instructor at the school during the last two years of his life. His pupils included many future leaders of Philadelphia's free black community, such as Absalom Jones, Richard Allen, and James Forten, Sr. His teaching experience firmly convinced Benezet that stereotypes of black intellectual inferiority were wrong.

Benezet worked on behalf of many causes, including the relief of refugees and the poor and the peace and temperance movements, but he made his greatest contributions in the realm of antislavery. In the 1740s, John Woolman's agitation among the Quakers stirred Benezet's interest. The two collaborated to write *An Epistle of Caution and Advice* (1754), which was adopted and published by the Philadelphia Yearly Meeting. In light of the colonies' rising slave population, the *Epistle* spoke out against slavery, basing its stance on the Golden Rule (do unto others as you would have others do unto you) and arguing that slavery "draws down the displeasure of Heaven; it being a melancholy but true reflection, that where slave-keeping prevails, pure religion and sobriety declines." Woolman and Benezet urged better care of the enslaved, especially their religious nurture.

From then until the onset of the American Revolution, Benezet issued several important antislavery tracts, progressing from arguments rooted in Quaker piety to ones based on broader themes of universal rights. In 1759, he published *Observations on the Inslaving, Importing and Purchasing of Negroes,* which likened African slaves to those captured by the Indians during the Seven Years' War. He quoted from several West African travel narratives in order to show that Europeans were guilty of instigating wars there for the purpose of producing captives for sale. In *A Short Account of That Part of Africa, Inhabited by the Negroes* (1762), Benezet expanded his use of travel narratives to refute stereotypes that Africa was a place of unmitigated barbarism. Instead, he described it as a land of natural abundance populated by decent, orderly people who "are equally intituled [sic] to the common Priviledges of Mankind with the Whites, that they have the same rational Powers; the same natural Affections, and are as susceptible of Pain and Grief as they, that therefore the bringing and keeping them in Bondage, is an Instance of Oppression and Injustice of the most grievous Nature." He called for an end to the slave trade and the passage of gradual emancipation legislation.

In 1766, Benezet wrote what some scholars consider his most influential work, *A Caution and Warning to Great Britain and Her Colonies on the Calamitous*

State of the Enslaved Negroes, which was distributed widely in England as a warning to landholders about the economic and social effects of slave rebellions. Benezet's use of travel literature culminated in his 1771 publication, *Some Historical Account of Guinea.* In this work, he fully developed his argument for Africa's natural fruitfulness and innocence and blamed Europeans for provoking African wars for the benefit of procuring slaves, thereby pinning the "savage" epithet on Europeans. The latter half of the book detailed the harsh punishments and deprivations of West Indian slavery, which he contrasted with Britain's vaunted love of liberty.

In addition to writing, Benezet worked toward abolition through other means. He lobbied in Quaker meetings for a firm antislavery posture, succeeding in 1758 when the Philadelphia Yearly Meeting denounced the buying and selling of slaves and ordered its members to prepare their slaves for freedom. In 1776, the Quakers finally declared slaveholders outside their fellowship. Benezet served on the committees that visited Quaker slaveholders and urged them to adhere to the denomination's position. He also tapped into networks of Quaker correspondents to disseminate his ideas to coreligionists in Britain and throughout the colonies.

Benezet organized legislative petition drives that led colonial Pennsylvania to restrict the slave trade by raising import fees. With the onset of the American Revolution, however, he withdrew from activism for fear of getting too entangled in revolutionary politics. After combat operations moved out of Pennsylvania, Benezet renewed his lobbying and helped achieve the passage of the state's Gradual Abolition Act of 1780, which outlined a plan to eradicate slavery over a period of several decades.

Finally, Benezet had a seminal influence on antislavery activists throughout the transatlantic world. Such American figures as Benjamin Franklin, Benjamin Rush, Moses Brown, and Samuel Hopkins all acknowledged his influence, as did British leaders such as Thomas Clarkson, Granville Sharp, and John Wesley. In France, the founders of the *Société des Amis des Noirs* (Society of Friends of the Blacks) promptly published a translation of *Some Historical Account of Guinea* in 1788, testifying to Benezet's international authority. He died on May 3, 1784, and was buried in Philadelphia.

Jonathan D. Sassi

See also: Forten, James, Sr.; Quakers (Society of Friends); Woolman, John.

Further Reading

Woodson, Carter G. "Anthony Benezet." *Journal of Negro History* 2 (January 1917): 37–50.

Berbice Slave Revolt (1763)

On February 23, 1763, a great slave revolt broke out in the Dutch colony of Berbice (today part of Guyana) at the Plantation Magdalenenburg on the Canje Creek; the revolt was prompted by the slaves' dissatisfaction with the work conditions associated with year-round sugarcane harvesting. The uprising, during which the slaves seized control of Berbice for eleven months, was led by Kofi (also known as Cuffy), a house slave and cooper on the Plantation Lilienburg who had conspired with other slaves in the area.

The revolt soon spread to the Berbice River region, where the rebels torched and plundered the Plantation Juliana, killing the wife of the plantation's manager and displaying her head on a pole. They continued on to Mon Repos, Essendam, Lilienburg, Elizabeth, and Alexandria, soon controlling most of the ninety-three private plantations on the Berbice River and twenty on the Canje Creek.

The rebels used the Plantations Hollandia and Zeelandia as their headquarters. As the white owners fled their plantations, the rebels set up government, designating Kofi as governor of the Negroes of Berbice and a slave named Akara as second in command. Kofi established strict discipline, drilling the soldiers and directing gangs of blacks to work in the field.

The rebels' immediate goal was to gain control of the plantations, and they succeeded easily. They were divided, however, as to their ultimate goal. Hardliners wanted to drive the white plantation owners from the colony. Kofi, however, sought to make a treaty that would partition the country, allowing blacks to live in freedom in the interior and giving whites control of the coast. He demanded almost exactly the same terms that Araby, a slave leader in neighboring Suriname, had won from the Dutch colonial government in 1761. But by negotiating the treaty, rather than attacking the whites quickly before reinforcements came, Kofi lost the advantage. Governor Wolfert Simon van Hoogenheim stalled for time, claiming that he had dispatched Kofi's terms to the metropolis and would have to wait two months for a reply.

While the governor and Kofi corresponded throughout April 1763, Dutch colonial reinforcements began to arrive from Suriname and Saint Eustatius, saving the remaining whites and eroding the rebels' position. In addition to rallying the support of neighboring Indian tribes, van Hoogenheim called on the governor of Barbados, who sent two well-armed barques with a total of 158 soldiers and many provisions.

Kofi realized van Hoogenheim's dishonorable intentions, and on May 13, he ordered an all-out attack on the Plantation Dageraad. Despite their numerical superiority (2,000 rebels to 150 Europeans), the insurgents were no match for the heavy guns on the Dutch ships anchored in the river, and they suffered their first major setback.

Kofi's Defeat

Although the Berbice rebels achieved some successes—reinforcing their troops with Suriname deserters and defeating van Hoogenheim's forces at Wikki Creek in December—a combination of internal division and external pressure ultimately defeated the rebellion. The movement was undermined by a lack of support from house slaves, many of whom opposed the uprising; divisions between the Creoles and the African-born slaves; and tribal rivalries, especially tensions between the Congo tribes and those from Asante and Dahomey. In a struggle for leadership, Akara rose to the command of the rebels; Kofi killed the members of his inner circle and shot himself.

Later that month, van Hoogenheim led an impressive flotilla up the Berbice River to retake the Plantation Peerboom, where the rebels had brought most of their ammunition and provisions. He launched a simultaneous attack from the Upper Demerara, pinching the rebel slaves between two fronts. The war of pitched battles turned into a guerrilla conflict. Ordinarily, the rebel slaves would have escaped into the bush to establish maroon communities (autonomous settlements of fugitives), as had occurred in Jamaica and neighboring Suriname. Surprisingly, these rebels began to surrender.

Indigenous resistance clearly played a major role in defeating the rebels and preventing the establishment of maroon communities as slaves fled into the interior. Indians from the neighboring Dutch colony of Demerara departed for Berbice to assist the whites. In February 1764, the chief of the Acuway tribe reported that he had subdued the rebels at La Savonette Plantation in Upper Berbice and claimed to have killed fifty-five black men, women, and children. In April, Governor Laurens Storm van Gravesande of Demerara reported that affairs in Berbice were "beginning once more to take a tolerably satisfactory turn there, to which

end our Caribs, both from these rivers and certainly from Barima, have loyally done their best and are yet doing it, constantly roving between the two Colonies."

Certainly, the Indians may have perceived the maroon communities settling in the hinterland as a threat, recalling the precedent set in Suriname. Or they may have seen an opportunity to gain advantage by allying themselves with the whites in exchange for arms, provisions, and favorable treatment. As the governors of the Dutch colonies exploited the enmity between the rebels and the colonies' indigenous population, the Indians of the Carib, Arawak, and Warouw nations banded together in a final effort to defeat the rebels.

Aftermath

The immediate outcome of the Berbice slave revolt was defeat and persecution. The total number of slaves executed was never tallied, but, in March and April 1764, forty rebels were sentenced to be hanged, twenty-four to be broken on the wheel, and twenty-four to be burned. Some twenty white deserters from Suriname were also caught, taken to Paramaribo, and executed.

No permanent changes in Berbice's slave trade, code, or treatment occurred as a result of the rebellion. No other large-scale rebellions erupted, nor did runaways establish major settlements in the bush, as they had in Suriname. Though it failed in the end, the rebellion imposed a high cost on the colony and the Berbice Association. It reduced the white population by half (to only 116 in 1764), interrupted trade, ruined the plantations, and burdened the association with the cost of expeditions sent from Holland, Saint Eustatius, and Suriname. If early the antislavery movement originated primarily in Europe, it also owes something to the forces of liberation undertaken by blacks in the Caribbean.

Today, Guyana commemorates the outbreak of the Berbice slave rebellion. The nation chose the date on which the revolt began, February 23, to become a cooperative republic in 1970, and it hails Kofi as a national hero.

Teresa M. Van Hoy

See also: Maroons.

Further Reading

Genovese, Eugene D. *From Rebellion to Revolution: Afro-American Slave Revolts in the Making of the Modern World.* Baton Rouge: Louisiana State University Press, 1979; New York: Vintage Books, 1981.

Betances y Alacán, Ramón Emeterio (1827–1898)

Born on April 8, 1827, to wealthy landowners in the western Puerto Rican town of Cabo Rojo, Ramón Emeterio Betances y Alacán was a radical abolitionist and separatist leader. He came of age at a time when race matters, anticolonial agitation, servile labor, and plantation agriculture dominated affairs in the Hispanic Caribbean.

His father, a native of Santo Domingo who emigrated to Puerto Rico in the aftermath of the Haitian Revolution, endured the injurious effects of a caste system that privileged both *peninsulares* (Spanish-born men) and lighter-skinned individuals. Although the elder Betances became a successful planter and merchant, in 1840, he was forced to suffer a degrading *limpieza de sangre*—a legal confirmation of his whiteness—before his daughter's marriage to a local Creole could be consummated. Fueled by the growth of the nonwhite population and white fears of race war, racial prejudice and discrimination contributed to the spread of abolitionist and separatist activity in Puerto Rico.

Betances took to the streets during the French Revolution of 1848 while studying in Toulouse and Paris. "When it comes to freedom," he later recalled of his support for the democratic revolt that culminated in the establishment of the Second French Republic, "all people are in solidarity." Across the Atlantic, the provisional French government abolished slavery in the French West Indies. When an island-wide uprising erupted in Martinique in response to the arrest and incarceration of an ex-slave, the Martiniquais government officials and planters, fearing for their lives, fled to Puerto Rico. Slaves in nearby Saint Croix also began to rebel.

As accounts of the widespread killing of whites, looting, and torching of plantations reached Puerto Rico, Governor Juan Prim issued a *código negro* (black code) in 1848, imposing stiff penalties against all people of color who threatened or attacked whites. The abolitionist crusade came on the heels of a devastating cholera epidemic that claimed nearly 30,000 lives, predominantly among slaves and people of color.

Betances devoted his life to combating the evils of colonialism, racial oppression, and human bondage, which he pursued with unyielding devotion. In the late 1850s, he joined a secret society that raised funds to purchase and free infant slaves upon their baptism, as allowed by colonial law under Governor Juan de la Pezuela. Another clandestine association reputedly sheltered and ferried runaway slaves to freedom in the nearby islands and the United States. The Spanish authorities expelled Betances from Puerto Rico on three occasions between 1858 and 1869 in an effort to silence his outspoken opposition to slavery and Iberian colonial domination.

In 1866, three Creole men—Segundo Ruiz Belvis, José Julian Acosta, and Francisco Mariano Quiñonez—boldly demanded the immediate abolition of slavery, with or without compensation for slave owners, before Spain's *Junta de Información* (Board of Inquiry). Their return to Puerto Rico coincided with rumors of an impending rebellion. Governor José María Marchesi seized the opportunity to crack down on political dissenters and ordered Betances, Ruiz Belvis, and seven other activists to appear before the Spanish overseas minister in Madrid to face charges of subversion. Betances and Ruiz Belvis escaped to Saint Thomas, where the former circulated a proclamation calling for the abolition of slavery and Puerto Rico's right to self-determination.

After Spain pressured the Danish to expel Betances from Saint Thomas, he and several associates relocated to Santo Domingo, where they founded the Puerto Rican Revolutionary Committee. The insurgents helped coordinate the ill-fated *Grito de Lares* (Cry/Proclamation of Lares) in 1868, the first systematic armed revolt against Spanish colonialism in Puerto Rico. Pressured by free traders at home, a war of liberation in Cuba, and growing social and political discontent in Puerto Rico, Spain abolished slavery on the island on March 22, 1873.

Though Betances was celebrated for his passionate and unwavering pursuit of freedom, he also cultivated other interests in medicine, science, and the humanities, studying ophthalmology, public health, botany, agronomy, history, literature, and journalism. In 1851, he cofounded the *Sociedad Recolectora*, which set about unearthing and cataloging primary documents on the history of Puerto Rico, culminating in the publication of Alejandro Tapia y Rivera's *Biblioteca Histórica de Puerto Rico* (1854).

Betances's 1853 novel, *Les Deux Indiens: Episode de la Conquéte de Borinquen*, was among the first works of Puerto Rican literature to focus on Spain's subjugation of the island's native Taino inhabitants. "El Antillano," as Betances became known in political circles, died in exile in France on September 16, 1898.

Jorge L. Chinea

See also: French West Indies, Abolition and Emancipation in the; Haitian Revolution (1791–1804).

Bevan, William (ca. 1800–ca. 1860)

The Reverend William Bevan was a Congregationalist minister who was an active member of the Liverpool Anti-Slavery Society in England during the 1830s. He was involved in several social reform movements in nineteenth-century Britain but devoted much of his attention to the antislavery movement and the campaign to eliminate prostitution.

Bevan was the minister of Liverpool's Newington Chapel, an independent congregation located near the waterfront. Ministering in a city that had an immediate connection to the transatlantic slave trade, Bevan was constantly reminded of the fruits that merchant capitalism had brought to his city. Nevertheless, his Christian charity and personal sense of the social gospel called on him to oppose the institution of slavery and to work toward its demise. He and James Cropper became founding members of the Liverpool Anti-Slavery Society, which published its manifesto in fall 1822.

The British Parliament's 1833 enactment of the Abolition of Slavery Act (commonly known as the British Emancipation Act) set in motion a compensated apprenticeship program and training regimen for freed slaves. The measure was designed to bring about the gradual abolition of slavery throughout the British West Indies. Although antislavery societies in Britain heralded the legislation, abolitionists realized that oversight would be necessary to guarantee that the steps prescribed by the act would be instituted.

Under Bevan's leadership, the Liverpool Anti-Slavery Society conducted its own investigation and published its findings in a report titled *The Operation of the Apprenticeship System in the British Colonies: A Statement, the Substance of Which Was Presented and Adopted at the Meeting of the Liverpool Anti-Slavery Society, Dec. 19th, 1837*. According to the report, "the conditions required of the Colonists have been, and continue to be, in the majority of cases, violated." On the basis of this report, Bevan wrote *A Letter to the Right Honorable Lord Brougham on the Alleged Breach of the Colonial Apprenticeship Contract* (1838) on behalf of the Liverpool Anti-Slavery Society. Published in pamphlet form, the text was widely circulated and helped to bring about Parliament's abolition of the apprenticeship system in 1838.

After Cropper's death in 1840, Bevan became the leading spokesman for the Liverpool Anti-Slavery Society. He was present at the 1840 World Anti-Slavery Convention in London, which was attended by delegates from the United States and Great Britain. He was one of the abolitionists who later sat for a portrait and was immortalized in Benjamin Robert Haydon's painting memorializing the event, *The Anti-Slavery Society Convention* (1841).

Under Bevan's leadership, the Liverpool Anti-Slavery Society made strenuous objections to Sir Thomas Fowell Buxton's plans to have the African Civilization Society establish "model settlements" along the Niger River in West Africa. Bevan specifically objected to the use of government funds to support what he perceived to be a poorly conceived effort with little chance of real success.

Bevan was also associated with other social causes in Liverpool. He presented a public lecture, *Prostitution in the Borough of Liverpool*, which was published as a pamphlet in 1843. Citing the need for a moral crusade against prostitution, he noted, "the force of licentious inclination has hurried a greater number into the commission of sin than I was prepared to expect."

Respected as a theological scholar, Bevan continued to lecture and write on religious topics, many of which were related to the theology and proper understanding of the Congregational Church in British religious history.

Junius P. Rodriguez

See also: Apprenticeship and Emancipation.

Bibb, Henry (1815–1854)

The fugitive slave Henry Bibb was the author of *Narrative of the Life and Adventures of Henry Bibb, an American Slave; Written by Himself* (1849). Bibb's narrative chronicled his life in servitude until he gained his freedom and settled in Michigan. Bibb was also the editor of *Voice of the Fugitive*, an influential abolitionist newspaper that he founded in Canada.

Born in Kentucky in 1815, Bibb endured bondage as a slave in the Upper South until he was sold to a slaveholder in Louisiana. He was later sold to a Native American slaveholder in Indian Territory.

At one point, he was separated from his family and sold to gamblers as punishment for his habitual attempts to escape.

Bibb's autobiography is unique among slave narratives, because, upon his successful escape to the North, he did not stay there and remain a free man. After his initial escape, Bibb returned to the South to rescue his wife and child, but he was captured and returned to slavery before he could complete his mission. Bibb made another escape from bondage to freedom in the North. He repeated this pattern of escape and recapture several times before finally settling in the North permanently in 1842, having given up hope of reuniting his family.

After making his final escape from servitude, Bibb settled in Detroit, Michigan. Slavery had denied him learning, so he resolved to find a teacher in Detroit who could provide him with a formal education. Soon, he began his career as an abolitionist and became active in antislavery politics. In 1844, he began campaigning on behalf of the Liberty Party, a new antislavery political party. His political activism put him at odds with the Garrisonian wing of the American abolitionists, who opposed political involvement.

Because his tale of repeated escape from slavery and recapture seemed so implausible, Bibb went to great lengths to authenticate his work. Slave narratives often included letters from well-known people who could vouch for the writer's character, but Bibb's extensive authentication included a letter from a former slave owner and several letters from members of the Liberty Party. A committee from the Liberty Party conducted an investigation that confirmed Bibb's story, which he repeated to audiences during his antislavery lectures. By 1849, Bibb's speeches on the abolitionist lecture circuit had made the story of his life in slavery and escape to the North famous, but his story reached an even larger audience when it was published in his narrative.

After the passage of the Fugitive Slave Law of 1850, African Americans began an exodus to Canada. Bibb also moved to Canada, where he started publishing the newspaper *Voice of the Fugitive* in 1851, making it the country's first black-owned newspaper. Like many African Americans at the time, Bibb had lost faith in the prospect that black people would ever gain equality in the United States. He used the pages of his newspaper to advocate African American emigration to Canada and the West Indies and to attack the American Colonization Society, which sought to settle former

Engraved by P.H Reason

Henry Bibb

Henry Bibb's *Narrative* (1849) is among the most moving accounts of the American slave experience. He escaped bondage several times, but returned to the South on each occasion to rescue his wife and child—never successfully. *(Library of Congress)*

slaves in Africa. Bibb and other African American leaders considered the society's efforts as a racist attempt to remove free blacks from the United States.

Voice of the Fugitive had a small circulation but great influence. Many of the foremost African American colonizationists contributed to its pages, including Martin Robison Delany and James Theodore Holly. Unlike some African Americans in Canada who advocated that blacks integrate into the mainstream of Canadian society, Bibb emphasized the importance of agriculture, and he urged blacks to become self-sufficient and build their own farms, businesses, and institutions. In fall 1851, he organized the North American Convention of Colored People in Toronto, with the goal of formulating strategies for blacks to become prosperous and self-sufficient.

To that end, Bibb also helped to organize the Refugees' Home Society in Canada, which bought land for the resettlement of black emigrants to Canada and distributed it in twenty-five-acre homesteads. By 1854, the Refugees' Home Society had distributed forty homesteads to settlers. Before his death in August 1854, Bibb also established a school for fugitive slaves and a Methodist church.

Kevin Butler

See also: Canada; Fugitive Slave Act of 1850; Fugitive Slaves.

Further Reading

Bibb, Henry. *Narrative of the Life and Adventures of Henry Bibb, An American Slave.* 1849. Madison: University of Wisconsin Press, 2001.
Hite, Roger W. "Voice of a Fugitive: Henry Bibb and Ante-Bellum Black Separatism." *Journal of Black Studies* 4 (March 1974): 269–84.

Birkbeck, Morris (1764–1825)

Morris Birkbeck, an early pioneer and promoter of frontier settlement in Illinois, was an antislavery advocate whose newspaper articles, penned in 1823 under the pseudonym Jonathan Freeman, helped defeat the Illinois legislature's proslavery proposal. As a result, Illinois was declared a free state.

Birkbeck was born on January 23, 1764, in Settle, England. When he was ten years old, his family moved to Wanborough, England, where Birkbeck worked as a farmer's boy and eventually leased his own farm. As a leaseholder, he felt oppressed by Britain's system of high taxation, which required him to support an established church but did not allow him to vote or hold office.

In 1814, Birkbeck and friend George Flower began to explore the possibility of relocating abroad, and they made a tour of France. They were intrigued by the agricultural opportunities there, but the ongoing Napoleonic Wars and the strong influence of the Roman Catholic clergy on French society deterred them. In 1816, Flower journeyed to the United States, surveyed potential sites for settlement, and purchased land in Virginia. Birkbeck, along with a small party of family and friends, met Flower at Richmond, Virginia, in May 1817. Birkbeck was horrified when he witnessed slavery firsthand, and he resolved to settle in free territory.

After traveling through Pennsylvania, Ohio, and Indiana, Birkbeck and Flower established a colony for English farmers on the Illinois prairie. They purchased adjoining tracts in Edwards County that came to be known as the "English Settlement" or "English Prairie." As a result of a falling-out between the two men, Birkbeck founded the separate town of Wanborough on his land, whereas Flower called his settlement Albion.

Birkbeck wrote two popular books, *Notes on a Journey in America* (1817) and *Letters From Illinois* (1818), that promoted the concept of English settlement to Britons who were considering emigrating to the United States. Although Birkbeck's main purpose was to encourage migration to the Illinois prairie, both works condemned slavery as an inhumane, unnatural practice that plagued the United States. On July 4, 1822, Birkbeck reiterated his opposition to slavery in a speech that urged Americans to fulfill the principles of the Declaration of Independence by abolishing slavery.

Given Birkbeck's strong feelings against slavery, he was alarmed when, in February 1823, proslavery members of the Illinois legislature sought to remove the restrictions on slavery contained in the state's 1818 constitution. Shortly after the passage of the convention resolution, Birkbeck wrote to Governor Edward Coles and informed his friend that he was prepared to dedicate the remainder of his life to preventing slavery in Illinois.

With Coles's encouragement, Birkbeck took up his pen and wrote a series of letters that were printed in local newspapers under the pseudonym Jonathan Freeman. In these letters, he argued that slavery was uncivilized, antirepublican, and un-Christian, and that it would especially harm yeoman farmers. Birkbeck also published a pamphlet under his own name that criticized the underhanded tactics that had been employed to pass the convention resolution. The widely circulated pamphlet asserted that the introduction of slavery in Illinois would lower the state's land prices, make the threat of slave rebellion a constant concern, and deter prospective settlers from Europe and the free states.

Despite vicious personal attacks from his political opponents, Birkbeck persevered. His devotion was rewarded in 1824 when a majority of voters rejected the convention proposal in a referendum that August.

Coles appointed Birkbeck secretary of state for Illinois in October 1824. He served in that capacity until a proslavery majority in the legislature rejected his nomination in January 1825. Birkbeck drowned on June 4, 1825, en route from a visit to New Harmony, Indiana.

Matt Norman

See also: Coles, Edward.

Birney, James Gillespie (1792–1857)

A two-time presidential candidate of the antislavery Liberty Party, James Gillespie Birney was one of the most influential and outspoken opponents of slavery in the United States. By encouraging the formation of a third-party political movement to confront the institution of slavery, Birney challenged the prevailing views of William Lloyd Garrison and other leading abolitionists, who did not support political action as a means to effect abolition. This ideological dispute eventually precipitated a schism in the American abolitionist movement.

Born on February 4, 1792, Birney was the only son of James and Martha Read Birney of Danville, Kentucky. At age six, he inherited his first slaves. His father, though a slave owner, believed that Kentucky should be a free state. As a youth, Birney was influenced by such notable antislavery religious leaders as David Barrow and David Rice, both Kentucky Methodists who had been expelled from their denomination for preaching abolitionism in 1806.

Birney received his formal education at Transylvania University in Lexington, Kentucky, the Priestly Seminary in Danville, Kentucky, and the College of New Jersey (now Princeton University), where he graduated in 1810. Birney went on to Philadelphia to study law in the office of Alexander Dallas. By 1814, he had returned to Danville to work as an attorney.

Within two years of his return to Kentucky, Birney was elected as a representative to the state legislature. While a member of that body, he opposed a resolution asking Indiana and Ohio to aid Kentucky in the return of runaway slaves. Although Birney's commitment to the antislavery movement remained strong, he did not immediately free his own slaves. Ironically, he obtained even more bondsmen in his marriage to Agatha McDowell in 1816.

Birney and his wife moved to a plantation in Madison County, Alabama, where he became involved in state politics and served as a member of the Alabama Constitutional Convention. His strong antislavery stance influenced convention delegates to pass a provision prohibiting the importation of slaves for sale into the state. He also supported the compensation of masters who freed their slaves. As an antislavery advocate in the Deep South, Birney's political career faced constant scrutiny. In 1819, he won a seat in the state legislature, where his antislavery rhetoric became even more intense; however, his downfall in Alabama politics came when he refused to support the presidential bid of the highly popular Andrew Jackson.

Birney continued to devote more time to public service than to his plantation. Financial troubles forced him to sell his land and his Alabama slaves. He moved to Huntsville, Alabama, where he established a lucrative law practice. The Cherokee Nation sought his legal expertise, as did many prominent Southerners. In addition, he helped found the University of Alabama, and, in 1819, he became a trustee of Centre College in his hometown of Danville.

By 1826, Birney had begun to promote the gradual emancipation of slaves. In August 1832, he accepted a position as agent of the American Colonization Society. Members of this society believed that emancipated slaves should be relocated to Africa and assisted free blacks in their emigration to settlements in present-day Liberia. Birney advocated his native Kentucky as an excellent place to test the removal and relocation of freed slaves. He traveled throughout the South, giving lectures and promoting the idea of resettling American blacks in Africa. In 1834, he felt that his stance on slavery might have cost him a position as professor of ancient languages at Centre College in Danville.

Eventually, Birney became disenchanted with the concept of gradual emancipation. In 1834, he broke with the American Colonization Society and decided that only the complete abolition of slavery would suffice. He wrote "Letter on Colonization," in which he explained his new position on human bondage. Emancipation did not work; abolition seemed to be the only viable remedy.

Southern attitudes toward slavery became more entrenched during the 1830s. Three years before Birney's decision to become an abolitionist, a slave rebellion in Virginia led by Nat Turner caused a panic throughout the South. In 1831, Turner and a number of other slaves went on a killing rampage that cost the lives of more than fifty whites. The state of Kentucky, along with the rest of the South, became terrified of a slave uprising, and many Southerners felt that the Turner rebellion had been precipitated by the antislavery movement.

By resigning from the American Colonization Society, Birney boosted his standing with the more radical antislavery forces. His hope of founding an abolitionist newspaper in Danville abruptly came to an end in 1835, however, when proslavery forces threatened his life and disrupted his mail. Feeling that Kentucky was no longer safe for himself or his family, he left the state and moved to New Richmond, Ohio. Birney's conversion to the abolitionist cause did not immediately prompt him to free his Kentucky slaves, though; not until 1839 did he emancipate his remaining twenty-one slaves, who were valued at about $20,000.

In January 1836, Birney founded *The Philanthropist* in New Richmond, Ohio. The publication not only attacked slavery as immoral, but it also gave advice to aspiring abolitionists on how to destroy human servitude through political action. Birney denounced both the Democrats and Whigs as ineffectual in dealing with the slavery question. His strong views on the destruction of slavery made him a number of enemies: After his relocating the paper to Cincinnati, a group of white Cincinnatians destroyed his printing press on several occasions, and his public appearances often suffered violent disruptions. Undaunted, Birney continued to publish there until December 1846, when he moved the paper to Washington, D.C., and renamed it the *National Era.*

In 1837, Birney left Ohio for New York to become director of the American Anti-Slavery Society. Although he was considered radical by many Americans, Birney held more conservative views than many of his colleagues in the abolitionist movement, including the society's leader, Garrison. Though some outspoken members of the American Anti-Slavery Society called for an end to human bondage by any means, including violence, Birney wanted to end slavery constitutionally. His views differed sharply from those of the Garrisonian abolitionists, who felt the U.S. Constitution was a proslavery document and favored secession. By taking a legal and peaceful approach to the abolition of slavery, Birney gained the support of many moderate Americans. Nevertheless, he and his followers split the abolitionist ranks, and when tensions arose within the society in 1839, he was among those who broke ties with the group. During the next few years, Birney spoke throughout the North, urging a legal end to slavery. He became a hero within certain factions of the antislavery move-

ment, and some politicians began to think of him as a potential presidential candidate.

In 1839, at a Liberty Party state convention in Warsaw, New York, delegates tentatively nominated Birney for president. In April 1840, the Liberty Party confirmed his nomination at its national convention in Albany, New York. Delegates from six states officially adopted the party name and announced the abolition of slavery as the single plank in its platform. In the November election, Birney received only 7,069 votes from six New England states, as well as Illinois, New Jersey, New York, Ohio, Michigan, and Pennsylvania (the states where he had been listed on the ballot).

Birney's reputation as a crusader against slavery continued to grow. He traveled to London as one of the vice presidents of the World Anti-Slavery Convention in 1840, and he spoke and wrote about the abolitionist movement. His best-known work, *The American Churches: The Bulwarks of American Slavery,* appeared in England that year; an American edition appeared two years later. In 1842, he moved to Bay City, Michigan, where he continued his work.

In 1843, Birney again received the Liberty Party's nomination for president at its convention in Buffalo, New York. This time, 148 delegates representing twelve states gathered to discuss the party's long and detailed antislavery platform, which included a passage calling the Fugitive Slave Law null and void.

The presidential race of 1844 was one of the most hotly contested elections in American history. The Democrats, led by James K. Polk, and the Whigs, led by Henry Clay, had to contend with the growing third-party movement and Birney's popularity as a presidential candidate. With the backing of influential men such as Ohio antislavery agitator Salmon P. Chase, Birney and the Liberty Party garnered more than 62,000 votes. The Whigs felt the Liberty Party votes had robbed them of the election, which they lost by fewer than 38,000 votes.

In summer 1845, Birney suffered severe injuries when he fell from his horse. He became partially paralyzed and withdrew from active participation in politics, although he continued to write pamphlets and tracts for the antislavery cause. Suffering from ill heath for a number of years, he became reclusive and somewhat bitter. He moved to Perth Amboy, New Jersey, where he died on November 25, 1857.

Ron D. Bryant

See also: Garrison, William Lloyd; Liberty Party.

Further Reading

Birney, James Gillespie. *Letters of James Gillespie Birney, 1831–1857.* 2 vols. Ed. Dwight L. Dumond. New York: D. Appleton-Century, 1938; repr. Gloucester, MA: P. Smith, 1966.

Borome, Joseph A. "Henry Clay and James G. Birney." *Filson Club History Quarterly* 35 (April 1961): 122–24.

Fladeland, Betty. *James Gillespie Birney: Slaveholder to Abolitionist.* Ithaca, NY: Cornell University Press, 1955.

Lamb, Robert Paul. "James G. Birney and the Road to Abolitionism." *Alabama Review* 47 (April 1994): 83–143.

Blackstone, William (1723–1780)

Sir William Blackstone was an English jurist, professor of common law at Oxford University, and author of *Commentaries on the Laws of England* (1765–1769), the first comprehensive treatise on English law and the English Constitution. His writings on slavery reflect the extent to which Enlightenment thought transformed English attitudes on the topic.

Born in London, Blackstone was formally educated at the Charterhouse School, Pembroke College at Oxford University, and the Middle Temple. He was called to the bar in 1746, but, in 1753, he chose to pursue his academic interests at Oxford. Blackstone immediately gained renown for his ability as a lecturer, leading to his appointment in 1758 as the first Vinerian Professor of English Law at Oxford. From 1761 to 1770, he sat in the House of Commons, but by most accounts, he was not effective as a Member of Parliament.

Blackstone's *Commentaries on the Laws of England*, based on his Oxford lectures, was enormously popular; this work became the authoritative text on common law and was circulated widely in Great Britain and America. The *Commentaries* were divided into an introduction and four books: Book I: "Of the Rights of Persons," Book II: "Of the Rights of Things," Book III: "Of Private Wrongs," and Book IV: "Of Public Wrongs." As a whole, the *Commentaries* was much more than a standard legal text; it provided a systematic and thorough account of the history of the English government, or "constitution." Blackstone remarked that he wished to give "a general map of the law, marking out the shape of the country, it's connexions and boundaries, it's greater divisions and principal cities." That meant, in part, tracing the English Constitution to its eighteenth-century terminus, in which sovereignty resided with the King-in-Parliament. For those in the eighteenth-century British Atlantic world,

Blackstone's *Commentaries* was often the first place to look when seeking to define questions about "rights" and "wrongs."

As commentators have long noted, Blackstone followed the French political philosopher Baron de La Brède et de Montesquieu in his position on slavery. Even Blackstone's definition of slavery appears to have come from Montesquieu. Particularly contemptuous of religious and racist justifications for slavery, Montesquieu stated, "The state of slavery is in its own nature bad." Indeed, Blackstone's *Commentaries* popularized for an English reading audience many of the ideas that Montesquieu had first put forth in a systematic way in *The Spirit of the Laws* (1748). That was the case with Montesquieu's critique of the Roman emperor Justinian's discussion of the foundation of slavery, which Blackstone addressed in similar terms. In the *Commentaries*, Blackstone argued that "the three origins of the right of slavery assigned by Justinian, are all of them built upon false foundations."

In "Of the Rights of Persons," Blackstone maintained, "the law of England abhors, and will not endure, the existence of slavery within this nation." He argued that the English were people who championed freedom and liberty. Indeed, he wrote, "this spirit of liberty is so deeply implanted in our constitution, and rooted even in our very soil, that a slave or a negro, the moment he lands in England, falls under the protection of the laws, and with regard to all natural rights becomes *eo instanti* a freeman."

Considering that of "master and servant" to be one of the "three great relations in private life," however, Blackstone weighed in on the legal basis of perpetual slavery. He thus maintained that American slaveholders had a right to perpetual service of their slaves: "Yet, with regard to any right which the master may have acquired, by contract of the like, to the perpetual service of John or Thomas, this will remain exactly in the same state as before: for this is no more than the same state of subjection for life, which every apprentice submits to for the space of seven years, or sometimes for a longer term."

Blackstone died on February 14, 1780. His *Commentaries* were long cited and quoted as an authoritative text, in part, because they were straightforward, lending themselves to easy reference.

Mark G. Spencer

See also: Montesquieu, Baron de La Brède et de.

Further Reading

Blackstone, William. *Commentaries on the Laws of England: A Facsimile of the First Edition of 1765–1769.* 4 vols. Introduction by Stanley N. Katz. Chicago: University of Chicago Press, 1979.

Davis, David Brion. *The Problem of Slavery in the Age of Revolution, 1770–1823.* Ithaca, NY: Cornell University Press, 1975; New York: Oxford University Press, 1999.

Fletcher, F.T.H. "Montesquieu's Influence on Anti-Slavery Opinion in England." *Journal of Negro History* 18 (October 1933): 414–26.

Jenkins, William Sumner. *Pro-Slavery Thought in the Old South.* 1935. Chapel Hill: University of North Carolina Press, 1960.

Blair, William Thomas (ca. 1800–ca. 1870)

William Thomas Blair was a member of the British and Foreign Anti-Slavery Society and a key proponent of the Free Produce movement in Great Britain during the 1840s. He believed that if his fellow countrymen used their collective purchasing power as an economic vote against slavery, they could hasten the day when abolition would become a reality worldwide. Blair's use of moral suasion to encourage British citizens to make intelligent purchases represented a true grassroots effort to convince consumers that everyone was capable of being an abolitionist.

An active member of the antislavery movement, Blair was present at the 1840 World Anti-Slavery Convention in London, which was attended by 500 delegates from the United States and Great Britain. He was one of the British abolitionists who later sat for a portrait and was immortalized in Benjamin Robert Haydon's famous painting memorializing the event, *The Anti-Slavery Society Convention* (1841).

Blair wrote a public letter, *On the Introduction of Slave-Grown Produce Into the British Markets*, which was published by the British and Foreign Anti-Slavery Society in 1844. In it, he argued that all British citizens were supporters of slavery and the slave trade by proxy because of the thoughtless economic choices that they made daily in markets throughout the country. By emphasizing the power and importance of British purchasing power, Blair advocated for the Free Produce movement that members of the Society of Friends (Quakers) had initiated earlier.

The Free Produce movement had supporters in Great Britain and the United States, but its influence tended to be limited to Quaker communities. For example, in the United States, the abolitionist editor Benjamin Lundy, who published the *Genius of Universal Emancipation*, operated a Free Produce store in the Quaker community of Mount Pleasant, Ohio. Blair and other advocates of the Free Produce movement hoped that this form of deliberate economic resistance to slavery would become mainstream and that more consumers would vote with their pocketbooks and refuse to purchase goods having any direct link to slave labor.

The Free Produce movement was especially popular among women, who did much of the purchasing at village markets throughout Great Britain. For those who otherwise might not have had the opportunity to join the moral crusade against slavery in a more formal sense, the conscious decision that many women made to boycott selected goods was a form of active resistance against slavery that could be maintained daily with relatively little discomfort. In particular, British consumers were urged to be wary of manufactured goods that might contain either sugar or cotton, two of the raw materials most likely to have been produced by slave labor in the Americas.

Blair spent most of his career in Great Britain, but he visited the United States on at least one occasion. In 1846, he and black abolitionist Alexander Crummell were in New York City, where they delivered a eulogy to mark the passing of Thomas Clarkson, the beloved champion of the British abolitionist movement. Their remarks were later published as a memorial pamphlet by a local antislavery society.

A champion of social justice causes, Blair later published a pamphlet criticizing the Inam Commission and its work in British Hindustan (modern-day India). Parliament had initiated the work of the Inam Commission in response to the Sepoy Mutiny (1857), an attack on British imperial interests in the region. Just as he had advocated for the rights of Africans who were enslaved, Blair wanted to ensure that the British government was treating the indigenous Hindu and Muslim peoples of the Indian subcontinent with civility and justice.

Junius P. Rodriguez

See also: Clarkson, Thomas.

Further Reading

Nuermberger, Ruth Ketring. *The Free Produce Movement: A Quaker Protest Against Slavery.* New York: AMS, 1970.

Blanchard, Jonathan (1811–1892)

Jonathan Blanchard was a pastor, educator, social reformer, and combatant for abolitionism for more than two decades. He wrote that slavery exhibited "all the worst principles of European despotism and Asiatic caste" and worked to change the proslavery mind-set through his writing and preaching.

Blanchard was born on January 19, 1811, in Rockingham, Vermont. He began studying for the ministry at the Andover Theological Seminary in Massachusetts but, having been introduced to abolitionist thought while an academy principal in Plattsburgh, New York, he became frustrated with Andover's equivocation on the issue of slavery.

He left the school in September 1836 to become a lecturer for the American Anti-Slavery Society as one of Theodore Dwight Weld's "seventy agents," a cadre of abolitionist agents who were sent out to attract more members to the society. After a year of travel and working alone as an abolitionist agent in Pennsylvania, where he was scorned, mobbed, and physically injured, he decided to return to his theological studies at the Lane Theological Seminary in Cincinnati, then a hotbed of abolitionist thought and action.

Upon completing his studies at Lane, Blanchard was ordained to the ministry by fellow abolitionists Calvin Stowe and Lyman Beecher. Blanchard stayed in Cincinnati and became pastor of the Sixth Presbyterian Church. He continued his abolitionist lecturing, describing the transforming influence of leading minds on the direction of churches, volunteer societies, and colleges. In 1845, he called for a "martyr-age of colleges and seminaries" where faculty would "lead their students, both by precept and example . . . into a zeal for reformation." His thoughts on this subject were reprinted widely in newspapers and tracts. Ultimately, Blanchard believed that "society is perfect where what is right in theory exists in fact; where practice coincides with principle and the law of God is the law of the land."

Blanchard was disinclined to support James Gillespie Birney, the abolitionist Liberty Party candidate for president in 1840, because of the detrimental effects he believed Birney's candidacy would have on the abolitionist cause in Ohio. Instead, he publicly supported William Henry Harrison against Martin Van Buren—a move that aroused the anger of the influential abolitionist and philanthropist Gerrit Smith. Blanchard's rationale was that a vote for Birney, who happened to be a member of Blanchard's church, was one less vote that Van Buren needed to defeat Harrison and be re-elected. For Blanchard, Harrison was the lesser of two evils.

As Blanchard's views on the abolitionist political party changed and he came to understand that political agency could advance the antislavery cause, he became more involved in shaping the direction of the Liberty Party in Ohio. He introduced attorney Salmon P. Chase to Thaddeus Stevens of Pennsylvania, while soliciting Stevens to speak at a convention in Ohio, which he hoped would convince him to join the Liberty Party. Stevens declined, but the introduction of Chase and Stevens was significant, as both men later moved on to national political careers.

Blanchard's involvement in the abolitionist cause reached its zenith in 1843, when he was selected as a delegate from the Ohio Anti-Slavery Society to the Second World Anti-Slavery Convention in London. He assumed a prominent role in the delegation and was elected a vice president of the convention. In that office and as a member of several committees, Blanchard had a number of opportunities to address the convention; some felt that he took undue advantage of those opportunities by expressing his personal views rather than those of the U.S. delegation.

In fall 1845, as his ministry at the Sixth Presbyterian Church was coming to an end, Blanchard debated the sinfulness of slavery for four days with the nationally known Reverend Nathan L. Rice. After assuming a new role as president of Knox College in Galesburg, Illinois, Blanchard used the position to further his status as an abolitionist spokesperson. His speech, *Public Men and Public Institutions,* which strongly called for a "martyr-age" of colleges, was republished for distribution to potential benefactors.

While at Knox, Blanchard remained a vocal champion of abolitionist thought. In 1850, he penned an open letter—spanning seven newspaper columns—to Stephen A. Douglas regarding his voting record on the Fugitive Slave Law. His repeated challenges culminated in a public debate in Knoxville, Illinois, on October 13, 1854, during which Blanchard highlighted Douglas's reversal of support for the 1820 Missouri Compromise and Douglas painted Blanchard as an extremist.

Nearing twenty years of outspoken opposition to slavery, Blanchard's agitation for abolition was causing friction and discord in Galesburg, and many had tired of the tensions and disunity. A rift began to develop between Blanchard and George Gale, the town's founder and a Knox College professor, culminating in Blanchard's departure in 1858.

In 1860, Blanchard assumed the presidency of the struggling Wheaton College in Illinois, and he fashioned it into a strong and vital institution. During his two decades as president of the college, he shifted his focus from the eradication of slavery to the elimination of secret societies. He died on May 14, 1892.

David B. Malone

See also: Kellogg, Hiram H.; Liberty Party; Weld, Theodore Dwight; World Anti-Slavery Convention (1843).

Further Reading

Blanchard, Jonathan, and Nathan L. Rice. *A Debate on Slavery: Held in Cincinnati, on the First, Second, Third, and Sixth Day of October, 1845, Upon the Question: Is Slave-Holding in Itself Sinful, and the Relation Between Master and Slave, a Sinful Relation?* Cincinnati, OH: William H. Moore, 1846; New York: Negro Universities Press, 1969.

Kilby, Clyde S. *Minority of One.* Grand Rapids, MI: Eerdmans, 1959.

Muelder, Hermann R. *Fighters for Freedom; The History of Anti-Slavery Activities of Men and Women Associated With Knox College.* New York: Columbia University Press, 1959.

Bloomer, Amelia Jenks (1818–1894)

Amelia Jenks Bloomer is best remembered for popularizing the female trousers that came to be known as "bloomers," but over the course of her long public life, she was involved in far more than dress reform. As a writer and orator, she lent her support to the causes of women's rights, temperance, and the abolition of slavery.

Amelia was born in Homer, New York, on May 27, 1818, the youngest of Ananias and Lucy Jenks's six children. She left home at the age of seventeen to work as a schoolteacher. For three years, she served as a governess in Waterloo, New York, and there she met Dexter Bloomer, a young lawyer and editor from nearby Seneca Falls. They married in April 1840, conspicuously omitting the word "obey" from their wedding vows.

With her new husband's encouragement, Bloomer began to contribute articles and essays on temperance and women's rights to his newspaper, the *Seneca Falls Courier.* In 1848, her associates in the Ladies Temperance Society asked her to help them start a "little temperance paper" to be called the *Lily,* but they lost interest in the project before the first issue was published. Although she disliked the name, Bloomer decided to honor the subscriptions that had already been taken, and the first issue rolled off the presses in January 1849.

Beginning as a modest paper dedicated to temperance issues and ladylike discussions of fashion, the *Lily* developed into a militant voice for a host of women's reform issues, including their access to higher education, the right of women to divorce abusive husbands, property rights for widows, and woman suffrage. In 1851, she stepped into the minefield of "rational dress reform" when she joined fellow feminists Elizabeth Smith Miller and Elizabeth Cady Stanton in wearing an outfit of full Turkish-style pantaloons under a short skirt. Her defense of this "shocking" form of dress was reprinted in the influential *New York Tribune,* and subscriptions to the *Lily* doubled almost overnight, ultimately reaching a circulation of 6,000.

Bloomer was never an active abolitionist, although she was sympathetic to the cause and made sure that the *Lily* was a staunchly antislavery newspaper. She contributed to the abolitionist cause by promoting the idea that women were capable of joining the struggle for abolition and giving them ample column space in her paper to share their views.

In 1853, the Bloomers emigrated westward, settling first in Mount Vernon, Ohio, and, in 1855, in the frontier town of Council Bluffs, Iowa. Realizing the impossibility of publishing a biweekly paper 300 miles away from the nearest railroad, Bloomer reluctantly sold the *Lily.* The publication folded less than two years later.

The Bloomers found prosperity in Council Bluffs. Dexter Bloomer made a fortune in land speculation and became active in local politics. The couple adopted two children. Amelia Bloomer continued to write and lecture throughout the 1860s and 1870s. In 1871, she became president of the Iowa Woman Suffrage Association, where she was instrumental in pushing through landmark married women's rights legislation in 1873.

Advancing years and declining health gradually curtailed Bloomer's public activities, and by the late 1880s, she had effectively retired. She died of a heart attack in Council Bluffs on December 30, 1894, at the age of seventy-six.

Heather K. Michon

See also: Women's Rights and the Abolitionist Movement.

Further Reading

Bloomer, Dexter C. *Life and Writings of Amelia Bloomer.* New York: Schocken, 1975.

Ginzberg, Lori D. *Women in Antebellum Reform.* Wheeling, IL: Harlan Davidson, 2000.

Bogle, Paul (1822–1865)

A national hero of Jamaica, Paul Bogle was a peasant farmer and deacon of the Native Baptist Church in Stony Gut, Saint Thomas parish. He is best known as the organizer and leader of the Morant Bay Rebellion of 1865, one of the most important events in Jamaican history. His resistance and struggle for justice during the postemancipation period affected not only the lives of the black population in Jamaica but also the racial consciousness of the British people and the Crown.

Little is known of Bogle's life before 1865. Born free in 1822, Bogle became an ardent supporter of George William Gordon, who was the son of a planter and a female slave, a member of the Jamaican House of Assembly, and a champion of the black cause. Although wage labor had replaced slavery in Jamaica thirty years earlier, an informal system of servitude largely remained in place. Discrimination, exploitation, and social injustice persisted after emancipation came in 1834. Access to land was severely restricted, the black population was poorly represented, and petitions for improvement or change had been denied. While Gordon defended the social and moral rights of the Jamaican people within the government, Bogle worked locally, educating and training the members of his congregation to rise above the stigma attached to Jamaican freedmen and the descendants of slaves.

In the hope of alleviating the conditions of servitude that persisted, Bogle traveled with the people of Stony Gut to Spanish Town, Saint Catherine, to meet with Governor Edward John Eyre in mid-1865. Their complaints about the exploitive conditions, however, fell on deaf ears. Eyre, not known for being sympathetic to the plight of the black peasantry, dismissed their claims for redress of grievances and sent them home.

Unsatisfied, Bogle led a march from Stony Gut to the parish capital of Morant Bay in a protest that he hoped would spread across the island. When the protesters reached the Morant Bay Courthouse on October 11, 1865, the local militia was waiting and opened fire on the group. Rioting occurred through-out the parish for several days, leading the governor to declare martial law on the island. Eyre sent troops to quell the uprising, resulting in the deaths of more than 400 participants; many others were flogged and imprisoned. With a £2,000 reward out for his capture, Bogle was arrested and hanged.

Bogle's struggle for justice was not insignificant. His objectives were realized and paved the way for changes in the social and economic conditions of the peasantry, not only in the parish of Saint Thomas but throughout the island. In Britain, public outcry against the "Governor Eyre controversy" and the brutal repression of the rebellion prompted the Crown to order a formal inquiry into the Morant Bay Rebellion and the measures that Eyre took to suppress it.

A year later, the Crown dissolved Jamaica's representative system of government and established a Crown colony government, taking power away from the local government in one quick action. The move increased the power of the British-appointed governor and replaced the old Legislative Council and House of Assembly with a single legislative council whose members were appointed by the British Crown. A century later, Bogle was recognized as a national hero of the independent nation of Jamaica.

Colleen A. Vasconcellos

See also: Gordon, George William; Jamaica, Emancipation in.

Further Reading

Heuman, Gad J. *The Killing Time: The Morant Bay Rebellion in Jamaica.* Knoxville: University of Tennessee Press, 1994.

Semmel, Bernard. *Jamaican Blood and Victorian Conscience: The Governor Eyre Controversy.* Boston: Houghton Mifflin, 1962.

Sheller, Mimi. *Democracy After Slavery: Black Publics and Peasant Radicalism in Haiti and Jamaica.* Gainesville: University Press of Florida, 2000.

Bolívar, Simón (1783–1830)

Known as "the Liberator" for his role in the independence struggles of Venezuela, Colombia, Bolivia, Panama, Ecuador, and Peru, Simón Bolívar also freed many slaves through his decrees of general manumission. Indeed, his efforts set in motion the end of slavery in much of South America.

Simón José Antonio de la Santísima Trinidad Bolívar was born on July 24, 1783, in Caracas, Venezuela. His parents, Juan Vicente Bolívar y Ponte and Maria de la Concepción Palacios y Blanco, were members of the Creole aristocracy.

Bolívar's first engagements in Venezuela began in 1810 and concluded in 1815 after Spanish forces routed his troops. He fled to Jamaica, seeking British support in the struggle against Spain. Preferring to maintain neutrality with Spain, Britain refused to directly support the cause of South American independence. Unabated, Bolívar sailed to Haiti, where he petitioned President Alexandre Sabés Pétion to assist the revolutionaries in New Spain.

Pétion agreed to support Bolívar in an undertaking to free the slaves in all lands liberated by revolutionary forces. After some deliberation, Bolívar agreed. His reasons were twofold. First, slave emancipation would provide additional troops needed for the revolutionary army. Second, emancipation was a necessary first step in the construction of a new Spanish American national identity.

In 1817, Bolívar returned to Venezuela to lead the revolutionary army. At Angostura, a congress elected him president of Venezuela, and he gave a speech urging radical land redistribution and the abolition of slavery. Bolívar promoted a constitutional form of government with an elected legislature, hereditary senate, and dictatorial executive. As *mestizos* (Venezuelans of mixed European and native ancestry) and *pardos* (manumitted slaves) were placed in leadership positions, Bolívar hoped that a republican commitment to civic equality combined with abolitionist sentiment would win support from the British.

Most *caudillos* (local elites) ignored calls for general manumission, fearing the policy would push slave owners into the royalist camp by unleashing racial revolts. They argued that rapid manumission would not bring greater numbers of recruits to the revolutionary army. Instead, they advocated a policy of selective and gradual manumission. A compromise called *military manumission* was reached; royalist-owned slaves who had fought in the forces of liberation were freed and their patriot planters entitled to compensation. The caudillos also held influential political posts enabling them to block or limit the conscription of slaves. General emancipation remained a point of conflict between Bolívar and the caudillos throughout his administration.

In 1821, manumission was officially achieved in South America by the Congress of Cúcuta in the Republic of Gran Colombia. The congress also adopted a constitution in which full citizenship was reserved for literate men with property worth 100 pesos. Children born to slave mothers were designated as free, although they were often required to labor for their mother's owner until the age of eighteen and to reimburse the owner for the supposed maintenance costs. The law also created locally administered and financed *Juntas de Manumisión* (Manumission Boards) that held the power to buy slaves' freedom from their owners.

After Bolívar's ally, General Antonio José de Sucre, occupied the city of Quito, Bolivar gained executive power in Ecuador. Bolívar increased enrollment in the revolutionary army by manumitting Ecuadorian slaves. Assisted by Sucre, Bolívar managed to liberate Peru in 1823. By February 1824, the Peruvian congress had appointed Bolívar dictator. In December 1824, Sucre, with an army if 8,000 men—half of them pardos—inflicted a crushing defeat of Viceroy José de la Serna at the Battle of Ayacucho. This was the death knell of Spain's South American empire and the beginning of Bolívar's short-lived "Gran Colombia."

Encouraged by the Chilean Constitution of 1823, Bolívar proposed new emancipatory measures in Peru and Bolivia. Bolívar's draft of the Constitution of the Republic of Bolivia declared that "all those who until now have been slaves are Bolivian citizens; and thereby freed by the publication of this constitution; a special law shall determine the amount to be paid as an indemnity to their former owners."

Bolívar's absence from Venezuela facilitated the consolidation of the republican resistance under the hegemony of the caudillos. The caudillos proved themselves highly committed to regional interests and autonomy; they frequently ignored Bolívar's decrees if they deemed his directives to be inconvenient. As a result, the domestic policy goals of Bolívar's weak central government struggled with the application of manumission on a local level by the Manumission Boards.

Bolívar was incensed that only 300 slaves had been manumitted by the Manumission Boards by 1821. In an 1827 decree, he attempted to strengthen the Manumission Boards and ordered that their funds be spent within one year on manumissions, starting with the eldest slaves. According to historian Robin Blackburn, "the failure of the juntas was rooted in the fact that they were beholden to the local possessing classes who had no interest in liquidating slave property." Although Bolívar was indeed angered by the intransigence of the juntas, he could not afford a confrontation with the caudillos or the slaveholders.

Disillusioned and in declining health, Bolívar resigned as president in 1830. After his death in

December 1830, the government of General José Antonio Páez made two modifications to the manumission law: First, the period of postemancipation obligatory service was lengthened from eighteen to twenty-one years, and *emancipados* were required to display proof of gainful employment to the Manumission Boards. Second, the new government confirmed Bolívar's wartime decrees freeing all the slaves in the provinces of Apure and Guyana.

Bolívar is said to have freed his slaves to show other wealthy landowners that he was earnest in his support for emancipation. The act also represented Bolívar's attempt to construct a distinct multiracial American identity. Other South American leaders, notably José Martí in Cuba and Getúlio Vargas in Brazil, made similar attempts.

Evan M. Daniel

See also: Manumission.

Further Reading

Belaúnde, Víctor Andrés. *Bolívar and the Political Thought of the Spanish American Revolution.* Baltimore: Johns Hopkins University Press, 1938.

Blackburn, Robin. *The Overthrow of Colonial Slavery, 1776–1848.* New York: Verso, 1988.

Bolívar, Simón. *The Liberator Simón Bolívar: Man and Image.* Ed. David Bushnell. New York: Alfred A. Knopf, 1970.

Bowditch, Henry Ingersoll (1808–1892)

A leading physician and prominent abolitionist in Massachusetts, Henry Ingersoll Bowditch was an energetic force in the state's radical antislavery activities from the early 1830s to the U.S. Civil War (1861–1865). He was also associated with a number of reforms in public health that improved the lives of countless Americans.

The son of Nathaniel Bowditch, one of early America's most prominent mathematicians, Henry Bowditch was born on August 9, 1808, in Salem, Massachusetts. He studied at Harvard University, where he graduated in 1828 and subsequently completed four more years of study to obtain a medical degree. He would later study with prominent physicians in London and Paris to further his medical expertise.

Bowditch was studying in Europe at the same time that the British Parliament was debating and enacting the 1833 Abolition of Slavery Act (commonly known as the British Emancipation Act), one of the most important legislative measures to affect the transatlantic antislavery movement. Bowditch followed the debates closely in the newspapers and began reading abolitionist literature regularly while he was in Europe. In particular, the American physician became so influenced by the abolitionist writings of William Wilberforce, the legendary antislavery leader in Great Britain, that he returned to Boston a committed abolitionist.

Bowditch became a disciple of William Lloyd Garrison's radical brand of abolitionism, and the doctor proved his value to the antislavery movement during two key episodes that took place in Boston. Each had a successful outcome, despite concerted efforts by proslavery advocates to enforce the Fugitive Slave Laws of 1793 and 1850.

In 1842, Massachusetts residents became outraged by the efforts of James B. Gray, a Virginia slave owner who traveled to Boston to seize a fugitive slave named George Latimer. The case quickly became the cause célèbre of the state, and the so-called Latimer Committee, consisting of Bowditch, William F. Channing, and Frederick Cabot, was organized to defend the fugitive against the threat of removal. Bowditch expressed the abolitionist position in the short-lived newspaper the *Latimer Weekly and North Star,* stating that the Fugitive Slave Act of 1793 was unconstitutional and that Latimer had the right to be a free man.

The Latimer Committee was so successful that a petition carrying 51,862 signatures was sent to Massachusetts congressman John Quincy Adams seeking a redress of grievances through congressional intervention in the Latimer case. Unfortunately, because the Gag Rule prohibited discussion of antislavery issues, such petitions were automatically tabled when they arrived at the U.S. House of Representatives. Annoyed with the large public outcry against his efforts, Gray sold Latimer to the abolitionists for $400 and returned to Virginia.

A decade later, Bowditch and other Massachusetts abolitionists repeated their acts of civil disobedience to win the release of Anthony Burns, another Virginia slave who had been captured as a fugitive in Boston. These efforts, too, bore success, but the passage of the federal Fugitive Slave Law in 1850 made such popular campaigns more difficult and their outcomes less certain.

Bowditch's support for the antislavery movement was eventually measured in real personal terms. His son Nathaniel fought with Union forces during the Civil War and was a casualty of that conflict. Bowditch found solace in knowing that his son had been an agent who had hastened the day of emancipation, but he also hoped that his son's death might serve a larger public purpose. Bowditch wrote *A Brief Plea for an Ambulance System for the Army of the United States, as Drawn From the Sufferings of Lieutenant Bowditch and a Wounded Comrade* (1863) in the hope that fewer families might have to grieve the death of a son on the battlefield.

Bowditch's antislavery efforts did not diminish his involvement in public health matters. He was associated with the Massachusetts General Hospital for fifty-four years, and through his writings and public advocacy, he was able to institute many public health measures—such as regular inoculations—that improved the lives of Massachusetts residents. Through his efforts, the Massachusetts Board of Health was organized to fight epidemic diseases (such as cholera) that plagued America during the nineteenth century.

His influence was not limited to Massachusetts. Bowditch also published *Public Hygiene in America* (1877), along with early medical reports on tuberculosis, a lung disease that was one of his specialties.

Junius P. Rodriguez

See also: Abolition of Slavery Act (1833); Fugitive Slave Act of 1793; Garrison, William Lloyd.

Further Reading

Bowditch, Vincent Yardley, ed. *Life and Correspondence of Henry Ingersoll Bowditch.* Freeport, NY: Books for Libraries, 1970.

Brazil, Abolition in

Brazil, the largest country in South America, ran a thriving sugar- and coffee-producing economy on the backs of African slave labor. By 1800, the nation had the largest slave population in the world, representing half of its population of 3 million.

Brazilian emperor Pedro I had signed a treaty with the British promising to end the slave trade to Brazil by 1830. Despite this agreement, Brazil continued to import African slaves, even increasing its imports during the 1830s and 1840s to meet the demands of its prospering economy.

As the abolitionist movement gained strength in England and the United States during the nineteenth century, British pressure finally forced Brazil to halt its 300-year-old transatlantic slave trade in 1850. By that time, there were approximately 3 million African slaves in a population that totaled nearly 7 million.

Early Efforts

Brazilian abolitionists had an ally in the succeeding emperor, Pedro II (also known as Dom Pedro). By the 1860s, Dom Pedro had become outspoken in his opposition to slavery—largely a response to popular opinion, which favored a move toward abolition. In 1864, he first suggested to his prime minister that the government begin a gradual process of abolition by freeing children born to slave mothers.

The conclusion of the U.S. Civil War in 1865 prompted the emperor to become even more vocal in his abolitionist views. By 1867, he had convinced his parliament to examine the abolition question.

The Paraguayan War of 1865–1870, also known as the War of the Triple Alliance, brought slavery to the forefront of Brazilian politics. The long and costly conflict saw Brazil, Argentina, and Uruguay fighting against Paraguay. When the war broke out, the Brazilian military was largely unprepared for the conflict and suffered heavy losses.

During this time, several factors brought attention to the issue of abolition. First, many political leaders and intellectuals saw the existence of African slavery in Brazil as the country's key vulnerability. Persistent rumors circulated that Paraguay would incite slave rebellions in Brazil. Second, as Brazilian political parties fought over the war, they also began to debate other key issues, including slavery. Third, the Brazilian military solicited the services of many slaves in the conflict, promising them freedom in exchange for military service; some 6,000 Afro-Brazilians gained their freedom in this way. Furthermore, their military service helped to integrate the freed slaves into society by teaching them valuable new skills.

In 1868, the opposition Liberal Party responded to the Conservative government with a reform program that included gradual abolition. By the end of war in 1870, slavery had become the key issue in Brazil. Liberal leaders and intellectuals debated abolition with Conservative politicians and slave owners. The discussion intensified in June 1870, when Spain took a first step toward complete abolition by freeing all newborn and aged slaves in Cuba and Puerto Rico. This move left Brazil isolated as the only remaining slave society in the Western Hemisphere.

In 1871, the Brazilian government passed the *Lei do Ventre Libre* (literally, the "Law of the Free Womb," or the "Free Birth Law," as it became known), which freed children born to slave mothers in Brazil. However, slave masters retained control of the children until the age of eight, at which point, the owners would receive compensation from the government. Slave owners also had the option of keeping these children until they reached twenty-one years of age by declining government compensation.

There was much opposition to the measure before its passage in the Brazilian Parliament: Slave owners defended their property rights, whereas abolitionists claimed that the law was too limited. At the time the law was passed, the Brazilian slave population had fallen to 1.5 million, and the free population numbered 8.6 million.

Abolitionist Movement Gains Momentum

Beginning in 1880, the abolitionist movement grew in strength. It was centered in Brazil's major cities, where many residents saw slavery as an outdated labor system that impeded their attempts to modernize the country.

In northern Brazil, many planters stopped relying on slave labor, as the sugar industry declined in relation to the booming coffee economy of the south. Many northern planters had already abandoned the region after the great drought of 1877–1879, selling their slaves or taking them to other parts of the country. Others had freed their slaves, and few remained in the region. Instead, they relied on the free labor of Afro-Brazilians and *sertanejos* (poor whites or *mestizos* from the interior of the country).

Furthermore, in 1884, the northern states of Amazonas and Ceará abolished slavery, although there were few African slaves in these areas by this time. The strongest resistance to the abolitionist movement came from the coffee planters in the southern states of Rio de Janeiro, São Paulo, and Minas Gerais.

The leadership of the abolitionist movement included both black and white Brazilians. Perhaps the best-known abolitionist was Joaquim Nabuco, the son of a prominent Brazilian politician. His opposition to slavery, articulated in his 1883 work *O abolicionismo* (Abolitionism), influenced many Brazilians. The mulatto journalist José do Patrocínio became known for his fiery propaganda against the institution of slavery. Another mulatto, the teacher and engineer André Rebouças, was a friend of the emperor and a leading organizer of the movement. These men and other abolitionists saw the end of slavery as a part of a larger movement to modernize Brazil that also included land reform, political democracy, and education.

In 1885, the Brazilian Parliament passed the Sexagenarian Law, freeing all slaves at the age of sixty. However, much like the earlier Free Birth Law, slaves had to serve their masters for three additional years and remain at their owners' residence for five years. In reality, though it affected some 120,000 slaves, the law had little real effect. Few slaves lived much beyond the age of sixty; often, planters were glad to be free of the burden of maintaining the old slaves. In addition, the government promised to purchase the freedom of all slaves within fourteen years.

At the same time, many slaves escaped via an informal Underground Railroad that linked the southern parts of the country, such as São Paulo, to Ceará in the north, where slavery had ended. As the abolitionist movement grew, there was much resistance to any attempt to forcibly return runaway slaves to their owners. Furthermore, the Brazilian military increasingly refused to capture escaped slaves.

In 1887, the city of São Paulo raised funds to purchase the freedom of slaves within the city. By this time, many slave owners in the coffee-producing regions of Brazil saw abolition as inevitable and had begun to free their slaves in exchange for promises that the freedmen would work for wages.

In the meantime, coffee plantation owners sought to attract foreign immigrants to labor on their estates. Such attempts were very successful—some 2.7 million immigrants, mainly from Spain, Portugal, and Italy, arrived in southern Brazil between 1887 and 1914—making slave labor unnecessary in the coffee region and leading many planters to accept the idea of abolition.

Slaves Freed

In May 1888, the Brazilian Parliament met to discuss the issue of abolition. Both houses of the legislature overwhelmingly passed a measure to end slavery.

On May 13, Princess Regent Isabel, acting on Dom Pedro's behalf, signed the *Lei Áurea* (Golden Law), granting freedom to Brazil's remaining 750,000 slaves, making it the last slave society in the Americas to abolish slavery.

In the country's large cities, such as Rio de Janeiro, the Golden Law met with much approval, and many Brazilians celebrated the end of slavery. However, in the countryside, many slave-owning planters blamed the monarchy for the end of slavery, a sentiment that contributed to Dom Pedro's fall in 1889 and the subsequent establishment of a republic.

Ronald E. Young

See also: Buxton, Thomas Fowell; Clarkson, Thomas; Fox, George; Quakers (Society of Friends); Wilberforce, William.

Further Reading

Burns, E. Bradford. *A History of Brazil.* 3rd ed. New York: Columbia University Press, 1993.

Conrad, Robert E. *The Destruction of Brazilian Slavery, 1850–1888.* Berkeley: University of California Press, 1972; 2nd ed., Malabar, FL: Krieger, 1993.

Reis, João José. *Slave Rebellion in Brazil: The Muslim Uprising of 1835 in Bahía.* Trans. Arthur Brakel. Baltimore: Johns Hopkins University Press, 1993.

Toplin, Robert Brent. *The Abolition of Slavery in Brazil.* New York: Atheneum, 1972.

Brazil, Emancipation in

The government of Brazil abolished the institution of slavery on May 13, 1888, with the signing of the *Lei Áurea* (Golden Law). However, the emancipation of the slaves was not accompanied by any social legislation to aid the *libertos* (freed slaves).

During the postemancipation period, political power remained in the hands of the wealthy landowners who had little interest in the humanitarian plans proposed by some abolitionists, which included subdividing large estates to provide land for ex-slaves. At the same time, other political concerns, such as the rise of republicanism and the end of the Brazilian monarchy, moved to the forefront. Thus, although the formal institution of slavery disappeared in Brazil, exploitation of and discrimination against blacks did not.

Former slave owners responded to emancipation in a number of ways. In more remote regions of the country, some slave owners simply ignored the law for as long as four years. Others refused to pay former slaves immediately, even when the freed blacks continued to work for them.

In the aftermath of abolition, planters sometimes complained about a lack of workers, as well as the fact that slaves who did remain seemed to work at a much more leisurely rate, as they were no longer compelled by force. The plantation owners worried that many ex-slaves would leave, even after they had agreed to continue working, and that the crops would suffer. In the end, after a brief period of celebration immediately following emancipation, many former slaves returned to work, and the transition to free labor was relatively smooth. Emancipation did not severely disrupt the Brazilian plantation economy, as many planters had feared.

The libertos also responded to emancipation in a variety of ways. In the immediate aftermath, many ex-slaves did leave their masters' estates. Some went to the cities to join in the many celebrations of the new law. There, they concentrated in the emerging *favelas*, or shantytowns. Others went in search of lost friends and relatives.

In some ways, the lives of the freed slaves did not change noticeably. Often, they performed the same physical work before and after emancipation. Few slaves were prepared to compete in the open labor market, as most had been field hands and possessed limited skills. Therefore, those who did not continue working in the fields were limited to temporary and difficult jobs. There were some former slaves who did well, such as domestic servants or artisans, but most Afro-Brazilians remained poor and malnourished.

Emancipation in the Sugar Region

Until the mid-nineteenth century, slavery in Brazil was concentrated in the sugar-producing regions of the northeast. By the time the Brazilian government abolished slavery in 1888, the northeast had begun to experience an economic decline, whereas the coffee-producing regions farther south continued to prosper. As a result of the regions' disparate economic situations, large-scale immigration to Brazil in the late nineteenth and early twentieth centuries centered on the southern part of the country. Because there were few immigrant workers in the northeast, sugar planters had to depend on the continued labor of freed slaves. Though the elite attempted to implement vagrancy laws to keep the former slaves on the plantations, in general, the northeastern planters had to attract and retain Afro-Brazilian workers by offering incentives.

Although the planters wanted to keep the freed slaves on their plantations as labor tenants, the Afro-Brazilians wanted land. Landowners in Brazil had a long tradition of allowing rural workers to occupy land. Known as *moradores* (dwellers), these rural Brazilians were labor tenants who provided work in exchange for their use of the land. In the immediate aftermath of abolition, many emancipated slaves depended on such traditional forms of labor instead of becoming full-fledged wage-earning workers. Although the moradores sometimes earned wages, they more often relied entirely on family production of small-scale market crops that they grew on the land owned by the wealthy planters. These crops included manioc and tobacco, which the former slaves sold to earn extra income.

Other factors limited the transition from slave labor to wage labor. The presence of seasonal workers from the interior backlands known as the *sertão* provided competition for jobs. In addition, by the 1880s, the sugar industry had become stagnant. The industry experienced no growth through the 1910s, making the demand for labor weak and wages low.

Although former slaves in the northeast remained largely dependent and poor, they also experienced some important changes. They had limited access to land, which allowed them to earn extra income and avoid dependence on wages determined by the plantation owners. By relying on family labor and exchanging labor with neighbors, the former slaves were able to create ties among poor, rural inhabitants.

The emancipated slaves also had more freedom to choose where they lived and worked. Although slaves lived in centralized and supervised quarters, moradores were more dispersed. Life was no longer geared toward the needs of the master, and Afro-Brazilians could dedicate more time to their families and neighbors.

Some took advantage of this freedom and relocated away from the sugar estates to areas with open land, such as the *agreste*, a dry region between the coastal sugar zone and the arid and desolate sertão. Traveling seasonally to the agreste, they raised cattle, grew cotton, and produced various food products.

Emancipation in the Coffee Region: The Case of São Paulo

By the late nineteenth century, Brazil's coffee economy was booming in the states of Rio de Janeiro, Minas Gerais, and São Paulo. The situation in São Paulo illustrates some of the difficulties that free Afro-Brazilians encountered after the abolition of slavery. On the one hand, there were no state-imposed racial controls or restrictions, as in the southern United States or South Africa. On the other hand, the government still greatly influenced the state's labor market by promoting European immigration to the coffee plantations.

The government and the coffee planters had already begun to discuss the possibility of attracting European immigrants as early as the 1850s, when the slave trade had come to an end. Immigration to the region was limited during the years leading up to abolition in 1888. After emancipation, the number of European immigrants in São Paulo increased dramatically. In 1888, there were three times as many Europeans in the state as there had been the previous year, and the state government subsidized most of these newcomers.

At the same time, the government chose not to invest in Afro-Brazilian workers, whom the planters viewed as lazy and irresponsible. Thus, although the government had no formal racial policy with regard to labor, its emphasis on foreigners at the expense of Afro-Brazilian workers clearly demonstrated its preference.

As a result of this preference for European workers, freed slaves in both urban and rural São Paulo held the least desirable jobs. Immigrant farmworkers acquired the best jobs in the most prosperous regions of the state. Rural Afro-Brazilians were concentrated in seasonal and low-paying jobs in poorer parts of the state. The situation was similar in the cities. The industrial labor force was largely made up of immigrants. There were relatively few black factory workers or artisans. Instead, Afro-Brazilians could be found in domestic service jobs or in the private sector of the urban economy.

The Brazilian elite also attempted to create a divide between black and white workers in São Paulo. As early as 1891, a dockworkers' strike in the port city of Santos brought to light the antagonisms encouraged among the working classes. When European immigrant dockworkers went on strike, management brought in Afro-Brazilians as strikebreakers. By effectively excluding Afro-Brazilians from jobs, the elite had created a willing force of black strikebreakers. Because so many former slaves were unemployed in the state, it was difficult for them to turn down such jobs.

Although most of the organized labor force in São Paulo was European born, some white workers attempted to eliminate the racial divide between blacks and whites. Influenced by egalitarian ideals of socialism and anarchism, some white labor leaders appealed to the former slaves to organize with them. But lingering racist attitudes among many white workers limited the success of such attempts. Thus, the state and the elite prevailed over labor unions.

The Black Guard

Some organizations attempted to continue the reform program. For example, shortly after the abolition of slavery, a group of Afro-Brazilians formed the Black Guard, a secret society dedicated to Princess Regent Isabel. Comprising hundreds of members, the Black Guard took a firm stance against republicanism in Brazil, as the republican movement was headed by elements dedicated to racial discrimination. Many republican supporters sought to implement new systems of forced labor, vagrancy laws, and forced military service. Soon, the Black Guard identified the Republican Party in Brazil as its main opponent.

Afro-Brazilians resisted many of the measures of republican supporters, sometimes violently. In December 1888, for example, hundreds of blacks gathered at a republican rally in Rio de Janeiro. Fighting erupted, shots were fired, and one republican died in the confrontation.

Republicans used such violence as "proof" that Afro-Brazilians intended to wage a race war, and they portrayed the Black Guard as a tool of monarchists who sought to destroy the planter class. Despite such opposition, the Black Guard movement spread throughout Brazil; however, once the Republican Party and the military took control of the government in 1889, the movement quickly died out.

Ronald E. Young

See also: Apprenticeship and Emancipation; Barbados Revolt (1816); Clarkson, Thomas; Jamaica Rebellion (1831–1832); Sharp, Granville; Wilberforce, William.

Further Reading

Andrews, George Reid. "Black and White Workers: São Paulo, Brazil, 1888–1928." *Hispanic American Historical Review* 68 (August 1988): 491–524.

Burns, E. Bradford. *A History of Brazil.* 3rd ed. New York: Columbia University Press, 1993.

Conrad, Robert E. *The Destruction of Brazilian Slavery, 1850–1888.* Berkeley: University of California Press, 1972; 2nd ed., Malabar, FL: Krieger, 1993.

Scott, Rebecca. "Defining the Boundaries of Freedom in the World of Cane: Cuba, Brazil, and Louisiana After Emancipation." *American Historical Review* 99 (February 1994): 70–102.

Toplin, Robert Brent. *The Abolition of Slavery in Brazil.* New York: Atheneum, 1972.

Brazilian Anti-Slavery Society

Founded in 1880 by the prominent antislavery politician Joaquim Nabuco, the Brazilian Anti-Slavery Society (*Sociedade Brasileira Contra a Escravidão*) was one of the first abolitionist organizations in Brazil to stimulate public interest in the antislavery cause. For a short period, it galvanized abolitionist sentiment in Brazil's capital city at that time, Rio de Janeiro, and its members and leaders included many of the prominent abolitionists of the day.

Antislavery sentiment had existed in Brazil since the early nineteenth century, but only in the late 1870s and early 1880s did a popular abolitionist movement emerge to mobilize widespread opposition to the Brazilian slave system. Social and economic changes created a favorable climate for the spread of antislavery ideas. From the mid-1800s on, Brazil had witnessed an expansion of capitalist enterprises, the development of large urban centers, and the growth of free labor. As a result, the country also saw the growth of sectors of society that were opposed to servitude and supported the diffusion of European ideas of civilization and progress. Many young professionals, mostly from affluent families, absorbed these cosmopolitan liberal ideas and formed the cadre of the abolitionist movement. They took the lead—both organizationally, in terms of leadership and involvement, and ideologically—as the strategists and formulators of the policies around which the movement rallied.

Abolitionist politicians such as Nabuco and Ruy Barbosa stressed the importance of protesting through legal channels and directed their message to the free masses, not to the slaves. They opposed the harsh condemnation of masters, politicians, and the emperor, maintaining that the only solution to slavery was gradual legal abolition. Other abolitionists, such as black antislavery activists José do Patrocínio and André Rebouças, were more openly critical of slavery and aimed their propaganda and agitation at a wider audience, including slaves.

Though most abolitionists had moved toward a more radical stance by the mid-1880s, early in the decade, there was a generalized belief in legal propaganda and agitation, and ideological differences were put aside to forge a united front. In the mid-1880s, an even more radical abolitionist wing emerged in São Paulo and Campos that advocated extralegal direct-action tactics.

Shortly after the defeat of his abolitionist legislation, Nabuco invited the foremost antislavery advocates of Rio de Janeiro to meet at his residence on Brazilian Independence Day, September 7, 1880. There he gave a rousing speech, exclaiming, "There is no liberty nor independence in a land with a million and a half slaves." He proposed the creation of the Brazilian Anti-Slavery Society as a moderate propaganda body devoted to the abolitionist cause. The assembled delegates enthusiastically took up Nabuco's call, electing him president and Rebouças as treasurer. The society was specifically modeled on similar propaganda clubs that had been established in England and the United States, and soon it would establish fraternal relations with the British and Foreign Anti-Slavery Society.

Nabuco wrote the group's manifesto, which denounced the "infinite cruelties" and backwardness of slavery and emphasized the eminently patriotic nature of the abolitionist mission. It was published in Portuguese, English, and French and distributed throughout Rio de Janeiro and the empire, as well as to interested groups internationally. On November 1, the first issue of the group's newspaper, the *Abolitionist*, was launched in Rio de Janeiro. It denounced the government for blocking abolition, concentrating on what Nabuco and others saw as the illegality of slavery. On the economic plane, the paper condemned slavery as the sole reason for the "industrial and economic backwardness" of Brazil. The Brazilian public, the paper strongly expressed, was sick of the "spectacle of riches accumulated criminally under the general misery and through the exploitation of a million and a half humans."

Together with a more moderate organization dedicated to raising money to buy freedom for selected slaves, the Central Emancipation Association, the Brazilian Anti-Slavery Society remained active during the first months of 1883, bringing its antislavery message to a wider audience. The society also organized public rallies in theaters and concert halls, devoting ample time to formal speeches, as well as to music and poetry with antislavery themes. Such events were closely covered by abolitionist newspapers such as the *Gazeta da Tarde* (Afternoon Gazette) and influenced the formation of like-minded clubs in other Brazilian cities. The society's forceful abolitionist message resonated with broad sectors of public opinion.

Nabuco resigned as president of the society in 1881, and thereafter the *Abolitionist* published only a handful of issues. Nevertheless, the society played a critical role in spurring abolitionist activity in the early 1880s. In 1883, it joined with the Central Emancipation Association and other clubs to form an even broader-based organization, the Abolitionist Confederation (*Confederação Abolicionista*), which was active during the last years before abolition was achieved in 1888.

Sean Purdy

See also: Nabuco, Joaquim; Patrocínio, José do; Rebouças, André.

Further Reading

Conrad, Robert E. *The Destruction of Brazilian Slavery, 1850–1888.* Berkeley: University of California Press, 1972; 2nd ed., Malabar, FL: Krieger, 1993.

Drescher, Seymour. *From Slavery to Freedom: Comparative Studies in the Rise and Fall of Atlantic Slavery.* London: Macmillan, 1999.

Nabuco, Carolina. *The Life of Joaquim Nabuco.* Palo Alto, CA: Stanford University Press, 1950.

Toplin, Robert Brent. *The Abolition of Slavery in Brazil.* New York: Atheneum, 1972.

British and Foreign Anti-Slavery Society

See Anti-Slavery International

British Emancipator, The

Published from 1837 to 1840, *The British Emancipator* was an abolitionist newspaper that served as the official organ of the London-based Anti-Slavery Society of Great Britain. The paper focused on efforts to end slavery throughout the transatlantic world.

Throughout the history of the transatlantic abolitionist movement, much of the leadership and direction of the antislavery cause was provided by abolitionists in Great Britain, who were among the first to take direct action against the slave trade and the institution of slavery. Fellow antislavery supporters in the United States and elsewhere were able to keep up to date on events transpiring within the British abolitionist movement by reading the bimonthly publication of the Anti-Slavery Society of Great Britain. The newspaper's name changed on occasion, often reflecting the specific focus or direction of the movement at the time.

Initially published as the *Anti-Slavery Reporter,* the publication was renamed *The British Emancipator* by the Anti-Slavery Society's Central Negro Emancipation Committee; it was published under this title from December 27, 1837, to January 10, 1840. The new title reflected the preeminent role that British abolitionists had played in bringing an end to slavery throughout the British Empire with the passage of the Abolition of Slavery Act (commonly known as the British Emancipation Act) in 1833.

In 1840, the publication changed its name again to *The British and Foreign Anti-Slavery Reporter,* reflecting the universal appeal of ending slavery and the slave trade in all places where it still existed. This change echoed the hope that British abolitionists sought to portray in 1840 as they hosted the World Anti-Slavery Convention in London.

The name change also reflected a schism within the ranks of the British abolitionist movement. A faction of British antislavery advocates that called themselves the British and Foreign Anti-Slavery Society (a pro-Garrisonian group that later became Anti-Slavery International) had taken the title of the *Anti-Slavery Reporter* with them and began publishing their own paper with that name in 1840. Out of necessity, the abolitionists who remained within the orthodox ranks of the Anti-Slavery Society of Great Britain needed to find another name for their group's publication so that it would not be confused with that published by their rivals. Thus, *The British Emancipator* was born.

Sixty-one issues of the bimonthly publication were published under the title *The British Emancipator.* The three-year period from 1837 to 1840 was a time of significant transition for the British antislavery movement, and the topics addressed in the newspaper were indicative of the changes that were taking place. Initially, a significant number of articles focused on the movement's success at ending the apprenticeship system in the British West Indies, which had been designed to smooth the transition from slave labor to free labor upon emancipation. Yet other important issues also began to appear in the pages of *The British Emancipator.*

For the first time, attention was paid to the problem of "coolie labor" (unskilled workers from Asia, especially India and China, in the British and French colonies), and British abolitionists began to see a need to expand the purpose and scope of the antislavery movement. Articles that advocated the Free Produce movement, which encouraged the exclusive purchase of goods produced by free laborers, emphasized the yet-unfinished work of abolitionists in bringing an end to slavery throughout the Americas.

During the 1837–1840 period, another organization, the British and Foreign Anti-Slavery Society, began to take shape as British abolitionists realized that the evils of slavery and the slave trade were universal problems that transcended national boundaries. Recognizing the abolitionist movement as a worldwide movement, British antislavery advocates formed an association that continues its work today under the name Anti-Slavery International, the world's oldest human rights organization.

Junius P. Rodriguez

See also: Anti-Slavery International; *Anti-Slavery Reporter.*

Further Reading

Fladeland, Betty. *Men and Brothers: Anglo-American Antislavery Cooperation.* Urbana: University of Illinois Press, 1972.

British West Indies, Abolition in the

Large-scale plantation slavery in the British Empire began in the West Indies, as did efforts to abolish slavery during the late eighteenth and early nineteenth centuries. Because the economic system of the area was based on slave labor, British planters from the West Indies developed a politically powerful bloc in Parliament to fight abolition.

The abolition of slavery in the British West Indies was achieved incrementally, as abolitionists were forced to pass legislation that eroded the institution but fell short of complete emancipation until 1834. As the British became the driving force behind the movement to end slavery worldwide, the pace of abolition in the West Indies became linked to global abolition.

Early Attempts

In 1671, George Fox, founder of the Society of Friends (Quakers)—which would drive the abolitionist movement over the next two centuries—visited Barbados and urged the plantation owners to free their slaves. The colonial legislature of Barbados responded by outlawing Quakerism in the island, and Fox's visit marked the beginning of a long dispute between planters on the island and abolitionists. The planters used their wealth and influence to delay abolition, while the Quakers highlighted the relatively harsh slave laws of the island to rally public support for their cause.

The Barbadian slave law of 1688 was one of the most stringent and restrictive slave statutes in the British Empire. For example, the slave law in

Barbados gave owners the right to kill or permanently maim slaves who misbehaved. Slaves who stole items valued at more than a shilling were also subject to execution. Slaves were forbidden to own property, marry, or even discipline their children, nor could they leave the plantation without a written pass. To prevent the rise of a free black class, there were restrictions on the process of manumission.

A key imperative driving the British abolitionists was the emergence of dichotomous laws on slavery. In 1772, Lord Mansfield held in the *Somersett* case that individuals could not be held as slaves in Great Britain. The West Indian planters tried to challenge Mansfield's ruling, to no avail. Consequently, this decision ended legal slavery in Great Britain. At the same time, the nation dominated the international slave trade, and plantations in the West Indies accounted for the majority of slaveholdings within the empire.

In 1776, David Hartley introduced the first motion in Parliament to end slavery; it was overwhelmingly defeated. Two years later, William Pitt introduced a measure to regulate the slave trade, and it, too, was defeated. The first organized British abolitionist movement was formed by the Quakers in London in 1783. The Quakers created the Committee on the Slave Trade, which petitioned Parliament to end the slave trade but not to abolish slavery. Initially, the abolitionist movement concentrated on making the slave trade illegal. Their hope was that by ending the trade, the value of individual slaves would rise dramatically, forcing owners to treat their slaves better and prompting colonial legislatures to enact laws for the humane treatment of slaves.

Public support for abolition began to build in the 1780s and 1790s as the movement was led by prominent British politicians and other public figures such as Thomas Clarkson, Granville Sharp, and William Wilberforce. They were aided by Pitt, who served as prime minister from 1783 to 1801 and from 1804 to 1806. Pitt was an astute politician who supported abolition but also allowed economic and geopolitical concerns to influence his level of support and willingness to expend political capital to achieve abolition. Within Pitt's cabinet, the majority of members were opposed to abolition, and more significantly, King George III opposed restrictions on both the slave trade and slavery. Consequently, during the 1790s—a time when Britain was almost continuously at war with revolutionary France—Pitt's support for abolition was lukewarm at best, and repeated motions to abolish the slave trade were defeated.

Within Parliament, the West Indian planters were able to develop a lobby that proved adept at defeating efforts to regulate or abolish slavery and the slave trade. Their bloc, known as the Society of West Indian Planters in Parliament, successfully promoted the planters' economic self-interest and equated slavery with Great Britain's financial health. In the House of Lords, the West Indian planters had a powerful ally in the king's son, William, Duke of Clarence (later King William IV), who emerged as the foremost opponent of abolition. The House of Lords defeated abolitionist resolutions passed in the House of Commons on several occasions in the 1790s, as well as bills introduced by Wilberforce and Pitt to end the slave trade in 1799, 1801, and 1802. In the House of Commons, measures to end the slave trade were passed in 1804 and 1805, but the bills were tabled.

Successes

The British abolitionist movement finally achieved a breakthrough when Parliament outlawed the slave trade in 1807. During the debate, the West Indian members of Parliament unanimously opposed the bill, and the colonial legislatures passed a variety of resolutions condemning the measure. The colonies drew up petitions to the king, the government, and both houses of Parliament. However, public opinion in Great Britain overwhelmingly favored abolition of the trade, and the planters had undermined their position by using their clout in the colonies to prevent the passage of legislation that made it a crime to kill a slave except in self-defense. The planters' economic might also had suffered a hit, as sugar prices had fallen precipitously over the previous few years. Although the planters petitioned the king, he gave the law Royal Assent in March 1807.

Initially, efforts to enforce the law and curtail the slave trade were sporadic and ineffective. Although the Royal Navy was given permission to stop and search suspected British slave ships, it did not have the ability to stop the slave ships of other countries. Slaves continued to be imported and exported from the West Indies on American, Spanish, or Dutch ships. The British government tried to negotiate treaties with other countries that would allow its representatives to search suspicious vessels, but the process was lengthy and complicated, as nations such as France, Spain, Portugal, and the United States resisted the treaties.

Meanwhile, many of the benefits that abolitionists had hoped to realize with the end of the slave

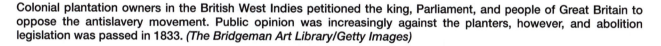

THE HUMBLE PETITION
Of the West India Planters to the People of England, with every Englishman's Answer.

Come, buy our rich produce, ye Englishmen, buy !
  We have excellent sugar, and coffee, and spice:
But we want a good market, so pray you draw nigh,
  (For we're nothing without you) and give us our price.

It is true that our fields are still cultured by slaves,
  And their sweat and their blood is aye wrung from their
    backs,
By the flesh-rending cart-whip, applied to the knaves ;
  For they wouldn't work else, all these indolent blacks.

It is true, they are flogged till their muscles are bare,
  And whenever they vex us—'tis all at our will;
You may see on their bodies full many a scar,
  Just excepting the few we may happen to kill.

And although they don't marry, together they live,
  Till it suits us the one or the other to sell;
Then the parents, or children, to market we drive,
  As we do other beasts, though they don't bear it so well.

When their kind-hearted friends have come over the main,
  To instruct them in virtue and care for their good,
We as promptly enjoin them to go back again ;
  If they don't, we soon let out their traitorous blood.

So we won't let them learn ; nay, we flog them for praying,
  And pull all their preaching shops down to the ground
Who would let such asses be constantly braying,
  Such dens of sedition be open around ?

But you will not, on this account, think of not dealing ?
  About such *mere brutes* you won't make a bother ?
You don't mean to resent the small sin of man-selling ?
  Or if you are *saints*, you won't feel for a brother ?

You'll not claim *their* freedom, because *you* are free ?
  You're not going for the rights of the *Negro* to care ?
Such days of romance we thought never to see,
  And we're ruined, quite ruined, at once, if you are.

O buy our slave produce, free Englishmen, buy !
  If you suffer such scruples, 'twill rot on the ground :
Of the twice-taxed free sugar the price is so high,
  You can't get it so cheap by a penny a pound.

EVERY ENGLISHMAN'S ANSWER.

Go, and loosen the captives ! No longer will I
  Spend a farthing, thou human-flesh-monger, with thee
For the sake of a penny, I never will buy
  E'en an ounce of thy sugar, *till Negroes are free.*

Printed and sold by B. WHITE, Binder, and Stationer, Broad-St. Reading. at 6d. per hundred or 1d. per doz.

Colonial plantation owners in the British West Indies petitioned the king, Parliament, and people of Great Britain to oppose the antislavery movement. Public opinion was increasingly against the planters, however, and abolition legislation was passed in 1833. *(The Bridgeman Art Library/Getty Images)*

trade did not materialize. The conditions and treatment of slaves did not improve on the islands and, in some cases, actually declined. A slave revolt in Barbados in 1816 dramatized the continuing plight of slaves in the West Indies and reinforced public calls for the abolition of slavery altogether.

New antislavery organizations with greater political clout and wider public appeal than the Quakers began to emerge. The most prominent group, formed in 1823, was known as the Society for the Mitigation and Gradual Abolition of Slavery throughout the British Dominions (more commonly called the Anti-Slavery Society). The group served as an umbrella organization for smaller groups, including the Quakers, and within a few years of its establishment, it had more than seventy chapters in Great Britain.

In Parliament, a new generation of leaders led by Thomas Fowell Buxton advanced the goal of complete abolition. Buxton tried to pass an abolition bill in 1823, but Parliament instead enacted a series of regulations designed to improve the condition of the slaves. The new rules gave slaves the right to purchase their freedom and to own property. The laws also limited the use of physical punishment and ordered that all punishments be recorded. Each colony was to appoint an ombudsman to oversee the safety and health of slaves throughout the colony. The planters reacted angrily to the measures, and the colonial legislatures were reluctant to adopt or support the new rules. By 1826, only Barbados, the Bahamas, Grenada, Saint Vincent, and Tobago had appointed officials to oversee the treatment of slaves. Some colonies, such as Jamaica and Antigua, simply refused.

In 1830, the ruling Tory Party splintered over the issue of Catholic emancipation in Ireland, and the Whig Party took control of Parliament and formed a government under Earl Grey. The Whigs signaled their intention to press ahead with full abolition. When the abolition of the slave trade and subsequent acts of Parliament failed to significantly improve the lives of slaves or lead to the gradual end of slavery, the Anti-Slavery Society and abolitionist leaders in Parliament began to push for immediate abolition throughout the British Empire. Opponents argued that the plantation owners would have to be compensated if their slaves were freed and used the cost issue to block legislation.

To increase public pressure on Parliament, the Anti-Slavery Society initiated a broad public relations campaign in 1831. The society sponsored lectures throughout the country and provided leading newspapers with accounts of the problems of slavery. Its efforts were bolstered by a new antislavery group, the Agency Committee, which was formed by abolitionists who were unhappy with the slow pace of legislation. Led by George Stephen, the Agency Committee aggressively lobbied members of Parliament and campaigned for pro-abolitionist candidates ahead of the 1832 general election. In that election, a combination of borough realignment and the slavery concerns caused sixteen West Indian planters to lose their seats.

In the new Parliament, 104 members pledged to the Agency Committee that they would support abolition, whereas the West Indian planter bloc amounted to only thirty-five. Additional pressure for abolition came from the Ladies' Anti-Slavery Society, which collected 187,000 signatures in favor of abolition. By May 1833, the House of Commons had received 500 petitions and the House of Lords 600 petitions in favor of emancipation.

When Parliament convened in 1833, abolition was simply a matter of time. The debate was no longer whether to abolish slavery but how to do so. The government sought an apprenticeship program that would replace slave labor with wage labor. They hoped the slaves could be coaxed into remaining on the plantations, where they would work for wages.

The West Indian lobby sought to ensure that the final abolition bill would be as generous as possible, and they had some notable successes. The bill originally called for £15 million in loans to compensate the planters for the loss of their slaves, but that figure was increased to £20 million in outright grants. In addition, many slaves would not gain immediate freedom but would have to serve a mandatory apprenticeship before emancipation.

The Abolition of Slavery Act (commonly known as the British Emancipation Act) was passed on August 29, 1833, and took effect August 1, 1834. By 1838, slavery was abolished in the British West Indies.

Tom Lansford

See also: Buxton, Thomas Fowell; Clarkson, Thomas; Fox, George; Wilberforce, William.

Further Reading

Craton, Michael. *Empire, Enslavement, and Freedom in the Caribbean.* Princeton, NJ: Markus Wiener, 1997.

Goveia, Elsa. *Amelioration and Emancipation in the British Caribbean.* Saint Augustine, Trinidad: University of the West Indies, 1977.

Higman, B.W. *Slave Populations of the British Caribbean, 1807–1834.* Baltimore: Johns Hopkins University Press, 1984.

Miers, Suzanne. *Britain and the Ending of the Slave Trade.* London: Longman, 1975; New York: Africana, 1975.

Temperley, Howard. *British Antislavery, 1833–1870.* London: Longman, 1972.

Turley, David. *The Culture of English Antislavery, 1780–1860.* London: Routledge, 1991.

Brown, Henry "Box" (1816–?)

Henry "Box" Brown, a fugitive slave who shipped himself to freedom in a crate, gained fame as the author of the widely read *Narrative of the Life of Henry Box Brown, Written by Himself* (1851). Brown's 1849 escape from Virginia to the free soil of Philadelphia demonstrated the extent to which some African Americans would go to rid themselves of the shackles of slavery.

Brown was born in 1816 to enslaved parents in Louisa County, forty miles outside Richmond, Virginia. As a child, many of his duties involved waiting on his master and mistress. Brown lived much of his early childhood surrounded by his parents and siblings. At the age of fifteen, following his master's death, Brown was separated from his family and became the slave of his former master's son. Brown moved with his new owner to Richmond, where he was forced to work in a tobacco factory.

In the mid-1830s, Brown met and married a young slave woman named Nancy, who was the property of Mr. Leigh, a clerk in the local bank. Following negotiations with Nancy's master and obtaining his assurance that the two would never be sold or separated, the couple was given permission to marry. Less than twelve months after their marriage, Brown's wife and children were abruptly sold to a saddler named Joseph Colquitt. On the advice of his wife, Colquitt sold Brown's family to Samuel Cottrell, another saddler in the Richmond area.

Amid this trauma, Brown sought to make negotiations to prevent the future sale of his family. To get them back, Brown was forced to loan Cottrell $50 to repurchase them, pay Cottrell $50 a year to keep them close, and finally buy a house for them. In August 1848, Cottrell burst into the Brown household and demanded immediate payment. Financially unable to provide the requested funds, Brown later learned that while he had been away at work, his family had been sent to an auction mart and sold to a North Carolina slave trader.

Devastated by the loss of his family, Brown sought the help of Samuel A. Smith, a white storekeeper in Richmond. Recounting his circumstances, Brown offered to pay the man $86 to help him escape from bondage. Influenced by a vision, Brown got the idea to ship himself in a box labeled as dry goods headed to a Northern free state. Desiring death over the hold of slavery, he injured his finger as a ruse to avoid having to work the next day.

On the morning of March 29, 1849, Brown, standing five feet eight inches and weighing 200 pounds, willingly placed himself in to a box measuring approximately three feet by two feet. Brown was equipped with a bladder of water and a gimlet to cut holes for air. Smith and a free black employee sent Brown by express mail to William A. Johnson, a friend of the store owner, in Philadelphia. In this manner, Brown traveled 350 miles, spending twenty-seven hours in the box, sometimes being forced to lie upside down on his head for hours at a time. Once delivered to Johnson, Brown emerged from his box a free man.

Throughout the remainder of his life, Brown was an active voice for the abolitionist movement in the Northern states. After the passage of the Fugitive Slave Law of 1850, which provided for the return of

A slave named Henry Brown spent twenty-seven hours in a dry-goods crate shipped to Philadelphia by a Virginia storekeeper in March 1849. Brown emerged a free man and became a featured speaker for antislavery groups. *(Library of Congress)*

escaped slaves to the South, Brown sought asylum in Great Britain, where his narrative was published to raise funds in order to purchase freedom for Brown's wife and children. The narrative concludes with an essay by Charles Stearns titled "Cure for the Evil of Slavery."

Sowandé Mustakeem

See also: Fugitive Slaves.

Further Reading

Brown, Henry Box. *Narrative of the Life of Henry Box Brown, Written by Himself.* 1851. New York: Oxford University Press, 2002.

Brown, John (1800–1859)

Recognized as a martyr to the antislavery cause, the radical abolitionist John Brown gave his life to end the "peculiar institution" of slavery in the United States. Through his failed efforts to foment a slave insurrection by capturing the U.S. Army arsenal at Harpers Ferry, Virginia, and distributing weapons to the slaves, Brown moved the nation closer to the precipice of civil war.

Brown was born into a devout Calvinist family in Torrington, Connecticut, on May 9, 1800. His father, Owen Brown, taught John and his five siblings that slavery was unjust and unacceptable. Brown developed an abiding hatred of the institution of slavery, and, in 1837, he took a public stand against it at a church service in Cleveland, Ohio. Moved by the minister's sermon, Brown rose to his feet, raised his hand, and pledged before God and man that he would devote the rest of his life to the destruction of slavery in America.

By 1847, Brown had become convinced that abolition could be attained only by the shedding of blood. That same year, he met Frederick Douglass in Springfield, Massachusetts, and informed him of his plan to begin a slave revolt by launching a surprise attack from the Allegheny Mountains with twenty-five well-armed men. Although this particular plan was never realized, Douglass came away from the meeting convinced of Brown's sincerity and abolitionist conviction.

Brown attempted to make a living in more than twenty different occupations, including working as a tannery operator, sheep raiser, and cattle driver, but he failed at all of them. In 1849, he moved his family—which consisted of thirteen children and Mary Day, his

John Brown's attack on a federal arsenal in Harpers Ferry, Virginia, in October 1859 was intended as the beginning of a massive slave insurrection. His capture and execution made him a martyr to the cause of emancipation. *(Library of Congress)*

wife—to North Elba, New York, a community founded by the wealthy abolitionist Gerrit Smith. At North Elba, Brown lived among black families, an uncommon choice at that time even for an abolitionist, and he taught them how to farm on rocky soil.

After the passage of the Kansas-Nebraska Act in 1854, several of Brown's sons settled in the newly organized Kansas Territory, where they encountered a firestorm between proslavery and antislavery men. After hearing the news from his sons, Brown left his wife and younger children in New York and traveled to the territory. He had no intention of settling there permanently; his only motivation was to lend a hand in the war against slavery in "Bleeding Kansas."

On May 24, 1856, Brown led a small party of men in an attack on proslavery families at Pottawatomie Creek. Armed with broadswords, the men stormed three houses and killed five men. In the months that followed, Brown and five of his sons fought proslavery groups in Kansas and Missouri.

In August, Brown successfully defended Osawatomie, Kansas, with his band of "Kansas Regulars," but he lost one of his sons in the conflict, giving him greater resolve to keep fighting against slavery. The victory at Osawatomie also gained him national fame. Shortly after the battle, for example, a play on Broadway told the story of "Osawatomie Brown."

In 1856, Brown devised a plan to attack the federal arsenal at Harpers Ferry, Virginia, which contained thousands of rifles and a plentiful supply of ammunition that could be used to arm freed slaves; he began a speaking tour in New England to raise funds for an army. In 1857, Franklin Sanborn, secretary for the Massachusetts State Kansas Committee, introduced Brown to several wealthy abolitionists in Boston. The "Secret Six," as they came to be called, were so impressed with Brown's earnestness that they secretly gave him enough money to raise a small army. In 1858, Brown used his new backing to make a brief excursion to Missouri, killing one master and freeing eleven slaves. In the weeks that followed, Brown transported the liberated slaves to freedom in Canada.

In 1859, Brown felt that the time had come to put his master plan into action. On the evening of October 16, Brown's army, which consisted of five blacks and thirteen whites, rode into Harpers Ferry with a wagonload of guns, cut the telegraph wires, and easily took control of the armory, arsenal, and engine house. Brown's men took hostages, including George Washington's great-grandnephew, Colonel Lewis Washington, and they issued a proclamation that invited Virginia's slaves to join Brown's army. Brown planned to lead the runaway slaves south along the Appalachian Mountains as he continued his war on slavery. However, no slaves came forward. Instead, angry townspeople took up arms and began firing on the invaders, forcing them to take cover.

By early the next morning, Harpers Ferry was surrounded by U.S. Marines under the command of Colonel Robert E. Lee. Lee ordered Lieutenant J.E.B. Stuart to approach Brown's men with a white flag and offer them their lives in exchange for surrender. Brown refused, and the daylong battle that followed resulted in the death of one marine and twelve of Brown's men, two of whom were his sons. Brown was seriously wounded and captured.

On November 2, a Charles Town, Virginia, jury found Brown guilty of murder, treason, and inciting a slave insurrection and sentenced him to death. Brown said nothing from his jail cell; however, on the day he was scheduled to be executed, he handed a note to one of his guards. In the note, Brown stated that he had come to the realization that much more bloodshed would be necessary to rid the nation of slavery.

Ironically, Thomas Jackson, later known as General "Stonewall" Jackson, and John Wilkes Booth, who would later be Abraham Lincoln's assassin, were among the troops who carried out the death sentence. On December 2, Brown, who believed that he was God's agent on earth, was hanged.

The immediate reaction to Brown's execution drew a visible line between the outspoken abolitionists of the North, who esteemed Brown as a martyred hero, and the proslavery men of the South, who regarded him as a treasonous lunatic. After the U.S. Civil War, which resulted in the abolition of slavery, historians pointed to Brown's crusade as an important factor in bringing about the war. It was because of Brown's attack on Harpers Ferry, for example, that Southerners began to build up their militia, which became the Confederate army.

Rolando Avila

See also: Douglass, Frederick; Harpers Ferry Raid (1859); Smith, Gerrit.

Further Reading

Abels, Jules. *Man on Fire: John Brown and the Cause of Liberty.* New York: Macmillan, 1971.

Oates, Stephen B. *To Purge This Land With Blood: A Biography of John Brown.* New York: Harper & Row, 1970.

Peterson, Merrill D. *John Brown: The Legend Revisited.* Charlottesville: University of Virginia Press, 2002.

Scott, Otto J. *The Secret Six: John Brown and the Abolitionist Movement.* New York: Times Books, 1979.

Brown, William Wells (ca. 1814–1884)

Born into slavery, William Wells Brown escaped to freedom and became the first African American to publish a novel and a play. Throughout his life, he fought against slavery as a writer and orator, gaining international fame.

Brown was born about 1814 in Lexington, Kentucky. He was the son of a slave woman named Elizabeth—according to oral tradition, she was the daughter of frontiersman Daniel Boone—and either a white relative of Brown's owner or the owner himself. William was hired out at a young age and held a variety of jobs, working as a printer's helper in the office of Elijah P. Lovejoy, a well-known abolitionist newspaper

editor, and as a handyman for James Walker, a Missouri slave trader. Brown later claimed to have made three trips aboard Walker's steamboat to the New Orleans slave market. Thus, Brown experienced slavery from several different perspectives, and this would influence his later literary and professional career.

In 1834, after twenty years as a slave, Brown fled to Canada with the help of a Quaker, for whom Brown renamed himself. After gaining his freedom, he worked on a steamboat on Lake Erie and helped fugitive slaves get safely into Canada. The same year, he married Elizabeth Spooner, a free black woman. Two years after his marriage, Brown moved to Buffalo, New York, where he worked as a conductor for the Underground Railroad and continued to hide slaves attempting cross the border into Canada. In Buffalo, Brown also began his career as an abolitionist, attending meetings of the Western New York Anti-Slavery Society and speaking at local abolitionist gatherings.

In 1843, a national antislavery convention and the National Convention of Colored Citizens took place in Buffalo. Brown attended both meetings and had the opportunity to meet other black abolitionists, including Frederick Douglass and Charles Lenox Remond. Brown soon became a lecturing agent for the Western New York Anti-Slavery Society. In his speeches, he appealed to the power of moral suasion, rejecting the type of antislavery violence advocated by Henry Highland Garnet in his "Address to the Slaves." In 1844, Brown's reputation in the antislavery community earned him an invitation to speak before the American Anti-Slavery Society at its annual meeting in New York City.

In 1847, Brown became a lecturing agent for the Massachusetts Anti-Slavery Society and moved to Boston, where he completed the first version of his *Narrative of William W. Brown, A Fugitive Slave* (1847). The autobiographical narrative was subsequently revised and expanded, and, by 1850, it had been reprinted in four American and five British editions, securing its author international fame. This work was rivaled in fame and sales only by the *Narrative of the Life of Frederick Douglass* (1845), whose model Brown had adopted. Brown retained the plot structure and chronological development of the antebellum slave narrative, but he resisted Douglass's highly rhetorical style, as well as his heroic characterization of the fugitive slave.

In 1849, Brown went to Europe as a representative of the American Peace Society, which chose him as its delegate to the Peace Congress in Paris. Letters of recommendation written by the American Anti-Slavery Society acquainted him with many eminent Europeans, such as British statesman Richard Cobden and French novelist Victor Hugo, and opened the doors of European intellectual circles.

After attending the Peace Congress, Brown went on to lecture in Britain and stayed in Europe until 1854, both for personal and for political reasons. He enjoyed his prestigious European social contacts and found European culture a fertile environment for his own literary efforts. While in Europe, Brown wrote the travel book *Three Years in Europe; or, Places I Have Seen and People I Have Met* (1852), which received positive reviews, and *Clotel, or The President's Daughter* (1853). The latter, which is prefaced by the lengthy "Narrative of the Life and Escape of William Wells Brown," is generally regarded as the first African American novel. The story is a commentary on interracial love, the first of many narratives inspired by the alleged affair between Thomas Jefferson and Sally Hemmings. Personally, Brown was also trying to recover from the failure of his marriage during his stay in Europe. Furthermore, the passage of the Fugitive Slave Law of 1850 made it dangerous for the escaped slave to return to America.

Upon his return to the United States, Brown settled in the Boston area, where he was protected by the community's antislavery activists, and continued to publish important fiction and nonfiction works that attest to his enduring antislavery militancy: *The Escape; or, A Leap for Freedom* (1858), the first drama by an African American; *The Negro in the American Rebellion* (1867), the first military history of African Americans in the United States; and *The Black Man: His Antecedents, His Genius, and His Achievements* (1863). He became the most prolific black literary figure of the mid-nineteenth century.

Brown continued to travel and give lectures, and he contributed to important antislavery papers such as William Lloyd Garrison's *The Liberator,* the *National Anti-Slavery Standard,* and the London *Daily News.* His last book, *My Southern Home: or, the South and Its People,* which focused on black–white relationships in the South, was completed in 1880, four years before his death on November 6, 1884.

Luca Prono

See also: Fugitive Slaves; Garrison, William Lloyd; Lovejoy, Elijah P.

Further Reading

Brown, William Wells. *From Fugitive Slave to Free Man: The Autobiography of William Wells Brown.* Ed. William L. Andrews. New York: New American Library, 1993.

Dorsey, Peter A. "De-Authorizing Slavery: Realism in Stowe's *Uncle Tom's Cabin* and Brown's *Clotel.*" *Emerson Society Quarterly* 41:4 (1995): 256–88.

Fabi, Giulia. "The Unguarded Expressions of the Feelings of the Negroes: Gender, Slave Resistance, and William Wells Brown's Revisions of *Clotel.*" *African American Review* 27 (Winter 1993): 639–54.

Farrison, William Edward. *William Wells Brown: Author and Reformer.* Chicago: University of Chicago Press, 1969.

Mulvey, Christopher. "The Fugitive Self and the New World of the North: William Wells Brown's Discovery of America." In *The Black Columbiad: Defining Moments in African American Literature and Culture,* ed. Werner Sollors and Maria Diedrich. Cambridge, MA: Harvard University Press, 1994.

Bruce, Henry Clay (1836–1902)

The lifetime of African American writer Henry Clay Bruce was almost evenly divided between slavery and freedom. In his autobiography, *The New Man: Twenty-Nine Years a Slave, Twenty-Nine Years a Free Man* (1895), he recounted his life and attempted to write an objective and unbiased view of the social mind-set of the slave system and post–Civil War America.

Born in Prince Edward County, Virginia, in 1836, Bruce was the son of slave parents; he carried the name of Kentucky senator Henry Clay and assumed his master's surname. By the age of eight, he had been moved to Chariton County, Missouri, and the following year began menial work in a tobacco factory where workers were whipped for sleeping or speaking. In 1847, he returned to a Virginia plantation, where his master's son taught him to read and write. By 1850, he had been sent to Mississippi to pick cotton and shortly thereafter rejoined his master's family in Brunswick, Missouri, where he worked in the tobacco industry until the U.S. Civil War.

Confederate support was strong in Brunswick, Missouri, at the outset of the war, but it had waned, along with the Confederate army, by 1864. Owners became unable to persuade slaves to work, and many slaves began to flee, including Bruce. On March 30, 1864, Bruce armed himself and narrowly escaped Missouri with his fiancée to Fort Leavenworth, Kansas. From Kansas, his life as a free man began. But newfound freedom created challenges for Bruce, as he had little understanding of how to manage money and was frequently cheated by white businessmen.

After the war, Bruce opened mercantile stores in Fort Leavenworth and Atchison, Kansas, both of which failed; in 1878, he was left in debt when a fire destroyed his business. Despite these setbacks, Bruce received the Republican nomination for the Fourth Legislative District of Kansas in 1880, but he was narrowly defeated.

Bruce found temporary employment until 1881 when his brother, Blanche K. Bruce (a Republican senator from Mississippi), offered him a position at the Post Office Department in Washington, D.C. After working for one year, Bruce found improved employment with the U.S. Pension Office. In Washington, he began writing the memoirs that would become his autobiography.

The publication of his slave narrative intrigued scholars, not just for his personal accounts of slavery but also for his perceptions of the institution. Bruce attempted to write an emotionless account of slavery, rationalizing its preservation on the basis of economics. Bruce confronted bloodlines and the emergent mixing of races, claiming that four-fifths of African Americans were white to some degree. He believed there was a social hierarchy beyond race: Bruce distinguished people as being of either "superior blood" or "inferior blood," and both whites and blacks fell into both categories.

Slaves of superior blood carried hope and aspirations, completed their work, and took pride in themselves, their family, and their workplace. Superior-blooded whites treated slaves morally, were religious, and, when the slaves' children misbehaved, had their parents punish them rather than delegating discipline to the slaves' master or overseer.

Slaves of inferior blood were characterized as being unreliable, having no self-respect, and taking no interest in helping their owners. Inferior-blooded whites, whom Bruce described as "poor white trash," were illiterate, lied, and ruthlessly beat slaves. Bruce believed these poor whites were virtually slaves themselves, because they were unable to attain upward mobility in society and because the slave-owning class shunned them. This frustration spurred poor whites' driving ambition—to create written and unwritten laws to keep African Americans from attaining rights. According to Bruce, it was members of this group who were responsible for the lynching of Southern blacks after the Civil War.

Despite years of slavery, Bruce felt little malice toward former slave owners; most, he believed, were decent people. He believed that owners treated slaves well because they were valuable property and recognized that mistreating their property would harm them economically. After publishing his autobiography, Bruce continued to work at the U.S. Pension Office until his death in 1902.

Nathan R. Meyer

See also: Civil War, American (1861–1865).

Further Reading

Bruce, Henry Clay. *The New Man: Twenty-Nine Years a Slave, Twenty-Nine Years a Free Man.* 1895. Lincoln: University of Nebraska Press, 1996.

Buffum, Arnold (1782–1859)

One of the first abolitionists in the United States to recognize the merits of establishing a regional anti-slavery organization, Arnold Buffum laid the foundation for the formation of the American Anti-Slavery Society in 1833. Initially a pro-Garrisonian advocate who believed that moral suasion rather than political action could end slavery, Buffum vehemently opposed any means of compromise with slave-owning interests, and the tone of his antislavery rhetoric placed him at odds with the Quaker (Society of Friends) community. Ever the pragmatist, however, he came to realize that political action and compromise might be necessary to hasten the end of slavery, a position that placed him in opposition to Garrisonian ideology.

Born into a Quaker family in Smithfield, Rhode Island, on December 13, 1782, Buffum came to recognize the conflict in the American Quaker community over slavery and the slave trade. For nearly a century, since the proclamation of the Germantown Protest in 1688, the Quaker community had disassociated itself from the evils of slavery, yet some individuals in the port cities of New England continued to profit from the slave trade. Buffum's father demonstrated his family's position on the issue by joining the ranks of the Providence Society for Promoting the Abolition of Slavery and by aiding fugitive slaves escaping from servitude in New York.

A gentleman farmer and a hat manufacturer, Buffum was fortunate in business and accumulated a substantial fortune. Throughout his life, he used his personal income to support many philanthropic causes, principally the antislavery movement. Buffum was a key organizer of the 1832 meeting in Boston at which the New England Anti-Slavery Society was formed, and he became the first president of this abolitionist organization. With the financial means to travel and speak on behalf of the antislavery cause, Buffum also became the society's primary lecturing agent; in this capacity, he helped establish many local abolitionist groups throughout New England.

Buffum supported the efforts of abolitionist educator Prudence Crandall to operate a school for black women in Canterbury, Connecticut. However, Crandall's school was forced to close as a result of residents' fear that the ideology of antislavery firebrands such as Buffum would find its way into the curriculum of the educational institution.

Buffum was one of the founders of the American Anti-Slavery Society, formed in 1833 in Philadelphia. In 1834, Buffum moved to Philadelphia, where he became a subscription agent for William Lloyd Garrison's antislavery newspaper, *The Liberator.* When the newspaper experienced financial difficulties in its early years, Buffum was asked to provide advance financial support based on the subscriptions that he had garnered in the Philadelphia area. Buffum provided funds to Garrison, but confusion about his accounting practices—whether the funds had come from subscriptions or from Buffum's personal funds—led to his dismissal as subscription agent. Still, it seems that his relationship with Garrison remained cordial after the incident.

Buffum's penchant for fiery rhetoric and liberal support for reform-oriented causes led to his dismissal from the New England Yearly Meeting of the Quakers. He moved to Indiana but soon found himself dismissed from that state's yearly meeting as well. Buffum and his associates formed their own organization, the Indiana Yearly Meeting of Anti-Slavery Friends.

As a young man, Buffum had had the opportunity to meet with the famous abolitionist Thomas Clarkson when he visited Britain in 1824, and that meeting influenced his early thoughts on the antislavery question. Buffum had a second opportunity to meet Clarkson when he traveled to London in April 1843 to attend the Second World Anti-Slavery Convention, organized by the British and Foreign Anti-Slavery Society. Buffum participated actively in the deliberations. The Reverend William Muhlenberg, an American Episcopal clergyman and a fellow delegate, described him as "an Old Hickory Quaker Abolition-

ist" with the bearing of a "tall, gray-headed, gold-spectacled patriarch."

After returning from London, Buffum realized that political action was likely the only effective means of ending slavery in the United States. By accepting this view, he opposed that of his mentor, Garrison, who believed that moral suasion alone was the proper approach to combating the sin of slavery. In 1844, Buffum delivered his "Lecture, Showing the Necessity of a Liberty Party," which was later printed as campaign literature, in an effort to convince others that political action—in addition to moral suasion—was a more reasonable means of fighting the abolitionist crusade.

Arnold Buffum died on March 13, 1859, having made a substantial contribution to the antislavery movement. Other members of the Buffum family also dedicated themselves to the abolitionist cause. His daughter, Elizabeth Buffum Chace, helped establish the Fall River Female Anti-Slavery Society in Massachusetts in 1837. Several of her children—Buffum's grandchildren—also took an active role in the cause of antislavery, continuing four generations of passionate New England abolitionists.

Junius P. Rodriguez

See also: American Anti-Slavery Society; Crandall, Prudence; Garrison, William Lloyd.

Burleigh, Charles Calistus (1810–1878)

Charles Calistus Burleigh's involvement as a young writer, editor, and agent of the antislavery movement made him one of the most influential abolitionists in New England. He became the editor of the *Pennsylvania Freeman*, a newspaper with a wide circulation among abolitionists in the United States.

A scion of one of America's first families, Burleigh was born in Connecticut on November 3, 1810, and grew up in a household in which the weight of history and the moral imperative of reform were keen. He was the son of Rinaldo Burleigh, who had been president of the first abolitionist organization established in Windham County, Connecticut. Burleigh's mother was Lydia Bradford, a direct descendant of Plymouth Colony governor William Bradford, who had come to America aboard the *Mayflower.*

Burleigh was a precocious child: He was admitted to a course of college studies at the Plainfield Academy when he was only eleven years old, and he began to teach at the age of fourteen. Burleigh eventually began studying law and was admitted to the Connecticut bar in 1835 at the age of twenty-five. He was recognized as an excellent extemporaneous speaker, and the power of his reasoned arguments implied a level of thought and insight far beyond his years.

American abolitionist Samuel Joseph May first recognized Burleigh's potential for the antislavery cause after reading an 1833 article on Connecticut's "Black Law" that Burleigh had published in William Goodell's *Genius of Temperance.* Even though Burleigh was only twenty-three years old at the time and still studying to be a lawyer, May convinced Arthur Tappan that the young writer would be an outstanding editor of the *Unionist,* an antislavery newspaper financed by Tappan and published by Prudence Crandall, a Connecticut educator who had been indicted for establishing a school to teach black girls. Burleigh served as editor for two years, during which time he earned a reputation for bold and opinionated writing.

Burleigh decided not to practice law but rather to continue his active involvement as an antislavery agent, lecturer, and writer, in particular for the Middlesex Anti-Slavery Society in Massachusetts. In addition to his antislavery work, Burleigh also lectured on other vital reform issues of his day, including pacifism, temperance, women's rights, and the abolition of the death penalty. He became widely recognized as a champion of sentencing reform when he published *Thoughts on the Death Penalty* (1845), a pamphlet that condemned the use of capital punishment in the United States.

Over the course of his involvement with the abolitionist cause, Burleigh was often at the center of some of the most dangerous conflicts that antislavery supporters faced. In 1835, he helped defend abolitionist William Lloyd Garrison from being attacked by a Boston mob of 2,000 people. The situation was so dangerous that Garrison was rescued and lodged in Boston's Leverett Street Jail for his own personal safety. Burleigh was lecturing at Pennsylvania Hall in Philadelphia when a proslavery mob attacked and burned that structure on May 17, 1838. Unwilling to be silenced, he remained a frequent contributor to Garrison's *Liberator* through the years.

In the late 1830s, Burleigh became the editor of the *Pennsylvania Freeman,* an abolitionist newspaper published in Philadelphia that was the voice of the Eastern Pennsylvania Anti-Slavery Society. He was arrested for selling abolitionist literature on a Sunday

in 1847 in West Chester, Pennsylvania, thus placing the antislavery reform movement at odds with the anti-Sabbatarian reform movement. In 1859, he was elected to serve as the corresponding secretary of the American Anti-Slavery Society; in that role, he wrote the society's annual report, *The Anti-Slavery History of the John Brown Year* (1861).

Burleigh continued to support the women's rights movement in the United States and attended several of the national conventions that were held in support of the cause. He lectured in behalf of the temperance movement into the 1870s and died on June 13, 1878.

Junius P. Rodriguez

See also: Crandall, Prudence; May, Samuel Joseph; *Pennsylvania Freeman;* Tappan, Arthur.

Further Reading

Burleigh, Charles Calistus. *Slavery and the North.* New York: American Anti-Slavery Society, 1855; Westport, CT: Negro Universities Press, 1970.

Butler, Benjamin Franklin (1818–1893)

A Union army general, U.S. congressman, and governor of Massachusetts, Benjamin Franklin Butler was one of the most colorful and controversial figures in American politics in the nineteenth century. He is best known for his unilateral decision during the U.S. Civil War to quasi-emancipate slaves escaping to Union lines by declaring them "war contraband." He is also remembered for less flattering actions, such as his harsh rule during the Union occupation of New Orleans—for which Southerners labeled him the "Beast"—and for leading the prosecution in the impeachment trial of President Andrew Johnson during Reconstruction.

Butler was born in Deerfield, New Hampshire, on November 5, 1818. His father, John, died when he was an infant, and his mother, Charlotte Ellison Butler, supported the family by working in a textile mill in Lowell, Massachusetts. After graduating from Maine's Waterbury Baptist College in 1838, Butler moved back to Lowell, where he was admitted to the bar and began practicing law in 1840, a vocation he would continue intermittently until his death.

In 1853, he was elected to the Massachusetts House of Representatives and six years later to the state senate. A Democrat, he distinguished himself in local politics by tirelessly crusading for the standardized ten-hour workday, an issue he held dear because of his mother's hard life as a factory worker.

Despite having no military training, Butler earned an appointment as a brigadier general in the Massachusetts militia when the Civil War erupted in 1861. He skillfully maneuvered the Eighth Massachusetts Regiment in eastern Maryland and occupied Baltimore. President Abraham Lincoln promptly enlisted his services, placing him in command of Fortress Monroe in eastern Virginia. When local slaves fled to the fort seeking refuge, they informed Butler that they had been compelled to labor for the Confederate army. Butler immediately declared all slaves under his control contraband of war and ordered that they be kept in Union army custody and not returned to their masters; he then compelled the former slaves to serve the Union army.

At the same time, Butler cooperated with the American Missionary Association in setting up the first school for liberated slaves; this institution became the forerunner of the more famous Freedmen's Bureau schools created after the war. He also helped establish one of the first banks for black freedmen, located in Norfolk. His forward-thinking policies were not sanctioned by the Lincoln administration, however; in June 1861, after suffering defeat in battle at Big Bethel, Virginia, the controversial general was relieved of his command.

Butler was transferred to North Carolina with the mission of taking Forts Hatteras and Clark on the coast. After succeeding in late August, he journeyed back to Massachusetts to raise a force especially for the purpose of capturing and occupying the city of New Orleans. Again he succeeded, and from May to December 1862, Butler became the military governor of the city of New Orleans. While there, he achieved infamy for his Draconian rule of the city. Locals called him "Beast Butler" for treating Confederate prisoners of war harshly; for executing a citizen who had torn down the American flag, for allegedly being a thief; and especially for his "Order No. 28," which authorized occupying troops to treat otherwise respectable Southern women as prostitutes should they in any way insult the Union army. Confederate president Jefferson Davis authorized Butler's immediate execution in the event of the general's capture.

After President Lincoln reluctantly made the decision to allow the enlistment of some blacks, Butler raised a total of thirty-seven regiments of black soldiers in Louisiana, which he called the Corps d'Afrique and staffed entirely with black officers. Because of the negative press that he received and the controversy his rule engendered, the Lincoln administration removed Butler from New Orleans in December 1862.

Butler remained inactive for the next few months, although many military and political leaders called for him to return to active duty. His next appointment came in November 1863 as head of the Department of Virginia and North Carolina, where he commanded the Army of the James and supervised prisoner exchanges. In the latter capacity, he sought the welfare of both black and white prisoners, counting some 3,000 black prisoners of war being held by the Confederates. He also created an office of black affairs to deal especially with black issues.

In May 1864, Butler suffered defeat at the Battle of Bermuda Hundred near Richmond during General Ulysses S. Grant's Wilderness Campaign. In November 1864, Secretary of War Edwin Stanton appointed Butler to lead the patrol of New York City during the presidential election season in order to prevent voter fraud and rioting, which he did successfully. Butler then returned to North Carolina, where he botched an attack on the Confederate defenses at Wilmington. Lincoln fired the general yet again.

After the war, Butler returned home to Lowell. Switching to the Republican Party in 1866, he was elected to Congress, where he represented his district of Massachusetts for the next nine years. Affiliating himself with the radical wing of his new party, he became one of the main proponents of the "forty acres and a mule" approach to land redistribution in the South, which gave forty-acre plots of abandoned and confiscated land and army mules to black freedmen and Southern white refugees who had been loyal to the Union during the war.

In 1868, Butler led the charge to impeach President Andrew Johnson, serving as chief prosecutor in the Senate impeachment trial. Critics blamed his incompetence in that position for the failure of the impeachment, although admirers noted his strong oration skills. Two years later, Butler played a leading role in the congressional hearings that outlawed the Ku Klux Klan and prosecuted Klansmen as terrorists; five years after that, he was instrumental in getting the Civil Rights Act of 1875 passed. While he lost a bid for re-election in 1875, he subsequently regained his seat two years later for one last term in Congress.

Butler ran for governor of Massachusetts three times, finally succeeding in 1882 on the Democratic Party ticket. In 1884, he ran for president of the United States as the candidate of the Anti-Monopoly Party, campaigning on a platform of national control of interstate commerce and an eight-hour workday, but his candidacy hardly made a dent in the outcome of the election.

Throughout the 1870s and 1880s, Butler was a common target for political satirists and cartoonists. He was easy to caricature—both physically and politically—because he had changed parties four times during his political career. Republicans considered him a traitor, Southern Democrats abhorred his presence in their party, and he remained largely insignificant. En route to Washington, D.C., where he was to argue a case before the U.S. Supreme Court, Butler died on January 11, 1893.

Thomas Adams Upchurch

See also: Civil War, American (1861–1865); Ku Klux Klan; Reconstruction.

Further Reading

Hearn, Chester G. *When the Devil Came Down to Dixie: Ben Butler in New Orleans.* Baton Rouge: Louisiana State University Press, 1997.
Holzman, Robert S. *Stormy Ben Butler.* New York: Macmillan, 1954.
Werlich, Robert. *"Beast" Butler: Biography of Union Major General Benjamin Franklin Butler.* Washington, DC: Quaker Press, 1962.

Buxton, Thomas Fowell (1786–1845)

Thomas Fowell Buxton was a British reformer and antislavery advocate who led the abolitionist movement in Great Britain during its successful campaign for emancipation within the empire. After the passage of the Abolition of Slavery Act (commonly known as the British Emancipation Act) in 1833, Buxton spent the remainder of his public career working to suppress the international slave trade.

Buxton was born on April 1, 1786, in Essex, England. Although he was raised in the Anglican Church, his mother was a Quaker, and she introduced the young man to prominent abolitionists within the Society of Friends. As a youth, Buxton had a religious experience that made him a staunch Christian for the rest of his life.

Buxton graduated with distinction from Trinity College in Dublin, Ireland, in 1807. While at college, Buxton began attending Quaker meetings, and he married Hannah Gurney, a member of a leading family of the church. After his graduation, Buxton became active in the social reform movement in Great Britain. He was particularly supportive of penal reform and worked to raise money for impoverished factory workers.

Buxton gained prominence in 1818 with the publication of his *Inquiry into Prison Discipline,* which exposed the deplorable conditions at Newgate Prison. He used his newfound fame to win a seat in the House of Commons in 1818, representing a borough in Dorset. Initially, Buxton concentrated on prison reform and, beginning in 1820, led a series of unsuccessful attempts to end capital punishment. Nonetheless, he was able to secure passage of legislation that reduced the number of crimes that were subject to the death penalty.

Buxton's initiatives gained the attention of William Wilberforce, the leader of the abolitionist campaign in Parliament. Wilberforce soon convinced Buxton to join the antislavery movement. In 1823, Wilberforce and Buxton helped form the Society for the Mitigation and Gradual Abolition of Slavery throughout the British Dominions (also known as the Anti-Slavery Society), which marked the start of an ultimately successful abolitionist movement.

In 1822, upon Wilberforce's retirement from Parliament, Buxton emerged as the leader of the parliamentary abolitionists. Although he campaigned vigorously to end slavery within the British Empire, Buxton proved to be a marginal parliamentary leader. Basing his arguments and tactics on appeals to humanitarianism and Christian virtue, he failed to garner widespread public support for abolition. He generally opposed efforts to appeal directly to the British people and instead insisted that antislavery forces concentrate their efforts on Parliament.

Buxton was repeatedly able to provide evidence of the role that slavery played in the economic decline in the Caribbean, contrary to the arguments of the proslavery faction in Parliament; however, his efforts at complete abolition were defeated. As a result, Buxton endeavored to pass measures to improve the standard of living for slaves and to provide them legal protections. Buxton's program included acts designed to encourage greater religious instruction and freedom for slaves, increased regulation of flogging, and

The Buxton Memorial Fountain, in London's Victoria Tower Gardens, was erected in 1865 to commemorate the 1834 emancipation of slaves in the British Empire and in memory of abolitionist leader Sir Thomas Fowell Buxton. *(©Victoria Tower Gardens, London, UK/The Bridgeman Art Library)*

an easement of laws regarding manumission. Again, he was unable to gain approval for these initiatives, although Parliament did pass on many of Buxton's proposals to the colonial legislatures, with the recommendation that they be enacted at the local level.

In 1831, the Anti-Slavery Society created a subgroup, the Agency Committee, and charged that body with a program designed to encourage public support for abolition through lectures and publications. Unhappy with Buxton's cautious approach, the Agency Committee eventually became independent of the Anti-Slavery Society, calling for immediate and unconditional emancipation throughout the British Empire.

Meanwhile, parliamentary elections in December 1832 resulted in an increase in the number of

abolitionists and reformers in the House of Commons. Buxton formed a coalition with proreform Members of Parliament and, in 1833, he finally triumphed with the passage of the Abolition of Slavery Act, which outlawed slavery throughout the empire. The new law reflected Buxton's caution and willingness to compromise. Although it abolished slavery, it did allow for a system of gradual emancipation by establishing a forced apprenticeship system.

Concurrent with the campaign to end slavery, Buxton also led an effort to secure and improve the rights of aboriginal peoples. He worked with the London Missionary Society to gain a legal decision in 1828 that gave the indigenous Khoikhoi people of southern Africa equal legal standing with white settlers. He also secured passage of a parliamentary motion that acknowledged African peoples' inherent sovereign right to their land. Partially because of this resolution, Buxton was able to convince the British government in 1835 to restore land that had been seized from the Xhosa people during a border war with colonial settlers.

After the passage of the Abolition of Slavery Act, Buxton concentrated his energies on ending the international slave trade. He left Parliament in 1837 after losing an election, but he remained an active lobbyist on behalf of efforts to completely end the slave trade. He provided monetary and public support for evangelical Christian missions to Africa and argued for government support for missionaries.

In 1839, he published *The African Slave Trade and its Remedy* in an attempt to revitalize the antislavery coalition. In his book, Buxton argued for increased anti–slave trade patrols and a system of international treaties to ban the trade, including agreements with indigenous African rulers. Buxton further argued that the European powers should foster the spread of Christianity in Africa as a method to "civilize" (as he perceived it) the continent and therefore end the trade at its roots. To accomplish the latter goal, Buxton founded the African Civilization Society in London in 1840. For his efforts to abolish slavery, Buxton was made a baronet that year.

Through his fame and the efforts of the new organization, Buxton was able to convince the British government to support an expedition to the Niger Valley to establish an outpost for missionaries and traders to spread European values and ideals among the native peoples. The expedition was vehemently opposed by many within Great Britain who believed that both the sponsors and participants of the operation were too idealistic and unprepared for the climate and conditions of the region. Launched in 1841, the expedition was an abysmal failure. A mission, farm, and trading post were all established in the Niger Valley, but disease quickly ravaged the expedition. Some 145 settlers and missionaries had embarked on the journey, but within a few months, one-third of the group was dead from tropical disease, and the remainder had to be rescued by traders using steamships.

The failure of the mission to Niger, for which Buxton held himself personally responsible, exacted a heavy toll on his health. Furthermore, the African Civilization Society disbanded amid public criticism of the expedition's management and an erosion of confidence in Buxton among members. The failure of the expedition, the demise of the society, and deteriorating health led Buxton to retire from public life. He died on February 19, 1845.

Tom Lansford

See also: Abolition of Slavery Act (1833); Wilberforce, William.

Further Reading

Barclay, Oliver. *Thomas Fowell Buxton and the Liberation of Slaves.* York, UK: William Sessions, 2001.

Davis, David Brion. *The Problem of Slavery in the Age of Revolution, 1770–1823.* Ithaca, NY: Cornell University Press, 1975; New York: Oxford University Press, 1999.

Fladeland, Betty. *Men and Brothers: Anglo-American Antislavery Cooperation.* Urbana: University of Illinois Press, 1972.

Temperley, Howard. *British Antislavery, 1833–1870.* London: Longman, 1972.

Cadbury, Richard Tapper (1768–1860)

Richard Tapper Cadbury, a leading British merchant and financier, served as a major patron of the British and Foreign Anti-Slavery Society for half a century. Having earned enormous profits from his drapery and silk business, Cadbury believed in the moral dictum that wealth must serve a higher calling. An early proponent of the social gospel, he worked tirelessly to promote the cause of abolition. He was the father of John Cadbury, who began importing and selling cocoa, thereby associating the family name with some of the world's finest chocolates.

Raised as a member of the Society of Friends (Quakers), Cadbury was attracted to the evangelical fervor of the antislavery movement. Buoyed by religious enthusiasm and blessed with business acumen, Cadbury devoted his time and treasury to bringing an end to the slave trade and slavery. Cadbury never wavered from the religious orthodoxy of the abolitionist crusade as he supported the movement for five decades.

Cadbury was present at the 1840 World Anti-Slavery Convention in London, which was attended by nearly 500 delegates from the United States and Great Britain. He was one of the prominent abolitionists immortalized in Benjamin Robert Haydon's painting memorializing that event, *The Anti-Slavery Society Convention* (1841).

Cadbury's association with the antislavery movement is representative of the stewardship and personal development that was associated with the crusade for social justice worldwide. The work of abolition was expensive, but donations from individuals such as Cadbury helped to finance the fight against slavery and keep the movement viable.

Junius P. Rodriguez

See also: World Anti-Slavery Convention (1840).

Further Reading

Cadbury, William A. *Richard Tapper Cadbury, 1768–1860.* Birmingham, UK: William A. Cadbury, 1944.

Caesar, John (ca. 1770–1837)

John Caesar was a Black Seminole military commander who lived as a free man in Florida. He helped many fugitive slaves from the Southern states emancipate themselves by assimilating among the Seminole and living as virtual maroons. Having liberated themselves, the Black Seminoles of Florida fought against the U.S. military to retain their freedom.

The United States fought two wars against the Seminole Nation. As part of the U.S. Army's efforts to stem anarchy and lawlessness in Spanish Florida, army forces attacked and destroyed Fort Blount on Apalachicola Bay on July 27, 1816. The fort, which had been renamed Negro Fort, was manned by nearly 300 escaped slaves and 20 Creek Indian allies who had sought asylum in the Spanish colony of East Florida. During the attack, the fugitive slaves and natives who defended the site suffered tremendous casualties—only forty defenders were still alive when the fort was surrendered to the American forces.

Having lived his entire life in Florida, growing up among the Seminoles, Caesar spoke both English, the language of his fugitive slave parents, and fluent Muskogee, the dialect of the Seminole Indians. He was about forty-five years old when the First Seminole War took place. He survived that conflict and helped the Black Seminole population regroup and reconstitute itself after suffering substantial losses. Considered one of the elders of the community, Caesar attained a position of respect within the tribe. He became a trusted adviser to the Seminole leader, King Philip (Emathca), and he eventually became principal chief among the Black Seminoles living along the Saint Johns River.

In December 1835, just before the start of the Second Seminole War, Caesar and fellow Black Seminole John Philip organized hundreds of fugitive slaves in an attack on the plantations of the Saint Johns River region in Florida. The coordinated attacks were designed to obtain provisions and to liberate additional slaves who might then join the Black Seminole ranks.

In December 1835, the American army prepared to move by force on Seminole country after New Year's Day to round up the American Indians for emigration. The Black Seminoles brought a military force of 250 fighters to augment the 1,650 Seminole warriors who resisted the American forces. When the Seminoles attacked the plantations along the east coast of Florida, they were joined by the Black Seminoles and approximately 300 slaves. The leaders of the raids included Caesar and Philip, both of whom had family members on the plantations.

On January 17, 1837, Caesar led a band of fourteen Black Seminoles in an attack on a plantation near Saint Augustine, Florida. Local militia routed the Black Seminoles, who retreated to their wilderness campsite to regroup. Militia members discovered Caesar's camp that night and attacked under cover of darkness. Three Black Seminoles, including Caesar, were killed.

Although Caesar's military skills had been extremely valuable, the Black Seminoles continued to fight. Finally, on December 25, 1837, the American forces defeated a Black Seminole band led by chief John Horse at the Battle of Okeechobee.

The U.S. military lost 1,500 men in a war that historians have described as "a slave catching enterprise for the benefit of the citizens of Georgia and Florida." It cost the U.S. government $20 million to sustain the seven-year struggle.

The eventual defeat of the Seminole Nation and the forced relocation of large numbers of Seminole Indians to Oklahoma proved to be the undoing of the Black Seminole presence in Florida. Fugitive slaves from nearby plantations no longer had a network of extended kinship to assist them if they attempted to escape and seek their freedom.

Junius P. Rodriguez

See also: Maroons.

Further Reading

Covington, James W. *The Seminoles of Florida.* Gainesville: University Press of Florida, 1993.

Heidler, David S., and Jeanne T. Heidler. *Old Hickory's War: Andrew Jackson and the Quest for Empire.* Baton Rouge: Louisiana State University Press, 2003.

Laumer Frank. *Dade's Last Command.* Gainesville: University Press of Florida, 1995.

McReynolds, Edwin C. *The Seminoles.* Norman: University of Oklahoma Press, 1988.

Rivers, Larry Eugene. *Slavery in Florida: Territorial Days to Emancipation.* Gainesville: University Press of Florida, 2000.

Canada

From the eighteenth century until the demise of slavery in the United States during the 1860s, thousands of freedom-seeking American blacks escaped, many via the Underground Railroad, to Upper Canada (present-day Ontario). Canadian terminals on the Underground Railroad were located in Niagara, Owen Sound, Collingwood, Oro, Sandwich, New Canaan, Colchester, Buxton, Chatham, Dresden, Dawn, London, Brantford, Wilberforce, Amherstburg, and Windsor. Refugees arrived at periodic intervals, often in small, isolated groups without family or friends. An estimated 20,000 black fugitives added to the population in Upper Canada, which primarily comprised English, American, French, and Irish immigrants.

Fugitives frequently referred to Canada as the "Promised Land," and Harriet Tubman, one of the charismatic conductors of the Underground Railroad, was affectionately known as "Moses." By the mid-nineteenth century, the Detroit River, used as a crossing by many blacks, had become associated with the biblical River Jordan.

From 1820 to 1865, American fugitives and free blacks joined an existing black population in Canada that had come during earlier migrations in the years after the American Revolution and the War of 1812. The newly arrived blacks quickly discovered, however, that there was an absence of any real or fictive kin relationships within the scattered black population of Upper Canada.

In addition to the horrors of the slavery system, a series of legislative and judicial developments in the United States provided further impetus for the migration of blacks to Canada. The second Fugitive Slave Law, passed in 1850, required citizens to assist in the capture of escaped slaves or be liable for fines or imprisonment. The legislation endangered the freedom of runaway slaves in the free states and increased the allure of Canada as a safe haven.

Likewise, the Kansas-Nebraska Act of 1854 jeopardized the status of blacks and contributed to the prevailing proslavery sentiment. Three years later, the U.S. Supreme Court's ruling in *Dred Scott v. Sandford* seemed to seal the fate of blacks in America. Under the ruling, blacks were not recognized as citizens of the United States and therefore did not enjoy protection under the Fifth Amendment. Thus, migration to Canada became increasingly appealing to blacks who desired personal freedom and protection from slave catchers.

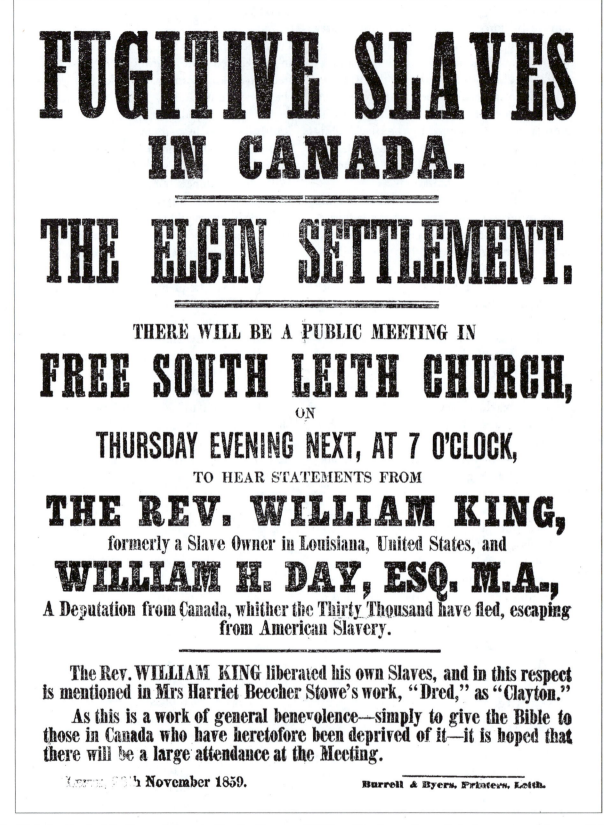

FUGITIVE SLAVES
IN CANADA.

THE ELGIN SETTLEMENT.

THERE WILL BE A PUBLIC MEETING IN

FREE SOUTH LEITH CHURCH,

ON

THURSDAY EVENING NEXT, AT 7 O'CLOCK,

TO HEAR STATEMENTS FROM

THE REV. WILLIAM KING,

formerly a Slave Owner in Louisiana, United States, and

WILLIAM H. DAY, ESQ. M.A.,

A Deputation from Canada, whither the Thirty Thousand have fled, escaping from American Slavery.

The Rev. WILLIAM KING liberated his own Slaves, and in this respect is mentioned in Mrs Harriet Beecher Stowe's work, "Dred," as "Clayton."

As this is a work of general benevolence—simply to give the Bible to those in Canada who have heretofore been deprived of it—it is hoped that there will be a large attendance at the Meeting.

Leith, 20th November 1859.   Burrell & Byers, Printers, Leith.

The Elgin (or Buxton) Settlement, founded by the Reverend William King in southern Ontario, was one of several black refugee communities in Canada that arose as a result of the Fugitive Slave Act of 1850. *(National Archives of Canada, MG 24 J 14, p. 863)*

In 1848, more than 5,000 fugitive blacks were living in Canada, including those who had come prior to 1830. By 1852, the country was home to a sizable population of 30,000 blacks. After the passage of the Fugitive Slave Law in 1850, Canada's fugitive population increased dramatically. The spurt coincided with the rapid spread of black churches and the renewed vigor of the Protestant mission.

The plight of fugitive slaves was indeed unfortunate, as the journey to Canada was accomplished with few belongings and little or no financial resources. During the 1850s, white and black women in Upper Canada made substantial contributions to alleviate the plight of the refugees.

Groups such as the Toronto Ladies' Association for the Relief of Destitute Coloured Fugitives and the West London Ladies' Association were dominated by sympathetic white women. Likewise, in the town of Cobourg, women interested in eradicating slavery banded together to form a ladies association that promoted a Christian mission among blacks. In 1854, a group of black wives in Chatham founded the Victoria Reform Benevolent Society to assist needy women. The Fugitives' Union and the Windsor Anti-Slavery Society represented small-scale efforts but nevertheless were instrumental in serving the needs of recently displaced refugees. Undoubtedly, these organizations helped foster a spirit of independence and created role models for the fledgling black communities in Upper Canada.

In Canada, white missionaries also worked among communities of fugitives and ensured that schools, settlements, and churches were properly organized. Among the Protestant denominations, the Presbyterians, Baptists, and African Methodist Episcopalians played pivotal roles. Their churches and missionaries received regular assistance from antislavery organizations and sympathetic humanitarians in the United States and Great Britain.

Fugitives from Maryland, Kentucky, and Virginia were generally better educated than those from other states, where slave masters denied education to their slaves. Those with little or no schooling were all the more appreciative of the church's educational efforts in Upper Canada—one of its great contributions to the emancipation movement.

Part of the enduring legacy of the Presbyterian Church was its missionary efforts among black refugees from the United States. The Reverend William King, supported by the Presbytery of Toronto, spearheaded the establishment of the Elgin Settlement in the township of Raleigh. There, black children were able to benefit from the school, and fifty settlers willingly accepted the religious and moral instruction provided by King.

Members of the American Missionary Association also worked to educate freed slaves. The Reverend David Hotchkiss, one of the association's missionaries, rendered outstanding service to small schools in Chatham, Mount Pleasant, and Puce. Similarly, Sabbath schools for blacks organized by the Protestant denominations flourished in Hamilton, Sandwich, Amherstburg, Chatham, and Dresden.

During the 1840s, the demand for separate schools intensified as blacks were excluded from public schools in towns such as Chatham. This prompted the American Baptist Mission to allocate money for a teacher in Chatham in 1843–1844. Despite this gesture of goodwill, the lone school was inadequate for the young blacks, and a separate common school was soon established.

The segregation of blacks also took place in the white churches. In some churches, whites referred to the separate pews reserved for blacks as "Nigger Heaven." Likewise, specific burial plots at Amherstburg, Windsor, Puce, and Colchester were allocated for blacks. In Normanby Township, there was a designated area for the burial of blacks, and similar areas existed in the Queen's Bush Settlement, Peel Township, and Oxford County.

Despite the minor difficulties that fugitive slaves faced in their new homeland, Canada played a significant role in protecting them and providing a refuge from slavery.

Jerome Teelucksingh

See also: American Missionary Association; Underground Railroad.

Further Reading

Bramble, Linda. *Black Fugitive Slaves in Early Canada.* Saint Catharines, Ontario, Canada: Vanwell, 1988.

Farrell, John. "Schemes for the Transplanting of Refugee American Negroes From Upper Canada in the 1840s." *Ontario History* 52 (December 1960): 245–50.

Hembree, Michael F. "The Question of 'Begging': Fugitive Slave Relief in Canada, 1830–1865." *Civil War History* 37 (December 1991): 314–27.

Hill, Daniel G. *The Freedom Seekers: Blacks in Early Canada.* Agincourt, Ontario, Canada: Society of Canada, 1981.

Candler, John (1787–1869)

As a deeply committed member of the Society of Friends (Quakers) who opposed the slave trade and slavery on moral principles, John Candler did journeyman's work for the British abolitionist movement as he visited plantation societies in Jamaica, Haiti, Brazil, and the United States to proselytize against the flesh trade. Equally important to the cause were his published accounts of these journeys, which provided valuable propaganda to support the work of British antislavery advocates.

Candler's first transatlantic journey took him to the West Indies in 1839–1840 on a fact-finding mission led by Joseph John Gurney, the noted British Quaker philanthropist, minister, and writer. The delegation of Quaker visitors was observing how effective the 1833 Abolition of Slavery Act (commonly known as the British Emancipation Act) had been at introducing an apprenticeship system that would prepare the former slaves for a wage labor system. Members of the delegation were especially interested in the availability of education, religious training, and the overall condition of the black population, particularly on the free islands as compared to those that still permitted slavery.

Candler kept detailed journals during his travels, and later, upon returning to London, he published two accounts of his experiences. *West Indies: Extracts From the Journal of J. Candler Whilst Travelling in Jamaica* (1840) and *Brief Notices of Hayti: With Its Condition, Resources, and Prospects* (1842) provided more than mere geographic literature to the British public; they also provided important commentary on what was possible when former slaves obtained economic and, in the case of Haiti, political freedom.

Candler's second expedition took him to Brazil, one of the most notorious slave societies in the Western Hemisphere during the nineteenth century. Candler and fellow Quaker Wilson Burguess met with Brazilian leaders to press for an end to the slave trade in the hope that reasoned arguments and moral suasion might produce a change of heart among the leaders.

While in Brazil, Candler and his party were occasionally transported in *cadeiras* (curtained sedan chairs) that were carried by specially selected slaves. Candler realized that within a slave society, different levels of status exist, and he noted that the cadeira carriers felt themselves special. He noted, "No one need suppose that [the use of cadeiras] was an oppression to the slaves: on the contrary, it was to them a coveted employment . . . a kind look, and a very small gratuity added to the fare, always made us welcome." He published these and other findings in *Narrative of a Recent Visit to Brazil; to Present an Address on the Slave-Trade and Slavery, Issued by the Religious Society of Friends* (1853), written with Burguess.

Candler's last transatlantic venture took him to the United States, where he traveled through twenty-three states in 1853 and 1854. Candler kept a journal, writing much on the topics of slavery and race, and he frequently corresponded with his wife, Marie Knight Candler, who had remained in Britain. Many of Candler's letters home were published a century later in the collection *A Friendly Mission: John Candler's Letters From America, 1853–1854* (1951).

The delegation to the United States included four Quakers: William Forster, his brother Josiah Forster, William Holmes, and Candler. In October 1853, the men were able to meet with President Franklin Pierce but felt that they received a cool response to the antislavery views they advocated. In addition, the group met with many governors during their travels.

While the British Quakers were in the United States, they experienced the political firestorm associated with the passage of the Kansas-Nebraska Act (1854), which permitted the possible expansion of slavery into previously free territory. Moved by circumstances to become more than antislavery missionaries, the Quaker visitors found themselves transformed into moral lobbyists as they mailed circulars and held private meetings with congressmen and senators.

Although the Quakers were unsuccessful in their efforts to curtail the passage of the act, Candler continued to believe that forthright dialogue with slave owners was one of the best means of bringing an end to slavery. He affirmed this hope in a letter to his wife: "There is something in [the slaveholder] . . . better than himself, to the authority of which he bows."

Junius P. Rodriguez

See also: Quakers (Society of Friends).

Further Reading

Candler, John. *A Friendly Mission: John Candler's Letters From America, 1853–1854.* Indianapolis: Indiana Historical Society, 1951.

Castlereagh, Lord (1769–1822)

As British foreign secretary at the Congress of Vienna in 1814–1815, Lord Castlereagh sought to encourage the European powers to end their involvement with the transatlantic slave trade. His success, although incomplete, helped to hasten the end of the slave trade.

Robert Stewart, second marquis of Londonderry and Lord Castlereagh, was born on June 18, 1769, in Dublin, Ireland, the second-born and eldest surviving son of the first earl of Hertford and Lady Sarah Seymour-Conway. A member of the Presbyterian Ulster elite, Castlereagh entered Saint John's College at Cambridge University after being confirmed in the Church of England, and he saw his father become one of the representative peers of Ireland in 1801.

By 1790, Castlereagh had begun a career in the Dublin Parliament, but he quickly shifted his ambitions to Westminster, where he served as a Whig Member of Parliament from County Down and then, in 1805, held a safe seat in Boroughbridge, England. Deeply sympathetic to Ireland's political problems, he worked to gain clemency for the 1798 rebels, supported Roman Catholic emancipation if it could be accomplished through peaceful means, and worked closely with Lord Charles Cornwallis to ensure a smooth transition through Ireland's union with Britain.

In the House of Commons, Castlereagh became a great advocate for the British Empire, serving as president of the Board of Control (India) and heading the defense of England against Napoleon's channel invasion plans in 1805. Castlereagh had a farsighted appreciation of global politics and advocated avoiding the War of 1812 against the United States while pushing for more attention to the Spanish theater in the Napoleonic Wars.

Many of Castlereagh's political allies, such as William Wilberforce, were committed abolitionists, and he leaned toward that policy because of their influence rather than personal inclination. In 1805, he pressed the House of Commons to limit slavery in the colonies that Britain had taken in the war; this recommendation later became an Order in Council, eliminating legal slavery in the Cape Colony.

In February 1812, Lord Perceval, head of the new government, asked Castlereagh to replace the marquis of Wellesley at the foreign office—a post he would hold until his death in 1822—as well as to manage the House of Commons on behalf of the peer prime minister. As foreign secretary, Castlereagh represented Britain at the Congress of Vienna, where he hoped to achieve moderate reforms but was forced to admit the intransigence of the conservative Spanish and Italian monarchs. Unable to prevent the Holy Alliance among Russia, Prussia, and Austria or the conservative and legitimist bent of the conference, Castlereagh chose

to leverage Britain's power to press for the abolition of the slave trade, using Napoleon's desperate anti–slave trade declaration, issued during the Hundred Days, as extra pressure on the allies.

At the Congress of Vienna, the Netherlands and Sweden agreed to abolish the slave trade in return for British retrocession of their East Indian possessions, and the restored Bourbon king of France, Louis XVIII, was convinced to honor Napoleon's declaration. The Austrians and Russians, who had little to lose from the end of the slave trade, joined Castlereagh in moving for a special condemnation of it as a declaration of the congress.

Spain, Portugal, and the United States, which was not a signatory at Vienna, proved less tractable to Castlereagh's plans. Spain finally agreed in 1817—after Castlereagh refused to mediate a territorial dispute between Spain and Portugal—to abolish the slave trade north of the equator immediately and to eradicate it south of the equator by May 30, 1820. In return, it received £400,000 and Britain's diplomatic mediation. The same year, Portugal agreed to abolish the trade north of the equator and to restrict it to Portuguese territory and Portuguese ships south of the equator in exchange for a £300,000 gift from Britain and forgiveness of a £60,000 war debt. The United States refused all British approaches and demanded repayment for slaves freed during the War of 1812.

Enforcement of the ban posed a significant problem, a subject that Castlereagh broached at the Congress of Aix-la-Chapelle in 1818, asking that the British navy have the right to search foreign vessels for slaves. Spain, the Netherlands, and Denmark granted these rights, but the Portuguese, French, and Americans refused outright.

Juggling three crises—the Greek declaration of independence from the Ottoman Empire, the fallout of the Peterloo Massacre of 1819, and the scandalous re-appearance of King George IV's wife in England—Castlereagh became severely depressed. Historians have suggested that Castlereagh, who had been married since 1794 to Lady Emily Hobart, may also have been blackmailed over a personal sexual scandal.

On August 12, 1822, Castlereagh cut his own throat. Buried in Westminster Abbey, he is generally acknowledged as a capable and forward-thinking British politician.

Margaret Sankey

See also: Congress of Vienna (1814–1815); Wilberforce, William.

Further Reading

Bartell, C.J. *Castlereagh*. New York: Scribner's, 1966.

Derry, John W. *Castlereagh*. New York: St. Martin's, 1976.

Webster, Charles K. *The Foreign Policy of Castlereagh, 1815–1822*. London: G. Bell & Sons, 1925, 1931.

Castro Alves, Antônio de (1847–1871)

Antônio Frederico de Castro Alves was the last of the prominent romantic Brazilian poets. His sympathy for the Brazilian abolitionist cause was expressed in his poetry, earning him the moniker "Poet of the Slaves." Although he died at the age of twenty-four, his social consciousness encouraged an outpouring of work that fed the antislavery sentiment in late-nineteenth-century Brazil.

Castro Alves was born in the state of Bahia, Brazil, on the family plantation close to Curralinho (now Castro Alves) in 1847. The son of a doctor, he moved with his family to Salvador, the capital of Bahia, in 1854. In Salvador, Castro Alves attended school, where he showed an interest in literary studies from an early age.

In 1862, Castro Alves moved with his oldest brother to Recife, Pernambuco, where he attended law school. As a law student, he became politically involved with groups of young intellectuals, such as Tobias Barreto and Ruy Barbosa, who supported liberal ideas, especially the abolition of slavery and the establishment of a republican government.

Castro Alves wrote several poems supporting liberal ideas and became more and more involved with his literary production. His personal experiences in Salvador and later in Recife, two important slave centers, ignited his interest in the social injustices of Brazil's slavery system. In 1863, Castro Alves published his first poem against slavery, "A Canção Africana" (The African Song), in the academic journal *A Primavera*. In this poem, he defended freedom for all slaves in Brazil.

The mid-nineteenth century was characterized by intense international pressure to end the transatlantic slave trade and slaving systems in the New World. In Brazil, it was a moment of intense political and economic instability. Discontent with the imperial regime led to many social upheavals and protests, including the Cabanagem (1835–1837), Sabinada (1837–1838), Balaiada (1838–1841), and Farroupilha (1845) revolts. It was in this social climate that Castro Alves lived and worked.

In 1850, the legal slave trade into Brazilian territory was suppressed by legislation; however, slave traders continued to operate illegally, bringing more Africans to Brazil. Together with another famous abolitionist, Ruy Barbosa, Castro Alves founded an abolitionist society, and both men assumed important roles in the abolitionist movement in Brazil. Castro Alves's writing activities took him to São Paulo and Rio de Janeiro, at that time the capital of the empire, where he was in touch with leading intellectuals, such as Machado de Assis and José de Alencar.

These experiences shaped Castro Alves as a writer, and he used his art to express his political opinions, mainly through short pieces published in newspapers and theater presentations. In one of his works, "Os Escravos" (The Slaves), he denounced the abuses of slavery. In what is perhaps his most famous poem, "O Navio Negreiro" (The Slave Ship), written in 1868, he criticized the use of slave labor to enrich the elite class in Brazil, as well as the use of slaves in the armed forces involved in the Paraguay War in exchange for their freedom. In many of his other poems—for instance, in the collection *Vozes d' Africa* (Voices of Africa)—he portrayed the African as a truly human figure, both hero and lover, in an effort to effect empathy from white readers.

In 1869, just two years before his death, Castro Alves witnessed the publication of a law prohibiting the public sales of slaves. He also saw the publication of one book, *Espumas Flutuantes* (Floating Foams), in 1870. Following an accident that resulted in the amputation of a foot, he contracted tuberculosis. Castro Alves died in Salvador on July 6, 1871.

Although he did not live to see the abolition of slavery, his literary contributions inspired and encouraged the approval of several bills. These included the *Lei do Ventre Libre* (Law of the Free Womb, or Free Birth Law, as it became known) of 1871, the Sexagenarian Law of 1885, and the *Lei Áurea* (Golden Law), which finally abolished slavery in Brazil in 1888.

Mariana P. Candido

See also: Brazil, Abolition in; *Lei Áurea* (Golden Law, 1888).

Further Reading

Castro Alves, Antônio de. *The Major Abolitionist Poems*. Ed. and trans. Amy A. Peterson. New York: Garland, 1990.

Goldberg, Isaac. *Brazilian Literature*. New York: Alfred A. Knopf, 1922.

Haberly, David T. *Three Sad Races: Racial Identity and National Consciousness in Brazilian Literature.* Cambridge, UK: Cambridge University Press, 1983.

Chace, Elizabeth Buffum (1806–1899)

Abolitionist and reformer Elizabeth Buffum Chace was an important fund-raiser and organizer for both the antislavery and women's rights movements in the United States. Though she was not as visible as other antislavery advocates, she nevertheless stood as a shining example of the core of the movement—middle-class wives and mothers who made their political and moral beliefs a vital part of their lives. She was, in the words of one scholar, the "quintessential feminist-abolitionist."

Elizabeth was born into a prominent Quaker family in Providence, Rhode Island, on December 9, 1806, the fourth of nine children. She attended schools in Smithfield and Providence, Rhode Island, and in Pomfret, Connecticut. After finishing her education, she joined her family in Fall River, Massachusetts, where she taught school until she married Samuel Buffington Chace in June 1828.

Although she had been, in her words, "born and baptized into the anti-slavery spirit," Elizabeth Chace spent most of the period between 1828 and 1837 focused on her growing family, bearing five children at regular intervals. Between 1837 and 1839, all five youngsters died of various ailments.

To assuage her grief, Chace turned her attention to antislavery work, which by then had become something of a family cause. Her father, Arnold Buffum, was the founder and president of the New England Anti-Slavery Society, and her mother, grandparents, sister, and brothers-in-law were all involved with the abolitionist cause. As vice president of the Fall River Female Anti-Slavery Society, Chace arranged speakers and lecturers, organized petition drives and fund-raising fairs, and even went door to door herself.

In 1840, the Chaces moved to Valley Falls, Rhode Island, where Samuel opened a cotton manufacturing factory and Elizabeth organized a new antislavery society. Their home, like that of her sisters and parents, became a well-known stop on the Underground Railroad. In her new home, Elizabeth Chace bore five more children between 1843 and 1852 (Samuel, Arnold, Lillie, Edward, and Mary), and she raised them as abolitionists. Her daughter, Lillie

Chace Wyman, later recalled her mother counseling them on "how they must behave if the constables should come and carry . . . father and mother off to jail."

After slavery was defeated, Chace shifted her focus to the cause of women's rights. In 1868, she founded both the New England Woman Suffrage Association and the Rhode Island Woman Suffrage Association, serving as president of the state organization from 1870 until her death. She also devoted considerable time to social reform, investigating almshouses, asylums, reform schools, and women's prisons as an appointed member of the Rhode Island Board of Lady Visitors.

An invalid during her final decade of life, Chace barely slowed her pace, spending her days writing and organizing. She held suffrage meetings in her bedroom until the last days of her life. She died on December 22, 1899, at the age of ninety-three. At her request, her funeral ceremony in Providence was conducted by the noted feminist minister Anna Garlin Spencer.

Heather K. Michon

See also: Buffum, Arnold; Underground Railroad; Women's Rights and the Abolitionist Movement.

Further Reading

Chace, Elizabeth Buffum. *Two Quaker Sisters.* New York: Liveright, 1937.
Salitan, Lucille, and Eve Lewis Perera, eds. *Virtuous Lives: Four Quaker Sisters Remember Family Life, Abolitionism, and Women's Suffrage.* New York: Continuum, 1994.
Stevens, Elizabeth C. *Elizabeth Buffum Chace and Lillie Chace Wyman: A Century of Abolitionist, Suffragist, and Worker's Rights' Activism.* Jefferson, NC: McFarland, 2003.

Chandler, Elizabeth Margaret (1807–1834)

One of the most outspoken women of the American antislavery movement, the poet and activist Elizabeth Margaret Chandler used her literary talents to advance the causes of abolition and women's rights.

Chandler was born in Centre, Delaware, on December 24, 1807. Her early life was marked by loss: Her mother died when she was an infant, and her father died when she was eight. She and her brothers were sent to Philadelphia, where they were educated and raised by their grandmother.

As a Quaker, Chandler absorbed the antislavery doctrine at a young age. She joined the Free

Produce movement, boycotting items produced by the slave trade, such as molasses, rice, cotton, and tea. She left the orthodox Quaker church in 1828 to join the more liberal and more vocally antislavery Hicksite movement.

A poet from childhood, Chandler naturally turned her antislavery passions into verse. In 1826, when she was eighteen, she penned "The Slave Ship," which won third prize in a local newspaper contest. Abolitionist Benjamin Lundy, editor of the *Genius of Universal Emancipation,* reprinted the poem.

Lundy met Chandler and invited her to become the editor of the "Ladies Repository" of the *Genius* in 1829. She accepted, becoming only the second American woman to be employed in journalism. For five years, Chandler edited the ladies' page and contributed most of its material; her antislavery poems, including "The Wife's Lament," "The Recaptured Slave," and "The Slave's Appeal," appeared regularly.

Her essays extolled not only the need for a strong antislavery movement but also a prominent role for women. The "Ladies Repository" urged women to follow the lead of female antislavery societies in England: "You deceive yourselves, American women! Your power is sufficient for its extinction. . . . We would have you exert your influence by instilling into the minds of your offspring a deep-felt sense of their duty as men and Christians to break the fetters of their oppressors!"

Chandler dismissed conservatives' criticism that she was encouraging women to step outside their proper sphere. Emancipation was not political, she contended, but "an outrage against humanity and morality and religion, because it is criminal." Some of her strongest work, a series of letters "To the Ladies of Baltimore," appealed directly to the women of the South such that "it is a dark and fearful wickedness to make merchandise of men" and encouraged them to start their own antislavery societies.

In 1830, Chandler moved with her brother to the Michigan Territory, where they settled in Lenawee Township, an outpost on the Raisin River about thirty miles southwest of Ann Arbor. She was delighted with both the climate and community. "I have chosen my lot," she wrote her aunt, "and *am satisfied* with it. I believe I am in my place and that we did well in coming here." She organized Michigan's first antislavery society and raised funds for a library.

Chandler continued her editorial work and steady production of poems, many of which became popular among antislavery societies and were adapted as hymns

sung at meetings. She maintained a constant correspondence with friends and family in the East, and Lundy kept her supplied with the latest antislavery books, pamphlets, and magazines.

In 1831, she began receiving William Lloyd Garrison's newspaper, *The Liberator.* Garrison had been a longtime admirer of Chandler's work and soon began his own "Woman's Department," made up almost entirely of reprints from the *Genius.* Chandler agreed wholeheartedly with Garrison's political views, though she was gentler in tone.

In spring 1834, Chandler fell ill and never recovered. She died on November 2, 1834, two months before her twentieth-eighth birthday. She was eulogized in the pages of *The Liberator* as "the first American woman who devoted her time and talents to the cause of the slave." In 1836, two volumes of her writings were published: *Essays, Philanthropic and Moral* and *Poetical Works of Elizabeth Margaret Chandler; With a Memoir of Her Life and Character.*

Heather K. Michon

See also: Lundy, Benjamin; Quakers (Society of Friends); Women's Rights and the Abolitionist Movement.

Further Reading

Dillon, Merton L. "Elizabeth Chandler and the Spread of Antislavery Sentiment to Michigan." *Michigan History* 39 (December 1955): 481–95.

Lutz, Alma. *Crusade for Freedom: The Women of the Antislavery Movement.* Boston: Beacon, 1968.

Channing, William Ellery (1780–1842)

Best remembered as the father of American Unitarianism and as a predecessor of and influence on the American Transcendental movement, William Ellery Channing lent his voice to the emerging abolitionist movement of the early nineteenth century. Though the magnitude of his philosophical teachings had become obvious by the time he published his treatise *Negro Slavery* in 1835, he had previously shied away from the highly politicized slavery debate. This publication signaled a turning point in Channing's public life, though his arguments against the institution were based on the religious principles that had guided him throughout his life: the value of all humankind and the right of all persons to fulfill their potential for the sake of their own development and happiness.

Moreover, as he had done time and again from the pulpit, he demonstrated the application of reason to scripture, showing that the biblical statements in favor of slavery were not applicable in modern times.

Channing was born on April 7, 1780, in the busy slave port of Newport, Rhode Island, to a Calvinist and slaveholding family. He studied at Harvard College, where he began an intellectual journey that would lead him to radically undercut the mainstream Christian teachings of postrevolutionary America.

After graduating from Harvard in 1798, Channing spent time as a tutor to a Virginia family, developing, among other traits, a passionate hatred of slavery. During this period, he became acquainted with the works of Jean-Jacques Rousseau and other French revolutionaries and thus developed a lens through which his radical Christian beliefs could be more clearly developed.

Upon his return to the North, and after an intense period of studying theology, he became the minister of the Federal Street Church in Boston in 1803. It was from this post, which he held until 1842, that he would denounce the doctrine of the Christian trinity and influence multitudes of religious liberals throughout the world.

Throughout his career, Channing emphasized the reformation of social establishments, including education, but he remained apprehensive about the use of government to bring about what he considered to be moral reforms. Additionally, he attempted to avoid the type of radical political action that was becoming more prevalent among reformers, especially in abolitionist circles. "We honor religion too much to give its sacred name to a feverish, forced, fluctuating zeal, which has little power over life," he said at an early point in his career.

By the mid-1820s, Channing had begun to speak out against slavery. Later, upon reading an antislavery tract by Lydia Maria Francis Child, he began an ongoing dialogue with the author to clarify his thinking on the subject. In doing so, he also imparted in her his prudence regarding the rising tide of abolitionism. She later commented, "I owe him thanks for preserving me from the one-sidedness into which zealous reformers are so apt to run. He never sought to undervalue the importance of Antislavery, but he said many things to prevent my looking upon it as the *only* question interesting to humanity."

After years of prodding from contemporaries, Channing published *Negro Slavery*. A broadside against the institution of slavery, the work proclaimed that human rights derive from one's moral nature, which is created by God, not society. The issue of slavery, Channing believed, called for an examination of "the foundation, nature, and extent of human rights." He went on to say that slavery was not only an insult to God, it thwarted the spiritual progress of slaves and slave owners alike. However, he condemned the sin, not the sinners.

Abolitionist William Lloyd Garrison was disappointed by such moderate antislavery sentiment and heavily criticized Channing's book. Others, such as Massachusetts attorney general James T. Austin and the Boston industrialists who sat in the pews of the Federal Street Church, disapproved of Channing's position, because they believed the minister was encouraging slave insurrection.

In 1840, Channing's friend, the Unitarian and abolitionist minister Charles Follen, died in a shipwreck. Channing presided over the funeral, delivering an impassioned sermon. Soon after, the Massachusetts Anti-Slavery Society asked, with Channing's support, if a memorial service for Follen might be held at the Federal Street Church. When the church elders denied the request, Channing responded by proclaiming his willingness to give up his post if the church deemed him expendable. Channing preached only once more from the Federal Street pulpit, though he continued his ministry.

In his waning years, Channing published a fervent antislavery article titled *The Duty of the Free States* (1842). In this publication, he refuted Daniel Webster's legal rhetoric about the necessity of obeying the slave laws of the United States. "No decision of the state absolves us from the moral law," Channing argued.

Channing's last public address, in Lenox, Massachusetts, on August 1, 1842, celebrated the anniversary of the emancipation of slaves in the British West Indies and called for an end to slavery in the United States using similarly peaceful means. He died on October 2, 1842.

Geoffrey A. Koski

See also: Child, Lydia Maria Francis; Garrison, William Lloyd.

Further Reading

Edgell, David P. *William Ellery Channing: An Intellectual Portrait.* Westport, CT: Greenwood, 1983.

Harwood, Thomas F. "Prejudice and Antislavery: The Colloquy Between William Ellery Channing and Edward Strutt

Abdy, 1834." *American Quarterly* 18 (Winter 1966): 697–700.

Mendelsohn, Jack. *Channing, The Reluctant Radical: A Biography.* Westport, CT: Greenwood, 1980.

Robinson, David, ed. *William Ellery Channing: Selected Writings.* New York: Paulist Press, 1985.

Chapman, Maria Weston (1806–1885)

As founder of the Boston Female Anti-Slavery Society and chief organizer of the many antislavery fairs that funded the abolitionist movement in the United States, Maria Weston Chapman was one of the staunchest allies and supporters of the abolitionist leader William Lloyd Garrison.

Born on July 25, 1806, she was the first of six children born to Warren and Anne Bates Weston. Originally from Weymouth, Massachusetts, Maria studied in England after moving there with her uncle, Joshua Bates, a prosperous London banker. In 1828, she returned to Massachusetts and served as principal of Ebenezer Bailey's Young Ladies' High School. She married businessman Henry Grafton Chapman in 1830, and the couple had four children: three girls and a boy.

Henry Chapman came from a family of abolitionists. Maria and her sisters, Caroline, Deborah, and Anne, soon dedicated themselves to the cause, aligning themselves with the Garrisonians and espousing the belief that moral suasion, not political action, was the best way to end slavery. In 1834, Maria Chapman and other like-minded women helped found the interracial Boston Female Anti-Slavery Society, "believing slavery to be the direct violation of the laws of God, and productive of a vast amount of misery and crime, and convinced that its abolition can only be effected by an acknowledgment of the justice and necessity of immediate emancipation."

On October 21, 1835, while she was serving as the society's corresponding secretary, the infamous "Boston Mob" protested the visit of English abolitionist George Thompson by interrupting a meeting of the society. Under Chapman's direction, members of the society relocated to her house without harm. The event inspired her to become an even more outspoken abolitionist.

Always willing to speak her mind, Chapman became an important, if controversial, figure in abolitionist circles and a critical ally of Garrison as tensions among the abolitionist groups intensified.

Beginning in 1835, Chapman was in charge of the annual antislavery fairs, which served as the abolitionists' primary source of funding. She authored the Boston Female Anti-Slavery Society's annual reports starting in 1836; served on the editorial committee of the *National Anti-Slavery Standard* from 1844 to 1848; and, along with Edmund Quincy, she edited *The Liberator* in Garrison's absence. She and her sisters also edited *The Liberty Bell,* an annual gift book comprising writings by prominent abolitionists, from 1839 through 1846.

In May 1838, a mob gathered around Pennsylvania Hall as Chapman delivered her only formal public speech to the Anti-Slavery Convention of American Women. The following day, the hall was burned down. An exhausted Chapman was briefly hospitalized after the event.

Even when Chapman's personal life pulled her away from Boston, her dedication to abolition remained unflinching. Because of her husband's tuberculosis, Chapman and her family spent much of 1841 and 1842 in Haiti. Maria kept up her antislavery work, serving as foreign corresponding secretary to the Boston Female Anti-Slavery Society.

Harry Chapman died in 1842, and from 1848 to 1855, Maria lived with her children in Europe. While abroad, she actively recruited donations to the American antislavery cause, including contributions from Harriet Martineau and Alexis de Tocqueville, and continued to write abolitionist material. She published *How Can I Help to Abolish Slavery?* in 1855.

Chapman was often at the center of controversy in the antislavery movement. Tensions between the Garrisonians and their rivals in the American and Foreign Anti-Slavery Society broke apart the Boston Female Anti-Slavery Society in 1840. Chapman was active in the fight, and even her ally, fellow abolitionist Lydia Maria Francis Child, believed that she had acted unfairly toward her opposition. Undaunted, Chapman led a campaign to found a new society with the same name. In 1843, the abolitionist Henry Highland Garnet, enraged by her suggestion that his actions were controlled by white anti-Garrisonian forces, accused her of being a racist in a letter published in *The Liberator.*

Chapman agreed with Garrison that the work of antislavery societies should end with abolition. Beginning in the early 1860s, therefore, she worked for her son's brokerage office in New York and later returned to Weymouth, Massachusetts. In 1877, she published a two-volume edition of abolitionist

Harriet Martineau's *Autobiography*. She died on July 12, 1885.

Katherine L. Culkin

See also: Anti-Abolition Riots; *Liberty Bell, The; National Anti-Slavery Standard.*

Further Reading

Hansen, Debra Gold. *Strained Sisterhood: Gender and Class in the Boston Female Anti-Slavery Society.* Amherst: University of Massachusetts Press, 1993.

Hassett, Constance W. "Siblings and Antislavery: The Literary and Political Relations of Harriet Martineau, James Martineau, and Maria Weston Chapman." *Signs* 21 (Winter 1996): 374.

Munsterberg, Margaret. "The Weston Sisters and the 'Boston Mob.'" *Boston Public Library Quarterly* 9 (October 1957): 183–94.

Taylor, Clare. *Women of the Anti-Slavery Movement: The Weston Sisters.* New York: St. Martin's, 1995.

Chase, Salmon P. (1808–1873)

"True democracy makes no inquiry about the color of the skin," Ohio attorney Salmon Portland Chase declared in 1854 upon accepting a gift in recognition of his defense of a fugitive slave. Perhaps no other words more accurately sum up the fundamental principle that guided Chase's life. His work on behalf of runaway slaves and those who aided them earned him the nickname "Attorney General of Fugitive Slaves," a derogatory moniker given to him by Kentucky slaveholders but one that Chase embraced wholeheartedly. Chase's ideals guided his work as a U.S. senator from Ohio (1849–1855, 1861), governor of Ohio (1855–1861), U.S. secretary of the treasury (1861–1864), and chief justice of the U.S. Supreme Court (1864–1873).

Chase's early life gave little indication of what he would later achieve. Born in Cornish, New Hampshire, on January 13, 1808, he suffered the loss of his father at age nine. The young boy went to live on the Ohio frontier with his uncle, Philander Chase, the foremost pioneer of the Protestant Episcopal Church in the West and the first bishop of Ohio. Chase returned to New Hampshire to enroll in Dartmouth College and graduated Phi Beta Kappa in 1826.

After a few years of teaching, Chase moved back to Ohio, opened a private law practice, and married Catherine Jane Garniss, the first of his three wives, all of whom died within seven years of marriage. He garnered his first public recognition by amassing a

three-volume annotated compilation of the Statutes of Ohio that became the authoritative reference in state courts.

Chase discovered his life's calling in 1837, when he defended the abolitionist editor James Gillespie Birney of Cincinnati, Ohio. Birney had hired a woman whom he believed was a white servant but turned out to be an escaped slave from Missouri. Charged with harboring a fugitive slave, Birney hired Chase to lead his court defense. In his argument, Chase disputed the constitutionality of the Fugitive Slave Law of 1793 and invoked the language of the Declaration of Independence, arguing that slavery was a violation of the natural right to liberty. Although he lost the case, it marked the beginning of his career as a defender of fugitive slaves and an opponent of the institution of slavery.

As an Episcopalian, Chase believed that slavery was a sin. His antislavery attitudes cost him many clients and friends, but his morals guided his every career move. Though he never won a case in defense of a fugitive slave, he never charged his clients a fee. He believed that blacks had the right to vote, the right to an education, and the right to testify in court against whites—views that prompted slavery proponents to pelt Chase with eggs and bricks during antislavery rallies.

Nevertheless, Chase persevered and became a figure of national importance, writing most of the platform of the Free Soil Party in 1848. The platform called for a ban on slavery in any newly admitted state, as well as an end to slavery in the Western territories. Although the Free Soil national candidate, Martin Van Buren, failed to garner much electoral support, Chase had sealed his nationwide reputation by authoring the party's platform.

Capitalizing on his success in organizing the Free Soil Party, Chase formed a coalition with the Ohio Democratic Party and won election as a U.S. senator, a post he assumed in March 1849. While in the capital, he opposed the idea of popular sovereignty, which allowed for the possibility of slavery in new U.S. territories, as well as both the Compromise of 1850 and the Kansas-Nebraska Act of 1854. In response to the latter, he helped organize Northern Whigs and other Democrats into the Anti-Nebraska Party, a faction that became a pillar in the new Republican Party in 1854.

Upon completion of his term in the Senate, Chase was elected governor of Ohio in 1855 as a

Free Soil Democrat and re-elected in 1857 as a Republican. During his terms as a reformist governor, Chase called for women's rights, better treatment of the incarcerated and the insane, and improvements in education.

After failing to win the Republican nomination for president in 1856 and 1860, Chase was elected to the U.S. Senate again in 1860. After taking his seat on March 4, 1861, he resigned only two days later to take a position in President Abraham Lincoln's cabinet as secretary of the treasury. In this position, not only did Chase see his face appear on the first dollar bills printed by the federal government, but he also tackled the monumental task of overseeing the wartime economy and suggested to Lincoln that the Emancipation Proclamation needed to acknowledge a supreme being ("And by this act . . . I invoke the considerate judgment of mankind and the gracious favor of Almighty God.").

In summer 1862, Chase quarreled with Lincoln over the case of Union General David Hunter. Operating in conquered districts of South Carolina, Hunter had enlisted black soldiers into the U.S. Army and issued a statement declaring all slaves owned by Confederates in the area free. Although Lincoln could not allow this action, Chase sided with Hunter and nearly resigned his post over the issue. Two years and many disagreements later, Chase did finally resign.

In December 1864, Lincoln appointed Chase chief justice of the Supreme Court, where he became highly critical of Lincoln's Reconstruction plans. Upon Lincoln's death, Chase sided with the Radical Republicans in Congress and continued to rule against Andrew Johnson's plans for Reconstruction. He presided over the Senate impeachment proceedings against Johnson in 1868. While on the Court, he interpreted the Thirteenth and Fourteenth amendments as protecting the rights of blacks. Chase died on May 7, 1873.

Geoffrey A. Koski

See also: Birney, James Gillespie; Free Soil Party.

Further Reading

Gienapp, William E. "Salmon P. Chase, Nativism, and the Formation of the Republican Party in Ohio." *Ohio History* 93 (Spring 1984): 5–39.

Luthin, Reinhard. "Salmon P. Chase's Political Career Before the Civil War." *Mississippi Valley Historical Review* 29 (March 1943): 517–40.

Child, David Lee (1794–1874)

One of the founders of the New England Anti-Slavery Society, David Lee Child devoted a lifetime of service to the antislavery cause as a lawyer, activist, and newspaper editor.

Child was born on July 8, 1794, in West Boylston, Massachusetts, to Zachariah and Lydia Bigelow Child. He graduated from Harvard in 1817. After serving as submaster of the Boston Latin School, he moved to Portugal to work as the secretary of the American legation. He later fought with the Spanish army against French forces before returning to America to study law in 1824.

In 1827, Child assumed editorship of the *Massachusetts Journal.* The next year, he was admitted to the Suffolk County bar, elected to the Massachusetts state legislature, and married the well-known author Lydia Maria Francis. Throughout their marriage, Lydia's writing provided most of the couple's income, whereas David devoted himself to fighting for social change and pursuing idealistic causes.

Soon after his marriage, Child turned his energy and idealism to abolition. He had met William Lloyd Garrison in 1828 while both were working on the campaign to re-elect President John Quincy Adams. In November 1830, Child wrote a column for the *Massachusetts Journal* defending Garrison, who had recently been jailed for libel. Child was one of the first to hear of Garrison's plans to publish *The Liberator,* and, late in life, Garrison would remember Child as one of his earliest supporters. The two men were not always in agreement, however; Child and his wife regularly exchanged opinions with Garrison through their writing, working out their philosophies on abolitionism in the process. The Childs eventually came to embrace Garrison's insistence on ending racial discrimination and immediate rather than gradual emancipation.

In the 1832, the two men, along with fourteen others, founded the New England Anti-Slavery Society in order to attract more supporters to the cause of abolition. Child published his first antislavery tract, *The Despotism of Freedom,* in 1833. In 1835, the members of the Massachusetts Anti-Slavery Society elected him vice president. The same year, Child agreed to help Quaker abolitionist Benjamin Lundy establish a free labor colony for freed slaves in Mexico; the colony never came to pass, however, as the Texas government claimed the land that the Mexican governor had given Lundy for the project.

Child set off on another idealistic project in 1836, hoping to alleviate the horrific conditions in which slaves on the Caribbean sugar plantations lived and worked by diminishing the tremendous demand for sugar from the region. He believed that free laborers in the North could produce sugar more economically from sugar beets than slaves could from sugarcane. He studied the cultivation and use of sugar beets for almost a year in Belgium and then purchased 100 acres in Northampton, Massachusetts, where he opened the first beet sugar farm and factory in the United States.

In 1841, Garrison asked the Childs to become co-editors of the *National Anti-Slavery Standard,* the official publication of the American Anti-Slavery Society in New York City. David remained in Northampton, tending the beet farm and sending in the occasional editorial, while his wife moved to New York to take over the paper. By the end of 1841, the farm and factory had failed.

David eventually joined Maria in New York and took over as editor of the *National Anti-Slavery Standard* in 1843. He resigned only a year later amid controversy over his support for the Whig Party, growing tensions among the abolitionist factions, and charges of mismanagement.

The couple moved to Wayland, Massachusetts, in 1852, where David farmed, practiced law, and continued to fight for abolition through his writing. The 1861 pamphlet *Rights and Duties of the United States Relative to Slavery Under the Laws of War* was his final publication. He died in Wayland on September 18, 1874.

Katherine L. Culkin

See also: American Anti-Slavery Society; Child, Lydia Maria Francis; Garrison, William Lloyd; Lundy, Benjamin; *National Anti-Slavery Standard.*

Further Reading

Clifford, Deborah Pickman. *Crusader for Freedom: A Life of Lydia Maria Child.* Boston: Beacon, 1992.
Karcher, Carolyn. *The First Woman in the Republic: A Cultural Biography of Lydia Maria Child.* Durham, NC: Duke University Press, 1994.
Meltzer, Milton, and Patricia G. Holland, eds. *Collected Correspondence of Lydia Maria Child, 1817–1880.* Millwood, NY: Kraus Microfilm, 1980.
———, eds. *Lydia Maria Child: Selected Letters, 1817–1880.* Amherst: University of Massachusetts Press, 1982.
Pease, Jane H., and William H. Pease. *Bound With Them in Chains: A Biographical Story of the Antislavery Movement.* Westport, CT: Greenwood, 1972.

Child, Lydia Maria Francis (1802–1880)

One of the most influential women in the American abolitionist movement, "Maria" Child used her talent as a brilliant essayist to advance the antislavery cause and to promote the rights of women. She blended these strands of reform when she edited Harriet Jacobs's memoir *Incidents in the Life of a Slave Girl* (1861), a powerful slave narrative that exposed the sexual exploitation of women who had been victimized within the institution of slavery.

Born in Medford, Massachusetts, on February 11, 1802, Lydia Maria Francis was raised in a household that esteemed the education of young girls, and she demonstrated her ability to write eloquently at an early age. At the age of twenty-two, she penned her first novel, *Hobomok* (1824), which examined the taboo subject of miscegenation (interracial sexual activity) and earned a reputation for its young author in New England literary circles. From 1826 to 1834, she gained acclaim as editor of the *Juvenile Miscellany,* one of the most popular children's magazines in nineteenth-century America.

Maria's marriage to Boston lawyer and abolitionist David Lee Child brought her into the center of the abolitionist movement, where she became a close personal friend of William Lloyd Garrison. Child's greatest literary productivity was associated with her antislavery nonfiction, which appeared after she became involved in the work of the American Anti-Slavery Society.

In 1833, she published *An Appeal in Favor of That Class of Americans Called Africans,* a work that demonstrated Child's abolitionist credentials, independent of her husband's reputation. Much of Child's literary outpouring reflected a growing awareness that the role of women in American society was not unlike that of the enslaved, and she dedicated her life to hastening the emancipation of both groups.

As one of the founding members of the Boston Female Anti-Slavery Society, Child worked tirelessly to attract more women to the antislavery cause. She maintained her prodigious writing career by publishing *Authentic Anecdotes of American Slavery* (1835), *The Evils of Slavery and the Cure of Slavery* (1836), and *Anti-Slavery Catechism* (1836). Few other abolitionist authors, male or female, amassed such an impressive record of antislavery publications.

During the early 1840s, Garrison recruited Maria and David Child to serve as co-editors of the *National*

Anti-Slavery Standard, the official journal of the American Anti-Slavery Society. Maria's influence on the *Standard* was particularly noticeable, as she incorporated contributions from some of the leading literary figures in the transatlantic world into the pages of the paper. In particular, she is credited with introducing American readers to the poetry of William Blake. In 1844, the Childs, differing with Garrison over matters of editorial control, both left the *Standard*.

Maria Child's passion for the antislavery movement and radical causes did not wane during the antebellum era. In the aftermath of John Brown's failed raid on Harpers Ferry in 1859, she requested permission of the Virginia authorities to tend to Brown's medical needs while he was awaiting trial in prison. In addition, Child raised money to support the families who had lost loved ones in the raid.

As the opening shots of the U.S. Civil War were being fired, Child began editing Jacobs's *Incidents in the Life of a Slave Girl*. Upon its publication, the scandalous nature of the subject matter made it clear to readers why slavery needed to be destroyed.

In the aftermath of the Civil War, Child worked to assist and educate freedmen in the South. She was present at the final meeting of the American Anti-Slavery Society in April 1870, when it decided to disband after the passage of the Fifteenth Amendment to the U.S. Constitution. Child died on July 7, 1880, in Wayland, Massachusetts.

Junius P. Rodriguez

See also: Child, David Lee; Garrison, William Lloyd; Jacobs, Harriet; Women's Rights and the Abolitionist Movement.

Further Reading

Baer, Helene G. "Mrs. Child and Miss Fuller." *New England Quarterly* 26 (June 1953): 249–55.

Karcher, Carolyn. "Censorship, American Style: The Case of Lydia Maria Child." *Studies in the American Renaissance* 9 (1986): 287–303.

———. *The First Woman in the Republic: A Cultural Biography of Lydia Maria Child.* Durham, NC: Duke University Press, 1994.

———. "Rape, Murder, and Revenge in 'Slavery's Pleasant Homes': Lydia Maria Child's Antislavery Fiction and the Limits of Genre." *Woman's Studies International Forum* 9 (1986): 323–32.

Meltzer, Milton, and Patricia G. Holland, eds. *Lydia Maria Child: Selected Letters, 1817–1880.* Amherst: University of Massachusetts Press, 1982.

Mills, Bruce. *Cultural Reformations: Lydia Maria Child and the Literature of Reform.* Athens: University of Georgia Press, 1994.

Church Missionary Society

Created as the missionary arm of the Church of England, the Church Missionary Society (CMS) played a significant role in efforts to Christianize Africans and prevent the re-emergence of slavery during the postemancipation and imperialist eras. Its missionary activity in West Africa gathered momentum during the early nineteenth century as it endeavored to repair the ills caused by centuries of European-led slave trade.

Missionaries redeemed slaves in the region by paying compensation to their owners, enrolled ex-slaves in mission schools, and equipped adults with economic skills. In addition, the missionaries provided homes for ex-slaves, clothed them, and guided them on the path to Christian conversion, with a larger goal of helping them gain self-sufficiency.

Early Years

The CMS, initially known as the Society for Missions to Africa and the East, was founded on April 12, 1799. Its first members comprised sixteen evangelical clergymen and nine laymen of the Church of England. The society recognized the importance of the laity in religious matters, emphasizing that laypersons should and must play a major role in the church's missionary endeavors. This group worked in collaboration with the Society for Promoting Christian Knowledge, founded in 1698, and the Society for the Propagation of the Gospel in Foreign Parts, founded in 1701, both of which had been established to work with British settlers overseas and the non-Christians among whom they lived.

During its early years, the activities of the CMS were informally directed by the society's secretary, who worked from his home. The society's public activities included an annual sermon and dismissal meeting, an event at which missionaries were commissioned for their work and sent into the field. Offerings were collected at these events and provided much of the society's income. Additional income came from special collections in Anglican churches, membership dues paid to the CMS, and membership dues paid by working people in the associated Church Missionary Associations.

At first, the CMS struggled to find lay missionaries who would carry out its work. English clergymen were not offering to act as missionaries for the CMS, so its first missionaries were two German Lutherans who served in South India. The first English-born lay missionaries for the CMS went to the field in 1809, and the first Anglican clergyman went to the field in 1815, the year the archbishop of Canterbury formally approved CMS. By 1813, fifteen missionaries had been sent by the CMS—twelve Germans to West Africa and three English laymen to New Zealand.

Beginning in 1824 with the establishment of the Church Missionary Institution, which would later become the Church Missionary College, missionary training took place in Britain. This activity was made possible by an act of Parliament in 1819 that made it legal to ordain men for overseas service. The number of missionaries sent by the CMS began to grow, as did the proportion of British missionaries compared to those from continental Europe.

The Reverend Josiah Pratt was the society's leader from its inception until his resignation in 1824. His successor, Henry Venn, who served as clerical secretary of the CMS from 1834 to 1873, provided strong leadership at a crucial time when the society's mission was being seriously questioned.

Venn believed that the CMS should be a voluntary society within the Church of England. He disagreed with the place of the episcopacy in the church's mission, and he strongly supported the idea that missionaries should preach the gospel and then move on to other locations, leaving behind indigenous leaders and pastors who could maintain self-sustaining churches. Venn's program of "Christianity, Civilization, and Commerce" involved conversion, education, industry, and self-sustaining communities; in particular, he advocated the introduction of new crops to replace the income lost with the end of the slave trade.

Later Years

During the mid-nineteenth century, the CMS gained recognition as the legitimate missionary arm of the Church of England. It also became known as a group representing the church's evangelical wing.

The CMS's fields of service included West Africa, New Zealand, India, Ceylon, Malta, Egypt, the West Indies, British Guiana, and Nigeria. West Africa—the area that would become Sierra Leone—was the focus of the society's first efforts. It was legally impossible for the British to enter India during the early nineteenth century, and because several CMS leaders were abolitionists who hoped to repatriate former slaves to Africa, work in West Africa made perfect sense. The earliest settlers in Sierra Leone

were freed slaves from Britain, Nova Scotia, and Jamaica.

Following Parliament's 1807 vote to abolish the slave trade, slaves rescued from illegal slave ships were brought to Freetown, the capital of Sierra Leone. These new settlers were uneducated, un-Christian, and unprepared for life in the colony. The town and its surrounding townships grew quickly, and the missionaries served not only as pastors but also as teachers and government administrators for the townships and the people in them.

Nigeria followed Sierra Leone as the CMS's next missionary field. The slave trade had removed thousands of people from their homes and placed them on ships. When these ships were intercepted by the British navy, the "recaptives," as they were called, were brought to Sierra Leone, where missionaries worked to teach the adults trades and to educate the children. The indigenous Africans eventually returned to their native homes, taking their new skills and the religion they had encountered with them.

Since its founding, the CMS has been at the forefront of pioneering mission work throughout the world. During its 200-year history, the CMS has attracted more than 9,000 men and women to serve as missionaries, boasting 150 mission partners in twenty-six countries in Africa, Asia, Europe, and the Middle East.

Mary J. Jarvis

See also: Sierra Leone.

Further Reading

Walls, Andrew F. *The Missionary Movement in Christian History: Studies in the Transmission of Faith.* Edinburgh, UK: T&T Clark, 1996.

——. *The Nineteenth Century Missionary Task and Continental Europe.* Cambridge, MA: North Atlantic Missiology Project, 1996.

Cinqué, Joseph (ca. 1815–ca. 1879)

Joseph Cinqué led an uprising aboard the Spanish slave vessel *Amistad* in 1839 in order to win his own freedom and that of fifty-three fellow West Africans who had been illegally traded as slaves. In 1841, the legal case involving the *Amistad* captives reached the U.S. Supreme Court, which ordered that the captives be set free and allowed to return to Africa.

Cinqué (also known as Sengbeh Pieh), a member of the Mende tribe in Sierra Leone, was kidnapped around the age of twenty-five. Cinqué was a rice planter who was married with two daughters and a son. At the time of his capture, he thought that he was being taken because he owed a debt. He was sold to a prince who, in turn, sold him to the Spaniards on Lomboko Island off the coast of Sierra Leone.

In 1839, Cinqué and the other Africans made the difficult journey from Africa to the Americas aboard the Spanish slaving vessel *Tecora*. During the voyage, one-third of the enslaved Africans died due to a lack of water. Although the slave trade had been made illegal under Spanish law, its practice persisted because of the lucrative profits that could be made transporting slaves to Cuba. When they arrived in Havana, the Africans were issued passports indicating that they were Cuban slaves born before 1820, the year the slave trade was outlawed by the Spanish. After being purchased by two Cuban plantation owners, Pedro Montes and José Ruiz, Cinqué and fifty-three others were placed on the *Amistad.*

Puerto Príncipe, Cuba, was the next stop for the Africans. Aboard the *Amistad,* they were treated poorly and given little food or water. Cinqué asked the cook, Celestino, what would become of them; Celestino led him to believe that they would be killed and eaten.

Cinqué told the others, and they developed a plan: Cinqué found a nail to pick the locks that chained them together. When the Africans rose in revolt, they killed the captain, who had slain one of the

JOSEPH CINQUEZ.
The brave Congolese Chief, who prefers death to Slavery, and who now lies in Jail in Irons at New Haven Conn. awaiting his trial for daring for freedom.

SPEECH TO HIS COMRADE SLAVES AFTER MURDERING THE CAPTAIN &C. AND GETTING POSSESSION OF THE VESSEL AND CARGO

"Brothers, we have done that which we purposed, our hands are now clean, for we have striven to regain the precious heritage we received from our fathers. We have only to persevere, Where the Sun rises there is our home, our brethren, our fathers. Do not seek to defeat my orders, if so I shall sacrifice any one who would endanger the rest, when at home we will kill the Old Man, the young one shall be saved he is kind and gave you bread, we must not kill those who give us water. Brothers, I am resolved that it is better to die than be a white man's slave, and I will not complain if by dying I save you. Let us be careful what we eat, that we may not be sick. The deed is done and I need say no more."

Joseph Cinqué, formerly Sengbeh Pieh of the Mende tribe of West Africa, led a historic slave revolt aboard the Spanish schooner *Amistad* in July 1839. This portrait was done while he awaited trial in New Haven, Connecticut. *(Library of Congress)*

Africans, as well as Celestino. The knife-welding Africans ordered Montes and Ruiz to take the ship back to Africa.

During the day, Montes and Ruiz sailed the *Amistad* slowly eastward, but at night, they sailed north toward the United States. They followed this routine for almost two months, during which time ten Africans died. Other ships saw the *Amistad* but were frightened by the sight of the armed men. When the ship ran out of supplies, a landing party went ashore at Long Island, New York, for supplements. In August 1839, the U.S. Coast Guard intercepted the *Amistad* and took it to New London, Connecticut, where slavery was still legal.

Whether the Africans were slaves was at issue in the United States. Technically, because they had been imported against Spanish law, upon arriving in Cuba, they should have been free automatically, but the false passports they had been issued in Cuba made this notion problematic.

American abolitionists came to Cinqué's assistance and sought to win the freedom of the captive Africans. Former president John Quincy Adams joined the legal defense team, arguing on behalf of the *Amistad* captives when the case reached the Supreme Court in February 1841. Ultimately, the Court freed the Africans, and it was decided that they would go back to Sierra Leone under the care of missionaries who had raised money for this endeavor. Cinqué believed the missionaries were there to assist him, whereas the missionaries believed that Cinqué would help them evangelize. Cinqué and his fellow Africans finally departed in November 1841 after spending two years in the United States.

When they arrived in Sierra Leone in January 1842, the missionaries faced a challenge: Although they established the Kaw Mende Mission, most of the Africans left to look for family members. A few stayed at the mission, including James Covey, who had served as a translator for the group while they were in the United States, and several African girls who had adopted Christian names.

When Cinqué returned to his home, he found that it, too, had fallen victim to the slave trade. His village had been burned, and his wife and children had likely been sold into slavery. Cinqué died sometime around 1879.

Denise Lovett

See also: Adams, John Quincy; *Amistad* Case (1841); Tappan, Lewis.

Further Reading

Cable, Mary. *Black Odyssey: The Case of the Slave Ship* Amistad. New York: Viking, 1971.

Jones, Howard. *Mutiny on the* Amistad*: The Saga of a Slave Revolt and Its Impact on American Abolition, Law, and Diplomacy.* New York: Oxford University Press, 1987.

McClendon, R. Earl. "The *Amistad* Claims: Inconsistencies of Policy." *Political Science Quarterly* 48 (September 1933): 386–412.

Osagie, Iyunolu F. *The* Amistad *Revolt: Memory, Slavery, and the Politics of Identity in the United States and Sierra Leone.* Athens: University of Georgia Press, 2000.

Civil Rights Act (1866)

The U.S. Congress passed the Civil Rights Act on March 16, 1866, granting the full rights of citizenship to African Americans in the aftermath of the U.S. Civil War and the Emancipation Proclamation. The measure was vetoed by President Andrew Johnson, who viewed it as an invasion of states' rights, but the U.S. Congress overrode his presidential veto on April 9.

The Civil Rights Act represented Congress's first attempt to define citizenship, and it was the first major law in U.S. history to be approved over a president's veto. As a consequence of Johnson's resistance to the measure, Congress passed the Fourteenth Amendment on June 13, 1866, and it was ratified by the states in 1868. Historians have suggested that the Fourteenth Amendment was a direct response to Johnson's negative reaction to the Civil Rights Act; both measures aimed to define the rights of persons born in or naturalized as citizens of the United States.

The Civil Rights Act was intended to prevent President Johnson and former Confederates in the South from continuing slavery-like practices under the Black Codes. The act remains important today—it has been amended several times throughout the years—because it prohibits racial discrimination in employment and the sale and renting of housing. The Civil Rights Act of 1866 was the first legislative attempt to ensure that African Americans had equal political and legal status, as was subsequent legislation in the Civil Rights Acts of 1870, 1871, and 1875.

When the Civil War ended in 1865 and slavery was abolished by the Thirteenth Amendment, the Southern states were so bitter over their defeat and the new legislation that they began passing state laws that restricted the rights of African Americans, hoping to regain control of the freedmen. These regulations, which became known as Black Codes, excluded

African Americans from many occupations, denied them the right to vote, and, in some places, forbade them to appear in any role except that of a servant. Some state codes went even further; Mississippi, for example, prohibited interracial marriage and imposed a penalty of death as punishment. Another state code restricted the area in which black people could live—for example, they could not own or rent land outside an incorporated town. The purpose of the Black Codes was to undermine the federal government's efforts to provide full citizenship to former slaves.

The enactment of the Black Codes and other such measures angered the Northern-allied Radical Republicans in Congress who had taken political power after the Civil War. The transition brought many legislative changes during the Reconstruction years, as Congress was led by individuals such as Senator Charles Sumner (R-MA) and Representative Thaddeus Stevens (R-PA), who first passed legislation to establish the Freedmen's Bureau. Despite President Johnson's efforts to stop legislation that would assist African Americans, Congress advanced several significant bills that proved advantageous to the former slaves.

With the installation of martial law in the South, which was eventually countered by the Ku Klux Klan, Congress enjoyed immense power. The rebellious states could not vote on measures that appeared before Congress, and there were enough votes to override President Johnson's vetoes. It was against this backdrop that Congress passed the Civil Rights Act of 1866. In effect, it mandated that the former slaves had the same rights enjoyed by white citizens.

All of the Southern states, except Tennessee, refused to ratify the Fourteenth Amendment. Congress passed the First Reconstruction Act on March 2, 1867, prohibiting the Southern states from participating in Congress until they passed the measure and revised their own state constitutions.

The passage of the Fourteenth Amendment and the First Reconstruction Act met with violent opposition as whites rioted in the streets. Despite the presence of the U.S. military to control white protestors, African Americans were beaten, burned, and lynched by the hundreds.

Fred Lindsey

See also: Amendments, Reconstruction.

Further Reading

Hyman, Harold Melvin. *The Radical Republicans and Reconstruction, 1861–1870.* Indianapolis, IN: Bobbs-Merrill, 1967.

Lindsey, Howard O. *A History of Black America.* Secaucus, NJ: Chartwell, 1994.

McKissack, Patricia, and Frederick McKissack. *The Civil Rights Movement in America: From 1865 to the Present.* 2nd ed. Chicago: Children's, 1991.

Civil War, American (1861–1865)

The abolition of slavery in the United States and the emancipation of nearly 4 million enslaved people was the most significant outcome of the U.S. Civil War, which lasted from 1861 to 1865. Although slavery was not the only matter at issue in the conflict, it was the *central* cause, and after President Abraham Lincoln issued the Emancipation Proclamation in 1863, the abolition of slavery became the chief objective of the war. In the history of slavery, the United States stands alone as the only nation that effected the abolition of slavery through civil war.

Seeds of Division

Although antebellum politicians such as New York senator William H. Seward described the war as "an irrepressible conflict," the war's roots can be traced to a series of deliberate policy choices made from the mid-1840s onward that polarized Americans' attitudes toward slavery. The nation had managed to suppress the divisive issue through legislative compromise throughout much of its early history, but the acquisition of vast territories in the Southwest after the Mexican-American War (1846–1848) and the vexing question of whether slavery should be allowed to extend into these territories made further compromise unlikely.

The political impasse was largely the result of increasingly vociferous discourse that began in the 1830s and grew more strident with time. Northern abolitionists, as represented by William Lloyd Garrison, criticized the U.S. Constitution for its support of slavery and suggested disunion as a viable alternative to the morally reprehensible act of remaining in a country that condoned slavery. Southern politicians and orators, such as William Lowndes Yancey, fashioned a proslavery ideology to counter the charges raised by the abolitionists. Whereas one group saw slavery as a sin, the other charged that it was a morally uplifting practice that benefited the slave.

Garrison's beliefs, which constituted a form of Christian anarchy, discouraged abolitionists from voting and from trying to effect a political solution to the slavery question. Those who supported this belief

After the Emancipation Proclamation on January 1, 1863, some 180,000 black troops joined the Union army. They served in all-black, segregated units such as the Fourth U.S. Colored Infantry; Company E was photographed at Fort Lincoln in Washington, D.C. *(Library of Congress)*

did not think that the same Constitution that protected slavery could be used to abolish the practice. Other more politically minded abolitionists who disagreed with Garrison formed political associations such as the Liberty Party and the Free Soil Party, which were associated with varieties of antislavery ideology. Although these movements were short lived and attracted little popular support, the formation of the Republican Party in 1854 marked the creation of a decidedly antislavery political party that had mass appeal among a large segment of the populace.

The election of Republican candidate Abraham Lincoln to the presidency in November 1860 set in motion the secession of seven Southern states. Believing that Lincoln and the Republicans were planning to destroy slavery, South Carolina and six other slaveholding states voted to leave the Union and form the Confederate States of America (commonly known as the Confederacy). In February 1861, the seceded states sent delegates to Montgomery, Alabama, where they created a constitution that enshrined the principle of states' rights over federal interference and selected Jefferson Davis as president of the Confederacy.

The War Begins

Lincoln stood firmly against the notion of disunion as he delivered his first inaugural address on March 4, 1861. He made it clear that reconciliation was still possible and that armed conflict was not a forgone conclusion, but he demanded that the Southern states rescind their ordinances of secession and work with their sister states to effect a political solution to the crisis at hand.

Although a group of senators worked to arrange a compromise that would protect slavery where it existed and preserve the Union, all efforts to find a negotiated settlement failed to achieve their desired objective. On April 12, 1861, Confederate forces opened fire on Fort Sumter, a federal garrison located in Charleston, South Carolina. The war had begun.

Abraham Lincoln immediately issued a call for 75,000 military volunteers to serve for ninety days, the limited time that many imagined would be required to whip the Rebel forces and bring an end to the secession crisis. Northern forces responded to Lincoln's call in patriotic fashion. At the same time, Southern volunteers flocked to the Confederate banner to defend their homeland and the "Southern way of life" from the threat of Northern aggression. Both sides believed that one decisive battle in what was expected to be a short war would settle the issue to their liking, but both sides were mistaken.

The earliest battles and campaigns of the war did not turn out as the federal forces had imagined, and the Confederates were emboldened by their early victories. Lincoln struggled to find a competent general to command the Union forces who would not be timid in the heat of battle. His failure to find such a commander during the early stages of the war, however, led many Northerners and some fellow Republicans to criticize the president as an ineffectual commander in chief.

Despite the growing chorus of criticism, Lincoln remained focused on the goal of preserving the Union. He was confident that the United States possessed more men and material than the Southern Confederacy could muster. In a war of attrition, the tide would eventually turn in the favor of Union forces.

Wartime Slaves and Emancipation

Neither side gave sufficient consideration to the impact that an extended war would have on the South's 4 million slaves. When federal forces entered Missouri in 1861, they immediately encountered hundreds of slaves who had escaped and made their way to the Union lines, where they sought refuge as free people.

No existing military protocol outlined procedures to be followed in such a case, so military commanders often made decisions in the field that were at odds with Lincoln's views. When General John Charles Frémont issued a field order emancipating the slaves in Missouri, Lincoln promptly rescinded the measure and removed the general from his post.

In similar fashion, the Confederate Congress soon realized that the peace and security of the South's large plantations would be endangered if slaveholders left the region en masse to join the war effort. Accordingly, the Confederate Congress enacted a measure exempting anyone who owned twenty or more slaves

from military duty. Later in the war, the measure was amended to reduce the number of slaves to ten.

The Union forces were able to clarify their position on the emancipation of slaves in the field after the U.S. Congress enacted two Confiscation Acts in 1861 and 1862, permitting the liberation of slaves who were viewed as military assets to the Confederate war-making effort. Many of the slaves liberated as "contraband of war" were employed by Union forces to assist the troops in a support capacity. Federal policy at the time did not permit the use of black troops.

As the war dragged on and the Union forces failed to achieve the decisive victory that would end the conflict, Northern morale began to decline, and the number of volunteers dropped precipitously. Lincoln was aware that asking troops to fight and possibly die for the abstract cause of a constitutional principle in order to preserve the Union was becoming difficult to promote. Federal forces had to resort to a military draft to keep the Union army filled with fresh recruits, and this practice was becoming increasingly unpopular in the North. Lincoln awaited an opportune moment to announce an executive proclamation that would redefine the war's primary aim and attract a heretofore untapped supply of fresh troops.

In issuing the Emancipation Proclamation on January 1, 1863, Lincoln transformed the Civil War into a moral crusade designed to produce a "new birth of freedom." By refocusing the war on the cause of righteousness, he aimed to revitalize the efforts of the republic.

In addition, Lincoln's decision to begin using black troops in the U.S. armed forces provided a tremendous supply of new recruits who would soon swell the ranks of the federal forces. By the end of the war, some 180,000 black troops would be employed in the military services. Their ability to fight for the emancipation of the slaves provided a tremendous demonstration of courage and valor for a noble cause.

Eventual Success

In summer 1863, the military turning point that Lincoln had been awaiting finally came. After an extended siege, federal forces were able to capture the fortified city of Vicksburg, Mississippi, which had been known as the "Gibraltar of the South." In the greatest battle of the war, the Union army repulsed efforts by Confederate General Robert E. Lee to take the war to the North as federal forces prevailed in the Battle of Gettysburg. From this point onward, the war of attrition was at work, and the inexorable outcome of Union victory was considered certain.

Although he was still fighting a war against a formidable enemy, Lincoln began to give some thought to the postwar settlement as early as 1864, when he began to formulate plans for the restoration of the Southern states and the incorporation of the emancipated freedmen into American national life. The preliminary battles that Lincoln fought with the U.S. Congress in 1864 over the management of postwar policy foreshadowed events that would transpire later during the Reconstruction era.

Confederate General Lee surrendered to U.S. General Ulysses S. Grant at Appomattox, Virginia, on April 9, 1865, marking the end of the bloody conflict. Some 620,000 casualties represented the physical costs of the Civil War, but they did not reflect the total cost of the war.

Many soldiers returned home with bodies badly broken in battle, and many carried deep psychic injuries. Because most of the fighting had taken place in the Southern states, the destruction of facilities and the region's commercial infrastructure was devastating, and it would take years to rebuild. Most notably, the war did not bring an end to the animosity that had existed between the North and the South during the conflict; instead, it simmered as subsequent generations sustained regional antagonisms.

For the 4 million emancipated slaves, the end of the Civil War marked a new beginning as freedmen, but the transition from slave labor to free labor would be difficult. Many of the civil liberties that had been promised with the coming of emancipation did not materialize, as new barriers took shape in the postwar South, denying true liberty to the freedmen. The protection of federal troops during the Reconstruction era helped freedmen obtain some of the rights guaranteed by new constitutional amendments and federal civil rights laws, but these liberties were largely lost after 1877, when the last federal troops left the South at the end of Reconstruction.

Junius P. Rodriguez

See also: Amendments, Reconstruction; Confiscation Acts (1861, 1862); Emancipation Proclamation (1863); Lincoln, Abraham; Massachusetts Fifty-Fourth Regiment.

Further Reading

Gerteis, Louis S. *From Contraband to Freedman: Federal Policy Toward Southern Blacks, 1861–1865.* Westport, CT: Greenwood, 1973.

Glatthaar, Joseph T. *Forged in Battle: The Civil War Alliance of Black Soldiers and White Officers.* New York: Free Press, 1990; Baton Rouge: Louisiana State University Press, 2000.

Potter, David Morris. *The Impending Crisis, 1848–1861.* Comp. and ed. Don E. Fehrenbacher. New York: Harper & Row, 1976.

Quarles, Benjamin. *The Negro in the Civil War.* Boston: Little, Brown, 1953.

Vorenberg, Michael. *Final Freedom: The Civil War, the Abolition of Slavery, and the Thirteenth Amendment.* Cambridge, UK: Cambridge University Press, 2001.

Clarke, Lewis G. (1815–1897)

Lewis G. Clarke was a Kentucky slave who escaped in 1841 and later became a frequent and popular lecturer on the abolitionist circuit in the United States. Editions of his autobiography were published in both the United States and Great Britain. The American writer Harriet Beecher Stowe, after meeting Clarke and hearing his personal narrative, is said to have modeled the character of George Harris in her antislavery novel *Uncle Tom's Cabin* (1852) after him.

In the language of his times, Clarke was considered a "quadroon" (the offspring of a white person and a mulatto). His father was a Scottish weaver who had fought for the American cause at Bunker Hill, and his mother, Letitia Campbell, was a mulatto slave, the daughter of her master. Despite his mixed parentage, Clarke was treated no differently than other Kentucky slaves, as the legal status of the child customarily followed that of the mother. For the first years of his life, Clarke's world was defined by the Madison County tobacco plantation of William Campbell, where he labored; his circle of acquaintances was largely confined to the slave quarters in which he lived.

Campbell transferred ownership of the young slave to his sister, Betsy Branton, when Clarke was only about seven years old. He was severely punished by Branton, whom Clarke believed had special animosity toward him because of his mixed ethnicity. After Clarke had proven himself a trusted slave, his new owner permitted him to hire himself out for odd jobs in the surrounding community, as long as he shared the bulk of his earnings with her. By earning income that he could keep and by working beyond the confines of the plantation, Clarke's world—and his options—began to expand.

Clarke's mother had been promised that she and her children would be manumitted when her husband died, but local authorities reneged on this agreement. Instead, Letitia and her nine children remained slaves. In August 1841, Clarke heard a rumor that he was going to be sold "down the river" to New Orleans so he escaped through Ohio (from Cincinnati up the river to Portsmouth, then by canal to Cleveland). From Cleveland, he crossed Lake Erie by steamer to reach freedom in Upper Canada (modern-day Ontario). Being very light skinned, Clarke was able to pass for a white man, and this made his escape somewhat easier. Clarke would later return to Kentucky to help three of his brothers escape.

After escaping from slavery, brothers Lewis and Milton Clarke told the story of their experiences to the abolitionist sympathizer J.C. Lovejoy, who published the tale as *Narratives of the Sufferings of Lewis and Milton Clarke, Sons of a Soldier of the Revolution, During a Captivity of More Than Twenty Years Among the Slaveholders of Kentucky, One of the So Called Christian States of North America* (1846). Clarke's story was initially published in Great Britain under the title *Interesting Memoirs and Documents Relating to American Slavery and the Glorious Struggle Now Making for Complete Emancipation* (1846).

Clarke noted the inhumanity inherent in slavery, writing that there existed "little more scruple about separating families than there is with a man who keeps sheep in selling off the lambs in the fall." He went on to note that in his twenty-six years of slavery, he had never met a single slave family who had not experienced the pain of separation through sale at the auction block. Despite these hardships, Clarke acknowledged that he considered Kentucky his home. He wrote, "people are very much afraid all the slaves will run up North . . . But I can assure them that they will run *back* again if they do. If I could have been assured of my freedom in Kentucky, then, I would have given anything in the world for the prospect of spending my life among my old acquaintances, and where I first saw the sky, and the sun rise and go down."

Clarke became a popular abolitionist speaker who attracted large audiences to hear his remarkable story. He became acquainted with many of the leading antislavery advocates of his day, and he married a daughter of William Storum, a prominent New York abolitionist. On September 30, 1851, Clarke narrowly avoided capture when a band of slave catchers, emboldened by the new Fugitive Slave Law (1850), descended on the Storum farmstead in Chautauqua County, New York.

Clarke received a special tribute at the time of his death in 1897. Kentucky governor William

O. Bradley ordered that his body lie in state in Frankfort's city auditorium so that citizens could pay their respects. His body was later taken for burial to Oberlin College in Ohio, where he had been a frequent lecturer. Carved onto Clarke's headstone is the inscription "The Original George Harris of Harriet Beecher Stowe's Book, *Uncle Tom's Cabin.*"

Junius P. Rodriguez

See also: Stowe, Harriet Beecher; *Uncle Tom's Cabin* (1852).

Further Reading

Logan, Rayford W., and Michael R. Winston, eds. *Dictionary of American Negro Biography.* New York: W.W. Norton, 1982.

Clarkson, John (1764–1828)

In 1792, the British naval lieutenant and abolitionist John Clarkson led a contingent of free blacks from Nova Scotia and New Brunswick in Canada to found the Sierra Leone colony in West Africa. As the colony's governor, he initiated a framework of governance that established precedents for peaceful relations with Africans and introduced efficient administration and the seeds of participatory government.

Born in Wisbech, Cambridgeshire, he was the younger brother of Thomas Clarkson, whose abolitionist career overshadowed John throughout his life. At the age of eleven, he joined the British navy, serving in the Caribbean during the American Revolution. After six years, he returned to Britain but failed to obtain a new commission. Meanwhile, the time he had spent in the West Indies had raised his consciousness about the evils of slavery and the usefulness of a military career.

Back in Britain during the late 1780s, Clarkson began to take part in abolitionist activities as secretary to his brother and confidant to William Wilberforce, a member of the House of Commons who was leading the parliamentary fight for the abolition of the slave trade. Clarkson joined the Abolition Society and helped establish the Sierra Leone Company, a commercial endeavor that aimed to resuscitate the colony of free black settlers and develop trade with West Africa.

Although the original settlement in Sierra Leone had been destroyed, prospects for its revival brightened in 1791, when Thomas Peters arrived in London to present a petition from 200 black Nova Scotians who wanted to settle in the West African colony. Originally slaves in the Southern American colonies, they had fought with the British army against the revolutionaries in exchange for their freedom and the promise of land. This promise was only partially kept, and they now complained of discrimination and new types of servitude in Canada. They dreamed of autonomy and freedom in Africa.

Clarkson volunteered to accompany Peters to Nova Scotia to recruit colonists for Sierra Leone and to prepare for their journey to West Africa. He spent four months in Nova Scotia in 1791, promoting the venture and organizing a fleet for the crossing. Whereas many abolitionists did not translate their intellectual beliefs into everyday behavior, Clarkson was not racist or patronizing in his treatment of others. He empathized with the deplorable conditions of the black community in Canada and with their grievances. Attracted by Clarkson's ebullient optimism and eloquence, many more black Nova Scotians signed up as colonists than expected.

Clarkson supervised every aspect of the planning—refitting the ships, finalizing the contracts, procuring the provisions, and drawing up instructions for the treatment of passengers. Just as the ships were about to leave, he fell ill from exhaustion and had to be carried on board. Finally, on January 15, 1792, a small convoy of fifteen ships set sail for Sierra Leone with 1,190 passengers on board. Although the voyage was relatively harmonious, illness was widespread and sixty-seven people died. Clarkson himself nearly died.

The settlers landed in Sierra Leone in March 1792, but they were dismayed to find that no preparations had been made for them. Instead of food and building materials, the company had sent industrial machines and trade goods—a signal of its priorities. They lost no time in unpacking their axes and beginning to cut trees. They organized makeshift housing of tents and huts and discovered what local crops were available.

Meanwhile, Clarkson learned that the company-appointed superintendent had resigned and that he had been designated as the replacement. A few months later, he was promoted to become the first governor of the new colony. He instituted a government of conciliation, combining idealism and pragmatism with genuine respect for the black settlers and the indigenous inhabitants. Despite his approachability, he found it difficult to meet Nova Scotian expectations for the new land of freedom and equity.

Because of the shortage of supplies and expertise, initial conditions were harsh. Sickness broke out among the settlers, resulting in a 14 percent loss of their population. Disputes soon arose among Clarkson, the Eu-

ropean employees of the company, and the Nova Scotian lieutenants over corruption and the slowness of land distribution. Although his efforts to mediate were not wholly successful, the settlers tempered their opposition in the interest of political harmony.

Clarkson's health continued to decline, and, in December 1792, eight months after his arrival in Africa, he was invalided to England. He arrived in England early in February 1793, just as war was declared with France. His reception was unexpectedly unfriendly. More interested in commercial success than altruism, the company directors, who had received several adverse reports from colonial employees (including Zachary Macaulay), publicly snubbed him. Within a short time, they dismissed him.

Undaunted by adversity, he retained his optimistic outlook on life and prospered in a series of business ventures. Shortly after his return, he married Susan Lee and settled in Essex. By now, his abolitionist ideas had led him to embrace pacifism. In 1793, he turned down the command of a ship on the grounds that he did not believe in war. Two years later, he resigned from the navy. In 1816, Clarkson joined William Allen and Joseph Price to found the Society for the Promotion of Permanent and Universal Peace, and he served as its treasurer until 1820.

Until his death on April 9, 1828, he continued to take an interest in West Africa, keeping up a correspondence with Sierra Leoneans and sometimes representing their interests to the British government. Sierra Leoneans remember Clarkson as the colony's most beloved governor, and many still adorn their walls with a framed copy of the prayer he said upon his departure.

LaRay Denzer

See also: Macaulay, Zachary; Sierra Leone.

Further Reading

Fyfe, Christopher. *A History of Sierra Leone.* New York: Oxford University Press, 1962.

Haliburton, Gordon McKay. "The Nova Scotia Settlers of 1792." *Sierra Leone Studies* NS:9 (1957): 16–25.

Wilson, Ellen Gibson. *John Clarkson and the African Adventure.* London: Macmillan, 1980.

Clarkson, Thomas (1760–1846)

Thomas Clarkson was the ideologue of the British antislavery movement who mustered the moral energy of the nation to oppose the trade in human flesh.

Born in Wisbech, Cambridgeshire, on March 28, 1760, he was the son of the Reverend John Clarkson, headmaster of the local grammar school. He was educated at Saint John's College at Cambridge University, where he received his bachelor's degree and was ordained as a deacon in 1785. In his final year as an undergraduate, Clarkson won first prize in an essay competition on the topic *anne liceat invitos in servitutem dare?* (Is it right to make men slaves against their will?). The topic soon dominated his intellectual curiosity.

At the time, the most important treatise against slavery in North America and Europe was Anthony Benezet's *Some Historical Account of Guinea* (1772), which emphasized the physical torment and suffering endured by the slaves on the African coast and at sea but provided little evidence about the scope of the trade and Britain's involvement in it. Once Clarkson had exhausted the published materials, he felt that more information was necessary, so he sought interviews with individuals who had personal experiences of slavery and the slave trade, an early instance of the use of oral research methodology in African history. Required to write his essay in Latin, he translated it into English, and, in 1786, used his prize money to publish it under the title *An Essay on the Slavery and Commerce of the Human Species, Particularly the African, Translated From a Latin Dissertation, Which Was Honoured With the First Prize in the University of Cambridge, for the Year 1785*. His goal was to raise general awareness about the evils of the slave trade.

Clarkson's *Essay* struck a responsive chord among the members of a small but growing network of intellectuals who believed that slavery went against English philosopher John Locke's social contract and the tenets of Christianity. It became instantly influential and soon brought him into contact with others who were campaigning against the slave trade. In May 1787, he joined forces with the veteran abolitionist Granville Sharp and others to establish the Society for the Abolition of the Slave Trade. Of the society's twelve members, nine were from the Society of Friends (Quakers), a religious society that promoted the idea of freedom for all humankind. Among the influential figures who supported the society's work were John Wesley, cofounder of the Wesleyan Methodist denomination, and Josiah Wedgwood, the famous pottery manufacturer. Later, the group persuaded William Wilberforce, the popular Member of Parliament for Hull, to be their spokesperson in the House of Commons.

An early advocate of the abolition of the British slave trade, Thomas Clarkson exerted his greatest influence as an essayist, pamphleteer, and itinerant spokesman during the 1780s and 1790s. *(Hulton Archive/Getty Images)*

The Abolition Society decided that the most effective campaign strategy was first to target the slave trade before tackling the institution of slavery itself. It soon realized, however, that it needed more information about the organization and scale of the slave trade and its effect on British society and economy. To remedy this, Clarkson undertook the task of collecting this information and preparing it for publication. Building on his undergraduate experience, he traveled all over England, visiting the major ports, particularly Bristol and Liverpool, and seeking eyewitness accounts of the facts and horrors of the slave trade. He interviewed hundreds of sailors and obtained samples of the equipment used on the slave ships, including branding irons, iron handcuffs, leg shackles, thumbscrews, and instruments for forcing open slave's jaws for forced feeding.

In gathering this material, he risked great danger, as his activities threatened the slavers, who sometimes hired men in the ports to harass him and discourage informants from talking to him. On one occasion, he narrowly escaped assassination. Undaunted, he amassed a voluminous amount of evidence, which he used to write his *Summary View of the Slave Trade, and the Probable Consequences of Its Abolition.* Published in 1787, it provided the ammunition needed to mobilize sympathetic parliamentarians, clergy, and members of the public against the slave trade.

From 1787 to 1794, Clarkson worked tirelessly to further the cause of abolition. He continued to collect evidence for the Abolition Society and its allies in Parliament to use in passing legislation to outlaw the trade. In February 1788, a committee of the Privy Council convened to take evidence on the state of the African trade. While Wilberforce organized the campaign in Parliament, Clarkson continued to produce new evidence, which Wilberforce used effectively in parliamentary debates. Notable politicians who were won over to the abolitionist cause included William Pitt, Thomas Grenville, Charles James Fox, and Edmund Burke. Although it was difficult to persuade eyewitnesses to appear before a commission of enquiry by the Privy Council, eventually Wilberforce and the Abolition Society marshaled enough credible witnesses to initiate a parliamentary debate against the slave trade in May 1787.

Political events in France, which culminated in revolution, turned Clarkson's attention to the Continent. In autumn 1789, he made an unsuccessful trip to Paris in an attempt to persuade the new government of France to abolish the slave trade. His letters to Comte de Mirabeau (Honoré-Gabriel Riqueti), a proponent of constitutional monarchy during the chaotic period before the revolutionary forces brought down King Louis XVI, emphasized that the revolutionary ideals of *liberté, égalité,* and *fraternité* meant nothing if they were not extended to the slaves.

After his return to London early in 1790, Clarkson redoubled his propaganda efforts, continuously traveling across Britain for several years. This hectic schedule affected his health, and, in July 1794, he suffered a physical breakdown that forced him to withdraw from the abolitionist campaign. In the meantime, the parliamentary campaign was not going well, and public interest in abolition declined.

Because the British elite feared the possibility of revolution at home, interest in the abolitionist campaign ceased in the 1790s, and it would not be revived until the turn of the century. In 1803, Clarkson rejoined the Abolition Society, which launched a vigorous new campaign against the slave trade the following year. Once again, Clarkson and Wilberforce worked as a team; Clarkson gathered evidence around the country, while Wilberforce renewed his campaign to introduce the abolition bill to Parliament. Finally, after two defeats, the bill was passed by the new Whig government in February 1807.

Clarkson was recognized as a national figure in the abolitionist movement and a model of philanthropy. In 1808, he published the comprehensive *History of the Rise, Progress and Accomplishment of the Abolition of the African Slave-Trade.* Since its publication, this work has been a significant source of information about the abolitionist campaign, although some scholars contend that Clarkson exaggerated his role, for he did not take part in the movement between 1794 and 1803.

The abolition of the slave trade raised new problems. Clarkson doubted the effectiveness of the measures enacted to end the slave trade. In 1807, he joined with Thomas Fowell Buxton to establish the Society for the Mitigation and Gradual Abolition of Slavery throughout the British Dominions, initiating the second phase of abolition, which sought to eradicate the institution of slavery itself. This campaign was waged for another twenty-five years, until 1833, when Parliament passed the Abolition of Slavery Act (commonly known as the British Emancipation Act), emancipating all of the slaves in the British Empire.

Slavery still continued to thrive in the United States, other European empires, Latin America, and Africa. In 1839, Clarkson became a founding member of the British and Foreign Anti-Slavery Society, which sought to extend the abolition campaign to the rest of the world.

Within a few years, Clarkson retired to Ipswich, Suffolk, where he died on September 26, 1846. On the 150th anniversary of his death, September 26, 1996, a monument to Clarkson and seven other abolitionists was unveiled at Westminster Abbey in recognition of their great service to humanity.

LaRay Denzer

See also: Buxton, Thomas Fowell; Wilberforce, William.

Further Reading

Clarkson, Thomas. *History of the Rise, Progress, and Accomplishment of the Abolition of the African Slave-Trade by the British Parliament.* 2 vols. 1808. London: Frank Cass, 1968.

Griggs, Earl Leslie. *Thomas Clarkson, the Friend of Slaves.* 1936. Westport, CT: Negro Universities Press, 1970.

Wilson, Ellen Gibson. *Thomas Clarkson: A Biography.* 2nd ed. New York: William Sessions, 1996.

Clay, Cassius Marcellus (1810–1903)

The American politician Cassius Marcellus Clay, who earned the sobriquet "the Lion of Whitehall" for his passionate denouncement of slavery and fierce oratory style, was a prominent abolitionist in his home state of Kentucky. Inspired by the radical antislavery mind-set of William Lloyd Garrison, editor of the abolitionist newspaper *The Liberator*, Clay launched his own efforts to emancipate African Americans while serving in Kentucky's state legislature. He published the antislavery newspaper the *True American* in 1845, penned numerous antislavery editorials and speeches, and is credited with encouraging President Abraham Lincoln to sign the 1863 Emancipation Proclamation, which freed all slaves in the United States.

Clay entered the world a child of privilege. Born to Green and Sallie Lewis Clay on October 19, 1810, at the family estate of Whitehall, Clay's family was antebellum Kentucky aristocracy. His father, General Green Clay, had served in the War of 1812 and helped found the town of Richmond, Kentucky. As wealthy slave owners in Madison County, Kentucky, the Clays were related to the illustrious Senator Henry Clay and became one of the most prominent families in the area.

Clay attended local schools including Madison Seminary, and he also studied under the supervision of a private tutor. In 1827, he enrolled in the Jesuit College of Saint Joseph in Bardstown, Kentucky, and later attended Transylvania University in Lexington, the state's oldest educational institution. In 1831, he entered Yale College in New Haven, Connecticut.

While a student at Yale, Clay heard a speech given by Garrison, whose impassioned plea for the destruction of slavery inspired Clay to become an abolitionist himself. As a Southerner and the son of a slave-owning family, as well as a new convert to the antislavery cause, he embarked on a controversial and dangerous phase of his life.

When Clay returned to Kentucky, he completed his law degree at Transylvania University and became active in local politics. In 1835, he successfully ran for a seat in the Kentucky legislature representing Madison County. During his term, he took every opportunity to criticize the institution of slavery. His outspoken nature and vehement temper led to his defeat in the next election, but, in 1837, he again won a legislative seat.

As a Whig, Clay infuriated the proslavery element of the party. His quick wit and sharp tongue made him a number of enemies. At times, his political and philosophical arguments provoked violence. In 1841, for example, he fought a duel with fellow Kentuckian Robert Wickliffe over the issue of slavery. Two years later, while attending a debate near Lexington, Clay was attacked by Samuel Brown, a paid assassin from New Orleans.

Although Clay decried slavery as an immoral practice, he did not free his own slaves until 1841. In 1845, he began publishing in Lexington an antislavery newspaper called the *True American*, which favored gradual emancipation. The first issue appeared on June 3 and proclaimed its motto, "God and Liberty." In the columns of his paper, Clay taunted not only slave owners but their families as well. He admonished the wives and daughters of slaveholders to "put their slaves away . . . if you want a drink go to the pump or the spring to get it; if you want to bathe, prepare your own bath."

Clay knew that many people in the community would be outraged by his words. To prepare for a possible attack on the office of the *True American,* he had the building's windows and doors sheathed in metal. He placed two small brass cannons at the entrance to the office and had the building rigged with enough gunpowder to blow it—and any intruders—to pieces. Some Lexington citizens began to refer to Clay as the "autocrat from hell."

In August 1845, while Clay lay ill from typhoid fever, a delegation of proslavery advocates led by James B. Clay, the son of Henry Clay, entered the newspaper office, dismantled the printing equipment, and shipped it to Cincinnati. Clay quickly relocated his newspaper, resuming publication thereafter from Cincinnati as the *Examiner.*

Clay remained one of the most outspoken men of his time. He campaigned for Henry Clay in the presidential election of 1844. When the Democrats elected James K. Polk, Clay blamed the extremists in the abolitionist movement for his cousin's defeat.

Clay served as a captain in the Mexican-American War and continued to agitate against slavery. In 1854, he aided abolitionist John Gregg Fee in establishing a racially mixed settlement and school at Berea in Madison County. Clay became active in the newly formed Republican Party, and, in 1860, he was mentioned as a possible presidential candidate. Instead of pursuing his own political career, however, he supported the successful candidacy of Abraham Lincoln.

The grateful Lincoln appointed Clay as minister to Russia, a post he held until 1869.

When he returned to America in 1869, Clay became a leading force in the liberal wing of the Republican Party. He worked for the nomination of Horace Greeley for president on a liberal ticket. However, Clay became disenchanted with the Radical Republicans and switched his political allegiance to the Democratic Party.

Throughout the rest of his life, Clay remained a controversial character. His marriage, already strained by long absences from home, came to an end when he asked for a divorce from his wife of more than forty years. While in Russia, he had fathered a son and saw no reason not to claim the child as his own. Mrs. Clay did not contest the divorce.

Controversy continued to surround Clay as he became more and more eccentric with age. He died at the age of ninety-three on July 2, 1903, and is buried in Richmond.

Ron D. Bryant

See also: Garrison, William Lloyd.

Further Reading

Carl'ee, Roberta Baughman. *The Last Gladiator: Cassius M. Clay.* Berea, KY: Kentucke Imprints, 1979.

Harrison, Lowell H. "The Anti-Slavery Career of Cassius M. Clay." *Register of the Kentucky Historical Society* 59 (October 1961): 259–317.

Harrold, Stanley C., Jr. "Cassius M. Clay on Slavery and Race: A Reinterpretation." *Slavery and Abolition* 9 (May 1988): 42–56.

McQueen, Keven. *Cassius M. Clay: Freedom's Champion.* Paducah, KY: Turner, 2001.

Sears, Richard D. *The Kentucky Abolitionist in the Midst of Slavery 1854–1864: Exiles for Freedom.* Lewiston, NY: Edwin Mellen, 1993.

Coffin, Levi (1798–1877)

The reputed "president" of the Underground Railroad—an elaborate network of safe houses that hid and assisted fugitive slaves as they made their way North to freedom—the Quaker merchant and abolitionist Levi Coffin helped more than 3,000 runaway slaves escape from bondage during his lifetime.

Coffin was born on October 28, 1798, in New Garden, North Carolina, to Levi and Prudence (Williams) Coffin, farmers who belonged to the Society of Friends (Quakers). The youngest of seven children, Coffin was educated primarily by his father

before entering school at the age of twenty-one. In his anecdote-laden autobiography, *Reminiscences of Levi Coffin* (1876), the only significant source on his life, Coffin dated his abolitionism from age seven, when he witnessed a slave coffle (a gang of slaves chained together during transport). His parents and grandparents opposed slavery, and he first assisted a runaway slave—a man named Stephen who had been kidnapped into slavery—at age fifteen.

In 1821, Levi and his cousin, Vestal Coffin, established a Sabbath school in New Garden to teach slaves to read the Bible. However, several area slaveholders soon insisted that the school be shut down. Coffin subsequently helped to organize the Manumission Society, but the New Garden group split from its regional organization over the issue of colonization, which Coffin perceived as a way for malicious slaveholders to rid the country of free blacks.

In 1824, Coffin married Catharine White. The couple moved to Wayne County, Indiana, in 1826, where Coffin and other Quakers established an antislavery library and would later form the Indiana State Anti-Slavery Society.

In the small town of Newport (now Fountain City), Indiana, Coffin established a successful mercantile store, pork business, and linseed oil manufactory. He soon discovered that the town was on a line of the Underground Railroad; several free blacks had settled in the area and were helping escaped slaves, but Coffin noted that the runaways were often recaptured. He encouraged local Quakers to follow the Bible rather than the law and to aid in assisting escaped slaves. In winter 1826–1827, fugitives began to appear at the Coffin house, as it had become known on different routes that slaves fleeing from bondage would find shelter there. As Coffin recounted in his *Reminiscences,*

> I soon became extensively known to the friends of the slaves, at different points on the Ohio River, where fugitives generally crossed, and to those northward of us on the various routes leading to Canada. . . . Three principal lines from the South converged at my house: one from Cincinnati, one from Madison, and one from Jeffersonville, Indiana. The roads were always in running order, the connections were good, the conductors active and zealous, and there was no lack of passengers.

Coffin did not feel compelled to hide his participation in the Underground Railroad, although he was not as outspoken as fellow abolitionist William Lloyd Garrison and other immediatists. "I and my wife were the veritable Simeon and Rachel Halliday"—the Quaker couple in Harriet Beecher Stowe's novel *Uncle Tom's Cabin* (1852)—Coffin commented in his autobiography. For more than twenty years, the Coffins provided food, shelter, clothing, and transportation to runaways in Wayne County; their home became famous throughout the "depots" of the Ohio River Valley. Levi learned to disregard proslavery threats against his business, and Catharine organized neighborhood women into a sewing society that made clothes for fugitives.

Initially, such abolitionist activity encountered strong opposition from the white workers in Indiana, but, by the 1840s, antislavery sentiment had become more prevalent in the northern and eastern portions of the state. Coffin claimed that Stowe's character Eliza Harris had been inspired by a slave woman who crossed the Ohio River on ice floes and was sheltered at the Coffin house before settling in Canada. In 1854, Coffin again met the woman on one of his tours of free black settlements in Upper Canada (present-day Ontario).

In the mid-1840s, the *Free Labor Advocate* was established in Newport, and Coffin became conscious of selling goods made by slave labor at his store. He instead began selling, at a lower profit margin, goods made in New York and Philadelphia. A convention of Midwestern abolitionists decided to establish a wholesale free labor goods depository in Cincinnati and urged Coffin to manage it. Initially he refused, but in 1847, he sold his store and moved his family to Cincinnati. Coffin received many orders, and he became influential in promoting the manufacture of free labor products.

The Coffins hoped to retire from active Underground Railroad duty in Cincinnati, but Levi once again found the efforts of the city's free blacks to be lacking. As in Indiana, the Coffin home often housed runaways and hosted weekly Anti-Slavery Sewing Society meetings. In 1856, Coffin sold his Cincinnati store, but he continued his wholesale business.

Coffin believed that the U.S. Civil War represented divine judgment for the national sin of slavery, and he was convinced that the conflict would not end until Americans abolished the "peculiar institution." A pacifist, Coffin refused to contribute to the war effort as a combatant, but he cared for the wounded, the Coffin house serving as a makeshift hospital. During the way, he also visited "contrabands" (escaped

slaves) in southern Illinois and helped to gather bedding, clothing, and books for freedmen.

From May 1864 to June 1865, Coffin traveled to Britain and Paris to solicit funds among philanthropists, including Quakers and Members of Parliament, for the Western Freedmen's Aid Commission. Coffin's speeches emphasized the transatlantic origins of American slavery, and his trip resulted in the founding of the London Freedmen's Aid Society. After the Civil War, he toured Southern freedmen's schools and supported the passage of the Fifteenth Amendment, which granted black men the right to vote. Coffin was a delegate to the International Anti-Slavery Conference in August 1867 in Paris.

Coffin was also a temperance activist, and he helped form the Newport Temperance Society in the 1830s. Incidents recounted in his autobiography indicate that, although he opposed slavery and colonization, he did not support interracial marriage or racial "mixing." Coffin died in Avondale, Ohio, on September 16, 1877.

Brian M. Ingrassia

See also: Quakers (Society of Friends); *Uncle Tom's Cabin* (1852); Underground Railroad.

Further Reading

Gara, Larry. *The Liberty Line: The Legend of the Underground Railroad.* 2nd ed. Lexington: University Press of Kentucky, 1996.

Hendrick, George, and Willene Hendrick, eds. *Fleeing for Freedom: Stories of the Underground Railroad, as Told by Levi Coffin and William Still.* Chicago: Ivan R. Dee, 2004.

Coles, Edward (1786–1868)

Edward Coles, the second governor of Illinois (1822–1826), was an abolitionist who prevented his state from amending its constitution to allow slavery.

Coles was born on December 15, 1786, into a prominent Virginia family that owned a large plantation in Albemarle County. Through both family ties and proximity, he became acquainted with such luminaries as Thomas Jefferson, Patrick Henry, James Madison, and James Monroe. Coles attended Hampden-Sydney College and the College of William and Mary.

Later in life, Coles attributed his antislavery convictions to the teachings of Bishop James Madison at William and Mary. Though the bishop was a slaveholder, he imbued Coles with the belief that slavery was an unjustifiable violation of natural rights. Following the death of his father, Coles inherited an estate and twenty slaves. He resolved to emancipate his slaves and move to an area where slavery was prohibited, but these actions were delayed as he served as President James Madison's private secretary from 1809 to 1815.

As Madison's secretary, Coles attempted to persuade the president to free his slaves. After failing to convince the founding father to set an example, Coles wrote to Thomas Jefferson on July 31, 1814, and urged the author of the Declaration of Independence to live up to the principles of that document by leading a movement for gradual emancipation in Virginia. Coles believed Jefferson's participation would lend such weight to the cause, so that even if the effort did not succeed immediately, his mere involvement would exert a profound influence on posterity. Much to Coles's disappointment, Jefferson responded that he was too old to be of any use—the problem of slavery, he said, was for the young to solve. Jefferson advised Coles to remain in Virginia and lead the antislavery movement.

Despite Jefferson's counsel, Coles was determined to leave his native state for free territory. After resigning as presidential secretary, he made two visits to Illinois and decided that the state would be a suitable place to relocate. Coles obtained an appointment from President James Monroe to serve as registrar of the land office at Edwardsville and set out for Illinois with his slaves in spring 1819. Though he had made the decision to emancipate his slaves years earlier, Coles did not inform them of their freedom until they were traveling down the Ohio River. Coles had purchased thousands of acres of land in Madison and Saint Clair counties; in addition to granting freedom to his slaves, he gave each family head 160 acres.

When Coles moved to Illinois, the state was home to more than 1,000 slaves and indentured servants. Although the state's 1818 constitution prohibited any further introduction of slavery, it permitted indentured servitude and did not free slaves who had been in Illinois since the territorial period. The constitution also allowed the temporary hiring of slaves to labor at the Shawneetown saltworks. Many Illinois settlers had come from slave states and hoped to spur economic prosperity by eliminating the constitutional restriction on slavery. Alarmed by this prospect, Coles ran for governor in 1822, winning the election with only 33 percent of the vote in a four-way contest.

In his inaugural address, Coles called on the legislature to pass measures to end the vestiges of slavery and to grant more equitable treatment to free blacks. The proslavery majority in the legislature responded by employing unethical tactics to obtain the two-thirds majority needed to put a referendum on the ballot at the next general election to determine whether a new constitutional convention should be assembled. If approved, the convention could draft a new constitution that allowed slavery.

The next general election was not until August 1824, so each side had eighteen months to present its case to the electorate. Coles assumed the mantle as leader of the anticonvention forces. When the legislature adjourned, he met with those who had voted against the convention resolution and drafted an impassioned appeal urging the people of Illinois to support the cause of freedom by opposing the convention. The address was signed by fifteen members of the legislature and published. Coles helped purchase a newspaper in Vandalia, Illinois, to which he contributed anticonvention editorials. Perhaps most significantly, Coles obtained the services of skilled antislavery writers such as Morris Birkbeck and Roberts Vaux, who penned persuasive essays for the cause. Coles's efforts were rewarded when 57 percent of the voters rejected the convention proposal.

This triumph marked the zenith of Coles's political career. Enemies sought revenge by prosecuting him for failing to post bonds for his emancipated slaves, a case that he eventually won. Coles also weathered an attempt by the lieutenant governor to usurp his power. His term as governor expired in 1826. After finishing last in a three-way race for a seat in the U.S. Congress, he moved to Philadelphia in 1832.

The remainder of his life was spent largely out of the public eye. He made a final, vain attempt to persuade Madison to emancipate his slaves, and, in the aftermath of Nat Turner's Rebellion in 1831, he presented a plan for gradual emancipation to Thomas Jefferson Randolph, President Jefferson's grandson. The plan recommended colonization, which Coles deemed imperative, yet he failed to convince his former slaves to emigrate to Liberia.

In 1854, Coles briefly re-entered the political arena when he publicly challenged Stephen A. Douglas's interpretation of the Northwest Ordinance of 1787. The experience prompted him to write a short history of the ordinance, titled *History of the Ordinance of 1787,* which he read before the Pennsylvania Historical Society in June 1856.

Though Coles supported President Abraham Lincoln, one of his sons was killed while serving in the Confederate army during the U.S. Civil War. Coles died in Philadelphia on July 7, 1868.

Matt Norman

See also: Vaux, Roberts.

Colored American, The

Launched in 1837 by Philip A. Bell and editor and publisher Samuel E. Cornish, *The Colored American* was the most influential African American newspaper published prior to the U.S. Civil War. Published from its New York City offices until December 1841, *The Colored American* was noted for its high editorial quality and militant call for black unity and full citizenship for African Americans. *The Colored American* was also published in Philadelphia, making it the first African American newspaper to operate in more than one city with two editions.

With Cornish, a Presbyterian minister, at the helm, the format of the newspaper (initially published as the *Weekly Advocate*) was established as a four- to six-page weekly. Using the motto "Righteousness Exalteth a Nation" as inspiration, the paper became an instrument of service for free black Americans, its primary readership.

Cornish, an important figure in the abolitionist movement, had twice edited newspapers in New York. In spring 1827, he established *Freedom's Journal,* the first black newspaper in the United States, with John B. Russwurm. After resigning in September of that year, the paper, under Russwurm's sole editorship, declined. In 1829, Cornish revived the paper and renamed it *The Rights of All,* which lasted nearly a year.

Early on, Bell and Cornish pronounced that the editorial mission of *The Colored American* was the moral, social, and political elevation of free blacks and the peaceful emancipation of the slave. *The Colored American* gave prominent coverage to abolitionist activity and to civil rights struggles in the North. During the presidential campaign of 1840, the paper declared itself in favor of the Liberty Party candidate, James Gillespie Birney, although the publication was not perceived as a partisan organ. From the start, *The Colored American* was to be a newspaper devoted to the interests of free black Americans. It would provide a forum in which they could communicate with each other and with their friends. More importantly, they could express their sentiments on the subjects of the day, such as abolition, colonization, emancipation, expatriation, the expression of prejudice, the enactment of equal laws, and their rights as men and women and as citizens.

By all indications, *The Colored American* was a progressive newspaper that quickly took on the antislavery personas of Cornish, part-time financial supporters Lewis and Arthur Tappan, white liberals who saw slavery as a social and political problem, as well as the African American abolitionist Charles B. Ray, who shared their views. Like some of the earliest black newspapers, such as *Freedom's Journal* and Frederick Douglass's *The North Star, The Colored American* actively endorsed and sought to increase literacy within the African American community. In addition to reporting daily news and political developments in black America, it was common for these publications to launch campaigns promoting reading and literary activity as a component of citizenship and a responsibility of all free blacks in the North.

When Cornish left the newspaper in 1839, Ray became its sole owner and editor. An African American, Ray was a native of Massachusetts who had briefly attended Wesleyan University, worked as a boot maker in New York City, and was an ordained minister. He became a prominent figure in the American Anti-Slavery Society, served as a conductor on the Underground Railroad, and participated in the New York Vigilant Committee, which protected the rights of fugitive slaves. He also supported missionary and temperance causes, as well as educational programs within New York's African American community. Ray's vision for *The Colored American* mirrored that of his predecessors.

Like other antebellum newspapers, *The Colored American* employed agents in various cities to solicit subscribers. It also used abolitionist organizations to market itself. *The Colored American* employed the executive committee of the American Anti-Slavery Society to urge its members to support the paper and used membership lists from other organizations to gain subscribers. Despite these efforts, the paper often teetered on the brink of financial ruin. When money was tight, the paper was published only sporadically; at times, several weeks passed between issues.

The paper raised donations from African American churches and local abolitionist societies. These efforts, supplemented by occasional cash donations from prominent white allies, enabled the paper to survive until December 25, 1841, when its last issue was published.

Fred Lindsey

See also: Birney, James Gillespie; Cornish, Samuel E.; Ray, Charles B.; Russwurm, John B.

Further Reading

Dunn, Martin E., ed. *The Black Press, 1827–1890: The Quest for National Identity.* New York: Putnam, 1971.

Horton, James Oliver, and Lois E. Horton. *In Hope of Liberty: Culture, Community, and Protest Among Northern Free Blacks, 1700–1860.* New York: Oxford University Press, 1997.

Hutton, Frankie G. *The Early Black Press in America, 1827 to 1860.* Westport, CT: Greenwood, 1993.

Jacobs, Donald M. *Antebellum Black Newspapers.* Westport, CT: Greenwood, 1997.

Quarles, Benjamin. *Black Abolitionists.* New York: Oxford University Press, 1969.

Commonwealth v. Aves (1836)

Argued before the Massachusetts Supreme Judicial Court, the case of *Commonwealth v. Aves* (1836) decided the freedom of an enslaved girl named Med who was allegedly the property of Samuel Slater of Louisiana. In its ruling, the Massachusetts court held that any slave brought within the state's borders by his or her master became legally free.

In a broader sense, the case reflected the responses of courts and legislators in the Northern states to the federal legislation on the status of fugitive slaves—the Fugitive Slave Law of 1793, enacted by the U.S. Congress to ensure the right of slave owners to reclaim runaway slaves. The doctrine of comity, the principle whereby states respect the laws of other states, was in jeopardy, as Northern states challenged Southern slave laws during the early nineteenth century.

The case involved Med, who resided in New Orleans, Louisiana, and was brought to Boston by her mistress, Mrs. Slater, in 1836 for a limited stay. A group of antislavery women, members of the Boston Female Anti-Slavery Society, discovered Med's enslaved condition and brought her situation before the court. A writ of habeas corpus was served on Slater's father, Thomas Aves, a resident of Boston. According to the petition for the writ, Med was being unlawfully restrained of her liberty by Aves. The court summoned Aves to defend himself against the claim that his custody of Med constituted an illegal restraint on her liberty.

Benjamin Curtis, counsel for Aves, maintained that the enslaved were simultaneously persons and property and that their status accompanied them when they traveled. In addition, Curtis stressed the preeminence of Louisiana law (*lex domicilli*) over local Massachusetts law (*lex loci*), for it was under Louisiana law that the child's enslaved status had been determined. The arguments advanced by Curtis centered on the doctrine of comity—that is, the constitutional principle that provides for the limited acceptance of laws from a foreign locale or state. Thus, Curtis argued, in the spirit of legal cooperation, Massachusetts should accept the laws of Louisiana as a foreign sovereign entity and uphold Med's status as a slave.

The counsel for Med, Ellis Gray Loring, argued against the principle of comity. He issued a lengthy challenge noting that comity was not meant to be exercised in doubtful circumstances or when specific regulations on a subject existed. In addition to the purely legal arguments, Loring emphasized the immorality of slavery, insisting that the court had determined such concepts. Loring's strategy was to establish the commonwealth's long-term commitment to liberty, as well as underscore Massachusetts's theoretical ability to carve out and maintain a moral high ground in the matter of slavery. Just as the *Somersett* case (1772) had focused on the undesirability of admitting slavery within specified precincts, Loring insisted that Massachusetts, like Somersett's England, was also a place that esteemed liberty and thus should not admit slavery.

Chief Justice Lemuel Shaw offered the opinion in the case, underscoring the fact that Massachusetts had a history of enlightened practice and enlightened law that tended toward liberty. The general rights of the master were not at issue; Shaw would not rule on that. Rather, Shaw emphasized the character of the Commonwealth of Massachusetts as it was derived from the operation of the state's laws.

Thus, although Shaw would not declare categorically by what act slavery had been abolished in Massachusetts, he maintained that it did indeed appear to have been abolished by law. By coming within the limits of that state, a person was subject to its municipal laws and entitled to the privileges those laws conferred. Med was granted her freedom.

T.K. Hunter

See also: Fugitive Slave Act of 1793; *Somersett* Case (1772).

Further Reading

Higginbotham, A. Leon, Jr. *In the Matter of Color: The Colonial Period.* New York: Oxford University Press, 1978.

Commonwealth v. Jennison (1783)

When the Massachusetts constitution went into effect in 1780, slavery was legal in the commonwealth. However, in the case of *Commonwealth v. Jennison* (1783), the Massachusetts Supreme Judicial Court applied the principle of judicial review to challenge the legality of slavery in that state. The court ruled that laws and customs that sanctioned slavery were incompatible with the new state constitution. Generally referred to as the *Quock Walker* case, the legal proceedings—actually a series of related cases—began in 1781.

The case involved a slave named Quock (also spelled Quaco) Walker, who had been purchased as an infant in 1754 by James Caldwell. In 1763, Caldwell died, and his widow married Nathaniel Jennison. Walker became the property of Jennison, who resided in central Massachusetts. In 1781, at the age of twenty-eight, Walker fled to the home of Caldwell's sons, Seth and John Caldwell, where he sought refuge. Jennison recaptured, severely beat, and re-enslaved Walker, claiming that the slave was his property.

The first case, *Walker v. Jennison,* was tried in the Worcester County Court of Common Pleas in April 1781. Walker sued Jennison for assault and battery, claiming that he had been injured without cause. Walker maintained that Caldwell, his first master, had promised him freedom by the age of twenty-five, and thus he was no longer a slave. The jury found Walker to be a free man and awarded him damages of £50.

In the second case, *Jennison v. Caldwell* (June 1781), Jennison sued the Caldwell brothers for "interfering" with his property; Jennison claimed the brothers had unlawfully enticed Walker away from him. The jury returned a verdict against the Caldwells and awarded Jennison damages of £25. Each side appealed the verdicts, and the two cases were placed on the docket of the Massachusetts Supreme Judicial Court in 1781, although the case did not come before the court until April 1783.

In the third case, *Commonwealth v. Jennison,* Jennison was charged with assault and battery against Walker. The Massachusetts attorney general argued that Jennison had attacked a free man, basing his argument on testimony that Jennison had been aware that Walker's former master had promised him freedom at the age of twenty-five. The attorney general

further argued that Walker was free by virtue of the declaration of rights ("All men are born free and equal") found in the Massachusetts constitution. Jennison's attorney argued that the state constitution did not specifically prohibit slavery. The jury convicted Jennison of assault and battery, and the court ordered him to pay a small fine.

Although no opinion was ever written, Chief Justice William Cushing held that slavery was indeed incompatible with the Massachusetts constitution: "Slavery is in my judgment as effectively abolished as it can be by the granting of rights and privileges wholly incompatible and repugnant to its existence. The courts are therefore fully of the opinion that perpetual servitude can no longer be tolerated in our government, and that liberty can only be forfeited by some criminal conduct or relinquished by personal consent or contract."

According to the 1790 Census, there were no slaves in Massachusetts, but historians disagree about the role that *Commonwealth v. Jennison* played in abolishing slavery in the state. Although changing economic conditions and abolitionists' persistent efforts certainly contributed to slavery's demise, at the very least, the *Quock Walker* case established that slave owners could not triumph in the state courts.

T.K. Hunter

See also: *Somersett* Case (1772).

Further Reading

Cushing, John D. "The Cushing Court and the Abolition of Slavery in Massachusetts: More Notes on the 'Quock Walker Case.'" *American Journal of Legal History* 5 (April 1961): 118–19.

Higginbotham, A. Leon, Jr. *In the Matter of Color: The Colonial Period.* New York: Oxford University Press, 1978.

Spector, Robert M. "The Quock Walker Cases (1781–83): Slavery, Its Abolition, and Negro Citizenship in Early Massachusetts." *Journal of Negro History* 53 (January 1968): 12–32.

Zilversmit, Arthur. *The First Emancipation.* Chicago: University of Chicago Press, 1967.

Compensated Emancipation

Plans for compensated emancipation were widely discussed in the United States during the late eighteenth and early nineteenth centuries, although they were rarely adopted. Proponents of compensated emancipation understood that the property claims of slaveholders were a major obstacle to bringing about the abolition of slavery. As a result, the concept of reimbursing slaveholders for their financial loss of slave property was introduced into public discourse.

In the late eighteenth century, Quaker abolitionists had already adopted the idea of purchasing the manumission of a slave, whereby an individual might buy the freedom of a slave by paying the market value of that slave to his or her master. In some cases, slaves worked to purchase themselves from willing masters. Plans for compensated emancipation took this idea one step further, stipulating that public funds be used to purchase the freedom of all slaves in a given state.

Connecticut clergyman Levi Hart formulated one early plan for compensated emancipation in 1775. Hart's proposal considered both the financial interests of the slaveholders as well as some of the communal concerns that states such as Connecticut had about inheriting large populations of free blacks. His plan called for the abolition of slavery, provided that each owner was reimbursed for the financial loss by the state of Connecticut. Hart even worked out a complicated formula for determining the monetary value of slaves, whereby a slave's value—thus the compensation the slave owner would receive for emancipation—was reduced by a certain amount for each year of the slave's service. Additionally, slaves under the age of twenty-five would work for their masters until they attained that age, at which time they would be freed. Slaves who were old or infirm would not be liberated and would remain the financial responsibility of their master.

Gradual emancipation would later be adopted in Connecticut and throughout the North; however, compensated emancipation schemes such as Hart's did not prove to be popular and were not adopted. "Even though whites in increasing numbers refused to take moral responsibility for slavery," one historian has noted, "they had no interest in taking on the financial responsibility for its dissolution."

During the late eighteenth century, proponents of compensated emancipation experimented with the idea of using public lands to provide the financing. Massachusetts congressman Elbridge Gerry proposed such a plan to the U.S. Congress in 1790, suggesting that the sale of public lands be used to finance the purchase of slaves. Though it was never put into a formal legislative proposal, Gerry's idea persisted well into the early nineteenth century. In 1819, for example, former president James Madison endorsed

compensated emancipation, and he also proposed that it could be financed through the sale of public lands.

Although the American Colonization Society, formed in 1816, provided a major impetus for the colonization of free blacks, some proponents of colonization dabbled with the idea of compensated emancipation. Indeed, many Southerners viewed the existence of the American Colonization Society as a mask for abolitionism. Many believed the society would lobby for public federal funding to colonize free blacks and then advocate the use of national funds to purchase and liberate slaves throughout the South.

Even before the rise of radical abolitionism in the 1830s, proslavery Southerners emphatically rejected compensated emancipation. First, the very mention of emancipation suggested that the institution of slavery was flawed, a fact that many Southern slaveholders refused to acknowledge. Second, in the opinion of many Southerners, the use of federal funds to finance emancipation was a blatant violation of states' rights, such that states should be entirely free of federal interference or pressures when it came to the regulation of domestic institutions, such as slavery.

With the rise of militant abolitionism, many antislavery advocates also rejected compensated emancipation altogether. Compensating slaveholders for liberating their slaves was considered the equivalent of rewarding criminals for their crimes.

Nevertheless, a handful of advocates of compensated emancipation remained. The wealthy New York abolitionist Gerrit Smith, for example, became involved with the National Compensation Society, an organization that tried to reinvigorate the idea of compensated emancipation during the 1850s.

During the U.S. Civil War, a number of plans for compensated emancipation were hatched, most of which involved President Abraham Lincoln. In fall 1861, Lincoln became involved in a plan for the gradual emancipation of slavery in the border state of Delaware. Working in conjunction with Congressmen George P. Fisher and Nathaniel Smithers, Lincoln called for the immediate emancipation of all slaves over the age of thirty-five and the liberation of all remaining slaves by 1872. Under the proposed plan, special assessors would evaluate the value of individual slaves, but most owners could expect to receive about $500 for each emancipated slave; funds appropriated by Congress would finance the plan. However, the Delaware General Assembly never acted on the measure, and as a result, the abolition of slavery in Delaware was not accomplished until the Thirteenth Amendment was ratified in December 1865.

Shortly thereafter, Lincoln sponsored a plan of compensated emancipation for all the border states. Lincoln's plan, introduced on March 6, 1862, called for Congress to pass a joint resolution promising federal aid for any border state that willingly initiated a plan of gradual emancipation. Though Congress approved the resolution and it received favorable support in the press, border state congressmen, who believed the measure was both unnecessary and an unwarranted interference in state affairs by the federal government, failed to support it.

By summer 1862, compensated emancipation had been realized only in the District of Columbia. Enacted by Congress on April 16, 1862, the measure compensated slave owners $300 for each slave who was manumitted. To address concerns about a large population of free blacks in the nation's capital, the bill also provided $100,000 to support the colonization of willing free blacks.

As the Civil War continued, so did plans for emancipation; however, compensated emancipation was no longer considered an option. With the passage of the Thirteenth Amendment, all states were required to abolish the institution of slavery with no compensation for emancipated slaves from the federal government.

Bruce Tap

See also: American Colonization Society; Civil War, American (1861–1865); Gradualism; Immediatism; Lincoln, Abraham.

Further Reading

Donald, David H. *Lincoln.* New York: Simon & Schuster, 1995.

Egerton, Douglas R. "Averting a Crisis: The Proslavery Critique of the American Colonization Society." *Civil War History* 43 (June 1997): 142–56.

Fladeland, Betty L. "Compensated Emancipation: A Rejected Alternative." *Journal of Southern History* 42 (May 1976): 169–86.

Harrold, Stanley L. *The Rise of Aggressive Abolitionism: Addresses to the Slaves.* Lexington: University Press of Kentucky, 2004.

Melish, Joanne Pope. *Disowning Slavery: Gradual Emancipation and "Race" in New England, 1780–1860.* Ithaca, NY: Cornell University Press, 1998.

Williams, William H. *Slavery and Freedom in Delaware, 1639–1865.* Wilmington, DE: Scholarly Resources, 1996.

Concert of Europe

The informal association of the major European powers throughout the nineteenth century—from the end of the Napoleonic Wars to the eve of World War I—was known as the Concert of Europe. In diplomatic language, the term "concert" originally defined a temporary agreement between two powers regarding a specific situation. The expression came to represent the informal relationship among the European powers, which was based on consultation regarding matters of common interest.

In 1815, representatives from Great Britain, Austria, Russia, and Prussia, the victors that had vanquished Napoleon, organized the Congress of Vienna to fashion a new international system. The Congress of Vienna was based on the principles of balance of power, the end of continuous conflict throughout Europe, and the suppression of revolution. Among the four powers, Great Britain, which had the financial and material resources, and Russia, which had the military power, were most in favor of the establishment of a new diplomatic order.

On February 18, 1815, as the framework for a new European order was being fashioned at the Congress of Vienna, the major powers made a statement calling for the abolition of the transatlantic slave trade throughout Europe, though there was little means of enforcement. By the beginning of the nineteenth century, some countries had already ended their trading in African slaves. Denmark was the first country to do so in 1802, followed by Great Britain and the United States in 1807 and Sweden in 1813. After 1807, Britain sought to bring an end to the practice throughout Europe. Convincing the rest of Europe to abolish the slave trade was more challenging, however, as Holland, France, Spain, and Portugal had profited heavily from the trade.

At the diplomatic forefront was Foreign Secretary Lord Castlereagh, the British representative to the Congress of Vienna, who worked to secure agreements with the other countries. In summer 1814, he negotiated a treaty with the Kingdom of the Netherlands to end its slave trade. He also approached papal representatives with the intention of imploring the pope to remind the Catholic rulers of Spain and Portugal of the sinfulness of slavery—to no avail. Securing French support proved particularly challenging for Castlereagh. France had barely emerged from the chaos of revolution and war, and the restored Bourbon monarchy, which had come to power on the heels of occupying armies, did not have popular support. Military defeat, not surprisingly, led to anti-British sentiments among the French public, who saw the move to abolish the transatlantic slave trade as merely another tactic for British commerce. It would take some time before any concrete effort was enacted.

In 1818, the Quadruple Alliance of Great Britain, Austria, Russia, and Prussia convened at the Congress of Aix-la-Chapelle, at which Castlereagh proposed the creation of an international police force to patrol the shores of Africa and to intercept slave traders. His proposal failed to gain support, however, chiefly because none of the European powers was willing to be subjected to searches by the Royal Navy. A second reason for the failure at Aix-la-Chapelle was Portugal's unwillingness to end trafficking. Third, France remained unwilling to end its slave trade.

Despite these initial setbacks, the following years brought gradual progress toward the abolition of the slave trade on a bilateral level. In 1817, Castlereagh secured a treaty with Spain that effectively ended its slave trade north of the equator between Africa and the West Indies by 1820. Both countries agreed to the right of search on each other's vessels, including the payment of an indemnity of £400,000 to Spain in that year alone. Likewise, Portugal entered into a similar agreement with Britain with a payment of £300,000. In exchange for recognition of its independence, Brazil, Portugal's former colony, entered into the same terms with Britain. In the 1830s, Foreign Secretary Lord Palmerston continued Castlereagh's work by negotiating agreements with Denmark, Sweden, Haiti, Uruguay, Venezuela, Mexico, and Argentina.

On November 30, 1831, the governments of France and Britain agreed to the right-of-search convention, which had been a constant sticking point with the previous Bourbon regime. That treaty required a French squadron along the West African coast and limited the right of search between the latitudes of 15° north and 10° south and between the longitudes of 0° and 30° west. The 1833 treaty was further supplemented by the treaties of 1834 and 1835, which widened the areas of search.

Britain continued to press other powers, including the United States, for full suppression of the slave trade. Of all the powers, Great Britain had the most resources with which to intercept illegal slave trading. In 1847, for example, the Royal Navy devoted thirty cruisers to patrolling the coast of West Africa, compared to seven cruisers by France and Portugal and five by the United States. By 1865, the transatlantic slave trade virtually ceased to exist.

For the rest of the nineteenth century, Britain focused on ending the slave trade along the east coast of Africa, where slaves were bound for the Middle East. Unlike the transatlantic slave trade, however, the move to abolish the slave trade clashed with late-nineteenth-century European ambitions in Africa.

At the Berlin Conference in 1884, Britain, France, Germany, Portugal, Spain, Turkey, Italy, Russia, Austria, the Scandinavian countries, Holland, Belgium, and the United States met to decide the fate of Africa and the slave trade. The representatives gathered at the conference condemned slavery and the slave trade, and they resolved not to allow their territories to be havens for such activities.

Ironically, it was the partitioning of Africa among the European powers that ended the slave trade. On July 2, 1890, the Brussels Conference, which was signed by fifteen nations, including almost all of Europe and the United States, officially brought the slave trade to an end.

Dino E. Buenviaje

See also: Congress of Vienna (1814–1815).

Further Reading

Albrecht-Carrié, René. *The Concert of Europe.* New York: Walker, 1968.

Holbraad, Carsten. *The Concert of Europe: A Study in German and British International Theory, 1815–1914.* London: Longman, 1970.

Kielstra, Paul Michael. *The Politics of Slave Trade Suppression in Britain and France, 1814–1818.* London: Macmillan, 2000.

Lloyd, Christopher. *The Navy and the Slave Trade: The Suppression of the African Slave Trade in the Nineteenth Century.* London: Longman, Green, 1949; London: Frank Cass, 1968.

Mathieson, William Law. *Great Britain and the Slave Trade, 1839–1865.* New York: Octagon, 1967.

Miers, Suzanne. *Britain and the Ending of the Slave Trade.* London: Longman, 1975; New York: Africana, 1975.

Condorcet, Marquis de (1743–1794)

Marie-Jean-Antoine-Nicholas Caritat, the Marquis de Condorcet, was one of the first eighteenth-century French *philosophes* involved in the abolitionist movement. As the protégé of the philosopher and mathematician Jean Le Rond d'Alembert and the French writer and historian Voltaire, Condorcet was well versed in the Enlightenment rhetoric of reason, tolerance, and justice, but he proved more radical than his mentors.

Eager to turn rhetoric into action, Condorcet sought public office in order to effect reform. In 1773, he became perpetual secretary of the Royal Academy of Sciences. From 1774 to 1776, during the finance ministry of his friend Anne-Robert-Jacques Turgot, Condorcet served as inspector of the mint and inspector-general of navigation; in these capacities, he fought for economic modernization.

During the French Revolution, he was a representative in the Legislative Assembly and the National Convention, promoting education reform and citizens' rights for oppressed groups such as women, Jews, and slaves. In 1789, he became president of the French abolitionist society *La Société des Amis des Noirs* (Society of Friends of the Blacks).

Condorcet's abolitionist activity dated to at least 1773. In letters to Benjamin Franklin, he requested information on the lives of freed slaves in the Americas, which he used to condemn slavery in his *Remarques sur "Les Pensées" de Pascal*, composed in 1774. Condorcet also appealed to Turgot, the newly appointed minister of finance, in 1774 to alleviate the fate of France's colonial slaves. After Turgot's dismissal from office in 1776, Condorcet took his antislavery campaign to the public arena. He published his *Remarks on "the Pensées" of Pascal* (1776) and, in 1777, denounced the slave trade in letters to the *Journal de Paris*. Appealing to the conscience of his readers, Condorcet insisted that the eighteenth century could not be called a "century of enlightenment" without hypocrisy if slavery were allowed to persist.

In 1781, he published his *Réflexions sur l'esclavage des nègres* (Reflections on the Slavery of Negroes) under the pseudonym Joachim Schwartz. In this piece, he argued that the slave trade must be abolished without paying damages to slave traders or owners, but emancipation should be accomplished in stages to avoid violence and to prepare former slaves to live under the rule of law.

By the end of the 1780s, pamphleteering gave way to direct action. In 1789, as president of the Société des Amis des Noirs, Condorcet led the French abolitionists against the slave owners. Together with Jacques-Pierre Brissot de Warville, founder of the abolitionist society, and Abbé Grégoire, an abolitionist bishop, Condorcet demanded that slaver traders and slave owners be excluded from the Estates-General. In an address to the electoral body of the Estates-General in February 1789, he insisted that the slave trade be abolished immediately and that slaves be prepared for emancipation.

Condorcet's demands alarmed the colonial planters and their allies, bringing them together as a powerful proslavery lobby called the *Comité Massiac* (Massiac Club, named for L'Hôtel Massiac where the members met). The Massiac Club virulently attacked the Amis des Noirs, to which Condorcet and Brissot angrily responded in the *Journal de Paris* and *Le Patriote Français* in November and December 1789. In heated exchanges, members of the Massiac Club even threatened to kill Condorcet. Undeterred, the Amis des Noirs continued their activities in January 1790, formally proposing that the National Assembly abolish the slave trade. Unwilling to risk losing valuable assets, however, the assembly voted to put colonial properties under national protection, implicitly guaranteeing the rights of slave owners.

Condorcet, Brissot, and Grégoire continued to advance the Amis des Noirs's agenda in the Constituent Assembly in 1791, leading to the compromise of May 15, which gave full political rights to free "men of color" born of free parents. In November and December, Condorcet published reports in the *Chronique de Paris* of Brissot's fight to have full citizenship granted to all free men of color, regardless of their parents' status. A law was passed to this effect in the Legislative Assembly on April 4, 1792.

Condorcet and the Amis des Noirs were too closely associated with Brissot, the leader of the modern Girondin faction, to survive the French Revolution intact. The battle between the Girondins and the radical Jacobins in late 1792 and 1793 over the form of the new constitution effectively silenced the Amis des Noirs. Brissot eventually went to the guillotine.

Condorcet initially survived the Jacobin purge of the Girondins on June 2, 1793, but his decision to publicly denounce the Jacobins for suppressing the proposed constitution—of which Condorcet was a primary author—proved fatal. The Committee of Public Safety retaliated with an arrest warrant on July 8. Forewarned, Condorcet went into hiding. Eight months later, he was captured in the suburbs of Paris and died in prison.

Gregory Matthew Adkins

See also: Enlightenment; *Société des Amis des Noirs, La.*

Further Reading

Baker, Keith Michael. *Condorcet: From Natural Philosophy to Social Mathematics.* Chicago: University of Chicago Press, 1975.

Confiscation Acts (1861, 1862)

The Confiscation Acts were laws enacted by Congress during the U.S. Civil War to address the vexing problem of how the property of Southerners—especially their property in slaves—should be treated by advancing Union forces. The legislation created a nebulous category called "contraband of war" to describe the fugitive slaves who sought refuge with the Union forces. In the months leading up to the issuance of the Emancipation Proclamation on January 1, 1863, thousands of contrabands maintained a curious existence, occupying a status somewhere between slave and fully emancipated freedman.

In a general sense, warriors throughout history have recognized that all goods and property seized during conflict are prizes of war if those items aid and abet the enemy's continued ability to make war. The U.S. Civil War was unique in this respect because the contraband "prizes" often included human beings, as Southern plantations were liberated by advancing Union forces and many slaves sought self-emancipation by rushing toward the advancing Union lines.

What to do with these individuals, who were ostensibly the chattel of Confederate sympathizers, and what status these liberated people should hold were perplexing questions that faced Union commanders in the field. Mixed signals and miscues between the administration of President Abraham Lincoln and the U.S. Army demonstrated that there was no clear policy regarding the treatment of former slaves as contraband of war, and the formulation of such a policy was a work in progress during the first months of the conflict.

Because Lincoln did not announce the Emancipation Proclamation until September 22, 1862, a carefully crafted veil of discomfiture shrouded the question of emancipation during the first year and a half of the conflict. Faced with the dilemma of keeping the proslavery border states of Missouri, Kentucky, Maryland, and Delaware in the Union, the Lincoln Administration believed that any rash action toward wholesale emancipation might drive these states to secede, augmenting the Confederacy and extending its ability and resources to make war. In such a world of high-stakes *Realpolitik*, all policies regarding the status of slaves as contraband of war were viewed as profound decisions that could affect the conduct of the war.

On May 24, 1861, only six weeks after the opening shots of the war had been fired at Fort Sumter, Union General Benjamin F. Butler reported to authorities in the War Department that he had put a group of fugitive slaves to work at Fortress Monroe, Virginia. In his dispatch, Butler described the fugitives as "contraband of war," and stated that some were employed on construction projects, while others picked cotton. Although the fugitive slaves were not considered legally emancipated, they were effectively free, and they received a small wage (usually 25 cents per day plus rations) from the federal treasury for the labor they performed for the Union forces.

Among Northern abolitionists, the catchphrase "contraband of war" became almost synonymous with emancipation. This practice became increasingly common after Congress passed the first Confiscation Act on August 6, 1861. This measure authorized the freeing of slaves who had previously been employed to aid the Confederate cause in areas that were already under Union army control.

Even with these policies in place, President Lincoln still proceeded cautiously on the issue of emancipation. In September 1861, Lincoln ordered General John Charles Frémont to revise a proclamation of martial law that he had issued. Frémont's initial proclamation had freed the slaves of all disloyal slave owners in Missouri.

In December 1861, Lincoln convinced Secretary of War Simon Cameron to delete several controversial passages in his annual report to Congress. It was Cameron's wish to urge emancipation as a wartime necessity and to advocate the use of former slaves as military laborers and soldiers. Shortly after Cameron submitted the revised report, Lincoln removed him from the War Department, naming him minister to Russia.

On July 17, 1862, Congress enacted the second Confiscation Act, which granted freedom to the slaves of masters who supported the Confederacy, but it did not provide for universal emancipation. With the passage of this measure, the president was authorized to employ "persons of African descent" in any fashion he deemed necessary, including their use as armed troops in military service. As part of the Militia Act, which Congress enacted on the same day, the use of blacks in "any military or naval service for which they may be found competent" was authorized. This measure granted freedom to any slave employed in such a capacity.

For many former slaves, their role as contraband of war was a part of the transition from slavery to freedom. When freedom finally came for the slaves in the South, Union lines swelled as tens of thousands of newly freed black men joined the camps and the ranks of their liberators. Coping with the demands of vast contraband camps that were teeming with displaced persons was a taxing obligation for the War Department; the solutions applied represent one of the first social welfare efforts sponsored by the U.S. government.

The provision of basic supplies of food, shelter, and clothing, the furnishing of rudimentary health services, and the establishment of schools were not skills traditionally associated with the military, but as the war progressed, efforts to assist the wards of the government in the contraband camps became more systematic. When Congress created the Bureau of Refugees, Freedmen, and Abandoned Lands (commonly known as the Freedmen's Bureau) in March 1865, the agency was placed under the auspices of the War Department, and General Oliver O. Howard was appointed its first director.

Junius P. Rodriguez

See also: Butler, Benjamin Franklin; Civil War, American (1861–1865); Emancipation Proclamation (1863); Frémont's Emancipation Decree (1861); Lincoln, Abraham.

Further Reading

Buker, George E. *Blockaders, Refugees, and Contrabands: Civil War on Florida's Gulf Coast, 1861–1865.* Tuscaloosa: University of Alabama Press, 2004.

Eaton, John. *Grant, Lincoln, and the Freedmen: Reminiscences of the Civil War, With Special Reference to the Work for the Contrabands and Freedmen of the Mississippi Valley.* New York: Longman, Green, 1907.

Swint, Henry L., ed. *Dear Ones at Home: Letters From Contraband Camps.* Nashville, TN: Vanderbilt University Press, 1966.

Congress of Vienna (1814–1815)

The Congress of Vienna was a diplomatic gathering of the major European powers held in the Austrian capital from September 15, 1814, to June 9, 1815. The original purpose of the congress was to restore the political structure of Europe after a generation of political upheaval and warfare wrought by the French Revolution.

Each of the major powers used every means to advance its position in the diplomatic arena. In particular, British diplomats applied pressure on the other European powers to end their involvement in the transatlantic slave trade. Despite the usual machinations that have so often been a theme in European history, the congress attempted to address the atrocities of slavery, serving as a foundation for human freedom.

Structure and Early Goals

A glittering assembly of nobles and rulers converged in Vienna, but the major decision makers of the congress were Chancellor Prince Klemens von Metternich from Austria; Viscount Robert Castlereagh, the foreign secretary from Great Britain; Chancellor Prince Karl August von Hardenberg from Prussia; and Czar Alexander I of Russia. Originally, the four victorious powers of the Napoleonic Wars intended to exclude France from the discussions, but the diplomacy of the French foreign minister, Charles-Maurice Talleyrand-Périgord, allowed French participation in the congress.

The defeat of Napoleon Bonaparte by the coalition forces and the resulting demise of his empire opened the door for the reconstruction of Europe and the creation of a new international order. The French Revolution had challenged the doctrine of monarchical rule by divine right by offering republicanism and political equality as an alternative. Napoleon's conquests had not only spread the revolution beyond France, but also deposed long-established dynasties throughout Europe, while unleashing warfare of unprecedented nature.

In the aftermath of Napoleon's defeat, legitimacy became the prevailing issue for the decision makers of the congress. For Austria, Prussia, and Russia, the conservative powers, the goals for Europe were to restore the rulers whom Napoleon had overthrown, to protect the idea of hereditary rule, to forge domestic alliances with the nobility and an established church, and to discourage the ideas of nationalism and liberalism that had been so identified with the French Revolution. While expressing the goals of restoration and legitimacy, the congress also exposed conflicting interests among the major European powers.

Alexander I envisioned the emergence of Poland under Russian influence, whereas Prussia's objective was to obtain Saxony in exchange for losing its Polish lands. Metternich, the strongest proponent of legitimacy and restoration, sought to re-establish Austria's predominance among the German states (in light of the demise of the 1,000-year-old Holy Roman Empire) and in northern Italy. Castlereagh's goal was to contain France, to establish Great Britain as a mediator in Continental affairs, and to draft a declaration ensuring freedom of the seas. Talleyrand supported the restoration of the Bourbons to the throne of France as a way of ensuring stability in postwar Europe.

Abolishing the Transatlantic Slave Trade

In addition to the reconstruction of Europe after the Napoleonic Wars, the Congress of Vienna also tackled the issue of the transatlantic slave trade. In 1814, Castlereagh aspired to have the practice abolished throughout Europe. During his political career, he allied himself with a group of abolitionists in Parliament known as the "Saints." This group was composed of Quakers and evangelical Christians who believed that slavery was a sin that ought to be erased from the face of the earth, lest humanity face the wrath of God. Influential figures of this bloc included William Wilberforce and Zachary Macaulay, who implored Castlereagh to push for the suppression of the transatlantic slave trade as part of the agenda of the congress.

Unlike many abolitionists of his time, Castlereagh was pragmatic in achieving the goal of abolishing the slave trade. In his capacity as foreign secretary, he was forced to consider Great Britain's national interests relative to those of other European powers. He realized that his Continental counterparts would not be moved by religious zeal. As a result, whatever measures he achieved were often overlooked and unappreciated by the British abolitionists.

By the beginning of the nineteenth century, some countries had already ended their trading in African slaves. Denmark was the first country to do so in 1802, followed by Britain and the United States in 1807, and Sweden in 1813. After 1807, Britain sought to

The Final Act of the Congress of Vienna, signed in June 1815, reorganized Europe upon the collapse of the Napoleonic Empire. At Britain's urging, the treaty also called for the suppression of the international slave trade on religious and humanitarian grounds. (*©Archives du Ministere des Affaires Etrangeres, Paris, France/Archives Charmet/The Bridgeman Art Library*) bring an end to the practice throughout Europe. Convincing the rest of Europe to abolish the transatlantic slave trade was more challenging, as Holland, France, Spain, and Portugal had profited heavily from the trade. Castlereagh had some successes, however. In summer 1814, he secured a treaty with the Kingdom of the Netherlands to end its slave trade. He also approached papal representatives with the intention of imploring the pope to remind the Catholic rulers of Spain and Portugal of the sinfulness of slavery—to no avail.

Securing French support proved particularly challenging for Castlereagh, for several reasons. First, French abolitionists had none of the political influence exercised by the Saints in Britain. Second, France had barely emerged from the chaos of revolution and war. Third, the restored Bourbon monarchy, which had come to power on the heels of occupying armies, did not have popular support. Finally, military defeat, not surprisingly, had led to anti-British sentiments among the French public, who saw the abolition of the transatlantic slave trade as merely another tactic for the advancement of British commerce.

In 1814, in conjunction with the French abolitionists, the Saints launched a pamphlet campaign, which included an open letter to Talleyrand, to convince the French to abolish the slave trade. In their pamphlets, the abolitionists argued the equality of blacks to Europeans in every respect, the cruelty of the Middle Passage, the economic strain on planters, and the religious ramifications of continuing the slave trade. French abolitionists such as Madame de Staël were instrumental in translating and circulating the pamphlets.

Talleyrand deftly prevented France from making any binding commitments regarding the abolition of the slave trade, which he saw as necessary to French national interests. He even negotiated for the return of most of the French colonies before the Napoleonic Wars. Castlereagh, however, convinced the French government to abolish the slave trade throughout its colonies within five years. His argument was greatly strengthened by Napoleon's brief return from Elba, which had already abolished the slave trade, thus precluding any chance the Bourbons had to reverse course.

Castlereagh also faced challenges from Spain and Portugal, which saw the slave trade as a lucrative market. In January 1817, he convinced representatives from Spain and Portugal to agree to partial abolition in exchange for economic concessions. He also realized that the only way to enforce any agreement

abolishing the slave trade was to create an international squadron of ships that would patrol the seas for slave ships and to secure for Britain the right to search any ship under suspicion of carrying slaves.

With the support of the other powers, particularly Russia, Castlereagh formed an eight-country commission on the transatlantic slave trade. After four meetings, the committee recommended that the slave-trading countries limit their traffic and issue a joint declaration calling for the end of the slave trade. In the short term, the conferences and the resulting declaration were of little substance, but they served as a foundation for human rights in succeeding generations.

Dino E. Buenviaje

See also: Concert of Europe.

Further Reading

Ferrero, Guglielmo. *The Reconstruction of Europe: Talleyrand and the Congress of Vienna, 1814–1815.* Toronto, Ontario, Canada: W.W. Norton, 1963.

Jennings, Lawrence C. *French Anti-Slavery: The Movement for the Abolition of Slavery in France, 1802–1848.* Cambridge, UK: Cambridge University Press, 2000.

Lockhart, J.G. *The Peacemakers, 1814–1815.* Freeport, NY: Books for Libraries, 1968.

Webster, Charles K. *The Congress of Vienna, 1814–1815.* New York: Barnes and Noble, 1963.

———. *The Foreign Policy of Castlereagh, 1815–1822.* London: G. Bell & Sons, 1925, 1931.

Conselheiro, Antônio (1830–1897)

Antônio Vicente Mendes Maciel, popularly known as Antônio Conselheiro ("the Counselor"), was the leader of a late-nineteenth-century religious community called *Canudos* in the northeastern Brazilian state of Bahia. He attracted as many as 35,000 devout followers, including ex-slaves, mulattoes, and indigenous people who were dissatisfied with the policies of the new Brazilian Republic, established in 1889. Canudos was regarded as a political and ideological challenge to the struggling republic, and it was eventually destroyed by government troops. Modern historians consider Canudos a religious movement caught up in the intense political, economic, and social conflicts of the Brazilian Republic.

Conselheiro was born on March 13, 1830, in a small town in the interior of northeast Brazil. In the 1860s, he developed a particularly pious version of Catholicism that he began to preach throughout

Brazil's economically underdeveloped interior. He wandered from town to town, conducting public prayers, preaching against ungodly behavior, and making apocalyptic prophecies.

In addition to his religious teaching, he also supported political issues that affected poor agricultural laborers in the region, especially after slavery was abolished in 1888 and the monarchy was deposed in favor of a republican government controlled by the powerful economic and military elite of the more developed urban centers. Conselheiro moderately supported the monarchy, but, most importantly, he opposed the secular laws emanating from the republic, especially the requirement for civil marriage and a series of onerous taxes.

The republican government and the local landed elites used Conselheiro's monarchism to attack the movement and to consolidate their political power, even though Conselheiro posed no threat to the government. Three attacks were launched, but the inhabitants of Canudos relied on guerrilla warfare to repel government forces. They held out for four months, but the city was eventually destroyed and many of its inhabitants were killed in battle, died of disease or starvation, or were summarily executed.

Most Brazilians saw Canudos as a symbol of the clash between urban progress and rural backwardness. Conselheiro's defeat was regarded as a national victory for civilization and against the ignorance and superstition of the isolated interior. This argument derived from the first classic account of the attacks, *Rebellion in the Backlands* (1902) by Euclides da Cunha. Though critical of the unrestrained violence that had been meted out to Conselheiro's followers, Cunha firmly believed the conflict to be between the immature economy and society of the northeastern interior and the modernizing projects of Brazil's coastal cities, such as Rio de Janeiro and São Paulo.

Modern historians have thoroughly revised this interpretation of Canudos. Several movements of disaffected peasants and rural laborers emerged during this period throughout Brazil and, compounded by the effects of rapid urban growth, resulted in widespread social and economic conflict. Moreover, Conselheiro was no fanatic: He faithfully abided by the laws, and he built a successful settlement based on cooperative farming and local commerce. Although he was a monarchist, he did not preach rebellion against the republican authorities. His followers comprised a wide range of poor agricultural laborers, including ex-slaves, indigenous peoples, mulattoes, and poor

whites, but during the period of slavery, Conselheiro never advocated abolition or spoke publicly about racial discrimination.

Racist opponents nevertheless saw the diverse composition of Conselheiro's community as emblematic of the uncivilized nature of rural Brazil. Historians have come to view the multiracial nature of the movement and its relative success against overwhelmingly superior state forces as an inspiring model for the struggles of contemporary popular movements in Brazil.

Sean Purdy

See also: Brazil, Emancipation in.

Further Reading

Cunha, Euclides da. *Os Sertões* [Rebellion in the Backlands]. 1902. Chicago: University of Chicago Press, 1944.

Levine, Robert M. *Vale of Tears: Revisiting the Canudos Massacre in Northeastern Brazil, 1893–1897.* Berkeley: University of California Press, 1995.

Reesink, Edwin. " 'Til the End of Time': The Differential Attraction of the 'Regime of Salvation' and the 'Entheotopia' of Canudos." *Journal of Millennial Studies* 2 (Winter 2000): 1–18.

Coolie Labor

See British Emancipator, The; Hibernian Anti-Slavery Society

Cornish, Samuel E. (1795–1858)

One of the leading black abolitionists in the United States, Samuel Eli Cornish was the editor of several prominent antislavery newspapers published in the 1820s and 1830s. He became a leading critic of colonization schemes that sought to return free blacks to the colony of Liberia in West Africa.

Cornish was born to free parents in 1795 in Sussex County, Delaware. At the age of twenty, he moved to Philadelphia, where John Gloucester, who had founded the first black Presbyterian church, provided him with an education and training for the ministry. In 1819, Cornish was licensed to preach, and he went to work in Maryland and Philadelphia as a missionary for the African Presbyterian Church; the following year, he was sent to New York City to establish a mission in the black community. By 1822, he was ordained as a minister and established the New Demeter Street Presbyterian Church. In 1824, he married Jane Livingston, with whom he had four children. In 1828,

Cornish resigned from the church to work as an itinerant preacher and missionary.

Cornish is best known for his commitment to a range of political issues, including abolition, colonization, and suffrage. In 1824, he, along with Peter Williams, Jr., founded the Haytien Emigration Society, an organization that actively recruited free blacks to relocate to the newly formed Haitian Republic.

Partly because of his commitment to emigration, Cornish (along with John B. Russwurm) was chosen as co-editor of first black newspaper published in New York City, *Freedom's Journal.* Cornish and Russwurm wanted *Freedom's Journal* to refute racist arguments that were designed to deny them equal justice. Although both men had originally been staunch emigrationists, the rising tide of racism within the colonization movement caused Cornish to reconsider his position. Russwurm continued to support emigration, however, and the two men's conflicting ideologies eventually collided. By September 1827, Cornish had resigned from the paper, and Russwurm continued to edit *Freedom's Journal* on his own. Cornish briefly edited another New York paper, the *Rights of All,* but financial problems caused it to fold within months.

In 1827 and 1828, Cornish became involved in the education movement as an agent for the African Free Schools in New York City. In 1831, he was selected by the delegates of the Colored Convention to collect funds for the creation of a black college in New Haven, Connecticut, a project that ultimately failed because of racist opposition. After the decline of the Colored Convention movement in the 1830s, Cornish was the only New Yorker to support the creation of a new organization, the American Moral Reform Society.

In 1832, Cornish briefly left New York to return to Philadelphia and to resume leadership of the First African Presbyterian Church, but he soon went back to New York City, where he assumed a position on the board of managers of the New York Anti-Slavery Society, a branch of the American Anti-Slavery Society. Following the internal division within the abolitionist movement, Cornish defected from the American Anti-Slavery Society and joined the American and Foreign Anti-Slavery Society, along with most black New Yorkers.

From 1837 to 1839, Cornish again became a newspaper editor, helping to establish *The Colored American* with Philip A. Bell. Although he lived in New Jersey at the time, he remained active in New York City politics, particularly in matters of suffrage and colonization. In February 1837, Cornish helped draft a petition arguing for the right to equal suffrage for blacks. The petition not only failed to pass the state legislature, but it was overwhelmingly defeated with only eleven affirmative votes. Later that year, Cornish helped create the United Anti-Slavery Society. In 1839, the black community convened the Great Anti-Colonization Meeting, and Cornish offered an unequivocal manifesto on the horrors of colonization. With Theodore Sedgwick Wright, he co-authored *The Colonization Scheme Considered* (1840), in which the authors challenged the American Colonization Society to resolve its prejudices and treat black people as equal citizens.

In 1844, Cornish's wife died, and he returned to New York City, where he organized the Emmanuel Church, which he led until 1847. He became active in the education movement again, helping to create the New York Society for the Promotion of Education Among Colored Children, which was designed to improve the educational environment for black youth.

In the 1850s, Cornish dedicated most of his attention to anticolonization and the cause of fugitives. In particular, he strongly opposed the Liberian Agriculture and Emigration Society, which was founded in 1851. Cornish argued eloquently against Liberian emigration, stating that there were too many problems in Liberia and that blacks had better hopes for a future in the United States. By 1855, Cornish was in declining health, and he moved to Brooklyn, where he died in 1858.

Leslie M. Alexander

See also: *Colored American, The;* Russwurm, John B.; Williams, Peter, Jr.; Wright, Theodore Sedgwick.

Further Reading

Andrews, Charles C. *The History of the New-York African Free Schools.* 1830. New York: Negro Universities Press, 1969.

Gross, Bella. "Freedom's Journal and the Rights of All." *Journal of Negro History* 17 (July 1932): 241–86.

Pease, Jane H., and William H. Pease. *Bound With Them in Chains: A Biographical History of the Antislavery Movement.* Westport, CT: Greenwood, 1972.

Sterling, Dorothy, ed. *Speak Out in Thunder Tones: Letters and Other Writings by Black Northerners, 1787–1865.* Garden City, NY: Doubleday, 1973; New York: Da Capo, 1998.

Crandall, Prudence (1803–1890)

Prudence Crandall became a controversial figure in 1833 after she admitted African American girls as students at her school in Canterbury, Connecticut. The legal challenges that ensued demonstrated the racial prejudice that existed in the Northern states and the limited opportunities that were available to free blacks in the United States.

Crandall, the daughter of a prosperous Quaker farmer from Westerly, Rhode Island, was born on September 3, 1803. She attended a Society of Friends school in Plainfield, Connecticut, and after she completed her studies, she became a teacher. In 1831, she was invited by the people of Canterbury, where her family had recently relocated, to start a school for young ladies in a mansion on the town green. The Canterbury Female Boarding School opened in January 1832.

Later that year, Crandall was approached by Sarah Harris, the daughter of one of Canterbury's most respected black farmers, who wanted to attend Crandall's academy to expand her education and prepare her for a career in teaching. Knowing the controversy this might unleash, Crandall hesitated, but her Quaker principles won out, and Harris was admitted. Consequently, several irate white parents pulled their daughters out of the school.

Her conscience awakened, Crandall wrote to the abolitionist editor William Lloyd Garrison in January 1833, asking his opinion on opening a school for free black girls. Garrison invited her to Boston and, with other antislavery leaders, enthusiastically backed the idea. In the April 1833 issue of *The Liberator,* Crandall announced her intention to open her doors to "young ladies and Little Misses of Color."

Residents of Canterbury reacted with outrage and threats before the first students ever arrived. The town revived old vagrancy laws prescribing fines and public whippings for outsiders; storekeepers refused to supply the school; and churches closed their doors to Crandall's pupils. Finally, Andrew T. Judson, a prominent politician who lived next door to Crandall's school on the green, pushed a law through the Connecticut state legislature making it illegal for people of color to come from out of state for the purpose of attending school. Many of Crandall's twenty students had come from prominent families in Boston, New York, and Philadelphia.

On June 27, 1833, Crandall was arrested under the new Black Law and taken to the county seat in nearby Brooklyn, Connecticut, for arraignment. Supporters were ready to post her bail, but, hoping to draw sympathy to her cause, she allowed herself to be jailed for one night in a cell last occupied by a convicted murderer.

Crandall was tried in August 1833, but the jury deadlocked on the verdict. Retried in October, she

Quaker schoolteacher Prudence Crandall opened a private school for free black girls in Connecticut in 1833. She was tried and convicted under the state's new "Black Law." *(©North Wind/North Wind Picture Archives)*

was found guilty, with sentencing delayed pending appeal. The case, which held that "slaves, free blacks or Indians" were not considered citizens under the U.S. Constitution, slowly made its way through the appeals process and was upheld throughout. It was cited as a precedent in the landmark *Dred Scott v. Sandford* case in 1857, which denied the African American Dred Scott any rights as a citizen.

Throughout her legal battles, Crandall continued to teach. "Love and union seemed to bind out little circle in the bonds of sisterly affection," she wrote of those days. She counseled her pupils not to hate their adversaries.

During this period, Crandall married a Baptist minister named Calvin Philleo, and they spent their honeymoon drumming up support from antislavery leaders. Shortly after their return to Canterbury, a mob descended on the school, demolishing the entire first floor. Looking at her traumatized students, some dazed and bleeding from flying glass, Crandall closed the school and left Canterbury.

The family lived for a time in upstate New York and then moved to Illinois. Crandall's husband suffered from mental illness, so she was left to support her stepchildren, mostly through farming and teaching. After his death in 1874, Crandall moved to Elk Falls, Kansas.

In 1885, Crandall and her supporters petitioned the Connecticut legislature to expunge her conviction and compensate her for property losses. The petition was granted in 1886, and she was given an annuity of $1,400. The sum allowed her to buy a tiny house in Elk Falls, where she spent her final years. She died on January 28, 1890, at the age of eighty-seven.

Heather K. Michon

See also: Quakers (Society of Friends).

Further Reading

Child, Alfred T., Jr. "Prudence Crandall and the Canterbury Experiment." *Bulletin of the Friends' Historical Association* 22 (Spring 1933): 35–55.

Fuller, Edmund. *Prudence Crandall: An Incident of Racism in Nineteenth-Century Connecticut.* Middletown, CT: Wesleyan University Press, 1971.

Small, Edwin, and Miriam Small. "Prudence Crandall, Champion of Negro Education." *New England Quarterly* 18 (December 1941): 506–39.

Strane, Susan. *A Whole-Souled Woman: Prudence Crandall and the Education of Black Women.* New York: W.W. Norton, 1990.

Creole Case (1841)

The mutiny of slaves aboard the vessel *Creole* in November 1841 and their subsequent arrival in the British possession of the Bahamas set in motion a diplomatic crisis between the United States and Great Britain. The matter would not be resolved until the negotiation of the Webster-Ashburton Treaty (1842), which sought to limit interference with the cargo of foreign vessels docking at British ports.

In October 1841, the *Creole* left port at Hampton Roads, Virginia, with 135 slaves and nineteen crew and miscellaneous passengers on board, bound for New Orleans. Approximately eleven days after setting sail, the ship was nearing the Bahamas when a group of slaves began to revolt.

On November 2, the slave cook, Madison Washington, was found by the ship's chief mate in the company of female slaves. Washington fled the chief mate and thwarted efforts to recapture him. While doing so, he encouraged other slaves to join his insurrection. Together with three other slaves, Washington recruited nineteen slaves to overtake the crew and the ship's brig. Historians believe that at least one member of the crew

was killed in the revolt. The slaves ordered overseer William Merritt to direct the *Creole* to the port of Nassau in the British colony of the Bahamas. It pulled into Nassau on November 9 and was immediately seized by the British military.

The nineteen participants were arrested, and the remaining slaves were removed from the *Creole* by a group of black islanders who had surrounded the ship. The islanders called for the release of the slaves and the granting of their freedom. The British complied, and the *Creole* was released to continue its journey to New Orleans on December 2.

Britain's actions were not well received in the United States. Southerners, in particular, resented the British for intervening in a situation that they believed to be an American issue. The U.S. government called for compensation. Everyone from politicians to average citizens believed that the circumstances of the event had condoned mutiny and violence. Still others speculated that another rebellion might explode as a result of the episode.

The Northern abolitionists became ardent supporters of the British, and Washington became a folk hero of the growing antislavery movement. Some abolitionists, such as Elizur Wright, likened Washington to Joseph Cinqué, the West African slave who had led the mutiny on the *Amistad* ship in 1839. John Quincy Adams used the *Creole* incident to once again call for an end to slavery. Ohio representative Joshua Giddings lauded the efforts of the *Creole* slaves and openly attacked the South's slave codes.

Although analogies were made to the *Amistad*, this case was different: In the former case, the U.S. Supreme Court had ruled that a group of Africans who had been illegally abducted from Sierra Leone could not be held as slaves and had the right to return to their homeland. In the case of the *Amistad*, a Spanish slave ship, the slaves had been released because Spain had made the slave trade illegal in 1820. In the *Creole* case, however, the slaves had been purchased in the United States, where slavery was still legal, for transport to another U.S. city. The British validated their actions by citing international law and the Abolition of Slavery Act of 1833 (commonly known as the British Emancipation Act), which prohibited slavery throughout the British Empire. In addition, the British had already behaved similarly with respect to the American slave ships *Comet*, *Encomium*, *Enterprise*, and *Formosa*.

Secretary of State Daniel Webster was forced to avert a crisis over the *Creole*, as well as to find a resolution to an existing boundary dispute with Great Britain over the border between the United States and Canada. According to international law, a slave revolt aboard a ship was considered a mutiny, and any such mutiny was subject to the laws, regulations, and punishment of the locality in which it occurred. Webster held that the prisoners in Nassau could not be tried for high crimes because the United States had no jurisdiction there; moreover, they should not be sent to America because the United States had no power to force extradition after the expiration of the 1794 Jay's Treaty in 1807. The stage was set for a show-down over the slaves, but chaos was avoided through Webster's diplomatic maneuvers.

The nineteen slave mutineers were released in Nassau. In April 1842, Lord Ashburton, the British foreign secretary, journeyed to the United States to forge the Webster-Ashburton Treaty (1842), which clearly defined the borders between Maine and New Brunswick and in the Great Lakes area; the treaty also included an extradition clause. According to Article 10, seven crimes could result in extradition (the legal process for returning fugitives to another jurisdiction), including murder, arson, piracy, and robbery. No mention was made of slave revolts or mutiny. In addition, Ashburton guaranteed that British officials would refrain from substantial interference on ships docking at British ports. The United States agreed to station ships off the African coast in an effort to detect Americans engaging in the slave trade.

The terms of the Webster-Ashburton Treaty appeased Southerners but angered Northerners. In the aftermath of the case, the U.S. Navy joined the Royal Navy in patrolling the seas to curtail the slave trade. In addition, in 1855, Great Britain paid $110,330 to the United States on the grounds that forcible seizure of a ship did not suspend the operation of U.S. law.

Philine Georgette Vega

See also: Amistad Case (1841).

Further Reading

Lee, R. Edward. "Madison Washington, Slave Mutineer." *Blackfax* (Winter/Spring 1998): 8.

Crowther, Samuel Ajayi (ca. 1806–1891)

Samuel Ajayi Crowther was the first African bishop to be consecrated in the Anglican Church (1841). One of the foremost Christian missionaries working in Africa during the nineteenth century, he was also an explorer and a pioneer linguist.

Born in the Yoruba town of Osogun, he was enslaved during the civil wars that followed the collapse of the Oyo Empire in 1817. Passing through the hands of six indigenous slave dealers, he was finally sold to a Portuguese transatlantic trader whose ship was intercepted by the British antislavery squadron in April 1822. Young Ajayi was taken to the Sierra Leone colony, which had been founded by British abolitionists in 1787 as a base for the spread of Christianity, trade, and "good government," as defined by the eighteenth-century philosophers of the Enlightenment.

Three years after landing in Sierra Leone, young Ajayi converted to Christianity. He chose Samuel Crowther as his new name, in honor of an eminent British clergyman in the Church Missionary Society (CMS). Church authorities in Sierra Leone quickly perceived that the young convert possessed the aptitude for learning and leadership that they wanted in African agents to spearhead mission work in West Africa. They first sent him to England for a brief period of training and, after his return home, admitted him to the foundation class of the Fourah Bay Institution (later Fourah Bay College), established in 1827 to train indigenous CMS clergymen.

At the institution, he came under the tutelage of the Reverend John Rahan, who believed that mastery of the Yoruba language would be a crucial tool for Crowther's evangelical work in the region. Eventually, Crowther became an important linguist in his own right, publishing a pioneer work on the Yoruba language, participating in the translation of the Bible into Yoruba, and initiating studies of the Hausa, Nupe, and Igbo languages.

After serving for some years as a mission teacher in Sierra Leone, Crowther's life went in a new direction in 1841 when he was invited to join the Niger Expedition, a scheme designed to fuse evangelism, commerce, and the abolition of the indigenous African slave trade. Although the expedition ended in failure, Crowther had so impressed his superiors that they decided to send him for further training in England. Ordained in 1845, he returned to West Africa as a missionary to Yorubaland, first serving in Badagry (1845) and then in Abeokuta (1846).

In the 1850s, Crowther became an influential figure in the spread of Christianity throughout what is today southern Nigeria. He accompanied William Balfour Baikie on his 1854 and 1857 expeditions up the Niger River, which succeeded where the 1841 expedition had failed. In 1857, Crowther was appointed head of the Niger Mission, which comprised only African CMS workers. They founded a native pastorate in Onitsha and its surrounding area that became the linchpin of indigenous mission work. Seven years later, Crowther was consecrated as bishop and appointed to the section of the Niger that covered a vast, diverse area comprising large Igbo polities in the east, Muslim emirates in the north, and city-states in the Delta that had long been involved in world trade.

From the 1850s to the 1870s, the CMS viewed Crowther as the epitome of their ideal African Christian leader. His outlook reflected the Victorian values of the age, but he was also well versed in the values and customs of indigenous African society. However, European expansion and the growth of racism in the 1880s changed the political and intellectual climate in West Africa. Opposition to Crowther developed among brash young British missionaries and traders who objected to African mission leadership. They masterminded the dismissal of a number of Crowther's agents on charges of misconduct and accused him of weak leadership.

Mild and unassuming, Crowther failed to counter the charges against his regime and tendered his resignation in 1890. His spirit broken, he died the following year of a stroke. Not until 1955 would the principle of a self-governing church and an indigenous episcopate be re-established in Nigeria.

LaRay Denzer

See also: Sierra Leone.

Further Reading

Ajayi, J.E. Ade. *A Patriot to the Core: Samuel Ajayi Crowther.* Ibadan, Nigeria: Anglican Diocese of Ibadan, 1992.

Crowther, Samuel Ajayi. "A Second Narrative of Samuel Ajayi Crowther's Early Life." Ed. A.F. Walls. *Bulletin of the Society for African Church History* 2 (1965): 5–14.

Mackenzie, P.R. *Inter-Religious Encounters in Nigeria: S.A. Crowther's Attitude to African Traditional Religion and Islam.* Leicester, UK: Leicester University Press, 1976.

Page, Jesse. *The Black Bishop.* London: Hodder and Stoughton, 1908.

Crummell, Alexander (1819–1898)

A nineteenth-century black nationalist, pan-Africanist, clergyman, author, and educator, Alexander Crummell is best known as the founder of the American Negro Academy, America's first major black learned society, which was established in Washington, D.C., in 1897. Although he certainly qualified as an abolitionist in his early years, he was always more interested in improving the plight of free blacks than in emancipating the slaves. Although he never rose to the same level of notoriety as his contemporaries Frederick Douglass and Booker T. Washington, Crummell was arguably just as important to the development of the African American mind in the late-nineteenth century. A highly original thinker, he expounded many of the ideas that civil rights leaders of the twentieth century would later adopt.

Born on March 3, 1819, in New York City to a free black mother and a father who claimed to be an African prince by lineage, Crummell grew up amid free blacks and abolitionists in New York. He attended the African Free School in Manhattan, the Oneida Institute in Whitesboro, New York, and the integrated Noyes Academy in New Hampshire (along with his friend Henry Highland Garnet) before local whites destroyed the latter school for racial reasons. As a young man, he worked in the New York office of the American Anti-Slavery Society and later as a newspaper correspondent.

In 1839, Crummell applied to the General Theological Seminary of the Episcopal Church in New York, but he was denied admission because of his race. He served the church faithfully nonetheless, first in the Rhode Island parish in 1841–1842. After private tutoring and unofficial studies at Yale College in New Haven, Connecticut, he received ordination in the Episcopal Church in Boston in 1844, becoming only the tenth African American to earn that distinction. He temporarily served parishes in Philadelphia and New York before moving to England in 1847. There, he studied at Cambridge University, graduating in 1853.

Crummell began the second phase of his life and ministry when he accepted an offer to enlist as a missionary for the Episcopal Church in Liberia. Initially, he served as principal of an agricultural school, but he eventually took a position as a professor of English at the newly founded Liberia College. However, the frontier life in Africa did not agree with either his own or his family's health and temperament. Over the years, he also became disillusioned with the racist tendencies of the people of Liberia, who favored light-skinned blacks over dark and American immigrants over indigenous Africans. After the government of Liberia was overthrown in a coup, Crummell fled the country and returned to the United States.

In 1873, Crummell became a domestic missionary to African Americans in the United States, making his home in Washington, D.C. Seven years later, he founded Saint Luke's Episcopal Church there. Experiencing the painful effects of segregation and proscription in the Episcopal Church, he organized the Union of Black Episcopalians to fight a proposal for separate missionary districts for black parishes. He retired from the ministry in 1894; for the better part of the last few years of his life, he taught at Howard University in Washington, D.C.

After a life spent in frustration and turmoil, Crummell made his greatest contribution to African American culture and race relations in 1897, when he founded the American Negro Academy. The first organization of its kind, the academy sought to bring together the best and brightest black intellectuals and academics for the purpose of publishing original scholarly works. Described in its constitution as "an organization of authors, scholars, artists, and those distinguished in other walks of life, men of African descent, for the promotion of Letters, Science, and Art," the academy served as a precursor to the National Association for the Advancement of Colored People, and it proved the validity of what W.E.B. Du Bois would later call "the talented tenth."

Crummell influenced not only Du Bois, but a whole generation of black leaders who would carry on his work through the dark days of Jim Crow in the twentieth century, including Booker T. Washington, Marcus Garvey, Mary Church Terrell, and many others. Throughout his life, Crummell believed that education and moral training were the keys to black progress. He advocated self-help in the same vein as Washington, but he did it for years before Washington became famous for it. Crummell also spoke at the 1895 Cotton States and International Exposition in Atlanta, where Washington delivered his famous "Atlanta Compromise" speech, although he received no acclamation for it. Despite his early disillusionment with Liberia, he remained a black nationalist and a pan-Africanist at heart, working with and supporting the mission of the American Colonization Society to the bitter end. Garvey, the most famous colonizationist of the twentieth century, later borrowed key ideas from Crummell for the charter of his Universal Negro Improvement Association.

In several of his discourses and publications, Crummell sought to identify the proper role of black women in a civilized Christian society, which he believed consisted mainly of charitable work and familial duties rather than public leadership. Terrell's National Association of Colored Women later reflected his ideas on that topic.

Unlike Douglass, Crummell could never bring himself to place enough faith in the U.S. government or the white leaders of the day to believe that racial integration and equality would ever be fully realized in America. He chose instead to work within the framework of a segregated society, deliberately seeking to demonstrate the equality and ability of blacks through action rather than mere rhetoric. In that sense, he was not so much a protester for civil rights as he was a leader who sought to transcend the unfavorable circumstances of his race by making intellectual achievements that would rival those of any white man. Crummell published three books in his lifetime—*The Future of Africa* (1862), *The Greatness of Christ* (1882), and *Africa and America* (1891)—and many of his individual sermons and speeches were published posthumously.

Thomas Adams Upchurch

See also: American Colonization Society; Garnet, Henry Highland; Liberia; Racism.

Further Reading

Moses, Wilson Jeremiah. *Alexander Crummell: A Study of Civilization and Discontent.* New York: Oxford University Press, 1989.

———, ed. *Destiny and Race: Selected Writings of Alexander Crummell, 1840–1898.* Amherst: University Press of Massachusetts, 1992.

Oldfield, John R. *Alexander Crummell (1819–1898) and the Creation of an African-American Church in Liberia.* New York: Edwin Mellon, 1990.

Rigsby, Gregory U. *Alexander Crummell: Pioneer in Nineteenth-Century Pan-African Thought.* Westport, CT: Greenwood, 1987.

Cuba, Abolition in

During the nineteenth century, outside forces, especially from Great Britain, pressured Spain to end the transatlantic slave trade within its empire as a step toward the abolition of slavery. This pressure focused on the Spanish colony of Cuba. Before 1835, Great Britain offered cash incentives to end the trade. After 1835, it relied increasingly on the threat of force. Change was slow, however, as Spain resisted outside pressure and officials in Cuba had difficulty executing orders.

When the Spanish government signed the Anglo-Spanish Treaty of 1835, it agreed to take measures to end slave trafficking to Cuba. The Spanish government agreed to search ships suspected of carrying slaves, punish subjects who engaged in the slave trade, and free any Africans found on captured slave ships. Although British cruisers were authorized to arrest suspected Spanish slavers and bring them before mixed commissions established at Sierra Leone and Havana, the treaty did little to slow the slave trade.

In 1845, Spain passed the Law of Abolition and Repression of the Slave Trade to avoid reprisal by Great Britain. The new law allowed for the detection, confiscation, and destruction of Spanish ships involved in the slave trade, and it called for fines, imprisonment, or exile for those guilty of trading slaves. Furthermore, government officials who were directly or indirectly involved in the slave trade could be suspended or lose their jobs. Because Spain wanted to respect property rights, however, government officials were not permitted to enter estates to determine the origins of slaves.

Cuban guerrilla leader Antonio Maceo Grajales continued fighting Spain after the Ten Years' War, because the truce of 1878 did not abolish slavery or grant full independence. He was killed by Spanish troops during the war of independence in 1896. *(Snark/Art Resource, New York)*

In response to the 1845 law and in anticipation of abolition, many Cuban planters panicked and sold their estates. Other Cuban planters and proslavery advocates protested the law, prompting the Spanish government to grant the planters the right to import slaves from Brazil and Puerto Rico until 1854. Despite this concession, the law virtually ended the slave trade to the island.

Events such as the Civil War in the United States fueled the abolitionist cause. Gradually, Cuban planters came to accept the idea of abolition, as long as it was accompanied by some form of compensation to the slave owners.

Ten Years' War

On October 10, 1868, the beginning of rebellion in Cuba was marked by *El Grito de Yara* (The Cry of Yara). This uprising marked the beginning of a decade of conflict known as the Ten Years' War (1868–1878), during which time Cuba sought to end Spanish rule on the island and establish itself as an independent republic. The rebels complained of discriminatory taxation, favored free trade, and called for universal male suffrage. By the 1870s, the rebel army comprised some 40,000 people, black and white, free and slave.

The abolition of slavery became a key issue during the Ten Years' War. Though the rebels supported the general idea of abolition, most leaders called for gradual abolition including compensation for slave owners. Furthermore, they proposed delaying abolition until they had achieved independence from Spain. At the same time, some rebels proposed immediate abolition.

Some planters freed their slaves during the war; however, many former slaves were simply forced into military service. On the other hand, rebel military leaders would not accept those who were still slaves as soldiers without the consent of their owners. They announced that the rebellion would respect slave property in order to gain the financial and material support of the elite. Indeed, the rebels announced in 1869 that they would apply the death penalty to anyone who attacked sugar plantations or slave property.

The rebels' ambiguous attitude toward slavery made the conduct of the war problematic. The wealthy, civilian leaders of the insurrection wanted to limit the war to the eastern part of the island so as to not alienate the sugar planters in western Cuba. They did not want to abolish slavery, disrupt sugar production, destroy property, or start a race war. At the same time, many rebel military leaders called for the expansion of hostilities to the west, along with the nationwide abolition of slavery. Such a strategy would allow them to freely add former slaves to the rebel army. It also would disrupt the sugar economy, in turn diminishing Spanish revenues from the island.

By 1878, the rebellion had come to an end as a result of desertions, dissension among rebel leaders, and declining morale. Hostilities ended with the signing of the Pact of Zanjón, in which Spain promised to implement reforms in Cuba, including general amnesty for the rebels and freedom for the slaves.

Despite Spanish concessions, many rebels were unhappy with the truce, as it did not call for outright independence or the abolition of slavery. Some rebel leaders, such as the Afro-Cuban Antonio Maceo Grajales, continued to fight for another ten weeks after the pact was signed.

Aftermath

Following the Ten Years' War, the abolition of slavery in Cuba was inevitable. Many slaves gained their freedom through the Moret Law of 1870, which granted freedom to children born to slaves, slaves over sixty years old, and slaves who had served in the Spanish army, particularly those who had fought during the Ten Years' War. Other slaves had escaped to the interior of the island during the war. Furthermore, the war had destroyed plantations in certain parts of the island, decreasing the economic need for slave labor. Under the new law, the Spanish government compensated slave owners 125 pesetas for each slave emancipated.

By 1878, the slave population of Cuba had decreased to 227,000 from 363,000 in 1869. The Moret Law, slave mortality, and the destruction of the sugar estates contributed to the decline in the number of slaves on the island.

In 1880, the liberal government in Spain decreed the abolition of slavery in Cuba, although it was accompanied by a six-year period of *patronato*, or unpaid tutelage, during which slave "apprentices" would receive a monthly wage. After 1880, many slaves sought to gain their freedom by filing grievances against their owners, purchasing their own freedom and that of family members, or simply deserting the estates of their former owners, accelerating the

end of slavery in Cuba. In response, the Spanish government effected the complete emancipation of slaves in Cuba in 1886.

Ronald E. Young

See also: Cuba, Emancipation in.

Further Reading

Knight, Franklin W. *Slave Society in Cuba During the Nineteenth Century.* Madison: University of Wisconsin Press, 1970.
Pérez, Louis A., Jr. *Cuba: Between Reform and Revolution.* 3rd ed. New York: Oxford University Press, 2006.
Scott, Rebecca. *Slave Emancipation in Cuba: The Transition to Free Labor, 1860–1899.* Princeton, NJ: Princeton University Press, 1985.

Cuba, Emancipation in

The final abolition of slavery in the Spanish colony of Cuba in 1886 was a watershed, as the Caribbean island's economy depended on the production of sugar traditionally grown by slave labor. Cuba's economic future would be determined by the reorganization of labor following emancipation. Further complicating emancipation, Cuba soon become involved in a war of independence against Spain, resulting in both independence from the mother country in 1898 and growing U.S. influence on the island.

Many sugar planters in the Spanish colony sought to expand production to supply North American refineries. Furthermore, many planters believed that former slaves would not provide a sufficient workforce for the growing industry. The postabolition system that emerged was known as the *colonato*. Under this system, cane farmers called *colonos* provided sugarcane to a central mill for processing. The colonos were a heterogeneous group: Some were former slaves who had received small parcels of land to cultivate, but many were new immigrants from Spain and the Canary Islands who relied on family labor to produce sugar, thus competing with the Afro-Cubans in the economy.

The living conditions of former slaves in Cuba varied by region. In the older sugar-producing regions of the west, emancipated Afro-Cubans had few alternatives to working for their former masters. Most ex-slaves became agricultural wage laborers, though few owned or even rented their own land. The situation was different outside the traditional sugar-producing regions, especially in the eastern part of the island. Here, the colonato system thrived, providing

Afro-Cubans with more opportunities to rent or own land. Nevertheless, at the end of the nineteenth century, most cane farmers in Cuba were white. In 1899, more than 11,000 whites owned or rented land for sugar production, whereas just over 3,000 nonwhite Cubans did so.

Spanish authorities considered a number of steps to socially control the former slaves. At first, officials contemplated vagrancy laws to force the freed slaves to continue to work on the plantations. However, they abandoned such plans for fear of fueling anticolonial sentiment among the Cuban population. Instead, Spain encouraged workers from the mother country to labor in Cuba. In the late nineteenth century, tens of thousands of Spanish workers went to Cuba seasonally or permanently to labor in the sugarcane fields.

In postabolition Cuba, former slaves sought to acquire animals, tools, and land. Sometimes they took advantage of a system of customary possession, whereas at other times they asserted their rights as free people. Before emancipation, it was common for slaves in Cuba to acquire, raise, and sell animals, particularly pigs. Though the animals sometimes provided a source of food, more importantly, they provided a source of income. After emancipation, some planters sought to limit access to animals such as pigs and horses. Selling the animals gave the freed slaves access to cash and mobility, making it more difficult for their former owners to continue to control them. However, Afro-Cubans resisted such attempts, sometimes even withholding their labor when the planters tried to limit their access to animals.

The former slaves also sought land and housing. Sometimes, freed slaves attempted to assert their right to the land and houses they had lived in while they were enslaved. Some planters allowed their former slaves squatter rights on plantations, as it made it easier to maintain a supply of labor. However, it was extremely difficult for former slaves to gain the legal title to land belonging to a plantation owner. Some planters chose to expel the freed Afro-Cubans, who often moved to nearby towns, where they looked for permission to build on empty lots. Some former slaves were able to save enough money to purchase land, often from their former owners. The Spanish colonial government made no formal provision for giving land or housing to the freed slaves.

In addition to plots for housing, the primary goal of many ex-slaves was to acquire rural land on which to grow subsistence and market crops. Such land provided a source of food, as well as a source of income, as Afro-Cubans often produced foodstuffs for local urban markets. This situation gave them a degree of autonomy from the sugar industry. As with housing plots, the former slaves claimed unoccupied land or made formal purchases of land. Planters sometimes willingly allowed the former slaves to settle and cultivate land on the fringes of their estates in order to define the boundaries more clearly and to prevent incursions by neighboring landowners. Generally, the former slaves cultivated poor-quality land on the fringes of plantations or in the foothills of nearby mountains.

In 1895, Cuban separatists rebelled against Spanish rule. Ex-slaves took advantage of the rivalry between Spanish loyalists and Cuban separatists as each side sought to gain the support of the freed Afro-Cuban population. The Spanish colonial government conceded a number of rights, granting Afro-Cuban men the right to vote. Despite the concessions, most ex-slaves joined the rebel cause after 1895. Thousands of Afro-Cubans joined the rebel army as both enlisted men and officers. Those who were not directly involved in the armed struggle contributed material aid to the rebels. Many Afro-Cubans hoped that the establishment of an independent republic would bring about the social changes that abolition had failed to achieve. Later, they used their role in the fight for independence as the basis for requesting citizenship rights after the defeat of Spain in 1898. Indeed, many Cuban nationalists of the late nineteenth century professed racial equality.

However, the intervention of the United States in 1898 impeded the struggle for racial equality. The presence of a U.S. military government on the island from 1899 to 1902 limited the gains that the Afro-Cubans had made, as U.S. authorities demanded respect for private property and offered limited suffrage. U.S. interests came to dominate the Cuban economy. U.S.-owned mills bought up large tracts of land, relegating Afro-Cubans to wage labor. Former slaves faced competition from immigrant workers from Spain, Haiti, and Jamaica.

After achieving independence from Spain in 1898, many Afro-Cubans sought to assert their rights and resist repression. Some turned to strikes and labor organization. In 1902, for example, urban strikes in south-central Cuba spread to the countryside. The anarchist-led Workers Guild included many Afro-Cubans among its ranks. Thus, many former slaves joined with poor whites to form a cross-racial alliance against the exploitation of workers.

By 1910, Afro-Cubans had begun to mobilize, creating *El Partido Independiente de Color* (Independent Party of Color) as a political vehicle to force the government to move toward racial equality. Instead, the government banned the party, and Cuban blacks were rounded up, jailed, or killed. In response, Afro-Cubans openly protested in 1912. The country's white elite labeled the protest as a "race war," and rumors circulated of a black uprising. The Cuban government provided white Cuban volunteers with arms to suppress the revolt by any means possible, and thousands of black Cubans, mostly unarmed, were massacred for "resisting arrest." This massacre quieted most future social protest among Afro-Cubans in the twentieth century.

Ronald E. Young

See also: Cuba, Abolition in.

Further Reading

Helg, Aline. *Our Rightful Share: The Afro-Cuban Struggle for Equality, 1886–1912.* Chapel Hill: University of North Carolina Press, 1995.

Pérez, Louis A., Jr. *Cuba Between Empires, 1878–1902.* Pittsburgh: University of Pittsburgh Press, 1983.

Scott, Rebecca. *Slave Emancipation in Cuba: The Transition to Free Labor, 1860–1899.* Princeton, NJ: Princeton University Press, 1985.

Scott, Rebecca, and Michael Zeuske. "Property in Writing, Property on the Ground: Pigs, Horses, Land, and Citizenship in the Aftermath of Slavery, Cuba, 1880–1909." *Comparative Studies in Society and History* 44 (October 2002): 669–99.

Cuffe, Paul (1759–1817)

One of the first financially and socially successful Americans of color, the seaman and philanthropist Paul Cuffe was an early advocate of resettling free blacks in West Africa. His ideas regarding emigration predated the American Colonization Society (1816), the first organized attempt to encourage African American emigration.

Cuffe was born on Cuttyhunk Island, Massachusetts, on January 17, 1759, to a former slave father who had purchased his freedom and a Native American mother. Like his nine brothers and sisters, Cuffe had no formal education—this was the norm in farming families at the time—but he was ambitious even as a youth. He and his older brother inherited the family farm, but he set out as a teenager to make his own way.

As a teen, Cuffe worked on whaling ships and was captured by the British just as the American Revolution was under way, spending three months in a British jail in New York. Upon his release, Cuffe became a maritime trader and blockade runner, bringing much-needed supplies to Nantucket Island. In 1783, he married Alice Pequit, a local American Indian woman. The couple had seven children.

Maritime New England was growing and developing rapidly in the early years of the republic, offering economic opportunities even for black men. In addition to purchasing a shoemaker's shop, Cuffe continued trading and did some whaling. The seagoing activities were dangerous in and of themselves, but in light of the newly enacted Fugitive Slave Law of 1793, even free blacks at sea were susceptible to capture.

Cuffe came to own several ships and personally sailed to destinations as diverse as Norfolk, Virginia; Vienna, Maryland; the Gulf of Mexico; and, later, Sweden and Denmark. Though the arrival of a black sea captain was often shocking enough (especially in places such as Vienna and ports located farther south), Cuffe's crews were predominantly composed of African American and Native American seamen. By 1800, Cuffe was financially stable, and, in his local community of Westport, Connecticut, he owned about 200 acres and a windmill, in addition to the cobbler's shop.

Cuffe was a respected and connected man in Westport. He set up a racially integrated school on his land, one of the first in the United States. He also maintained close connections with friends in New York who belonged to the African Methodist Episcopal Church and moved in the circles of the Westport Society of Friends (Quakers). Despite his affluence, the respect he commanded, and his philanthropic activities (he paid for a large portion of the Westport Friends Meeting House, which is still in use today), there would always be a color divide between Cuffe and his white Quaker counterparts.

Naval and diplomatic tensions between the new nation and Britain provoked several incidents on the high seas in which U.S. vessels were searched and cargoes seized. In 1807, President Thomas Jefferson's Embargo Act essentially prevented any foreign trade. This law, which was violently condemned in New England, curtailed maritime activity in the region.

On voyages to Wilmington, Delaware, and elsewhere, Cuffe began to speak with local abolitionists, including members of the Delaware Abolition Society, who saw in Cuffe a successful, ambitious, hardworking, and self-made man. These traits formed a powerful combination that matched what most abolitionists were looking for in advocates for their cause. In 1807, the Delaware Abolition Society published Cuffe's biography in a British magazine, and

British antislavery agitators began to see Cuffe as a useful figure. One group that was especially interested in Cuffe was the African Institution, a new antislavery organization founded in 1807 in Britain.

News of West African affairs was relatively easy to come by in the ports of New England, but Cuffe initially showed little interest in any particular area. In 1803, one of Cuffe's ships began regular transatlantic trading, whaling off the African coast and trading with the West Indies. Through these activities, Cuffe became familiar with the British colony of Sierra Leone, which had been established in 1787 as a refuge for London blacks.

Meanwhile, Cuffe formally applied for admission to his local Friends meeting. He soon indicated that he was considering a journey to Sierra Leone to evaluate the merits of establishing a settlement there for free blacks, and he suggested that he and his family might relocate to the West African colony. These thoughts were relayed to the African Institution, which encouraged Cuffe's plans in its correspondence.

Finally, in December 1810, Cuffe departed for Sierra Leone, arriving in March 1811. Cuffe met with the colony's governor, local settlers, and native rulers, and then he sailed on to Britain. In Britain, he visited several cities and met with members of the African Institution, who were eager and willing to facilitate Cuffe's efforts to develop Sierra Leone. A delegation from the group met with the British secretary of state to request a land grant for Cuffe.

Amid such difficulties as embargoes between Britain and the United States, which made it problematic for a citizen of one nation to travel from one territory to another, Cuffe eventually brought thirty-four immigrants to Sierra Leone. By 1817, however, his health was quickly declining, and on September 9 of that year, he died in the presence of his family and friends in Connecticut. His estate was valued at approximately $20,000.

Wayne Ackerson

See also: African Institution; American Colonization Society; Sierra Leone.

Further Reading

Ackerson, Wayne. *The African Institution (1807–1827) and the Antislavery Movement in Great Britain.* Lewiston, NY: Edwin Mellen, 2004.

Harris, Sheldon. *Paul Cuffe: Black America and the African Return.* New York: Simon & Schuster, 1972.

Thomas, Lamont. *Paul Cuffe: Black Entrepreneur and Pan-Africanist.* Urbana: University of Illinois Press, 1988.

Cugoano, Quobna Ottobah (ca. 1757–ca. 1791)

Quobna Ottobah Cugoano, a native African and former British West Indian slave, was one of the few British abolitionists of the eighteenth century to call for immediate abolition of the slave trade and slavery. With his own money, he published his thoughts and experiences under the title *Thoughts and Sentiments on the Evil and Wicked Traffic of the Slavery and Commerce of the Human Species, Humbly Submitted to the Inhabitants of Great Britain by Ottobah Cugoano, a Native of Africa* (1787). His account is especially valuable, as it not only describes the horrors of slavery and the fateful Middle Passage but also gives the point of view of a slave who survived the experience.

Born about 1757 in the small Fante village of Agimaque on the coast of present-day Ghana, Cugoano was kidnapped by African traders and sold into slavery around 1770. The thirteen-year-old found himself in Grenada, where he worked as a field laborer on an estate owned by Alexander Campbell. After making several stops on various West Indian islands, Campbell took Cugoano to Great Britain in 1772.

The following year, at age sixteen, Cugoano was baptized John Stewart, "so that I might not be carried away and sold again." His life thereafter is unknown until the 1780s, when he worked for the painter Richard Cosway and his wife in Pall Mall. While in their employ, Cosway paid for Cugoano's education and eventually freed him.

Although it is unknown when Cugoano gained his freedom, he was working as an active abolitionist by 1786. Associating with other Afro-Britons such as William Green, Olaudah Equiano, and Ignatius Sancho, Cugoano participated in the cause in every way possible. He signed petitions, appealed to British abolitionist Granville Sharp on behalf of others who had been sold into slavery in the West Indies, and published letters and statements describing the horrors of slavery and the slave trade in periodicals and newspapers.

Cugoano financed and published his first book, *Thoughts and Sentiments,* with the support of Richard Cosway. In it, he argued that "every man in Great Britain [was] responsible, in some degree" for the enslavement and oppression of Africa. Translated into French in 1788, with an abridged edition appearing in 1791, it became the first abolitionist book to be published by an African. Advocating the abolition of the slave trade and the emancipation of slaves in all British dominions, Cugoano wrote, "It is as much the duty of a man [who is enslaved] to get out of the hands of his enslaver." In a postscript to the 1791 edition, a thoroughly Anglicized Cugoano announced that he planned to establish a school for "all of his complexion" where they could learn Christianity and the "Laws of Civilization." There is, however, no evidence that he ever opened such a school.

Cugoano dropped out of sight in 1791. Although he was still employed by the Cosways, it is unlikely that he lived with them any longer. Around this time, Cugoano had made a request to Sharp that he be sent to Nova Scotia to participate in the settlement efforts of the British colony in Sierra Leone; he may have gone to recruit freed Afro-Britons to relocate in that African colony. It also is possible that he made his way back to his family in Agimaque, a desire that he hinted at in his 1791 edition: "I wish to go back as soon as I can hear any proper security and safe conveyance can be found." It is generally believed that Cugoano died soon after or within a few years following the publication of this edition.

Despite all that is not known about his life, Cugoano left his mark on history. He was one of the few Africans to be involved in bringing about the Mansfield Judgment of 1772, a piece of legislation that granted freedom to as many as 20,000 slaves living in Britain. The ruling decreed that slaves brought to Britain from other colonies had the right to freedom if they fled their masters and chose to stay in England. In addition to being the first abolitionist work written by an African (though many historians argue that he was helped by Equiano), *Thoughts and Sentiments* was also the first Anglo-African work on the history of slavery and the slave trade.

Colleen A. Vasconcellos

See also: Equiano, Olaudah; Sancho, Ignatius; Sharp, Granville; *Somersett* Case (1772); Sons of Africa.

Further Reading

Cugoano, Quobna Ottobah. *Thoughts and Sentiments on the Evils of Slavery and Other Writings.* 1787, 1791. Ed. Vincent Carretta. New York: Penguin, 1999.

Edwards, Paul, and James Walvin, eds. *Black Personalities in the Era of the Slave Trade.* London: Macmillan, 1983.

Curaçao Slave Revolt (1795)

The Curaçao revolt of 1795 was the largest slave insurrection to occur in the Dutch colonies of the Caribbean. The rebellion spread quickly, and it took the Dutch authorities two weeks to subdue the rebels and another month to capture all of the slaves. In response to the revolt, stricter slave laws were passed in an effort to improve the lives and working conditions of the slaves and thus prevent future insurrections.

The Haitian Revolution, which began in 1791, inspired the slaves of Curaçao to rise up against their white owners. The slaves were also motivated by the French defeat of the Dutch during the Napoleonic Wars and the subsequent establishment of the French-dominated Batavian Republic (1795). The French Republic had abolished slavery in 1794, and the slaves of Curaçao believed that the Batavian Republic would follow suit, as they had noticed increased tensions between local leaders and plantation owners and the government in Amsterdam. The leaders of the revolt genuinely believed that if they could gain control of the island, the Batavian Republic would not have the resources to retake it or any interest in doing so. They had a lengthy list of violations and abuses perpetrated by owners that violated Dutch colonial law on the treatment of slaves.

The revolt was led by Tula and Bastian Carpata, both slaves on one of the island's larger plantations. For several months before the rebellion, they gathered items that could be used as weapons—even if they were only farm tools—and worked to convince more slaves to join the revolt. The slaves were assisted in their preparations by free blacks, who could move between plantations and carry messages between the leaders.

The revolt began on August 17, 1795. That morning, Tula and forty to fifty slaves gathered at the main house on their plantation. They refused to work and presented the estate's owner with a list of grievances. He told the slaves that they were free to present their grievances to the island's governor at Fort Amsterdam. Under Tula's command, the slaves freed their compatriots who had been locked up or were under punishment and left the plantation with their weapons. Meanwhile, the plantation owner's son went by horseback to inform the residents of the other plantations and the government of the uprising.

Tula freed twenty-two slaves from a nearby plantation and went to meet Carpata, who had escaped from his owner with an equal number of slaves. The two dispatched a runaway French slave, Louis Mercier, with a force to attack plantations in the countryside and free more slaves. During his attacks, Mercier was able to capture a small cannon and a number of muskets.

Mercier used the cannon and guns to defeat a small Dutch force, taking its leader and mulatto soldiers captive. Tula defeated a Dutch force of about sixty men who had been sent to subdue the rebellion. Meanwhile, another slave leader, Perdro Wacaww, captured the Plantation Fontein and killed the plantation's owner—the first white victim of the rebellion.

The colonial government responded by calling up the militia and sending in a military force of free blacks, known as the Corps of Free Coloreds and Blacks. Another force was sent into the countryside to attack Tula. The militia troops found Tula's forces on August 19, but before attacking, they sent Father Jacobus Schink to try to negotiate an end to the rebellion. Tula and Carpata were offered amnesty, but they demanded total freedom for themselves and their followers. The Dutch attacked and defeated the poorly armed slaves, most of whom fled into the jungle. There were no Dutch fatalities in the battle, but the conflict claimed the lives of about twenty slaves.

To end the rebellion and capture its leaders, the Dutch authorities offered a blanket pardon to all slaves, with the exception of the revolt's top leadership. They offered a cash payment to free blacks who helped suppress the insurrection and freedom to any slave who helped capture other slaves involved in the revolt. The authorities decreed that any escaped slave with a weapon could be shot.

The escaped slaves continued their rebellion for a few days and even poisoned the wells of whites and conducted small raids. However, the Dutch were able to capture more and more of them. Mercier was captured while on the run. Tula was on captured on September 18 after he was betrayed by a slave at a plantation where he sought to hide. One day later,

Carpata and Wacaww were taken after they were betrayed by slaves loyal to their owners.

With the capture of the two main leaders, the rebellion ended. The leaders, including Tula, Carpata, and Wacaww, were publicly tortured and put to death. Mercier and other prominent leaders were hanged. In all, twenty-six slaves were executed, while others were forced back into bondage. Free blacks who had participated in the revolt were deported and banned from the island.

The colonial government of Curaçao tried to force the plantation owners to address some of the slaves' concerns, passing new laws to prevent another rebellion. For example, the owners were prohibited from giving slaves firearms and required to report runaway slaves immediately. To ease the conditions of the slaves, the owners were ordered to clothe and feed their slaves and to limit punishment. In addition, the laws mandated that field slaves would not work on Sundays and that the workday would not begin before five o'clock in the morning or extend past dusk.

Tom Lansford

See also: Haitian Revolution (1791–1804).

Further Reading

Craton, Michael. *Empire, Enslavement, and Freedom in the Caribbean.* Princeton, NJ: Markus Wiener, 1997.

Geggus, David, ed. *The Impact of the Haitian Slave Revolt in the Atlantic World.* Columbia: University of South Carolina Press, 2001.

Genovese, Eugene D. *From Rebellion to Revolution: Afro-American Slave Revolts in the Making of the Modern World.* Baton Rouge: Louisiana State University Press, 1979; New York: Vintage Books, 1981.

Postma, Johannes. *The Dutch in the Atlantic Slave Trade.* New York: Cambridge University Press, 1990.

Danish West Indies, Abolition in the

The Danish West Indies consisted of three small, adjacent islands in the Caribbean: Saint Thomas, established as a colony in 1672; Saint John, established in 1718; and Saint Croix, established in 1734. From the beginning of the Danish colonial period until 1848, abolitionism on the islands found expression in a variety of individual, group, and institutional forms. Significantly, religion was not connected with abolitionism in the Danish West Indies, a result of the accomodationist mind-set of the denominations that were permitted to settle on the islands.

For individuals and small groups, the most feasible recourse to slavery was *grand marronage*, or permanent escape from the slave owner. Police journals attest that marronage was the most common form of antislavery resistance between 1672 and 1848. In the early years of colonization, extensive forest cover provided ample opportunity for individuals to escape. In later years, hideouts in cane fields and inaccessible caves, neighboring islands, and the islands' towns offered havens for fugitives. Grand marronage became particularly acute and effective after the 1833 emancipation of the neighboring British islands, located only a few miles from Saint John.

Early Resistance

Slaves on the islands sought freedom through organized revolt on several occasions, with varying degrees of success. A slave revolt occurred on each island within twenty years of colonization, when the labor force was primarily African born and the ratio of blacks to whites was heavily weighted toward the former.

The first reported slave rebellion in the Danish West Indies occurred in 1691 on Saint Thomas; it was readily quelled. The first large-scale revolt took place on Saint John in 1733; it proved one of the most successful slave rebellions in Caribbean history. Rebel factions were able to take control of the island, and slavery ceased for more than six months, from November 1733 until May 1734. Rebel conspiracies were discovered and squelched in 1746 and 1759 on Saint Croix; the instigators of the 1759 attempt were tortured and executed.

The formal abolition of the Danish slave trade in 1792 was only a gesture toward the true abolition of the institution of slavery. Danish involvement in the slave trade predated their colonization of the West Indies. The Danish trade involved extensive collaboration with other slave-trading nations and accounted for less than 2 percent of the total African trade. In 1791, a committee formed to investigate the Danish slave trade determined that it was not profitable and suggested that the Danish West Indian slave community could replenish itself through reproduction (with improved social conditions) rather than importation. The Danish Crown abolished the slave trade by ordinance in 1792, with a grace period lasting until 1803. The grace period allowed for accelerated importation of slaves, with an emphasis on the importation of females, to stabilize the labor force.

Denmark holds the distinction of being the first nation to abolish its transatlantic slave trade. However, the considerable gap between its decision to abolish the slave trade in 1792 and the emancipation of Danish West Indian slaves in 1848—fifty-six years—suggests that abolition was motivated by economic and political reasons rather than humanitarian ones.

The abolition of the slave trade indirectly influenced the abolition of slavery in an ideological sense. Cross-culturally, a slave is defined as an outsider. Prior to 1804, approximately 46 percent of all plantation slaves were born in Africa. By the 1840s, only 10 percent were African born, and many of them were elderly. The demographic transition to a locally born slave community diminished the slaves' status as outsiders, increased their social and kinship networks, and strengthened their demands for rights and freedom.

Abolition by Royal Decree

On July 28, 1847, King Christian VIII of Denmark issued a royal proclamation declaring that all unfree persons in the Danish West Indies would gain their freedom twelve years from the decree's date of issue, and all children born after that date would be born free. Governor General Peter von Scholten reached the islands in September and immediately had the proclamation read throughout the islands, particularly in the churches.

The proclamation was not a spontaneous humanitarian action; rather, it was the end result of years of negotiation between Danish officials and von Scholten, encouraged by the emancipation of the British islands in 1833. The colonial administration had made few attempts to reform the conditions of slavery while the slave trade persisted. Afterward, reforms became necessary to prevent depletion of the slave population. Accordingly, von Scholten initiated a sequence of ameliorative reforms in 1828 that eventually came to be regarded as an emancipation plan.

During the 1830s, von Scholten's reforms strictly regulated the length of the workday, curtailed slave owners' arbitrary powers over the use of corporeal punishment, banned public auctions of slaves, gave slaves some property rights, granted legal validity to slave testimony under certain circumstances, and required the maintenance of plantation journals for regular inspection. In the 1840s, the word "slave" was officially replaced with the term "unfree," Saturday became an institutionalized day off for all slaves, and elementary schools for slave children were opened.

These reforms, though they made steps toward reversing the dehumanization of the enslaved, had a causal relationship with the 1848 revolt. Von Scholten promoted what he termed an "eventual emancipation," with definite provisions for a necessarily long period of transition to prepare the enslaved for the conditions of freedom. He strongly opposed the free birth policy enacted by Christian VIII, realizing that it would be unacceptable to both parents and planters. Indeed, historians have identified the free birth policy as the most significant contributor to the 1848 revolt.

The 1848 Revolt

Other critical factors influenced the timing of the rebellion. Christian VIII died unexpectedly in January 1848, and, by March of that year, news of a new Danish constitution and revolution in France had reached the Danish West Indies. In May, reports of insurrection and emancipation in the French West Indies and news that Germany had declared war against Denmark reached the islands. Von Scholten felt the slaves were certain that the change in the Danish constitution would result in their immediate emancipation and that the proclamation had only been delayed. Those enslaved on Saint Croix decided to take action by forcing the issue of emancipation through a carefully planned and concealed rebellion.

The revolt began as enslaved laborers blew conch shells—the signal to assemble—on July 2, 1848, in Frederiksted, Saint Croix. Slaves Moses Robert, Martin Williams, and John Gottlieb were the main leaders of the rebellion. Their plan was to obtain their freedom by initiating a work strike and entering town en masse to demand their freedom. Thousands gathered in town on July 3, awaiting von Scholten's response and threatening to set fire to the town if they were not appeased.

Von Scholten declared the emancipation at 4 P.M., ending sixteen hours of rioting with minimal bloodshed. Von Scholten cited weak colonial institutions, particularly the insufficient military and police force, as concerns when he made his decision to emancipate the enslaved rather than attempt to suppress the rebellion. Von Scholten resigned on July 6, 1848. King Frederick VII issued a royal decree on September 22, 1848, recognizing the emancipation and officially ending slavery in the Danish West Indies.

Lori Lee

See also: Danish West Indies, Emancipation in the; Von Scholten, Peter.

Further Reading

Hall, Neville. *Slave Society in the Danish West Indies: St. Thomas, St. John, and St. Croix.* Ed. B.W. Higman. Baltimore: Johns Hopkins University Press, 1992.

Lawaetz, Hermann. *Peter von Scholten.* Trans. Anne-Luise Knudsen. 1940. Herning, Denmark: Poul Kristensen, 1999.

Tyson, George, ed. *Bondmen and Freedmen in the Danish West Indies.* Saint Thomas: Virgin Islands Humanities Council, 1996.

Von Scholten, Peter. "Letter of December 22, 1849." In *Emancipation in the U.S. Virgin Islands: 150 Years of Freedom*, ed. Arnold Highfield. Saint Croix: Virgin Islands Emancipation Commission/Virgin Islands Humanities Council, 1998.

Danish West Indies, Emancipation in the

The Danish West Indies comprised three small, adjacent islands in the Caribbean—Saint Thomas, Saint John, and Saint Croix—colonized by Denmark between the late seventeenth and early eighteenth century. An island-wide slave rebellion that took place on July 3, 1848, on Saint Croix resulted in the emancipation of all slaves in the Danish West Indies, ending nearly two centuries of plantation-based slave labor.

The freed slaves forged new lives for themselves during a period characterized by social turbulence and economic recession. Emancipation sparked a transition to a new social system in the Danish West Indies, though the form, speed, and process of the transition varied from island to island—a reflection of the diversity of social structures and traditions that had developed on the islands since the earliest days of colonization.

Economic Life

The Danish islands were strategically located near the traditional points of entry from North America and Europe to and from the West Indies. This location was desirable for the establishment of a trading entrepôt. Saint Thomas, in particular, was a prime location and quickly became a successful free port. Because Saint Thomas had limited agricultural potential, the Danish also colonized Saint John and Saint Croix, which were more hospitable to plantation agriculture. In the 1840s, more than 80 percent of the population of Saint Thomas was engaged in nonagricultural occupations, primarily in positions related to trade in the island's commerce-based social system. In comparison, Saint John and Saint Croix were dependent on sugar production and had plantation-based social systems.

After emancipation, the planters were eager to organize a new means of retaining labor on their plantations. The colonial assembly established the labor regulations of 1849, which were among the most restrictive in the West Indies. The regulations stipulated a mandatory yearly contract with fixed wages for fixed hours of work. Wages, hours, and the length of the contract were established by law rather than by negotiation between workers and planters. Workers were required to enter into contracts each October, and notice of non-renewal could only be given in August. A vagrancy law ensured compliance. Employers were required to provide free housing and a cultivation plot.

Some workers perceived the regulations as an attempt to return them to slavery. Workers from seventy-seven Cruzan plantations organized a strike on July 2, 1849, but the police quickly forced them back to work. Later that month, workers on Saint John began boycotting work in the cane fields.

Thus, the postemancipation era began with conflict. Some Cruzan workers migrated into the towns to seek work, attracted by these centers of trade with their consonant need for service-related labor. Workers from Saint John and Saint Croix migrated to Saint Thomas. Officials attempted to halt migration by creating a mandatory (though limited) passport system. Even with tight social controls in place, the labor force continued to decline. This lack of labor was a central concern among planters throughout the postemancipation era, and it shaped their volatile relationships with the workers. The planters chose to solve the labor problem by using their resources to import immigrant workers rather than improve social conditions for local workers. Immigrant workers were primarily recruited from the surrounding islands.

Revolt

In 1878, Cruzan workers demonstrated their long-term dissatisfaction with the labor regulations and living conditions by mounting another rebellion against the plantation system. An investigative committee formed that year identified three primary factors contributing to the workers' dissatisfaction: the planters' abuse of the penalty fining system, frustration with the short period of time allowed to annul annual contracts, and obstacles that prevented workers from leaving the island. Discontent over wage inequalities and differential employment opportunities created by the opening of a central factory and the hiring of day laborers also fueled the protest.

The so-called Fireburn rebellion lasted four days, resulting in extensive damage and vicious suppression by the government. The labor regulations were repealed on August 1, 1879, and another general strike took place on October 1, 1879. As a result, government concessions allowed workers the freedom to choose the length and location of their employment.

Workers began referring to 1848 as the "first free" and 1878 as the "second free." Many workers left their plantations for the towns to work as porters or day laborers. Sugar production remained the predominant industry on Saint Croix, constituting more than 90 percent of the crops as late as 1917.

Aftermath

Emancipation brought a dramatic increase in estate expenses compared to the size of the labor force. On Saint Thomas and Saint John, for example, it was impossible to produce sugar without a large labor force, and so emancipation had a devastating economic effect as sugar production declined there. On Saint Thomas, plantation wages could not match those paid at the harbor, prompting workers to migrate into the towns; sugar production was largely abandoned by 1860.

By the 1850s, Saint Thomas had become an important shipping and distribution center for the West Indies and a locus of transit trade between Haiti and several South American republics. Charlotte Amalie, the main harbor and town, employed thousands of workers in service-related jobs, as well as many artisans. These workers received high pay and were rarely limited by the 1849 labor regulations. Trade and commerce continued to be central pursuits in the second half of the nineteenth century, though they were adversely affected by natural disasters and the increasing use of steamships.

Sugar production on Saint John became increasingly unprofitable and ceased around 1880 as a result of a lack of capital to modernize the sugar plantations, emigration from the island, serious disease epidemics, and natural disaster. On Saint John, agriculture was the only means of subsistence aside from fishing and production of charcoal. Plantation cultivation continued after the production of sugar ceased, but instead focused on bay oil, lime trees, and cattle. When the sugar plantations failed, many prominent estate owners sold their estates and left Saint John. Several African West Indians from other islands purchased these estates to raise stock and became the core of a new upper class on the island.

On Saint John, the peasant society that emerged after emancipation developed out of the social structure that had existed there during slavery. The enslaved became largely self-sufficient through subsistence activities, cultivating crops, raising livestock, and fishing. After emancipation, they sought to establish their own independent society of small, self-sufficient farmers outside the plantations, whereas the owners attempted to retain them as a dependent labor source. In July 1848, an injunction limiting the sale of land to workers was enacted in order to prevent squatting. It succeeded but also prompted considerable emigration. When sugar cultivation ceased, the planters no longer considered small holdings a threat. By 1915, the majority of residents on Saint John were living on such small holdings, and the population had stabilized.

The postemancipation communities that developed in the Danish West Indies were based on social systems and practices that had been initiated during slavery. A subsistence-based social structure developed on Saint John, a trade- and service-based system on Saint Thomas, and a rural proletariat on Saint Croix. The postemancipation era was a difficult period of adjustment as former slaves, planters, and officials negotiated strategies for the provision of labor and freedom. Social instability combined with natural disasters and economic decline. Denmark lost interest in the unprofitable islands as colonial possessions, and they were sold to the United States in 1917.

Lori Lee

See also: Danish West Indies, Abolition in the; Von Scholten, Peter.

Further Reading

Dookhan, Isaac. *A History of the Virgin Islands of the United States.* 1974. Kingston, Jamaica: Canoe, 2002.

Highfield, Arnold, ed. *Emancipation in the U.S. Virgin Islands: 150 Years of Freedom.* Saint Croix: Virgin Islands Emancipation Commission/Virgin Islands Humanities Council, 1998.

Jensen, Peter. *From Serfdom to Fireburn and Strike: The History of Black Labor in the Danish West Indies, 1848–1916.* Saint Croix, Virgin Islands: Antilles, 1998.

Olwig, Karen. *Cultural Adaptation and Resistance on Saint John: Three Centuries of Afro-Caribbean Life.* Gainesville: University Press of Florida, 1984.

Davis, Paulina Wright (1813–1876)

As a lecturer, editor, antislavery activist, and suffragist, Paulina Kellogg Wright Davis spent a lifetime working for America's reform causes. Although she once wrote, "I hate organizations. They cramp me," she worked with fellow suffragists Elizabeth Cady Stanton and Susan B. Anthony to organize the National Woman Suffrage Association in 1869.

Born Paulina Kellogg on August 7, 1813, near Niagara Falls, New York, she was orphaned at the age of seven and grew up in the care of her aunt. As a young woman, she developed a zeal for helping the disadvantaged, but the Presbyterian Church, of which she was a faithful member, did not allow women to become missionaries.

Her passion won the attention of Francis Wright, a young merchant from Utica, New York. They wed in 1833 and settled in Utica, where they joined the local reform movement. When the Presbyterian Church took a proslavery position, the Wrights resigned their membership and became active in the antislavery movement.

Together, the Wrights organized Utica's first antislavery convention in October 1835. On the day the convention was to start, word came that a mob had organized to stop them. They hastily moved the meeting to the nearby home of fellow activist Gerrit Smith. The mob descended on the Wright home, tearing down fences and demolishing porches. They piled hay around the house to burn it down, but before lighting the fire, the rioters looked inside the parlor window to see a group of women who had stayed behind calmly kneeling in prayer. The crowd slowly drifted away.

After her husband's death, Paulina Wright moved to New York City to continue her amateur study of human anatomy. She acquired an anatomically correct female mannequin from France, called a *femme modele*, and embarked on a lecture tour of the eastern United States to teach women about the construction of their own bodies, a taboo subject at the time. This had never been done before, and the effect was shocking: News accounts reported that women would "drop their veils, [run] out of the room, or even [faint]."

A charming, intelligent young woman, Paulina Wright did not stay a widow for long. In 1849, she married Thomas Davis, a Rhode Island jeweler and antislavery politician. The couple adopted two daughters and moved to the outskirts of Providence. Unlike her first husband, Davis had no objection to his wife speaking in public, and Paulina Wright Davis began an active schedule of lecturing on antislavery and women's rights.

Increasingly, Davis began to focus her energies on women's rights. With Lucy Stone, she organized the first women's rights convention in Worcester, Massachusetts, in 1850; two years later, she founded a newspaper dedicated to the education of women. Called *Una*, the monthly paper was acknowledged as the first publication of the women's rights movement to "discuss the rights, sphere, duty and destiny of women, fully and fearlessly." After her husband was elected to the U.S. House of Representatives in 1854, Davis began to share control of *Una* with feminist Caroline Healy Dall, but the two women clashed over the editorial direction, and, by 1855, the paper had ceased publication.

Like many women abolitionists, Davis faced a choice after the U.S. Civil War. Some, such as Stanton and Anthony, felt they could not support suffrage for freed male slaves if women were not also enfranchised.

Like many leaders of the women's rights movement, Paulina Wright Davis was an active abolitionist. Like some, however, she could not support suffrage for freed male slaves until women, too, were enfranchised. *(Hulton Archive/Getty Images)*

Others felt that every effort should be made to raise up the former slaves, regardless of whether women were enfranchised.

Davis had already foreseen this possibility. As early as 1854, she had written, "[T]he harmony, unity, and oneness of the race cannot be secured while there is class legislation; while one half of humanity is cramped within a narrow sphere and governed by arbitrary power." In 1869, she said goodbye to many of her old abolitionist friends and joined Stanton and Anthony's wing of the movement, helping to organize the National Woman Suffrage Association. In 1871, she was chosen to write the history of the first two decades of the women's rights movement for the association.

Davis's final years were spent mostly in Europe, where she indulged her love of art and painting until her hands became crippled by arthritis. In 1876, she returned to Rhode Island and died at her home in Providence on August 24 of that year.

Heather K. Michon

See also: Anthony, Susan B.; Stanton, Elizabeth Cady; Stone, Lucy; Women's Rights and the Abolitionist Movement.

Further Reading

Ginzberg, Lori D. *Women in Antebellum Reform.* Wheeling, IL: Harlan Davidson, 2000.

Lutz, Alma. *Crusade for Freedom: The Women of the Antislavery Movement.* Boston: Beacon, 1968.

Dawes, William (1799–1888)

The abolitionist William Dawes worked tirelessly to ensure that African Americans would one day enjoy the same liberties as all other Americans. As the grandson of an American patriot (also named William Dawes) who rode with Paul Revere and Samuel Prescott to alert Massachusetts farmers of the advance of British troops out of Boston in 1775, Dawes inherited a storied name and a sense of history. Two generations later, the grandson Dawes would become an important abolitionist and an educational reformer who spent his life defending the liberties that his famous forefather had helped to initiate.

From 1839 to 1851, Dawes served as a trustee of Oberlin College in Ohio (known as the Oberlin Collegiate Institute before 1850), and he was a major financial benefactor of the institution throughout his life. He was best known for his fund-raising activities on behalf of the school. Founded in 1833, Oberlin had earned a special place in the American abolitionist movement as the first institution of higher education in the United States to accept black students on an equal basis with white students. Though this was a noble action on the part of the institution, Oberlin still struggled for financial survival in its early years. Already in a precarious situation, the young institution faced especially difficult times after the financial panic of 1837, and it looked as though the antislavery school might go bankrupt.

In 1839, having been appointed soliciting agent for the institution, Dawes was sent to Great Britain with John Keep, president of Oberlin's board of trustees, to conduct a fund-raising campaign on behalf of the college. They were able to raise $30,000 (then £6,000), enough to retire the institutional debt and keep Oberlin afloat.

In addition to conducting their fund-raising meetings, the two American abolitionists lectured on antislavery themes during their visit to Britain. The two men were able to meet some of the most influential leaders in the transatlantic antislavery movement. While Dawes was in London, he attended the 1840 World Anti-Slavery Convention, which drew nearly 500 delegates from the United States and Great Britain. Dawes was one of the American abolitionists who later sat for a portrait, and he was immortalized in Benjamin Robert Haydon's famous painting memorializing that event, *The Anti-Slavery Society Convention* (1841).

Like many other nineteenth-century American abolitionists, Dawes was drawn into other social reform movements of his era. A committed pacifist, he was actively involved in the U.S. antiwar movement and served as president of the Lorain County Peace Society in Ohio.

Junius P. Rodriguez

See also: World Anti-Slavery Convention (1840).

Further Reading

Fletcher, Robert Samuel. *A History of Oberlin College from Its Foundation Through the Civil War.* Oberlin, OH: Oberlin College, 1943.

Day, Thomas (1748–1789)

One of the first individuals to harness literature as a tool in the fight against slavery, the English writer and social reformer Thomas Day, wrote publications ranging from poetry to political tracts. He is remembered primarily as the author of the three-volume *History of Sandford and Merton* (1783–1789), one of the earliest novels written for children.

Day was born in London on June 22, 1748, the only child of a prosperous merchant who died when Day was only one year old, leaving him financially independent. He received his formal education at the Charterhouse School and later at Corpus Christi College at Oxford University.

Day became a proponent of the natural education espoused by Jean-Jacques Rousseau in his novel *Émile* (1762), and part of his interest in slavery stemmed from a romanticized view of the natural existence of Africans before being sold into slavery. Day was a member of the Lunar Society, an informal group of men of letters who met in Birmingham; some of the most prominent figures in the abolitionist cause came from the organization's ranks.

Day's active involvement in the antislavery crusade began after he read a newspaper article about an escaped slave, recently baptized and engaged to a white servant, who had shot himself in London after being recaptured by his master. Although Lord Mansfield had ruled in 1772 that escaped slaves in England could not be returned to their owners by force, little effort was being made to enforce the decision.

With John Bicknell, an old school friend, Day wrote "The Dying Negro" (1773), a highly sentimental poem about a man on the verge of suicide who recounts his natural existence in Gambia, a bucolic life interrupted by the arrival of Europeans. Hospitality is extended to the white men, who return it by inviting the tribesmen aboard their ship for a supposed feast that turns out to be a trap. On board, the captured African falls in love with a white female servant and, upon arrival in England, is baptized in order to be free from slavery and to marry her. His plans are interrupted by his brutal owner, and the African feels he has no choice but to kill himself.

Although Day refused to keep any of the proceeds, the poem sold many copies and was reprinted several times. It received critical praise in the pages of the *Monthly Review* and the *English Review.* The piece inspired a growing genre of antislavery poems, including Hannah More's *Slavery, a Poem* (1788).

Day became involved in the political issues of the day and was active in reform organizations such as the Society for Constitutional Information, which worked for universal male suffrage and annual parliaments. Beginning in 1776, he published a series of pamphlets, speeches, and poems in favor of the American cause. Though he supported the Americans in their struggle for liberty, he noted the contradiction of leaders who talked about their oppression by the British yet supported the institution of slavery.

After meeting John Laurens, the son of a South Carolina plantation owner who was considering whether to free his slaves, Day wrote *Fragment of an Original Letter on the Slavery of Negroes* (1784). He worked on the pamphlet with enthusiasm, believing that it could persuade Laurens to free his slaves. Using an excerpt from the Declaration of Independence, Day argued that, just as America had the right to break off its ties to Great Britain, slaves also possessed an inalienable right to live in freedom. "If there be an object truly ridiculous in nature," he noted indignantly, "it is an American patriot signing resolutions of independence with one hand, and with the other brandishing a whip over his affrighted slaves."

In 1783, Day published the first volume of the work for which he is best remembered, the children's novel *History of Sandford and Merton*, in which slavery is a peripheral issue. In the book, the spoiled child Tommy Merton is the son of a rich West Indian planter who owns slaves; both title characters are saved by a kind African who rescues the boys from a bull that has been baited. The novel was a tremendous success and continued to be read at the end of the nineteenth century. Day died on September 28, 1789, at the age of forty after falling off a horse that he thought he could tame through kindness.

Kenneth Pearl

See also: Somersett Case (1772).

Further Reading

Rowland, Peter. *The Life and Times of Thomas Day, 1748–1789: English Philanthropist and Author: Virtue Almost Personified.* Lewiston, NY: Edwin Mellen, 1996.

Day, William Howard (1825–1900)

William Howard Day was a noted African American newspaper editor, printer, educator, orator, abolitionist, and minister of the nineteenth century. He was a supporter of the radical abolitionist John Brown and his failed Harpers Ferry raid in 1859.

Day was born on October 19, 1825, in New York City to John and Eliza Dixon Day. After his father died, leaving the family destitute, he was adopted by a white man, J.P. Williston of Northampton, Massachusetts. Williston, an ink manufacturer and social reformer, provided for Day's education and apprenticed him to a local newspaper, *The Hampshire Herald.* In time, these skills would provide Day with a means to champion his many reform and abolitionist ideas. Day entered Oberlin College in 1843, graduating in 1847; he later received an honorary doctor of divinity degree from Livingston College in Salisbury, North Carolina, in 1887.

After graduating from Oberlin, Day settled in Cleveland, Ohio, where he worked as a journalist and then editor of the Cleveland *True Democrat.* In 1853, he established his own newspaper, *The Aliened American*, which ranked among the first black newspapers in the Midwest.

Politically, he led campaigns for black suffrage and against Ohio's oppressive Black Laws. He was also active in the local and national Black Convention movement, which provided a forum for leaders to discuss African American issues and considered Canada a potential location for emigration. In 1852, Day was elected secretary of the National Council of Colored People, an advocate of black interests, and, in 1853, he represented Ohio at the organization's national convention. Originally opposed to colonization and emigration, Day eventually came to support Martin Delany's "back-to-Africa" movement. He also advocated armed resistance to bring an end to slavery, a position that brought him much criticism.

After *The Aliened American* failed in 1855, Day grew frustrated by the prejudice and discrimination that free blacks faced in the North. Suffering from poor health, he moved to Ontario, Canada, in 1857 and began writing occasional articles for Mary Ann Shadd Carey's newspaper, the *Provincial Freeman*, in nearby Chatham. When his health improved, Day began to teach and developed educational programs for freedom seekers in Canada.

By 1858, Day had set up his own print shop in Saint Catharines, Ontario. A supporter of John Brown, he secretly printed Brown's *Provisional Constitution,* which outlined the visionary free state for former slaves that Brown hoped to establish in the South. Brown presented this document to a small group of black men who met secretly in Chatham in May 1858 and adopted Brown's "Declaration of Liberty." The following autumn, Day was in Britain with William King, founder of the Elgin Settlement in Buxton, Ontario, to raise funds for black schools when Brown led his failed raid at Harpers Ferry, Virginia. During the U.S. Civil War, Day remained in Britain, lecturing and gathering support for the Union cause and the freedmen.

After returning to the United States, Day worked for the Freedmen's Bureau (formally, the Bureau of Refugees, Freedmen and Abandoned Lands), the government agency responsible for aiding the former slaves in their transition to freedom, and he committed himself to establishing schools for black children throughout the South. He was appointed inspector general of schools for refugees and freedmen in Maryland and Delaware in 1867, overseeing approximately 140 schools in the region. Day risked his life registering black voters in Wilmington, Delaware, in 1869. In 1878, he became the first African American elected to the school board in Harrisburg, Pennsylvania. He eventually became president of the board, representing the nearly all-white school system until his retirement in 1899.

In 1866, Day was ordained as a minister in the African Methodist Episcopal Zion Church, and in 1886, he was elected general secretary of its General Conference, a post he held until his death. Throughout this period, he remained active in missionary and educational work. Day co-edited the *Zion Church Herald and Outlook*, the church's first paper to be published, with John E. Price.

After a long illness, Day died on December 3, 1900, in Harrisburg, Pennsylvania. A member of the Freemasons and the Odd Fellows, Day was buried in Lincoln Cemetery in Harrisburg.

Kate Clifford Larson

See also: Brown, John; Delany, Martin Robison; Freedmen's Bureau.

Further Reading

Quarles, Benjamin. *Black Abolitionists*. New York: Oxford University Press, 1969.
Ripley, C. Peter, et al., eds. *The Black Abolitionist Papers*. 5 vols. Chapel Hill: University of North Carolina Press, 1985–1992.
Sterling, Dorothy, ed. *Speak Out in Thunder Tones: Letters and Other Writings by Black Northerners, 1787–1865*. Garden City, NY: Doubleday, 1973; New York: Da Capo, 1998.

De Gouges, Marie Olympe (ca. 1748–1793)

One of the most influential French women of the Enlightenment era, Marie Olympe de Gouges established her home as a salon where leading *philosophes* (writers) could gather to discuss the events of the day. As such, her home was the center of the early antislavery debates held in France during the late eighteenth century. Also a playwright, de Gouges is best known for her political writings in support of the French Revolution and her advocacy of women's rights, which she put forth in her *Declaration of the Rights of Woman and Citizen* (1791).

Born sometime around 1748 in southern France, Marie Gouze was the daughter of a butcher from Montauban. At the age of sixteen, she married Louis Yves Aubrey, a much older man with whom she had a son. In the early 1780s, she arrived in Paris, where she claimed to be a widow (although she may have fled her husband). She changed her name to Olympe de Gouges, taking her mother's middle name, adding the aristocratic "de," and altering the spelling of Gouze to Gouges. She also asserted that her father was the notable playwright Marquis Le Franc de Pompignan, who refused to accept her paternity. As a free woman in Paris, de Gouges embarked on a career as a playwright herself, penning works for the Comédie Française and working as an actress, though without any great success.

In one of her nontheatrical works, an open letter titled *Lettre au peuple, au projet d'une cause patriotiqe* (Letter to the People, or Project for a Patriotic Bank by a Female Citizen, 1788), she demanded that women, the key to national regeneration and reform, needed the ability to act legally and control their own finances. She outlined changes such as legalized divorce, rights for illegitimate children, maternity hospitals, a national theater, clean streets, and the abolition of slavery, and she called for an end to the monarchial government in order to achieve such reforms. Her ideas were met with ridicule.

The early days of the French Revolution offered de Gouges a new outlet for her ideas. She became outspoken in defending the monarchy against Jacobin radicalism and dedicated her September 1791 *Déclaration des droits de la femme et de la citoyenne* (Declaration of the Rights of Woman and Citizen) to the queen, Marie Antoinette.

The new political climate offered de Gouges an audience for her plays, which were written so that the audience's true nature would be revealed through strong emotion; as a result, they featured histrionic and melodramatic plots and acting. On December 26, 1789, the Théâtre de la Nation, subsidized by the antislavery *Société des Amis des Noirs* (Society of Friends of the Blacks), produced her play *L'Esclavage des noirs* (Slavery of the Negroes), subtitled "The Happy Shipwreck." In it, de Gouges refuted the stereotypes of black and white by introducing noble black characters to illustrate the way in which whites had usurped human rights through their monopoly on technology and education. For de Gouges, equality was a state of nature, whether between men and women, black and white, eldest and youngest children, or legitimate and illegitimate children. The play ran only three nights, as the actors playing the slaves refused to wear blackface.

De Gouges began to concentrate on the rights of women, which she saw as the cornerstone of a successful social revolution. A proper place in public affairs would ensure that women could promote the preservation of order and the common good through benevolent and paternalistic government. In October 1789, she presented a full program of feminist reforms to the French National Assembly that included the elimination of dowries, freedom for women to enter any occupation, and legal gender equality. Additionally, she advocated the total abolition of slavery in the French Empire, even at the cost of the colonies.

Slavery's corruptive influence, she argued, threatened both women and the revolution through its insidious immorality and promotion of bigotry.

De Gouges never belonged to any of the women's revolutionary clubs. She preferred instead to write pamphlets and speak publicly, especially in light of her monarchist views, which extended to volunteering to defend King Louis XVI at his trial.

Increasingly the enemy of Maximilien de Robespierre, leader of the Jacobin political party—whom she suggested should throw himself into the Seine River as a public service—de Gouges began to annoy the more radical Committee of Public Safety with her insistence on women's participation in the revolution. Believing that women had been cheated of liberty, equality, and fraternity, she pointed out that women could be tried and executed for their political beliefs but could not exercise them publicly.

The final straw came in July 1793, when de Gouges suggested that the public vote on a form of government—republic, federal union, or monarchy—in order to repudiate Robespierre, the radical Jacobins, and the Committee of Public Safety. Arrested immediately for treason, she was tried and convicted on November 1. Despite her claim that she was pregnant and her plea to delay the sentence, she was executed by guillotine two days later.

Slavery and abolition were never primary issues for de Gouges; rather, she advocated a crucial recognition of equality among all people, including women, illegitimate children, and black slaves. Her plays made a forceful and emotional case for human dignity and a revolution that embraced the ideals of natural law and the common good. Instead, she was destroyed by a revolution of men who disdained her participation and humanist goals.

Margaret Sankey

See also: Enlightenment.

Further Reading

Kadish, Doris Y., and Françoise Massardier-Kenney, eds. *Translating Slavery: Gender and Race in French Women's Writing, 1783–1823.* Kent, OH: Kent State University Press, 1994.

Melzer, Sara, and Leslie W. Rabine, eds. *Rebel Daughters: Women and the French Revolution.* New York: Oxford University Press, 1991.

Proctor, Candice. *Women, Equality, and the French Revolution.* Westport, CT: Greenwood, 1990.

Roessler, Shirley Elson. *Out of the Shadows: Women and Politics in the French Revolution 1789–95.* New York: Peter Lang, 1996.

Declaration of Independence (1776)

The Second Continental Congress approved the Declaration of Independence, the document that asserted the independence of the thirteen North American colonies from British rule, on July 4, 1776, in Philadelphia, Pennsylvania. The document was written and endorsed amid disagreements between Great Britain and the colonies over taxation and the abuse of traditional English liberties by Parliament since the end of the French and Indian War in 1763.

The Declaration of Independence announced a new nation and set forth a philosophy of human freedom. Although language of the slave trade was struck from its original draft, the document's fundamental tenets of equality and "Life, Liberty and the pursuit of Happiness" would be referenced by abolitionists to usher in the end of slavery.

Origins

In summer 1776, amid a tense political climate filled with open warfare between the colonies and Britain, the Continental Congress met in Philadelphia with the intention of voting for independence. On June 11, 1776, the Congress appointed a committee of five men to draft a document declaring independence for a pending vote in three weeks. The committee consisted of Thomas Jefferson representing Virginia, John Adams from Massachusetts, Roger Sherman from Connecticut, Benjamin Franklin from Pennsylvania, and Robert R. Livingston from New York.

The Declaration of Independence was modeled on the English Bill of Rights, promulgated in 1689 after the Glorious Revolution, which replaced King James II with William and Mary as the new rulers of England. The English Bill of Rights affirmed the liberties shared by all Englishmen that had been endangered by James II. It also listed the offenses of James II as causes for his removal. On the eve of the American Revolution, some colonies had drafted their own declarations of independence based on the English Bill of Rights; examples include Virginia's Declaration of Rights (May 1776).

The Declaration of Independence, drafted by Jefferson, begins with a preamble outlining the "inalienable rights" based on "self-evident truths" held by all men, followed by a list of grievances committed by King George III upon the colonies. It concludes with a pledge by all members of the Continental Congress to continue the cause of independence.

Congress approved the Declaration of Independence on July 4, and by July 19, all the colonies had approved it. The Continental Congress approved an official copy, which was signed by all its members on August 2, bringing the struggle against Britain to a whole new level.

Slavery Language

In a preliminary draft of the declaration, Jefferson cited the African slave trade as one example of British oppression. He included a paragraph denouncing King George III for the spread of slavery throughout the colonies that read: "He has waged cruel war against human nature itself, violating its most sacred rights of life and liberty in the persons of a distant people who never offended him, captivating [and] carrying them into slavery in another hemisphere, or to incur miserable death in their transportation thither . . . Determined to keep open a market where men should be bought and sold, he has prostituted his negative for suppressing every legislative attempt to prohibit or to restrain this execrable commerce."

Knowing that condemning slavery would alienate proslavery colonists and force them to give their support to the king, Franklin and Adams urged Jefferson to delete this language. When Jefferson submitted his draft on June 28, Congress rejected the paragraph, mostly because of sectional sensitivities. Southerners did not want to confront the reality of human bondage in their own midst as they struggled for liberty against an oppressive government, and Northerners did not want to be seen as complicit in the trafficking of human beings. Most Southern plantation owners were economically dependent on slave labor; specifically, South Carolina and Georgia resolved to vote against the declaration if the slavery language remained. In order to keep all the colonies united, Congress withdrew the paragraph.

The words "all men are created equal" and the overarching concept of equality raised contradictions about Jefferson, a lifelong owner of slaves. As a man of the Enlightenment, he subscribed to the ideas of philosophers John Locke and Baron de La Brède et de Montesquieu regarding the fundamental equality among all human beings. In his writings, Jefferson railed against the disfranchisement of 4 million Americans by 160,000 electors in Great Britain whose vote could affect the colonies. In the realm of race relations, however, Jefferson wrote of the supposed inferiority of Africans to Europeans in terms of intelligence, skill, and physical beauty. In his *Notes on the State of Virginia* (written in 1780–1781 but not published until 1785), Jefferson declared that, by nature, blacks and whites were too different from one another to live together in peace. Such contradictions would continually haunt the new nation and forever be a part of Jefferson's reputation.

Legacy and Meaning

During the first years of the republic, the declaration's promise of equality was championed to gain rights for all white men to hold elected office, to have political representation, and to have access to opportunity, regardless of class. However, the promise of equality enshrined in the declaration stung deeper in America's conscience. Americans of all political stripes found it difficult to reconcile the words of the declaration with the reality of slavery. As the colonists achieved freedom from King George III, American slaves repeatedly petitioned the colonial assemblies and courts for their freedom, questioning how the Declaration of Independence could state that "all men are created equal" when at least half a million individuals remained enslaved.

Moreover, people of diverse religious denominations saw the declaration and the Revolution it had wrought as more than a political struggle; it was a religious struggle against the evils of slavery. In 1820, clergyman Samuel Hopkins observed that the Declaration of Independence went further than the Bible in declaring slavery a sin. Quakers and other Protestants saw the abolition of slavery as a way to purify the nation and to fulfill its promise as the proverbial "city upon a hill."

During the years following the Revolution, the leaders of the early republic made earnest efforts to address the question of slavery. By the end of the 1780s, an abolitionist movement had taken hold among the Northern states. In 1783, the Superior Court of Massachusetts declared slavery incompatible with its constitution. Vermont and New Hampshire ended the institution outright, and Connecticut, Rhode Island, and Pennsylvania gradually abolished it. The generation that had led and fought the American Revolution seemed hopeful that the stain of slavery might be removed in their lifetimes.

The cause of abolitionism, however, suffered major setbacks. At the 1787 Constitutional Convention, the "three-fifths compromise," which determined how slaves would be counted, protected the status of slavery in the Constitution to appease Southern states that wanted to include their slave populations in apportionment representation. Second, the Constitution granted the American slave trade twenty years of protection, causing much consternation among abolitionists. Additionally, the economic impact of abolishing slavery weighed heavily in the minds of the leaders of the postrevolutionary era, as they debated whether slave owners would be compensated for the loss of their "property."

As the revolutionary era slipped into history, those wishing to eliminate slavery continued to employ the words of the Declaration of Independence. On December 30, 1799, a delegation of seventy-four African Americans from Philadelphia petitioned the U.S. House of Representatives to bring an end to the slave trade so that their people might "be permitted to partake in the liberties and inalienable rights" to which they were entitled. The petition was rejected by a vote of eighty-five to one.

In the decades before the U.S. Civil War, orator Frederick Douglass continually reminded the nation of the promises contained in the Declaration of Independence. He denounced the hypocrisy of a society that claimed to espouse a belief in equality while holding one class of people in bondage. After the Civil War brought about the official end of slavery, Douglass continued to argue that it still had not fulfilled the promises contained in the Declaration of Independence.

Dino E. Buenviaje

See also: American Revolution (1775–1781); U.S. Constitution (1789).

Further Reading

Fehrenbacher, Don E. *The Slaveholding Republic: An Account of the United States Government's Relations to Slavery.* New York: Oxford University Press, 2001.

MacLeod, Duncan J. *Slavery, Race, and the American Revolution.* Cambridge, UK: Cambridge University Press, 1974.

Maier, Pauline. *American Scripture: Making the Declaration of Independence.* New York: Alfred A. Knopf, 1997.

Miller, Keith D. "Frederick Douglass, Martin Luther King Jr., and Malcolm X Interpret the Decoration of Independence." In *The Declaration of Independence: Origins and Impact,* ed. Scott Douglas Gerber. Washington, DC: CQ, 2002.

Quarles, Benjamin. "The Revolutionary War as a Black Declaration of Independence." In *Slavery and Freedom in the Age of the American Revolution*, ed. Ira Berlin and Ronald Hoffman. Charlottesville: University of Virginia Press, 1983.

Wills, Garry. *Inventing America: Jefferson's Declaration of Independence.* New York: Vintage Books, 1979.

Declaration of the Rights of Man and of the Citizen (1789)

The Declaration of the Rights of Man and of the Citizen is a manifesto that was adopted by the French National Assembly on August 26, 1789. The declaration served as the preamble to the French constitution, ratified in 1791.

The document upheld the ideals of human rights and equality, not just for the French people but for all humanity, and it became a model for future revolutions. In addition, the statement served as a banner for the cause of French abolitionism throughout the nineteenth century.

Origins and Significance

By 1789, the old regime of the absolutist monarchy had reached a crisis point. The eighteenth century had witnessed population growth and the rise of the economic influence of the middle class. Although the French economy was expanding during this period, most of the workers and the peasants were not partaking in the wealth generated by commerce and industry. France remained largely feudal in its outlook, and the church and the nobility held privileges that exempted them from taxation and other burdens borne by most of French society.

Conditions worsened toward the end of the eighteenth century. The 1770s were a period of economic recession. The years between 1787 and 1789 were plagued by bad harvests, causing starvation among the poor. Additionally, the economic policies of the monarchy had created a fiscal crisis that could no longer be ignored.

It was a budgetary crisis that precipitated the events of 1789. A century of war had left the government on the brink of bankruptcy. There were calls for King Louis XVI to make drastic reforms in the budget. Anne-Robert-Jacques Turgot, the finance minister, proposed a major revamping of the tax system, strict economy by the royal family, the easing of restrictions on commerce, and the end of monopolies.

Pressure mounted for the king to convoke the parliaments, which had long been marginalized since the establishment of absolutism. In 1787, Louis XVI called for an Assembly of Notables, which was composed of the nobility, the clergy, and the commons, in order to address the financial crisis. The nobility opposed any measures to end its privileged status and instead called for new taxes.

On May 1, 1789, the king assembled the Estates-General, representing the church, the nobility, and everyone else; the body had not met since 1614. When it first assembled, the Estates-General was confronted with a controversy over whether votes would be cast by each of the three estates or by each individual. Facing opposition from the king and the nobility, the Third Estate, which renamed itself the National Assembly, gathered at a tennis court on June 20, 1789, vowing not to dissolve until it had drafted a constitution limiting royal prerogatives. On July 14, 1789, a mob gathered in Paris and stormed the Bastille, bringing the French Revolution to a significant turning point.

The revolution gathered speed after the storming of the Bastille. All over France, peasants and townspeople targeted nobles and agents of the old regime as they stormed churches and chateaus, ransacking their contents and destroying feudal records. On August 4, 1789, in a measure to restore order, the National Assembly voted to bring an end to feudalism and redefined the monarch's relationship to the people. It declared: "The National Assembly hereby abolishes the feudal system. It decrees that the existing rights and dues . . . and all those originating in or representing real or personal serfdom should be abolished without indemnification. All other dues are declared redeemable, the terms and mode of redemption to be fixed by the National Assembly. Those of the said dues which are not extinguished shall continue until indemnification shall take place." With such a broad declaration, the National Assembly began the process of drafting a new constitution.

The Declaration of the Rights of Man and of the Citizen was based on drafts written by the Marquis de Lafayette, who had served in the American Revolution. He consulted Thomas Jefferson, who had served as the American resident in Paris. The declaration owed its origins to the Virginia Declaration of Rights and the American Declaration of Independence. Additionally, the intellectual antecedents of the declaration can be traced to the Enlightenment ideas of philosophers John Locke, Baron de La Brède et de Montesquieu, and Jean-Jacques Rousseau. In structure, the declaration echoed both the English and the American Bill of Rights, which made explicit the rights guaranteed to all citizens. In essence, the declaration served as a manifestation of the exchange of ideas during the Age of Enlightenment.

Language

The declaration consists of a preamble and eighteen articles that delineate the rights of each citizen. It begins, "The representatives of the French people, organized as a National Assembly, believing that the ignorance, neglect, or contempt of the rights of man are the sole cause of public calamities and of the corruption of governments, have determined to set forth in a solemn declaration of the natural, unalienable, and sacred rights of man, in order that this declaration, being constantly before all the members of the Social body, shall remind them continually of their rights and duties . . . ."

The first article affirmed equal rights for all men. The second article listed the inalienable rights of the citizen, such as liberty, property, security, and resistance to oppression. Article III placed sovereignty in the nation. Article VI gave citizens the right to due process by protecting them from arbitrary arrest. Articles XI, XV, and XVI protected freedom of speech and freedom of the press, and Article X protected freedom of religion.

The framers of the declaration intended to educate the French people in liberty and provide a system by which the new government could be held accountable. The National Assembly adopted the declaration on August 26, 1791.

Relevance to Abolitionism

Slavery was a particularly contentious issue in 1780s France. A powerful current of antislavery opinion was swelling, fueled in part by the influential antislavery tracts of the French Catholic clergyman Abbé Raynal. Raynal denounced slavery, along with most European commerce with the colonies. With the promulgation of the declaration came calls to liberate the slaves in the French colonies in the Caribbean. Organizations such as *La Société des Amis des Noirs* (Society of Friends of the Blacks), whose members included Abbé Mirabeau, Abbé Grégoire, and the Marquis de Lafayette, petitioned the National Assembly to abolish the slave trade and slavery.

In 1790, the National Assembly abolished slavery in France, but abolition did not apply to its colonies. In 1791, the National Assembly granted citizenship to mulattoes in the Caribbean, increasing tensions in the French colony of Saint-Domingue, where a slave revolt led by Toussaint L'Ouverture was in its initial stages. In 1794, the National Convention granted emancipation to the colonies in the hopes of enlisting the support of blacks in a war against Great Britain.

After emancipation, *La Société des Amis des Noirs* fought for the rights of freed slaves. The rise of Napoleon Bonaparte dealt a serious blow to the cause of abolitionism and the spirit embodied in the declaration, however, as he restored slavery in the colonies in 1802 and attempted to reconquer what is today known as Haiti. Toussaint and his slaves successfully achieved independence and formed the republic of Haiti, freeing all slaves on the island. Several images portray revolutionaries extending the Declaration of the Rights of Man and of the Citizen to freed slaves.

During Napoleon's reign, *La Société des Amis des Noirs* was persecuted for its efforts to restore emancipation and ultimately was marginalized. The Napoleonic government stifled any discussion of abolition until its fall in 1815. When Napoleon returned from Elba during the "Hundred Days," however, he abolished the transatlantic slave trade as a means of winning popular support. But the restoration of the Bourbons did not appease the abolitionists, who equated them with republicanism and the excesses of the revolution that toppled it.

Dino E. Buenviaje

See also: Lafayette, Marquis de; *Société des Amis des Noirs, La.*

Further Reading

Breunig, Charles, and Mathew Levinger. *The Revolutionary Era, 1789–1850.* New York: W.W. Norton, 2002.
"The Declaration of the Rights of Man and of the Citizen." In *The Great Documents of Western Civilization*, ed. Milton Viorst. New York: Barnes & Noble, 1965.
Jennings, Lawrence. *French Anti-Slavery: The Movement for the Abolition of Slavery in France, 1802–1848.* Cambridge, UK: Cambridge University Press, 2000.
Seeber, Edward Derbyshire. *Anti-Slavery Opinion in France During the Second Half of the Eighteenth Century.* Baltimore: Johns Hopkins University Press, 1937.

Delany, Martin Robison (1812–1885)

Martin Robison Delany's life and work as a political activist embodied the spirit of black nationalism in the United States. His ideas contributed to the evolution of the Afrocentric philosophy and the ideas of black separatism and black self-reliance. Delany had a multifaceted career as a physician, abolitionist, editor, writer, orator, organizer, explorer, soldier, and politician. No matter the occupational context, his focus was constant: equal opportunity for black people and the right to their place in history. Known for plain speaking and courage, Delany defied unjust laws, fearlessly promoted projects for racial uplift, and traveled on fact-finding missions.

Born free on May 6, 1812, in Charles Town, Virginia (now West Virginia), Delany was a third-generation American. All of his grandparents had come from Africa to the United States as slaves; his father's father had been a Mandingo prince, and his mother's father had been the chieftain of a Golah village. Delany grew up in an atmosphere of resistance against racist laws and the slave code.

Delany was determined to pursue a medical career, which turned out to be a long and frustrating experience because of racist proscriptions against the admission of African Americans to medical school. He attended Jefferson Medical College in Philadelphia in 1832, after which his medical training consisted of apprenticeships with several physicians. All of his efforts to continue in medical school failed. Although Harvard Medical School eventually admitted him in November 1850, it rescinded his admission because of pressure from racist students. His apprenticeships finally enabled him to set up a medical practice.

Organizer

Delany became an inveterate organizer for groups devoted to abolition, temperance, and African repatriation. In the 1830s and 1840s, he was a member of the executive committee of the Philanthropic Society, a front organization for the activities of the Underground Railroad in Pennsylvania. Later, he extended his work with fugitive slaves to Canada, where he felt there was less discrimination against blacks. He also played a key role in organizing black emigration conventions.

Throughout this period, Delany promoted his ideas concerning African American progress through his work as an editor, beginning in 1843 with the founding of *The Mystery*, a black-controlled newspaper in Pittsburgh. His views attracted the attention of William Lloyd Garrison, who published two of Delany's articles in his journal, *The Liberator.* In Au-

gust 1847, he met the great African American leader Frederick Douglass, and the two collaborated in founding and co-editing the *North Star.* He traveled throughout the Midwest, promoting the newspaper, lecturing, and reporting on racial conditions.

Proponent of Emigration

In 1831, Delany began to explore ideas about black emigration to a new land beyond the boundaries of racist oppression, considering, in turn, the east coast of Africa, Texas (when it was still independent), Canada, Haiti, the West Indies, Central America, and South America as possible locations. Although the colonies of the American Colonization Society (which would become Liberia in 1847) had already been established, Delany adamantly opposed emigration there, because so many of the society's founders were slaveholders or their Northern allies. The publication of his *Condition, Elevation, Emigration, and Destiny of the Colored People of the United States, Politically Considered* (1852) established Delany as one of the leading proponents of African American emigration from the United States. From 1854 to 1858, he worked with J. Theodore Holly to promote a black empire in the American tropics, but the publication of new works on missionary travels in Africa revived his interest in that continent.

In 1858, Delany was commissioned to organize the Niger Valley Exploring Party at the National Emigration Convention (held in Chatham, Ontario, Canada) and to report on the prospects for black emigration there. Delany sailed for West Africa and arrived in Liberia on July 10, 1859. After about nine weeks, he resumed his voyage down the coast, finally reaching Lagos in mid-September.

In Liberia, Cape Coast, Lagos, and Abeokuta, Delany was well received by local authorities and the emergent coastal elite, including former heads of state and incumbent ministers (in Liberia), merchants, civil servants, teachers, missionaries, and professionals, many of whom were themselves emigrants from the United States, Sierra Leone, and Brazil. His goals of a settlement for repatriates and modernization coincided with their ideas about black agency and socioeconomic development. He spent significant time with Edward Blyden, Alexander Crummell, Captain James Davies, and the Reverend Samuel Ajayi Crowther—all major figures in African coastal society during the second half of the nineteenth century.

Born a free black in Virginia, Martin Robison Delany was trained as a physician and commissioned as the first African American field officer in the U.S. Army. He is also regarded as the founder of the black nationalist movement in America. *(Hulton Archive/Getty Images)*

Abeokuta, a new town founded in 1830 in south-western Yorubaland, seemed an ideal location for an African American settlement. There, Delany found a community that was already using modern methods introduced by the large number of Sierra Leonean repatriates who had established missions, trade, and schools. There was also prosperous trade between the northern and southern areas, important indigenous industries, the beginning of modern cotton cultivation, and good relations between the traditional authorities and the educated elite. The *alake* (king) and council of Abeokuta signed a treaty with Delany and his co-commissioner, Robert Campbell, granting the commissioners the right to settle a group of skilled African American emigrants on unoccupied land.

On their journey home in May 1860, the two travelers stopped in England. They found that the African Aid Society, which advocated black emigration and promoted modern agricultural and industrial methods, particularly cotton growing, was very interested in their Abeokuta project. Unfortunately, the scheme never materialized because of the outbreak of war on two fronts: the Civil War in the United States and frequent warfare between Abeokuta and Dahomey in West Africa. In West Africa, the alake and council renounced the treaty with the Americans and the British government discouraged African American emigration in its spreading sphere of influence in West Africa.

Delany continued to advocate for emigration, authoring two key publications: *Blake; or the Huts of America* (1859), a novel about a slave rebellion, and *The Official Report of the Niger Valley Exploring Party* (1861). For the remainder of the 1860s and the following decade, Delany turned his attention toward the struggle for black equality and integration in the United States.

Army Officer

During the U.S. Civil War, Delany organized the recruitment of thousands of African Americans to serve in the Union army. Toward the end of the war, in February 1865, he succeeded in arranging a meeting with President Abraham Lincoln, who was acquainted with his career and writings. Lincoln liked Delany's ideas, assertive demeanor, and pragmatism. As a result, Lincoln recommended him for an army commission, and Delany became the first African American major in the U.S. Army.

After the war, Delany gave his support to Reconstruction, which he believed might promote equal rights and peaceful integration in a multiracial society. By then, he had taken up residence in South Carolina, where he was an officer in the Freedmen's Bureau, a position he held until August 1868.

Later Years

Delany's optimism about better opportunities for African Americans turned sour. For a while, he cooperated with the state branch of the Republican Party, but he became disillusioned with the high level of corruption and dirty politicking. In 1874, he broke with the party and joined with other dissidents in creating the Independent Republican movement, which sponsored him as its candidate for lieutenant governor in the forthcoming election; the party lost.

Two years later, Delany switched party allegiances again, this time endorsing the Democratic candidate for governor—Wade Hampton, a former slaveholder. This turned out to be a serious miscalculation on Delany's part: African Americans in South Carolina abused him as a turncoat, and, on one occasion, he narrowly escaped assassination amid the violence associated with the campaign. Although Hampton won and Delany was rewarded for his support with an appointment as a trial justice, the events that followed the election brought Reconstruction to an abrupt end, along with Delany's hopes for better conditions for his people.

Bitter and disappointed, Delany once again turned his attention to Africa as a land of equal opportunity and political autonomy. In summer 1877, he helped organize the Liberia Exodus Joint Stock Steamship Company in Charleston, serving as chair of its finance committee and leading its recruitment of Southern emigrants to Liberia.

Delany continued to practice medicine in Charleston. In 1884, he decided to move to Ohio, where he died of consumption on January 24, 1885.

LaRay Denzer

See also: Freedmen's Bureau; Liberia.

Further Reading

Delany, Martin R. *The Condition, Elevation, Emigration, and Destiny of the Colored People of the United States, Politically Considered.* 1852. New York: Arno, 1968.
———. "Official Report of the Niger River Valley Exploring Party." In *Search for a Place*, ed. Howard Bell. Ann Arbor: University of Michigan Press, 1969.

Levine, Robert S., ed. *Martin R. Delany: A Documentary Reader.* Chapel Hill: University of North Carolina Press, 2003.

Ullman, Victor. *Martin R. Delany: The Beginnings of Black Nationalism.* Boston: Beacon, 1971.

Demerara Revolt (1823)

Slaves in the Demerara River region of Guyana (formerly British Guiana) in South America revolted in August 1823 when it was rumored that the British government had granted emancipation but that implementation was being withheld by the local planter elite. The uprising—initiated by 9,000 to 12,000 slaves from about sixty plantations on the eastern cost of Guyana—was met with violent resistance by the local militia.

The revolt began on August 18 on the plantation Success, which belonged to John Gladstone, father of future British prime minister William Gladstone. Beginning around 6 P.M. and continuing through the night, the slaves rose to the sound of shell horns and drums. Slaves across the Demerara region surrounded planters' houses, put overseers in stocks, and seized their guns and ammunition. When the slaves met resistance, they used force—some even commanding their masters' whips—to fight back.

Over the next several days, the slaves broke doors and windows, destroyed furniture, and set buildings on fire. By the end of the revolt, three whites had lost their lives, one accidentally from fire. By contrast, army and local militia units killed more than 200 slaves while restoring order.

The slave-based plantation economy of Guyana had been officially incorporated into the British Empire at the beginning of the nineteenth century. At the time, the institution of slavery in the overseas colonies faced increasing challenges in Great Britain, including a growing abolitionist presence and an evangelical religious movement, along with a strong antislavery sentiment. Planters strove to maintain slavery, despite abolitionist pressure in Great Britain and the orders of colonial officials, whom they often regarded as unsympathetic to their interests.

The colony's master–slave culture was fraught with tension as well. An aging and decreasing slave population of approximately 77,000 was working longer and harder after sugar replaced coffee and cotton as Guyana's major export crop. With the removal of their customary free time, slaves complained that they were being denied rights they had once enjoyed. The antislavery rhetoric of the era and the example of the Haitian Revolution (1791–1804) further contributed to the restlessness among Demerara's slaves.

The activities of the London Missionary Society in Demerara profoundly influenced the events leading up to the revolt. Paranoid planters who hoped Christian missionaries would sanction slave subordination and passivity, thereby augmenting plantation management, approved the Reverend John Wray's first London Missionary Society chapel amid the Demerara plantations. However, Wray also encountered hostile and intransigent planters who declined to give their slaves Sundays off or allow them to attend religious meetings. The society eventually sent to Demerara a number of missionaries who endorsed the principles of equality and abhorred slavery. The planters perceived the missionaries as undermining their influence and interfering in their affairs.

In 1817, the Reverend John Smith succeeded Wray in Demerara. Wray had struggled to assure planters that his mission posed no threat to the colony's social order before being transferred to another region of Guyana. Like Wray, Smith complained of planter resistance to his mission. Smith's regular protestations provoked the planters, who suspected him of intentionally promoting subversion among their slaves. Slavery necessitated the humiliation of slaves and the prevention of group solidarity among the oppressed. When Smith preached human dignity and encouraged a community of brethren, the planters inferred that Smith's teaching had contributed to slave discontent. When the revolt took place, the planters assumed that Smith was blameworthy.

In the aftermath of the revolt, the alleged leaders, including prominent members of Smith's congregation, were captured and put on trial. Twenty-seven were put to death; others were flogged or evicted from the colony. Smith, who had neglected to inform the authorities of his knowledge that some form of protest was being planned, spent seven weeks in prison while he awaited trial. He was found guilty of instigating the revolt and condemned to death by hanging. Lingering in jail, Smith died in February 1824, nearly two months before his anticipated reprieve from King George IV arrived.

David M. Carletta

See also: Haitian Revolution (1791–1804).

Further Reading

Costa, Emilia Viotti da. *Crowns of Glory, Tears of Blood: The Demerara Slave Rebellion of 1823.* New York: Oxford University Press, 1994.

Dillwyn, William (1743–1824)

William Dillwyn was a noted antislavery campaigner in the United States and Great Britain. A contributor to antislavery pamphlets such as *Brief Considerations on Slavery, and the Expediency of Its Abolition* and *The Case of our Fellow Creatures the Oppressed Africans*, he was one of the early abolitionists in the transatlantic world who helped bring together the American and British antislavery traditions.

Born in Philadelphia in 1743 to affluent second-generation Welsh Quaker immigrants, Dillwyn was a favorite pupil of the Quaker abolitionist Anthony Benezet, who educated his classes in antislavery principles. Benezet later employed Dillwyn as an editorial secretary, giving him a wide knowledge of slavery and the slave trade.

In 1772, Dillwyn, working as a merchant, visited South Carolina (with letters of introduction from Benezet), and the suffering of the slaves he observed there strengthened his feelings. In 1773, living in Burlington, New Jersey, he co-authored the pamphlet *Brief Considerations on Slavery*, which explained how the freeing of slaves could be organized financially. The same year, Dillwyn published and cowrote a preface to Granville Sharp's *Essay on Slavery* and was a member of an abolitionist Quaker deputation to the New Jersey legislative assembly.

In 1774, Dillwyn first visited Britain to establish stronger links with British abolitionists. His diary recounts a busy trip during which he served as Benezet's representative, meeting notables such as Sharp and John Wesley, as well delivering letters to the Queen and Parliament. Dillwyn stayed with leading abolitionist Quakers—often men of wealth—such as Joseph Woods, George Harrison, the noted bookseller and publisher James Philips, and bankers Samuel Hoare and John Lloyd.

Dillwyn moved to Britain in 1777 during the American Revolution. His established acquaintances introduced him to his second wife, the wealthy Quaker heiress Sally Weston, soon after arriving. He settled at Higham Lodge at Walthamstow, Essex, and joined his father-in-law's merchant firm, making Dillwyn part of the British Quaker elite.

In 1783, transatlantic trade recommenced, and Dillwyn and Woods became partners in supplying books to the Library Company of Philadelphia. Dillwyn was committed to ensuring that British abolitionist Quakers matched the recent success of their American brethren in separating themselves from all business associations with the slave trade.

In April 1783, Dillwyn contacted Sharp and exchanged ideas and information about a new campaign. Dillwyn and his Quaker friends succeeded in forming the London Abolition Committee in June 1783, a subcommittee of the Committee of Sufferings. Dillwyn was one of its hardest working members. One of the committee's first acts was to commission Dillwyn and Lloyd to write the antislavery pamphlet *The Case of Our Fellow Creatures the Oppressed Africans*, which was published in October 1783. The pamphlet raised significant publicity, and 15,000 copies were published, one being donated to every British public official.

In July, Dillwyn and others formed a small, informal group with ties to non-Quaker abolitionists who were willing to circulate more controversial publicity. In 1785, Dillwyn befriended Member of Parliament and abolitionist Thomas Clarkson, whose first work had been published by Philips and who praised Dillwyn highly for educating him in the complexities of slavery through his firsthand experience. These connections culminated in 1787 with the formation of the Society for Effecting the Abolition of the African Slave Trade, which teamed several Quaker groups with Clarkson and Sharp.

In 1788, Dillwyn helped bring out a new edition of Benezet's *Some Historical Account of Guinea*, and aided Clarkson in preparing antislavery evidence for a Privy Council committee that was investigating the slave trade. The ongoing campaign in Parliament proceeded slowly, and Dillwyn looked for other weapons against slavery. Thus, he was prominent in calling for the boycott of West Indian sugar in 1792. He campaigned against slavery until his death in 1824.

Gwilym Games

See also: Benezet, Anthony; Clarkson, Thomas; Quakers (Society of Friends); Sharp, Granville.

Further Reading

Davis, David Brion. *The Problem of Slavery in the Age of Revolution, 1770–1823.* Ithaca, NY: Cornell University Press, 1975; New York: Oxford University Press, 1999.

Jennings, Judith. *The Business of Abolishing the Slave Trade, 1783–1807.* London: Frank Cass, 1997.

Klingberg, Frank J. *The Anti-Slavery Movement in England: A Study in English Humanitarianism.* New Haven, CT: Yale University Press, 1926.

Merrill, Louis Taylor. "The English Campaign for Abolition of the Slave Trade." *Journal of Negro History* 30 (October 1945): 382–99.

Williams, Eric. "The British West Indian Slave Trade after Its Abolition in 1807." *Journal of Negro History* 27 (April 1942): 175–91.

Dolben's Act (1788)

At the peak of the transatlantic slave trade, abolitionist activists in Great Britain pressured Parliament to impose restrictions on the importation of Africans into the British colonies. Although the trade would not end for another two decades, the manner and method of carrying slaves aboard British ships was scrutinized and limited for the first time.

An answer to concerns about the increasing mortality on board British slavers, Dolben's Act of 1788 was the first parliamentary measure to regulate the importation of slaves by limiting the number of Africans on board ship to the ship's tonnage. The measure was an early success for British abolitionists, as it not only lowered the number of African slaves transported to the British colonies but also signified the beginning of legislative efforts that would eventually bring an end to the British slave trade in 1807.

Increased demand for slaves in the British colonies brought the transatlantic slave trade to its peak by the mid-eighteenth century. By the 1780s, British slavers were carrying an average of 400 Africans per ship across the Atlantic. With such overcrowding aboard British ships, mortality reached drastic numbers. In addition to being packed tightly below deck with barely enough food and water to survive—a common practice on such vessels—slaves perished as dysentery and fevers raged aboard the ships. Occasionally, epidemic diseases such as smallpox and yellow fever claimed the lives of entire cargoes. Although most slavers claimed that only about 5 percent of slaves died aboard their ships, many experienced mortality rates as high as 50 percent.

In May 1788, Sir William Dolben, Member of Parliament for Oxford University, proposed the "Africa bill," which was designed to regulate the transportation of slaves from Africa to the British colonies. Although it met with strong opposition from British merchants, examinations and debates were held in Parliament the following month. Ship captains and surgeons were questioned on every detail of their voyages. British merchants objected to the bill, arguing that it would destroy the local economy in seaports such as Bristol and Liverpool, which depended heavily on the trade. They were also concerned that such a bill would open the door for other European countries to develop trade relationships with Africa in what previously had been British areas. Preferential relationships would form among competing European nations and African

states trading along the coast of the continent, and Britain's economy would suffer.

Proponents of the bill, however, argued that mortality would decrease and healthier slaves would be imported into the British colonies. With healthier slaves, they argued, production would increase. In July 1788, Dolben's Act—officially called An Act to Regulate, for a Limited Time, the Shipping and Carrying of Slaves in British Vessels from the Coast of Africa—easily passed the House of Commons by a vote of fifty-six to five. It had a more difficult time in the House of Lords but passed later that month by a vote of fourteen to twelve.

Beginning August 1, 1788, the capacity of each British ship was reduced by limiting the number of slaves to 2.6 slaves per ton. As a result, more African women and children entered the slave trade, as Dolben's Act limited the number of African men on each ship to one per ton. Furthermore, children and slaves under four feet four inches tall could compose no more than two-fifths of any ship's cargo. To ensure that the regulations were upheld, certificates of tonnage were carried in each ship and presented upon arrival in the West Indies under penalty of £30. Captains faced penalties of £30 for every slave—adult or child—over these limits.

In an attempt to alleviate the causes of mortality, each ship's surgeon was required to keep a journal during the voyage in which he recorded the number of deaths and the causes of death among both slaves and crew during the voyage. These journals were to be presented at the port of arrival under penalty of £100. At the same time, a reward system was put in place that offered a bounty of £100 to each master and £50 to each surgeon upon proof that no more than two slaves in each hundred had died while crossing the Atlantic. For three deaths out of every one hundred, the bounties were reduced to £50 and £25, respectively.

Dolben's Act was renewed and revised eleven years later, but neither act's restrictions did much to reduce losses in the Middle Passage. The 1799 act further limited each ship's capacity, using space measurements below deck rather than tonnage to restrict the number of slaves carried on each ship, thereby reducing capacity to approximately one slave per ton, regardless of the slave's age or gender. By 1800, slave ships averaged about 300 slaves per ship.

Although both acts dictated an increase in the space provided for each slave aboard ship, they did not address the conditions aboard British ships.

African slaves still received a meager amount of food and water, harsh treatment and punishment, and limited medical care. Though fewer slaves traveled from Africa to the British colonies than had been transported earlier in the eighteenth century, unhealthy conditions and epidemic disease still caused high mortality rates aboard ship. As a result, the effectiveness of Dolben's Act has been the subject of debate among historians.

Colleen A. Vasconcellos

See also: Porteus, Beilby.

Further Reading

Donnan, Elizabeth. *Documents Illustrative of the History of the Slave Trade to America.* New York: Octagon, 1965.

Klein, Herbert S. *The Atlantic Slave Trade.* Cambridge, UK: Cambridge University Press, 1999

LoGerfo, James W. "Sir William Dolben and 'The Causes of Humanity': The Passage of the Slave Trade Regulation Act of 1788." *Eighteenth-Century Studies* 6 (1973): 431–51.

Douglass, Frederick (1818–1895)

An exceptional orator, writer, and activist for the cause of black liberation, Frederick Douglass is a towering figure in the history of African Americans. Through his courage, determination, and unrelenting pursuit of knowledge, he rose from slavery to freedom. Upon gaining his own freedom, Douglass passionately fought for the abolition of slavery and became a spokesperson for millions of enslaved blacks.

Born Frederick Augustus Washington Bailey in Tuckahoe, Maryland, around 1818, Douglass's black ancestry can be traced back to 1746, when the name of his great-grandmother, Jenny (or Jeney), was recorded in an inventory of slaves owned by Richard Skinner, a tobacco planter in Talbot County. Uncertain of the actual date of his birth, Douglass placed it somewhere between 1817 and 1818 at Tuckahoe Farm. Believed to be the son of his white master, who never acknowledged him, and a slave, Harriet Bailey, Douglass was very light skinned and seems to have been a relatively carefree, spirited, and precocious boy.

In summer 1824, his grandmother took him on a journey to Wye to visit Colonel Lloyd's plantation and left him there to live with his other siblings. The Lloyds were known for their harsh overseers, who enforced severe discipline, and for never granting their slaves manumission. Although Douglass did not personally suffer ill treatment at Lloyd's plantation, the experience heightened his awareness of the evils of slavery, and he became sensitive to the devastating effect of the abuse of others. Douglass's exceptional abilities were identified at a young age, and he was chosen to be the companion of Daniel Lloyd, the colonel's youngest son.

Douglass's autobiographies—*The Narrative of the Life of Frederick Douglass, An American Slave* (1845), *My Bondage and My Freedom* (1855), and *Life and Times of Frederick Douglass* (1881)—provide an authentic account of slavery from an insider whose indomitable spirit and thirst for knowledge kindled his desire not only to gain his own freedom but also to fight passionately for other slaves' freedom using his oratorical and writing skills. Having witnessed the brutal flogging of Hester, an exceptionally beautiful teenager, Douglass traced the evil of slavery to the absolute power that the institution conferred upon one human being over

Born a slave in Maryland, Frederick Douglass became the most widely respected spokesman of the African American community. He advanced the cause of emancipation with his writings, oratory, and work as an organizer, editor, and political adviser. *(Taxi/Getty Images)*

another. He wrote, "The slaveholder, as well as the slave, is the victim of the slave system."

After hearing about the successful escape of Aunt Jenny (his mother's sister) and an uncle, Douglass started to think seriously about his own escape from slavery. He was sent to Baltimore as a house servant, and there he learned to read and write at the hands of a sympathetic master's wife. In 1838, he escaped to New York, and, as a free man, Frederick Douglass built a new life for himself.

He gradually rose to prominence as a gifted orator, writer, and newspaper editor, speaking and writing about his firsthand knowledge of the horrors of slavery. Employed as a lecturer by the Massachusetts Anti-Slavery Society, Douglass began speaking for freedom and abolition, eventually taking the podium on more than 1,000 occasions. He participated in the Rhode Island campaign against a new state constitution that proposed the disfranchisement of blacks. In 1842–1843, he became the central figure in the famous "One Hundred Conventions" of the New England Anti-Slavery Society, which were intended to spread the antislavery conviction and to combat the rising influence of the American and Foreign Anti-Slavery Society.

After settling in Rochester, New York, and purchasing his freedom, in 1847, Douglass founded and began editing the abolitionist newspaper *The North Star* (after 1851, *Frederick Douglass' Paper*). During this time, he gained a reputation as a moderate abolitionist.

His autobiography *Narrative of the Life of Frederick Douglass* was a resounding success, selling more than 30,000 copies in the United States, Britain, France, and Germany by 1850 and laying a solid foundation for his international acclaim and recognition. In both his newspaper and in his books, Douglass addressed topics such as women's suffrage, the Fugitive Slave Laws, the stereotype of black inferiority, the American Colonization Society, the West Indian emancipation law, and other contemporary issues. Opposed to the radical abolitionism espoused by William Lloyd Garrison, Douglass counseled against John Brown's raid on the Harpers Ferry arsenal in 1859. At the outset of the U.S. Civil War, Douglass helped recruit the Fifty-fourth and Fifty-fifth Massachusetts colored regiments and served as an adviser to President Abraham Lincoln.

Widely traveled, Douglass won many honors, awards, political posts, and nominations. In 1876, he was appointed U.S. marshal for the District of Columbia, the highest office ever held by a black man at that time. From 1889 to 1891, he served as U.S. minister to Haiti. Douglass died on February 20, 1895, in Washington, D.C.

Kokila Ravi

See also: Fugitive Slaves.

Further Reading

Burke, Ronald K. *Frederick Douglass: Crusading Orator for Human Rights.* New York: Garland, 1996.
McFeely, William S. *Frederick Douglass.* New York: W.W. Norton, 1991.
Preston, Dickson J. *Young Frederick Douglass: The Maryland Years.* Baltimore: Johns Hopkins University Press, 1980.
Washington, Booker T. *Frederick Douglass.* 1907. New York: Haskell House, 1968.

Douglass, Sarah Mapps (1806–1882)

One of the first African American women to hold office in a national antislavery organization, the noted educator and abolitionist Sarah Mapps Douglass worked to improve conditions for women and girls throughout her lifetime. During her abolitionist career, Douglass held a number of posts in the Philadelphia Female Anti-Slavery Society, contributed to publications such as William Lloyd Garrison's *Liberator* and the *Anglo-African Magazine*, gave many public lectures, and served as vice president of the women's branch of the Pennsylvania Freedmen's Relief Association.

Born in Philadelphia on September 9, 1806, Douglass grew up in a prosperous family that valued education, faith, and work for reform. Her maternal grandfather, Cyril Bustill, was a freed slave; he joined the Free African Society, the first African American benevolent society, early in its existence. Her mother, Grace Bustill Douglass, was a milliner, teacher, founder of the Philadelphia Female Anti-Slavery Society, and, like Cyril, a devoted Quaker. Sarah's father, Robert Douglass, served as elder of the First African Presbyterian Church and was a member of the Philadelphia Vigilant Committee and the Pennsylvania Augustine Society, which supported schools for African Americans.

Douglass first studied at the Quaker Arthur Donaldson's school in Philadelphia. She later attended the school for African American children that her mother had opened with entrepreneur and abolitionist James Forten in 1819; Douglass was teaching there by 1825. In 1831, she helped found the Female Literary Association, a venue for African American women to share their literary works and support anti-slavery causes.

Douglass moved to New York City in 1833 to teach in a free African school for girls, but she returned to Philadelphia, where she opened a school for girls, the Institute for Colored Youth, within a year. The Philadelphia Female Anti-Slavery Society began to underwrite the institution in 1838. Douglass ended the arrangement two years later, however, as she felt it was wrong to take funds away from the antislavery cause.

Douglass resented the racism that she encountered within the Society of Friends. When she attended the Arch Street Meeting and North Meeting with her mother, they had to sit on a bench apart from the white Friends. Douglass's anger prompted her to stop going to meetings for a time, but her mother continued to attend regularly. When Douglass befriended the white abolitionists Sarah and Angelina Grimké, the sisters insisted on sitting with Grace at the Arch Street Meeting in 1837, an action for which they were reprimanded.

The following year, the press expressed horror when Sarah and Grace Douglass attended Angelina Grimké's marriage to Theodore Dwight Weld in Philadelphia. The wedding was held on the eve of the second Anti-Slavery Convention of American Women; a mob formed to protest the two interracial events—the wedding celebration and the convention—and burned Pennsylvania Hall, which housed the convention, to the ground.

In May 1838, Douglass was elected treasurer of the Anti-Slavery Convention of American Women, one of the first African American women to hold such a post. In 1840, Sarah Grimké used information obtained from Douglass as evidence of racism in the American Society of Friends in a pamphlet that she printed with the English abolitionist Elizabeth Pease.

Douglass continued to expand the scope of her reform work throughout her life. She was an active member of the Philadelphia Female Anti-Slavery Society, holding positions such as secretary and librarian and serving on the education committee and board of managers. From 1837 to 1839, she and her mother served as delegates to the annual Anti-Slavery Convention of American Women. In 1852 and 1853, Douglass attended lectures at the Female Medical College of Pennsylvania in order to educate African American women about their health.

In 1855, she married the Reverend William Douglass, an Episcopal priest with nine children. The marriage proved to be an unhappy one, and Douglass became even more devoted to her reform work. She raised money for the Women's Central Branch of the Pennsylvania Freedmen's Relief Association and, in 1865, was the association's vice president. She also founded the Stephen Smith Home for the Aged and Infirm Colored Persons in 1864. She continued her work with the Institute for Colored Youth in 1853 and did not retire until 1877. Douglass died on September 8, 1882.

Katherine L. Culkin

See also: Forten, James, Sr.; Grimké, Angelina Emily; Grimké, Sarah Moore; Weld, Theodore Dwight; Women's Rights and the Abolitionist Movement.

Further Reading

Bacon, Margaret Hope. *Sarah Mapps Douglass, Faithful Attender of Quaker Meeting: View from the Back Bench.* Philadelphia: Quaker Press, 2003.

Lerner, Gerda. *The Grimké Sisters from South Carolina: Pioneers for Woman's Rights and Abolition.* New York: Schocken, 1983; Chapel Hill: University of North Carolina Press, 2004.

Winch, Julie. *Philadelphia's Black Elite: Activism, Accommodation, and Struggle for Autonomy, 1787–1848.* Philadelphia: Temple University Press, 1988.

Downing, George Thomas (1819–1903)

A successful businessman from Newport, Rhode Island, and a crusader for African American rights in the mid-1800s, George Thomas Downing labored to improve the social condition of blacks in the United States.

Downing was born in New York City in 1819. The son of the noted black activist Thomas Downing, he attended New York City's African Free School and graduated from Hamilton College. By the late 1830s, he had become part of the new, young black leadership in New York City.

Downing's first known political participation centered on the issue of suffrage; in 1837, he helped draft a petition to the New York State Assembly calling for the unrestricted right of blacks to vote. The petition spoke directly to the issue of citizenship, asking for the "abolition of an odious distinction" that denied black men the full rights of citizenship. Although the petition was denied, black New Yorkers held a series of statewide conventions in 1840 and 1841 to address the issue of suffrage.

Toward the end of 1841, frustrated by setbacks, Downing helped establish the American Reform Board of Disfranchised Commissioners. The language of the organization tended toward the militant, as members demanded the immediate extension of citizenship rights. Later in the 1840s, Downing moved to Rhode Island, where his property included the Atlantic House in Newport, site of the U.S. Naval Academy during the U.S. Civil War.

Throughout the nineteenth century, Downing remained active in New York City politics, especially regarding the issues of education, fugitives, and anticolonization. In 1850, he helped form the American League of Colored Laborers, which advocated for education and training in mechanical skills to improve conditions for blacks. The following year, Downing became a member of the Committee of Thirteen, an organization dedicated to the protection of fugitives in New York. He was particularly concerned about the Fugitive Slave Act of 1850, which required authorities and citizens in the Northern states to assist in the recapture of fugitives, and he publicly denounced his white pastor at Saint Phillip's Episcopal Church for not opposing the law.

Although he remained committed to a range of issues, Downing was most outspoken on the colonization question. At a community meeting in 1851, he vehemently condemned the activities of the Liberian Agricultural and Emigration Society and declared that the black community's future was in the United States. In 1852, he organized a meeting to oppose New York governor Washington Hunt's procolonizationist views. Downing eloquently argued that the destiny of the black community was inextricably linked with the future of the United States.

Downing was also a delegate to the National Negro Conventions in 1853 and 1855, where he continued his denunciation of colonization. In 1855, he condemned Harriet Beecher Stowe's novel *Uncle Tom's Cabin* as a procolonization treatise and demanded that a letter supporting colonization be burned on the convention floor.

In 1858, Downing again asserted his opposition to colonization, but this time, the target was childhood friend Henry Highland Garnet and the African Civilization Society. Both Downing and Frederick Douglass wrote extensively about Garnet's scheme, arguing that it should be dismissed as another plot to remove the free black population from the United States. The conflict culminated in a public debate between Garnet and Downing in April 1860, which resulted in a fistfight.

Beyond the issue of colonization, Downing was most committed to desegregation. From the late 1850s to the mid-1860s, he led a series of desegregation efforts, specifically targeting public schools in Rhode Island and streetcars on the Baltimore & Ohio Railroad. He even forced the U.S. Senate to open its gallery to black people and protested curfews for blacks in Washington, D.C.

Upon his death in New York City in 1903, the *Boston Globe* eulogized Downing as "the foremost colored man in this country. . . . He fought not only for his own race, but his purse strings were always open in helping all races who were oppressed."

Leslie M. Alexander

See also: Garnet, Henry Highland.

Further Reading

Grossman, Lawrence. "George T. Downing and Segregation of Rhode Island Public Schools, 1855–1866." *Rhode Island History* 36 (November 1977): 99–105.

Drayton, Daniel (ca. 1802–1857)

Daniel Drayton is best known for orchestrating the attempted escape of seventy-six slaves in the Washington, D.C., area in 1848. Drayton, who operated a small coastal vessel, named the *Pearl,* for Captain Edward Sayres, had begun to transport slaves from Washington to freedom in the Northern states. On April 18, 1848, the ship was seized in Chesapeake Bay, and Drayton and Sayres were arrested and charged with attempted slave theft. The two men were convicted and sentenced to prison in Maryland.

Drayton and Sayres had smuggled fugitive slaves before but never on the grand scale of their April 1848 venture. Although Drayton later wrote that he had always believed in the nobility of the abolitionist cause, it was the lure of spectacular profit—$100 for a brief voyage—that convinced the men to fill the hold of the *Pearl* with fugitives.

The plan to sail down the Potomac River, through the Chesapeake Bay, and up the coast to Frenchtown, New Jersey, seemed straightforward enough, but Drayton and Sayres did not know that their plans had been reported to local authorities. A free black cab driver who had delivered two fugitives to the vessel had realized what was taking place and notified the police.

The vessel was stopped near the mouth of the Potomac River by armed vigilantes who had given chase in a steamboat. The fugitives wanted to resist capture, but at the urging of Drayton and Sayres, who feared the bloodbath that might result, they decided against that course of action. Although some of the captors wanted to lynch everyone on board the vessel, this did not come to pass either. Some of the slaves were returned to their owners, but most were sold at auction to plantations downriver. Drayton and Sayres were arrested and charged under Maryland law for attempting to steal the slaves.

The case against the men was a veritable who's who of early American history. The prosecutor who brought charges against the men was Francis Scott Key, the lawyer who had penned the future national anthem during the bombardment of Fort McHenry in the War of 1812. Massachusetts senator Charles Sumner wanted to make sure that the men had the best possible defense against the charges; Sumner convinced fellow abolitionist Horace Mann, the father of American public education, to defend Drayton and Sayres.

Despite his best efforts, however, Mann was unable to secure the release of the two men. He was able to win a reduction in the punishments that they received, but when neither Drayton nor Sayres could pay the fines that they owed, the men ended up in prison in Washington, D.C.

Senator Sumner continued to work behind the scenes to find a way to free the two men. Believing that it would be impossible to win their freedom through any type of congressional action, Sumner decided instead to lobby President Millard Fillmore to issue a presidential pardon. This finally occurred in August 1852, but only after the men had served four years and four months in prison. Senator Sumner hired a special driver to take the men to Baltimore, where they boarded a train for the Northern states to ensure their personal safety.

Little is known of Sayres's activities after his release, but Drayton became a heroic figure within the abolitionist movement. His story, a jailhouse conversion experience, was published by the American and Foreign Anti-Slavery Society as the *Personal Memoir of Daniel Drayton* (1854). Drayton became a frequent guest of honor at abolitionist events.

Junius P. Rodriguez

See also: Fugitive Slaves; Mann, Horace.

Further Reading

Drayton, Daniel. *Personal Memoir of Daniel Drayton, for Four Years and Four Months a Prisoner (for Charity's Sake) in Wash-ington Jail, Including a Narrative of the Voyage and Capture of the Schooner Pearl.* New York: Negro Universities Press, 1969.

Dred Scott Case (1857)

The U.S. Supreme Court case *Dred Scott v. Sandford* took up the fate of Dred Scott, a slave who had lived in the free state of Illinois and the free territory of Wisconsin before moving back to the slave state of Missouri, at which time, he sued for his freedom. In the case, which reached the Supreme Court in 1856, proslavery Chief Justice Roger B. Taney denied Scott's freedom on the grounds that both slaves and free blacks were not citizens of the United States and therefore could not sue in federal court. The Court also determined that the section of the Missouri Compromise of 1820 that had banned slavery in U.S. territories north and west of the state of Missouri was unconstitutional, thus permitting slavery in all of the U.S. territories. The *Dred Scott* decision intensified the country's ongoing debate over slavery and was a catalyst of the U.S. Civil War.

After traveling with his master, John Emerson, an army surgeon, and spending years in Missouri, Louisiana, Illinois, and Wisconsin, Scott returned to Saint Louis, Missouri, in February 1846. At that time, he attempted to buy his freedom and that of his wife and daughters. Emerson's widow, Irene Emerson, refused his offer, so Scott sued for his freedom. The sons of Scott's former master, Peter Blow, came to Scott's aid and helped finance his legal action—a case that was first filed in April 1846 and continued until the Supreme Court ruled on it in 1857.

Historians have argued that, based simply on the fact of the Scotts' residence in free territory, there was no need for Scott to sue for his freedom at all, let alone for that process to take some twelve years. Additionally, the Scotts' formal marriage in the free Wisconsin Territory set several precedents for Scott's claim that he was not a slave—specifically, a recognized slave marriage such as the Scotts' would have, by its existence, undermined the property rights of one or the other's master to freely transfer or relocate his property. At the outset, the fact of the family's time in Illinois and in Minnesota and Wisconsin should have been easily accepted by the Missouri courts, which were considered fairly liberal at the time of Scott's initial suit.

Scott's case, however, was thrown out on a technicality in June 1846. A new trial, ordered and upheld

FRANK LESLIE'S ILLUSTRATED NEWSPAPER

Entered according to Act of Congress, in the year 1857, by FRANK LESLIE, in the Clerk's Office of the District Court for the Southern District of New York. (Copyrighted June 22, 1851.)

No. 82.—VOL. IV.]   NEW YORK, SATURDAY, JUNE 27, 1857.   [PRICE 6 CENTS.

TO TOURISTS AND TRAVELLERS.

We shall be happy to receive personal narratives, of land or sea, including adventures and incidents, from every person who pleases to correspond with our paper.

We take this opportunity of returning our thanks to our numerous artistic correspondents throughout the country, for the many sketches we are constantly receiving from them of the news of the day. We trust they will spare no pains to furnish us with drawings of events as they may occur. We would also remind them that it is necessary to send all sketches, if possible, by the earliest conveyance.

VISIT TO DRED SCOTT—HIS FAMILY—INCIDENTS OF HIS LIFE—DECISION OF THE SUPREME COURT.

WHILE standing in the Fair grounds at St. Louis, and engaged in conversation with a prominent citizen of that enterprising city, he suddenly asked us if we would not like to be introduced to Dred Scott. Upon expressing a desire to be thus honored, the gentleman called to an old negro who was standing near by, and our wish was gratified. Dred made a rude obeisance to our recognition, and seemed to enjoy the notice we expended upon him. We found him on examination to be a pure-blooded African, perhaps fifty years of age, with a shrewd, intelligent, good-natured face, of rather light frame, being not more than five feet six inches high. After some general remarks we expressed a wish to get his portrait (we had made

ELIZA AND LIZZIE, CHILDREN OF DRED SCOTT.

efforts before, through correspondents, and failed), and asked him if he would not go to Fitzgibbon's gallery and

have it taken. The gentleman present explained to Dred that it was proper he should have his likeness in the "great illustrated paper of the country," overruled his many objections, which seemed to grow out of a superstitious feeling, and he promised to be at the gallery the next day. This appointment Dred did not keep. Determined not to be foiled, we sought an interview with Mr. Crane, Dred's lawyer, who promptly gave us a letter of introduction, explaining to Dred that it was to his advantage to have his picture taken to be engraved for our paper, and also directions where we could find his domicile. We found the place with difficulty, the streets in Dred's neighborhood being more clearly defined in the plan of the city than on the mother earth; we finally reached a wooden house, however, protected by a balcony that answered the description. Approaching the door, we saw a smart, tidy-looking negress, perhaps thirty years of age, who, with two female assistants, was busy ironing. To our question, "Is this where Dred Scott lives?" we received, rather hesitatingly, the answer, "Yes." Upon our asking if he was home, she said,

"What white man arter dad nigger for!—why don't white man 'tend to his own business, and let dat nigger 'lone? Some of dese days dey'll steal dat nigger—dat are a fact."

HIS WIFE, HARRIET.   PHOTOGRAPHED BY FITZGIBBON, OF ST. LOUIS.

A popular magazine of the time reports on the *Dred Scott* case of 1857, in which the U.S. Supreme Court affirmed the constitutional principle that black slaves could not become citizens—even if they had been freed—and thus could not sue in federal court. *(Hulton Archive/Getty Images)*

by the state supreme court, was postponed for nearly two years by the great Saint Louis Fire and a devastating cholera outbreak in the area. The new circuit court jury sided with Scott, but because she was reluctant to lose her slaves, Mrs. Emerson, with the help of her brother, John F. Sanford, appealed the decision to the Missouri Supreme Court. (A clerical error resulted in the misspelling of Sanford's name—thus the title *Scott v. Sandford* has come down through legal history.)

The state supreme court ruled in 1852 that Scott was indeed still a slave, reversing the lower court's ruling. By this time, however, the Scotts' condition made it worthwhile for them to continue seeking their freedom: The Scott family had been held in court custody during the entire six years of legal proceedings to this point, and the sheriff had rented out their services and received payment for their work. Therefore, either Scott or his owner would receive this money.

In 1854, Scott's lawyers sued Sanford in the federal court system for battery and wrongful imprisonment, seeking $9,000 in damages. The damages and battery charge were immaterial: Scott's lawyers were seeking a judgment that Sanford was illegally holding Scott prisoner (in slavery); the awarding of any damages would mean, by definition, that Scott was free, because only (free) citizens could receive such awards. After protracted wrangling over jurisdiction, the federal court agreed to hear the case.

Sanford admitted to the truthfulness of all of Scott's claims; however, Sanford also maintained that Scott had not been damaged by these actions because, as a slaveholder, he was entitled to treat his slaves as he saw fit. When the case officially went to trial in 1854, it was determined that Missouri law would rule; Scott was therefore determined to be a slave.

Montgomery Blair, a Free Soil attorney, took Scott's case for free and led the appeal before the U.S. Supreme Court. When *Dred Scott v. Sandford* came before the Court in February 1856, several points were up for discussion: whether blacks could be considered U.S. citizens; whether Congress could prohibit the spread of slavery into the territories; and whether the Missouri Compromise—legislation that restricted slavery in certain territories—was constitutional. The Court delayed its decision, maintaining that it did not wish to influence the outcome of the upcoming presidential election, during which the expansion of slavery was a hot-button issue. By the time arguments were heard in December 1856, even Northerners who opposed abolition began to express support for Scott because of the case's larger implications.

The Supreme Court's decision, rendered on March 6, 1857, sent shock waves throughout America's judicial system. Writing for the majority, Chief Justice Taney effectively ruled that a dual citizenship system was in place in the United States: Although blacks might be considered citizens of the state in which they lived, they could never be recognized as U.S. citizens. Rather than dismissing the case, as this ruling would imply, Taney declared the Missouri Compromise unconstitutional because, according to his reading of the Fifth Amendment, it unjustly nullified citizens' rights to due process and the control of their own property.

Justices John McLean of Ohio and Benjamin R. Curtis of Massachusetts wrote scathing dissenting opinions to Taney's decision. The outcome of *Dred Scott v. Sandford* prompted widespread outrage among legal observers and common citizens across the North.

A short time after the case concluded, Blow's sons purchased Scott's family and gave them their freedom. Scott himself lived less than a year after the landmark decision and did not have the satisfaction of benefiting from the Emancipation Proclamation some seven years later.

Dred Scott v. Sandford was overturned in 1865 by the Thirteenth Amendment, which ended slavery, and, in 1868, by the Fourteenth Amendment, which made all persons born in the United States citizens of both the nation and the state in which they lived. These two amendments effectively reversed Taney's assertions that the U.S. Constitution protected slavery and that African Americans could not be citizens of the United States.

Barbara Schwarz Wachal

See also: Amendments, Reconstruction; Civil War, American (1861–1865); Missouri Compromise (1820).

Further Reading

Ehrlich, Walter. *They Have No Rights: Dred Scott's Struggle for Freedom.* Westport, CT: Greenwood, 1979.

Fehrenbacher, Don E. *The* Dred Scott *Case: Its Significance in American Law and Politics.* New York: Oxford University Press, 1978.

———. *Slavery, Law, and Politics: The* Dred Scott *Case in Historical Perspective.* New York: Oxford University Press, 1981.

Kutler, Stanley I., ed. *The* Dred Scott *Decision: Law or Politics?* Boston: Houghton Mifflin, 1967.

Wilson, Charles Morrow. *The* Dred Scott *Decision.* Philadelphia: Auerbach, 1973.

Du Bois, W.E.B. (1868–1963)

A historian, educator, author, and social activist, William Edward Burghardt Du Bois was the leading African American intellectual of the late nineteenth and early twentieth century, a time when the United States struggled to provide and guarantee civil rights to former slaves and their descendants. His efforts as a scholar and activist would lead him to confront racism and the role that it played in American institutional life. Described by civil rights activist Martin Luther King, Jr., as "a tireless explorer and a gifted discoverer of social truths," Du Bois lectured and wrote on black–white race relations and the need for full equality for blacks.

Born on February 23, 1868, in Great Barrington, Massachusetts, Du Bois was a mulatto of African and French descent. At the age of fifteen, as a local correspondent for the *New York Globe*, he wrote editorials about the need for blacks to politicize themselves. Du Bois attended the all-black Fisk University in Nashville, Tennessee, earning his bachelor's degree in 1888. He then attended Harvard University in Cambridge, Massachusetts, where he became the first black in America to earn a doctorate. His 1895 doctoral dissertation, *The Suppression of the African Slave Trade to the United States of America, 1638–1870*, was later published as the first volume in the Harvard Historical Monograph series.

In 1896, after a brief stint as a professor of classics at Wilberforce University in Ohio, Du Bois accepted a position as an assistant professor of sociology at the University of Pennsylvania. There, he conducted a pioneering sociological study of Philadelphia's slum district, which was published as *The Philadelphia Negro: A Social Study* (1899).

Next, Du Bois accepted a position as a professor of economics and history at Atlanta University in order to further his study and teachings in African American sociology. With Atlanta as his base from 1897 to 1910, Du Bois studied and wrote about issues pertaining to black American society, including morality, urbanization, business, spirituality, and crime.

During this period, he published his first major work, *The Souls of Black Folk* (1903), a compilation of essays in which he conveyed "the strange meaning of being black here in the dawning of the Twentieth Century." He explored the effects of emancipation, examined race relations, and discussed the role of the leaders of his race. The book included an attack of Booker T. Washington, founder of the Tuskegee Insti-

Born after the Civil War, W.E.B. Du Bois was the first African American to earn a doctorate at Harvard and the leader of the activist approach to civil rights, social equality, and the fight against segregation in the early twentieth century. *(Hulton Archive/Getty Images)*

tute, for his gradualism and accommodationist views on black civil rights, which Du Bois believed encouraged blacks to give up their political power and civil rights in favor of economic advancement. The two men would continue their ideological debate until Washington's death in 1915—Du Bois leading a radical protest movement for black civil rights, Washington advocating industrial education and economic independence as a means of African American advancement.

Maintaining that only persistent agitation and political action would bring about full citizenship rights for black Americans, in summer 1905, Du Bois solicited the help of other leaders "who believe in Negro freedom and growth." Twenty-nine men from fourteen states answered the call in Fort Erie, Ontario, where the Niagara movement was formed to advocate an end to segregation and the realization of full civil and political rights for blacks. In his August 15 speech at the group's second meeting, Du Bois clearly stated the movement's mission: "We will not be satisfied to take one jot or tittle less than our full manhood rights. We claim for ourselves every single right that belongs to a free-born American, political, civil and social; and until we get these rights we will never cease to protest and assail the ears of America."

Although thirty local branches were established across the country, the group suffered from organizational weakness and lacked funding and mass support. In 1909, members of the movement formed the multiracial National Association for the Advancement of Colored People (NAACP), an organization dedicated to advancing the civil rights of blacks in America. Du Bois was the only black man elected to the board of directors; among his other duties as director of research and publications, he would edit and write for the organization's magazine, the *Crisis*, for the next twenty-five years.

As editor of the *Crisis*, Du Bois was known for his editorials denouncing lynching, restrictive Jim Crow laws, racial segregation, and sexual inequality. In addition, the *Crisis* became the primary vehicle for literary criticism and for poems and fictional stories written by black Americans. Du Bois recognized that a publication devoted to the literature of black Americans was part of his calling, and, in 1912, he developed humble guidelines for the journal that stated it would publish literature set in black life but not so directly propagandistic that it ignored the principles of art. The *Crisis* was responsible for showcasing the poetry of Langston Hughes, Countee Cullen, and Claude McKay; the race-centric fiction of Charles Chestnutt and Jessie Fauset; and the artistic work of Aaron Douglas and John Henry Adams, who illustrated the *Crisis* covers.

Du Bois produced a number of works on the African American race and social prejudice, including *John Brown* (1909), a biography of the radical Kansas abolitionist and his raid on Harpers Ferry; *The Gift of Black Folks: The Negroes in the Making of America* (1924), a chronicle of African American contributions to civilization; *Black Reconstruction in America* (1935), a revisionist interpretation of blacks during the Reconstruction era; *Black Folk Then and Now* (1939), a historical look at blacks in America and in Africa; and the *Encyclopedia of the Negro and Democracy: Colonies and Peace* (1945). He also wrote novels, poems, and memoirs.

Under intense criticism from NAACP board members for his increasingly radical views, Du Bois resigned as editor of the *Crisis* in 1934. For the next decade, he chaired the sociology department at Atlanta University.

Although Du Bois felt that his destiny was intertwined with his writings and political activism and that he could change the fate of his fellow black citizens, he later became disgruntled with America. In 1960, he joined the Communist Party and moved to Accra, Ghana, where he obtained citizenship. He died on August 27, 1963, on the eve of the civil rights march on Washington, D.C.

Imelda Hunt and Gina Misiroglu

See also: Washington, Booker T.

Further Reading

Andrews, Williams L. *Critical Essays on W.E.B. Du Bois.* Boston: G.K. Hall, 1985.

Aptheker, Herbert. *The Literary Legacy of W.E.B. Du Bois.* White Plains, NY: Kraus International, 1980.

Byerman, Keith. *Seizing the Word: History, Art, and the Self in the Work of W.E.B. Du Bois.* Athens: University of Georgia Press, 1994.

Du Bois, W.E.B. *The Souls of Black Folk.* Chicago: A.C. McClurg, 1903; ed. David Wright and Robert Williams, New York: Bedford/St. Martin's, 1997.

Rampersad, Arnold. *The Art and Imagination of W.E.B. Du Bois.* New York: Schocken, 1990.

Dunmore's Emancipation Decree (1775)

Issued in November 1775, early in the American Revolution, Dunmore's Emancipation Decree was an effort by the British colonial governor of Virginia to enlist the support of slaves in the struggle against the American rebels. Most of the rebels were middle-class men of property who owned slaves, who were viewed as chattel property. One of the most direct means by which the British could adversely affect the American colonial economy—and thereby suppress its rebel leaders—was to liberate some or all of the slaves. This course of action, however, was fraught with controversy and danger.

On November 14, 1775, John Murray, fourth earl of Dunmore and British governor of the Virginia colony, issued a decree that would affect the course of the war. Attempting to raise a local Loyalist army, Dunmore promised to free any male slaves who deserted their plantations or farms and joined the British forces in the effort to suppress the rebellion among the American Patriot forces. During the course of the American Revolution, some 800 Virginia slaves accepted Dunmore's invitation and joined the king's forces, but this success came at a tremendous cost to the British. White Loyalists, both Tidewater planters and Piedmont farmers, were infuriated with the governor's actions, and many found themselves drawn to the Patriot cause as a result of Dunmore's proclamation.

Dunmore's intent can be understood in a variety of ways. Some whites believed that the governor's decree was largely a preemptive measure meant to end the rebellion by hinting that the slaves would be emancipated if rebel forces did not put down their arms. In this light, Dunmore's promise of emancipation was merely a ploy, motivated more by political pressure (or perhaps hypocrisy) than by ethics. Others believed the governor's actions were sincere and were aimed to reveal the hollow promise of liberty that echoed in the patriotic rhetoric of rebel leaders such as Patrick Henry. If this were the case, Dunmore's actions would have revealed the falsehood of the American argument for freedom by demonstrating that freedom and slavery were incompatible within Virginia.

The greatest risk that Dunmore's proclamation posed was that it added a decidedly racial element to an already uncertain conflict. To many white Virginians, the notion of arming blacks to fight against Patriot forces was anathema. Doing so would not only violate the slave codes that were in place within the colony, but it would also, many feared, foment a racial war the likes of which the world had never seen. To some Virginians, a policy of arming blacks to fight white troops would set in motion a course of action from which there could be no return. Although these fears may seem hyperbolic to modern-day sensibilities, they were considered real and present dangers in eighteenth-century Virginia.

Dunmore's action had a long-term effect on the course of abolition and emancipation in the transatlantic world. In response to Dunmore's proclamation, George Washington, as commanding general of the Continental army, announced on December 31, 1775, that free blacks would be permitted to enlist in the Patriot cause, but he did not extend this invitation to slaves. In making this announcement, Washington reversed a decision that he had made only six weeks earlier prohibiting all blacks—slave or free—from joining the Continental army. Black troops would indeed serve with distinction in support of the American cause. The marquis de Lafayette, who fought with Washington throughout the war years, later noted that his abolitionist sympathies largely stemmed from his admiration and appreciation of black troops during the American Revolution.

For slaves who did abandon their plantations and join the British cause during the Revolution, the promise of emancipation did come with the end of the conflict. One of the terms of the Treaty of Paris (1783), which ended the American Revolution, allowed for the emigration of black Loyalists to points of resettlement within the British Empire at the conclusion of the war. Many black Loyalists were taken aboard British ships to the Canadian maritime provinces of New Brunswick and Nova Scotia, to Sierra Leone, Africa, or to Barbados and other locations within the British West Indies.

Junius P. Rodriguez

See also: American Revolution (1775–1781).

Further Reading

Pulis, John W., ed. *Moving On: Black Loyalists in the Afro-Atlantic World.* New York: Garland, 1997.
Quarles, Benjamin. *The Negro in the American Revolution.* Chapel Hill: University of North Carolina Press, 1961.
Wilson, Ellen Gibson. *The Loyal Blacks.* New York: Capricorn, 1976.

Dutch West Indies, Abolition in the

The government of the Netherlands ceded its monopoly on the African slave trade to the Dutch West India Company in 1621. Using its exclusive right, Dutch traders furnished most of the slaves to the American mainland colonies until 1660.

By 1630, the Dutch West India Company occupied several Caribbean islands, including Saba, Saint Eustatius, and Saint Martin in the Antilles and a second group off the coast of South America consisting of Aruba, Bonaire, and Curaçao. In addition, the Dutch gained control of an area called Suriname in 1667.

During the late seventeenth century and into the eighteenth century, Dutch traders became the major suppliers of slaves to planters in the Caribbean. As the cultivation of sugarcane spread throughout the Caribbean, Dutch traders increased the volume of slaves introduced into the region. Between 1700 and 1800, the Dutch brought approximately 50,000 slaves into the Caribbean and imported another 500,000 Africans into Suriname. During the peak period of 1700 to 1760, some 280,000 slaves arrived in Suriname. The traders did not discriminate; they sold slaves to the English, the French, and the Spanish.

The Dutch slave trade declined after 1680, but it remained competitive with foreign traders, particularly the English, who had begun to infringe on the exclusive right to the slave trade that the Dutch possessed by holding the *asiento* (contract) to conduct the slave trade. The Dutch focused their attention on the Lesser Antilles, introducing about 225,000 slaves during the eighteenth century. Curaçao, with its excellent harbor, became a major port for Dutch traders. From there, Dutch traders carried slaves into other Caribbean ports. Saint Eustatius was also an important location, as slave traders furnished the French with slaves on Guadeloupe, Martinique, and elsewhere from this tiny island. The increased demand for slaves on the sugar-producing islands of the Caribbean allowed Dutch traders to profit from the transatlantic trade in human cargo throughout the eighteenth century.

Although the Dutch were still enjoying a brisk profit by the late eighteenth century, the British withdrew from the trade in 1807 and began pressuring other European nations to do the same. During the early decades of the nineteenth century, the Dutch faced a challenging question: Should they continue to engage in the slave trade or bow to British pressure to abolish the traffic? A strong abolitionist movement in Britain influenced the Dutch participation in the slave trade; however, even though profits from the traffic declined, most traders remained in the business.

Without an abolitionist movement in Holland, the Dutch felt little internal pressure to leave the transatlantic trade. Dutch slavery supporters argued that the profits far outweighed any moral consideration and contended that ending the trade would disrupt the labor market, believing that their withdrawal would prompt the Africans to demand high wages for their labor. British pressure on the Dutch to discontinue the slave trade increased during the early years of the nineteenth century; however, with little or no push from domestic groups, the Dutch resisted these efforts.

In 1806, another British anti–slave trade law affected all of the Caribbean islands, as it applied to any islands conquered by the British. The Dutch refused to abide by the treaty, which called for the British to search all vessels, and, if they contained slaves, the British navy would escort the ships into port to determine what action they might take. Dutch officials refused to agree to the terms and conditions of the treaty. Because of increased British efforts to stop the trade and disruptions in the traffic after 1807, Dutch capitalists began to lose money. Some traders relocated to Spanish American colonies such as Cuba, where they continued to smuggle slaves into ports.

As profits continued to spiral downward, the British increased pressure on the Dutch to end the trade. The final strike in the abolitionist movement in the Dutch West Indies occurred as the British occupied possessions in the Antilles, as well as Aruba, Bonaire, and Curaçao from 1807 until 1815. Dutch traders who continued to engage in the slave trade after this time did so outside the reach of the British.

The abolition of the Dutch slave trade came without much opposition. The trade in slaves had spiked during the eighteenth century and steadily declined thereafter. In the end, external pressures on Dutch traders forced most to accept the abolition of what had been a profitable trade.

Jackie R. Booker

See also: Dutch West Indies, Emancipation in the; Wilberforce, William.

Further Reading

Conniff, Michael L., and Thomas J. Davis. *Africans in the Americas: A History of the Black Diaspora.* New York: St. Martin's, 1994.

Craton, Michael. *Empire, Enslavement, and Freedom in the Caribbean.* Princeton, NJ: Markus Wiener, 1997.

Dorsey, Joseph C. *Slave Traffic in the Age of Abolition: Puerto Rico, West Africa, and the Non-Hispanic Caribbean.* Gainesville: University Press of Florida, 2003.

Stinchcombe, Arthur L. *Sugar Island Slavery in the Age of Enlightenment: The Political Economy of the Caribbean World.* Princeton, NJ: Princeton University Press, 1995.

Dutch West Indies, Emancipation in the

The British occupation of the Dutch West Indies between 1807 and 1815 ended the slave trade to the region, but it did not bring emancipation to thousands of Africans remaining in bondage. In 1815, the British returned the islands of the Dutch West Indies and Suriname to the Netherlands but made little effort to emancipate the slaves in their possession.

From 1828, the Dutch ruled their overseas possessions from Holland. In the Dutch West Indies and Suriname, laws were enforced by governors general who were dispatched from Holland. Later, Holland appointed two governors general: One presided over Suriname, while the other administered the colonies in the Leeward Islands—Saba, Saint Martin, and Saint Eustatius—plus Aruba, Bonaire, and Curaçao, near South America. The Dutch government had no desire to move toward the emancipation of the slaves in its overseas colonies. Moreover, the Dutch public did not exhibit much inclination to end slavery in the Caribbean or in Suriname. Thus, the few in Holland who favored emancipation were dependent on outside leadership. More often than not, those advocating emancipation looked to Britain for support.

British abolitionists began pushing for emancipation after 1823, and most advocated a gradual approach. William Wilberforce supported the movement and tried to position his government somewhere between the British planters and the abolitionists. Thus, the government imposed rules intended to limit beating, improve living conditions, give slaves more rights in court, and even allow slaves to have bank accounts. A decade after British abolitionists began supporting gradualism, only 50,000 slaves had been freed in the British Caribbean. According to one estimate, at that rate, it would take another fifty years to end slavery in all possessions. Gradualism fell out of favor with most abolitionists, and they increased pressure on Parliament to end slavery at once. Finally, in 1833, the British Parliament voted to end slavery throughout its colonies, but emancipation was not immediate. After studying the impact of emancipation, slaves were freed throughout the British Caribbean in 1836 and 1837. The move encouraged Dutch abolitionists, who agreed that slavery should be ended in the Dutch West Indies as well.

The course of Dutch emancipation was strongly influenced by the British drive to end slavery in its colonies. Leaders in Holland first acknowledged some support for emancipation in 1841. Petitions from British antislavery groups were presented to the Dutch government the next year to end slavery in Suriname. In 1841, the Dutch government made a commitment—in principle—to emancipate the slaves in its possessions; however, the actual decree was delayed.

Looking at the postemancipation experience in British Guyana, the Dutch government had second thoughts about liberating the slaves in its colonies. A major slave insurrection had occurred there in 1823, and with emancipation, many ex-slaves refused to work for the low wages offered by former masters. Foreign workers had to be imported to fill the labor demand. Thus, the Dutch struggled with the dilemma of liberating their slaves while still earning a profit.

Between 1841 and 1848, British antislavery groups submitted more petitions for emancipation to the Dutch government. Holland promised the British that it would move toward the abolition of

slavery in its possessions, except in Saint Martin. The Dutch delayed emancipation until military garrisons could be improved, fearing a possible slave insurrection. Although the Dutch authorities had planned to exempt Saint Martin from the decree, in fact, slaves there received their freedom before those elsewhere in the Dutch West Indies. A system of education was established, and wage labor replaced the slavery system on Saint Martin by 1848.

After 1848, continued discussions within the Dutch government focused on compensation for slave masters. According to one plan, the emancipated slaves would contribute to the compensation of their former owners. The estimated compensation would be higher for slaves on sugar plantations than for those who labored on cocoa and coffee estates. Masters in Suriname, who held the largest number of slaves, stood to benefit more than those elsewhere in the Dutch West Indies.

In 1858, the Dutch Reformed Church petitioned the government to emancipate the slaves in its colonies. Without a significant abolitionist organization, the church led the emancipation movement. Proslavery advocates argued that ending slavery would create a labor market in which ex-slaves would demand high wages for their labor, and without a low-wage labor market, few would earn profits. Despite the objections of the proslavery forces, the Dutch government moved ahead with plans to emancipate all slaves in its possessions.

Emancipation for slaves in the Dutch West Indies and Suriname finally came in 1863. On the morning of July 1, a twenty-one-gun salute at 6 A.M. signaled the end of slavery in Suriname and throughout the Dutch West Indies. To the surprise of the planters, who had anticipated rioting, the ex-slaves spent three days celebrating their freedom, after which they returned to work.

In Suriname, a system of apprenticeship replaced slavery. Emancipation had little impact in Bonaire, and in Aruba and Curaçao, the end of slavery had no impact on the economy. Likewise, the smaller islands of Saba and Saint Eustatius were not seriously affected by the emancipation decree.

Jackie R. Booker

See also: Dutch West Indies, Abolition in the.

Further Reading

Conniff, Michael, and Thomas J. Davis. *Africans in the Americas: A History of the Black Diaspora.* New York: St. Martin's, 1994.

Craton, Michael. *Empire, Enslavement, and Freedom in the Caribbean.* Princeton, NJ: Markus Wiener, 1997.

Emmer, Pieter C. "Between Slavery and Freedom: The Period of Apprenticeship in Suriname (Dutch Guiana), 1863–1873." *Slavery and Abolition* 14 (April 1993): 87–113.

Shepherd, Verene, ed. *Slavery Without Sugar: Diversity in Caribbean Economy and Society Since the Seventeenth Century.* Gainesville: University Press of Florida, 2002.

Williams, Eric. *From Columbus to Castro: The History of the Caribbean, 1492–1969.* New York: Vintage Books, 1984.

Education of Former Slaves

The period of emancipation in the American South held great promise for African Americans. Free from enslavement, black people set out to obtain land and gain political and economic equality. Many set education high among their priorities, viewing literacy as a means to gain entry into the civil society that included voting, serving on juries, holding political office, and establishing businesses.

Early Efforts

During the U.S. Civil War and immediately afterward, many blacks continued their quest to proceed with education that had begun during slavery. Black regiments of the Union army formed classes for enlisted men when they were not in combat. Chaplains and officers' wives often taught those classes, but some black soldiers, such as Elijah Marrs, a former slave from Kentucky, also taught classes for fellow soldiers.

Those who had learned to read and write during slavery soon established small schools to teach other adults and children. Sometimes they held those schools in local black churches, sometimes outside on a makeshift bench, and sometimes in their homes.

When white federal employees and Christian missionaries went to the areas that first came under Union control during the war, they were overwhelmed with requests from freedmen and women for teachers. The missionaries had gone to the South expecting to establish churches; instead, the former slaves, who already had churches, were far more interested in asking the missionaries to recruit well-trained teachers from the North.

In response to these requests, white Northern men such as Edward L. Pierce, a U.S. Treasury agent working on the Sea Islands of South Carolina, and Calvin C. Lockwood, a Congregationalist minister who represented the American Missionary Association (AMA), wrote letters to their contacts in the North, imploring them to send teachers. The AMA established its first school in Hampton, Virginia, in 1861, appointing a black woman named Mary Peake as its teacher. As the Union army opened new areas, more teachers were sent, and, by 1863, the AMA had placed 83 teachers in the South. By 1868, it had sent more than 500 teachers to the Southern and border states.

Early in 1862, Pierce helped found the New York National Freedmen's Relief Association, the first organization to send teachers from the North to teach former slaves. The organization worked specifically in the South Carolina Sea Islands; by 1865, the organization was cooperating with other societies to support black schools across the South. Most of the Northern teachers who went to teach in the South were white women who had been trained as teachers; however, some African Americans from the North also went south, including Charlotte Forten, Sara Stanley, and Rebecca Primus.

Reconstruction

Fundamental changes took place in education in the South during Reconstruction (1866–1877), when Southern states were re-admitted to the Union upon acceptance of the Thirteenth Amendment, which abolished slavery.

In 1865, the federal government created the Bureau of Refugees, Freedmen and Abandoned Lands (commonly known as the Freedmen's Bureau). The bureau invested more than $5 million in schools for Southern African Americans. The bureau often paid for the transportation of missionary teachers, and sometimes it subsidized the building of schools. African Americans, although usually employed at low wages, raised funds and contributed their labor to build many of the schools themselves. The bureau worked directly with Northern aid societies, such as the American Tract Society and the Freedman's Union Commission, which helped locate teachers and contributed funds, schoolbooks, and supplies. By 1870, 4,000 schools were operating with an attendance of 200,000 students; by 1876, 40 percent of Southern black children were in school.

Both adults and children attended these schools, where they were taught by other local African Americans or Northern missionaries. Most schools charged tuition of $1 per month per student, but, in some areas, African Americans formed educational associations that took up subscriptions from those in the community who could afford to give so that school attendance would be open to all.

Males and females attended school in approximately equal numbers. Some adults attended day schools and sat alongside children, whereas other adults attended night classes that teachers held especially for those who had to work during the day. As soon as some students learned the rudimentary elements of reading and writing, they went out and held classes of their own. In this way, lessons taught by one teacher spread far beyond the original classroom.

Isaac and Rosa, emancipated slave children from Louisiana, attend a free school in New York in 1863. At this time, various organizations were sending teachers to the South to run black schools for children as well as adults. *(Library of Congress)*

In most areas of the South, both teachers and students of freedmen's schools faced great hostility from members of white society who were outraged at the idea that former slaves should have access to education. Conservatives, who attempted to reinstate the servile status of blacks through "Black Codes," opposed any form of education. Like slaveholders before the war, these whites perceived black education as a threat to the social systems of the South, which placed white people above black people in all interactions and transactions. They feared that once African Americans achieved some degree of education, they would no longer provide the manual labor on which the Southern economy—indeed, the economy of the United States—relied. Although other groups, such as large plantation owners and small farmers, marginally supported or were ambivalent about the education of blacks, most Southern whites skirted the issue of education altogether.

Young white children threw stones at black children as they walked to school. Adult whites threatened white teachers who taught blacks with physical violence or death, beat and killed black teachers, and burned down freedmen's schools. Some Southern newspapers published virulent editorials attacking the notion of African Americans attending schools. In Louisiana and South Carolina, where blacks and whites attended schools together, violence or boycotts by whites resulted.

The Freedmen's Bureau was established at the same time that the clamor for universal free public education was growing. In the border states, as well as some sections of Florida and Louisiana, there existed aggressive efforts to establish black public school systems. Border areas such as Washington, D.C., supported black public schools with taxes paid by African Americans. In 1865, Missouri included blacks in its public school system.

West Virginia, which became a separate state in 1863, was the first Southern state to provide for a "separate but equal" education clause for blacks in its constitution. The issue was not so much support for the schools but whether black and whites should attend school together. Although segregation in public schools had ended in some states, there were major obstacles to school integration. Although some whites attended the schools established for blacks, or requested that missionary teachers establish separate schools for them, most of the missionary schools that were established had exclusively black enrollments throughout much of the Reconstruction period.

Higher Education

Early in the education movement, it became clear that freedmen and women would need schools of higher education. General Oliver Howard, director of the Freedmen's Bureau, maintained, "Academies and colleges, universities, and normal [teacher training] schools had long been a necessity in all sections where the free schools had been continuously sustained." Therefore, Freedmen's Bureau officials and missionary associations, including the AMA, placed special emphasis on the idea of developing "normal" schools, teacher training schools that would produce well-trained Southern African American teachers.

Both organizations provided initial funds for the establishment of several early schools of higher education, including Fisk University in Nashville, Tennessee, founded in 1866; Howard University in Washington, D.C., founded in 1867; Talladega College in Talladega, Alabama, founded in 1867; and Hampton University in Hampton, Virginia, founded in 1868. After the Freedmen's Bureau was eliminated in 1868, higher education became a reality for blacks in America through the efforts of churches, missionary societies, and black ministers.

Heather A. Williams

See also: American Missionary Association; Freedmen's Bureau.

Further Reading

Anderson, James. *The Education of Blacks in the South, 1860–1935.* Chapel Hill: University of North Carolina Press, 1988.

Butchart, Ronald E. *Northern Schools, Southern Blacks, and Reconstruction: Freedmen's Education, 1862–1875.* Westport, CT: Greenwood, 1980.

Cornelius, Janet Duitsman. *"When I Can Read My Title Clear": Literacy, Slavery, and Religion in the Antebellum South.* Columbia, SC: University of South Carolina Press, 1991.

Jones, Jacqueline. *Soldiers of Light and Love: Northern Teachers and Georgia Blacks, 1865–1873.* Chapel Hill: University of North Carolina Press, 1980.

Morris, Robert C. *Reading, 'Riting, and Reconstruction: The Education of Freedmen in the South, 1861–1870.* Chicago: University of Chicago Press, 1981.

Richardson, Joe M. *Christian Reconstruction: The American Missionary Association and Southern Blacks, 1861–1890.* Athens: University of Georgia Press, 1986.

Webber, Thomas L. *Deep Like Rivers: Education in the Slave Quarter Community, 1831–1865.* New York: W.W. Norton, 1978.

Williams, Heather Andrea. *Self-Taught: African American Education in Slavery and Freedom.* Chapel Hill: University of North Carolina Press, 2005.

Emancipation Proclamation (1863)

The Emancipation Proclamation, which was issued by President Abraham Lincoln and took effect on January 1, 1863, was an attempt to abolish slavery in the United States through executive decree. Lincoln believed the action to be constitutional, as he viewed it as emanating from the war-making powers that the president holds as commander in chief of the nation's armed forces. The document created tremendous discord from its initial promulgation, and much debate has centered on the purpose, meaning, and intent of the proclamation ever since.

When the U.S. Civil War began in April 1861, it was clear that the U.S. government believed the conflict to be centered on the constitutional question of whether the Union could be dissolved. Although many Northern abolitionists and a few strident leaders within the Republican Party wanted to make the abolition of slavery the central focus of the conflict, Lincoln resisted these efforts, preferring to focus on the preservation of the Union as the primary aim of the war. Thus, the president's initial call for 75,000 volunteers in April 1861 was a call to arms to fight—and possibly to die—for the settlement of a constitutional question.

Lincoln did not suggest that the abolition of slavery was his goal when he delivered his first inaugural address on March 4, 1861. He did make clear that the defense of the U.S. Constitution and the preservation of the Union was essential to any settlement of differences that might be effected between the Northern and Southern states. During the early months of his presidency, Lincoln continued to stress that the preservation of the Union was central to his goal, and any policy regarding slavery—that is, whether to abolish it, retain it, or end it in some states but keep it in others—would be considered if it could achieve the war's primary objective.

In 1861 and early 1862, the U.S. military experienced a series of setbacks against the Confederate forces during the first battles and campaigns of the war. These initial failures on the battlefield and the astonishing number of casualties that resulted caused Northern support for the conflict to wane, and it became increasingly difficult to muster troop strength through volunteers alone. The thought of fighting and dying for a constitutional principle was insufficient motivation for some after the horrors and brutality of

The Emancipation Memorial, erected in 1876 in Washington's Lincoln Park, commemorates the Emancipation Proclamation of January 1, 1863. The bronze sculpture depicts President Abraham Lincoln and a slave breaking the chains of bondage. *(©Nancy Carter/North Wind Picture Archives)*

the battlefield became apparent. Some Northern residents began to suggest that the South should be permitted to secede without any further cause for fighting.

As president, Lincoln was not unaware of the growing chorus of protest against the war, but he had to find a way to balance his public statements about the conflict with his private thoughts and actions. In August 1862, newspaper editor Horace Greeley of the *New York Tribune* published a public editorial titled "The Prayer of Twenty Millions," in which he called on the president to abolish the institution of slavery as a means of rejuvenating the Northern war effort by turning the conflict into a moral crusade in which Union victory would mean the defeat of the evils of slavery. Lincoln's response to Greeley, published shortly after the editorial appeared, reflected

the public Lincoln's carefully chosen words, while not revealing the policy initiatives that he was privately considering at the time.

At the same time Lincoln was responding to Greeley's call for emancipation, he was also revealing privately to members of his cabinet his plan to issue a proclamation of emancipation shortly after the next Union military victory. When he polled the members of his cabinet on this idea, Lincoln found that they unanimously opposed declaring emancipation, believing that it would be too divisive a policy. In typical fashion, Lincoln sized up their opinions and, after announcing that he supported the idea, declared that his side had won the debate.

Lincoln wanted to issue the proclamation after the Union forces won a significant victory so that he could speak from a position of authority when he made the first public announcement of the policy initiative. To that end, he traveled to the field in Maryland to meet privately with General George B. McClellan and to urge him to engage Confederate forces in battle soon. McClellan, who had a reputation for avoiding a fight, apparently understood the urgency of Lincoln's request.

On September 17, 1862, Union and Confederate forces clashed along Antietam Creek near Sharpsburg, Maryland, in what would become the bloodiest single day of the Civil War. By the end of the battle, both armies had suffered combined casualties of 25,000 troops. The Northern forces declared the day a victory, as Confederate General Robert E. Lee retreated into northern Virginia with his depleted forces.

Five days after the Battle of Antietam, on September 22, 1862, Abraham Lincoln issued a preliminary draft of his Emancipation Proclamation. The document stated what the president's intent would be if the war was not concluded by January 1, 1863, 100 days after the preliminary draft was issued. Lincoln stated that he would end slavery in areas that remained in rebellion against the U.S. government on January 1, 1863, but the proclamation carefully avoided freeing slaves in the border states or in regions of the Southern Confederacy that were already under the control of Union forces.

The Emancipation Proclamation offered the Confederacy the option of retaining slavery if it ended armed conflict against the United States during the 100-day window that Lincoln had provided. After that time, Lincoln promised only to free slaves in the areas that remained in rebellion. The document carefully listed the states (and parts of states) where the proclamation would have no effect, as the inhabitants of those enumerated regions were no longer in rebellion against the government.

Confederate leaders did not give serious consideration to Lincoln's offer, believing they would achieve victory in the war on the field of battle. Any thoughts of a negotiated settlement were anathema to the heady nationalism that permeated Southern thought in the fall and winter of 1862.

In his selective application of emancipation, some argued that Lincoln was not really freeing anyone. He claimed that he would free slaves in the areas that remained in rebellion against the United States, but he was not in a position of political authority to enforce this. In areas where Union forces already were in control of portions of the Confederacy—and where Lincoln's presidential authority could be enforced—he had opted not to emancipate. According to this reading of the document, Lincoln promised to free slaves in areas where he had no authority to do so and denied freedom to slaves in those areas where he could have done so.

The Emancipation Proclamation also provoked a serious constitutional debate. Lincoln's action of abolishing slavery by executive fiat criminalized an entire class of property in the United States that had previously been recognized as legitimate, despite the moral aspects of the South's "peculiar institution." The financial implications of emancipation were huge. It is estimated that 80 percent of the United States' gross domestic product in 1860 was tied to slavery, and billions of dollars worth of investments were linked to the ownership of slaves in the Southern states. Although some questioned whether such a bold move could be accomplished through executive proclamation alone, others believed the policy would spell financial ruin for the nation. In fact, denying Southerners the benefits accrued through the labor of their slaves was key in Lincoln's thinking as he approached the idea of emancipation.

Even though Lincoln believed that his action was justified by his war-making powers, he did not block congressional efforts to enact a Thirteenth Amendment to the U.S. Constitution, which would officially abolish slavery. He understood that the passage of such an amendment to the Constitution would quell any dispute over the constitutionality of emancipation. In January 1865, Congress approved the Thirteenth Amendment to the U.S. Constitution that abolished slavery. The measure took effect in December 1865.

Another provision of the Emancipation Proclamation, the decision to recruit and use black troops within the U.S. armed forces, reflected a change of heart in Lincoln's prior position. During the final years of the Civil War, some 180,000 black troops would serve with distinction as the war became a moral crusade to end slavery, and black troops became symbolic of African American pride, courage, and valor.

As the Emancipation Proclamation transformed the Civil War, it also served to transform perceptions of Lincoln among observers in both the Southern Confederacy and the Northern states. To Southerners, Lincoln's action was proof that he was an abolitionist and a "black Republican," charges that had been made ever since Lincoln had become a presidential candidate in 1860. In the North, the view of Lincoln as the "Great Emancipator" began to form, and this concept gained further credence after the president's assassination in April 1865. The process of deifying Lincoln began when Julia Ward Howe wrote the lyrics to the "Battle Hymn of the Republic," in which a Christ image merges with a personification of Lincoln.

Although some slaves became free on January 1, 1863, when they were released from servitude or ran away from the plantations and farms where they had been enslaved, final emancipation came gradually to the slaves in many parts of the South. The news of emancipation did not reach the slaves of Texas until Union forces arrived in Galveston on June 19, 1865, and as a result, the "Juneteenth" celebration commemorating that event has become a Texas state holiday and has been noted elsewhere as a celebration of freedom.

The Emancipation Proclamation energized the Union cause by making the abolition of slavery central to the war effort. Because the idea of freedom had resonated with Americans since the time of the American Revolution, Lincoln's association of emancipation with the idea of freedom itself—as he stated eloquently in his Gettysburg Address—was a masterful use of rhetoric to sway the public consciousness to support a difficult war that measured costs in lives and in treasure.

By making the ideals of 1776 the ultimate goal of the Civil War, Lincoln's Emancipation Proclamation initiated the "new birth of freedom" that would be necessary for survival as a reunified nation.

Junius P. Rodriguez

See also: Amendments, Reconstruction; Civil War, American (1861–1865); Juneteenth; Lincoln, Abraham.

Further Reading

Franklin, John Hope. *The Emancipation Proclamation.* Wheeling, IL: Harlan Davidson, 1995.

Guelzo, Allen C. *Lincoln's Emancipation Proclamation: The End of Slavery in America.* New York: Simon & Schuster, 2004.

Quarles, Benjamin. *Lincoln and the Negro.* New York: Oxford University Press, 1962.

Wiggins, William H., Jr. *O Freedom! Afro-American Emancipation Celebrations.* Knoxville: University of Tennessee Press, 1987.

Emancipation Act of 1833

See Abolition of Slavery Act (1833)

Enlightenment

The Enlightenment of the eighteenth century was an era of intellectualism during which philosophers and authors sought to popularize a new mode of thinking among the masses. Although this new mode of thought was not specifically antireligious in its intent, it seemed to resist the formulaic patterns of thinking that had traditionally been associated with church doctrine and teachings. In many respects, the ideas that became popular among abolitionists and the earliest formulations of emancipation rhetoric were rooted in the vibrant new forms of secular discourse made fashionable during the Enlightenment.

The earliest stirrings of antislavery thought represented a radical departure from the staid conventions of reliance on the authority of the ancients and the long-standing precedent of custom and tradition. Our present-day perception of modernity, which purports the mutual existence of faith and reason within the human condition, was an idea that was fashioned through a very difficult birth. For many, the emergence of rationalism was perceived as the product of an ongoing battle between faith and reason, a zero-sum game in which the affirmation of one mode of thought could only be accomplished through the denial, sublimation, or outright destruction of the other. In truth, elements of both faith and reason animated and inspired abolitionist thought in the transatlantic world.

It is impossible to deny the significance of the Enlightenment for the growth and development of the abolitionist movement. This historic intellectual revolution that began in the early eighteenth century in Western Europe supported not only the belief that slavery was an irrational custom and practice but also the concept that abolition was a moral imperative for all who claimed the blessings of civilized society.

It was organized religion's tacit endorsement of slavery that fueled much of the intellectual antislavery rhetoric, which condemned any faith that would not openly equate slavery with evil. The failure of scripture to condemn and the propensity of church leaders to condone the institution of slavery was understood by Enlightenment thinkers as evidence that a higher moral authority vested within the conscience of the individual was superior to the teachings and practices of Judeo-Christian thought.

Church leaders did not remain silent on the question of slavery, but their pronouncements on the topic never questioned the moral legitimacy of the institution. They only addressed the proper ethical relationship that should exist between master and slave. The notion of faith as an activist agent that could transform the existing structures of society was alien to most believers, but it was this unquestioning reverence for the status quo that motivated Enlightenment thinkers to challenge those who practiced faith without works in an error-filled world that was in need of ethical cleansing. The failure of organized religion to acknowledge the evils of slavery and to recognize it as sin was understood as a ringing endorsement of the institution and the societal ills that it engendered.

Perhaps an earlier age might have accepted the silence of the gods without question, but the growing awareness that pure, unaided reason could lead one to discern right from wrong fashioned a new understanding—a secular humanism that found a moral compass within the human capacity to think and act on the basis of knowledge. Any institution, the church included, that sought to diminish the power of human reason and thereby limit the perfectability of humankind was perceived as irrational and archaic.

Despite the best intentions of French *philosophes* (thinkers) such as Jean-Jacques Rousseau, Voltaire, and Baron de La Brède et de Montesquieu, as well as others who ascribed to the principles of Enlightenment thought, rationalism was no panacea that could guarantee the moral perfectability of human society. Notwithstanding the heady rhetoric that espoused common cause with the "brotherhood of mankind," modern notions of racial equality and the natural rights of man were not universally accepted by all who wore the mantle of Enlightenment thought. Even during the Age of Reason, a belief persisted among many that true equality was theoretical but not practical. Just as Saint Paul had admonished early Christians to hate sin but love the sinner, some eighteenth-century rationalists readily came to hate the sin of slavery, but they could not bring themselves to recognize the true equality of the slave. From the very beginning, there were mixed messages within the ideals and rhetoric of the abolitionists.

For many eighteenth-century European intellectuals, slavery was an artificial construct that existed in a colonial *cordon sanitare*, out of sight and frequently out of mind of those living within the metropole. Some recognized that everyone living in a slaveholding society was sullied by the institution, but this understanding was by no means universal.

Only a few writers of the Enlightenment era personally ventured to the West Indies, where they could experience and sense the true conditions of slavery and come to understand how the practice degraded the slave, the slave owner, and, by association, all who profited in any fashion from the benefits of a slave-based economy. These authors, such as Abbé Raynal, offered a more realistic and candid assessment of the evils of the system of slavery. Such accounts began to put a human face on the slave.

Essential to the rationalists' arguments against slavery was an understanding of the "natural rights" philosophy, which theorist John Locke had first articulated in the late seventeenth century. This belief was both compelling and troubling to the Enlightenment thinkers, a fact suggested by Montesquieu's acknowledgment, "If they [African slaves] are, indeed, human, then we [whites] are not Christian." Montesquieu voiced his criticism of slavery in *The Spirit of the Laws* (1748), in which he asserted, "The state of slavery is bad of its own nature: it is neither useful to the master nor the slave."

Even among British intellectuals, a belief in African inferiority was commonly accepted, leading some to argue that slavery was a morally and culturally uplifting experience. In the 1754 edition of his work *Of National Characters*, the philosopher David Hume argued that Africans were culturally inferior to whites, noting, "No ingenious manufactures among them, no arts, no sciences."

Not all of the Enlightenment authors arrived at similar conclusions on the question of slavery, but the process of open dialogue that was encouraged by the *philosophes* generated a variety of thought on the topic. For example, *On the Natural Variety of Mankind* (1776) was published in Germany by the zoologist and anthropologist Johann Friedrich Blumenbach. This work was the first of its kind to challenge the prevailing racist assumptions that viewed blacks as racially inferior and thus prone to enslavement by superior peoples. Blumenbach's work challenged "enlightened" thinkers such as Voltaire and Hume, who argued that blacks were somehow related to apes. The first to classify the human species into Caucasians, Mongolians, Ethiopians, Malayans, and Americans, Blumenbach proved that the skulls and brain sizes of both blacks and Europeans were similar.

Abolitionist rhetoric was troubling, because it augured a denial of self that was not readily accepted by a skeptical and less than introspective society. Writers such as Voltaire might proclaim their desire to "crush infamy" (*Ecrasez l'infame!*), but the desire to do so was diminished by the understanding that when applied to slavery, this battle would be an internal struggle within the hearts and minds of men and women. Abolition would entail an immense amount of moral courage, but it would also necessitate a humbling sense of spiritual awakening within many that would compel them to action. Thus, the battle against slavery would be joined by adherents of both faith and reason, as individuals began to understand clearly the societal costs and consequences of continued silence and inaction.

Junius P. Rodriguez

See also: De Gouges, Marie Olympe; Montesquieu, Baron de La Brède et de; Religion and Abolitionism.

Further Reading

Carrithers, M., Steven Collins, and Steven Lukes, eds. *The Category of the Person: Anthropology, Philosophy, History.* Cambridge, UK: Cambridge University Press, 1985.

Nederveen Pieterse, Jan. *White on Black: Images of Africans and Blacks in Western Popular Culture.* New Haven, CT: Yale University Press, 1992.

Tiainen-Anttila, Kaija. *The Problem of Humanity: The Blacks in the European Enlightenment.* Helsinki: Finnish Historical Society, 1994.

Equiano, Olaudah (1745–1797)

Olaudah Equiano is one of the best-known figures in the history of the transatlantic slave trade. A former slave and world traveler, he became an active participant and activist in the abolitionist movement. His autobiography remains one of the most popular and widely published narratives of the slave trade era.

Born in 1745 in the Igbo village of Isseke in present-day Nigeria, Equiano was the son of a highly respected elder. In 1756, Equiano and his younger sister were kidnapped and sold to a nearby slave market.

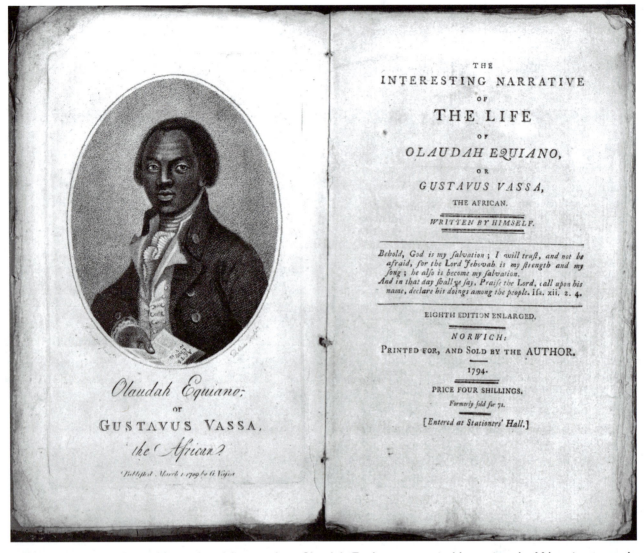

The best-selling 1789 autobiography of former slave Olaudah Equiano recounts his capture in Africa, ten years in bondage, and spiritual awakening. Equiano and his narrative came to play a vital role in the British antislavery movement. *(Library of Congress)*

The siblings traveled together for the next two months but were soon separated. Sold from village to village, Equiano eventually found himself in a coffle, or caravan of slaves, and marched to the sea for destinations unknown. His sister remained a slave in West Africa, and he never saw her again. On the coast, a slave ship captain purchased Equiano, along with hundreds of other Africans, and set sail for Barbados.

When the captain was unable to find a buyer for the boy, Equiano was shipped to Virginia, where he was purchased by a tobacco planter named Campbell. His stay there was brief, however, as he was soon sold to Michael Pascal, a British naval officer who renamed him Gustavus Vassa. Although Equiano learned to read and write between voyages, his life revolved around

the sea. As a slave to a naval officer, he lived a life of adventure, traveling the Americas and the Mediterranean, witnessing battles in the Seven Years' War, participating in an Arctic expedition, and watching open-mouthed as Mount Vesuvius erupted.

At the end of the Seven Years' War, Equiano expected to be granted his freedom, but instead he was sold to a ship bound for Montserrat. Purchased by Quaker merchant Robert King, Equiano left his naval ventures behind for the world of colonial trade. In Montserrat, he saw firsthand the horrors of West Indian slavery. Gradually, he earned enough money to buy his freedom in 1766, ten years after his initial capture.

Incensed by his slave experience and motivated by his newfound Christian beliefs, Equiano traveled the West Indies and the American South, observing and preaching along the way. He eventually settled in England, where he joined the abolitionist movement. In the midst of the political backlash following the infamous *Somersett* decision (1772), in which Lord Mansfield had ruled that slavery was illegal in England, Equiano worked on behalf of his friend John Annis, who was embroiled in a similar legal case. Annis, a slave from Saint Kitts who had been brought to England by his owner, was trying to enforce the *Somersett* decision to obtain his freedom. Equiano hired a lawyer, who did nothing to help his friend; Annis was taken back to Saint Kitts and tortured to death.

Equiano blamed himself for his friend's death and set out on a spiritual journey through the Middle East and Spain. At one point, he contemplated a conversion to Islam; however, an epiphany and spiritual vision in Cadiz, Spain, brought him back to his Christian faith with renewed belief and direction. By the 1780s, he had joined the British abolitionist movement once again.

Equiano worked behind the scenes to spread news and propaganda throughout Great Britain and the Americas. He became an open advocate of racial mixing, noting that mixed marriages would eventually destroy racism by eliminating color barriers. It was Equiano who alerted abolitionist Granville Sharp to the atrocities of the slave ship *Zong*, which had filed an insurance claim for 132 drowned slaves who had, in fact, been murdered by the ship's captain in November 1781.

He became a philanthropist in the late 1780s, joining the Committee for Relief of the Black Poor, an organization that was bent on relocating British freedmen in Sierra Leone. Despite his own protests, he was appointed the expedition's commissary and was its only black official. That position was short-lived, as Equiano uncovered corruption in the Sierra Leone colonization efforts and reported the committee to officials in the British Treasury. This motivated Equiano, along with his fellow Afro-Britons, to organize the Sons of Africa, a powerful voice for the black community in England.

Inspired by the autobiography of friend and fellow abolitionist Quobna Ottobah Cugoano, *Thoughts and Sentiments on the Evil and Wicked Traffic of the Slavery and Commerce of the Human Species*, which was published in 1787, Equiano began writing his own narrative the following spring. In 1789, *The Interesting Narrative of the Life of Olaudah Equiano, or Gustavus Vassa, the African* was published.

In this book, Equiano recounted his life story, replete with recollections of his childhood in Africa, his experiences as a slave, his travels around the world, and his own spiritual journey and awakening. He interspersed his life story with an abolitionist platform that proclaimed the horrors of slavery. He argued that slavery was a sin that could be eradicated through economic change. Thus, he called for an end to the trade and slavery, stating that such a move would spark economic progress and industrialization. Equiano's autobiography appealed to a diverse audience in Britain and became one of the most popular works of its time.

In 1792, Equiano married an Englishwoman, Susan Cullen, and they had two daughters. Cullen died in 1795, a few months after the birth of their second child, and Equiano followed two years later. Although he did not live to see the end of the slave trade or slavery in the Western world, he did live to see his book become an international best-seller. Before his death in 1797, his *Interesting Narrative* went through twelve printings in four languages.

Until the end of American slavery in 1865, Equiano's narrative was used as a political tool in the struggle against slavery. Today, it stands as an important educational tool for the study of slavery and the slave trade.

Colleen A. Vasconcellos

See also: Cugoano, Quobna Ottobah; Sharp, Granville; *Somersett* Case (1772); Sons of Africa; *Zong* Case (1781).

Further Reading

Acholonu, Catherine Obianuju. *The Igbo Roots of Olaudah Equiano.* Owerri, Nigeria: AFA, 1989.
Edwards, Paul, and James Walvin, eds. *Black Personalities in the Era of the Slave Trade.* London: Macmillan, 1983.
Equiano, Olaudah. *The Interesting Narrative of the Life of Olaudah Equiano.* 1789. Ed. Robert J. Allison. Boston: Bedford, 1995.

Estlin, John Bishop (1785–1855)

John B. Estlin, a noted eye surgeon from Bristol, became one of the staunchest pro-Garrisonian abolitionists in Great Britain. His daughter, Mary Anne Estlin (ca. 1820–1902), also became an important advocate for the cause of abolition.

The son of Joseph Prior Estlin and Edith Stuckey, John was raised in a freethinking household. The elder Estlin, a Bristol Unitarian minister, was a friend and frequent correspondent of the poet Samuel Taylor

Coleridge. John would devote much of his life to supporting a range of social causes, including the abolition of slavery, temperance, instruction of the poor, and religious toleration.

Not surprising for a man of science, Estlin was also a proponent of vaccination as a public health initiative, and he campaigned vigorously for the suppression of medical quackery. In addition to his private practice, he operated the Frogmore Street Ophthalmic Dispensary in Bristol for more than forty years.

The American abolitionist Samuel May, an associate of William Lloyd Garrison, met with Estlin when he visited Great Britain in 1843. Although many within the British and Foreign Anti-Slavery Society did not support Garrison's extremism, the two men became allies. Despite the rift between abolitionists on both sides of the Atlantic, Estlin tried to present a balanced view of both positions when he published *A Brief Notice of American Slavery, and the Abolition Movement* (1846).

During the 1850s, Estlin personally financed the operation of an abolition newspaper, the *Anti-Slavery Advocate*, which became the public voice of the Anglo-American Anti-Slavery Association. William Tweedie edited the newspaper from London until the time of Estlin's death, after which the publication moved to Dublin under the editorial leadership of Richard and Hannah Webb.

Although Estlin was considered one of the most liberal-minded and philanthropic men of his time, elements of his personality reflected an intolerant nature with respect to race. Estlin's comments to American abolitionists when Frederick Douglass, the noted black abolitionist, made a triumphant visit to Great Britain suggest that the Bristol surgeon was troubled that a line of interracial sexual indiscretion seemed to have been crossed. Estlin wrote, "You can hardly imagine how he is noticed—petted I may say by the ladies. Some of them really exceed the bounds of propriety or delicacy, as far as apearances [sic] are concerned; yet Frederick Douglass's conduct is most guardedly correct, judicious and decourous [sic]." He further commented, "My fear is that after associating so much with white women of education and refined taste and manners, he will feel a craving void when he returns to his own family."

Estlin's discomfort with matters of sexual propriety became evident again in 1845, when he censored portions of a British edition of Douglass's classic narrative that related specifically to the "breeding" of slave women in the United States. Though Estlin defended his action as a means of protecting English womanhood from a tawdry subject, some historians have noted that the reservations characterized by his editorial discretion were personal and reflected his discomfort in addressing issues involving mixed races and sexuality.

Estlin continued to articulate the pro-Garrisonian view among abolitionists in the British Isles. He responded sharply to an 1850 effort by the Glasgow (Scotland) Association for the Abolition of Slavery to discontinue efforts aimed at supporting the Boston Anti-Slavery Bazaar. Yet sensing that abolitionists from competing camps had more similarities than differences among them, Estlin finally became a member of the British and Foreign Anti-Slavery Society in 1853, just two years before his death.

Junius P. Rodriguez

See also: Garrison, William Lloyd; May, Samuel Joseph.

Further Reading

Fisch, Audrey. *American Slaves in Victorian England: Abolition in Popular Literature and Culture.* New York: Cambridge University Press, 2000.

Taylor, Clare. *British and American Abolitionists: An Episode in Transatlantic Understanding.* Edinburgh, UK: Edinburgh University Press, 1974.

Fairbanks, Calvin (1816–1898)

Known as one of the most daring abolitionists, Calvin Fairbanks became legendary for his exploits in freeing slaves and sending them to safety in the North. His forays into the slave state of Kentucky earned him the hatred of slaveholders throughout the nation during the mid-1800s.

Fairbanks was born on November 3, 1816, in Pike, New York, to Chester and Betsey Abbott Fairbanks. In 1844, he graduated from Oberlin College in Ohio. Trained as a Methodist minister, he dedicated his life to the abolition of slavery. Not content to decry the evils of slavery from the pulpit, Fairbanks personally helped liberate slaves. Among the first abolitionists to go into the South and lead runaway slaves to freedom, he soon mastered the often dangerous role of conductor on the Underground Railroad.

A man of passionate beliefs, Fairbanks wanted to see an immediate end to slavery and devised a number of ways to evade slave catchers, such as using simple disguises and dressing men as women and women as men. He hid slaves in wagons under old furniture and quilts and helped ferry them on logs across rivers. He later noted, "I piloted them through forests, mostly at night . . . on foot and on horseback, in buggies, carriages, common wagons, in and under loads of hay, straw, old furniture, boxes and bags or in boats or skiffs; on rafts and often on a pine log." During his twenty-year career as a conductor, not one of his fugitives was ever captured and returned to bondage.

Fairbanks's association with Oberlin College encouraged other Ohio abolitionists to become active in the Underground Railroad. The school had a reputation as a hotbed of abolitionist sentiment, and Fairbanks made the acquaintance of many antislavery advocates there. Among them was Delia Webster, a schoolteacher from Vermont with whom he worked tirelessly in the abolitionist cause. He also became acquainted with Sojourner Truth, whom he admired as a kindred spirit who had dedicated her life to the betterment of those around her.

Fairbanks's antislavery work in Kentucky gained national attention. The state's proximity to free territory made it ideal for abolitionist activities. One incident in particular that took place in Lexington, Kentucky, earned him respect and condemnation, respectively, from free and slave states.

In May 1843, Fairbanks, financially backed by other abolitionists, attended a slave auction in Lexington. Known as a center for the slave trade in the Upper South, the town drew slave buyers from throughout the slave states. Fairbanks had heard that a girl named Eliza, the daughter of a recently deceased slave owner, was to be sold to the highest bidder. Although her father was white, her mother had been a slave. Under the law, Eliza also was a slave and was to be sold as part of her father's estate. Instructed by fellow abolitionists to bid as high as $2,500 for her, Fairbanks attended the auction, ready to make an example for the antislavery cause. He outbid a New Orleans slave trader for the girl, offering $1,485. Although the majority of the crowd attending the auction remained proslavery in sentiment, they applauded Fairbanks's actions. He immediately took Eliza to the courthouse to obtain her freedom papers; that night, she crossed the Ohio state line.

In December 1844, Fairbanks was arrested in Kentucky for helping slaves flee their masters. Found guilty, he began serving a prison term in February 1845 in the penitentiary at Frankfort, Kentucky's state capital; four years later, Governor John J. Crittenden pardoned him.

In 1851, he was arrested again, this time in Louisville, Kentucky, for helping a female slave escape her master. Sent back to the Frankfort prison for a sentence of fifteen years of hard labor, Fairbanks suffered beatings and ill treatment for a number of years. Although many Southerners wanted him to stay in prison for the rest of his life, in 1864, during the closing months of the U.S. Civil War, President Abraham Lincoln pardoned him. Altogether, Fairbanks spent a total of seventeen years and four months in prison.

He wrote his life's story in the *Autobiography of Calvin Fairbanks* (1890). He did not sell many copies of the work, however, and soon the memory of his exploits in the abolitionist movement began to fade. He lived the rest of life in relative obscurity and died in Angelica, New York in 1898.

Ron D. Bryant

See also: Underground Railroad.

Further Reading

Coleman, J. Winston, Jr. "Delia Webster and Calvin Fairbanks: Underground Railroad Agents." *Filson Club History Quarterly* 17 (July 1943): 129–42.

Federal Writers' Project, Slave Narrative Collection

Created in 1935 as part of the New Deal, a set of public programs designed to counter unemployment, the Federal Writers' Project collected more than 2,300 interviews with former slaves between 1936 and 1938. Part of the project's Slave Narrative Collection, the interviews constitute a crucial—if not entirely unproblematic—document of American history. As historian David Brion Davis has pointed out, the number of documented slave narratives that are available in the United States is "indisputably unique among former slaveholding nations."

The Federal Writers' Project was part of the Works Progress Administration (WPA), which provided jobs for the unemployed through public works. Some WPA funds were allocated to support projects in the arts, a result of the federal government's decision to grant subsidies to writers and artists.

Although the public remained skeptical about the necessity of funding writing with federal money, the Federal Writers' Project, headed by former journalist and theater director Henry Alsberg, created jobs for thousands of writers and produced important publications on American topics. In addition to collecting slave narratives, writers in the program created volumes on folklore; guides to states, cities, and regions; and the monumental series *Life in America*. Comprising 150 volumes, the series included studies of ethnic groups, such as *The Italians of New York* and *The Negro in Virginia*.

Origins of the Collection

The Slave Narrative Collection originated in a belief that those who had endured slavery could depict it with a sense of immediacy that was lacking in other reconstructions. Compiled in seventeen states, the collection consists of first-person testimonies on slave life. The identities of the former slaves who were interviewed vary greatly in terms of their age at the time of emancipation (from one to fifty), occupation, the size of the slave groups in which they lived, and the treatment they received. Almost all had experienced slavery in the former slaveholding Southern states and still lived there.

All the major categories of the slave population seem to be represented in the collection, thus offering a more balanced perspective than autobiographies written by runaway male slaves before the U.S. Civil War. To what degree the narratives are representative of the slave population, however, remains uncertain. The official documents and correspondence regarding the collection do not specify the criteria according to which interviewees were chosen.

In literary terms, the Slave Narrative Collection symbolizes the culmination of a tradition that dates back to the eighteenth century, when the earliest American slave narratives began to appear. These narratives challenged the notion of slavery as a benevolent institution, a common argument among propagandists. The image of the happy slave who was safer in the caring plantations of the South than in the industrial North was contradicted by the many fugitive slaves who produced narratives about their bondage and their flight from it. These narratives formed the core of abolitionist propaganda and were widely published and distributed. Many of these publications proved to be financially successful.

After the Civil War and the abolition of slavery, however, interest in slave narratives declined. The harsh realities described in the narratives were at odds with national efforts toward reconciliation. The public did not want to be reminded of the division that had existed between North and South before the war. The fewer number of slave narratives that appeared from the end of the Civil War to the early decades of the twentieth century coincided with a shift toward local color depictions of the South, with their nostalgic and sentimental reaffirmations of the "plantation legend." This new perspective on slave life was obviously irreconcilable with the unsentimental recording of actual life under slavery. This emphasis, together with the disappearance of many former slaves, endangered the possibility of preserving the "inside view" of slavery.

Renewed interest in the genre was not simply a function of the sudden realization that the chances of

A group of ex-slaves gathered in 1937 at Southern Pines, North Carolina, to be interviewed for the Slave Narrative Collection of the Federal Writers' Project. The collection includes stories from more than 2,300 former slaves in seventeen states. *(Library of Congress)*

a sociological awareness of the typical and ordinary aspects of slave life rather than the dramatic and sensational aspects that distinguished the antebellum autobiographies. The Slave Narrative Collection of the Federal Writers' Project should be viewed in this historical and cultural context and represents the most important and comprehensive of these endeavors.

Collecting Stories

Before the creation of the Federal Writers' Project, other private institutions had tried to secure the records of former slaves. For example, independent projects were undertaken at Fisk University (under the supervision of black sociologist Charles S. Johnson), Southern University, and Prairie View State College in 1929.

The collection of slave narratives of the Federal Writers' Project did not start as a coherent and coordinated plan but as a spontaneous effort among the project's African American employees. The central folklore office of the project—headed in Washington, D.C., by the ethnomusicologist and folklorist John Lomax, a white Southerner—did not issue a formal directive to collect the narratives until April 1937. Washington's interest was aroused by the submission of interviews with former slaves collected by the Florida branch of the project. The active black unit of the Florida project, which included the novelist and anthropologist Zora Neale Hurston, had conceived these interviews as part of its research on African American folklore in the state.

The value of preserving such narratives soon became apparent to the project's national directors, who immediately gave instructions to the Southern states to begin a more systematic compilation. Thereafter, however, black interviewers were rarely employed, and the research was conducted largely by white employees. The Washington directors were unable to ensure equal employment opportunities for African Americans, especially in the Southern states.

Ultimately, the interviews took place in all of the Southern states, the majority of border states, and New York and Rhode Island. The largest achievement was realized in Arkansas, where almost 700 narratives—one-third of the entire collection—were collected. Former slaves were given detailed questionnaires that aimed to collect information on their daily routines and catalogue their experiences of slavery.

recording direct perspectives on slavery were endangered by the decreasing numbers of surviving slaves. Racism and a distorted view of slavery had gained a surprising academic respectability during the first decades of the twentieth century, and the preservation of first-person accounts of slavery was perceived as a much-needed corrective.

The 1920s also witnessed a renewed interest in African American art and literature, which found its best-known expression in the Harlem Renaissance and was affirmed by the increasing academic respectability of sociology and anthropology. These disciplines challenged racist assumptions and established a receptive scientific and cultural climate in which personal testimonies were valued as important historical documents.

During the late 1920s and early 1930s, several independent projects started to collect the testimonies of former slaves. These efforts were characterized by

Legacy

The need to focus on the production of other materials, the repetitiveness detected in the narratives, and the erroneous conviction that all surviving slaves had been contacted brought the project's work on the Slave Narrative Collection to an end in 1938. The material remained unpublished, and when the Federal Writers' Project was disbanded in 1939, its interviews were stored in the Library of Congress.

In 1941, folklorist Benjamin A. Botkin, who succeeded Lomax as head of the folklore office of the Federal Writers' Project, supervised the acquisition of the material from the states and arranged for it to be archived in the Rare Book Room of the Library of Congress. The material became part of the permanent collection "A Folk History of Slavery in the United States."

The collection was publicized in Botkin's volume *Lay My Burden Down* (1945) and in Norman R. Yetman's *Voices From Slavery* (1970), which contained a selection of slave narratives. But it was not until 1972 that the entire series was published under the title *The American Slave: A Composite Autobiography*, edited by George P. Rawick.

Scholars have pointed out several weaknesses of the Federal Writers' Project collection, noting potentially inaccurate testimonies and poor transcriptions of interviews. Most of the former slaves who were interviewed were old and impoverished during the 1930s, which may have led them to present a more positive and nostalgic picture of the Southern plantation system and the way slaves were treated. The presence of a white interviewer also led some African Americans to believe that they were talking to a government official, and this may have influenced them to present slavery in a more acceptable light. Despite these criticisms, the narratives provide a glimpse into a period of American history that otherwise would be lacking.

Luca Prono

Further Reading

Bailey, David Thomas. "A Divided Prism: Two Sources on Black Testimony on Slavery." *Journal of Southern History* 46 (August 1980): 381–404.

Botkin, Benjamin A., ed. *Lay My Burden Down: A Folk History of Slavery.* Chicago: University of Chicago Press, 1945.

Mangione, Jerre. *The Dream and the Deal: The Federal Writers' Project, 1935–1943.* Boston: Little, Brown, 1972.

Rawick, George P., ed. *The American Slave: A Composite Autobiography.* Westport, CT: Greenwood, 1972–1979.

Soapes, Thomas F. "The Federal Writers' Project Slave Interviews: Useful Data or Misleading Source." *Oral History Review* 2 (1977): 33–38.

Spindel, Donna J. "Assessing Memory: Twentieth-Century Slave Narratives Reconsidered." *Journal of Interdisciplinary History* 27 (1996): 247–61.

Yetman, Norman. "The Background of the Slave Narrative Collection." *American Quarterly* 19 (Fall 1967): 534–53.

Fedric, Francis (ca. 1810–ca. 1870)

Francis Fedric was a slave who escaped from his Kentucky owner by means of the Underground Railroad. He published a narrative of his experiences, *The Life and Sufferings of Francis Fedric While in Slavery* (1859), which was widely read by abolitionists on both sides of the Atlantic.

Fedric was born a slave on a tobacco plantation in Fauquier County in northern Virginia. When he was about fourteen years old, his master relocated to Mason County, in northeastern Kentucky, and established a tobacco plantation twenty miles south of Maysville. Moving from one plantation to another was more than a real estate transaction for the slaves. Fedric noted, "Men and women down on their knees begging to be purchased to go with their wives or husbands, who worked for my master, children crying and imploring not to have their parents sent away from them; but all their beseeching and tears were of no avail. They were ruthlessly separated, most of them for ever."

Befriended by his master's wife, Fedric became a well-treated house slave in Kentucky. After attending a secret prayer meeting, however, Fedric was so badly beaten that he decided to run away. His initial attempt at escaping was unsuccessful: He was free for only nine weeks before he was captured. His punishment for attempting to escape was 107 lashes with a rawhide whip.

The brutality of Fedric's beating provided the cause that would lead to his second—and successful—attempt to escape from his master in Kentucky. Assisted by a local abolitionist planter, a member of the Society of Friends (Quakers) who opposed slavery on moral principle, Fedric was transported to Maysville, along the Ohio River, where he was delivered to a fellow abolitionist who was associated with the Underground Railroad. Fedric was passed from one abolitionist to another until he was kept for the winter (from November to mid-May) before being sent on to Sandusky, Ohio. Using this network as a means of escape, a series of Underground Railroad conductors managed to get Fedric to Upper Canada (modern-day Ontario), where he became a free man.

The abolitionists who aided Fedric's escape were acting in violation of the new Fugitive Slave Law (1850), which made their actions a federal crime. Fedric had great respect for the abolitionists, later describing them as "heroes of the highest stamp . . . [who] would willingly lay down their lives rather than allow one fugitive slave to be taken from them." This passion, he believed, stemmed from their "having seen over and over again slaves dragged back chained through their country, and having heard the tales of horrible treatment of the poor hopeless captives, some having been flogged to death, others burnt alive, with their heads downwards, over a slow fire, others covered with tar and set on fire"—potent observations that made abolition a moral imperative for these courageous individuals.

Fedric was employed by the Anti-Slavery Society in Toronto and given the task of assisting escaped slaves who arrived in the region. In this work, he met a British woman from Devonshire who was living in Toronto, and the two were soon married.

After living in Canada for several years, Fedric and his wife moved to Great Britain, where antislavery advocates published his autobiography, *Slave Life in Virginia and Kentucky; Or, Fifty Years of Slavery in the Southern States of America* (1863). The Reverend Charles Lee, vicar of Holy Trinity in London, wrote the preface to the narrative and assisted in the preparation of the text. Fedric settled in Manchester, England, and continued to give antislavery lectures to support the cause of transatlantic abolitionism.

Junius P. Rodriguez

See also: Fugitive Slaves; Underground Railroad.

Further Reading

Chapman, Abraham. *Steal Away: Stories of the Runaway Slaves.* New York: Praeger, 1971.

Franklin, John Hope, and Loren Schweninger. *Runaway Slaves: Rebels on the Plantation.* New York: Oxford University Press, 1999.

Fee, John Gregg (1816–1901)

The pastor John Gregg Fee was an abolitionist and the founder of Kentucky's racially mixed Berea College in 1855. An outspoken agitator, he boldly spoke from his pulpit, rallying support for the antislavery cause in a border state that was known for its support of slavery.

The eldest child of John and Elizabeth Bradford Fee, he was born on September 9, 1816, in Bracken County, Kentucky. Growing up in a slaveholding family gave Fee a firsthand knowledge of human bondage. He later stated that as a child, he had not seen the wrongs committed in the name of slavery. Fee's father owned thirteen slaves and remained a staunch defender of the South's "peculiar institution."

Fee was educated at Miami University of Ohio and Augusta College in Bracken County, but his greatest inspiration as a youth came from a local schoolteacher, Joseph Corliss, who boarded with the Fee family. Deeply religious, Corliss influenced Fee's decision to join the ministry. From 1842 to 1843, Fee attended the Lane Theological Seminary in Cincinnati, where he came to believe that slavery was a sin that must be eradicated. He realized that, as a matter of conscience, he must become an abolitionist, a choice that would eventually cost him the support of his family and friends. On September 26, 1844, Fee married Mathilda Hamilton, a devoted abolitionist.

Fee first thought he would become a minister with the Methodist Episcopal Church. Instead, he joined the New School Presbyterians, who favored the mutual development of faith and reason. He became a forceful preacher known for his rational arguments and sometimes controversial sermons on the social topics of the day; his support of the abolitionist cause made him all the more controversial. Desiring a religious calling that would satisfy his needs as an abolitionist, Fee decided to begin his ministry in Kentucky, a state that he strongly believed needed to be enlightened on the slavery issue, and settled in Bracken County.

Fee's outspoken support of the abolitionist cause soon made him an object of concern within the synod of the New School Presbyterians of Kentucky. The church told Fee that if he did not cease his agitation as an abolitionist he would be removed from its financial support. He refused and left his church, moving to Lewis County, Kentucky. There, he began another ministry within the denomination. Despite threats of violence from angry slave owners, Fee continued to speak out against slavery.

In October 1845, the New School Presbyterians again demanded that Fee cease advocating abolitionist doctrines. He defended himself by invoking the Bible and the church constitution, adamantly maintaining his stand that slavery was immoral and had to be destroyed. The synod passed four resolutions condemning Fee and his preaching, removing all church support for his ministry. Undeterred by the Presbyterians' rejection, Fee continued to advocate an end to slavery. He suffered attacks from outraged mobs and had his life threatened. His stubborn dedication to the cause gained him the attention of a number of prominent antislavery advocates, such as Salmon P. Chase of Ohio and Cassius M. Clay of Kentucky. He also won the financial support of the American Missionary Association, which provided him with an extra income of $200 per year.

Fee's 1851 work on the abolitionist cause, *An Anti-Slavery Manual, or the Wrongs of American Slavery Exposed by the Light of the Bible,* found a wide audience and impressed many in the abolitionist movement. Clay sent for a copy of the book, and some residents of his home county of Madison, Kentucky, invited Fee to preach for them. In 1853, Clay, a wealthy landowner, encouraged Fee to stay in Madison County and gave him ten acres of land out of a plot of 600 that would become the town of Berea, named for a biblical town whose residents were open-minded and receptive to the Gospel. The following year, Fee built his home there, and, in 1855, he established an integrated school and a church on the grounds, where he preached against slavery.

The school, which would eventually become Berea College, began as a one-room schoolhouse. Teachers were recruited from Oberlin, and blacks and whites were educated together. Fee envisioned his fledgling school as the beginning of a sister institution "which would be to Kentucky what Oberlin is to Ohio, anti-slavery, anti-caste, anti-rum, anti-sin." In December 1859, four years after the school opened, a mob of sixty proslavery sympathizers attacked Berea while Fee was away. The residents of the town fled, and Fee lived in exile in Ohio until 1864. He retuned to Kentucky and offered his services at Camp Nelson in Jessamine County, a Union camp that had become a haven for former slaves. There, he cared for and educated the masses of displaced blacks who came seeking refuge.

After the U.S. Civil War, Fee had the satisfaction of seeing the school at Berea become successfully integrated. In 1873, the first bachelor's degrees were awarded to both blacks and whites, and, by 1892, blacks made up half the student population. This trend would not continue, however, and, by the time of Fee's death on January 11, 1901, America had adopted the racial philosophy of separate but equal.

In 1904, integrated education was legally ended in Kentucky with the passage of the state legislature's Day Law, which forbade racial mixing in schools. In 1950, when the Day Law was amended to allow integration above the high school level, Berea was the first Kentucky college to reopen its doors to black students.

Ron D. Bryant

See also: Clay, Cassius Marcellus.

Further Reading

English, Philip Wesley. *John G. Fee: Kentucky Spokesman for Abolition and Reform.* Lanham, MD: University Press of America, 1986.

Howard, Victor B. *Evangelical War Against Slavery and Caste: The Life and Times of James G. Fee.* Selinsgrove, PA: Susquehanna University Press, 1996.

Sears, Richard D. "John G. Fee, Camp Nelson, and Kentucky Blacks, 1864–1865." *Register of the Kentucky Historical Society* 85 (Winter 1987): 29–45.

———. *"Practical Recognition of the Brotherhood of Man": John G. Fee and the Camp Nelson Experience.* Berea, KY: Berea College Press, 1986.

Fifteenth Amendment

See Amendments, Reconstruction

Finney, Charles Grandison (1792–1875)

Charles Grandison Finney was the American religious leader most closely associated with the Second Great Awakening, an evangelical revival that swept the United States in the 1820s. Many who experienced spiritual rebirth through Finney's preaching found special meaning in the social calling of the gospels and became active in social reform movements such as abolitionism. Biographer Keith Hardman portrayed Finney as a practical theologian, crafting a "theological framework upon which abolitionist ideas could be made to interface with Christian doctrine."

Finney was born in Warren, Connecticut, on August 29, 1792, to Sylvester and Rebecca Finney. When he was two years old, the family moved to Oneida County, New York, where Finney had little access to religion. As he stated in his memoirs, "My parents were neither of them professors of religion, and, I believe, among our neighbors there were very few religious people. I seldom heard a sermon, unless it was an occasional one from some traveling minister, or some miserable holding forth of an ignorant preacher who would sometimes be found in that country."

From 1806 to 1808, Finney attended the Hamilton Oneida Academy (later Hamilton College). Then, after a brief teaching stint in New Jersey, he moved to Henderson, New York, in 1818 to study law. In 1821, his life and career underwent a profound change when he had a personal religious experience and, in response to the energetic preaching of George W. Gale, converted to Presbyterianism. In 1824, he was ordained as a Presbyterian minister.

During the 1820s, Finney became a prominent revivalist in the western New York area known as the "Burned-Over District," so-called because of the many revivals that had taken place there. Believing that God offered himself to everyone and that men and women could be saved only through an active acceptance of God's invitation to grace, Finney began an effort to reach as many people as possible with his message. He was especially successful in the burgeoning commercial city of Rochester, located at the Great Lakes terminus of the Erie Canal. The abolitionist Theodore Dwight Weld was converted at an 1826 revival in Utica, New York, and became an ally of Finney's before branching off into radical abolitionism. In 1832, Finney established the Chatham Street Chapel in an old theater in New York City, and from its pulpit, he spoke on issues such as the equality of all people, free will, and personal self-governance.

Finney was convinced that converting individuals through revivals was the best way to bring about social reform. Although some conservative clergymen considered him somewhat radical in his practices, such as encouraging prayer among women in mixed-sex audiences, Finney was an antislavery moderate. For example, in 1833, he advised *New York Evangelist* editor Joshua Leavitt not to promote abolitionism too stridently. As a result of Finney's association with New York abolitionists Arthur and Lewis Tappan, however, his church was used for antislavery gatherings. When the Tappan brothers founded the New York Anti-Slavery Society in October 1833, they moved the gathering to Finney's church to avoid proslavery violence. While Finney was on a six-month sea voyage to the Mediterranean in 1834 (to recoup his health after contracting cholera), Lewis Tappan invited the city's blacks to the Chatham Street Church for an Independence Day reading of William Lloyd Garrison's "Declaration of Sentiments."

While Finney was away, Weld led a group of Lane Theological Seminary students in the notorious "Lane debates," which addressed whether the slaveholding states should immediately abolish slavery. The trustees of the Cincinnati school, including President Lyman Beecher, were mostly advocates of colonization and

Finney Memorial Chapel at Oberlin College was built in memory of Charles Grandison Finney, a professor of theology and president of the college from 1851 to 1866. As a leader of the Second Great Awakening, he inspired many to the abolitionist cause. *(Library of Congress)*

silenced the students. However, Weld and the so-called Lane Rebels—many of whom, like Weld, had been converted during Finney's revivals—concluded that slavery was a sin and that the American Colonization Society's plan to send blacks to Africa was ineffective. Instead, they resolved to establish an institution that would admit blacks and encourage free speech. Thus, they founded Oberlin College with the financial backing of the Tappan brothers and other abolitionists, especially Gerrit Smith. Weld had first met Lewis Tappan in 1831 at Gale's Oneida Academy after Finney had recommended the school for Tappan's sons.

Weld recommended Finney for the professorship of theology at Oberlin. Although his health was still poor, Finney accepted the position on the Ohio frontier in 1836. From its founding, Oberlin was a base for the abolitionist movement, but Finney did not share this antislavery zeal. He referred to slavery as a "great national sin," but he saw it as merely one manifestation of a more pervasive American sinfulness. Slavery would not end, his sermons and books argued, unless religion eliminated sin itself. Finney forbade slaveholders from taking communion at the Chatham Street Chapel, but he also opposed the election of a black church trustee and opposed "amalgamation," or mixing of the races. Seating in Finney's New York church was segregated.

Initially, Finney served both the Chatham Street Chapel and Oberlin. In April 1836, however, he resigned from the Presbyterian Church and moved his New York ministry (thereafter Congregationalist) to the new Broadway Tabernacle. In early 1837, with the dual role of teaching and preaching weighing heavily on Finney's health, he severed ties with the church and began teaching and ministering full-time at Oberlin.

Finney, who was not college educated, saw religion as an integral part of the school's educational mission and taught courses in practical theology. By 1852, Oberlin's enrollment had grown to 1,000 students, making it one of the largest colleges in the country. Finney's emphasis on moderation and Christian ministry—especially when Weld's influence at Oberlin diminished after 1839—helped keep the antislavery school from becoming as zealous as Garrison and his followers, who often diminished the importance of religion.

Over time, Finney became more radically abolitionist. He participated in the founding of the Oberlin Anti-Slavery Society in 1835 and condemned the act of owning another human being in his 1847 *Lectures on Systematic Theology*. Writing to Smith in 1864, he declared that President Abraham Lincoln's antislavery position was too conservative.

Finney traveled to Britain in 1849, ministering widely. He returned to Oberlin in 1851 and was elected president of the college in August, replacing Asa Mahan, who had resigned the previous year. Until he stepped down in 1866, Finney served as president of the Oberlin faculty and preached throughout the United States and Britain. After retiring, he returned to teaching theology and continued his ministry. He died in Oberlin, Ohio, on August 16, 1875.

Brian M. Ingrassia

See also: Religion and Abolitionism; Tappan, Arthur; Tappan, Lewis; Weld, Theodore Dwight.

Further Reading

Essig, James David. "The Lord's Free Man: Charles G. Finney and His Abolitionism." *Civil War History* 24 (March 1978): 25–45.

Hardman, Keith J. *Charles Grandison Finney, 1792–1875: Revivalist and Reformer.* Syracuse, NY: Syracuse University Press, 1987.

Follen, Eliza Lee Cabot (1787–1860)

Eliza Lee Cabot Follen is best known for her antislavery writings, which include *Anti-Slavery Hymns and Songs* and *A Letter to Mothers in Free States.* Known as an ardent and devoted abolitionist and a proponent of women's rights, Follen used her social standing and literary connections to support the growing antislavery movement in Boston.

The daughter of a prominent Boston family, Eliza was born on August 15, 1787, to Samuel Cabot and Sarah Barrett. The fifth of thirteen children, her parents were Unitarians who held strong abolitionist views and believed in an expanded role for females. A product of her upbringing, Eliza expressed liberal and progressive views that would later draw her to the outspoken German refugee Charles Follen. Follen had fled Germany in 1825 because of his radical beliefs; after arriving in the United States, he became a staunch Garrisonian abolitionist.

Although her family considered marriage to Follen beneath Eliza's position in society, they welcomed him into the family and financed a professorship in German for him at Harvard University. The two were married on September 15, 1828, and their only son, Charles Christopher, was born two years later. It did not take long for Follen's radical beliefs to have a detrimental effect on his position in Boston, however, both in social circles and within the Unitarian Church. By the time of his death in a steamboat explosion and fire in 1840, Eliza's family had rescinded their financial support and Boston's Unitarian ministers refused to officiate at his funeral.

Eliza Follen started a school and began writing publicly in the 1820s, primarily concentrating on songs, poems, and stories that provided moral lessons for children. She was best known for her antislavery writings, including *Anti-Slavery Hymns and Songs* and *A Letter to Mothers in Free States*, both published in 1855. In *A Letter,* she wrote, "What can we mothers do? . . . everything; I repeat, you can abolish slavery. Let every mother take the subject to heart, as one in which she has a personal concern. In the silence of the night, let her listen to the slave-mothers crying to her for help. . . ."

At a time when many women abolitionists joined local antislavery organizations and began speaking out in public, Follen joined the Boston Anti-Slavery Society. She used her popularity as an author to distribute her abolitionist viewpoints, writing articles for the society's local publication, *The Liberty Bell*, and continued to do so for more than twenty years. With such titles as "Women's Work," "Song for the Friends of Freedom," and "Conscious," the intent and purpose of her articles was clear.

Like many of the mid-nineteenth-century women abolitionists, she focused her appeal on the virtuous nature of women and motherhood. Follen believed that because women were excluded from both the political and the commercial realm—and thus uncorrupted by money and the power of lawmaking—they were better positioned to uphold the tenets of truth and justice.

Although the 1820s and early 1830s were dangerous and tumultuous times for many within the abolitionist movement in the United States, the 1840s was a turning point in Northern sentiment. Follen's continued devotion to her beliefs and the desire to see slavery abolished secured her position as a well-respected member of the Boston elite. She remained active as an abolitionist and writer throughout her life, yet she did not live long enough to see the slaves emancipated. She died in 1860 in Brookline, Massachusetts.

Robin Hanson

See also: Liberty Bell, The; Women's Rights and the Abolitionist Movement.

Further Reading

Hansen, Debra Gold. *Strained Sisterhood: Gender and Class in the Boston Female Anti-Slavery Society.* Amherst: University of Massachusetts Press, 1993.

Foreign Slave Trade Act (1806)

The British Parliament enacted the Foreign Slave Trade Act (1806) as part of a sustained campaign to inflict economic distress on the French and their allies during the Napoleonic Wars (1799–1815). The far-reaching measures of this act met with the approval of the liberal Members of Parliament, who had been advocating the abolition of the slave trade for nearly two decades. Nevertheless, the institutionally conservative body had been moved to enact the measure not out of enlightened benevolence but out of military necessity: It was a critical aspect of the economic war against Napoleon Bonaparte.

In response to Napoleon Bonaparte's decision to extend his conquests across Europe, an alliance of European powers, with Britain as their titular head, formed a coalition that used the combined efforts of military action and economic sanctions to deny France further territorial claims and the financial means to conduct extended warfare. The British effort to close elements of the transatlantic slave trade aimed to hasten the end of armed conflict in Europe by denying Napoleon and his allies the means to finance their armed forces with the lucrative profits of colonial sugar.

The legislation that became commonly known as the Foreign Slave Trade Act was fully titled "An Act to prevent the Importation of Slaves, by any of His Majesty's Subjects into any Islands, Colonies, Plantations, or Territories belonging to any Foreign Sovereign, State, or Power; and also to render more effectual a certain Order, made by His Majesty in Council on the Fifteenth Day of *August* One thousand eight hundred and five, for prohibiting the Importation of Slaves (except in certain Cases), into any of the Settlements, Islands, Colonies, or Plantations on the Continent of *America*, or in the *West Indies*, which have been surrendered to His Majesty's Arms during the present War; and to prevent the fitting out of Foreign slave Ships from *British* Ports."

The Foreign Slave Trade Act, enacted on May 23, 1806, placed into positive legislation an Order in Council that had been issued on August 15, 1805, by the British War Cabinet. The measure was vigorously advocated by Prime Minister William Pitt the Younger and had the support of King George III. Although the measure was not universally accepted by all British subjects—those directly associated with the African slave trade would suffer economic hardships—it was understood among the general populace that the restrictions would be more onerous for the French, and thus the greater good necessitated that Parliament take such actions.

The act criminalized the involvement of any British citizen in efforts to provide slaves to those portions of the West Indies and North America that remained under the control of France or its allies and those that had come under British possession as a consequence of the war. The measure carefully enumerated all aspects of the trade that were illegal. These included the shipping of slaves, the financing of such a voyage, and any type of labor associated with the business of the slave trade. Moreover, slaving vessels, regardless of whether they were British, were not permitted to embark from any British port.

The act authorized the British government to seize any vessels captured while engaged in activities that were contrary to the intent of the legislation.

In such cases, both the slave ships and the slaves they carried became the property of the British Crown. In addition, the Foreign Slave Trade Act authorized severe fines and penalties for those who sought to violate the legislation and voided all insurance policies issued to guarantee the security of a slaving expedition.

The act authorized British Customs, Excise, and Navy officers and agents to prosecute those who violated the law as necessary. This provision of the legislation foreshadowed the Courts of Mixed Commission that would become common along the western coast of Africa as the African Squadron patrolled the region to enforce the abolition of the transatlantic slave trade when this became British law in 1807. Such judicial proceedings permitted a form of universal extraterritoriality, in which British law, custom, and policy could be implemented by courts in multiple venues, thus forming a tacit British juridical hegemony in the process.

The actual economic effects of the Foreign Slave Trade Act on France and its allies were slight. The French had already lost control of their sugar colony on Saint-Domingue as a result of slave insurrection, and the former colony had declared itself the independent republic of Haiti in 1804, taking it out of the French economic orbit. France's control over the Spanish and Portuguese colonies in the Americas became tenuous at best, as homegrown independence movements formed in several of these settings when Napoleon placed his brother Joseph on the Spanish throne. Creole elites who resisted the control of Bonapartist Spain did so not as liberal reformers but rather to preserve the rights and prerogatives they had acquired under previous imperial control.

The successful implementation of the Foreign Slave Trade Act paved the way for further action by Parliament to curtail the transatlantic slave trade. In 1807, Parliament outlawed the transatlantic slave trade altogether and instituted a sustained campaign to convince other nations in Europe and the Americas take a similar stance.

Junius P. Rodriguez

See also: Abolition of the Slave Trade Act (1807).

Further Reading

Craton, Michael. *Sinews of Empire: A Short History of British Slavery.* Garden City, NY: Anchor, 1974.

Fladeland, Betty. *Men and Brothers: Anglo-American Antislavery Cooperation.* Urbana: University of Illinois Press, 1972.

Kriegel, Abraham. "A Converging of Ethics: Saints and Whigs in British Antislavery." *Journal of British Studies* 26 (October 1987): 423–50.

Forten, James, Sr. (1766–1842)

One of the first prominent black abolitionists in the United States, James Forten became an early opponent of the American Colonization Society's efforts to send free African Americans to Liberia.

Forten was born a free man in Philadelphia, Pennsylvania, on September 2, 1766. A firm believer in the ideals of the Declaration of Independence, he served as a crew member on an American privateer during the American Revolution. After his release from a British prisoner-of-war ship, Forten returned to Philadelphia and learned the trade of sailmaking. He later became master of his own sailmaking loft, where he employed white and African American workers; he established strong relationships with prominent men in the region and ultimately became one of the wealthiest African Americans of the period. Because of his wealth and reputation, Forten quickly emerged as a leader of Philadelphia's African American community.

Forten's political activism began early in the nineteenth century, predating the American Anti-Slavery Society. In 1800, he signed a petition asking the U.S. Congress to modify the Fugitive Slave Act of 1793 and to take steps toward emancipation. When the Pennsylvania legislature debated whether to prevent free African Americans from entering the state, Forten published an eloquent plea in defense of the rights of free and enslaved African Americans. His pamphlet, *Letters From a Man of Colour* (1813), invoked the ideals of the Declaration of Independence and argued that African Americans deserved access to freedom, equality, and opportunity.

Forten further developed his abolitionist credentials in 1817, when he chaired (along with African American ministers Absalom Jones, Richard Allen, and John Gloucester) a meeting of Philadelphia blacks to discuss the newly formed American Colonization Society. The African Americans of Philadelphia unanimously rejected the society, arguing that they intended to stay in the country of their birth and refused to turn their backs on slaves. Forten became a spokesman for this point of view and remained a staunch opponent of the American Colonization Society throughout his life. His anticolonization stance ultimately would be embraced by William Lloyd Garrison and members of the American Anti-Slavery Society.

As a prominent figure in the Northern free black community, Forten was active in a number of organizations and institutions established to improve the status of African Americans, both free and enslaved.

He attended the early National Negro Conventions and contributed letters to the *Freedom's Journal*, the first newspaper created by African Americans. A friend of William Lloyd Garrison, Forten helped raise African American support for Garrison's journal, *The Liberator*. Forten's letters to the editor were often published in the paper, as was the antislavery poetry of two of his daughters, Margaretta Forten and Sarah Forten Purvis. He served on the board of managers of the American Anti-Slavery Society, and his home was a gathering place for members of the organization, both white and black.

Throughout his life, Forten was a vocal advocate for emancipation and racial equality in America. When he died on March 4, 1842, he left an important legacy to the American abolitionist community. His wife and children would continue to be active in antislavery circles, and his granddaughter, Charlotte Forten Grimké, would become well-known for her work with freed men and women in the South Carolina Sea Islands during the U.S. Civil War.

Forten himself would be lionized by both white and black abolitionists as a symbol of free African American morality, intelligence, and success. Forten's name and his achievements would remain essential weapons in the arsenal of antislavery advocates who hoped to disprove the rhetoric of African American degradation.

Erica L. Ball

See also: American Colonization Society; Grimké, Charlotte Forten.

Further Reading

Douty, Esther M. *Forten the Sailmaker: Pioneer Champion of Negro Rights.* Chicago: Rand McNally, 1968.

Horton, James Oliver, and Lois E. Horton. *In Hope of Liberty: Culture, Community, and Protest Among Northern Free Blacks, 1700–1860.* New York: Oxford University Press, 1997.

Nash, Gary. *Forging Freedom: The Formation of Philadelphia's Black Community, 1720–1840.* Cambridge, MA: Harvard University Press, 1988.

Winch, Julie. *A Gentleman of Color: The Life of James Forten.* New York: Oxford University Press, 2002.

"Forty Acres and a Mule"

The phrase "forty acres and a mule" has resonated since the end of the U.S. Civil War as the unfulfilled promise of land reform and opportunity made to freedmen. Popularized by freed slaves after the war, the phrase became a call for agricultural self-sufficiency. In the modern era, the phrase has been invoked by those calling for slave reparations.

Origins

During the final stages of the Civil War, as General William Tecumseh Sherman marched through the South with little opposition from Confederate forces, he was accompanied by thousands of freed slaves. The destruction caused by the war had displaced African Americans, who followed their liberators in droves. Concerned about their plight, Sherman asked the freedmen what was needed to identify them as *free men*.

After meeting with black leaders, Secretary of War Edwin M. Stanton and Sherman recommended that parcels of land be given to all freedmen. Sherman issued Field Order No. 15 on January 16, 1865, setting aside more than 400,000 acres, including the South Carolina Sea Islands region. The land was divided into forty-acre tracts, and Sherman distributed land titles to the head of each family of freedmen. He also ordered that mules and horses that were no longer useful to the Union army be distributed to each of the households.

On March 3, 1865, weeks before the end of the Civil War and almost a year prior to the ratification of the Thirteenth Amendment, which abolished slavery as a legal institution, the U.S. Congress created the Bureau of Refugees, Freedmen and Abandoned Lands, known colloquially as the Freedmen's Bureau. Among the responsibilities of the new agency was the task of supervising and managing all abandoned and confiscated land in the South and continuing to assign tracts of land to former slaves. Records indicate that by June 1865, approximately 40,000 freedmen had been allocated the designated 400,000 acres of land.

By September 1865, however, the former owners of the land that Sherman had reserved demanded the same rights afforded the returning rebels in other states. Exempted from the general amnesty, the former rebels secured special pardons from President Andrew Johnson, who broke the government's promise to redistribute the abandoned lands to the freedmen. Legal scholars have consistently maintained that Sherman's order was a military one and valid only during wartime.

Reparations

A variety of plans were presented to Congress and to President Johnson in order to secure land for the freedmen. One proposal suggested transporting former slaves to the West, where there was plenty of free land. The Homestead Act of 1862 had given 160 acres of land to each person or family, provided they stayed and worked the land for at least five years. Johnson, however, vetoed every proposal that provided land to the former slaves. Under the Southern Homestead Act of 1866, freedmen were allowed to purchase land at low prices, but few had any money, particularly after years of unpaid labor in the plantation system.

Introducing the 1867 slave reparations bill in the U.S. House of Representatives, Representative Thaddeus Stevens (R-PA) told his congressional colleagues that a grant of family homesteads of forty acres, with $100 to build a dwelling, was more valuable to freedmen at the time than the promise of suffrage. Although civil rights legislation was passed by Congress in 1866, 1871, and 1875, none of the measures included reparations for slavery, and few of the measures were enforced, especially in the South.

At the turn of the twentieth century, black organizations revived the phrase "forty acres and a mule" as they sought compensation for slavery and unsuccessfully lobbied Congress for pensions for former slaves and their families. The phrase arose in the context of Marcus Garvey's African nationalism movement of the 1920s and again in the 1930s, when writers were farmed out across the South and interviewed more than 2,300 former slaves as part of the Federal Writers' Project of the Works Progress Administration.

Many black nationalist groups took up the reparations debate in the 1960s, as organizations such as the Black Panther Party, the Black Muslims, and the Student Non-Violent Coordinating Committee demanded financial reparations for slavery. In the twenty-first century, an abundance of mainstream black assemblages have revisited the topic. In the quest of political activism, several organizations have promoted the idea of reparations for African Americans, espousing their "forty acres and a mule" or equivalent value.

Beginning in 1989 and every year since, Representative John Conyers (D-MI) has introduced legislation to establish a commission to study reparations and make recommendations. The bill would acknowledge the injustice, cruelty, brutality, and inhumanity of slavery in the United States and the original American colonies between 1619 and 1865 and establish a commission to examine the institution of slavery. The bill has never made it to the House floor, and African Americans have yet to receive their "forty acres and a mule."

Fred Lindsey

See also: Reconstruction.

Further Reading

Bardolph, Richard. *The Civil Rights Record: Black Americans and the Law, 1849–1970.* New York: Crowell, 1970.

Bennett, Lerone. *Before the Mayflower: A History of Black America, 1619–1962.* Chicago: Johnson, 1961.

Foner, Eric. *Politics and Ideology in the Age of the Civil War.* New York: Oxford University Press, 1980.

Oubre, Claude F. *Forty Acres and a Mule: The Freedmen's Bureau and Black Land Ownership.* Baton Rouge: Louisiana State University Press, 1978.

Foster, Abigail Kelley (1810–1887)

The abolitionist lecturer and fund-raiser Abigail ("Abby") Kelley Foster became one of the most influential women in the antislavery movement in the United States. In 1840, her controversial appointment to a committee of the American Anti-Slavery Society caused a rift in the U.S. abolitionist movement, which remained divided until the U.S. Civil War.

Kelley was born on January 15, 1810, in Pelham, Massachusetts, the fifth of seven children in an Irish Quaker family. She grew up near Worcester and attended the Friends Boarding School in Providence, Rhode Island, where her classmates included such future antislavery luminaries as Prudence Crandall and Elizabeth Buffum Chace.

In 1835, she went to work as a teacher at a Quaker school in Lynn, Massachusetts. She joined the Lynn Female Anti-Slavery Society and was elected secretary, bringing her into contact with antislavery workers across the Northeast. A passionate, impromptu speech at the 1838 Anti-Slavery Convention of American Women in Philadelphia brought her to the attention of national antislavery leaders, who began cajoling her to join their lecture bureau. Theodore Dwight Weld went so far as to tell her, "Abby, if you don't, God will smite you!" After much reflection, she resigned her teaching post and began lecturing in May 1839.

The novelty of this pretty young Irishwoman speaking before a "promiscuous" or mixed audience of men and women inspired both curiosity and hostility. It took her years to develop a skin tough enough to ignore the slanders and insults lobbed at her, along with rotten eggs and garbage. Although she resigned from the Quakers in 1841, she never abandoned plain clothing and plain speech. She often spoke in the extemporaneous style of a Quaker minister.

In 1840, Kelley found herself at the center of a political firestorm when she was nominated to join the business committee of the American Anti-Slavery Society. Conservatives, already inflamed by the radical position taken by William Lloyd Garrison and his ilk, did not want a woman on the committee, and when they were outvoted, they walked out of the convention and established their own society. This left Garrison in control of the American Anti-Slavery Society and Kelley as its chief lecturer.

For fifteen years, Kelley traveled back and forth across New England, New York, Pennsylvania, Ohio, Michigan, and Indiana, making speeches, raising funds, and building networks among local antislavery societies. Along the way, she cultivated a whole new generation of female speakers, including Lucy Stone, Paulina Wright Davis, and Susan B. Anthony.

She married fellow abolitionist Stephen Symonds Foster in December 1845 following a four-year courtship. In May 1847, they had their only child, a girl named Paulina Wright Foster, nicknamed Alla. Foster took a year off to care for the newborn and then shocked every female in her circle by "abandoning" her child to go back on tour.

At the annual meeting of the New England Anti-Slavery Society in 1856, the Fosters' relationship with Garrison finally splintered over their dissatisfaction with the direction he was taking the organization. They supported the creation of an independent abolitionist political party, whereas Garrison supported the newly launched Republican Party. Garrison lost his temper and publicly accused Abby of dishonesty and mishandling of funds.

The charges were baseless, but Garrison refused to apologize. Realizing that the accusation of financial impropriety, however false, had destroyed her ability to raise funds, and sick and exhausted from seventeen years of almost constant activity, Foster began to curtail her speaking activities. After the U.S. Civil War, she worked on a variety of causes, including freedmen's rights, women's rights, and temperance, but mostly at the local level.

Her last appearance on the national stage came in 1880, at the women's rights convention in Worcester. In her speech, she denounced the new law that gave Massachusetts women the right to vote in school elections as an insult, saying that half a loaf was worse than none at all. She accused men of being responsible

for the political disenfranchisement of women, and, to the delight of the crowd, at one point she turned to a gentleman standing on the platform with her and said, "*You* are my enslaver!"

Foster died on January 14, 1887, one day before her seventy-seventh birthday. "She who fought this dreadful battle is now at rest," wrote Lucy Stone. "She had no peer, and she leaves no successors."

Heather K. Michon

See also: American Anti-Slavery Society; Foster, Stephen Symonds; Garrison, William Lloyd; Weld, Theodore Dwight.

Further Reading

Bernard, Joel. "Authority, Autonomy, and Radical Commitment: Stephen and Abby Kelley Foster." *Proceedings of the American Antiquarian Society* 90 (1981): 347–86.
Sterling, Dorothy. *Ahead of Her Time: Abby Kelley and the Politics of Anti-Slavery.* New York: W.W. Norton, 1991.

Foster, Stephen Symonds (1809–1881)

Stephen Symonds Foster, an antislavery activist and lecturer, is best known for his scathing criticism of organized religion as tacitly supporting slavery.

Foster was born in Canterbury, New Hampshire, on November 17, 1809, the ninth child in a family of twelve. At the age of twenty-two, he decided to become a missionary. He entered Dartmouth College and began a course of study that emphasized Greek, Latin, rhetoric, and public speaking. He also became active in the Dartmouth Young Men's Anti-Slavery Society, and, in his junior year, he arranged a visit by the noted abolitionist lecturer Angelina Grimké.

In the spring of his senior year, Foster was arrested for an unpaid debt of $12.14 to a local merchant. Unable to come up with the money, he was sent to state prison as a debtor. In the two weeks that it took for friends to arrange his bail, he wrote an impassioned letter to the editor of the local newspaper, denouncing both the horrible living conditions and the injustice of minor criminals being incarcerated with murderers and thieves. His letter raised such a public outcry that within two years, the state prison system had been reformed, and the state legislature had passed a law abolishing imprisonment of debtors.

Foster graduated third in his class in 1838 and went on to complete his missionary training at the Union Theological Seminary in New York City, where he clashed with seminary officials over his strident criticism of slavery. Although they went so far as to offer him a scholarship in return for his restraint, he announced that he "could not be bought to hold his peace" and left not only the seminary but also the Congregational Church itself. He took a position as a lecture agent for the New Hampshire Anti-Slavery Society.

Foster was a powerful, passionate speaker. He did not hide his feelings regarding the horror of slavery, nor did he spare his listeners' feelings when he condemned what he believed was their complicity in a corrupt system that permitted the institution to continue. Often, his audiences were so angered by his aggressive statements that they turned on him with threats of violence. The movement itself was divided between those who thought he was a crackpot fanatic and those who saw him as a stalwart defender of liberty.

In September 1841, Foster adopted a new tactic: going into churches that had refused to hold antislavery meetings and interrupting the sermon with a plea to speak to the congregation. Within four months, he reported, he had been physically dragged from twenty-four separate churches.

> [Twice] my countrymen have thrown me with great violence from the second story of their buildings. Once they gave me an evangelical kick in the side that left me for weeks an invalid. Times out of memory they have hunted me with brick-bats and bad eggs. Four times they have opened their dismal cells for my reception.

In 1843, he wrote a scathing seventy-five-page tract titled *The Brotherhood of Thieves, or, a True Picture of the American Church and Clergy,* in which he castigated both Southern congregations for supporting slavery and Northern churches and clergy for segregating black church members. The booklet remained a best-seller in antislavery circles until the U.S. Civil War.

After his marriage to fellow lecturer Abigail ("Abby") Kelley in 1845, Foster slowly drifted out of the mainstream abolitionist movement. With the birth of their daughter Paulina in 1847, the Fosters took turns going on the road. Over the next twenty years, he turned much of his attention to farming, taking a run-down property on the outskirts of Worcester, Massachusetts, and turning it into a profitable farm and comfortable home for his extended family.

Like many of the old abolitionists, the Fosters found themselves marginalized during the Reconstruction period and slowly reduced their public speaking schedules. Taking up the Revolutionary War battle cry, "no taxation without representation," Foster refused to pay the tax on his farm as long as Abby was not permitted to vote. The farm was sold at auction several times, only to be bought back by friends and supporters. The Fosters were unable to win much attention for their efforts, however, and finally they abandoned the protest.

Foster died on September 8, 1881, at the age of seventy-two. At his memorial two weeks later, colleagues remembered him as a true original, "an agitator at a time when nothing but an agitator could serve."

Heather K. Michon

See also: Foster, Abigail Kelley.

Further Reading

Bernard, Joel. "Authority, Autonomy, and Radical Commitment: Stephen and Abby Kelley Foster." *Proceedings of the American Antiquarian Society* 90 (1981): 347–86.

Sterling, Dorothy. *Ahead of Her Time: Abby Kelley and the Politics of Anti-Slavery.* New York: W.W. Norton, 1991.

Fourteenth Amendment

See Amendments, Reconstruction

Fox, Charles James (1749–1806)

Charles James Fox, a celebrated British statesman and orator, led the Whig Party in opposition from 1784 to 1797. He publicly declared his thoughts on the moral depravity of trading in slaves and, when appointed secretary of state in 1806, became a leading force for legislation to abolish the slave trade in Britain.

Fox was born in Westminster on January 24, 1749, and raised with many advantages for a career in politics. His first private tutor was the Reverend Philip Francis, a translator of Demosthenes, the Greek orator to whom Fox would later be compared. Fox received his formal education at the academy at Wandsworth and Eton, the latter a school famous for its parliamentary tradition, and at Hertford College at Oxford University, where he was an avid reader of literature, a lifelong passion. In 1769, at the age of twenty, Fox took a seat as Member of Parliament for Midhurst.

During his long career in opposition politics, Fox championed many liberal causes for which he has been celebrated, particularly by Victorian scholars. At first a court supporter, by 1772, he had come to oppose the policies of King George III. Famously, he lent his support to the grievances of the American colonies against the administration of Lord North. Fox's speeches to Parliament on that subject gained him a reputation for oratory and quickened his friendship with other renowned speakers, such as Edmund Burke. Unlike Burke, Fox sympathized with the revolution in France, but like his contemporary, Fox spoke against slavery and the slave trade.

In the aftermath of the heightened political tensions that characterized the late 1780s, the Whig Party split into liberal and conservative branches. Fox's attempts at reconciliation were unsuccessful and unpopular with both factions. Fox did not think Britain was justified in going to war against France and fought against the counter-revolutionary spirit that caused the Habeas Corpus Act to be suspended in Britain.

English politicians also were divided over the issue of abolition, and during these years, Fox increasingly came to support William Wilberforce's championing of the abolitionist cause. By all accounts, Fox ranked with Burke and William Pitt in the eloquence of his speeches, which were delivered with an eye to ending slavery. He came to believe that British parliamentarians had an onus to take into account public opinion about slavery. While Parliament debated and passed a series of acts in the 1780s and 1790s to regulate the slave trade, Fox thought that approach wrongheaded. He maintained that the slave trade's destruction—rather than its mere regulation—should be the ultimate goal. In 1797, Fox withdrew from Parliament, largely a disappointed man.

Following Pitt's death in 1806, Fox was appointed secretary of state, a post he would occupy for only a few months before his death. He aimed to negotiate peace with France, but he found that impossible, given Napoleon's designs.

Fox supported Catholic emancipation and continued to press for the abolition of slavery. He worked closely with Wilberforce, to whom he reported that although abolition measures would carry in the House of Commons, any legislation for ending the slave trade would be defeated in the House of Lords. In his last parliamentary speech, delivered on June 10, 1806, Fox moved, "That this House, conceiving the African slave trade to be contrary to the principles of justice, humanity, and sound policy, will with all practicable expedition, proceed to take effectual measures for abolishing the said trade, in such manner, and at such periods, as may be deemed advisable."

In summer 1806, his health failing, Fox was forced to give up attendance at Parliament. He died on September 13, 1806, and was buried at Westminster Abbey. His speeches inspired many later reformers, including Frederick Douglass, who often quoted "the eloquent Fox."

Mark G. Spencer

See also: Wilberforce, William.

Further Reading

Davis, David Brion. *The Problem of Slavery in the Age of Revolution, 1770–1823.* Ithaca, NY: Cornell University Press, 1975; New York: Oxford University Press, 1999.

Derry, John W. *Charles James Fox.* New York: St. Martin's, 1972.

Drinkwater, John. *Charles James Fox.* London: Ernest Benn, 1928.

Eyck, Erich. *Pitt Versus Fox: Father and Son, 1735–1806.* Trans. Eric Northcott. London: G. Bell & Sons, 1950.

Fox, George (1624–1691)

The founder of the Society of Friends (Quakers), George Fox was born in July 1624 in Fenny Drayton, Leicestershire, England. He was raised as a Puritan but began to move away from the teachings of the church during his youth. By his mid-teens, he was living an isolated existence as a sheepherder and itinerant shoemaker and spending much of his time in meditation.

In 1647, after years of spiritual searching, Fox began preaching a simple yet revolutionary message to people in the small towns and villages of central England: "Every man [is] enlightened by the divine Light of Christ," he maintained, believing that communication with the Divine is direct and personal, accessible to anyone by listening inwardly.

His ministry quickly caught on, especially among the landless, the powerless, and the poor of society. First known as the Children of the Light, then the Friends of Truth, and later the Society of Friends, he and his followers spread out across the country. They preached simplicity in speech and dress and eschewed vices such as dancing and gambling. More provocatively, they withheld church tithes and refused to bow or doff their caps to those of higher social status. "Oh, the blows, punchings, beatings and imprisonments we underwent for not putting off our hats to men!" Fox wrote in his autobiography.

Laws passed in 1662, 1664, and 1670 criminalized Quaker practices, and hundreds of Friends were imprisoned at any given time; Fox himself was jailed eight times between 1649 and 1675 on various charges. Despite widespread persecution, the movement continued to grow, and the organizational foundation of the religion was complete by 1660.

George Fox, the founder of the Society of Friends (Quakers) in England, visited North America in the 1670s and planted the seeds of antislavery sentiment among his followers. Within a century, Quakers were openly denouncing the ownership and trade of slaves. *(Hulton Archive/Getty Images)*

Missionaries first arrived in the New World in 1655, and they won many converts, both in North America and on the islands of the West Indies. Many of these followers were slave owners, and, in 1657, Fox sent an epistle titled "To Friends Beyond the Sea That Have Black and Indian Slaves," encouraging them to treat their slaves mercifully but not condemning the practice itself.

In 1671, Fox announced it "was upon me from the Lord to go beyond sea, to visit the plantations in America," and he boarded a ship for the West Indies. He arrived in October, sick and weak from the strenuous crossing. Once he was able to tour the islands, he was stunned by what he saw. Slaves on the sugar and tobacco plantations worked in hellish conditions; they lived in strictly segregated societies; they were treated as animals, their lives and deaths unimportant except as property gain or loss. This was nothing like the indentured servitude he was familiar with in England, and it caused him to meditate on the nature of slavery.

During a meeting on November 2, 1671, just three weeks after his arrival, Fox told his followers that "Christ died for them all, both Turks, Barbarians, Tartarians, and Ethiopians; he died for Tawn[i]es and for the Blacks, as well as for you that are called whites." In other sermons on the islands over the next three months, he challenged the faithful to put themselves in the slaves' place to consider how they would feel. Though he did not explicitly call for an end to the practice, he urged slave owners to consider giving their slaves freedom after thirty years of service. Fox also encouraged owners to set a good moral example for their slaves, to allow them to marry and maintain their family groups, and to record marriages, births, and deaths as they would in their own families. In a few instances, he was able to speak to the slaves directly, and he won some converts among them.

Fox did not follow up on this message when he moved on to the mid-Atlantic colonies in 1672, nor are there records of him speaking out against slavery later in life. But this brief period of ministry laid the foundation for the antislavery sentiment that would live within the Society of Friends for the better part of two centuries.

Fox returned to England in 1672. His remaining years were punctuated by persecution of and dissent within the Society of Friends, but he maintained an active traveling ministry and spiritual search until his death near London on January 13, 1691, at the age of sixty-seven. The first edition of Fox's *Journal,* with a preface by William Penn, was published in 1694.

Heather K. Michon

See also: Quakers (Society of Friends).

Further Reading

Carroll, Kenneth. "George Fox on Slavery." *Quaker History* 86 (Fall 1997): 16–25.

Fox, George. *The Autobiography of George Fox.* Grand Rapids, MI: Christian Classics Ethereal Library, 2000.

Gragg, Larry. "A Heavenly Visitation: Larry Gragg Recounts the Reasons for a Visit of the Quaker George Fox to Barbados in 1671, and the Significance of His Presence There." *History Today* 52 (February 2002): 46–51.

Ingle, H. Larry. *First Among Friends: George Fox and the Creation of Quakerism.* New York: Oxford University Press, 1994.

Free Enquirer, The

The *New Harmony Gazette* was a specialized, reform-oriented weekly newspaper that was established to promote the experimental utopian-socialist community at

New Harmony, Indiana, founded in 1825 by Robert Owen, a Welsh manufacturer, social reformer, and philanthropist. Robert L. Jennings, Frances "Fanny" Wright, and two of Owen's sons were the chief editors of the newspaper during its three years of publication (1825–1828). The *Gazette* featured articles on Owen's social theories, as well as other topics of interest to its reform-minded subscribers. It provided a thorough—albeit one-sided—view of the history of the New Harmony experiment.

After the New Harmony experiment failed in fall 1828, the publication was re-invented and given a new focus. Operating under a new name, the *New Harmony and Nashoba Gazette, or the Free Enquirer,* the paper began to focus on another social experiment that Wright was associated with. Wright had established the Nashoba Plantation near Memphis, Tennessee, as an experimental community in order to demonstrate the effectiveness of wage labor for black workers over slavery. When Wright's experiment failed in 1829, the newspaper's title was shortened to *The Free Enquirer,* and the publication was relocated to New York City. Wright and Owen continued to serve as editors of the publication until 1835.

Wright and Owen were also the chief contributors to *The Free Enquirer.* The publication quickly gained a degree of notoriety for its advocacy of social policies that were considered radical in early-nineteenth-century America. Wright and Owen espoused the rights of women, championed the merits of socialism, universal suffrage, free secular education, and birth control, and challenged the social mores of the time. Among their radical views, they supported the immediate rather than gradual abolition of slavery without any financial compensation to slave owners.

Publications such as *The Free Enquirer* relied on the financial support of subscribers to remain viable as business enterprises. Like most other abolitionist publications, the editors found this situation financially untenable, and, as a result, few remained in operation for many years. The extreme freethinking views of Wright and Owen also contributed to the demise of *The Free Enquirer,* as their social advocacy often extended beyond the pale of what many reform-minded readers accepted as appropriate during the antebellum era.

Junius P. Rodriguez

See also: Owen, Robert Dale; Wright, Frances ("Fanny").

Further Reading

Lane, Margaret. *Frances Wright and the "Great Experiment."* Totowa, NJ: Rowman & Littlefield, 1972.

Leopold, Richard William. *Robert Dale Owen: A Biography.* Cambridge, MA: Harvard University Press, 1940.

Morris, Celia. *Fanny Wright: Rebel in America.* Cambridge, MA: Harvard University Press, 1984.

Free Soil Party

The Free Soil Party was formed in the United States in 1848 to oppose the expansion of slavery into the territories acquired from Mexico following the Mexican-American War (1846–1848). The new party was made up of three distinct political factions: (1) members of the antislavery Liberty Party, (2) Conscience Whigs (those motivated by their moral opposition to slavery), and (3) Barnburner Democrats (a faction that opposed slavery's expansion into the territories).

Since the election of 1840, the small, fledgling Liberty Party alone represented politically minded radical abolitionists. Its success at the polls, however, was insignificant at the national level. After the election of 1844, leading Liberty Party activists, such as Ohio's Salmon P. Chase, actively reached out to antislavery factions of the Whig and Democratic parties in an effort to form a broader and more successful antislavery party. When the Mexican War brought slavery to the forefront of national politics, conditions were ripe for the creation of a coalition of antislavery activists. In August 1848, the Free Soil Party emerged as the product of those conditions.

For nearly two decades, antislavery Whigs and Democrats had remained committed to their political organizations, convinced that the parties eventually would take more pronounced antislavery positions. At the conclusion of the Mexican War, however, Conscience Whigs felt betrayed when Zachary Taylor, a Southern slaveholder, was nominated as the Whig candidate for president. Led by such antislavery luminaries as Charles Sumner, Joshua R. Giddings, and Charles Francis Adams, Conscience Whigs met in Worcester, Massachusetts, during summer 1848. Denouncing the national Whig Party for its subservience to the "slave power," the Conscience Whig convention recommended participation in a national antislavery convention that was planned for Buffalo, New York, on August 9–10, 1848.

Similarly, some Democrats were upset with their party on the slavery issue. Some Democrats perceived that too much of the party's direction was dictated by the South and the interests of slavery. Accordingly, in

FREE SOIL.—FREE LABOR.—FREE SPEECH.

TEMPLE OF LIBERTY

MARTIN VAN BUREN　　CHARLES F. ADAMS

GRAND DEMOCRATIC FREE SOIL BANNER.

Martin Van Buren and Charles Francis Adams represented the new Free Soil Party in the presidential election of 1848. Free Soilers opposed the expansion of slavery into territories acquired by the United States from Mexico. *(Library of Congress)*

August 1846, many of these Democrats supported the Wilmot Proviso, which would have prohibited the spread of slavery into any territories acquired from Mexico during the war. At the New York Democratic convention in September 1847, radical "Barnburner" Democrats walked out when the more conservative "Hunker" faction took control of the convention and refused to support a resolution prohibiting the spread of slavery into the territories of the United States.

The younger Barnburners urged a permanent break with the party, but older leaders, such as Martin Van Buren, recommended reconciliation. When the national Democratic convention did not accept the Barnburner faction as solely representative of New York's Democratic Party, angry Barnburners answered the call to attend the Buffalo convention.

For several years, the principal leaders of the Liberty Party, including Chase, Joshua Leavitt, and Henry B. Stanton, had actively tried to increase the influence of their party. It was largely through the efforts of Chase that the Buffalo convention was organized. Liberty Party leaders were pleasantly surprised when more than 10,000 delegates crowded into Buffalo in 1848 for what would prove to be the formation of the Free Soil Party.

From the beginning, tensions and mutual suspicions needed to be overcome. Because the Liberty Party had stressed the immorality of slavery and the absolute necessity of separating the power of the national government from the protection of slavery, its delegates were concerned that its message might be diluted into a movement whose only concern was to prevent the spread of slavery into the federal territories. Moreover, early on, there was talk of a Van Buren presidential nomination, a rumor that made Conscience Whigs and Liberty delegates suspicious given Van Buren's less than stellar antislavery credentials. The resultant political platform diluted the message of the Liberty Party; nevertheless, it managed to satisfy all factions.

Chase played a major role in creating the Free Soil platform, which contained something for each faction. For the Whigs, there was an internal improvement plank. For the Democrats, there was a tariff reform plank. Though the platform neither condemned slavery on moral grounds nor attacked the Fugitive Slave Law, it did speak out against the spread of slavery in the federal territories, as well as denounce the use of federal power to protect slavery—something dear to Liberty Party members. Avoiding the issue of black political rights, Free Soil Party members took a long view of events. They were not Garrisonians who demanded the immediate abolition of slavery; rather, they believed that slavery, although immoral, could only be abolished gradually—largely through the adoption of a political strategy mapped out in their party's platform.

Van Buren edged out John P. Hale as the first Free Soil presidential nominee. Critical to the nomination was his endorsement of abolition for the District of Columbia, something he had not favored previously. In the 1848 elections, the new party was much more successful than the Liberty Party. Although Van Buren did not carry a single state, his popular vote total was 291,000, almost five times more than Liberty Party candidate James G. Birney had polled in 1844. At the same time, twelve Free Soil representatives were sent to the 31st Congress, and Free Soil delegations held the balance of power in key state legislatures. In both Ohio and Massachusetts, this arrangement led to the election of Chase and Sumner to the U.S. Senate.

The party had a promising beginning, but, by 1852, its prospects had diminished significantly. Although it adopted a much more radical platform at its national convention in Pittsburgh, its presidential nominee, Hale, garnered fewer than half the votes of Van Buren. There were a number of reasons for the party's decline. The adoption of the Compromise of 1850 temporarily quelled the slavery controversy and diminished the electoral fortunes of the new party. Disgruntled Barnburner Democrats made their peace with their former party and supported Franklin Pierce for president in 1852. Similarly, some Conscience Whigs were attracted to Whig presidential nominee Winfield Scott and migrated back into the Whig fold.

The 1852 election would be the last presidential election for the Free Soil Party. The decline of the Free Soil Party, however, did not mean the demise of antislavery sentiment. Although Free Soilers believed that the demise of the Whig Party after 1852 and the confusion generated by the Kansas-Nebraska Act in 1854 would revive their party, instead, antislavery and anti-Nebraska factions slowly coalesced under the mantle of the Republican Party between 1854 and 1856. Wiser and stronger, the new political party nonetheless endorsed many of the political positions held by the Free Soil Party.

Bruce Tap

See also: Chase, Salmon P.; Liberty Party; Van Buren, Martin.

Further Reading

Blue, Frederick J. *The Free Soilers: Third Party Politics, 1848–54.* Urbana: University of Illinois Press, 1973.

Foner, Eric. *Free Soil, Free Labor, Free Men: The Ideology of the Republican Party Before the Civil War.* New York: Oxford University Press, 1970.

Sewell, Richard H. *Ballots for Freedom: Anti-Slavery Politics in the United States, 1837–1860.* New York: Oxford University Press, 1976.

Free Soil Pioneer

The *Free Soil Pioneer* was one of several short-lived abolitionist newspapers that appeared during the antebellum era in the United States. The paper and others like it aimed to rally support for the antislavery movement by publishing articles, letters, and proceedings of abolitionist gatherings for the widest possible audience. The *Free Soil Pioneer* was created as the political organ of the Free Soil Party, and it served largely as a campaign vehicle for Martin Van Buren during the 1848 presidential election.

The *Free Soil Pioneer* was published weekly in Norwich, Connecticut, and edited by J.G. Cooley under the auspices of the Norwich Free Soil League. At the time the newspaper was founded, Norwich was a growing manufacturing community located at the confluence of the Yantic and Shetucket rivers in central Connecticut. The area of New London County, where Norwich is located, had a sizeable free black population, and the community had a reputation for its abolitionist sentiments; several homes were known as safe houses on the Underground Railroad.

The first issue of the *Free Soil Pioneer* appeared on July 27, 1848, a heady time in the antislavery movement. The United States had acquired substantial territory at the conclusion of the Mexican-American War, and the question of the day was whether slavery would be allowed to expand into these newly acquired territories. Particularly troubling to many was the realization that the United States might be re-introducing slavery into the region, as Mexico had effectively abolished the practice there in 1829. This concern sparked the formation of the Free Soil movement in the United States.

Like the party that it represented, the *Free Soil Pioneer* operated under a masthead that stated, "Free soil, Free labor, Free men." The party held its nominating convention in Buffalo, New York, where it selected Van Buren as its candidate for the presidency; Charles Francis Adams, the son of former president John Quincy Adams, was chosen as the vice presidential candidate. Although the Free Soil ticket was able to garner 10 percent of the popular vote in the November election, it won no electoral votes. Ironically, the Free Soil candidates polled enough votes in New York to put that state—and effectively, the election—in the hands of Whig candidate Zachary Taylor.

Publications such as the *Free Soil Pioneer* relied on the financial support of subscribers to remain viable as business enterprises. Most abolitionist presses found this situation financially untenable, and as a result, few remained in operation for many years. Though the *Free Soil Pioneer* had a limited circulation, its articles were reprinted in many other newspapers of the day, including William Lloyd Garrison's *The Liberator.* Through these means, the small abolitionist newspaper gained a larger national following.

Junius P. Rodriguez

See also: Free Soil Party.

Further Reading

Blassingame, John W., Mae D. Henderson, and Jessica M. Dunn. *Antislavery Newspapers and Periodicals.* 5 vols. Boston: G.K. Hall, 1980–1984.

Freedmen's Aid Societies

Freedom, though welcomed and celebrated by former slaves in the South, also brought poverty, uncertainty, and discrimination to many. Former slave masters did not assist in the transition from slavery to freedom, and the pressures of living outside bondage—such as illiteracy, lack of economic opportunity, and resulting poverty and hunger—proved formidable obstacles.

Following the U.S. Civil War, a number of social welfare organizations in the North began sending white teachers, missionaries, and charitable aid to assist former slaves with the transition to freedom. Motivated by religious and abolitionist zeal, these social reformers came to the South as soon as the guns fell silent. Their work in providing education, religious training, food, clothing, and other assistance had a profound effect on the welfare of former slaves for more than a decade.

The American Missionary Association (AMA) was the largest and most influential of the freedmen's aid societies. Formed in 1846, the AMA pursued a number of different social and religious causes during the years before the Civil War, including education reform and temperance. Abolition, however, was the AMA's chief concern. Its antebellum activities included supporting antislavery missionaries in the South, printing and distributing abolitionist literature, and promoting antislavery as a religious cause. Led by George Whipple, the AMA began to play a role in Reconstruction as early as 1863, sending missionaries to serve black Southerners in areas under the control of the Union army. By summer 1865, the AMA had dispatched workers to every state of the former Confederacy, attempting to meet the social and religious needs of newly freed slaves. The AMA was officially aligned with the Congregational Church, but it espoused an ecumenical philosophy that encouraged most evangelical Protestants to take up the mantel of social uplift under its sponsorship. Though religious conversion was an important component of the AMA's work, the education and social welfare of former slaves was paramount.

Other freedmen's aid societies shared similar origins and purposes but differed in the role that religion played in uplift efforts. For some groups, such as the Freedmen's Aid Society of the Methodist Episcopal Church, the conversion of former slaves and their acceptance of specific religious doctrines was a cornerstone of their reform agenda. Other groups took a secular path, such as the American Freedmen's Union Commission, which focused on education, charitable activities, and other causes without an official religious agenda. Differences in religious outlook and approach caused tension among the aid societies, and, as a result, they seldom cooperated on projects even though they sought to help the same people. The aid societies were not alone in their work among former slaves.

In 1865, the U.S. Congress established the Bureau of Freedmen, Refugees and Abandoned Lands within the War Department to address the same social and economic issues that the aid societies were targeting. Private aid societies and the Freedmen's Bureau sometimes cooperated in educational endeavors, but, again, their different agendas and approaches to relief often put them at odds.

Regardless of their ideological stance, the freedmen's aid societies approached their work in similar ways. After emancipation, former slaves entered a world for which they were unprepared. Freedom meant unrestricted movement and self-determination. But black Southerners carried the legacy of their bondage in the form of illiteracy, often limited skills beyond agriculture, and unfamiliarity with the daily challenges that their newly won freedom presented. Freedmen's aid societies attempted to help black Southerners make the transition in a number of ways, the most important of which was education.

Following the Union victory, these organizations dispatched thousands of teachers to the South to create schools for blacks. Most teachers were white Northern women in their early twenties who felt a personal call to missionary work, though white men sometimes found work as principals, administrators, or ministers in the schools formed by the societies. Aid society workers received support from Northern sponsors, such as wealthy philanthropists or local congregations who were interested in the freedmen's welfare. They traveled South and established black schools, most often in cities or towns, meaning that rural blacks benefited little from these educational efforts.

Teaching slaves to read and write had been illegal in the Southern states before the Civil War, so the vast majority of slaves had never become literate. In taking up this cause, the teachers faced a difficult challenge. Nevertheless, these institutions filled a critical gap in the South's education structure, and countless former slaves received at least a rudimentary education through them. Some, such as Shaw University in Raleigh, North Carolina; Fisk University in Nashville, Tennessee; and Morehouse College in Atlanta, Georgia, became prominent institutions of higher learning.

By 1875, the number of aid society workers in the South had declined, as changing political realities, financial difficulties, and waning interest among workers undermined support for such efforts. Five years later, aid society work among former slaves had all but vanished.

For more than a decade, however, the freedmen's aid societies played a crucial role in easing the transition to freedom for former slaves across the South. Though their religious agendas sometimes clashed with those of the people whom they were trying to help, by providing educational opportunities, food, clothing, and other assistance, the freedmen's aid societies improved the lives of countless black Southerners at a critical time in American history.

Richard D. Starnes

See also: American Missionary Association; Education of Former Slaves; Freedmen's Bureau; Howard, Oliver Otis.

Further Reading

Jones, Jacqueline. *Soldiers of Light and Love: Northern Teachers and Georgia Blacks, 1865–1873.* Chapel Hill: University of North Carolina Press, 1980.
Richardson, Joe M. *Christian Reconstruction: The American Missionary Association and Southern Blacks, 1861–1890.* Athens: University of Georgia Press, 1986.

Freedmen's Bureau

Created by an act of Congress on March 3, 1865, the Bureau of Refugees, Freedmen and Abandoned Lands—commonly known as the Freedmen's Bureau—was established within the federal War Department to educate and rehabilitate more than 4 million former slaves in the South and to ease their transition from slavery to freedom.

Although laws passed in 1863 and 1864 gave U.S. Treasury officials the responsibility of leasing abandoned lands for periods not exceeding twelve months, the Department of War took control of labor relations and the rehabilitation of former slaves toward the end of the U.S. Civil War and the subsequent Reconstruction period. The Freedman's Bureau was given the authority to supervise and manage all affairs pertaining to refugees, freedmen (slaves who were emancipated after Congress passed the Confis-

cation Act in 1862), and abandoned lands and to oversee the distribution of provisions, clothing, fuel, temporary shelter, and the allocation of forty acres of land for three years at an interest rate not to exceed 6 percent per year.

In May 1865, General Oliver O. Howard, a thirty-five-year-old soldier from Maine who was well versed in the intricacies and details of the task at hand, was appointed commissioner of the bureau, with about 900 agents working under him. The bureau often worked with other relief organizations, such as the Northern relief societies, the freedmen's aid societies, the American Missionary Association, the National Freedmen's Relief Association, the American Freedmen's Union, the Western Freedmen's Aid Commission. These and other organizations had sent food, clothes, and supplies to freedmen and refugees during the Civil War.

Foreseeing the difficulty of creating a judicial system that would be fair to the newly released slaves, the bureau set up temporary courts to settle disputes between white employers and black employees, with local agents serving as three-man courts. However, unable to meet the increasing demands for such arbitration, the bureau eventually took charge of monitoring state and local legal affairs, with a view toward expanding the rights of the freedmen within the context of the unabated racism that prevailed at that time.

The bureau aimed to help black workers obtain plantation work by arranging land sales at cheap prices, distributing essential livestock and farming equipment, and empowering them with the potential to move up and out of the labor class through education and entrepreneurship. The slogan "forty acres and a mule" originated during Reconstruction, as the bureau envisioned distributing 400,000 acres of confiscated or abandoned lands among the newly freed slaves. In reality, only 1 percent of the 4 million ex-slaves in the South received the promised forty acres and a mule, as President Andrew Johnson subsequently pardoned Confederates and returned the lands to their pre–Civil War owners.

Health care was another area in which the bureau sought to improve conditions by strengthening the few existing medical facilities and expanding the services available by establishing clinics in rural areas. The final report of the American Freedmen's Inquiry Commission to the Secretary of War claimed that the bureau had provided medical attention to an estimated 500,000 freedmen in approximately 100 hospitals.

THE MISSES COOKE'S SCHOOL ROOM, FREEDMAN'S BUREAU, RICHMOND, VA.—FROM A SKETCH BY JAS. E. TAYLOR.

MISSES COOKE'S SCHOOL-ROOM,

Chimborazo Hospital, Richmond, Va.

One of our illustrations last week showed an office of the Freedmen's Bureau, at Richmond. This week, as a continuation of the interesting series, we give a picture of the school-room for the freed children of larger and smaller growth) at Chimborazo Hospital, on a high bluff overlooking the James River, at the extreme southern part of the city of Richmond. The whole of the buildings of this hospital were assigned for the reception of colored refugees after the evacuation of the city by the Confederates; and this school, founded under the auspices of the National Freedmen's Relief Association, tells its own story in the order prevailing, and the promise which it gives of permanent benefit to that colored race which could not have been so long kept in slavery if it had not likewise been kept in *ignorance.*

MRS. D. P. BOWERS AND "LADY AUDLEY'S SECRET."

It was a remark of an acute critic, many years ago, that "scarcely an *artiste* could be found on any stage incapable of playing some part with rare perfection, if only the *artiste* or his friends could be induced to understand what was the peculiar part;" and many instances, on both the American and the foreign stage, illustrate the truth of the statement. When Mr. Sothern, a pleasant actor, but by no means a great one in other lines, picked up Lord Dundreary, he found the prize of his life. Mr. Owens, a more uniformly excellent actor, but never before within the reach of the celebrity which was his due, found a correspondingly excellent chance in Solon Shingle; and Mr. John S. Clarke discovered his measure almost equally well as Major Wellington de Boots; just as Mr. Jefferson had done as Asa Trenchard. Miss Jean Margaret Davenport struck a corresponding "placer" in fame if not in wealth as Peg Woffington; Mr. Chanfrau found it in the Mose characters; Mr. Blake had it (among other excellencies) as Jesse Rural; Mr. Couldock struck it as Abel Murcott; perhaps Mr. Davidge rivaled either as Solomon Probity. The most notable instance, after all, previous to the success of the subject of this sketch, was Miss Maggie Mitchell's Fanchon—not only alone, but beyond approach. To this same class of *peculiar excellencies, toward which all others may gaze in despair,* belongs the Lady Audley of Mrs. Bowers, in John Brougham's play from Miss Braddon's "Lady Audley's Secret." The character of the subtle, handsome, versatile, bewitching "diamond woman," without one particle of heart, but with a world of simulated caressing fondness to atone for the lack, is hers, hers alone, and no other person can hope to approach it. She may play it when and where she will, and it will always draw, from the subtle reality of the personation. Elsewhere we give an excellent portrait of the lady (a highly pleasing general actress in all appropriate lines, and deservedly popular)—a face worth studying, though even better on the stage than pictorially.

THE MOZIER STATUES.

Mr. Mozier, the distinguished American sculptor, resident of Rome, and so well and favorably known by American travelers, has just placed on exhibition seven of his splendid statues in marble, at the Gallery of the Tenth Street Studio Buildings. It is very seldom that we have an opportunity to see such a collection of rare works. They were all modeled and done in marble at Rome. Mr. Mozier is now on a visit to the land of his birth, and brings the marbles with him, at the urgent request of a large number of Americans who had been at his studio in Italy.

The most important work in the collection is called:

THE RETURN OF THE PRODIGAL SON.

It is an illustration of the following familiar passage:

"And he arose and came unto his father. But when he was a great way off, his father saw him and had compassion and ran and fell on his neck and kissed him."

The figures are life-size: the returned prodigal has flung himself into the arms of his father. The old man holds him tenderly to his bosom and bends over to kiss him on the cheek. The figure of the father represents one of those grand old patriarchs described by the Bards of the Bible; compassion, paternal affection and forgiveness are depicted in every feature of the face; on his head he wears an Hebraic turban; the drapery is grand, and must have cost the artist months of study and labor; the whole figure is full of power; every part thereof having been carefully considered. The figure of the son is that of a youth from eighteen to twenty years of age; his attenuated form shows the privations he has undergone; famished, weary and exhausted, he returns; all is rendered by a master-hand. It is in the face, however, that we discover the triumph of the artist. As the penitent youth reclines his head on his father's bosom and looks up, a calm smile overspreads his care-worn face. Seeing the forgiveness of his father, gratitude wells up from his heart and wreaths his features with the utmost tenderness. Any one who can look on this great group, unmoved by either compassion or pity, must have a heart as hard and cold as granite.

We have never seen any modern group that so completely illustrated the uses and beauty of the sublime art of sculpture. It is a poem, a moral lesson, and an imperishable illustration of one of the most beautiful and touching scenes in the sacred Scriptures.

The next figure that attracted our attention was

UNDINE RISING VAILED FROM THE CASTLE WELL.

This is a most beautiful figure; it is fully draped, with the face averted, and most ingeniously vailed, as if to prevent recognition. She stands on the water in a very graceful attitude, with one hand over her head, hold-

MRS. D. P. BOWERS, THE POPULAR ACTRESS, AND GREAT REPRESENTATIVE OF "LADY AUDLEY."

FRANK PIGEON, OF THE BEDFORD B. B. CLUB, BROOKLYN, N. Y.

ing up the vail, which is exquisitely managed. Her lithe and agile form shows through the airy folds of the drapery, giving the impression of a lovely molded creature. Whoever may be fortunate to get this statue will have one worthy of any collection in the country. It is life

Schools established by the Freedmen's Bureau after the Civil War provided the first formal public education for African Americans in the South. As depicted in this 1866 newspaper, classes were open to children and adults, males and females alike. *(Library of Congress)*

Despite these milestones, the education of emancipated slaves and their children received most of the bureau's attention. Serving as a liaison between Northern relief societies and local governments and philanthropists, the bureau facilitated the establishment and operation of about 4,000 new schools, serving more than 150,000 newly emancipated slaves, and spent more than $400,000 to establish training institutions for teachers. With the intent to establish a system in which black educators would eventually take charge of black children's education, the bureau collaborated with American Missionary Association and the American Freedman's Union Commission to found the first black colleges of the South.

In 1866, the chairman of the Judiciary Committee, Lyman Trumball of Illinois, introduced a bill that not only increased the bureau's powers but also guaranteed comprehensive civil rights to blacks. Although the bill passed the Senate and the House, President Johnson vetoed it on the grounds that such a law would infringe on states' rights and might be perceived as an unconstitutional extension of military powers after the war. During his presidency, several Black Codes were passed that allowed the freed slaves to be treated like serfs on the plantations and, in certain instances, denied them the right to lease or rent farmland. Over Johnson's veto, Congress passed the Civil Rights Act of 1866, which guaranteed citizenship to blacks and declared it illegal for states to restrict or deny them rights to hold property and testify in court.

Many activists supported the bureau's efforts to provide blacks with equal opportunities in the civic arena, arguing that the creation of a permanent bureau would not only assist former slaves in finding gainful employment but also would guarantee suffrage. Opponents believed that any institution favoring one group of people was unconstitutional; they claimed that the Thirteenth Amendment, which legally abolished slavery in the United States in 1865, was sufficient to establish equality.

The bureau's weak organization and lack of funding contributed to critics' growing disenchantment with the organization. By 1869, it ceased to play an active role. Under pressure from hostile white Southerners, Congress terminated the Freedmen's Bureau in 1872.

Kokila Ravi

See also: Civil War, American (1861–1865); "Forty Acres and a Mule"; Reconstruction.

Further Reading

Drake, Richard B. "Freedmen's Aid Societies and Sectional Compromise." *Journal of Southern History* 29 (May 1963): 175–86.

Du Bois, W.E.B. *The Souls of Black Folk.* Chicago: A.C. McClurg, 1903; ed. David Wright and Robert Williams, New York: Bedford/St. Martin's, 1997.

Morison, Samuel Eliot, and Henry Steele Commager. *The Growth of the American Republic.* 2 vols. New York: Oxford University Press, 1942.

Freedom Celebrations, International

Since the late eighteenth century, the Atlantic world has witnessed movements to abolish slavery and to establish independent black republics. Beginning with the Haitian Revolution (1791–1804), these efforts encompassed international abolitionism during the nineteenth century and movements for national independence in Africa during the mid-twentieth century. Public celebrations commemorate many of these events, from the independence of Haiti in 1804 (celebrated there each January 1) to the independence of Zimbabwe in 1980 (celebrated April 18).

Beginnings and Evolution

The act of emancipation that generated the most widespread commemorative activity was Great Britain's Abolition of Slavery Act of 1833 (commonly known as the British Emancipation Act), which marked the demise of slavery in all British colonies and throughout the empire. Public festivals commemorating the act were widely observed during the nineteenth century in the United States and in the West Indian colonies; both observed the August 1 date when the legislation took effect in 1834. Widespread celebrations did not take place until after 1838, when an interim apprenticeship system was terminated.

In the United States, both black and white abolitionists held annual celebrations in the free states and territories during the antebellum decades. West Indian emancipation celebrations solidified a vibrant commemorative tradition among Northern free blacks, a tradition that continued to be celebrated beginning in the 1860s on different dates commemorating U.S. emancipation.

In Canada, celebrations were held primarily in Ontario, where many fugitives from American slavery had settled during the mid-nineteenth century. The celebrations largely followed the U.S. pattern, featuring orations, parades, balls, and banquets. Nineteenth-century celebrations served an important social and activist function, but in the early twentieth century, they became more segregated and purely festive rather than political.

In South Africa, the Emancipation Act took effect on December 1, but no comparable tradition of annual commemoration developed. An Emancipation Centenary Celebration was held at Johannesburg in June 1934. This event featured performances of American Negro spirituals and Zulu folk songs, speeches by American missionaries and black South African nationalists, and a drama depicting the life of American slaves, including extracts from speeches by President Abraham Lincoln and African American orator Frederick Douglass, along with elements of minstrelsy.

In the West Indies, the patterns of celebration were complicated by competing interests, as white landowners, clergy, and government officials attempted to maintain control over the liberated population. The erratic patterns of commemoration in the British West Indies suggest the contested meanings of slavery, freedom, and political independence in the region.

The August 1 celebrations in the West Indies evolved from structured, largely religious events featuring lectures from white clergymen on proper behavior to become populist jubilees that were increasingly secular and political. Celebrations held in the Bahamas between 1834 and 1838, for example, were subdued events organized by white missionaries who were interested in maintaining social order, whereas later celebrations sponsored by secular lodges and self-help organizations created greater upheaval. In Barbados, former slaves celebrated August 1 in an orderly way between 1834 and 1838, with large contingents of local militia and imperial soldiers keeping watch. Jamaican celebrations of August 1 incorporated aspects of the traditional "crop-over" slave festival, in which slaves and whites marked the harvest of the sugar crop. White participation soon dwindled, though, as former slaves celebrated August 1 during two weeks of revelry featuring drumming and fireworks.

As time passed, the August 1 commemorations in some Caribbean countries focused less on emancipation and more on political and social change. In the urban areas of Trinidad, for example, August 1 was observed mainly by educated, free-born coloreds and white liberals, whereas ex-slaves used the carnival season as a venue to celebrate freedom. Until the mid-nineteenth century, celebrants held public dinners featuring political speeches that emphasized racial pride; over time, the holiday came to focus on outdoor entertainments, with little reference to emancipation until the 1888 jubilee. That year, politically active middle-class Trinidadians in the large cities restored the original focus of the public dinners, stressing the importance of self-help in racial uplift. Popular celebrations featuring toasts, dances, and athletic events took place in Trinidad's small towns and villages.

Contemporary Celebrations

During the 1980s and 1990s, scholars and activists succeeded in reviving Emancipation Day, and August 1 is once again a widely supported national holiday in Jamaica, Guyana, the Bahamas, and throughout the anglophone Caribbean. By the late 1990s, a pan-African element was added when the government of Ghana adopted the celebration of August 1, and the nation's Ministry of Tourism held a weeklong festival to attract cultural and historical tourism among blacks throughout the diaspora. Since 1995, blacks in Britain have observed August 1 as African Remembrance Day, a commemoration that they hope to popularize as a global day of grief, healing, and unity among African peoples.

Freedom celebrations in other parts of the Atlantic have not been observed so consistently. Cuba and Brazil, for example, have no national holiday commemorating emancipation. However, some scholars have identified the *Festa da Boa Morte* (Feast of the Good Death) in Brazil as the oldest ongoing vernacular celebration of emancipation in the Americas. This syncretic religious festival combines elements of Afro-Brazilian Candomble and Catholicism. Its nineteenth-century founders, a sisterhood of enslaved women, vowed to hold an annual procession and feast to express their gratitude for the Virgin Mary's intercession in their efforts to save money to purchase their freedom. These public festivals continued at least until the 1980s.

The liberation of African nations has generated a tradition of Independence Day or National Day celebrations, beginning with the 1847 independence of Liberia, where July 26 continues to be observed annually. As decolonization accelerated in the mid-twentieth century, other African nations established similar national holidays. Though they do not explicitly celebrate the end of slavery, these occasions continue the African peoples' annual tradition of commemorating the expansion of freedom and self-determination.

In addition to these official and vernacular holidays, monuments commemorating the end of slavery have been established in a number of Atlantic nations, including the Netherlands, Ghana, Martinique, Antigua, and Barbados.

Mitch Kachun

See also: Freedom Celebrations, U.S.

Further Reading

Higman, B.W. "Remembering Slavery: The Rise, Decline, and Revival of Emancipation Day in the English Speaking Caribbean." *Slavery and Abolition* 19:1 (1998): 90–105.

Kachun, Mitch. *Festivals of Freedom: Memory and Meaning in African American Emancipation Celebrations, 1808–1915.* Amherst: University of Massachusetts Press, 2003.

Walker, Sheila. "The Feast of Good Death: An Afro-Catholic Emancipation Celebration in Brazil." *Sage: A Scholarly Journal on Black Women* 3:2 (1986): 27–31.

Freedom Celebrations, U.S.

People in the transatlantic world, including the United States, have celebrated the demise of slavery since early in the nineteenth century. Although diversity across time and place characterizes the freedom celebrations, these annual events have included public rejoicing, political agitation, racial consciousness-raising, ethnic and socioeconomic discord, and collective history making.

On January 1, 1808, the official end of the transatlantic slave trade in the British colonies and United States prompted the first widespread freedom celebrations. Until about 1830, free blacks in the northern United States held services of thanksgiving, most often in black churches; these services generally included prayers, anthems, formal addresses, and sermons. Participants acknowledged the importance of celebrating on New Year's Day, as, under slavery, that date had signified the end of the Christmas holidays followed by widespread slave sales.

Emancipation in the British West Indies between 1834 and 1838 led to the most significant freedom commemorations in the transatlantic world during the first half of the nineteenth century. From Liberia to Ohio, former slaves and their supporters made August 1—the date that all slaves in the British Empire were emancipated—a day of celebration and agitation for worldwide abolition.

Free blacks in North America, including settlements of ex-slaves in Ontario, Canada, also held celebrations, with the largest taking place in Toronto and Hamilton. The annual rituals included church services, speeches, parades, fireworks, banquets, and military balls, and these events featured public demands for an end to slavery in the United States. Throughout the North, free African Americans and white abolitionists organized hundreds of August 1 celebrations. Though they were less likely to be held in churches than the New Year's Day celebrations, the formal exercises in August similarly featured orations, songs, prayers, and readings.

Some free blacks criticized the August 1 celebrations as a waste of time and money and for commemorating an act of emancipation that compensated slaveholders. Participants, though, expressed their solidarity with slave and free blacks throughout the diaspora, emphasized the contributions to history made by African Americans, pointed out how the United States was falling short of its ideals of freedom, and asserted their citizenship in the face of legislative gains by proslavery advocates.

The diaspora-wide commemorations of August 1 were not repeated when slavery was dissolved in the United States between 1861 and 1865. In the South, as a result of local and regional disparities in the granting of freedom, African Americans held annual celebrations on a range of dates—January 1, June 19, and August 1—drawing on the antecedents of slave holidays and free black freedom celebrations.

Emancipation Day was always a community affair featuring speeches, fellowship, events, and food. The public nature of Emancipation Day celebrations had tremendous political significance, as former slaves claimed free assembly and active citizenship in the face of violent opposition from whites. Former slaves created an oral, visual collective history of their triumph over slavery, even as they called for deliverance from continued oppression.

During the twentieth century, attention to freedom celebrations waxed and waned throughout the United States, as urbanization and popular culture provided new diversions. People of African descent debated how best to spend their limited resources and whether to publicly acknowledge their slave past. Renewed interest in emancipation throughout the transatlantic world in the late twentieth century spurred movements for governmental recognition of emancipation through the designation of official holidays.

In the twenty-first century, a movement proposed celebrating a new national holiday in the United States on June 19, or "Juneteenth." This freedom celebration began in the 1860s as blacks in eastern Texas, western Louisiana, southwestern Arkansas, and southern Oklahoma adopted the date as the official and celebratory date of their independence.

Antoinette G. van Zelm

See also: Juneteenth.

Further Reading

Fabre, Genevieve. "African-American Commemorative Celebrations in the Nineteenth Century." In *History and Memory in African-American Culture*, ed. Genevieve Fabre and Robert O'Meally. New York: Oxford University Press, 1994.

Gravely, William B. "The Dialectic of Double-Consciousness in Black Freedom Celebrations, 1808–1863." *Journal of Negro History* 67 (Winter 1982): 302–17.

Van Zelm, Antoinette. "Virginia Women as Public Citizens: Emancipation Day Celebrations and Lost Cause Commemorations, 1863–1890." In *Negotiating Boundaries of Southern Womanhood: Dealing With the Powers That Be*, ed. Janet L. Coryell, et al. Columbia: University of Missouri Press, 2000.

Wiggins, William H., Jr. "Juneteenth: Tracking the Progress of an Emancipation Celebration." *American Visions* 8 (June/July 1993): 28–31.

———. *O Freedom! Afro-American Emancipation Celebrations.* Knoxville: University of Tennessee Press, 1987.

Frémont, John Charles (1813–1890)

As a military officer and explorer of the Rocky Mountain region, John Charles Frémont became a well-known figure in early-nineteenth-century America. He earned his antislavery credentials as the presidential candidate of the newly established Republican Party in 1856 and furthered his reputation by issuing a controversial proclamation during the early stages of the U.S. Civil War in which he attempted to emancipate the slaves in Missouri.

Born on January 21, 1813, in Savannah, Georgia, Frémont spent his early years in Charleston, South Carolina, where he was raised by his mother until he entered Charleston College in 1829. In 1838, as a lieutenant in the U.S. Army Corps of Topographical Engineers, he set out on a number of wilderness explorations for which he would become famous, earning the moniker "the Pathfinder."

A number of factors helped shape Frémont's early antislavery views. As a key figure in conquering California during the Mexican-American War (1846–1848), he shared a distrust of slavery and slaveholders along with most of the Westerners with whom he associated. His explorations in the Rocky Mountains and his friendship with the Indian agent and scout Kit Carson contributed to his personal views of democracy and freedom.

Frémont's marriage to Jessie Benton—the daughter of Thomas Hart Benton, a representative and later senator from Missouri—brought an antislavery perspective to his immediate family. Senator Benton was an outspoken critic of the Kansas-Nebraska Act of 1854 (which established the territories of Kansas and Nebraska, with the slavery question to be determined by popular sovereignty), and Frémont opposed the spread of slavery into the territories.

The first national convention of the Republican Party convened in Philadelphia on June 17, 1856, for the purpose of writing the party's platform and nominating a candidate for the presidency. The Democratic incumbent, Franklin Pierce, had fallen out of favor because of his support of the Kansas-Nebraska Act. The Democrats seemed vulnerable, and it looked as if a strong Republican thrust could elect a Free Soiler (a member of the party opposing the extension of slavery into newly acquired territories) to the White House. The chairman of the Republican National Executive Committee, E.D. Morgan of New York, opened the meeting with words that would set the tone for the party's future: "You are here today to give direction to a movement which is to decide whether the people of the United States are to be hereafter and forever chained to the present national policy of the extension of human slavery."

No Southern states sent representatives to the Republican convention. Many of the delegates held extremely radical views, and abolitionists outnumbered Free Soilers. The convention was filled with the famous and some who would shortly become so. It became obvious that the new party was opposed to the territorial expansion of slavery and little else when Platform Committee Chairman David Wilmot, author of the infamous Wilmot Proviso, read the planks early the second morning. Five resolutions were devoted to slavery in the territories and in Kansas. It was, the platform said, the duty of the U.S. Congress to prohibit in the territories "those twin relics of barbarism—Polygamy and Slavery."

The delegates then turned their attention to the selection of a candidate to run for the presidency. A strong young party needed a strong young hero, and Frémont filled the bill admirably. His adventurous career, close family connection to Thomas Hart Benton, association with California politics (he had represented the state in the U.S. Senate from 1850 to

A political cartoon during the presidential campaign of 1856 ridicules Republican candidate John C. Frémont (riding the "Abolition Nag") and his supporters for their opposition to the spread of slavery into the Kansas and Nebraska territories. (*Hulton Archive/Getty Images*)

1851), and well-known Free Soil views all made him the perfect candidate for the nomination.

Frémont's supporters included a long list of important Washington personages, both within and outside the government, and he was clearly the front-runner as early as spring 1856. But it was the antislavery wing of the American (Know-Nothing) Party that most worried the Republicans and Frémont's backers. The Know-Nothings also had considered nominating Frémont as their presidential candidate. If he consented to go with them, then the Republican support would dwindle as Free Soilers defected to join the Know-Nothings. To counter this possibility, Frémont drafted a letter to one of that party's leaders, Thomas Ford of Ohio, disclaiming any interest in joining the Know-Nothing Party or becoming its nominee. Eventually, the two parties merged for the sake of strength, and the Republican ticket of Frémont and Senator William Dayton of New Jersey went forward.

Frémont's letter accepting the nomination of the Republican Party stressed his antislavery perspective and angered those in the South who might have voted for him. Many Southern slaveholders viewed Frémont as the leader of a conspiracy that was designed to tear the Union apart, and Senator John Slidell of Louisiana predicted disunion in the event of a Republican victory.

Frémont was not the first to speak out against slavery, but he was certainly the first presidential candidate of a major party to do so. Although he lost the 1856 presidential race to James Buchanan, Frémont's role as an antislavery supporter was far from finished.

When the Civil War began in 1861, Frémont was placed in command of Union forces in the border state of Missouri. He soon faced the difficult challenge of deciding what to do with slaves who approached Union forces seeking their freedom. Acting on his own initiative and without the backing of officials in Washington, D.C., on August 30, 1861, Frémont invoked martial law in Missouri and issued a proclamation that freed the slaves of all disloyal owners in the state. President Abraham Lincoln effectively nullified the order by asking Frémont to revise the proclamation so that it did not overstep congressional laws regarding emancipation. On September 11, when Frémont refused to comply with Lincoln's request, the president ordered the general to comply and then re-assigned him to a different department in Wheeling, West Virginia.

Thereafter, Frémont's career dwindled, and he never fully re-established himself in politics, although he served as territorial governor of Arizona from 1878 to 1883. He died in New York on July 13, 1890.

Henry H. Goldman

See also: Frémont's Emancipation Decree (1861).

Further Reading

Chaffin, Tom. *Pathfinder: John Charles Frémont and the Course of American Empire.* New York: Hill and Wang, 2002.

Nevins, Allan. *Frémont: Pathmarker of the West.* Lincoln: University of Nebraska Press, 1992.

Randall, J.G. *Civil War and Reconstruction.* Boston: D.C. Heath, 1953.

Rolle, Andrew. *John Charles Frémont: Character as Destiny.* Norman: University of Oklahoma Press, 1991.

Frémont's Emancipation Decree (1861)

Slaves in the border state of Missouri were emancipated, if only briefly, for several weeks in August and September 1861 by a military proclamation. The proclamation was subsequently rescinded by President Abraham Lincoln, who feared the measure might encourage Missouri to leave the Union and join the eleven other slave states that had formed the Confederate States of America.

It was U.S. Major General John Charles Frémont who struck the first blow against slavery during the U.S. Civil War. Frémont, who had run unsuccessfully as the Republican candidate for president in 1856, was placed in command of the Union forces at Saint Louis, Missouri, early in the war. There, pro-Union citizens were being harassed by Confederate supporters, and a full-scale guerrilla war was in progress. It was rumored that a rebel army of 10,000 was en route to the state.

Several of Frémont's closest friends and advisers were vocal antislavery advocates. These included the well-known abolitionist Owen Lovejoy, then a congressional representative from Illinois; John A. Gurley, who represented the Cincinnati area in the U.S. Congress; and Jessie Benton Frémont, Frémont's wife and the daughter of the late Senator Thomas Hart Benton of Missouri.

For reasons of military necessity, Frémont issued a proclamation of martial law throughout the state of Missouri early in August 1861. On August 30, the decree was expanded to include the confiscation of property from those who resisted the United States and their "slaves . . . declared [to be] freemen."

Frémont always maintained that he had issued the proclamation as a result of the guerrilla warfare within the Union lines. Whatever his motives, Frémont had exceeded his military authority in dealing with matters that properly belonged to officials in Washington, D.C. Indeed, President Lincoln quickly ordered him to modify the rule of martial law and to change the orders regarding the confiscation of property and emancipation so as to conform with existing legislation.

Frémont's emancipation decree had widespread consequences. Lincoln worried that Kentucky would not support the Union unless the proclamation was completely rewritten and the emancipation clause removed. The president even suggested, "on the news of General Frémont having actually issued deeds of manumission, a whole company of our volunteers threw down their arms and disbanded."

Lincoln further complained that "Genl. Frémont's proclamation, as to confiscation of property, and the liberation of slaves, is *purely political,* and not within the range of *military law,* or necessity. . . . If the General needs them [slaves], he can seize them, and use them; but when the need is past, it is not for him to fix their permanent future condition. . . . The proclamation in the point in question is simply 'dictatorship.'"

Lincoln's overruling of the proclamation was not intended to be a rebuke of Frémont, much less his dismissal. In Washington, however, Frémont's action was viewed as an embarrassment and a usurpation of power. The decree, taken together with charges of military incompetence raised by fellow officers, prompted the president to remove Frémont from his command at Saint Louis. The general was reassigned to the newly created Mountain Division, with headquarters in Wheeling, West Virginia. By then, Frémont's career had deteriorated, and he did not play a role in the remainder of the war.

Historians have suggested that Frémont's problems were political rather than military. Disgruntled from his loss in the presidential race of 1856, Frémont perhaps believed that he was due a greater role in the early years of the war. He ran afoul of the powerful, politically connected Blair family of Missouri, who viewed him as an opportunist and had distrusted him for years. With Montgomery Blair serving as postmaster general in the Lincoln administration, the president received a one-sided critique of Frémont's tenure in Missouri.

After the Frémont incident, Lincoln made certain that the government's policy of not permitting military commanders to issue orders of emancipation was enforced. In May 1861, for example, he overruled Frémont's successor, Brigadier General David Hunter, when he freed slaves in Georgia, Florida, and South Carolina.

Henry H. Goldman

See also: Frémont, John Charles.

Further Reading

Chaffin, Tom. *Pathfinder: John Charles Frémont and the Course of American Empire.* New York: Hill and Wang, 2002.

Nevins, Allan. *Frémont: Pathmarker of the West.* Lincoln: University of Nebraska Press, 1992.

Rolle, Andrew. *John Charles Frémont: Character as Destiny.* Norman: University of Oklahoma Press, 1991.

French Emancipation Declaration (1794)

On February 4, 1794, the French legislature, the National Convention, outlawed slavery in all of the nation's colonies. This momentous decision, coming five years after the start of the French Revolution, was the first of its kind by a European power. Although First Consul Napoleon Bonaparte re-established slavery in 1802, the Emancipation Declaration of 1794 set a historic precedent. The declaration represented the culmination of several historical developments—most notably, the successful slave revolt in the French colony of Saint-Domingue (Haiti), which began in 1791.

Slavery was a key component of the economic system of the *ancien régime,* not only fueling the commercial activity of France's overseas empire but also enriching the aristocratic and bourgeois families who owned the colonial plantations and had ties to French trading ports. For this reason, slavery became a contentious issue early in the French Revolution.

After the National Assembly was formed in June 1789, mulattoes and free blacks, supported by the French abolitionists, sought equal status with white colonists. Abolitionists associated with the *Société des Amis des Noirs* (Society of Friends of the Blacks) believed that securing civil rights for free people of color was the first step in their antislavery struggle. However, delegates representing colonial planters and merchant interests gained control of the Committee on the Colonies, the body charged with the administration of France's overseas colonies. The delegates used their influence to block attempts at social and political reform in the slave colonies of the West Indies.

While delegates to the National Assembly debated these issues, they also discussed a proposed declaration of rights that would define the terms of French citizenship. Although the Declaration of the Rights of Man and of the Citizen, which had been adopted in August 1789, stated, "men are born and remain free and equal in rights," the National Assembly declined to extend the vote to either mulattoes or free blacks.

Because the abolitionists supported the civil rights struggle for nonwhites, defeat on this point proved to be a setback for their larger goal of attacking slavery. Facing powerful opposition from both commercial and nationalist interests in the National Assembly, members of the *Société des Amis des Noirs* were unable to garner political support for the abolition of the slave trade. Rather than curtail the trade, the National Assembly voted to end the monopoly of the Senegal Company on January 18, 1791, thereby opening up the French slave trade to competition.

Frustrated by their exclusion from the electorate, a group of mulattoes led by Vincent Ogé arose in armed rebellion against the white planters in Saint-Domingue in October 1790. The rebellion was quickly defeated and the leaders executed. However, in August 1791, the black slaves of Saint-Domingue rebelled against their masters again in a much larger armed insurrection.

Events in Saint-Domingue quickly escalated to all-out war between the racial and political factions. The mulattoes were divided: Some created their own militias, some associated themselves with both royalist and revolutionary factions, and some joined the slaves in revolt. The white planters fled Saint-Domingue or joined royalist forces allied with Spain and Great Britain, the two European powers seeking to take control of the French colony.

Faced with the deteriorating situation in Saint-Domingue, the Legislative Assembly dispatched a new Civil Commission to the colony in July 1792. Headed by Léger-Félicité Sonthonax, the commission brought news that the Girondin-dominated National Assembly had finally granted full citizenship to all free men of color. The decree allowed Sonthonax and the other commissioners to actively recruit and promote mulattoes and free blacks within the ranks of the republican forces in the colony.

A passionate revolutionary with abolitionist sympathies, Sonthonax worked closely with the mulattoes, free blacks, and slaves who were fighting British, Spanish, and royalist forces. Faced with a divided colonial society that was hostile to the revolutionary cause, Sonthonax recognized that support from Saint-Domingue's slave population was the key to retaining French republican control of the colony.

In March 1793, France formally declared war on Britain and Spain, and in June 1793, the two remaining civil commissioners, Sonthonax and Étienne Polverel, granted freedom to all slaves who would fight for the republic. Sonthonax announced an end to slavery in Saint-Domingue's northern province in August 1793, and in fall 1793, the commissioners formally abolished slavery in the entire colony. Sonthonax organized elections for three new delegates from Saint-Domingue who would take the news of the general slave emancipation to the French legislature.

The Saint-Domingue delegation, composed of a white colonist, a mulatto, and a freed slave, arrived in France in January 1794. The deputies presented a proposal to the National Convention that the Saint-Domingue emancipation decree be extended to all French colonies in the interests of justice and military necessity. The National Convention responded positively to this proposal.

Since the emergence of the Jacobin faction in August 1792, the merchant and landed classes within France had come under attack and the country had become embroiled in a global war with Britain and Spain. Thus, the question of slave emancipation emerged at a critical point when revolutionary France was facing both internal and external enemies.

Support for abolition among the convention's deputies was seen as affirmation of the revolutionary ideology expressed in the Declaration of the Rights of Man and of the Citizen and as a bold strategic move intended to preserve the republic. As a result, on February 4, 1794, the National Convention issued the Emancipation Declaration, freeing all slaves in the French colonies and granting full citizenship rights to all men regardless of color.

In the following years, the former slaves of Saint-Domingue were able to retain their freedom and eventually secured independence from France after defeating Napoleon's attempts to regain political control of the colony. Slaves in the other French Caribbean colonies were not as fortunate. Slavery persisted in the territories that were captured by the British and finally returned to France after the end of the Napoleonic Wars in 1814. After ascending to power, Napoleon, no friend to the abolitionist cause, reinstated slavery in the remaining French colonies. So great was his suppression of French abolitionism that it did not re-emerge as an organized movement until the 1820s.

Melinda Marie Jetté

See also: Declaration of the Rights of Man and of the Citizen (1789); Haitian Revolution (1791–1804); *Société des Amis des Noirs, La;* Sonthonax, Léger Félicité; Toussaint L'Ouverture, François-Dominique.

Further Reading

Blackburn, Robin. *The Overthrow of Colonial Slavery, 1776–1848.* New York: Verso, 1988.

Doyle, William. *The Oxford History of the French Revolution.* New York: Oxford University Press, 1989.

Resnick, Daniel P. "The Société des Amis des Noirs and the Abolition of Slavery." *French Historical Studies* 7 (Autumn 1972): 558–69.

French West Indies, Abolition and Emancipation in the

The French were late arrivals in the Caribbean, preceded by the Spaniards, British, and Dutch during the sixteenth century. With the introduction of sugarcane cultivation on the island of Hispaniola, African slaves soon followed, becoming the workers of choice in the developing sugarcane industry. By 1700, the socioeconomic pattern that would dominate the Caribbean for the next 200 years had been established: Sugar, slavery, and the plantation system had arrived.

Early Settlement

The French gained a firm foothold in the Caribbean during the seventeenth century. The small island of Saint Kitts functioned as the administrative capital of the French West Indies. From Saint Kitts, French colonists gained control of Martinique and Guadeloupe during the middle of the century. Saint-Domingue (present-day Haiti) was added to the French possessions in 1681. With sugar as the major export of the French colonies, slavery soon became entrenched. Between 1664 and 1681, more slaves arrived in the French colonies; Martinique had the largest number, importing 13,126 slaves in 1696 alone.

The French claimed additional territories in the Caribbean during the seventeenth century, including Saint Lucia, Grenada, the Grenadines, Saint Christophe, Tortuga, Saint Croix, and Saint Barthelemy. The ascendancy of King Louis XIV to the French throne in 1661 and his appointment of Jean-Baptiste Colbert as finance minister signaled a change not only in political power but also in economic interests, particularly in the Caribbean. Louis XIV and Colbert desired to make the French West Indies more productive.

First, the French gave an exclusive monopoly to the Dutch West India Company to introduce more slaves into the French West Indies. Then, governors were appointed to rule over each of Caribbean colonies. Although Louis XIV attempted to exercise royal authority over his Caribbean possessions, the powerful planter class in the French colonies generally controlled all aspects of government.

Warfare, piracy, and international competition were major themes in the Caribbean during the late seventeenth century into the eighteenth century. Possessions changed hands, and the number of slaves increased exponentially. Three wars that pitted the Dutch against the English—during which France joined the English as allies—did little to alter the landscape of the region. The wars did, however, disrupt trade, allowing pirates to raid ships and plunder the smaller islands, often capturing gold, slaves, and other cargo.

The War of the Spanish Succession proved to be the last major conflict in the region. In 1713, the Treaty of Utrecht settled the conflict, in which Spain and France opposed England, Austria, and the Netherlands. Though the war resolved little, it ushered in a prolonged period of peace. The French used the eighteenth century to expand their Caribbean empire and to introduce more slaves into the region.

Following the signing of the Treaty of Utrecht, the French government opened the African slave trade to its Caribbean possessions, permitting any Frenchman with a ship to legally engage in the trade. Although the French method of slave trading did not introduce as many slaves as the monopoly system still in use at that time by the British, it nevertheless proved more than adequate in supplying the French colonies.

During the first five decades of the eighteenth century, the number of slaves in all French possessions increased dramatically. On Martinique, the slave total reached 147,000 in 1760, and the number of slaves on Guadeloupe reached 160,000. Saint-Domingue saw

a spike in its number of slaves, increasing from just 75,000 in 1700 to 481,000 on the eve of the Haitian Revolution in 1791. Sugarcane cultivation drove this exponential increase. In fact, during the eighteenth century, Saint-Domingue quickly became France's most important Caribbean jewel, accounting for more than 40 percent of all imports.

Few in France discussed emancipation during the eighteenth century. Many French merchants on the Continent benefited from sugar cultivation, and planters in the Caribbean reaped significant profits from sugar and slavery. Sugar production boomed during the middle and late decades of the eighteenth century, with Guadeloupe leading the way in the output of sugar. Despite repeated slave rebellions, there was still little discussion of emancipation.

Major slave rebellions took place throughout the French West Indies during the eighteenth century. In Saint-Domingue, thousands of slaves rebelled periodically between 1752 and 1758. Slaves joined forces with mountain maroons (communities of runaway slaves) and thus threatened to undermine the stability the French enjoyed in their most important possession.

Slave rebellions also took place in the smaller colonies. A revolt took place on Guadeloupe in 1737, and in 1752, a minor insurrection caused concern on Martinique. These and other local revolts helped set the stage for the Haitian Revolution, but the French Revolution provided the spark that set emancipation into motion.

Revolutionary Ideology

The French Revolution provided the impetus for emancipation in the French West Indies. The overthrow of the French government in 1789 and the execution of Louis XVI marked the beginning of more than twenty years of unrest in France and throughout Europe. Although the French revolutionaries wanted a new government with more rights for themselves, few said or paid any attention to the hundreds of thousands of French slaves in the Caribbean who also wanted their freedom. Of the early decrees issued by the new French government, none freed the slaves in the West Indies. Thus, inspired by events in France, the slaves in the West Indies, especially in Saint-Domingue, demonstrated their own desire for freedom.

Events in France had a dramatic impact on slavery in the French West Indies. On the eve of the French Revolution, Saint-Domingue was not only the most valuable French colony but also the most productive possession of any European power: More than 40 percent of the all the sugar produced in the world came from colony. The nearly half-million slaves there, however, wanted their freedom. The brutal system of slavery in Saint-Domingue exacted misery and caused thousands of deaths annually. With little consideration from the French revolutionary government, the slaves took matters into their own hands.

Beginning in 1791, there was some movement toward emancipating the slaves in Saint-Domingue. In May, a decree granted equality to free people of color but not to slaves, and an August decree proclaimed a general emancipation of all slaves in the northern province. However, the French revolutionary government was reluctant to free all slaves in the colony, as it needed some slaves in the struggle against Britain and Spain. The emancipation order called for slaves to continue working for one additional year, at which time, they would be granted their freedom; slavery would end, but a system of apprenticeship would replace the plantation labor.

In September, the revolutionary government extended the Declaration of the Rights of Man and of the Citizen to the western and southern provinces, eliminating slavery in those regions. This document effectively ended slavery throughout Saint-Domingue, instituting a wage labor system in its place. When the planters did not pay, revolts broke out among wage laborers on some plantations. Real emancipation did not take hold in the colony until 1793–1794.

Events in 1793 offered some encouragement for permanent emancipation in the French West Indies. In September, the British attacked Saint-Domingue. After most French planters surrendered, the British controlled western and southern regions of the colony. But, in the north, a Creole slave named Toussaint L'Ouverture initiated an uprising that would eventually bring about the true emancipation of the slaves in Saint-Domingue. Although the French revolutionary government issued another decree declaring that all slaves who took up arms would be emancipated, Toussaint led slaves in a massive revolt against the planters.

An emancipation decree issued by the French revolutionary government on February 4, 1794, was enforced in Saint-Domingue, but the document never reached Martinique. In a new constitution written by Toussaint in 1801, the slaves were again emancipated. The French made an effort to recapture their Caribbean jewel in 1802. After several months of brutal warfare, Toussaint signed a truce; however, Toussaint was tricked, captured, and returned to France, where he soon died. Napoleon Bonaparte then reestablished the slave trade to Guadeloupe and Martinique. Another constitution written in 1804 finally emancipated all slaves without compensation to the former masters. Thus, the Haitian Revolution that Toussaint initiated led to true emancipation in Haiti, but both Guadeloupe and Martinique retained the brutal institution.

The slave trade to Guadeloupe and Martinique reinforced slavery on those islands. Despite British efforts to suppress the trade, more than 80,000 slaves arrived in the remaining French possessions. After defeating Napoleon, the British forced an agreement on the French to abolish the slave trade in 1814. The illegal traffic to the French colonies of Martinique and Guadeloupe, however, continued until 1831.

Final Emancipation Efforts

French abolitionists became more outspoken against slavery during the 1830s. In 1834, they formed the Abolition Society and campaigned against slavery in books, pamphlets, and other literature. Abolitionists often pointed to the slave revolt in Haiti as a reason to end the practice. Pressuring the French government, abolitionists gained small victories, putting an end to the whipping and branding of slaves. Still, slavery persisted in the last two French Caribbean colonies.

On the eve of the 1848 French revolution, Martinique was home to more than 67,000 slaves and Guadeloupe more than 87,000. Planters were concerned about a labor force that would replace the slaves, if freed. But the French revolution of 1848 gave abolitionists additional support. The provisional government issued a decree to abolish slavery in Martinique and Guadeloupe and appointed an administrator to carry out the order. News of the decree prompted thousands of slaves to abandon the sugar plantations. Slaves rebelled on Martinique, killing many of the planters. French slavery in the Caribbean had finally ended.

Emancipation came to the last two French possessions in much the same way it did in Haiti. Violence rather than peaceful freedom proved to be the dominant theme in emancipation throughout the French West Indies.

Jackie R. Booker

See also: Haitian Revolution (1791–1804).

Further Reading

Brereton, Bridget. "Review Essay: Abolition and Its Aftermath." *Slavery and Abolition* 7 (December 1986): 299–306.

Emmer, Pieter C. "The Price of Freedom: The Constraints of Change in Post-Emancipation America." In *The Meaning of Freedom: Economics, Politics, and Culture After Slavery,* ed. Frank McGlynn and Seymour Drescher. Pittsburgh: University of Pittsburgh Press, 1992.

Fick, Carolyn. "Emancipation in Haiti: From Plantation Labour to Peasant Proprietorship." *Slavery and Abolition* 21 (August 2000): 11–40.

James, C.L.R. *The Black Jacobins: Toussaint L'Ouverture and the Saint-Domingue Revolution.* New York: Vintage Books, 1989.

Stinchcombe, Arthur L. *Sugar Island Slavery in the Age of Enlightenment: The Political Economy of the Caribbean World.* Princeton, NJ: Princeton University Press, 1995.

Fugitive Slave Act of 1793

When the U.S. Constitution took effect in 1789, it included a fugitive-from-labor clause that was meant to protect the right of slave owners to recover their property in slaves who had escaped. The U.S. Congress enacted the Fugitive Slave Law of 1793 to create a federal law that would describe the obligations between and among states for the recovery and return of slave fugitives. In the years after its passage, many Northern states enacted legislative measures that were designed to make the terms of the Fugitive Slave Law of 1793 largely ineffective.

In the years following the American Revolution, the existence of both slave states and free states in the Union posed significant problems for the United States. One challenge involved the interstate rendition (return) of fugitive slaves. Although slaves were considered the property of their owners, they also possessed the ability to resist chattel slavery and did so in many cases by means of escape.

To satisfy slave owners' right to property, the constitutional framers included a fugitive-from-labor clause that required fugitive slaves to be returned to their owners, but they failed to specify where the burden of enforcement fell, to whom claim should be made, and in what manner. To resolve any disputes arising from the ambiguous clause, the U.S. Congress passed the Fugitive Slave Law in 1793.

By the time lawmakers ratified the Constitution, all states north of Maryland had enacted measures to abolish slavery within their borders. In this climate, the Commonwealth of Pennsylvania passed its Act for the Gradual Abolition of Slavery in 1780. Rather than create unnecessary tension with the neighboring slave states of Maryland, Delaware, and Virginia, Pennsylvania lawmakers passed a relatively conservative emancipation act. However, conflicts soon arose over disputed claims of territory in the West. Both Pennsylvania and Virginia claimed present-day Westmoreland and Washington counties in western Pennsylvania, and the matter was not settled until 1784. Unlike Pennsylvania, the Virginia legislature did not pass any act of gradual emancipation, placing slave owners in the disputed area in a legal state of limbo.

In 1788, a scenario presented itself to both states that provided the impetus for the enactment of the Fugitive Slave Law. A slave owner named Davis who had previously resided in Maryland moved into the disputed territory in 1782. Davis failed to register his slave John in accordance with Pennsylvania law. After some time, Davis took his slave to Virginia to rent him out. Neighbors in Pennsylvania, acting on their abolitionist beliefs, found John in Virginia and took him back to Pennsylvania. Eager to regain his property, Davis authorized three men to capture John and bring him back to Virginia. The three agents set out for Pennsylvania, where they captured the slave and forcibly removed him to Virginia in 1788.

Believing that John had been emancipated by the Gradual Abolition Act of 1780, officials in Pennsylvania indicted the three Virginians for kidnapping in November 1788. Safely within the borders of Virginia, the men remained out of the reach of Pennsylvania officials. Over the next three years, the Virginians remained at large, despite several attempts to bring them to justice. With few legal options left, abolitionists appealed to Pennsylvania governor Thomas Mifflin, who sent copies of the indictment and a request for extradition to his Virginia counterpart, Governor Beverly Randolph. Instead of responding immediately, Randolph forwarded the request to his attorney general, James Innes. On the recommendation of Innes, who believed that no crime had been committed in Virginia, Randolph refused to extradite the three men to Pennsylvania.

Mifflin appealed to President George Washington, asking him to present the case before Congress in the hope that federal lawmakers could settle the matter. Instead, Washington sent all correspondence to Edmund Randolph, attorney general of the United States, who found fault with the arguments of both states. Pennsylvania, he argued, had failed to adequately explain the charges against the three men and failed to demonstrate that the men had, in fact, fled the state. Virginia officials, Randolph believed, were erroneous in their assumption of the severity and jurisdiction of the offense. The fact that the three men had not violated any Virginia law was of no consequence in the matter—Pennsylvania held jurisdiction in the case. Randolph suggested that Mifflin send a more complete description of the offense and subsequent indictment, thereby legally compelling Virginia to extradite the men. The attorney general further advised President Washington not to place the issue before Congress.

Washington complied with Randolph's recommendation, forwarding the attorney general's decision to both governors. At the same time, however, he also sent copies of Randolph's findings to Congress, perhaps anticipating the continued struggle between the two states. Congress, in turn, appointed a committee of three to investigate the matter and to render a bill that best provided for the interstate extradition of fugitives from justice and labor.

The investigative committee presented a bill to Congress in 1791, but the proposal never came up for a final vote. In 1793, an expanded committee of five presented another bill to Congress. After some debate, the new bill passed both houses of Congress. On February 12, 1793, Washington signed the measure into law.

The new law permitted the capture of fugitive slaves in any territory of the United States. Slave owners and their agents needed only to provide oral proof before a federal or state judge or magistrate in order to reclaim their property. The law further authorized a penalty of $500 for anyone harboring a fugitive slave. Despite its efforts to resolve ambiguity in the rendition of fugitive slaves, the law still failed to account for the personal liberties of free blacks. Fugitives were not guaranteed a trial by jury, and the judge's decision was final.

Consequently, many Northern states began passing concurrent legislation to protect the rights of free blacks. These state measures, known as "personal liberty laws," frequently interfered with the federal act of 1793, and the U.S. Supreme Court ultimately ruled them unconstitutional in the case of *Prigg v. Pennsylvania* (1842).

Rather than settle any ambiguities, the uneven enforcement of the law created more tension between slave states and free states. This led to the passage of a second Fugitive Slave Law in 1850.

Timothy Konhaus

See also: Fugitive Slave Act of 1850.

Further Reading

Finkelman, Paul. "The Kidnapping of John Davis and the Adoption of the Fugitive Slave Law of 1793." *Journal of Southern History* 56 (August 1990): 397–422.

Hildreth, Richard. *Despotism in America: An Inquiry Into the Nature, Results, and Legal Basis of the Slave-Holding System in the United States.* New York: John P. Jewett, 1854; New York: Negro Universities Press, 1968.

Morris, Thomas D. *Free Men All: The Personal Liberty Laws of the North, 1780–1861.* Baltimore: Johns Hopkins University Press, 1974.

Way, R.B. "Was the Fugitive Slave Clause of the Constitution Necessary?" *Iowa Journal of History and Politics* 5 (July 1907): 326–36.

Fugitive Slave Act of 1850

Passed after extensive debate in the U.S. Congress, the second Fugitive Slave Act was signed by President Millard Fillmore on September 18, 1850. The law was part of a series of measures known as the Compromise of 1850, which sought to put an end to divisive sectional debates about the extension of slavery into newly acquired territories that erupted following the Mexican-American War (1846–1848). Ironically, the Fugitive Slave Law of 1850 had the opposite effect, as it stoked the fires of sectional tension by enraging both abolitionists, who thought the law encroached on civil liberties, and proslavery forces, who were upset by widely publicized antislavery efforts to subvert the law through both legal and illegal means.

The Fugitive Slave Law of 1850—and the more lenient Fugitive Slave Law of 1793 that it replaced—sought to enforce measures endorsed by the U.S. Constitution. When it was first drafted, the Constitution stipulated, "No person held to Service or Labour in one State, under the Laws thereof, escaping into another, shall, in Consequence of any Law or Regulation therein, be discharged from such Service or Labour, but shall be delivered up on Claim of the Party to whom such Service or Labour may be due." Yet the Constitution did not provide any means by which to enforce this provision.

Thus, Congress passed the first Fugitive Slave Law in 1793. The measure authorized masters or their agents to apprehend purported fugitive slaves and to bring them before state or federal judges or magistrates to determine the validity of the claim. Those who interfered with the prosecution of the law were liable for a $500 fine. In addition, masters could sue those providing assistance to fugitive slaves for the value of all slaves lost, as well as expenses.

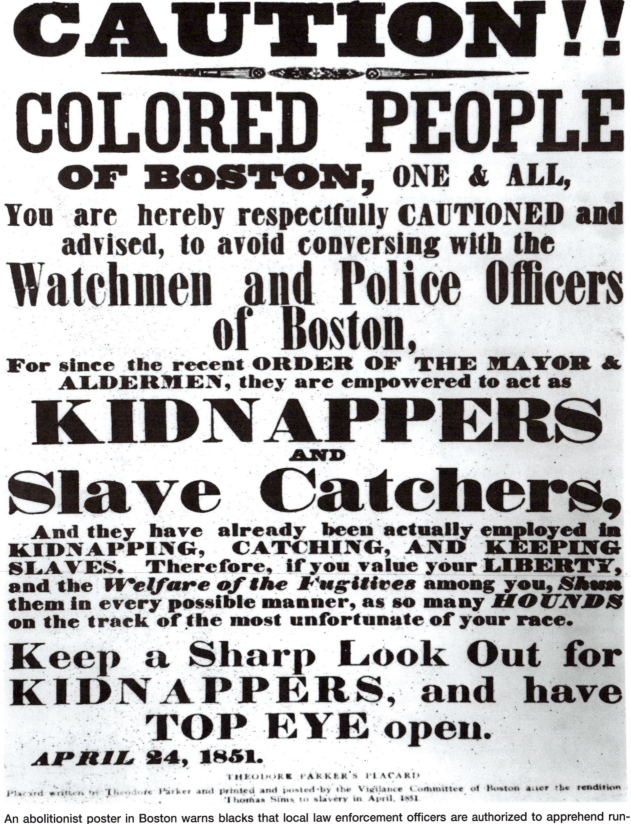

An abolitionist poster in Boston warns blacks that local law enforcement officers are authorized to apprehend runaways under the Fugitive Slave Act of 1850. In New England and elsewhere, the measure was vehemently denounced. *(Schomburg Center/Art Resource, New York)*

The Fugitive Slave Law of 1793 had evoked little protest. By the mid-nineteenth century, however, a number of Northern states had passed measures known as "personal liberty laws" that made it more difficult for masters to apprehend fugitive slaves by requiring cases to be heard by judges—who tended to be more attentive to the rules of evidence than local magistrates—and instituting penalties for illegal seizure.

The tension between these personal liberty laws and the Fugitive Slave Law of 1793 came to a head in 1837, when Edward Prigg, an agent for a Maryland slave owner, captured purported fugitive slave Margaret Morgan and her children in Pennsylvania and returned them to Maryland. The seizure violated an 1826 Pennsylvania personal liberty law, under which Prigg was tried and convicted.

Prigg appealed his case first to the Pennsylvania Supreme Court and then to the U.S. Supreme Court, which ruled that the Pennsylvania law was unconstitutional, because it impeded the enforcement of the federal Fugitive Slave Law. The ruling in *Prigg v. Pennsylvania* (1842), written by Massachusetts Justice Joseph Story, held that the federal government was responsible for enforcing the Fugitive Slave Law, adding that state governments were not legally bound to assist in the effort. The latter stipulation prompted the passage of a series of new personal liberty laws across the North that forbade the use of state officials and buildings in the capture and rendition of fugitive slaves.

By the late 1840s, sectional tensions were coming to a boil over the extension of slavery into the territories acquired in the Mexican cession. Senator Henry Clay of Kentucky proposed several measures to cool the waters, North and South. After more than six months of debate, Congress passed a series of laws known as the Compromise of 1850. Among other stipulations, the Compromise of 1850 admitted California as a free state, ended the slave trade in the District of Columbia, established the territories of New Mexico and Utah without forbidding slavery there, and enacted a more stringent fugitive slave law.

The Fugitive Slave Law of 1850 authorized the U.S. circuit courts to appoint commissioners to enforce the new law. The commissioners could summon the help of marshals and deputy marshals or even organize a posse to ensure the return of fugitive slaves. Officials who refused to assist in the apprehension or return of fugitive slaves were subject to a $1,000 fine, and anyone who aided a fugitive faced a similar fine, as well as up to six months imprisonment.

The law was designed to ensure quick verdicts for claimants, who needed only to have their claim authenticated in a local or state court in order to win their case. Accused fugitive slaves, by contrast, faced daunting procedural barriers: They could neither testify on their own behalf nor ask local or state courts to assist them by issuing a writ of habeas corpus.

Almost immediately, the Fugitive Slave Law was denounced vehemently by abolitionists. The Reverend Charles Beecher, for example, declared, "It is the monster iniquity of the present age, and it will stand forever on the page of history, as the vilest monument of infamy of the nineteenth century."

Opponents created vigilance committees that sought to combat the law. The Boston Vigilance Committee, for example, declared its intention to "endeavor by all just means to secure the fugitive slaves and colored inhabitants of Boston and vicinity from any invasion of their rights by persons acting under this law."

The first major test of the legislation came in Boston, where Frederick Wilkins (also known as Shadrach), an escaped Virginia house slave, was arrested in February 1851. Wilkins was saved by a group of African Americans who burst into the courtroom where his case was being heard. A similar rescue took place in Syracuse later that year.

Violence often followed such attempts to resist the law: A master and three African Americans were killed during a shootout in Christiana, Pennsylvania, sparked by an attempted arrest in September 1851. Three years later in Boston, a guard died during a conflict with white and black abolitionists who were trying to save fugitive slave Anthony Burns.

Although most of the high-profile fugitive slave cases took place in the early and mid-1850s, the law was enforced as late as June 1863. The U.S. Civil War ended efforts to return fugitive slaves to the former Confederate states, but citizens from border states such as Maryland, Kentucky, Missouri, and Delaware continued to initiate claims for much of the war. Enforcement largely halted after President Abraham Lincoln issued the Emancipation Proclamation in 1863, and Congress finally repealed the law on June 28, 1864.

Although the Fugitive Slave Law of 1850 was not widely enforced—only about 200 slaves were returned in more than a decade, and attempts to prosecute those who had assisted fugitive slaves rarely met with success—it had enormous symbolic importance in both the North and the South. Antislavery forces insisted that it exemplified the efforts of the "slave power" to wrest control of the North, and they effectively used the law's passage to mobilize support for their cause.

Many supporters of slavery, in turn, attached great significance to the legislation as well, decrying the resistance it engendered in the North. Indeed, several of the Confederate states that seceded from the Union in 1861 and 1862 listed the failure to enforce the law as one of their chief grievances.

Although it was intended to assuage sectional tensions that arose in the aftermath of the Mexican-American War, the Fugitive Slave Law of 1850 did just the opposite. It aroused the ire of proslavery and antislavery forces alike.

Ethan J. Kytle

See also: Fugitive Slave Act of 1793.

Further Reading

Campbell, Stanley W. *The Slave Catchers: Enforcement of the Fugitive Slave Law.* Chapel Hill: University of North Carolina Press, 1970.

Gara, Larry. "The Fugitive Slave Law: A Double Paradox." *Civil War History* 10 (September 1964): 229–40.

Pease, Jane H., and William H. Pease. *The Fugitive Slave Law and Anthony Burns: A Problem in Law Enforcement.* Philadelphia: J.B. Lippincott, 1975.

Way, R.B. "Was the Fugitive Slave Clause of the Constitution Necessary?" *Iowa Journal of History and Politics* 5 (July 1907): 326–36.

Fugitive Slaves

As long as slavery has existed as a social and economic institution, there have been those who have sought to escape. Some of the first fugitives were African captives who revolted aboard the ships taking them to a new world of lifelong enslavement. In the United States, fugitives came from every sector of society and had a profound effect on the culture of the societies that enslaved them. Fugitives directly affected workplace productivity, increased fears about slave revolts, challenged the concept of "property," and threatened the institution of slavery itself.

Although the great majority of fugitives were of African descent, some were Native Americans, and others white indentured servants. They used every imaginable means, both legal and illegal, in their pursuit of freedom. Fugitive slaves took their destinies into their own hands and initiated a self-liberation social movement that became known as the Underground Railroad. In contrast to short-term runaways, who would eventually return to their masters, the objective of the fugitive slaves was freedom from bondage.

Fugitive Profiles

The fugitive movement spanned the period from about 1640 to the end of the U.S. Civil War in 1865. Slaves escaped from the Southern plantation system, and the majority fled to the Northern states or Canada; others fled to Mexico, joined colonies of former slaves, or were assimilated into Native American tribes.

According to newspaper ads placed by slave owners attempting to recapture their runaway slaves, the youngest fugitive reported was a six-year-old boy who ran off alone. The oldest was a fugitive in Canada who reported that she was more than ninety years old. Preteens and teens constituted a notable portion of the runaway population. Family and community groups were not uncommon.

Some, with little or no knowledge of English, would leave within days of arriving on a plantation, without knowing where they were going or how they would provide for themselves along the way. Others were deliberate in their actions, and conscious planning characterized their escape attempts; to avoid being recognized, many used disguises. Members of the two groups sometimes ran away together. Current research suggests that 15 percent to 20 percent of fugitives were women; some were pregnant, and others took very young children with them. Men were much less likely to be accompanied by children.

It is not possible to know how many slaves attempted to run away and how many actually succeeded. The fugitive most often advertised in slavery-era newspaper ads was a male in his early to mid-twenties. Historians believe that families were more likely to flee together when they had a specific destination in mind and a clear sense of how they would meet their needs in the process. Some of these families were interracial.

The two reasons most often cited for running away were the threat of being sold and incidents of physical abuse. Physical assaults included whipping, branding, cutting off ears, salting open wounds,

A slave family crosses the Rappahannock River into Union-held territory in Virginia in 1863. Even after emancipation, slaves who attempted to leave the South were hunted down as fugitives until they reached safety. *(Hulton Archive/Getty Images)*

castration—all meant to "correct" the slave—and execution.

Slaves generally did not accept their lot; they tolerated it in order to survive and resisted by running away when circumstances allowed. In Canada, fugitives formed self-help organizations called *true bands* to assist new arrivals. Some fugitives signed on with whaling and other ocean-going vessels with the clear intention of deserting. The most determined fugitives armed themselves and sometimes killed those who pursued them.

Underground Railroad

Although dedicated and determined abolitionists and station masters operated from the relative safety of the free states, fugitives almost always negotiated the hazards of passing through slave states on their own. The enslaved community was the primary supporter of fugitives—hiding, feeding, clothing, sheltering, and transporting them. Free blacks and white abolitionists, including Quakers, functioned as secondary and tertiary levels of support. Though most

whites were empathetic toward the fugitive slave's flight, some charged a fee for their help.

By the 1830s and 1840s, hundreds—perhaps thousands—of slaves were escaping from Southern plantations every year. The Underground Railroad, an elaborate system of safe houses (called *stations*) manned by empathetic individuals (*conductors*) hid escaped slaves and assisted them in their journey North, the farthest destination being free Canada. Canada did not view escaped slaves or those who aided their escape as criminals; therefore, it had no treaty for the extradition of slaves with the United States.

Some historians estimate that the Underground Railroad helped as many 100,000 slaves escape from the South between 1810 and 1850. Determination and ingenuity characterized the stories of many escaped slaves: Henry "Box" Brown shipped himself from Richmond to Philadelphia in a specially built crate. Josiah Henson, who fled from Maryland in 1825, returned several times to help others escape. And Henry Bibb, who first escaped from a Kentucky plantation in 1838, made six unsuccessful attempts before reaching freedom; after 1850, Bibb settled in Canada, where he published the first antislavery newspaper, *Voice of the Fugitive.*

Individuals who became conductors on the railroad were often former slaves themselves, such as Calvin Fairbanks, who had reached freedom with the help of a white woman from Vermont known as "Miss Webster," and Harriet Tubman, who had escaped in 1849 from a Maryland plantation to freedom in Philadelphia. Tubman secretly returned to the South nineteen times. During these journeys, she led hundreds slaves to freedom, piloting "them North, traveling by night, hiding by day, scaling the mountains, fording the rivers, threading the forests, lying concealed as the pursuers passed them," as biographer Sarah Bradford described in 1886. Dubbed "Moses" by her people, Tubman was considered such a serious threat to the plantation slave system that landowners offered a $40,000 reward for her capture.

Levi Coffin, whom scholars estimate helped more than 3,000 slaves escape to freedom over a period of thirty-five years, employed freed slaves in his routes, mainly as drivers during late-night rides. His *Reminiscences*, published in 1876, is one of the most comprehensive accounts of the workings of the Underground Railroad.

Risks

In 1793, the first Fugitive Slave Law gave slaveholders the legal right to recapture their slaves in the free states and return them to bondage. In practice, however, it was a difficult and expensive process for slaveholders to locate runaways; methods that were commonly employed included posting advertisements in newspapers, hiring slave catchers (some of whom had trained dogs), and even personally pursuing their "property." In 1851, a Maryland slave owner named Edward Gorsuch was killed in Christiana, Pennsylvania, while attempting to recapture four fugitive slaves. Slaves and white neighbors banded together to fight off Gorsuch, and gunfire and violence ensued. The Christiana Riot, as it was called, resulted in a number of treason trials in which the slaves were acquitted; they ultimately reached their destination in Canada.

With the passage of the second Fugitive Slave Law in 1850, the process for recapturing escaped slaves became slightly easier, as slaves could be reclaimed upon the oath of a slave owner, and federal officials and everyday citizens were required by law to assist them.

Financial penalties were imposed on those who aided in an escape or hindered a recapture. In addition, there was no time limit on the recapture of a runaway, so even those who had long settled in free communities were at risk of recapture.

Some fugitives were declared outlaws, and reward notices offered more for their heads than for returning the slave alive. Enslaved persons would sometimes try to negotiate the terms of a fugitive slave's treatment. Many would simply "lie out" in the immediate vicinity of the plantation. Owners tacitly acknowledged that they were negotiating by offering to forgive the runaway if the person would return on his or her own.

Simple forgiveness, however, was rare. Slaves who were caught by their masters or by the men they hired typically faced punishment or death upon return. Masters viewed a slave's escape as a personal offense and often sold the slave into the Deep South, where harsh conditions and backbreaking workloads meant little chance of escape.

Francis Fedric recalled in his *Fifty Years of Slavery in the Southern States of America* (1863) the steps that his master had taken just one day after Fedric fled his plantation in Kentucky: "He had offered $500 reward—had placed a watch all along the Ohio River—had informed all the neighboring planters, who had cautioned all their slaves not to give me any food or other assistance, and he had made it known, that, when I should be caught, he would give me a thousand lashes."

Freedom

Fugitive slaves played a significant role in the American Revolution. Many of them served the British in fighting units called Black/African Brigades. Those who served in engineering and logistical capacities were called Black Pioneers.

All those slaves who thus served were promised freedom by the British, and some were eventually taken to Nova Scotia, then to England, and finally to Sierra Leone in West Africa. Others were not so fortunate. Some were sold to British plantation owners in the West Indies, and others were returned to their American claimants during the negotiations conducted by George Washington to end the war.

Some fugitive slaves and their descendants established self-governing, self-sustaining, independent settlements referred to as "maroon" communities deep in the woods and swamps. Maroons lived in North Carolina, Virginia, Florida, George, and Louisiana. From these settlements, individuals raided plantations, freeing other enslaved persons in the process. In the Southern colonies, the fugitives allied with Native Americans and posed a strong military threat to the stability of the region. In the North, more traditional towns were often founded. For instance, Timbuctoo, New Jersey, was established in 1820 by runaway slaves.

Once free, former slaves' personal accounts fed the abolitionist movement. Men such as William Wells Brown, Henry Bibb, Anthony Burns, and Josiah Henson recounted their stories in writing and in speeches. Their eyewitness accounts provided ammunition for abolitionists aiming to relate accounts of the horrors of slavery. Slave narratives were published in newspapers, in pamphlet form, and as comprehensive autobiographies, such as Brown's *Narrative of William W. Brown, a Fugitive Slave* (1847) and Bibb's *Narrative of the Life and Adventures of Henry Bibb, An American Slave* (1849). The celebrated abolitionist Frederick Douglass, an escaped slave, became recognized as one of America's first great black speakers. His *Narrative of the Life of Frederick Douglass* (1845) remains one of the most widely read slave narratives.

Despite the many stories of slaves who made it to freedom, the fugitive slave movement did not appreciably reduce the enslaved population, which still numbered 4 million according to the 1860 U.S. Census. A largely unlettered, dispossessed, and physically exploited group of people took steps to liberate themselves. Their actions and stories of horrors helped to fuel the sectional conflict that led to the Civil War and the abolition of slavery in the United States.

Prince Brown, Jr.

See also: Fugitive Slave Act of 1793; Fugitive Slave Act of 1850; Tubman, Harriet; Underground Railroad.

Further Reading

Bontemps, Alex. *The Punished Self: Surviving Slavery in the Colonial South.* Ithaca, NY: Cornell University Press, 2001.

Brown, Prince, Jr. *Runaway Enslaved Person Database (REPD).* Highland Heights: Institute for Freedom Studies, Northern Kentucky University, 2004.

Franklin, John Hope, and Loren Schweninger. *Runaway Slaves: Rebels on the Plantation.* New York: Oxford University Press, 1999.

Meaders, Daniel. *Dead or Alive: Fugitive Slaves and White Indentured Servants Before 1830.* New York: Garland, 1993.

Thomas, Hugh. *The Slave Trade.* New York: Simon & Schuster, 1997.

Windley, Lathan A. *Runaway Slave Advertisements: A Documentary History from the 1730s to 1790.* Westport, CT: Greenwood, 1983.

Gag Resolution

The adoption of the "gag resolution"—a procedural vote in the U.S. House of Representatives in 1836 that automatically tabled all slavery-related concerns directed to the House—indicated the shrill level to which the antislavery debate had risen in the U.S. Congress.

Many members of Congress believed that the use of such self-imposed censorship to stifle debate on a vital issue of the day was anathema to the democratic principles on which the United States had been founded. Supporters of the measure maintained that the primary role of Congress—to conduct the people's business—could not be accomplished if it was constantly embroiled in pointless debate over each abolitionist petition and memorial that was addressed to the legislative body. The resolution also was a sign of growing resistance to the abolitionist movement, as the measure was approved at the same time that anti-abolition riots were occurring in many Northern cities.

South Carolina congressman Henry L. Pinckney first proposed the gag resolution in the House of Representatives on May 18, 1836. Pinckney hoped that the measure would alleviate discord in Congress by automatically tabling all antislavery petitions upon arrival without having them read aloud in the House. The measure produced a vehement discussion in the House of Representatives and indirectly gave renewed urgency to antislavery supporters in the United States.

The Congress adopted and began using the so-called Gag Rule on May 26, 1836. The rule effectively prevented the reading and circulation of all antislavery petitions and memorials that were received by Congress. As a parliamentary maneuver, the House of Representatives had to renew the Gag Rule at the start of each year's congressional session.

John Quincy Adams, former president and Whig congressman from Massachusetts, had not been a vocal opponent of slavery before the passage of the Gag Rule, but this measure moved him toward solidarity with the antislavery advocates. Adams believed that the measure was "a direct violation of the Constitution of the United States (Amendment I), of the rules of this House and of the rights of my constituents." One of the most basic civil liberties of a free people—the right to petition their government for a redress of their grievances—was being denied to all who shared antislavery sentiments. Despite appeals from his political opponents that he remain silent, Adams fought relentlessly for the repeal of the Gag Rule.

On February 15, 1838, Congressman Adams introduced 350 antislavery petitions in defiance of the Gag Rule that the House of Representatives had instituted. The petitions opposed slavery and the annexation of Texas. Adams continued to be one of the most vocal congressional opponents of the Gag Rule. Ohio congressman Joshua R. Giddings, the first abolitionist to be elected to Congress, took his seat in the House of Representatives on December 3, 1838, and he, too, became a vocal opponent of the rule.

The House of Representatives voted to renew the Gag Rule on December 11, 1838. The measure had been introduced by Congressman Charles G. Atherton, a New Hampshire Democrat, and the policy thereafter became known as the "Atherton gag." Despite the unpopularity of the measure, the Gag Rule continued to win support, and it remained in effect for eight years until the rule was eventually repealed in December 1844 by a House vote of 108 to 80.

During these eight years, the Gag Rule did not stop antislavery supporters from addressing petitions and memorials to Congress. Under the direction of the American Anti-Slavery Society, a sustained effort in 1837–1838 sent more than 130,000 petitions to Congress calling for the abolition of slavery within the District of Columbia. The magnitude of this campaign made proslavery congressmen confident that they had acted wisely by prohibiting any consideration of these proposals.

Despite intense protests against the policy, in 1840, the House of Representatives made the Gag Rule even more restrictive. It was modified to state that antislavery petitions would no longer be accepted by Congress. Although the measure was never challenged in the courts, it appears to have been a legislative attempt to restrict the constitutionally protected First Amendment rights of a significant portion of the American population.

During the years in which it was in effect, the Gag Rule applied only to the House of Representatives and not to the Senate, which had rejected such an option. Despite the concerns of some congressmen that they could not conduct the people's business without the presence of the Gag Rule, the Senate seemed to function normally without resorting to such self-imposed censorship. Yet even without the Gag Rule, Senate procedures did not permit the automatic reading of antislavery proposals that were received by that body.

It is almost inconceivable to us today that self-imposed censorship in the House of Representatives prohibited the consideration of materials related to the slavery question from 1836 to 1844. A number of issues, ranging from the proposed annexation of Texas to the *Amistad* case, all had a direct bearing on the institution of slavery, and the Gag Rule made it impossible for the rich debate that is the hallmark of democracy to occur during this era.

Junius P. Rodriguez

See also: Adams, John Quincy; Anti-Abolition Riots; Giddings, Joshua Reed.

Further Reading

Miller, William Lee. *Arguing About Slavery: The Great Battle in the United States Congress.* New York: Alfred A. Knopf, 1996.

Gage, Frances Dana (1808–1884)

A writer who often lectured on abolitionism and women's rights, Frances Dana Gage was one of the most radical American female reformers of the early nineteenth century. She gained national attention in 1850 when she drew up a petition to the Ohio legislature asking that the qualifying words "white" and "male" be omitted from the new state constitution. Her well-reasoned arguments on women's rights and women's suffrage made her a sought-after speaker on the lecture circuit during a time when few women made a living from public speaking.

Frances Dana Barker was born on October 12, 1808, in Marietta, Ohio, to a farming and antislavery family. Her maternal grandmother served as a conductor on the Underground Railroad from her home

The abolitionist, temperance reformer, and women's rights advocate Frances Dana Gage petitioned the Ohio legislature to remove the words "white" and "male" from the state constitution. *(Library of Congress)*

in Belpre, Ohio. Frances attended a log cabin schoolhouse but was largely self-educated.

In 1828, she married James L. Gage, a lawyer from McConnelsville, Ohio. The couple had eight children, including six sons who enlisted in the Union army during the U.S. Civil War. Perhaps because of the threats made against Frances for advocating abolition—or simply out of wanderlust—the Gages moved frequently. They left McConnelsville for Saint Louis, Missouri, in 1853, then headed to Carbondale, Illinois, where James went bankrupt, and finally moved to Columbus, Ohio, in 1861.

A tall woman with brown hair, gray eyes, and an impulsive nature, Gage was part of the radical wing of most reform movements of her day, including women's rights, temperance, and antislavery. She promoted her causes in a series of speaking tours; her speeches at women's rights conventions, such as the 1851 convention in Akron, Ohio, attracted much attention to the movement.

She wrote frequently under the pen name "Aunt Fanny" on the topic of slavery for a number of religious, feminist, and agricultural magazines in the 1850s and 1860s, including the New York *Indepen-*

dent and the *Ohio Cultivator.* The editor of a state journal, possibly in Ohio, engaged her to write for his paper, but a few negative words about the Fugitive Slave Law of 1850 brought a note in the mail that her services were no longer required. In 1858, she was fired from the *Missouri Democrat* because she had appeared on the platform of the Boston Anti-Slavery Society.

In 1862, Gage sailed from New York City to Hilton Head, South Carolina, with the intention of teaching blacks, but she returned to Ohio a year later, possibly because of her husband's failing health. Widowed in 1863, Gage returned to the lecture circuit with the hope of making a substantial contribution to the end of the war by removing racial prejudice and inspiring confidence in the Emancipation Proclamation. Accordingly, she lectured on "Home Life Among the Freedmen" to impress whites with the real character and condition of blacks.

Disheartened by continuing Northern prejudice, Gage became a nurse and returned to the South. In 1864, as an agent of the Western Sanitary Commission, she worked in Memphis, Tennessee, Vicksburg, Mississippi, and Natchez, Louisiana. During the Civil War, she spent much of her time in hospitals for contraband (slaves who had escaped to or had been brought within Union lines) and black soldiers. In her writings, she described the suffering and needs of the black soldiers in the hope of getting them aid.

After the war, Gage moved to Lambertsville, New Jersey. In 1867, a stroke ended her days of lecturing. She died in Greenwich, Connecticut, on November 10, 1884.

Caryn E. Neumann

See also: Truth, Sojourner; Women's Rights and the Abolitionist Movement.

Further Reading

Hersh, Blanche Glassman. *The Slavery of Sex: Feminist-Abolitionists in America.* Urbana: University of Illinois Press, 1978.

Yellin, Jean Fagan, and John C. Van Horne, eds. *The Abolitionist Sisterhood: Women's Political Culture in Antebellum America.* Ithaca, NY: Cornell University Press, 1994.

Gama, Luís (1830–1882)

Brazil's foremost abolitionist, Luís Gonzaga Pinto da Gama was born free in São Salvador in the state of Bahia, Brazil, on June 21, 1830. His father was a Portuguese nobleman and his mother, Luiza Mahin, was a notorious rebel slave leader born in the Mahi region of West Africa (present-day Benin). Gama would become a self-taught lawyer, renowned orator, journalist, poet, and armed liberation fighter.

The Brazilian slave trade was abolished in 1831, but chattel slavery in the country and illegal shipments of captives from Africa persisted. During the slave revolts that ensued, Mahin was hounded from Salvador for her involvement. In 1840, to pay off his gambling debts, Gama's father sold him as a slave. Gama arrived in São Paolo as the property of a trader named Antonio Pereira Cardoso. As a houseboy, he was befriended by a law student who was boarding in the household and taught him to read and write. Gama's literacy was essential to his self-liberation: Using government documents, he was able to gain his freedom by proving the illegality of his enslavement based on the status of his birth.

In 1848, he fled and became a secretary in the São Paolo Guarda Urbana, a military police force in public service, and a clerk in the legal office of attorney Francisco Maria de Sousa Furtado de Mendonça, who helped further Gama's understanding of the judicial process. In 1854, Gama was dismissed from the police force for threatening an officer who had insulted him. For the next two years, he worked as a copyist in police stations in São Paolo. The education he gained in Mendonça's library and in the police headquarters developed his abolitionist emancipator spirit. He began organizing manumissions of regional slaves as he interacted with people from all classes, from slaves to slaveholders, poor freedmen to officers.

While working as a scribe, Gama developed his prodigious literary talent, publishing poems in a number of newspapers. In 1859, his first volume of poetry, *Primeiras Trovas Burlescas,* appeared under the pseudonym Getulino. These satirical poems mocked the hypocrisy of Brazilian society and politics. His radical yet entertaining attacks on subjects such as mulattos' denial of their black origins gained him both notoriety and public acclaim. Gama's lyrical poetry is also one of the first Brazilian literary expressions of "negritude," or the positive depiction of African physical and cultural features.

In 1858, Gama met Claudina Fortunata Sampaio, and their son was born the following year. Like many slaves and freed slaves, they were obliged to wait in order to register their union formally. They married on October 25, 1869.

During the 1860s, Gama's writings, mainly newspaper articles and poetry, focused on abolition. In the 1860s and 1870s, he founded a series of papers and magazines—*O Diabo Coxo* (Lame Devil), *Cabrião* (Billy Goat, the name used for mulatto slaves), and *O Coaraci* (named for the Tupi sun god)—and edited *O Polichinelo,* in which he voiced his abolitionist and republican arguments. As Gama wrote biting exposés of the "slavocratic" officials in government, police harassment eventually force him to close his journals.

Gama offered his legal services to slaves seeking to gain their freedom, and he became known as a fearsome lawyer with a powerful rhetoric for defending fugitive slaves. Although he did not have a law degree, Gama's passion and oratory skills persuaded judges to free more than 1,000 slaves during his career. In addition, Gama collected funds so that he might personally purchase the freedom of individual slaves. He operated at the heart of the abolitionist movement, but his credentials were particular: Among white abolitionists, he was an ex-slave who was not only antislavocratic but also antiracist.

In 1868, when the Conservative Party took power in Brazil, Gama lost his job as a secretary in the police department. The following year, he began working at the *Radical Paulistano* newspaper as a typesetter and writer, joining other abolitionists such as Ruy Barbosa, Joaquim Nabuco, and Antônio de Castro Alves in voicing antislavery sentiment. He engaged in abolitionist speaking tours, lecturing to widely diverse groups, such as black Catholic brotherhoods and radical antislavery groups.

As the abolitionist movement gained momentum in the 1870s, the movement's radical elements separated from its more conservative members. Gama was convinced that no progress could be made as long as chattel slavery and monarchy existed; he left the Paulista Republican Party in 1873, having lost the battle to exclude slave owners from its ranks. His pragmatic efforts to assist slaves continued, as his home became a haven to fugitives; from there, he transported them to free zones in Santos and surrounding areas.

According to biographer Sud Mennucci, Gama wrote only one autobiographic sketch, in 1880. Ill with diabetes, he died on August 24, 1882, six years before Princess Regent Isabel promulgated the *Lei Áurea* (the Golden Law), fully abolishing slavery in Brazil.

Polly Rossdale

See also: Brazil, Abolition in.

Further Reading

Kennedy, James H. "Luiz Gama: Pioneer of Abolition in Brazil." *Journal of Negro History* 59 (July 1974): 255–67.
Pescatello, Ann M. "Prêto Power, Brazilian Style: Modes of Re-Actions to Slavery in the Nineteenth Century." In *Old Roots in New Lands: Historical and Anthropological Perspectives on Black Experiences in the Americas,* ed. Ann M. Pescatello. Westport, CT: Greenwood, 1977.

Garner, Margaret (ca. 1834–1858)

On January 28, 1856, Margaret Garner, a fugitive slave from Kentucky who was facing recapture and return to slavery, killed her two-year-old daughter and attempted to kill her three other children in order to prevent them from being re-enslaved. Upon arrival in Ohio, she was captured by a posse that included her master and sheriff's officers, arrested under the terms of the Fugitive Slave Law of 1850, and jailed. The Quaker abolitionist Levi Coffin, who was present at Garner's trial, detailed the case of "the slave mother, who killed her child rather than see it taken back to slavery" in his *Reminiscences* (1876). In that work, he referred to Garner's case as one that "aroused deeper interest and sympathy" than any other.

Identified in the 1850 slave census as an unnamed mulatto, Garner was an enslaved domestic on the farm of Archibald K. Gaines in Richwood (Boone County), Kentucky. Twenty-two years old and pregnant at the time of her escape, she was accompanied by her husband Robert, his parents, and her four children, who ranged in age from nine months to six years. The family fled from Kentucky in record-cold temperatures, crossing the frozen Ohio River into Cincinnati.

The family's escape plan was aided by Robert's familiarity with Cincinnati, which was less than twenty miles away. Robert was enslaved on the farm of James Marshall, near the Gaines estate, but he had been hired out as a laborer and helped with the sale of hogs in Cincinnati. Upon arriving in the city, the Garners took refuge with Margaret's cousin, Elijah Kite, who was to obtain instructions from Coffin for the family's passage to the North via the Underground Railroad.

Before the family could proceed with their escape plans, the Kite home was surrounded by a U.S. marshal's party that included Gaines and Marshall's son. As they broke down the front door, Garner killed her daughter by slitting her throat. She was captured immediately, and the fugitives were jailed.

Garner was subject to the terms of the Fugitive Slave Law and liable for murder in the state of Ohio. The federal law mandated that escaped slaves be returned to bondage and imposed stiff fines and possible prison sentences on anyone who abetted or refused to help recapture runaway slaves. The law also sought to address whether enslaved persons who had traveled on free soil were entitled to their freedom.

In February 1856, the Garners' lawyer, John Jolliffe, argued that the family members were entitled to their freedom, as both Margaret and Robert had previously been taken to Cincinnati and given permission to work there by their respective owners. Jolliffe argued that the Garners' children were legally free, because they had been born after that time. He proposed that Margaret Garner be charged with murder and the other fugitives charged with complicity; this charge would guarantee that they could remain in a free state and be judged as people, not as property. Jolliffe also reasoned that the jury in a murder trial would sympathize with allegations that Margaret had been subjected to long-standing sexual abuse by Gaines.

Despite these arguments, the Garners, who were considered property under federal statute, were first subject to a fugitive slave hearing. Gaines's and Marshall's attorneys argued that federal law had supervening authority over Ohio's homicide statutes. In reply, Jolliffe and the Ohio attorneys general argued that any state willing to defer on cases involving the killing of its own citizens would accept the nullification of its statutory and constitutional authority to govern. Thus, the Garner case unfolded as a states rights debate, though it reversed the regional thinking of the era: Southern proslavery advocates claimed the overriding authority of the federal government, whereas Northern antislavery advocates argued for state sovereignty.

As the arguments unfolded, the courtroom drama riveted the nation for weeks. Although the insinuations of sexual abuse against Gaines were never formalized, in a speech delivered in the courtroom, Lucy Stone, a feminist abolitionist, pointed to the appearance of Garner's children as evidence of the abuse and Gaines's paternity. Steven Weisenburger, in his study *Modern Medea: A Family Story of Slavery and Child-Murder From the Old South* (1998), theorized that sexual violation explained Garner's motivation for running away and committing infanticide, finding that her pregnancies occurred after Archibald Gaines had arrived in Richwood and followed his wife's pregnancies. Furthermore, Gaines's extreme reaction to seeing the murdered toddler and his refusal to release her remains to the Cincinnati coroner were also indicative of his paternity.

Garner was never tried for the child's murder. John Pendery, the federal commissioner who tried the case, overruled the state's right to prosecute for murder and ruled that federal fugitive warrants had supervening authority, thus upholding the Fugitive Slave Law. Consequently, Garner and her family were returned to their Kentucky slaveholders and sold to a plantation in Mississippi. There, Margaret Garner died of typhoid fever sometime in 1858.

Garner's story was immortalized in several nineteenth-century interpretations, including Frances E.W. Harper's "The Slave Mother, a Tale of the Ohio," Elizabeth Barrett Browning's "The Runaway Slave at Pilgrim's Point," and Thomas Satterwhite Noble's 1867 painting *The Modern Medea.* The power of Garner's actions has captured the attention of contemporary artists and scholars as well. Toni Morrison's Pulitzer Prize–winning novel *Beloved* (1987), which was made into a motion picture in 1998, explores child murder as a solution to the horrors of slavery, as does Weisenburger's nonfiction account. Morrison also wrote the libretto for *Margaret Garner,* an opera with music by Richard Danielpour.

Delores M. Walters and Gina Misiroglu

See also: Fugitive Slave Act of 1850; Fugitive Slaves; Stone, Lucy.

Further Reading

Morrison, Toni. *Beloved.* New York: Alfred A. Knopf, 1987.
Weisenburger, Steven. *Modern Medea: A Family Story of Slavery and Child-Murder From the Old South.* New York: Hill and Wang, 1998.

Garnet, Henry Highland (1815–1882)

The noted African American clergyman Henry Highland Garnet was an antislavery activist who is best remembered for delivering the militant speech "An Address to the Slaves of the United States of America" in 1843. Two decades later, Garnet became the first African American to deliver a public address to the U.S. Congress.

Born on December 23, 1815, on a plantation near New Market, Maryland, Garnet escaped slavery as a child. Having experienced a plight like that of many slaves, he and his entire family fled to freedom via the Underground Railroad. The grandson of a Mandingo chieftain, Garnet seemed destined for leadership. In spite of a severe injury to his right leg that necessitated amputation in 1840, he rose to become a bold, outspoken advocate for self-determination among African Americans, insisting that blacks take their destiny of freedom into their own hands.

Garnet's preparation for leadership began when he assumed the role of class leader and exhorter in the Bethel African Methodist Episcopal Church on Mott Street in New York City, where his family had moved in 1825. In 1826, he received his early education at the African Free School. Several of his classmates there would later become prominent men, including Alexander Crummell, an Episcopalian priest and widely published intellectual; Ira Aldridge, the Shakespearean actor; and Samuel Ringgold Ward, a noted abolitionist. Together, as ardent abolitionists, they formed the Garrison Literary and Benevolent Association, an organization that organized political activities and spoke out against social injustice. Garnet and Crummell studied theology together at the Oneida Institute in New York, the training ground for their ministries of social activism.

Garnet rose to the forefront of national politics after delivering "An Address to the Slaves of the United States of America" at the National Negro Convention in Buffalo, New York. Continuing the tradition of militancy that David Walker had established in his *Appeal to the Colored Citizens of the World* (1829), Garnet's rousing speech, delivered to a mostly male audience, sought to incite men of the North to speak out against the oppression of their Southern brothers and sisters who were still physical and mental slaves.

In the speech, Garnet echoed Patrick Henry's emphasis on freedom: A recurring line throughout the speech was, "Rather die freemen than live to be slaves." He invoked the names of heroes who had fought for black liberation, such as Toussaint L'Ouverture, the leader of the Haitian Revolution; Nat Turner and Denmark Vesey, who had led slave rebellions in the United States; and Joseph Cinqué, the leader of the *Amistad* uprising. Garnet called on bound slaves to rise up against their masters and take up arms as a means of gaining their freedom, rather than waiting for political solutions. He reminded them that it was their "solemn and imperative duty to use every means, both moral, intellectual, and physical" to achieve the goal of freedom. The speech challenged audience members to maintain a continuous and steadfast fight: "Let your motto be resistance! Resistance! Resistance!"

Garnet's oratorical skills held those attending the convention spellbound, but his platform of radical action failed by one vote, largely because of abolitionist Frederick Douglass's firm counterargument, which denounced violent rebellion. Although Garnet's speech was written in 1843, no one would publish it until 1848 because of its incendiary tone. With abolitionist John Brown as financial backer, it was finally published, together with Walker's *Appeal*, the controversial tract that had encouraged blacks to foment rebellion.

Garnet began a long career as a Presbyterian minister, assuming his first pastorate at the Liberty Street Presbyterian Church in Troy, New York, beginning in 1834. In the early 1850s, he accepted a post as pastor of the Shiloh Presbyterian Church in New York City, a beacon for several black organizations engaged in political activities.

In 1854, Garnet accepted an appointment from the United Presbyterian Church of Scotland to serve as pastor of the Stirling Presbyterian Church in Jamaica. He served in that capacity for two years until 1856, when he returned to the United States after an illness. While in Jamaica, he began to formulate an economic plan to assist former slaves who were newly emancipated. In addition to his duties as a member of the Presbyterian clergy, he became a chaplain to a regiment of African American troops during the U.S. Civil war.

Known for his political and religious activism, Garnet, a popular, charismatic speaker, was invited by President Abraham Lincoln to address Congress on Sunday, February 12, 1865. His historic sermon, "A Memorial Discourse Delivered in the Hall of the House of Representatives, February 12, 1865," was the first delivered by an African American to that arm of the government.

In the speech, he gave firsthand testimony of the evils of slavery and quoted passages from Plato, Socrates, and Saint Augustine. He emphasized the urgency of endowing newly freed slaves with the same social and political rights that every American had. His motivational message urged Congress to "Emancipate, Enfranchise, Educate, and give the blessings of the gospel to every American citizen." The well-received speech thrust Garnet into national popularity, having appropriately taken place during the ratification of the Thirteenth Amendment, which abolished slavery as a legal institution.

Garnet moved to Liberia to serve as minister resident and consul general in 1881. He died in Africa, his ancestral homeland, on February 12, 1882. At his funeral, longtime friend Alexander Crummell delivered the eulogy.

Lena Ampadu

See also: Brown, John; Lincoln, Abraham; Walker's *Appeal* (1829).

Further Reading

Garnet, Henry Highland. "An Address to the Slaves of the United States of America." In *The Norton Anthology of African American Literature,* ed. Henry Louis Gates, Jr., and Nellie Y. McKay. New York: W.W. Norton, 1997.

———. "A Memorial Discourse Delivered in the Hall of the House of Representatives, February 12, 1865." In *Black Writers of America,* ed. Richard Barksdale and Keneth Kinnamon. New York: Macmillan, 1972.

Hill, Patricia Liggins. "Henry Highland Garnet." In *Call and Response: The Riverside Anthology of the African American Literary Tradition,* ed. Patricia Liggins Hill, et al. Boston: Houghton Mifflin, 1998.

Miller, Ruth. "Henry Highland Garnet." In *Black American Literature 1760–Present,* ed. Ruth Miller. Beverly Hills, CA: Glencoe, 1971.

Garrett, Thomas (1789–1871)

Thomas Garrett was a Quaker, merchant, abolitionist, and Underground Railroad agent who provided leadership, time, and financial support to assist antislavery efforts in and around Wilmington, Delaware. He believed in equality for African Americans and women, a stand that sometimes put him in conflict with his friends and neighbors.

Born to Quaker parents on August 21, 1789, on a farm in Upper Darby (Delaware County), Pennsylvania, Garrett learned the iron merchant business from his father, a blacksmith. Garrett married Mary Sharpless in 1813, and the couple lived with his family in Upper Darby. The Garrett family had long supported the abolition of slavery, and their home was a haven for runaway slaves making their way out of Maryland, Delaware, and Virginia.

In 1822, Thomas, Mary, and their three children moved to Wilmington, where Garrett established his own hardware and iron merchant business on Shipley Street, a short distance from his home. The Garretts continued their antislavery and Underground Railroad activities in Wilmington despite Delaware's status as a slave state. After Mary died in 1828, Thomas married Rachel Mendinhall, also a Quaker and an antislavery sympathizer, in 1830.

A close friend and supporter of the abolitionist William Lloyd Garrison, Garrett believed in the principles of nonresistance. He found it increasingly difficult, however, to adhere to that standard, especially in the face of sometimes violent actions of slave catchers in the course of their pursuit of runaway slaves. It was well known in the Wilmington area that Garrett was an Underground Railroad agent, a fact that often placed him at risk of arrest or physical harm. In fact, he was once accosted by several proslavery men who threw him from a train in Wilmington, where Garrett had been attempting to save a young free black woman who was being forcefully—and illegally—taken into slavery. Garrett turned his outrage into a lifelong commitment to assisting fleeing slaves and ending the slave system.

In 1848, Garrett was brought to trial in Delaware for aiding and abetting a fugitive slave family from Maryland. During the Christmas holiday of 1845, Garrett and two friends—John Hunn of Middletown and Samuel Burris, a free black—had succeeded in securing the freedom of the enslaved family of a free man named Samuel Hawkins. Garrett and his associates were charged, but, by the time the trial took place two and a half years later, Wilmington had become a notorious way station on the road to freedom for many escaped slaves. Public sentiment was mixed, though many Wilmington residents disapproved of Garrett's activities. He was found guilty and fined $1,500. Ever defiant, he proclaimed in open court that he would continue his illegal activities and redouble his efforts on behalf of runaway slaves.

Although he remained a marked man—most slave catchers knew to watch Garrett's house in anticipation of fugitives arriving there—he also was remarkably successful in this work. His Underground Railroad network employed agents from Virginia, Maryland, and Delaware, and his Quaker connections throughout southeastern Pennsylvania and northern New Jersey provided multiple avenues to freedom and safe havens for freedom seekers. Garrett's close working relationship with Harriet Tubman and other members of the black community helped ensure his remarkable success in helping slaves to escape the region.

After the passage of the Fugitive Slave Law of 1850, Garrett redoubled his commitment to the antislavery cause and the work of the Underground Railroad. In 1854, he traveled to Boston to witness the trial of Anthony Burns, a fugitive slave who had been convicted in a Massachusetts court under the 1850 legislation.

Garrett's close relationship with black abolitionists William Still and James Miller McKim and the Philadelphia Vigilant Committee proved to be one of the most important of his career. Their letters reflect a tireless network and organization that funneled hundreds of runaway slaves through Wilmington and Philadelphia and beyond during the 1850s. Garrett claimed to have assisted nearly 2,700 enslaved people to freedom over a forty-year period.

His correspondence with sisters Eliza Wigham and Mary Edmundson, Quakers living in England, also revealed intimate details of some of his Underground Railroad efforts, as well as Garrett's penchant for dramatic rescue stories that helped pique public interest and badly needed financial aid. The U.S. Civil War brought an end to his career as an Underground Railroad and antislavery activist, and his pacifist views and advanced age kept him out of the public eye.

In 1870, during celebrations in Wilmington following the passage of the Fifteenth Amendment, which granted African American men the right to vote, African Americans carried Garrett along the parade route, calling him their Moses. Garrett died on January 25, 1871, at his home in Wilmington.

Kate Clifford Larson

See also: Fugitive Slave Act of 1850; Underground Railroad.

Further Reading

Drake, Thomas E. "Thomas Garrett, Quaker Abolitionist." In *Friends in Wilmington, 1738–1938,* ed. Edward P. Bartlett. Wilmington, OH: Clinton County Historical Society, 1938.

McGowan, James A. *Station Master on the Underground Railroad: The Life and Letters of Thomas Garrett.* Moylan, PA: Whimsie, 1977; rev. ed., Jefferson, NC: McFarland, 2005.

Thompson, Priscilla. "Harriet Tubman, Thomas Garrett, and the Underground Railroad." *Delaware History* 22 (September 1986): 1–21.

Garrison, William Lloyd (1805–1879)

William Lloyd Garrison was one of the leading radical voices in the U.S. abolitionist movement during the final three decades of the struggle to eradicate slavery. Through his weekly antislavery newspaper *The Liberator,* which he published from 1831 until 1865, Garrison became one of the most famous abolitionists in the United States—a man celebrated by opponents of slavery and vilified by its supporters. In the process, Garrison, along with a handful of black and white colleagues, transformed the antislavery movement in the United States, challenging both the gradualism of earlier antislavery activists and the program of the American Colonization Society, which sought to emancipate slaves and "return" them to Africa. Garrison, in contrast, demanded the immediate emancipation of slaves, rejected any thought of compensation for slaveholders, and founded his appeal on a commitment to racial justice. In doing so, Garrison changed both the tenor and the terms of the antislavery debate, contributing significantly to the ultimate destruction of the institution of slavery.

Born in Newburyport, Massachusetts, on December 10, 1805, Garrison grew up in an impoverished household. His family suffered an economic blow when President Thomas Jefferson's 1807 embargo on trade with Britain and France crippled New England's shipping economy. The following year, Garrison's father Abijah, a sailor, abandoned his wife and three children; thereafter, Garrison's mother Fanny, a deeply pious Baptist, raised and supported the family single-handedly. Searching out employment opportunities, Fanny eventually moved her family from Newburyport to Lynn, Massachusetts, and later to Baltimore, Maryland.

At the age of thirteen, Garrison returned to his home state to work as an apprentice printer for the *Newburyport Herald.* As Garrison learned the printing trade, he proved himself far more his mother's child than his father's, regularly observing the Sabbath and attending Baptist services. After serving a number of printing apprenticeships, Garrison was able to combine his religious faith and his new trade when he assumed control of a Boston temperance newspaper, the *National Philanthropist,* in January 1828.

Garrison's columns in *National Philanthropist* denounced a wide range of vices—from the sale and consumption of liquor to dueling, infidelity, and mail delivery on the Sabbath—that the young editor believed corrupted the Christian republic. While writing for this paper, Garrison also began to cultivate the aggressive, uncompromising style that would later characterize his radical approach to abolitionism.

After attending an 1828 lecture by Quaker Benjamin Lundy, editor of the antislavery paper the *Genius of Universal Emancipation,* Garrison decided that slavery was the worst manifestation of moral corruption in America. Thereafter, he devoted his life to its eradication. The following year, Garrison left New England for Baltimore to co-edit the *Genius* with Lundy. At first, Garrison embraced the Quaker editor's moderate antislavery position, supporting gradual emancipation and colonization. Soon, however, Garrison began considering more radical solutions to the problem of slavery.

Garrison's shift toward radical abolitionism owed a good deal to the ideas of the black abolitionists whom he met in Baltimore and Philadelphia. James Forten, among others, helped convince the young antislavery editor that colonization ultimately reinforced, rather than challenged, the racist culture that was the backbone of the system of slavery. In 1832, Garrison formally rejected colonization in his publication *Thoughts on African Colonization*, a vigorous attack on the morality and practicality of the plan. He insisted that the American Colonization Society's plan was unfeasible, founded on dubious racial distinctions, and, worst of all, helped shore up the institution it purported to oppose. Garrison instead embraced

As publisher of *The Liberator* and a founder of the American Anti-Slavery Society, William Lloyd Garrison of Massachusetts came to personify the radical wing of the American abolitionist movement. *(Hulton Archive/Getty Images)*

immediate, unconditional emancipation and the complete assimilation of blacks into American society.

Garrison continued to develop his radical antislavery philosophy in the weekly antislavery newspaper *The Liberator*, which he founded in Boston in January 1831. "I do not wish to think, or speak, or write with moderation," he announced in the first issue of *The Liberator*. "I will not equivocate—I will not excuse—I will not retreat a single inch—AND I WILL BE HEARD."

Garrison's new paper demanded the complete destruction of the institution of slavery, refused to consider compensation for slaveholders, and denounced gradual abolition and political compromise on the issue of slavery. Although the circulation of *The Liberator* was limited at first, eventually, the paper earned a devoted audience of antislavery sympathizers, particularly among African American communities in the North.

Garrison played a pivotal role in the creation of the New England Anti-Slavery Society in 1832 and the American Anti-Slavery Society in 1833; for the latter, he wrote the official "Declaration of Sentiments." In this document, Garrison framed the struggle against slavery in light of America's revolutionary struggle for independence from Britain. But for all his rhetorical militancy, Garrison did not endorse the violent methods of the American colonists. Instead, the abolitionist editor insisted that the antislavery struggle must reject "the use of all carnal weapons for deliverance from bondage—relying solely upon those which are spiritual, and might through God to the pulling down of strongholds."

This pacifist stance was premised on the doctrine of nonresistance; nonresistants such as Garrison condemned violence categorically and rejected all governments created by humans, tracing America's flaws to its foundation in force. Garrison instead endorsed moral suasion, believing that to thoroughly rid America of the sin of slavery, individuals had to be convinced of the immorality of the institution. Garrison embraced "come-outerism," a practice in which individuals separated themselves from institutions that had been corrupted by slavery, ranging from individual churches to the American republic. He labeled the U.S. Constitution "the most bloody and heaven-daring arrangement ever made by men for the continuance and protection of a system of the most atrocious villainy every exhibited on earth" and, in the mid-1840s, began calling for the dissolution of the Union because it was founded on the corrupt compact.

Garrison's uncompromising militancy endeared him to radical abolitionists, particularly African American reformers, who proved his most loyal supporters in the early years of *The Liberator*. Yet it also alienated many antebellum Americans, both in the North and in the South. Some opponents of the antislavery movement blamed Garrison for Nat Turner's 1831 slave insurrection in Virginia, which happened shortly after Garrison started publishing *The Liberator*. Garrison also estranged fellow antislavery activists by rejecting efforts to work for the destruction of slavery through traditional political and religious channels.

Eventually, Garrison's unwillingness to compromise contributed to several highly visible divisions within the American antislavery movement. In 1840, his refusal to endorse political antislavery methods and commitment to ensuring that women played a significant role in the American Anti-Slavery Society spurred a major split in the organization that led to the formation of the Liberty Party and the American and Foreign Anti-Slavery Society. A decade later, Garrison had a public falling-out with his one-time protégé Fredrick Douglass, sparked by the latter's decision to endorse political abolitionism in his antislavery newspaper *The North Star*.

During the turbulent decade of the 1850s, Garrison began to soften his strident stances. He showed an increasing willingness to work with political abolitionists and even equivocated on the use of violence to destroy the institution of slavery. During the U.S. Civil War, Garrison abandoned his pacifism and threw his support behind President Abraham Lincoln and the Union war effort.

After the passage of the Thirteenth Amendment and the surrender of the Confederacy in 1865, Garrison decided that his thirty-year crusade had finally succeeded, and he ceased publication of *The Liberator*. Afterward, he retired to Roxbury, Massachusetts, and occasionally wrote editorials. He died in New York City on May 24, 1879.

Ethan J. Kytle

See also: American Anti-Slavery Society; American Colonization Society; Douglass, Frederick; Gradualism; Immediatism; Lundy, Benjamin.

Further Reading

Kraditor, Aileen S. *Means and Ends in American Abolitionism: Garrison and His Critics on Strategy and Tactics, 1834–1850*. New York: Pantheon, 1969.

Mayer, Henry. "All on Fire: William Lloyd Garrison and the Abolition of Slavery." *New England Quarterly* 73 (June 2000): 335–36.

Merrill, Walter M. *Against Wind and Tide: A Biography of William Lloyd Garrison*. Cambridge, MA: Harvard University Press, 1963.

Perry, Lewis. *Radical Abolitionism: Anarchy and the Government of God in Antislavery Thought*. Ithaca, NY: Cornell University Press, 1973; Knoxville: University of Tennessee Press, 1995.

Van Deburg, William L. "William Lloyd Garrison and the 'Pro-Slavery Priesthood': The Changing Beliefs of an Evangelical Reformer." *Journal of the American Academy of Religion* 43 (June 1975): 224–37.

Wyatt-Brown, Bertram. "William Lloyd Garrison and Antislavery Unity: A Reappraisal." *Civil War History* 13 (March 1967): 5–24.

Gatch, Philip (1751–1834)

As an itinerant Methodist preacher during the American Revolution, Philip Gatch faced the fury of many by supporting theological views that were contrary to both public opinion and Anglican orthodoxy. Such training prepared Gatch for his role as an early American abolitionist. A statesman, revivalist, and Ohio justice of the peace, Gatch consistently applied his faith to the denouncement of slavery and the pressing political issues of his day.

Gatch was born in Baltimore County, Maryland, in 1751 to a family of immigrant Prussian farmers. He was educated in local schools and received his religious training at Saint Paul's Anglican Church in the city of Baltimore. When he was twenty years old, he had the opportunity to hear the Methodist preacher Nathan Perigo speak, and, as a result, he became attracted to the Methodist movement that was taking root on both sides of the Atlantic. Gatch felt a special affinity with the logical purity of the new theology, and he began training to become a minister in the Methodist Church. By 1774, he was officially recognized as an itinerant Methodist minister, the first native-born American to earn this distinction.

Because of their suspected Loyalist sympathies, itinerant Methodist preachers were not entirely safe as they traveled during the years of the American Revolution. On one occasion, Gatch was preaching in Frederick County, Maryland, when he was attacked by a mob that attempted to tar and feather him. He sustained permanent injury when hot tar burned one of his eyes.

After two years of serving as a circuit-riding preacher, Gatch relocated to Richmond, Virginia, to settle down and restore his health. In 1778, he married

Elizabeth Smith, with whom he would raise eight children.

The religious climate of Virginia was more welcoming to Methodism, and the revivalism associated with camp meetings brought more adherents to the faith. Increasingly, however, many Methodists were being drawn into the cause of abolitionism, which John Wesley supported in Britain, although the cause was at odds with the social realities of Tidewater Virginia. At the Baltimore Christmas Conference of 1784, where the Methodist Episcopal Church was officially established, slave-owning Methodists were given a year to execute a legal instrument that would effectively emancipate all of the slaves they possessed. In 1785, Methodist ministers campaigned for signatures on a petition addressed to the Virginia General Assembly urging the "immediate or gradual emancipation of all slaves."

For the Gatch family, this was more than a mere theoretical debate. Elizabeth Smith Gatch had inherited several slaves upon the death of her parents, Thomas Smith and Martha Stovall of Powhatan County, Virginia. Philip Gatch emancipated these slaves through legal manumission on December 18, 1788, because he believed that "all men are by nature equally free." He later elaborated on his decision to free the slaves, writing, "Was I a slave to the Algereans [sic] I am sure I should want them to set me free."

Gatch was a founding member of the Humane Society of Richmond for the Abolition of the Slave Trade. Members of this society, largely consisting of Quakers and fellow Methodists, presented an antislavery memorial to the U.S. Congress in 1791.

Sensing the growing influence of the proslavery majority in Virginia, the Gatch family decided to relocate to the Ohio Territory in 1798. Gatch recounted his justification for moving: "I could not feel satisfied to die and leave my offspring in a land of slavery." He purchased property along the Little Miami River in Clermont County (near present-day Milford), became a justice of the peace, and, by 1802, was serving as a delegate to the Ohio Constitutional Convention. The document written by that body, which established statehood for Ohio in 1803, maintained the antislavery stipulation that the Northwest Ordinance of 1787 had created by prohibiting slavery in the state of Ohio.

Gatch lived for the next thirty years in southern Ohio as a farmer, local justice, and part-time preacher. He died at his home in 1834.

Gatch's papers were edited and published by fellow abolitionist John McLean, who later served as an associate justice on the U.S. Supreme Court and cast one of the two dissenting votes in the 1857 case of *Dred Scott v. Sanford*. Gatch's writings—including his autobiography, handwritten minutes of the conferences of early American Methodism (1774–1777), sermons, and letters—provide a rich insight into Methodists of his time and their role in abolitionism.

Junius P. Rodriguez

See also: Religion and Abolitionism.

Further Reading

Boase, Paul H. "Philip Gatch, Pioneer." *Bulletin of the Historical and Philosophical Society of Ohio* 13 (October 1955): 286–96.
Connor, Elizabeth. *Methodist Trail Blazer: Philip Gatch, 1751–1834, His Life in Maryland, Virginia, and Ohio.* Cincinnati, OH: Creative Publishers, 1970.

Gay, Sydney Howard (1814–1888)

Sydney Howard Gay was a noted American journalist, historian, and abolitionist who advocated the immediate emancipation of slaves. He also was a close friend and confidant of William Lloyd Garrison. In his later years, Gay produced a number of popular history works and biographies.

Gay was born and raised in Hingham, Massachusetts, but he lived in New York for most of his life. As a young man, he considered a career in law but decided against it after studying in his father's law office for a number of years. Gay was more inspired by the "higher law" that he had discovered in his reading of antislavery literature, and he soon found his calling in the American abolitionist movement.

Gay joined the American Anti-Slavery Society as a young man and became a lecturing agent for the organization in 1842. The following year, he became the editor of the pro-Garrisonian *National Anti-Slavery Standard*, the New York City–based newspaper that was the official organ of the society. Remaining true to his pro-Garrisonian ideology during the various schisms that occurred within the abolitionist movement, Gay remained steadfast as he edited the abolitionist newspaper until 1857.

In 1845, Gay married fellow abolitionist Elizabeth J. Neall, the daughter of Daniel Neall, a prominent Quaker abolitionist from Philadelphia. Elizabeth had been one of the American women who traveled to London in 1840 to attend the World Anti-Slavery Convention.

A true believer in the abolitionist cause, Gay was identified as one of the Northern abolitionists (the other was James Miller McKim) who assisted in the famous escape of Virginia slave Henry "Box" Brown, who shipped himself to freedom in 1849. When Brown arrived in the North, Gay helped him find employment by sending him to Joseph Rickford in New Bedford, Connecticut. Rickford later wrote of Brown, "The man appears to be a fine fellow, has found considerable employment—he has worked several days for me & if I commence manufacturing oil again I think I can give him constant employment."

In 1857, Gay left the *National Anti-Slavery Standard* after fifteen years at its helm and joined the *New York Tribune*, where he quickly rose through the ranks. Gay was managing editor of that paper during most of the U.S. Civil War years (1862–1865), and, in his capacity as a journalist of national importance, Gay corresponded with Abraham Lincoln. Still an avid abolitionist, it was common for Gay to hide fugitive slaves in the pressroom of the *Tribune*. The presence of an abolitionist as editor of one of New York's primary newspapers did much to influence the pro-emancipation editorial slant of the *Tribune*.

Gay left the East Coast for a brief time to become the managing editor of the *Chicago Tribune* in 1867. He left Chicago soon after the devastating fire of 1871, however, and returned to New York, where he wrote for the *New York Evening Post* from 1872 to 1874.

Gay made the transition from journalist to historian during his final years as he labored feverishly to write a multivolume history of the nation and several biographies of famous Americans. He is best remembered for co-authoring (with William Cullen Bryant) the four-volume *A Popular History of the United States, From the First Discovery of the Western Hemisphere by the Northmen, to the End of the First Century of the Union of the States, Preceded by a Sketch of the Prehistoric Period and the Age of the Mound Builders* (1876–1881). Gay also authored the biography *James Madison* (1884), part of the noted American Statesmen series.

Junius P. Rodriguez

See also: Brown, Henry "Box"; *National Anti-Slavery Standard*.

Further Reading

National Anti-Slavery Standard. In *The Black Experience in America: Negro Periodicals in the United States, 1840–1860*. Series I. Westport, CT: Negro Universities Press, 1970.

Still, William. *The Underground Railroad*. 1872. Chicago: Johnson, 1970; Medford, NJ: Plexus, 2005.

German Coast Rebellion (1811)

The largest slave insurrection in the history of the United States occurred in January 1811 about forty miles west of New Orleans, Louisiana. Referred to as the German Coast Rebellion or Deslondes' Revolt, it took place along the river road in Saint John the Baptist and Saint Charles parishes, a region of Louisiana called the German Coast (*Côte des Allemands*). As many as 500 slaves took part in the uprising as they sought to liberate themselves through the force of arms.

The rebellion began on the sugar plantation of Manual Andry when Charles Deslondes, a mulatto refugee from Saint-Domingue who worked as a slave driver on a nearby plantation, attacked and killed Andry's son on the evening of January 8. Deslondes organized the other slaves on the plantation, seized weapons, and fled to New Orleans. Deslondes led a slave force of 180 to 500 men, their numbers increasing with the liberation of additional plantations. Many of the white inhabitants of the German Coast region fled to New Orleans after learning of the attack at Andry's plantation, allowing the advancing slave force to burn plantations and seize food, supplies, and wine from the locations they pillaged.

Accounts of the incident suggest that there was a type of military style and discipline associated with the slave army that advanced eastward toward New Orleans. Slaves marched with leaders on horseback, waving battle flags as they advanced. The rebels were armed with crude weapons—primarily cane knives and axes—along with a small number of firearms. They shouted "On to Orleans!" as their battle cry, though it appears that their ultimate goal was simply self-emancipation.

The authorities of the Orleans Territory took action immediately when they learned of the revolt. Territorial governor William C.C. Claiborne issued orders calling the territorial militia into action, and he also called on the services of General Wade Hampton of the U.S. Army, who happened to be in New Orleans at the time with a company of troops. The presence of Hampton's forces, along with those of Major Homer Virgil Milton, who advanced with other troops from Baton Rouge, marked the first time that the U.S. military was involved in the active suppression of a slave revolt. The army and militia initiated a nighttime march in the rain to locate the rebels.

During the night of January 9 and the morning of January 10, local militia and U.S. troops attacked the slaves at Jacques Fortier's plantation in Saint Charles Parish, stopping the advance on New Orleans. Manual Andry also attacked the slaves with a local vigilante force he led. Several slaves were killed during the initial assault, and many fled into the nearby swamps and woodlands to escape the onslaught. Over the course of several weeks, vigilantes continued to hunt down these "outliers." Those who were captured alive were brought before a judicial tribunal of plantation owners that sat in judgment at the plantation of Jean Noel Destrehan. Nearly 100 slaves lost their lives in the attack, during the sweep of the countryside that followed, and in the judgments of the tribunal. The decapitated heads of the victims were placed on poles positioned along the river road to discourage any further thoughts of revolt among the region's slave population.

Governor Claiborne and others in New Orleans, especially the native whites, blamed the transplanted slaves from the West Indies for instigating the revolt; Deslondes was from Saint-Domingue, where slaves had launched a successful and brutal revolution against their masters in 1791. It is possible that the large population of migrant slaves who entered Louisiana, either directly from Saint-Domingue or indirectly through Cuba, had been supporters of the insurrection.

The bloody rebellion cost many lives and destabilized the region, but once suppressed, the revolt was viewed primarily as an embarrassment to the Orleans Territory, which was seeking statehood at the time. Some opponents of statehood argued not only that the possibility of establishing civil government in a former French and Spanish colonial setting would be difficult, but also that the large, unstable slave population threatened the creation of a state so distant from the other states in the Union.

In spite of these concerns, the U.S. Congress admitted the Orleans Territory into the Union as the state of Louisiana in April 1812. The Louisiana legislature, as well as those in several other slaveholding states and territories, passed new and tougher slave control laws.

Junius P. Rodriguez

See also: Prosser, Gabriel; Turner, Nat; Vesey, Denmark.

Further Reading

Aptheker, Herbert. *American Negro Slave Revolts.* New York: International Publishers, 1993.

Carroll, Joseph Cephas. *Slave Insurrections in the United States, 1800–1865.* 1938. New York: Negro Universities Press, 1968.

Dormon, John H. "The Persistent Specter: Slave Rebellion in Territorial Louisiana." *Louisiana History* 18 (1977): 389–404.

Germantown Protest (1688)

The Germantown Protest, a document published in 1688 denouncing the practice of slavery in colonial Pennsylvania, was the first known antislavery protest in the history of the United States.

The community of Germantown (a part of present-day Philadelphia) was settled by a group of thirteen Mennonite Quaker families from the Lower Rhine Valley of Germany in 1683. The first slaves had arrived in Pennsylvania a year earlier to provide the cheap labor needed to get the young colony started. Unlike the British colonists, the Germans settlers had no previous exposure to the African slave trade, and they were appalled by the immorality of stealing people from their homeland to live in bondage.

In April 1688, several leading Germantown Quakers assembled at the home of Thomas Kunders, which served as the local meetinghouse. Francis Daniel Pastorius, the lawyer and scholar who had founded the town, wrote the text of the protest, which was to be read before the Dublin Monthly Meeting, a gathering of several Quaker meetinghouses in the Germantown area. It began, "These are the reasons why we are against the traffic of men-body, as followeth."

Their argument was simple and logical: The practice of slavery was a violation of both common decency and Biblical injunctions. Paraphrasing the Golden Rule, Pastorius wrote, "There is a saying that we shall doe to all men like as we will be done by ourselves; making no difference of what generation, descent of colour they are. And those who steal or rob men, and those who buy or purchase them, are they not alike?"

Having suffered religious persecution in Europe, the Quakers could not understand the racial oppression of Africans in their new homeland. If it continued, they believed, the reputation of the Pennsylvania colony would be damaged. "This makes an ill report in all those countries of Europe, where they hear off, that ye Quakers doe here handel men as they handle there ye cattle."

Pastorius concluded, "Now consider well this thing, if it is good or bad? And in case you find it to be good to handel these blacks at that manner, we desire and require you hereby lovingly that you may inform us here in, which at this time was never done, viz., that Christians have such a liberty to do so." The document was signed by Pastorius, Garret Hendricks, Derick up den Graeff, and Abraham up den Graeff.

The protest slowly moved up the ranks of the Quaker organizational structure. The Dublin Monthly Meeting claimed that the issues were "so weighty that we think it not expedient to meddle with it here." They passed it on to the Philadelphia Quarterly Meeting, which deemed it "a thing of too great a weight for this meeting to determine." Finally, it was given to the Burlington Yearly Meeting, which tabled it, arguing that it "would not be so proper for this Meeting to give a Positive Judgement in this case, It having so General a Relation to many other Parts, and therefore at present they forbear it." The Quaker hierarchy was mostly made up of English settlers who saw slavery as a necessary evil. They were unready and unwilling to question the institution that was so quickly becoming a key part of the colonial economy.

The Germantown Protest failed in the sense that it did not force the Quakers to morally justify their decision to permit slavery in Pennsylvania. However, Pastorius and his followers established an antislavery sentiment that would grow over the following decades. By the early nineteenth century, Pennsylvania Quakers would become the moral center of the American antislavery movement.

Heather K. Michon

See also: Quakers (Society of Friends).

Further Reading

Furer, Howard B. *The Germans in America, 1607–1970: A Chronology and Fact Book.* Dobbs Ferry, NY: Oceana, 1973.

Gibbons, Abigail Hopper (1801–1893)

An abolitionist, prison reformer, and social activist, Abigail ("Abby") Hopper Gibbons was active in the New York City antislavery movement during the mid-nineteenth century. Her Quaker upbringing helped lay the groundwork for her socially conscious works, which included sheltering fugitive slaves, caring for displaced African American soldiers, and forming the Women's Prison Association of New York City in 1845. Her willingness to stand firmly on her principles of pacifism and equality characterized her life.

Hopper was born in Philadelphia on December 7, 1801, to Isaac Tatem Hopper and Sarah Tatum Hopper. Isaac was active in the antislavery movement—advocating tirelessly on behalf of escaped slaves and working on the Underground Railroad—and influenced Abby's desire to seek justice for those suffering from inhumane treatment. Abby's mother also fought for the rights of blacks and served on a Quaker committee that oversaw schools for black children. On February 14, 1833, Abby married James Gibbons, also a significant figure in the antislavery movement; the couple had six children.

In 1837, Abby Gibbons attended the first Anti-Slavery Convention of American Women in New York City, where she met prominent female abolitionists such as Lucretia Mott and Angelina and Sarah Grimké. After the convention, Gibbons became even more dedicated to the abolitionist cause. In 1841, she joined the Manhattan Anti-Slavery Society, which was composed primarily of blacks, in part to protest the all-white membership policy of the Ladies' New York City Anti-Slavery Society. In 1853, after the dissolution of the Manhattan Anti-Slavery Society, Gibbons and her family were instrumental in creating the New York Anti-Slavery Society.

During the U.S. Civil War, Gibbons became active as a nurse for the Union army and took on the role of advocate for slaves kept at the Union army camps. These slaves, referred to as "contraband of war," performed menial and arduous tasks, often in situations similar to those they were seeking to escape. Gibbons visited their camps and assisted them with family problems and childbirths. Her family and friends in the Northern states regularly shipped food, clothing, and medicine to her to be given to the contraband prisoners. Although she was entitled to army pay for her work, she requested that the payment be used to provide medical care for patients at the camps.

Gibbons was strongly opposed to the U.S. government policy that allowed slaves from border states to be returned to their owners if the owners signed an oath of allegiance to the United States. She was aware that many slave owners took the oath without any intention of abiding by it. Therefore, she worked diligently to prevent as many slaves as possible from being returned. She successfully encouraged many of her Northern supporters to hire ex-slaves as servants. After the war, she continued to maintain contact with former slaves, as well as other black abolitionists, helping to form the Labor and Aid Society to assist returning soldiers in finding employment.

In addition to condemning slavery, Gibbons actively supported other humanitarian causes. She played a significant role in the prison reform movement and was involved in the creation of America's first halfway house for women prisoners and an industrial school for German immigrant girls.

Gibbons died of pneumonia on January 16, 1893, at the age of ninety-one. Her daughter, Sarah Emerson, published her biography, *Life of Abby Hopper Gibbons,* in 1896.

Sharon Hill

See also: Civil War, American (1861–1865); Hopper, Isaac Tatem; Women's Rights and the Abolitionist Movement.

Further Reading

Bacon, Margaret Hope. *Abby Hopper Gibbons: Prison Reformer and Social Activist.* Albany: State University of New York Press, 2000.

Jeffery, Julie Roy. *The Great Silent Army of Abolitionism: Ordinary Women in the Antislavery Movement.* Chapel Hill: University of North Carolina Press, 1998.

Meaders, Daniel, ed. *Kidnappers in Philadelphia: Isaac Hopper's Tales of Oppression, 1780–1843.* New York: Garland, 1994.

Sterling, Dorothy. *Ahead of Her Time: Abby Kelley and the Politics of Antislavery.* New York: W.W. Norton, 1991.

Gibbons, James Sloan (1810–1892)

James Sloan Gibbons was a prominent Quaker, abolitionist, banker, and publisher during the mid-nineteenth century. With his wife, Abigail ("Abby") Hopper Gibbons, he spent his life fighting for the abolition of slavery and bringing national attention to the plight of blacks in America.

Gibbons was born in Wilmington, Delaware, on July 1, 1810. He was one of fourteen children born to William Gibbons, a physician, and Rebecca Donaldson Gibbons. He married Abigail Hopper on February 14, 1833; the couple had six children.

In 1835, the family moved to New York City, where Gibbons became a member of the executive committee of the American Anti-Slavery Society. So devoted was he to the society and its newspaper, the *National Anti-Slavery Standard,* that he used his own money to save the publication from its creditors and mortgaged his furniture to raise money for it. In 1842, Gibbons and his father-in-law, Isaac T. Hopper, were disowned by the New York Monthly Meeting of the Society of Friends for their support of the *Standard* and the American Anti-Slavery Society; nevertheless, Gibbons continued to attend meetings.

Gibbons contributed countless articles and letters on the U.S. Civil War to the New York papers. In 1860, he began publishing a magazine, the *Century,* which was devoted to the cause of abolition. One of his most significant writings was a poem published in July 1862 based on President Abraham Lincoln's request for 300,000 new recruits. The poem, titled "Three Hundred Thousand Strong," was published in the *New York Evening Post* and went on to become popular in the Northern states. (James did not sign his name to the poem, so it was generally credited to William Cullen Bryant; not until a number of years later did James establish his authorship of the poem.) During the Civil War, James oversaw the shipping of provisions to Union army outposts, while Abby and daughter Sarah served as nurses.

In addition to publishing materials pertaining to the Civil War and the antislavery movement, Gibbons wrote works on financial issues, among them *The Banks of New York, Their Dealers, the Clearing House, and the Panic of 1857* (1859) and *The Public Debt of the United States, Its Organization, Its Liquidation, Administration of the Treasury, the Financial System* (1867). In 1870, Gibbons was financially involved in the building of the Delaware Railroad, and in 1871, he became its president.

In his later years, he devoted himself to a national movement to save the forests that resulted in the celebration of Arbor Day. Gibbons also recorded observations of meteorological conditions several times a day and eventually gave his notes and charts to the Smithsonian Institution. He died on October 17, 1892, at the age of eighty-two.

Sharon Hill

See also: Gibbons, Abigail Hopper; Hopper, Isaac Tatem.

Further Reading

Bacon, Margaret Hope. *Abby Hopper Gibbons: Prison Reformer and Social Activist.* Albany: State University of New York Press, 2000.

Dyson, Zita. "Gerrit Smith's Effort in Behalf of Negroes in New York" *Journal of Negro History* 3 (October 1918): 354–59.

Jeffery, Julie Roy. *The Great Silent Army of Abolitionism: Ordinary Women in the Antislavery Movement.* Chapel Hill: University of North Carolina Press, 1998.

Ruchames, Louis, ed. *The Letters of William Lloyd Garrison.* Vol. 2., *A House Dividing Against Itself, 1836–1840.* Cambridge, MA: Belknap Press, 1971.

Winch, Julie. "Philadelphia and the Other Underground Railroad." *Pennsylvania Magazine of History and Biography* 61 (January 1987): 3–25.

Gibbs, Mifflin Wistar (1823–1915)

An abolitionist, merchant, judge, activist, and U.S. consul to Madagascar, Mifflin Wistar Gibbs enjoyed a diverse career as a black man in antebellum America. He attained prominence in Philadelphia, California, British Columbia, and Reconstruction-era Arkansas, where he was a leading figure in Republican Party politics and became the first black to be elected as a municipal judge in the United States. Gibbs left a substantial legacy as a champion of political rights and an advocate for black business.

Gibbs was born in Philadelphia on April 17, 1823, to free black parents, Jonathan Clarkson Gibbs, a Methodist minister, and Maria Jackson Gibbs. His formal education ended after the second grade, as he had to work to help support the family after his father's death. He was first exposed to slavery as a child during a trip to Delaware with his employer, and the image of oppression stuck with him throughout his life.

As a teenager, the self-taught Gibbs read voraciously and joined Philadelphia's Philomatheon Institute, a black literary society, through which he became acquainted with abolitionists Isaiah Wear and Robert Purvis. As a young man, Gibbs aided fugitive slaves in Philadelphia, and, in 1849, he joined the prominent abolitionist Frederick Douglass on the lecture circuit in New York for a year.

When the lecture tour was over, Gibbs, still feeling unfulfilled, found inspiration from Julia Griffiths, a black abolitionist who advised him to "Go do some great thing." In 1850, Gibbs decided to go to California and make his mark in life. His career blossomed in San Francisco, where, in partnership with another Philadelphian, Peter Lester, Gibbs started what would become one of the largest mercantile establishments in the city, the Pioneer Boot and Shoe Emporium.

Success in business did not end Gibbs's work as an activist, however; he became one of the most outspoken African Americans in California on issues of civil rights. In 1850–1851, he led an unsuccessful fight to abolish a provision of California law that did not allow black testimony in court. The ban affected Gibbs personally when a white man severely beat Lester over an incident in their store. Gibbs could only watch as the man's friend kept him at bay with a gun. Because there had been no white witnesses to the crime, Gibbs and Lester had no legal recourse. Gibbs participated in several state conventions held in 1854, 1855, and 1857 to protest the second-class status of blacks in Califor-

nia, and he helped establish the city's black newspaper, the *Mirror of the Times,* in 1856.

Disgusted with the discrimination in California, Gibbs joined the African American exodus from California to British Columbia, Canada, during the gold rush of 1858. There, he quickly made a small fortune as a merchant and became the most prominent member of Victoria's black community, forming a black militia in 1861. Blacks enjoyed more freedom in Canada than in California, but they still had to fight discrimination to win full legal equality. Gibbs twice won election to Victoria's city council in its most affluent ward but, like many other African Americans in Canada, he chose to return to his homeland when the U.S. Civil War was over.

In 1870, Gibbs moved to Little Rock, Arkansas, where he studied law and soon became active in Republican Party politics. In 1873, he won election as a municipal judge, becoming the first African American to be elected to a judgeship. In the ensuing years, he served as a representative to several national Republican Party conventions.

After losing re-election to the judgeship, Gibbs never regained electoral office, but he benefited from patronage appointments and remained active in Republican Party affairs, becoming secretary of the Republican State Central Committee in 1887. He championed the cause of industrial education and was prominent in Booker T. Washington's National Negro Business League, which was dedicated to improving the economic status of African Americans and building up the black community. Gibbs also remained active in the cause of civil rights for African Americans.

Gibbs political career peaked in 1897, when President William McKinley appointed him U.S. consul to Madagascar, where he served for four years. He published his memoir, *Shadow and Light,* in 1902, and died on July 11, 1915, in Little Rock.

Kevin Butler

See also: Canada.

Further Reading

Gibbs, Mifflin Wistar. *Shadow and Light: An Autobiography With Reminiscences of the Last and Present Century.* Lincoln: University of Nebraska Press, 1995.

Kilian, Crawford. *Go Do Some Great Thing: The Black Pioneers of British Columbia.* Vancouver, British Columbia: Douglas & McIntyre, 1978.

Lapp, Rudolph M. *Blacks in Gold Rush California.* New Haven, CT: Yale University Press, 1977.

Giddings, Joshua Reed
(1795–1864)

A Whig and Free Soiler who served as one of Ohio's representatives in the U.S. Congress from 1838 to 1859, Joshua Reed Giddings held radical antislavery views and became one of the first individuals to join the new Republican Party.

Giddings was born on October 6, 1795, in Bradford County, Pennsylvania, the youngest of seven children of farmers Joshua Giddings and Elizabeth Pease. Giddings had an unsettled and poverty-stricken childhood. The family moved to Canandaigua, New York, a week after his birth; there, Giddings did not attend school but instead worked on the failing family farm. In 1805, the family moved to Wayne, in Ohio's Western Reserve region, an area filled with poor New Englanders. Giddings continued to forego education in order to help with farm chores, but he did manage to obtain a grammar book and taught himself the rudiments of reading and writing. After six months' service in the War of 1812, Giddings returned home to discover that his father had gone bankrupt.

Rather than pursue a future in farming, in 1814, Giddings accepted a part-time teaching position at a local grammar school and devoted himself to study. In 1818, he joined the law office of the socially prominent Federalist Elisha Whittlesey. Upon passing the bar, Giddings settled in Jefferson, the seat of Ashtabula County.

The success of Giddings's law practice prompted him to take a partner in Benjamin Wade, a future U.S. senator. However, the two men became estranged at about the same time that Giddings lost his considerable investments in Western lands during the panic of 1837. In 1838, Giddings ran successfully on the Whig ticket, succeeding Whittlesey as the congressman from Ohio's Sixteenth District.

Like many former Federalists, Giddings held a deferential view of government. He believed that men of social standing and conservative habits should make decisions for the good of the nation. Giddings was never a fan of Andrew Jackson; his heroes were John Quincy Adams, Henry Clay, and Daniel Webster. In Congress, he joined Adams in his campaign against the congressional "Gag Rule," a measure enacted in the House of Representatives to silence floor discussion of slavery. Believing slavery to be exclusively a state matter, he opposed any federal measures that could be construed as supporting it.

Engraved by Jos. I. Pease.

A Whig from Ohio, Joshua Reed Giddings resigned as a U.S. congressman in 1842, after being censured for introducing a series of antislavery resolutions. Re-elected that same year, he served until 1859 as a key figure in the House debate over slavery. *(Hulton Archive/Getty Images)*

Giddings's views on slavery can be traced to his religious background. Like many New Englanders, the Giddings family belonged to the Congregational Church. But Giddings participated in the Second Great Awakening, a religious revival that swept through Ohio in the 1820s. By the time he entered Congress, Giddings felt a religious imperative to work for the moral improvement of the people around him. In his writings, he dwelled on the spiritual peace to be derived from acting on one's Christian duty to humanity. Giddings abandoned his support for sending African American to colonies in Africa and became a militant abolitionist. Like many other abolitionists, he also embraced the temperance movement wholeheartedly.

During the 1830s, the people of the Western Reserve became rampantly anti-Southern in their opinions, and Giddings reflected the views of his constituents. He had little interest in compromising with Southerners and angered party chieftains by voicing his antislavery views. In Congress, Giddings argued against the Second Seminole War (1835–1842), which he believed the government had waged at the South's behest in order to protect slavery.

In 1842, Giddings introduced his "Creole resolutions," which asserted the right of slaves on the high seas to rebel. In response, an angry House censured him and Giddings resigned. Within a month, his district overwhelmingly re-elected him. Giddings's return to Congress demonstrated that antislavery politicians could not be stifled, nor could sectional politics be prevented. Although Giddings was pressured to moderate his stance by the Whig leadership, he continued to embrace his radical antislavery views, becoming the political spokesman for abolitionist leader William Lloyd Garrison and his followers.

Giddings opposed the annexation of Texas and the Mexican-American War (1846–1848). In the House, he argued that annexation would destroy the old Union and, as a result, the familiar constitutional defense of slavery as a state's right would no longer applied. At this time, he based his antislavery stance on religious law rather than man-made legislation. He often spoke of the justice of slave insurrection and the duty of Northerners to aid rebel slaves.

Giddings failed in his lengthy effort to convert the Whig Party to his own advanced antislavery position. In 1848, he left the Whigs when the party chose General Zachary Taylor, hero of the Mexican-American War, as its presidential candidate. Giddings joined the new Free Soil Party; after the passage of the Kansas-Nebraska Act in 1854, he helped lead the Free Soilers to the Republican Party.

Declining health forced Giddings to retire from Congress in 1859. In 1861, President Abraham Lincoln rewarded him with an appointment as consul general to Canada. Giddings held this position until 1864; he died in Montreal on May 27 of that year.

Caryn E. Neumann

See also: Free Soil Party; Second Great Awakening.

Further Reading

Stewart, James Brewer. *Joshua R. Giddings and the Tactics of Radical Politics.* Cleveland, OH: Press of Case Western Reserve University, 1970.

Gilbert, Ann Taylor (1782–1866)

Best known as the author of children's nursery rhymes and songs, British author Ann Taylor Gilbert also wrote a number of poems and songs with a decidedly antislavery theme. In addition, she was one of the founding members of the first abolitionist society in Nottingham, England.

Ann Taylor was born in London on January 30, 1782, the eldest daughter of Ann Martin Taylor and Isaac Taylor. Her father, an engraver by trade, apprenticed his children in the same profession so that they could later support themselves, and Ann enjoyed scribing at an early age. At age four, she moved with her family from London to Lavenham, Suffolk, where her father taught the children at home while serving as a minister to a Nonconformist congregation. By age seven, Ann was occupying herself with literary projects, writing a new version of several *Psalms* and the *Iliad.*

In 1798, she published her first volume of poetry, *The Minor's Pocket Book,* and began developing a longstanding relationship with the publishers Darton and Harvey. In 1804, the same publisher printed *Original Poems for Infant Minds,* a compilation of poems by Ann and her sister Jane. In addition to becoming two of England's best-known and most widely read children's poets, together they produced two published essays, several short stories, an autobiography, and a novel.

Ann, known for her humor and love of puns, revealed her childlike spirit in her poems. Subsequent poetry works followed *Original Poems,* including *Rhymes of the Nursery* (1806) and *Hymns for Infant Minds* (1810). Among the sisters' most remembered works are Jane's 1804 classic "The Star," better known as the children's song "Twinkle, Twinkle Little Star," and Ann's 1806 poetic tribute to the slave mother. In "The Mother," Ann used attributes of white femininity and masculinity to construct the image of a female slave. She advocated Christian conversion and emancipation while extolling the importance of marriage, motherhood, and family. In *Rhymes of the Nursery,* Ann published an antislavery verse, "The Little Negro," about a young boy stolen from his home and taken into slavery.

Ann moved with her family to Ongar, Essex, in 1811 and took up writing articles. She had stubborn religious convictions but was considered even-tempered and had a charitable disposition that contributed to her love and talent for children's writing. Admiring Ann's poetic skills, the Reverend Josiah

Gilbert wrote to her in 1812 and asked to meet her. The two were married a year later.

Josiah Gilbert worked as a classics tutor in Rotherham before taking a position as a Congregationalist pastor in Hull, where the pair moved in 1817, eventually settling in Nottingham in 1825. For forty years, Ann and Josiah had busy religious, social, and domestic lives.

Although raising a family cut into the time she could dedicate to writing, Ann Gilbert maintained a relationship with literary circles in Sheffield, Hull, and Nottingham. Her personal and public writing reflected her local and national activism in political and social movements, such as the abolition of British and colonial slavery; the repeal of the Corn Laws, which protected wealthy landowners by encouraging the export of corn when prices fell; and the establishment of free libraries.

After the passage of the Slave Trade Act in 1807, new antislavery organizations sprang up across England. On April 8, 1825, a meeting held to discuss the role of women in the antislavery movement led to the founding of the Birmingham Ladies' Society for the Relief of Negro Slaves. Independent groups formed across the country, and Gilbert organized the antislavery organization in Nottingham. She published several pamphlets on abolitionism and contributed to *The Bow in the Cloud* (1834), a 1,400-page volume of antislavery essays and prose edited by Mary Anne Rawson.

Widowed in 1852, Gilbert continued to live in Nottingham until her death on December 20, 1866. Her son, Josiah Gilbert, Jr., finished her autobiography using a collection of her letters, and it was published as *Autobiography and Other Memorials of Mrs. Gilbert (Formerly Ann Taylor)* posthumously in 1874.

Howell Williams

See also: Women's Rights and the Abolitionist Movement.

Further Reading

Hubert, Miriam Blanton. *Story and Verse for Children.* 3rd ed. New York: Macmillan, 1965.

Kunitz, Stanley J., ed. *British Authors of the Nineteenth Century.* New York: H.W. Wilson, 1936.

Gordon, George William (1820–1865)

A minister, businessman, and political leader of postemancipation Jamaica, George William Gordon inspired—though he did not take part in—the Morant Bay Rebellion of 1865, during which Jamaicans resisted the power and authority of the colonial government.

Gordon was born in 1820 in Saint Andrew, Jamaica. He was the son of Joseph Gordon, a Scottish planter who came to the island in the early nineteenth century, and a slave woman who bore him several children. After Joseph Gordon married, he refused to allow any of these children to enter the great house on his estate. It does appear, however, that he bought the freedom of his common-law wife and their children.

Joseph Gordon nevertheless recognized that his son was a highly intelligent and gifted student. He gave George schoolbooks from which the boy taught himself to read and write. George Gordon showed promise as an orator, and from an early age he participated in religious debates. Although he was raised in Jamaica as an Anglican, Gordon eventually joined the Presbyterians and was baptized by the Baptists. In the early 1840s, he started an independent Baptist organization and built the Kingston Tabernacle, where he often preached.

Early in life, Gordon established himself as a successful businessman. He concentrated on buying and leasing lands, which he divided and sold or rented cheaply to the black peasants, as most whites refused to sell lands to them.

Gordon's entered public life in 1844 when he became a member of the Jamaican House of Assembly, the colonial legislature, where he often spoke on behalf of the poverty-stricken black peasants. This advocacy alienated many of his black middle-class peers. He was also instrumental in the establishment of the Jamaica Mutual Life Society, an insurance company, of which he became a trustee. Gordon was regularly appointed to committees on matters of finance, and more than once he was deputized as mayor.

Gordon's prominent role in Jamaican history, however, stems from his association with Paul Bogle, whom Gordon had ordained as a deacon in the Baptist church and who would later lead the Morant Bay Rebellion of 1865. By that time, the social and economic crisis in Jamaica had peaked: The black peasantry and laboring class had many complaints against the colonial government, which they believed was ultimately responsible for the discrimination and exploitation that were rampant in Jamaica's black wage labor system.

Access to land was severely restricted among the black working class, and any petitions for improvement or change were denied. When the peasants in Saint Ann's Bay sent a letter to Britain's Queen

Victoria asking for Crown lands to be rented, Victoria's answer nonchalantly recommended steady and continuous work on the plantations rather than "any such schemes" (i.e., the renting of land).

Gordon was among those who vigorously criticized the colonial administration and Governor Edward John Eyre for injustices and wrongful conduct. In a manifesto credited to Gordon and published in reaction to Queen Victoria's response, the following call was posted to the peasantry:

> People of St. Ann's, Poor People of St. Ann's, starving people of St. Ann's, you who have no sugar estates to work on nor can find other employment, we call on you to come forth, and protest against the unjust representations made against you by Governor Eyre and his band of Custodes. You don't require custodes to tell your woes; but you want men free of government influence—you want honest men—you want men with a sense of right and wrong who can appreciate you.

The term "unjust representations" suggests there was a general belief among the poor that the colonial government had framed the peasants' complaint in such way as to lead Victoria to answer in stark terms, which many actually thought were not her own words. Following the rebellion and violence in Morant Bay, the manifesto gave Eyre an excuse to have Gordon arrested and illegally court-martialed in 1865.

Gordon was nowhere in sight during the violent events that unfolded in the eastern part of the island. He was in ill health in the capital city of Kingston, and he privately and publicly protested all accusations of his guilt. Although he supported the protest, his politics would not have permitted the use of violence.

On October 21, 1865, Gordon was tried for treason, and, two days later, he was hanged. He was posthumously bestowed with the title of National Hero, Jamaica's highest honor, and Gordon House, the seat of Jamaica's legislature in Kingston, was named for him.

Holger Henke

See also: Bogle, Paul; Morant Bay Rebellion (1865).

Further Reading

Heuman, Gad J. *The Killing Time: The Morant Bay Rebellion in Jamaica.* Knoxville: University of Tennessee Press, 1994.
Semmel, Bernard. *Jamaican Blood and Victorian Conscience: The Governor Eyre Controversy.* Boston: Houghton Mifflin, 1962.
Sheller, Mimi. *Democracy After Slavery: Black Publics and Peasant Radicalism in Haiti and Jamaica.* Gainesville: University Press of Florida, 2000.

Gradualism

Abolitionists in the transatlantic world were never of a single mind regarding the most efficient and effective means of bringing an end to slavery. The most radical antislavery advocates supported the notion of instant emancipation, or "immediatism," whereas conservative abolitionists favored a more moderate notion of emancipation over time, or "gradualism."

Even among those who advocated a gradual approach, opinions varied widely. The gradualists as a group—and the abolitionist movement as a whole—no doubt suffered as a consequence of such dissent.

Ideological Roots

Many advocates of gradualism rooted their ideology in the belief that society could not cope with the social, political, and economic consequences that would result from the immediate emancipation of the slaves. Such a change, proponents argued, could be more effectively managed by allowing time to permit the kinds of adaptation necessary for the transition from a slave-based economic system to one based entirely on free labor.

In addition, racist notions prevailed among some antislavery advocates who genuinely opposed the horrors of slavery yet did not consider themselves the social and political equals of the emancipated slaves. The gradualist ideology thus sought to soften the fear of racial amalgamation that prevailed among many in the transatlantic world.

The notion that society copes better with evolutionary change than with revolutionary change was the primary underpinning of the gradualist philosophy. The lessons of history supported such an idea: Slavery had disappeared in ancient societies such as Greece and Rome, gradualists argued, only when it became economically disadvantageous and socially untenable. Such historical precedents, rooted in the ideology of change over time, made the gradualist approach appealing to many in the antislavery movement.

The gradualists also believed that some type of education and training would be necessary to prepare emancipated slaves for life and labor beyond slavery. Advocates argued that some form of tutorship or apprenticeship would be necessary to complete the social and economic transformation from slavery to freedom, and they believed that doing so over a period of time was more manageable than doing it at once. Proponents believed that a corps of trained freedmen could become effective teachers and mentors to others who would be freed in subsequent waves. This was the thinking behind the efforts of the British government when it abolished slavery throughout its colonial possessions in 1833 but in its place instituted a five-year system of apprenticeship to shepherd the freedmen to their new lives as wage laborers.

Methods

The roots of gradualist thought can be found in the methods that several states employed to abolish slavery at the end of the American Revolution. All states from Pennsylvania north ended slavery, but each—with the noticeable exception of New York—incorporated elements of gradualism into its emancipation scheme. New Jersey, for example, announced the date on which emancipation would take effect but allowed slave owners within the state to sell their slaves to owners in the South, where slavery persisted.

Methods varied as to how slavery might be ended according to a gradualist model. Some argued that passing a law freeing all children born to slave mothers might be an effective means of ending slavery. Others believed that setting a target age at which slaves would become free was a better approach. Brazil, for example, passed a law that freed all slaves at the age of sixty. However, both methods belied the hypocrisy of gradualism, as the purported emancipation of infants and the elderly did nothing immediately to free the many adults who labored as slaves during the prime of life.

In the United States, some abolitionists who subscribed to the gradualist approach were also active supporters of the American Colonization Society, founded in 1816. The idea of liberating slaves over the course of time while encouraging free blacks to emigrate to Liberia seemed to work well for the gradualists but this approach was vehemently criticized by the more radical abolitionists who opposed both gradualism and colonization. Opposition to colonization was so intense that by the 1830s, many antislavery supporters had distanced themselves from the American Colonization Society.

The battle between gradualism and immediatism became especially heated in the 1820s. In 1824 and 1825, legislatures in eight of the twelve free states passed measures urging the federal government to take steps to bring an end to slavery. All eight proposals called for a gradualist approach that combined elements of compensated emancipation and colonization outside the United States as components of national emancipation. Although the U.S. Congress took no action on any of these proposals, the measures had the unanticipated consequence of energizing the radical abolitionists who favored immediate emancipation and believed gradualism to be anathema.

Immediatists charged that if slavery was indeed evil, it was inconceivable that one could oppose the institution while working to prolong it. The question of gradualism versus immediatism quickly divided the abolitionists, and passions on both sides were charged by polemical attacks. In England, the Quaker Elizabeth Heyrick wrote an influential pamphlet titled *Immediate, Not Gradual Emancipation* in 1824, as Parliament began to consider the fate of slavery in the British colonies. In America, radical abolitionists such as William Lloyd Garrison believed that gradualists were effectively in league with slaveholders, as both groups sought to perpetuate an institution that was rooted in sin.

Though other questions also divided abolitionists—most notably, the role of women and their rights in the abolitionist movement and in society at large—the long-standing debate between the gradualists and the immediatists created a chasm within the antislavery movement that made unified action impossible. Although the abolitionists were a small but vocal minority in the early nineteenth century, the clarity of their message and the overall effectiveness of their efforts were diminished by factional infighting.

When emancipation did come in the United States, it was based on the immediate, uncompensated model that Garrison and other radical abolitionists had long promoted.

Junius P. Rodriguez

See also: Apprenticeship and Emancipation; Heyrick, Elizabeth; Immediatism.

Further Reading

Davis, David Brion. *From Homicide to Slavery: Studies in American Culture.* New York: Oxford University Press, 1986.

Gellman, David. "Pirates, Sugar, Debtors, and Slaves: Political Economy and the Case for Gradual Abolition in New York." *Slavery and Abolition* 22 (August 2001): 51–68.

MacLeod, Duncan J. "From Gradualism to Immediatism: Another Look." *Slavery and Abolition* 3 (September 1982): 140–52.

Stirn, James R. "Urgent Gradualism: The Case of the American Union for Relief and Improvement of the Colored Race." *Civil War History* 25 (December 1979): 309–28.

Grandy, Moses (ca. 1786–?)

Moses Grandy labored for more than forty years as a slave in North Carolina before he was able to purchase his freedom in 1833. Abolitionist supporters later published his autobiography, *Narrative of the Life of Moses Grandy; Late a Slave in the United States of America* (1843), which describes in detail his experience as a former slave in Camden, North Carolina, and southeastern Virginia. The title page of the autobiography promises readers that the work was "published and sold for the benefit of his relations still in slavery." Grandy planned to use the profits from the book to assist him in purchasing the last of his children who were still enslaved near New Orleans. Grandy became a popular lecturer on the abolitionist circuit in the United States and Great Britain, often referencing experiences from his autobiography.

Grandy was born in Camden County, North Carolina, about forty miles from the Atlantic Ocean. He was owned by Bill Grandy and later by his son James Grandy, who hired Moses out as a day laborer on the area waterways. Over the course of several years, Grandy became an experienced waterman. Working from the port of Camden on the Pasquotank River, he plied the waters as a river ferryman, pilot, and sailor on schooners on the Albemarle Sound and as captain of a canal boat in the Dismal Swamp. As a slave possessing these specialized skills, Grandy was able to find much work and earned profits for his owner, as well as for himself.

Grandy begins his autobiography by noting that he never had a true family, because he was the youngest child and his older brothers and sisters had been sold to other plantations. He mentions nothing of his parents, so it is likely that he never knew them. Grandy later recounted the heartbreak he experienced seeing his own wife and children sold to other owners, perhaps never to be seen again. Grandy would spend much of his adult life trying to purchase the freedom of his wife and children, one by one, so that he could reunite his family.

In his narrative, Grandy recounts that he purchased his own freedom three times before he was finally emancipated in 1833. On the first two occasions, unscrupulous owners took $600 from him and then sold him to another owner. Slaves such as Moses Grandy had no legal recourse, because they did not have the right to sue their owners in a court of law.

When he finally obtained his freedom, Grandy moved to Providence, Rhode Island, and later Boston, Massachusetts, where he found work as a merchant seaman. He traveled to the West Indies and the Mediterranean. He saved his earnings and began the process of locating lost family members and buying them out of slavery.

Grandy visited Great Britain in 1842 on an abolitionist speaking tour. He was highly recommended to the British abolitionists by several Maine and Massachusetts abolitionists, including Ellis Gray Loring, who wrote letters of introduction on his behalf. British abolitionists George Thompson and John Scoble became his patrons, and Grandy was well received at all of the venues at which he spoke on behalf of the British and Foreign Anti-Slavery Society.

Grandy's autobiography was a hugely successful and influential work of antislavery literature. One edition was published in London and another in Boston; the latter edition went through three printings and became one of the most popular antislavery accounts of the 1840s.

Junius P. Rodriguez

See also: Manumission.

Further Reading

Andrews, William L., ed. *North Carolina Slave Narratives: The Lives of Moses Roper, Lunsford Lane, Moses Grandy, and Thomas H. Jones.* Chapel Hill: University of North Carolina Press, 2003.

Grandy, Moses. *Narrative of the Life of Moses Grandy; Late a Slave in the United States of America.* 1843. Chapel Hill: Academic Affairs Library, University of North Carolina, 1996.

Great Awakening

The term *Great Awakening* refers to a series of religious revivals that took place among Protestant Christian communities throughout the transatlantic world during the eighteenth century. Taken as a whole, these moments of religious awakening drastically altered Protestant American styles of preaching and worship.

The first localized movements of the evangelical spirit occurred among the Dutch Reformed and Presbyterian churches in New Jersey and the Congregational churches in Connecticut. In 1740, however, these isolated revivals began to coalesce around the "Grand Itinerant" George Whitefield. Whitefield, a contemporary of John Wesley at Oxford, toured the New England colonies spreading a message of repentance and conversion. He used his mastery of speaking and acting to express his idea of "new birth," an emotional reorientation of an individual's soul toward God.

James Davenport, a resident of Connecticut and a Yale graduate, elaborated on Whitefield's preaching style, compelling worshippers to convey their experiences of rebirth through extreme emotional outbursts. By 1743, Charles Chauncy and other conservative ministers were condemning the fanaticism of Davenport and his followers. Jonathan Edwards, a friend of Whitefield's and a pre-eminent theologian of the mid-eighteenth century, responded more moderately, combining the emotion of conversion with the discipline of formal worship and clerical authority.

The Great Awakening coincided with an escalation in the transatlantic slave trade. The radical relocation of slaves from Africa to the Americas put untold stress on African religious systems—or, as historian Jon Butler put it, created an "African spiritual holocaust."

Many colonists of European descent, particularly the Anglicans of Virginia, relied on church institutions to validate their planter ethic of total superiority over slaves through violent and paternalistic means. When preachers such as Whitefield introduced slaves to the spiritually liberating concept of new birth, slaveholders responded with suspicion and malevolence. Although fewer slaves lived in New England than in the middle and Southern colonies, Whitefield and other itinerant preachers of the 1740s took special consideration of black participation at revivals. "God will highly favour them," Whitefield wrote, "to wipe off their reproach, and shew that He is no respecter of persons."

By 1755, Samuel Davies and Shubal Stearns had taken the lead among itinerant preachers in saturating Virginia with the message of new birth, regardless of gender or race. Opponents of religious enthusiasm viewed the mixed gatherings as a "promiscuous" affront to the social order. Proponents regarded the

George Whitefield, the English evangelist and founder of Methodism, carried the revivalist message of the Great Awakening to the American colonies in the 1740s. Black slaves joined in revival meetings with whites and were treated as religious equals. *(Hulton Archive/Getty Images)*

meetings as an opportunity to free souls from the bondage of worldly transgressions.

For the first time since their enslavement, some African Americans achieved a sense of spiritual equality with their white counterparts. Blacks and whites shared the spiritual experiences of conversions, sacraments, and ecstatic visions. Mechal Sobel, a historian of colonial America, dubbed the product of such racial interaction "the world they made together." The Christian ideas of sin, Trinitarian God, afterlife, and prayer made sense to many slaves who subscribed to traditional African religions. Moreover, African styles of worship, which relied heavily on dancing and singing, altered the staid European expressions of religious sentiment.

The racially mixed gatherings of Protestant evangelicals, however important their effects were to the introduction of spiritual equality in the American religious landscape, garnered only limited support from a society that was heavily invested in the institution of slavery. Many masters allowed missionaries to catechize their slaves, but they doubted the positive effects of slave conversions on plantation productivity. It was in their interest to reduce the collective and individual autonomy of slaves. Religious gatherings and personal religious experiences threatened the slaveholders' ideas of white superiority. While some white evangelicals retained the belief that blacks deserved equal status under God, the strong planter elites convinced most Protestant Christians to support the slave regime. As a result, the missionary message of new birth shifted to emphasize the doctrine of absolute obedience, thus increasing the level of violence and punishment that the slaves endured.

White evangelicals tried to separate the ideas of worldly equality and spiritual equality, but it was only a matter of time before slaves made their own, more empowering interpretations of Christianity. Slaves chose either to challenge the Christian system of beliefs and practices or to accept them as a vehicle for group solidarity and individual sovereignty. Those who defied the oppressive message of absolute obedience, as historian Ira Berlin has argued, were a testament to the slaves' ability to insulate themselves from complete domination. Those who accepted American Protestantism changed it to convey their own understanding of their position in the world. Christianity produced a new sense of inner freedom among slaves and compelled them to identify themselves as a separate community, a distinct people with their own past,

present, and future. The Great Awakening thus sowed the seeds of group identity and self-validation among African Americans.

By 1760, with the introduction of the evangelical message of new birth and the rise of the slave regime, two kinds of Christianity consumed the American colonies—a white Christianity and a black Christianity. The Christianity of white Protestants did not promote the abolition and emancipation of slaves. The Christianity appropriated by blacks, however, focused on the ideas of racial equality, individual dignity, and group solidarity. Blacks sowed their own seeds of abolition and emancipation.

Michael Pasquier

See also: Religion and Abolitionism.

Further Reading

Berlin, Ira. *Many Thousands Gone: The First Two Centuries of Slavery in North America.* Cambridge, MA: Belknap Press, 1998.

Butler, Jon. *Awash in a Sea of Faith: Christianizing the American People.* Cambridge, MA: Harvard University Press, 1990.

Gaustad, Edwin Scott. *The Great Awakening in New England.* New York: Harper, 1957.

Sobel, Mechal. *The World They Made Together: Black and White Values in Eighteenth-Century Virginia.* Princeton, NJ: Princeton University Press, 1987.

Great Postal Campaign

The Great Postal Campaign, initiated by the American Anti-Slavery Society in May 1835, was a massive effort to disseminate antislavery literature across the nation, using the U.S. postal system as the means of distribution. The controversy associated with the plan polarized views of both pro- and antislavery advocates, doing little to stimulate the informed discussion that abolitionists had hoped to spark through their efforts. The campaign also raised questions of states' rights, as local authorities in the South sought to censor the mail to prohibit the distribution of any propaganda that supported the antislavery cause—literature that they believed endangered the public peace and the security of their region.

Designed "to sow the good seed of abolition thoroughly over the whole country," in the words of abolitionist Lewis Tappan, the Great Postal Campaign involved the expenditure of $30,000 by the American Anti-Slavery Society to distribute more than 1 million pieces of abolitionist literature. The vast majority of items were sent to Northern churchmen in the hope that they would join the antislavery cause and proselytize the merits of the movement to their congregations. Only about 20,000 items were sent to the Southern states, but it was not the intent of the abolitionists to place the materials into the hands of slaves and free blacks in the South. Instead, these items were specifically addressed to people of influence throughout the South, including ministers, elected officials, and newspaper editors.

Only two years old, the American Anti-Slavery Society was still a fledgling organization seeking to expand its membership and attract financial backers to the cause of abolition. The Great Postal Campaign was largely a public relations effort designed to attract converts to the cause and engender a national dialogue on the question of slavery.

The American Anti-Slavery Society developed a wide array of abolitionist literature to appeal to readers in the South. These publications included the small folio newspaper *Human Rights*; a magazine called the *Anti-Slavery Record*; copies of *The Emancipator*, an abolitionist newspaper; and a reader for children titled *The Slave's Friend*. Despite the best plans and intentions of the Northern abolitionists, however, few of these items were ever delivered to the persons to whom they had been addressed.

The abolitionists had unreasonable expectations for the Great Postal Campaign. Many antislavery advocates believed in the power of moral suasion to make individuals see the error of their ways and change their attitudes. Many early Quaker abolitionists had courageously traveled into the South, where they conducted person-to-person conversations with slaveholders and tried to use the power of reasoned argument to convince these individuals to emancipate their slaves through manumission. The abolitionists believed, somewhat naively, that the arrival of unsolicited abolitionist literature in the mail would influence the opinions of individuals whose views had become ever more strident.

Southern officials lambasted the abolitionists for sending "incendiary literature" through the mail and charged that the real purpose of the campaign was to foment slave insurrection throughout the South. In cities all across the South, local postmasters took it upon themselves to censor the mail that had been sent by the Northern abolitionists. A mob raided the post office in Charleston, South Carolina, on July 29, 1835, and removed the suspected abolitionist materials from the premises. The following evening, a Charleston mob burned effigies of William Lloyd Garrison and Tappan, using the stolen abolitionist newspapers as bonfire material.

In his 1836 Message to the Congress, President Andrew Jackson sided with the Southern advocates of states' rights, who maintained that they were entitled to censor the mail and remove the abolitionist literature. Jackson urged the passage of "such a law as will prohibit, under severe penalties, the circulation in the Southern states, through the mail, of incendiary publications intended to instigate the slaves to insurrection." When Postmaster General Amos Kendall, a proslavery advocate, was questioned about the extralegal measures taken by Southern postmasters, he replied, "We owe an obligation to the laws, but we owe a higher one to the communities in which we live."

Free blacks living in the South became the unintended victims of the Great Postal Campaign as Southern legislatures enacted stricter codes regulating the liberties that were afforded that group. Many in the South feared that the true purpose of flooding the mail with abolitionist literature was to get it into the hands of free blacks, who could then place it—or the radical ideas contained therein—into the hands and hearts of slaves. There was rampant fear in many parts of the South in 1835–1836 that conspiracies between free blacks and slaves might be afoot. In several states, authorities placed militias on alert to mitigate the likelihood of a slave insurrection.

The high-minded abolitionist plan that moral suasion through the dissemination of abolitionist literature would sway the minds of Southern slaveholders failed. Nevertheless, the abolitionists may have gained ground as a result of the national controversy catalyzed by the Great Postal Campaign.

The campaign was more successful in the Northern states. Many individuals who had not previously subscribed to Garrison's newspaper, *The Liberator*, began to do so, and the membership rolls of the American Anti-Slavery Society experienced a growth spurt.

Junius P. Rodriguez

See also: American Anti-Slavery Society; Garrison, William Lloyd; Tappan, Arthur; Tappan, Lewis.

Further Reading

Filler, Louis. *The Crusade Against Slavery, 1830–1860.* New York: Harper & Row, 1960.

Stewart, James Brewer. *Holy Warriors: The Abolitionists and American Slavery.* New York: Hill and Wang, 1996.

Wyatt-Brown, Bertram. "The Abolitionists' Postal Campaign of 1835." *Journal of Negro History* 50 (October 1965): 227–38.

Wyly-Jones, Susan. "The 1835 Anti-Abolition Meetings in the South: A New Look at the Controversy Over the Abolition Postal Campaign." *Civil War History* 47:4 (2001): 289–309.

Greeley, Horace (1811–1872)

The American journalist and political leader Horace Greeley is perhaps best known as the founder of the influential *New York Tribune*. A crusader for the moral improvement of the United States, Greeley spoke out in favor of modest social reform and against slavery in the pages of the *Tribune* and, as a member of the House of Representatives, in the halls of the U.S. Congress. Throughout his life, Greeley's nationalism and liberal economic ideology guided his antislavery beliefs. Even though he was a professed abolitionist, he consistently favored industrial and commercial development over drastic social experimentation.

Greeley was born in Amherst, New Hampshire, on February 3, 1811, to Zaccheus and Mary (Woodburn) Greeley, poor farmers who moved several times during Horace's youth. His formal education ended at age fifteen, when he apprenticed himself to a printer in East Poultney, Vermont. During this time, Greeley became interested in the antislavery and temperance movements. When the paper closed in 1830, he headed west to Pennsylvania to work for the *Erie Gazette.* The next year, he moved to New York, where he and Jonas Winchester eventually founded the weekly *New Yorker* in 1834.

Raised in Federalist New England, Greeley was an early supporter of the Whig Party, which New Yorkers such as William Seward had formed in opposition to the Jacksonian Democrats. In the pages of the *New Yorker,* Greeley supported the national bank, industrialization, and African colonization; he decried abolitionism and the women's movement. Keenly aware of the centrality of industrialization to American social problems, he also began to promote Western migration as a "safety valve" for the urban classes. Greeley briefly published two Whig papers, the *Jeffersonian* and the *Log Cabin,* and wrote for the *Daily Whig.* He first published the *New York Tribune* in April 1841; within a year, it was selling more than 10,000 copies daily.

Greeley's editorials promoted moderate economic reforms such as manual training, Western settlement, and Fourierism (a social reform movement that promoted small, self-sustaining communes). Initially not an abolitionist, the ambivalent reformer feared that immediatism would make slavery a nationally divisive issue. For the most part, he simply wanted to eliminate the plantation system from the American economy in order to facilitate the development of railroads and westward expansion.

Greeley later claimed in his autobiography, *Recollections of a Busy Life* (1868), that Texas's independence and the assassination of Elijah P. Lovejoy in 1837 had converted him to abolitionism: "It was thenceforth plain to my apprehension, that Slavery and true Freedom could not coexist on the same soil." However, in the early 1840s, the *Tribune* clearly valued national unity over antislavery activism. Greeley argued against the acquisition of Texas and Oregon in 1844 in order to preserve the Union, and only the impending war with Mexico pushed him to argue for abolition. At an 1851 antislavery conference in London, Greeley contended that the best way to eliminate slavery was to reform the Southern economy and raise the status of white workers throughout Europe and the United States.

As founder and editor of the *New York Tribune*, Horace Greeley brought his antislavery message to hundreds of thousands of readers. The *Tribune* became the unofficial organ of the Republican Party, which Greeley helped found in 1854. *(Library of Congress)*

After his election to the House of Representatives in 1848, Greeley proposed (among other measures) a bill to eliminate the slave trade in the District of Columbia. He supported Henry Clay's 1849 omnibus bill, which aimed to keep Texas from claiming the New Mexico Territory. He was less enthusiastic, however, when Senator Stephen Douglas transformed the bill's provisions into the Compromise of 1850, which contained the notorious Fugitive Slave Law. Greeley also opposed the Douglas-sponsored Kansas-Nebraska Act of 1854, which repealed the Missouri Compromise. In response, the *Tribune* lambasted Southern economic backwardness and the institution of slavery.

Following the passage of the Kansas-Nebraska Act, Greeley and other Whigs began agitating for a new political party to support free labor and to repudiate the expansion of slavery. The new Republican Party formed in summer 1855, while Greeley was in Europe. The party opposed Douglas's Democrats, and Greeley vocally promoted the admission of Kansas to the Union as a free state.

In 1856, he supported John C. Frémont for the Republican nomination rather than the veteran William Seward, with whom he had developed an antagonistic relationship. Greeley wrote *History of the Struggle for Slavery Extension or Restriction in the United States* to support the ticket. Although the Republicans did not win the presidency, the new party garnered 114 of 296 electoral votes.

Greeley's antislavery stance became even more pronounced during the years of President James Buchanan's administration, especially after the U.S. Supreme Court made its ruling in the *Dred Scott v. Sandford* case in 1857. His editorials maligned Chief Justice Roger B. Taney and rhetorically warned that the decision would result in New York slave markets. Greeley also opposed the proslavery Kansas (Lecompton) Constitution, and the *Tribune* collected more than $20,000 to relieve the sacked antislavery stronghold in Lawrence. After the 1859 raid on the federal arsenal at Harpers Ferry, Virginia, and radical abolitionist John Brown's subsequent execution, Greeley advocated the peaceful abolition of slavery to curtail the encroaching federal influence of slave owners. Never a staunch supporter of Abraham Lincoln, in 1860, Greeley promoted Edward Bates of Missouri for the Republican presidential nomination over both Seward and Lincoln.

At the outset of the U.S. Civil War, Greeley declared that the government should not try to "coerce" the seceding states. He privately believed that they would remain in the Union and publicly claimed that the federal compact was irrevocable. His compromise called for both sides to agree not to spread slavery into the territories.

After the fall of Fort Sumter, however, the *Tribune* vigorously supported the war and began advocating the end of both slavery and the "slave power." In 1862, Greeley even chided Lincoln for hesitating to emancipate the slaves. Greeley began writing a history of the war, titled *The American Conflict* (published in two volumes in 1864 and 1866). In early 1864, he lobbied for peace so that American economic prosperity could once more claim top priority, and he reluctantly supported Lincoln's 1864 re-election campaign.

Greeley was a long-standing proponent of the antislavery movement who ultimately endorsed abolitionism, but his ideas about race were fairly moderate. His biographer noted that during the war, the *Tribune* editor fought discrimination and supported black suffrage in New York, but he saw it as "primarily a national rather than a humanitarian interest." During Reconstruction, Greeley opposed the radical program of Thaddeus Stevens; instead, he favored universal amnesty and sectional reconciliation, as well as gradual suffrage for freed slaves. Freedmen could best help themselves, he argued, by purchasing land or taking advantage of the Homestead Act, which gave vast amounts of public land to citizens who were willing to settle it. With the election of Ulysses S. Grant in 1868, Greeley proclaimed Reconstruction a success, even though he simultaneously acknowledged that social equality was probably not a realistic eventuality for Southern blacks, even if political equality was.

In 1872, Greeley became a compromise presidential candidate under the banner of the Liberal Republicans and the Democrats, who both opposed the corruption and perceived anti-Southern inclination of Grant's presidency. Greeley, called "Old Honesty," campaigned on a platform of nationalism, but he won only six states and 44 percent of the popular vote. He died on November 29, 1872, in Pleasantville, New York.

Brian M. Ingrassia

See also: Lincoln, Abraham.

Further Reading

Fahrney, Ralph R. *Horace Greeley and the Tribune in the Civil War.* 1936. New York: Da Capo, 1970.

Greeley, Horace. *Recollections of a Busy Life.* 1868. Port Washington, NY: Kennikat, 1971.

Isely, Jeter Allen. *Horace Greeley and the Republican Party, 1853–1861: A Study of the New York Tribune.* New York: Octagon, 1965.

McPherson, James M. "Grant or Greeley? The Abolitionist Dilemma in the Election of 1872." *American Historical Review* 71 (October 1965): 43–61.

Van Deusen, Glyndon G. *Horace Greeley: Nineteenth-Century Crusader.* New York: Hill and Wang, 1953.

Grégoire, Abbé Henri (1750–1831)

Abbé Henri Grégoire was a Catholic priest and radical activist who supported efforts to reform the Roman Catholic Church and French society that began during the French Revolution. In the process, he developed arguments for the emancipation of all oppressed peoples and the abolition of the slave trade. Both Europeans and Americans, according to Grégoire, debased the humanity of Jews and people of African descent. He took great strides toward reducing racial and religious prejudices by promoting the natural rights of all people. Despite his humanitarian positions, Grégoire believed that the social and economic uplift of oppressed peoples required their assimilation into European republicanism and Christianity. He attacked the institutions of slavery and anti-Semitism but disrespected many of the cultural and religious traditions of Jews and blacks.

The son of a peasant, Grégoire was born on December 4, 1750, in Vého, near Lunéville, France. Educated at the Jesuit college at Nancy, Grégoire became a Jesuit priest, and, in 1789, he was elected to the Estates-General, a French congress comprising different classes (or estates) of French citizens. He quickly established himself as a supporter of the French Revolution and a proponent of the union of the three estates.

Although the pope had condemned it, Grégoire took the oath of the Civil Constitution of the Clergy, becoming the first constitutional bishop of Blois in 1791. The following year, during the first session of the National Convention, France's legislative assembly, Grégoire proposed that kingship be abolished, stating that "kings are in the moral order what monsters are in the natural."

Jews and blacks represented two of the most oppressed peoples in the transatlantic world during the eighteenth and nineteenth centuries. In the 1780s and 1790s, Grégoire argued for the full incorporation of Jews into French society, blaming Christians for their social and economic persecution. To "regenerate" the humiliated religious minority, he proposed the equal-ization of civil rights regardless of religious tradition. The process of regeneration, however, also included an expectation of ultimate conversion to Christianity.

Grégoire considered the United States an ideal arena for the inclusion of Jews into society because its constitution separated church and state. During the 1820s, Grégoire joined American Jews in the promotion and founding of a Jewish state on an island near Buffalo, New York, called Ararat. The settlement failed, but Grégoire sealed his reputation as an ally of the Jewish community.

A passionate advocate for the emancipation of slaves and the abolition of the transatlantic slave trade, Grégoire argued in the French National Convention and National Assembly for racial equality. He also participated in the *Société des Amis des Noirs* (Society of Friends of the Blacks) as a supporter of gradual abolitionism and a correspondent with the Anti-Slavery Society of Philadelphia.

After Napoleon Bonaparte re-instated the institution of slavery in the French Caribbean colonies in 1802, Grégoire supported the establishment of an independent Haitian nation from 1815 to 1827. The small island state represented a tabula rasa for the full integration of blacks into society and, in his words, a "beacon elevated from the Antilles towards which slaves and their masters, oppressed and oppressors, turn their regards." The process of "civilizing" the previously enslaved black population, however, required that the island's unique culture and racial mix be replaced by Grégoire's paternalistic version of European society.

Following the re-establishment of slavery, Grégoire published his *De la litterature des negres* (1808), which was translated into English in 1810 as *An Enquiry Concerning the Intellectual and Moral Faculties and Literature of Negroes.* In this work, Grégoire maintained that differences among the races did not result from any sort of natural racial superiority but from climate and historical events and circumstances. His work profiled great people of African descent in order to convey that blacks, given the opportunity, were capable of extraordinary intellectual achievement. Though it was mocked by Napoleon's circle, the book was well received among the black and mixed-race leaders of the newly independent Haiti, and a popular American version published in the 1830s helped rally a new generation of Americans to the abolitionist cause.

Grégoire espoused a universal conception of humankind in which all people share a common human race. It was the obligation of Christians and republican governments, he maintained, to affirm fundamental human rights through movements toward liberation, emancipation, and enlightenment. "All men have an innate right to liberty and happiness," Grégoire wrote, "but nevertheless the annals of the globe offer only the picture of unfortunate people in chains." The Catholic priest's ideas of universal equality, however, were limited by his intolerance for multiculturalism. As a result, he promoted a system of assimilation to curb diversity and to homogenize the cultural and political dimensions of the Jewish and black communities.

When he died on May 20, 1831, the Catholic Church treated the republican reformer as a schismatic. On the bicentennial of the French Revolution in 1989, the French government transferred Grégoire's remains to a national monument as a symbol of church–state support for human rights activism.

Michael Pasquier

See also: Enlightenment; French West Indies, Abolition and Emancipation in the; Haitian Revolution (1791–1804).

Further Reading

Briere, Jean-Francois. "Abbé Grégoire and Haitian Independence." *Research in African Literatures* 35 (Summer 2004): 34–43.

Grégoire, Henri. *On the Cultural Achievements of Negroes.* Trans. Thomas Cassirer and Jean-Francois Briere. Amherst: University of Massachusetts Press, 1996.

Popkin, Jeremy D., and Richard H. Popkin, eds. *The Abbé Grégoire and His World.* Dordrecht, Netherlands: Kluwer Academic, 2000.

Griffing, Josephine (1814–1872)

Josephine Sophie White Griffing is best known for her work as a freedmen's aid reformer, though she also had an active career as an abolitionist in her adopted state of Ohio. Like many women who worked with former slaves, Griffing was also an advocate for women's rights. She was active in the movement for women's suffrage and, albeit briefly, in the National Woman Suffrage Association.

Born in Hebron, Connecticut, on December 18, 1814, Josephine moved to Ohio in 1842, five years after her marriage to Charles Stockman Spooner Griffing. Their home in Litchfield, Ohio, was a stopping point on the Underground Railroad, and both she and her husband were active in the Western Anti-Slavery Society. She was a popular antislavery lecturer in the Midwest and wrote articles for the Western Anti-Slavery Society's newsletter, the *Anti-Slavery Bugle.*

During the U.S. Civil War, Griffing joined the Loyal League, a group of women who petitioned the U.S. Congress to free the slaves after the war had started. The work for which she is most noted—supporting former slaves and lobbying on their behalf in Washington, D.C.—grew out of her efforts as an abolitionist.

Griffing moved to Washington with her three daughters in 1863 and began working with the former slaves who had migrated there. As a member of the National Freedmen's Relief Association, she campaigned tirelessly for passage of the Freedmen's Bureau bill, which established the federal agency to address all matters concerning refugees and freedmen within the states under Reconstruction. After its passage in 1865, she became an assistant to the assistant commissioner of the Freedmen's Bureau for the District of Columbia. Her appointment was revoked in November of that year, however, because of her private attempts to raise funds for former slaves who found themselves destitute in Washington. She continued her efforts to assist former slaves by establishing and running a school for freedwomen and by overseeing the distribution of food, clothing, and fuel to freedmen and women.

Griffing transported former slaves to the North, where she had friends who helped them find jobs and places to live. In 1867, she went back to work as an employment agent for the Freedmen's Bureau and, in support of women's suffrage, helped organize the Universal Franchise Association of the District of Columbia, later becoming its president. She died in Washington, D.C., on February 18, 1872.

Mary J. Jarvis

See also: Freedmen's Bureau; Women's Rights and the Abolitionist Movement.

Grimké, Angelina Emily (1805–1879)

Born into an affluent slaveholding family in Charleston, South Carolina, Angelina Emily Grimké became a leading opponent of slavery during the late 1830s. Outspoken by nature and endowed with a charismatic personality, she was a woman of many firsts: She was the first female to publicly debate a man on the issue of slavery and, in 1837, she became the first woman to speak before a state legislature (Massachusetts) on behalf of women. Accompanied by her older sister, Sarah, she became a successful female abolitionist agent, addressing audiences of men and women throughout New York and New England as she agitated for the cause.

Angelina Grimké was outraged by the treatment of women within the abolitionist movement—specifically, the prohibition against women speaking publicly—and she joined Sarah in speaking out for women's rights. Grimké's husband, Theodore Dwight Weld, a noted abolitionist and leader of the New York Anti-Slavery Society, later joined the sisters in their antislavery crusade.

Early Life

When Angelina was born on February 20, 1805, Sarah, who was thirteen years old at the time, was named her godmother. In the large household of eleven children, Sarah took responsibility for caring for the baby, and the sisters became so close that Angelina frequently called Sarah "Mother." When Sarah moved to Philadelphia in 1821, Angelina remained behind in Charleston. She frequently embarrassed her family and astonished her friends and neighbors by speaking her mind on all subjects, particularly slavery, and by refusing to accept her assigned place as a young, upper-class Southern woman.

In April 1826, Angelina left the Episcopal Church to join the Presbyterian Church, where she continued to cause discontent. Uncomfortable with Presbyterianism and influenced by Sarah's conversion to Quakerism, Angelina visited the local Quaker meetinghouse; she was expelled from the Presbyterian Church for having been so outspoken. Not knowing how to react to her daughter's unconventional boldness, in late 1829, Mary Grimké agreed to let Angelina join her sister in Philadelphia, where Angelina was accepted into Sarah's meetinghouse. In Philadelphia, Angelina was exposed to abolitionist newspapers for the first time, and, in February 1835, she attended her first meeting of the Pennsylvania Female Anti-Slavery Society.

In August 1835, a mass antislavery meeting was set to take place in New York City. Approximately 17,000 white Southern men converged on the city in response to the growing opposition to slavery. Afraid for their lives—there were rumors that paid assassins had been imported from New Orleans—many prominent abolitionists barricaded themselves inside their homes. The radical abolitionist William Lloyd Garrison called it a "reign of terror."

After reading about the events in New York, Grimké realized that she had to speak out against slavery. She wrote to Garrison, expressing her own strong, abolitionist views. Garrison, who owned the influential abolitionist newspaper *The Liberator,* realized the value of having a white Southern woman speak out against slavery, and he published her letter without her knowledge. Within a few months, she was known throughout the abolitionist movement. In fact, her name became so well known that she was banned from Charleston and never returned home.

Abolitionist Agent

Angelina Grimké had a gift for public speaking. Her powerful, well-modulated voice often swayed her audience with her enthusiasm for the abolitionist cause. In 1836, the Grimké sisters set out on a lecture tour, Angelina assuming the role of public speaker and Sarah working behind the scenes to research and write their speeches and abolitionist pamphlets. Unused to women in such public roles, newspapers described Angelina as "a pretty Quaker" who was "in need of a [male] protector."

Though they originally addressed only groups of women, the sisters soon began speaking to mixed audiences, stirring more controversy as they challenged the accepted norms of female behavior. On November 28, 1838, during the last speech of one of their tours in Philadelphia, an angry mob did not deter Angelina from speaking. When Pennsylvania Hall was emptied of antislavery delegates after her speech, the proslavery mob broke down the doors and set the building on fire. Others tried to attack the abolitionists in their own homes. As their lecture tour drew to a close, Angelina became ill with typhoid. Despite these personal upsets, the Grimké sisters established themselves as prominent abolitionists, and dozens of antislavery societies were formed in the wake of their lecture tour.

Neither Angelina nor Sarah was happy in their Quaker meetinghouse, whose conservative leaders frequently prevented them from speaking. The sisters left Philadelphia, and, in October 1836, they moved to New York City and became active in the New York Anti-Slavery Society. They quickly recognized the irony of a movement that advocated the rights of black men while denying rights to women within its ranks. Both sisters began to speak out for women's rights, influencing young feminists such as Elizabeth Cady Stanton, Lucretia Mott, Susan B. Anthony, Lucy Stone, and Abby Kelley Foster, who became part of the nascent women's rights movement.

Though Angelina and Sarah agreed in their views on slavery and women's rights, their approaches were different. Angelina formed her arguments along political lines, whereas Sarah presented her points along moral and theological lines. Angelina saw it as immoral and irrational that Christians should advocate slavery, claiming a biblical basis for their actions. She pointed out that separating families and destroying marriages were particularly un-Christian behaviors. These arguments were the backbone of their speeches and writings.

In 1836, Angelina Grimké's abolitionist pamphlet, *Appeal to the Christian Women of the South,* called for Southern women to read about slavery, pray about the subject, talk with others about how they felt, and then act on their convictions. Grimké suggested that women who owned slaves should free them and pay them wages if they retained them as servants. She asked Southern women to question what they had been taught about the biblical basis of slavery: "I would just ask whether American slaves have become slaves in any of the ways in which the Hebrews have become servants." Whereas the Hebrew people had been subjugated as a result of their own actions, she argued, the American slaves had been victimized. South Carolina officials publicly burned the document. In 1837, Grimké wrote its companion pamphlet, *Appeal to the Women of the Nominally Free States.*

That year, the Grimké sisters toured Congregational churches in the Northeast, where they not only denounced slavery but also spoke out against racial prejudice and argued that white women had a natural bond with black female slaves. These two concepts were extreme even for radical abolitionists, and their public speaking continued to draw criticism, making the Grimkés more zealously feminist.

Responding to an attack by Catherine Beecher, daughter of the radical Presbyterian minister Lyman Beecher, Angelina Grimké wrote a series of letters, later published as *Letter to Catherine Beecher* (1838), in which she challenged Beecher's traditional views on women's roles: "I believe it is a woman's right to have a voice in all the laws and regulations by which she is to be governed, whether in Church or State." She cited Miriam, Deborah, and Huldah as biblical examples of women who had participated in the public sphere.

Grimké's second letter to Beecher summarized her objections to slavery. Laws that legitimized slavery were "flagrant violations" of basic democratic principles because slavery "subverts justice, promotes the welfare of the few to the manifest injury of the many, and robs thousands of the posterity of our forefathers of the blessings of liberty." Grimké completed the yearlong speaking tour with an address to the Massachusetts legislature.

The sisters' antislavery efforts culminated in the publication of *American Slavery As It Is: Testimony of a Thousand Witnesses* (1839), which was edited by Weld and contained firsthand testimony by Angelina and Sarah. Angelina wrote that growing up in Charleston, she had "felt that there could be no rest for me in the midst of such outrage and pollution." She recalled their next-door neighbor whipping a young female slave so badly that, in her efforts to escape, she fell from a second-story window to the sidewalk and broke her hip. Another horror story concerned a child who had died after being beaten and falling from a table where she had been placed with her feet fastened in stocks. Another child had been blinded in one eye from a savage beating. Harriet Beecher Stowe later named *American Slavery As It Is* as the most important influence on her antislavery novel *Uncle Tom's Cabin.* Stowe wrote to Angelina that she slept with the book beside her bed.

After the publication of *American Slavery As It Is,* the Grimké sisters continued to circulate antislavery petitions, but they did not embark on any further speaking tours on behalf of the antislavery cause. Instead, they took various teaching positions and worked in the women's rights and temperance movements.

Marriage and Later Life

In May 1938, Angelina married fellow abolitionist Theodore Dwight Weld, a Presbyterian. The sisters were read out of the Society of Friends after the marriage: Angelina was disowned for marrying outside her faith, whereas Sarah was rejected for attending Angelina's wedding.

Angelina gave birth to her first son, Charles Stuart Weld, on December 14. Two years later, her husband purchased a fifty-acre farm in New Jersey, and the Welds, accompanied by Sarah, took up residence there. After giving birth to Theodore Grimké Weld in January 1841 and Sarah Grimké Weld in March 1844, Angelina's health began to suffer.

Because of this, Sarah took over caring for the children, and they looked to her rather than to their mother for nurturing. Although she encouraged the close relationship between her sister and her children, Angelina's jealousy created a rift between the sisters. Nonetheless, they lived together for most of their lives and retained a close bond.

In 1848, Weld established the Bellville Boarding School, where the Grimké sisters became teachers. After the school closed, Weld was asked to take charge of the Eagleswood School at the Raritan Bay Union, a utopian community, and Angelina and Sarah returned to the classroom. In 1863, the entire family moved to West Newton, Massachusetts, where the sisters taught at Diocletian Lewis's Young Ladies' Boarding School until it burned down in 1867.

After the birth of her children, Angelina Grimké continued to experience health problems that curtailed her activities. Despite her virtual retirement from public life, she continued to exercise an influence on the abolitionist and women's movements. In 1863, she gave her last public lecture at the convention of the Women's National Loyalty League. Six years after Sarah's death, Angelina died on October 26, 1879.

Elizabeth Purdy

See also: Grimké, Sarah Moore; Weld, Theodore Dwight.

Further Reading

Birney, Catherine H. *Sarah and Angelina Grimké: The First American Women Advocates of Abolition and Women's Rights.* New York: Haskell House, 1970.

Ceplair, Larry, ed. *The Public Years of Sarah and Angelina Grimké.* New York: Columbia University Press, 1989.

Lerner, Gerda. *The Grimké Sisters From South Carolina: Pioneers for Woman's Rights and Abolition.* New York: Schocken, 1983; Chapel Hill: University of North Carolina Press, 2004.

Lumpkin, Katherine Du Pre. *The Emancipation of Angelina Grimké.* Chapel Hill: University of North Carolina Press, 1974.

Grimké, Charlotte Forten (1837–1914)

One of the most prominent African American women in the abolitionist movement, Charlotte Forten Grimké used her talents as a journalist to advance the antislavery cause. During the U.S. Civil War, she spent time in the Sea Islands of South Carolina helping former slaves make the transition to freedom and economic independence.

The granddaughter of the wealthy African American sailmaker James Forten, Charlotte was born in Philadelphia on August 17, 1837. Both her father, Robert Forten, and her grandfather were ardent abolitionists. In addition, her grandmother, Charlotte Vandine Forten, and aunts were founding members of the Philadelphia Female Anti-Slavery Society, the country's first biracial organization of women abolitionists, and her uncle, Robert Purvis, had achieved fame as an antislavery lecturer. Because of the Forten family's long-standing commitment to abolitionist activism, leading spokesmen for the abolitionist movement such as William Lloyd Garrison, Harriet Martineau, and William C. Nell, regularly visited the Forten and Purvis homes. Such an atmosphere undoubtedly shaped Charlotte Forten's commitment to the cause.

In 1854, after being excluded from the whites-only Philadelphia private schools, Forten moved to Salem, Massachusetts, where she attended the Higginson Grammar School and Salem Normal School. There, she boarded with the family of Charles Lenox Remond, one of the most well-known African American abolitionist orators of the period. His house was a hotbed of abolitionist activity, and she established friendships with several of the prominent figures in the movement who came to visit, including a longtime friend of her family, John Greenleaf Whittier.

In Salem, Forten also took part in organized antislavery activities. She attended abolitionist meetings and lectures and joined the Salem Female Anti-Slavery Society, where she worked to promote abolitionism through raising money and discussing the subject with others. She also had the opportunity to hear other prominent speakers and writers of the day, such as Ralph Waldo Emerson and Massachusetts senator Charles Sumner.

An aspiring writer, Forten worked as a correspondent for the *National Anti-Slavery Standard* newspaper. She also composed a musical anthem for the March 5, 1858, festival held both to commemorate the death of African American Revolutionary War hero Crispus Attucks and to denounce the 1857 *Dred Scott* decision. Her works were published in antislavery publications such as *The Liberator* and *Anglo African* magazine.

Deeply concerned about the plight of enslaved African Americans, Forten traveled to the South in 1862 to play a more active role in the process of emancipation. Later that year, she arrived at Port Royal, South Carolina, territory that was then controlled by the Union army and home to thousands of African Americans who resided on nearby plantations.

As a member of what was called the Port Royal "experiment," Forten was charged with the task of proving to a skeptical white Northern populace that former slaves could be educated.

Ignoring the health problems that had long plagued her, Forten taught large classes of children during the day and equally large classes of adults in the evening. She recorded her experiences in her diary and in letters that she wrote to Whittier, confessing, "I long to inspire them with courage and ambition (of a noble sort), and high purpose." Her descriptions of freedmen and women who were bright, hardworking, and eager to learn were published in a lively essay, titled "Life on the Sea Islands," in the *Atlantic Monthly* in 1864.

As she began teaching, Forten found that many of the students spoke only Gullah, a Creole blend of Elizabethan English and African languages that had developed in the slave communities of the coastal South. Most were unfamiliar with the disciplines of formal schooling. Although she strived to forge a bond with the islanders, her upbringing and education set her apart, and she had to work at integrating herself into the community. Under physical and emotional stress, Forten contracted smallpox in 1864 and left South Carolina.

Forten returned to Massachusetts, where she convalesced and then worked as a secretary for the teacher's committee of the New England branch of the Freedmen's Aid Society. Her poor health prevented her from returning to the South in the 1860s; however, during the 1870s, she spent time working in Charleston, South Carolina, and Washington, D.C., where she became a clerk in the U.S. Treasury Department. In 1878, Forten met and married Francis J. Grimké, a former slave and Presbyterian minister who was the nephew of white Quaker abolitionists Sarah and Angelina Grimké.

Charlotte Forten Grimké spent the rest of her life traveling with her husband, ministering to freedmen and women in the South, and publishing essays that were critical of American racism. She died on July 23, 1914.

Erica L. Ball

See also: Forten, James, Sr.; Port Royal Experiment; Purvis, Robert.

Further Reading

Bethel, Elizabeth Rauh. *The Roots of African-American Identity: Memory and History in Free Antebellum Communities.* New York: St. Martin's, 1997.

Billington, Ray Allen. *The Journal of Charlotte L. Forten: A Young Black Woman's Reactions to the White World of the Civil War Era.* New York: W.W. Norton, 1981.

Stevenson, Brenda, ed. *The Journals of Charlotte Forten Grimké.* New York: Oxford University Press, 1988.

Winch, Julie. *A Gentleman of Color: The Life of James Forten.* New York: Oxford University Press, 2002.

Yee, Shirley. *Black Women Abolitionists: A Study in Activism, 1828–1860.* Knoxville: University of Tennessee Press, 1994.

Grimké, Sarah Moore (1792–1873)

At a time when most Southern white women were content to focus on domestic matters, Sarah Grimké became a leader in the abolitionist movement and laid the groundwork for the early women's right movement, which would be launched by Elizabeth Cady Stanton and Lucretia Mott at the Seneca Falls Convention in 1848. Along with her younger sister, Angelina, she dared to stand up for what she thought was right, even when it meant forsaking her home in Charleston, South Carolina, or speaking out in public in places where women had never raised their voices before.

Early Life

Grimké was born on November 26, 1792, to a wealthy Charleston family that owned a number of slaves. Her father, Judge John Fauchereau Grimké, was a member of the South Carolina Supreme Court and known throughout the state for his independent views. Rejecting the prevalent notion that women did not need an education, Judge Grimké allowed Sarah to be taught by tutors alongside her brother Thomas; she learned mathematics, geometry, world history, Greek, natural science, and botany.

Grimké was also required to learn the skills that were considered proper for upper-class Southern white women: spinning, weaving, fancywork, beadwork, reading, writing, arithmetic, and French. When she expressed a desire to become a lawyer, however, her father refused. She began studying the law in secret and continued to think about attending law or medical school until a few years before her death. Despite her wide-ranging instruction, Sarah always regretted her lack of formal education. Although her mother, Mary Grimké, was more traditional in her view of women's roles than either of her daughters, she was an intelligent, independent thinker and served as a role model for her daughters. The whole family frequently took part in lively debates about contemporary issues.

At loose ends after Thomas's departure for Yale when she was thirteen years old, Sarah concentrated her energies on her newborn sister, Angelina, and asked to be her godmother. She served as a maternal figure for her sister, so much so that Angelina called Sarah "Mother" for much of their lives. Sarah was shy and never made decisions without thinking about the consequences of her actions; Angelina was more outgoing and self-confident. Each sister lent her own strengths to the relationship, which remained unusually close throughout their lives. In their public lives as reform advocates, Angelina would become better known as a public speaker, whereas Sarah took responsibility for the greater part of their research and would establish herself as a gifted writer.

As a young woman, Sarah Grimké experienced the only frivolous period of her life, enjoying Charleston's social life. When her father became ill in 1818, she believed that her own sinfulness had been the cause and accompanied him to Philadelphia to see a specialist who was a Quaker. Knowing that Judge Grimké's condition was hopeless, the doctor sent him to the New Jersey seashore, where he died in 1820. On the way home to Charleston, Sarah met Israel Morris, a Quaker who would have a strong influence on her life; she later converted to the Quaker faith.

In May 1821, Sarah left Charleston for Philadelphia to pursue what she believed was a calling to become a Quaker minister. She would return to Charleston only for visits, the last of which took place in 1831. In Philadelphia, Sarah moved in with Morris's sister and became a member of the Fourth and Arch Street Meeting of the Pennsylvania Society of Friends.

Even at an early age, Grimké realized that slavery was wrong. Any time a slave was punished in the Grimké household, the family found her weeping. At the age of five, she inadvertently saw a slave being beaten and was later found at the Charleston docks with the idea of running away to a place that was free of the evils of slavery. Shortly before her death, she wrote to a friend that she had always found slavery "a millstone about my neck, and it marred my comfort from the time I can remember myself."

The only slave Grimké ever owned was a young girl who was given to her as a personal servant. She taught the slave to read and write, even though such an act was punishable in South Carolina by a fine of £100. When the young girl died, Grimké was inconsolable and vowed never to own another.

Rise to Prominence

Grimké became a leader in the abolitionist movement at a time when women had few legal rights. The system of coverture dictated that a married woman ceded her legal identity to her husband. Though single women had more legal rights than married women, they were often placed under the guardianship of their fathers. Throughout the United States, women lacked the right to vote and were expected to embrace wholeheartedly the domestic realm of hearth and home.

Believing that God had called her to be a minister in the Society of Friends, Grimké was devastated when her local meetinghouse refused to let her speak in meetings. Philadelphia was home to two separate groups of Quakers, and Sarah and Angelina were members of the orthodox group, which wanted to keep women in traditional roles. Lucretia Mott, who also lived in Philadelphia, was a well-known minister of the Hicksite sect, a more liberal group of Quakers.

The Grimké sisters were attracted to William Lloyd Garrison's radical antislavery movement, which called for the immediate emancipation of slaves, the education of former slaves, and an end to all racial prejudice. The Grimkés refused to stop speaking out publicly for women's rights, and some historians have argued that they precipitated a break in the antislavery movement between those who wanted to focus on black rights and those who saw the two causes as interrelated. The radical element of the antislavery movement fell in behind Garrison, whereas the orthodox members followed Lewis Tappan, Henry Stanton, and James G. Birney. The Grimkés had already developed close ties with Garrison's group, but Theodore Dwight Weld, whom Angelina married in 1838, was more in tune with the traditionalists. As a result of the schism, the three temporarily withdrew from their active roles in the abolitionist movement.

Though Angelina was devoted to the women's rights movement, the antislavery movement remained her focus. Sarah, on the other hand, developed a well-researched theory on women's rights and called attention to women's legal inequality. With the modern feminist movement more than a century off, she called for equal pay for women doing equal work. Like the English philosopher John Stuart Mill, she argued that society paid a great price for failing to recognize the contributions of half the human race. At one point during their first lecture tour, more than 500 people crowded into city hall in Lowell, Massachusetts, to hear Sarah and Angelina speak on abolitionism and women's rights.

In 1836, after a Quaker elder told her to sit down when she rose to pray in a meeting, Grimké felt that she had been released from the call to ministry. She and her sister moved to New York City and became the first female agents of the New York Anti-Slavery Society. In May 1837, they attended the first Anti-Slavery Convention of American Women in New York.

The sisters soon became engrossed in separate writing projects: Angelina began work on *Letter to Catherine Beecher*, a scathing rejection of slavery and women's traditional roles. Sarah worked on *Letters on the Equality of the Sexes and the Condition of Women*, a well-researched theoretical perspective on the legal status of women. Both works were published in 1838.

In her *Letters*, Sarah Grimké argued that the patriarchal system was a result of tradition rather than scripture. She challenged men to refrain from contributing to the tyranny of women: "All I ask our brethren is that they will take their feet from off our necks, and permit us to stand upright on that ground which God designed us to occupy." Grimké referred her readers to the creation story in Genesis, in which, she noted, "there is not one particle of difference intimated as existing between" male and female. On the contrary, both were "made in the image of God, dominion was given to both over every other creature, but not over each other." She further contended that because women had suffered from men's teachings for centuries, they were no longer bound to follow their instructions.

In *An Epistle to the Clergy of the Southern States* (1836), Grimké called particular attention to Psalm 8, which, she maintained, "affords irrefragable proof that God never gave to man dominion over his own wife." In verses 6 through 8, she noted that the psalmist acknowledges man's dominion over "all things under his feet, All sheep and oxen, And also the beasts, The birds of the heavens and the fish of the sea." Woman, however, is not identified as being under the dominion of man. Grimké denounced the notion that Abraham had been a slaveholder, maintaining that the basis for American slavery could be found not in the Bible, as so many Southerners proclaimed, but in England, where slave trading began in 1563.

In 1839, Sarah and Angelina Grimké helped Weld compile *American Slavery As It Is: Testimony of a Thousand Witnesses*. As part of her contribution, Sarah recalled growing up in South Carolina in the midst of slavery, noting that "the lashes and shrieks of tortured victims" continued to "come over my memory like gory specters." She had never forgotten seeing the head of an executed slave mounted on a pole, intended to serve as a deterrent to other errant slaves.

She told of beatings and other ill treatment at the hands of Charlestonian elites who read the Bible on a daily basis and attended church regularly yet saw no contradiction between their professed Christian beliefs and their ill treatment of slaves. One of Sarah's more harrowing tales concerned the practice of forcing a slave to stand on one foot while holding the other foot in hand for hours at a time. In addition to being beaten, slaves were sometimes starved into submission while the law and Charleston society pretended not to notice.

Though Grimké's contributions to the abolitionist movement were most prominent between 1836 and 1838, her influence continued to be felt in both the women's rights and antislavery movements. Her writings were a direct influence on feminists of her day and continue to provide an understanding of the abolitionist movement and the theoretical and theological foundations of feminism. She died on December 23, 1873.

Elizabeth Purdy

See also: Grimké, Angelina Emily; Weld, Theodore Dwight.

Further Reading

Birney, Catherine H. *Sarah and Angelina Grimké: The First American Women Advocates of Abolition and Women's Rights.* New York: Haskell House, 1970.

Ceplair, Larry, ed. *The Public Years of Sarah and Angelina Grimké.* New York: Columbia University Press, 1989.

Lerner, Gerda. *The Feminist Thought of Sarah Grimké.* New York: Oxford University Press, 1983.

———. *The Grimké Sisters From South Carolina: Pioneers for Woman's Rights and Abolition.* New York: Schocken, 1983; Chapel Hill: University of North Carolina Press, 2004.

Grinnell, Josiah B. (1821–1891)

As a journalist, abolitionist, social reformer, and political figure, Josiah Bushnell Grinnell helped to advance the antislavery cause in the decades prior to the U.S. Civil War. By the 1850s, he had become one of the most prominent abolitionists in the Midwest.

Grinnell was born in New Haven, Vermont, on December 21, 1821. Although his early education was scanty, he started teaching school at a young age. In 1841, Grinnell entered Yale College. Daunted by Yale's classical curriculum and conservatism, Grinnell transferred to the Oneida Institute in Whitesboro, New York, where he entered the manual labor seminary.

The school's manual labor ideology purported that combining productive physical activity with evangelical spirit would bring about the Christian millennium. In 1834, Oneida had provided the Lane Seminary of Cincinnati, Ohio, with its famous class of antislavery "rebels," which included Theodore Dwight Weld and other prominent abolitionists. At Oneida, Grinnell participated in lively student debates on abolitionism and temperance.

After completing his studies at Oneida in 1843, Grinnell moved to Milwaukee, Wisconsin, where he distributed literature for the American Tract Society and wrote for Horace Greeley's *New York Tribune.* However, the restless Grinnell soon decided to pursue a ministerial education, and he entered the Auburn Theological Seminary in Auburn, New York. The school was known for its conservative Presbyterian tenor, but the increasingly radical Grinnell nonetheless graduated in 1846.

Grinnell became pastor of a Congregationalist church in the integrated upstate New York town of Union Village, where he remained for five successful years. In 1851, he moved to Washington, D.C., and organized the new Trinity Church. Grinnell disdained the city's slave society, President Millard Fillmore's administration, and Congress's recent passage of the Fugitive Slave Law, which gave slave owners the right to recapture runaway slaves and mandated that both civil servants and private citizens must assist them. He quickly gained disfavor by delivering antislavery sermons, and rumor spread throughout the capital that he had helped slaves escape. Grinnell was soon forced to depart for New York City.

In New York, Grinnell once more worked as a writer for the *Tribune,* during which time he was a recipient of Greeley's famous advice to "Go West." While covering the Illinois State Fair for Greeley, Grinnell befriended Henry Farnham of the Rock Island Railroad, who made Grinnell a director of his new Mississippi and Missouri Railroad.

Upon settling in Iowa, Grinnell began advertising in New York newspapers for a planned utopian community and college. In March 1854, he and several other investors and future colonists began surveying a 5,000-acre site in central Iowa. Situated on the route of Farnham's railroad, this land became the town of Grinnell.

In February 1856, Grinnell was instrumental in forming Iowa's Republican Party in response to the imminent threat of slavery's expansion. Grinnell served as a state senator from 1856 to 1860. During his two

The Congregational minister and journalist Josiah Grinnell heeded the advice of Horace Greeley to "Go West, young man" and settled in Iowa. He founded the town of Grinnell and became a leading figure in the Midwestern abolitionist movement. *(Library of Congress)*

terms, he advocated free soil, equal education for blacks, temperance legislation, and the founding of a state agricultural college in Ames. He was not renominated in 1860, possibly because of the widespread unpopularity that he gained by harboring radical abolitionist John Brown and his men overnight in early 1859.

In 1860, Grinnell initially supported presidential hopeful William Seward, but the Iowa delegate met Abraham Lincoln at the Chicago convention and soon became the nominee's friend and proponent. Grinnell served in Chicago as an agent of the Post Office Department during the first two years of the Civil War and acted as a confidant to President Lincoln.

In 1862 and 1864, Grinnell was elected as an Iowa representative to the U.S. House of Representatives. In Congress, Grinnell was influenced by Thaddeus Stevens and became a member the Radical Republicans. He promoted railroad expansion, advocated the enlistment of blacks in the Union army, and supported the Thirteenth Amendment, which abolished slavery as a legal institution. However, Grinnell's alliance with the Radical Reconstruction faction, which demanded that 50 percent of the Southern states' voters pledge loyalty to the Union before being re-admitted and that former slaves be allowed to vote, likely cost him his political career.

On June 14, 1866, following venomous floor debates over the Freedmen's Bureau Bill, representative Lovell H. Rousseau (R-KY) mockingly caned Grinnell on the steps of the U.S. Capitol. Several observers noted that Grinnell did not strike Rousseau, which made him appear weak and unmanly to many voters; he was not renominated for the congressional seat.

Indeed, Grinnell was unable to successfully navigate politics for the rest of his life. He sought the Republican gubernatorial nomination in 1867 and Iowa's senatorial seat in 1869 but achieved neither. Grinnell left the mainstream Republican Party in the 1870s; he supported Horace Greeley's failed Liberal Republican bid for the presidency in 1872 and ran for an Iowa state legislature seat as a member of the Greenback Party in 1879. In 1880, he returned to the Republicans, supporting James Garfield's successful presidential election.

Ultimately, Grinnell represented the Republican Party's early devotion to free soil and railroads. He died in Grinnell, Iowa, on March 31, 1891.

Brian M. Ingrassia

See also: Greeley, Horace.

Further Reading

Payne, Charles E. *Josiah Bushnell Grinnell.* Iowa City: State Historical Society of Iowa, 1938.

Gronniosaw, James Albert Ukawsaw (ca. 1712–1775)

Following his enslavement in Africa, transportation across the Atlantic, and service in the French West Indies, James Albert Ukawsaw Gronniosaw, a native of west-central Africa, became an influential abolitionist throughout the transatlantic world. Gronniosaw is best known as the author of *A Narrative of the Most Remarkable Particulars in the Life of James Albert Ukawsaw Gronniosaw, An African Prince, As Related By Himself* (1772). This account of the self-styled "James Albert" influenced the genre of black abolitionist literature, which exposed Europeans to the atrocities of slavery while revealing the humanity of the native Africans.

Gronniosaw's *Narrative* influenced many notable black abolitionists, including John Marrant, Quobna Ottobah Cugoano, and Olaudah Equiano. Although Gronniosaw introduced himself to the literate public as a man who had been wrongfully enslaved, he opened the door for others to broaden the abolitionist debate by considering the immorality of slavery, its inconsistency with Christianity, and the economic expense of a mercantilist system dependent on coerced labor.

Gronniosaw's life is shrouded in mystery, and the details are related primarily in his autobiography. As the work's title suggests, his royal background ("an African Price") was exceptional. As the grandson of the king of Bornu and a member of a large royal household, Gronniosaw experienced great privilege. His status as the king's grandson undoubtedly provided him access to travel and educational opportunities; in his autobiography, he notes that he was "a curious turn of mind." Although he identifies his mother as the eldest daughter of the king of Zarra, he provides no further details of his country's history. During Gronniosaw's lifetime, Bornu was the principal city and political center of the Kanem-Bornu Empire, which achieved great prosperity and stability beginning in the sixteenth and continuing to the early eighteenth century.

Gronniosaw's enslavement appears to have been motivated by political rather than economic reasons. According to his account, he departed the city of Bornu to travel to Guinea as the guest of an ivory merchant from the Gold Coast (present-day Ghana), who had well-established ties to the royal court. Though he relates his departure as the result of personal unhappiness with his family situation, his family undoubtedly believed that his travels would provide the young Gronniosaw with access to education and a chance to develop better diplomatic relations with Guinea. Once he arrived in Guinea, however, the local king threatened to execute him as a spy and enslaved him. In subsequent weeks, he was sold to a European merchant and transported across the Atlantic, where he was sold in Barbados and then carried to New York.

In New York, Gronniosaw worked as a kitchen servant; he was manumitted shortly before his second master's death, around 1748. After working as a cook on an American privateer and serving as a soldier in the British army in Martinique in 1762, he moved to London, eventually settling in Kidderminster, England.

Gronniosaw related his story to an unidentified young Englishwoman, who later helped arrange for its publication in Bath, England, in December 1772. At least twelve editions of Gronniosaw's *Narrative* had appeared by 1800, including printings in Dublin, New York City, and Rhode Island.

Although Gronniosaw's was not the first account by an African to be published in Western Europe, the narrative had an influence on both the abolitionist movement and the genre of black abolitionist writing. In contrast to works by former slaves such as Ignatius Sancho and Phillis Wheatley, Gronniosaw's work did not aim to prove the intellectual equality of Africans to Europeans but to evidence the immorality of slavery. Although critics have often cited Gronniosaw's use of themes such as the "noble savage," others have cited its universal appeal and depth of history, containing "matter well worthy the notice and attention of every Christian reader," as its preface states.

After its publication, Gronniosaw's *Narrative* encouraged other Africans residing in London, most notably Cugoano and Equiano, to agitate more forcefully for the abolition of the slave trade. After more than two centuries, his account remains one of the most important surviving black narratives of the transatlantic slave trade.

Mark S. Quintanilla

See also: Cugoano, Quobna Ottobah; Equiano, Olaudah; Sancho, Ignatius.

Further Reading

Andrews, William L., and Henry Louis Gates Jr., eds. *Slave Narratives.* New York: Library of America, 2000.
Taylor, Yuval, ed. *I Was Born a Slave: An Anthology of Classic Slave Narratives.* Chicago: Lawrence Hill, 1999.

Grosvenor, Cyrus Pitt (1792–1879)

The Reverend Cyrus Pitt Grosvenor was a noted Baptist minister, abolitionist crusader, and educational innovator who lectured and wrote on his antislavery views. He edited the *Christian Reflector*, a religious newspaper published in Worcester, Massachusetts, that supported the abolitionist cause.

Grosvenor graduated from Dartmouth College in 1818 and later attended Princeton Theological Seminary, graduating in 1822. He accepted a position as pastor of the First Baptist Church of Boston, where he led his congregation from 1827 to 1830. During that time, he participated in the first antislavery meeting held in Boston in 1828.

Slavery was a divisive issue within the ranks of the Baptist Church in the United States and ultimately led to a schism within the denomination in 1845. Grosvenor was one of the leading advocates for the abolitionist cause in the antislavery wing of the antebellum Baptist Church. He held offices in both the American Anti-Slavery Society and the American Baptist Home Mission Society, and he repeatedly demanded that the latter society sever its ties with Southern slave owners.

Grosvenor delivered an address before the Anti-Slavery Society of Salem, Massachusetts, on February 24, 1834, that was widely circulated in the abolitionist press and helped make him a popular lecturer on the abolitionist circuit in the Northeastern states. Rather than ignoring the divergent views on slavery within the Baptist Church, Grosvenor presented a reasoned argument that supported the cause of abolition. He published *Slavery vs. the Bible: A Correspondence Between the General Conference of Maine, and the Presbytery of Tombecbee, Mississippi, With a Brief Appendix* (1840) to present the argument within a biblical exegesis.

Following the schism within the Baptist Church, Grosvenor published *A Review of the "Correspondence" of Messrs. Fuller and Wayland on the Subject of American Slavery* (1847). This work examined the debate on slavery that had been waged between the Reverend Richard Fuller of Beaufort, South Carolina, and the Reverend Francis Wayland of Providence, Rhode Island.

In 1848, Grosvenor founded an educational institution that was remarkably innovative for its time. The New York Free Central College was established in central New York's Cortland County near McGrawville (now McGraw). The school opened its doors to all students, regardless of gender or race, making it the first academic institution of higher education in the United States to have such an open admissions policy. It also had an integrated faculty that included Charles Lewis Ransom, the first black college professor in the nation.

According to Grosvenor, the purpose of the institution was the "literary, scientific, moral, and physical education of both sexes and of all classes of youth." Grosvenor served as president of the college from 1849 to 1850, and he remained on its staff as a professor for several years thereafter. Unfortunately, the venture had failed by 1858, when it had to close its doors because of bankruptcy.

Grosvenor retired from active ministry in 1867 and moved to Albion, Michigan. He died there in March 1879.

Junius P. Rodriguez

See also: Religion and Abolitionism.

Guerrero, Vicente (ca. 1782–1831)

Vicente Guerrero was a notable Mexican soldier and statesman during the movement for independence from Spain and the early national period, serving as commander in chief of the Mexican army during the last years of the 1810–1821 war for independence. He served briefly as president of Mexico in 1829 and is best remembered for abolishing slavery throughout Mexico.

Guerrero was born into a *mestizo* (mixed-heritage) family in the village of Tixtla, located near Acapulco, in southern Mexico. As a mestizo, Guerrero was rumored to have some African ancestry, and throughout his life, the nickname "El Negro" followed him. By all accounts, his family was poor and thus he had no formal education, though he did learn much from his work and travels as a mule driver.

When the first attempts at revolution against Spanish colonial control began in 1810, Guerrero joined the forces of Father José María Morelos and fought in the revolutionary army. After the execution of Father Morelos in 1815, Guerrero assumed command of the rebel forces in southern Mexico, which continued to fight the Royalist forces.

In 1821, Guerrero joined forces with Augustín de Iturbide, his former adversary, and agreed to the Plan of Iguala, whereby Mexico became independent of Spain in a bloodless, conservative revolution. According to this plan, Mexico remained unified, Catholicism was maintained, and the new nation developed as a limited constitutional monarchy. Despite his alliance with Iturbide, Guerrero continued to believe that Mexico would be best served by a republican government.

Guerrero served in several governmental offices during the administrations of Iturbide and his successor, President Guadalupe Victoria. In the elections of 1828, Guerrero sought the presidency but lost to Manuel Gómez Pedraza. Believing that the election had been stolen from him, Guerrero conspired with General Antonio López de Santa Anna to stage a coup d'état that removed Pedraza from power. Guerrero assumed the presidency in April 1829.

On September 15, 1829, Guerrero signed a decree that freed all of the slaves in Mexico. He promised that at some future date, when Mexico's national treasury would permit, the owners of the emancipated slaves would be compensated in some form for their loss.

Guerrero's actions caused settlers in the province of Texas to begin questioning whether their property rights were secure under Mexican law. In December 1829, Guerrero rescinded his emancipation decree with respect to Texas only. Thus, in the remainder of northern Mexico—the lands that became the Mexican cession territory in 1848—slavery was abolished by Guerrero's 1829 decree. This issue was a catalyst for the formation of the Free Soil Party, which argued in U.S. politics against the extension of slavery outside the boundaries outlined in the Wilmot Proviso.

In December 1829, Guerrro was overthrown by an alliance of conservative political leaders. He was executed on February 14, 1831, in Cuilapan, Mexico.

Junius P. Rodriguez

See also: Free Soil Party; Wilmot Proviso (1846).

Further Reading

Sprague, William. *Vicente Guerrero, Mexican Liberator: A Study in Patriotism.* Chicago: R.R. Donnelley, 1939.
Vincent, Theodore G. *The Legacy of Vicente Guerrero: Mexico's First Black Indian President.* Gainesville: University Press of Florida, 2001.

Index

Note: Numbers in bold are volumes.
Page numbers in italics indicate
images.

A

Abbot, W.W., 3:633–34

Abdülhamid II, Sultan, Ottoman
Empire, 2:409

Abdulmecid, Sultan, Ottoman
Empire, 2:409

Abdy, Edward Strutt, 1:5

Abdy, Thomas, 1:3

Abeokuta, West Africa, 1:149, 172,
174

Aberdeen, Scotland, 1:62; 2:446

Aberdeen Act (1845), Great Britain,
1:15

Aberdeen University, Scotland,
1:62

Abington, Pennsylvania, 2:334

Ableman, Stephen V.R., 1:4; 2:424

Ableman v. Booth (1859), 1:4; 2:424

*Abolicionista Español, El. See Spanish
Abolitionist, The*

Abolition, evolution of
classical civilizations, 1:xxvii–xxviii
colonialism, 1:xxxii–xxxix, *xxxiii,
xxxviii,* xli–xlii, xlv–xlvii, xlviii,
xlix, l, lii
Enlightenment, 1:xxix–xxxvi
evangelicalism, 1:xxxix
France, 1:xxx–xxxii, xxxvii–xxxix,
xlviii, l, lii
French Revolution (1789–1799),
1:xxxvii–xxxix
gradual emancipation, 1:xxxiv–
xxxv, xlii–xliii, xliv–xlv, xlix
Great Britain, 1:xxxii–xxxvii, xxxix,
xli–xlii, xlv–xlviii
intellectual origins, 1:xxix–xxxi
modernity, 1:xli, lii
natural rights philosophy,
1:xxxiv–xxxvi
New England, North America,
1:xxxii, xxxiv–xxxv, xxxvi
proslavery ideology, 1:xxvii–xxviii,
xxix
racism, 1:xxxi, xxxvii, xli, lii

Abolition, evolution of *(continued)*
religious reformation, 1:xxxi–xxxii
slave revolts, 1:xli, xxxviii, *xxxviii,*
l, lii
theological ideology, 1:xxvii–xxxiv,
xlii–xliii, xlv, xlvii
transatlantic legislation, 1:xxxii,
xxxiii–xxxiv, xxxv–xxxvi,
xxxvii, xl, xlii, xliv, xlv,
xlvii–xlix, l, *li*
transatlantic war, 1:xxxii, xxxiv,
xxxix–xl, xlviii, l
United States, 1:xxxvii, xxxix–xli,
xlii–lii
See also Chronology of emancipation
and abolition

Abolition, official
Antigua, 1:91
Argentina, 1:139
Bahamas, 1:91
Barbados, 1:91
Brazil, 1:83–85, 87–88, 110, 139;
2:442–43; 3:761
Caribbean, 1:187–88
Cuba, 1:83, 151–53, *152*
Denmark, 1:6, 138, 139, 143,
159–60
Great Britain, 1:4–8, 50, 52,
53, 71, 82, 89–92, 101, 102,
108, 129, 138, 143, 148, 223;
2:296, 307, 313, 315, 352,
420, 478, 507, 580, 582, 589;
3:689–705
Grenada, 1:91
Haiti, 1:139, 171
Jamaica, 1:91; 2:310–12, *311*
Mexico, 1:139
Netherlands, 1:187–88
New Granada, 2:390–92, *391*
Puerto Rico, 1:70–71, 83
Saint Croix, 1:159–60
Saint John, 1:159–60
Saint Thomas, 1:159–60
Saint Vincent, 1:91
Spain, 1:139; 2:494
Suriname, 2:510–12, *511*
Sweden, 1:138, 139, 143
Tobago, 1:91

Abolition, official *(continued)*
United States, 1:23–25, *24,* 30, 45,
116, 121–22, 137–38, 143,
184, 191–92, 195, 211, 223,
250; 2:316–18, 320–21, 343,
426, 457, 460, 498, 502,
543–44, 557; 3:739
Uruguay, 1:139
Venezuela, 1:139
West Africa, 2:574–76
West Indies
British colonialism, 1:4–8,
89–92
Danish colonialism, 1:159–60
Dutch colonialism, 1:187–88
French colonialism, 1:230–33
See also Emancipation; *specific
legislation*

Abolition documents, 3:646, 762
Address to Spanish Monarchy
(1870), 3:664–65
Afghanistan slave trade (1874),
3:666–67
African Institution objectives
(1807), Great Britain, 3:762,
763
Anti-Slavery Jubilee (1884),
England, 3:667–69
Anti-Slavery Society prospectus
(1823), Great Britain, 3:652–54
British and Foreign Anti-Slavery
Society, 3:664–65, 666–67,
742–43, 769–70
constitution (1873), 3:764–65
cotton plantations (1863), Great
Britain, 3:663–64
Free Produce movement (1857),
United States, 3:662–63
Free Soil Party principles (1852),
United States, 3:661–62
German Society for the Abolition of
Slavery prospectus (1848), 3:763
Germantown Protest (1688),
Pennsylvania, 3:647
New York slave address (1843;
Garnet), 3:657–60
slaves' petition (1773),
Massachusetts, 3:647–48

Curaçao
    Corps of Free Coloreds and Blacks,
        1:158
    Dutch colonialism, 1:157–58,
        187–90
    slave revolt (1795), 1:157–58
"Cure for the Evil of Slavery" (Stearns),
    1:93
*Cursory Remarks Upon the Revd. Mr.
    Ramsay's Essay on the Treatment
    and Conversion of African Slaves in
    the Sugar Colonies, By a Friend to
    the West India Colonies and Their
    Inhabitants* (Tobin), 2:448
Curtis, Benjamin, 1:135, 184
Curtis, George Ticknor, 2:473
Cushing, William, 1:136
Cuttyhunk Island, Massachusetts,
    1:155
Cuyahoga Anti-Slavery Society, Ohio,
    2:354
Cuyo, Argentina, 2:466

D

Dade, Francis, 2:412
Dahomey, West Africa, 1:174
Daily Free Democrat, Milwaukee,
    Wisconsin, 1:4
Daily Richmond Whig, Virginia, 3:756
Daily Whig, New York, 1:266
D'Alembert, Jean Le Rond, 1:139–40;
    3:805
Dall, Caroline Healy, 1:163
Dallas, Alexander, 1:74
Danielpour, Richard, 1:245
Danville, Kentucky
    educational institutions, 1:74
    newspapers, 1:75
    religious institutions, 1:74
Danville, Vermont, 2:497
Darien, Georgia, 2:325; 2:368
Darlington, England, 1:60
Dartmouth College, Vermont, 1:213,
    278; 2:497
Dartmouth Young Men's Anti-Slavery
    Society, Vermont, 1:213
D'Arusmont, Sylvia, 2:594
D'Arusmont, William Phiquepal, 2:594
Darwin, Charles, 2:483; 3:644–45
Darwin, Erasmus, 2:432
Davenport, James, 1:263
Davie County, North Carolina, 2:293
Davies, James, 1:172
Davies, Samuel, 1:263–64; 2:463
Davis, David Brion, 1:202
Davis, H. Winter, 3:757
Davis, Jefferson, 1:100, 123; 2:343,
    482; 3:757, 810

Davis, Nelson, 2:534
Davis, Paulina Wright, 1:162–64,
    163, 213
Davis, Thomas, 1:163
Dawes, William, 1:164; 2:351
Dawn Settlement, Ontario, Canada,
    2:295; 2:472, 585–86
Day, Eliza Dixon, 1:165
Day, John, 1:165
Day, Mary, 1:93–94
Day, Thomas, 1:164–65; 2:432, 463
Day, William Howard, 1:17, *106*,
    165–66
Day Law (1904), Kentucky, 1:206
Dayton, William, 1:227
De Gouges, Marie Olympe,
    1:166–67
*De la France et des États-Unis. See Of
    France and the United States* (Brissot
    and Clavière)
*De la litterature des negres. See Enquiry
    Concerning the Intellectual and Moral
    Faculties and Literature of Negroes,
    An* (Grégoire)
De Witt, Alexander, 1:xlix
"Death: A Poetical Essay" (Porteus),
    2:428
Debree, John, 2:473
Declaration of Independence
    Liberia (1847), 2:338
    New England (1776), 1:36, 73,
        115, 133, 168–70, 210; 2:319,
        463, 464
"Declaration of Mental Independence"
    (Owen), 2:410
Declaration of Rights (1776),
    Virginia, 1:168, 170
"Declaration of Sentiments" (American
    Anti-Slavery Society; AASS),
    1:207, 249; 2:368, 383, 430, 438,
    496
Declaration of the Rights of Man and
    of the Citizen (1789), France,
    1:170–71, 229, 230, 232; 2:282;
    3:677–78
*Declaration of the Rights of Woman and
    Citizen* (De Gouges), 1:166, 167
*Deeper Wrong, The. See Incidents in the
    Life of a Slave Girl* (Jacobs)
Deerbrook (Martineau), 2:366
Deerfield, New Hampshire, 1:99
Defense for Fugitive Slaves, A (Spooner),
    2:495
Del Monte, Domingo, 2:360, 546,
    547–48
Delany, Martin Robison, 1:72, 166,
    171–75, *173*; 2:384–85, 397–98,
    399, 472, 578; 3:809

Delaware
    African American education, 1:166
    compensated emancipation,
        1:137–38
    Confiscation Acts (1861/1862),
        1:141
    fugitive slaves, 1:236, 247–48;
        2:472, 501, 533, 539
    General Assembly, 1:138
    manumission, 2:357
    political representation, 1:137–38
    Underground Railroad, 1:247–48;
        2:472, 501, 539
    See also specific city
Delaware Abolition Society, 1:155–56
Delaware Railroad, 1:255
Delondes' Revolt. *See German Coast
    Rebellion (1811), Louisiana*
Demerara, Guyana
    Dutch colonialism, 1:69
    slave revolt (1823), 1:69, 175
Democracy in America (Tocqueville),
    2:365, 366, 525–26
Democratic Clarion, Princeton, Indiana,
    2:410
Democratic Party, United States
    Amistad (Spanish ship), 1:39
    Barnburner Democrats, 1:217–19
    Conscience Democrats, 2:342
    Copperheads, 2:395
    Hunker Democrats, 1:218
    New York convention (1847), 1:218
    popular sovereignty, 2:583–84
    presidential elections
        1840, 2:340
        1844, 1:75, 130
        1848, 1:217–19
        1856, 1:226–27
        1860, 2:342–43
        1872, 2:482
    Reconstruction (1866–1877),
        1:25–26; 2:457–58
    state representation, 1:99–100, 101,
        115–16; 2:333, 471, 508, 546,
        547, 556, 583–84
Denham, Elizabeth, 1:66
Denmark, 3:807
    abolition, 1:6, 138, 139, 143,
        159–60
    Congress of Aix-la-Chapelle (1818),
        1:13, 109, 139
    Horsa (Danish ship), 2:337
    monarchy, 1:159–60; 2:554
    West Indies colonialism, 1:159–62
Denver, Colorado, 1:23
Deptford, England, 2:334
Deptford Township, New Jersey,
    2:300–301